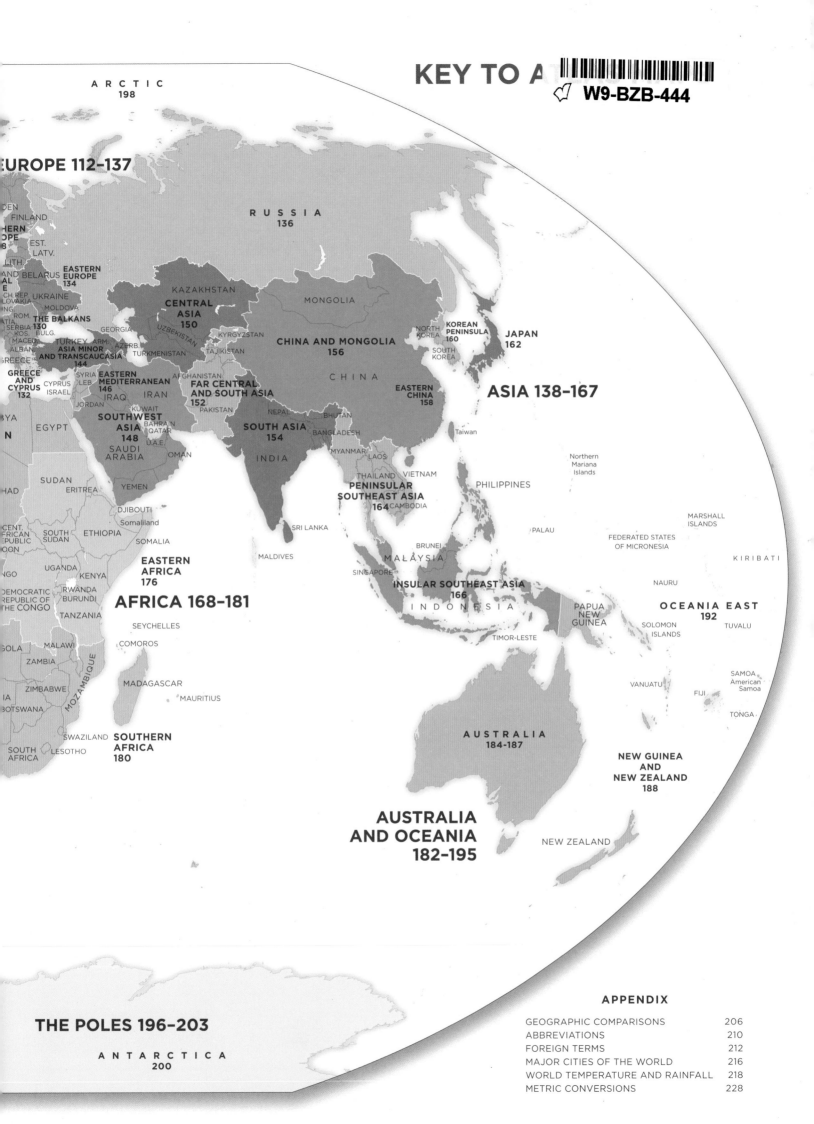

ARCTIC
198

EUROPE 112–137

RUSSIA
136

FINLAND

HERN
OPE
8

EST.
LATV.
LITH
BELARUS
EASTERN
EUROPE
134

CH REP.
LOVAKIA
UKRAINE
MOLDOVA

KAZAKHSTAN

MONGOLIA

NORTH
KOREA
KOREAN
PENINSULA
160

JAPAN
162

ING.
THE BALKANS
130
SERBIA
KOS.
MACED.
BULG.
GEORGIA
CENTRAL
ASIA
150
UZBEKISTAN
KYRGYZSTAN

CHINA AND MONGOLIA
156

SOUTH
KOREA

ALBAN.
TURKEY ARM.
ASIA MINOR
AND TRANSCAUCASIA
144
AZERB.
TURKMENISTAN
TAJIKISTAN

CHINA

ASIA 138–167

GREECE
GREECE
AND
CYPRUS
132
CYPRUS
SYRIA
LEB.
ISRAEL
EASTERN
MEDITERRANEAN
146
JORDAN
IRAN
IRAQ
AFGHANISTAN
FAR CENTRAL
AND SOUTH ASIA
152
PAKISTAN

EASTERN
CHINA
158

Taiwan

YA
EGYPT
KUWAIT
BAHRAIN
SOUTHWEST
ASIA
148
QATAR
U.A.E.
SAUDI
ARABIA
OMAN
NEPAL
SOUTH ASIA
154
INDIA
BHUTAN
BANGLADESH
MYANMAR
LAOS

Northern
Mariana
Islands

SUDAN
ERITREA
YEMEN
THAILAND
VIETNAM
PENINSULAR
SOUTHEAST ASIA
164
CAMBODIA
PHILIPPINES

MARSHALL
ISLANDS

PALAU

DJIBOUTI
Somaliland

SRI LANKA
BRUNEI

FEDERATED STATES
OF MICRONESIA

CENT.
RICAN
EPUBLIC
OON
SOUTH
SUDAN
ETHIOPIA
SOMALIA

MALDIVES

MALAYSIA

KIRIBATI

NGO
UGANDA
KENYA
EASTERN
AFRICA
176
SINGAPORE

INSULAR SOUTHEAST ASIA
166
INDONESIA

NAURU

EMOCRATIC
REPUBLIC OF
THE CONGO
RWANDA
BURUNDI
TANZANIA

AFRICA 168–181

PAPUA
NEW
GUINEA

OCEANIA EAST
192

SEYCHELLES

SOLOMON
ISLANDS

TUVALU

OLA
MALAWI
COMOROS

TIMOR-LESTE

ZAMBIA

ZIMBABWE
MADAGASCAR

MOZAMBIQUE

MAURITIUS

VANUATU

SAMOA
American
Samoa

FIJI

IA
BOTSWANA

SWAZILAND
SOUTHERN
AFRICA
180

AUSTRALIA
184-187

TONGA

SOUTH
AFRICA
LESOTHO

NEW GUINEA
AND
NEW ZEALAND
188

AUSTRALIA
AND OCEANIA
182–195

NEW ZEALAND

THE POLES 196–203

ANTARCTICA
200

APPENDIX

NATIONAL GEOGRAPHIC
Global Atlas

NATIONAL GEOGRAPHIC
Global Atlas

NATIONAL GEOGRAPHIC, WASHINGTON, D.C.

Land Cover (see key pp. 28-29)

Transverse Winkel Tripel Projection

Introduction

Presenting and representing the geographical state of the world in as unfiltered and unbiased a manner as possible has transformed into the pages that follow. These graphic depictions of Earth in lines, colors, points, numbers, and letters—ultimately in the form of pixels—paint a vivid, present-day review of our planet and its momentous trends. This compelling story of geographic evolution and the processes that ebb, flow, and remain in constant flux is illustrated by a comparison of the natural, physical world before the impact of human footprints with the current world political map. Today's map is densely dotted and plotted with thousands of towns and city spots and illuminated by colorful country boundary tints surrounding conquered lands where humankind has planted flags.

This comprehensive compendium of world, continental, and detailed regional maps covering every digital dot of Earth from the North Pole to its antipode—the South Pole—seeks to bring about a meaningful, visual portrayal and explanation of the physical, the political, and the endless variety of thematic landscapes in our world today. Humankind and nature are inextricably intertwined in a complex, dynamic web of cause and effect that makes ever greater demands on finite resources and on a growing population. As planetary stewards, we must manage and plan our environmental and humanitarian policies responsibly and sustainably. With empirical, unbiased data, and the guidance of internationally respected experts and consultants, we endeavor to bring you a clear and accurate picture of the facts and stats. The *Global Atlas* utilizes completely new, innovative, and updated sources that tap into the most reliable information available from the most recognized and authoritative scientific organizations—institutions of dedicated individuals who continually strive to collect, distill, and share with the world their findings from focused areas of their expertise, observation, and study. This approach, which includes the practice of gathering geographic information with technologically advanced processing and graphic projection tools, assists us in our aspirations to acquire, record, and report to you a myriad of topics concerning aspects of our intricate, intriguing, ever changing world.

It was more than a half century ago that John Glenn, flying a Mercury capsule, Friendship 7, became the first American to orbit Earth three times during a five-hour mission. Yuri Gagarin aboard Vostok I had surpassed this feat nearly a year earlier in the Cold War's space race. Regardless of nationality, both explorers in their extraterrestrial solitude aboard their spacecraft likely pondered the future of their world and the fragile balance between nature and humanity in the constant struggle for conflict resolution, equitable coexistence, and preservation and management of Earth's natural resources and riches. At the time of his historic 1962 flight, Glenn looked down from his spaceship's tiny portal at a planet then inhabited by 3.1 billion people. Today, the world's population exceeds 7 billion. Who, aside from demographers, would have thought the human population of billions would more than double in number in so brief a span of time? With such incredible population growth, issues of poverty, health, availability of food and fresh water, pollution, deforestation, and desertification—to name a few—become exacerbated. This dynamic and complex world calls for a better understanding, appreciation, and conservation of our finite lands and interconnected ocean, as well as our precious, limited resources—natural and human. In this new, robust collection of journalistic graphics, we devote detailed coverage to world population—including growth, density, distribution, fertility, urbanization, life expectancy, and migration. Other salient world trends covered in this new, world thematic collection include digital connectivity and globalization.

With topics ranging from plate tectonics to transportation, paleogeography to protected areas, climate to carbon emissions, human impact to health and education, this assemblage of earthly marvels depicts a gripping story of the pulse of a resilient yet very delicate planet. Comprehensive coverage of the planet's geographic superlatives will entertain and amaze readers of all cultures.

We hope that these pages will inspire, engage, and enrich your understanding of the world today and enhance the prospect for a more sustainable and verdant planet and peaceful existence for its inhabitants—human, animal, and plant—great and small.

At stake is the destiny of a balanced, responsibly managed world for present and future generations. Shared efforts and technologies bring tremendous possibilities and opportunities to seek greater resource management, conservation, and international peace and stability—and thus to have an impact on solving economic, social, and humanitarian issues.

As astronaut John Glenn wisely stated, "We have an infinite amount to learn both from nature and from each other." With this in mind, we aim in this atlas to disseminate—through meaningful, realistic illustrations—the natural wonders and treasures with which we are gifted and endlessly in awe.

CARL MEHLER
PROJECT EDITOR AND DIRECTOR OF MAPS
NATIONAL GEOGRAPHIC GLOBAL ATLAS

Contents

WORLD THEMATICS 20

NORTH AMERICA 82

EUROPE 112

SOUTH AMERICA 100

Contents continued on next page ▶

Using This Atlas

Map policies: Maps are a rich, useful, and—to the extent humanly possible—accurate means of depicting the world. Yet maps inevitably make the world seem a little simpler than it really is. A neatly drawn boundary may in reality be a hotly contested war zone. The government-sanctioned, "official" name of a provincial city in an ethnically diverse region may bear little resemblance to the name its citizens routinely use. These cartographic issues often seem obscure and academic. But maps arouse passions. Despite our carefully reasoned map policies, users of National Geographic maps write us strongly worded letters when our maps are at odds with their worldviews.

How do National Geographic cartographers deal with these realities? With constant scrutiny, considerable discussion, and help from many outside experts.

EXAMPLES

Nations: Issues of national sovereignty and contested borders often boil down to "de facto" versus "de jure" discussions. Governments and international agencies frequently make official rulings about contested regions. These de jure decisions, no matter how legitimate, are often at odds with the wishes of individuals and groups, and they often stand in stark contrast to real-world situations. The inevitable conclusion: It is simplest and best to show the world as it is—de facto—rather than as we or others wish it to be.

Africa's Western Sahara, for example, was divided by Morocco and Mauritania after the Spanish government withdrew in 1976. Although Morocco now controls the entire territory, the United Nations does not recognize Morocco's sovereignty over this still-disputed area. This atlas shows the defacto Moroccan rule but includes an explanatory note.

Place-names: Ride a barge down the Danube, and you'll hear the river called *Donau, Duna, Dunaj, Dunărea, Dunav, Dunay*. These are local names. This atlas uses the conventional name, "Danube," on physical maps. On political maps, local names are used, with the conventional name in parentheses where space permits. Usage conventions for both foreign and domestic place-names are established by the U.S. Board on Geographic Names, a group with representatives from several federal agencies.

Physical Maps

Physical maps of the world, the continents, and the ocean floor reveal landforms and vegetation in stunning detail. Created with digital elevation models and land cover data, the maps provide a generalized picture of each region's physiography. Patterns indicate specific landscape features such as sand, glaciers, and swamps. Blue lines indicate rivers; boundaries and political divisions are shown in red.

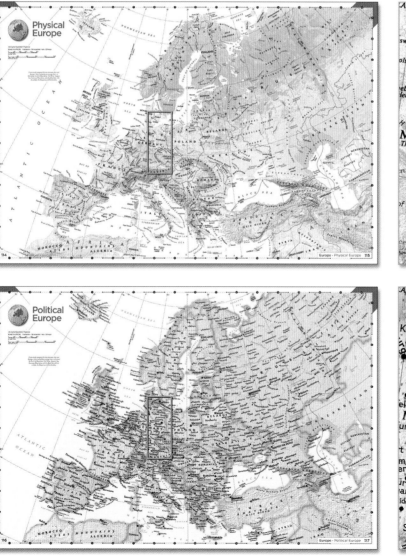

Physical Features Colors and shading Illustrate variations in elevation, landforms, and vegetation. Patterns indicate specific landscape features, such as sand, glaciers, and swamps.

Water Features Blue lines indicate rivers; other water bodies are shown as areas of blue.

Boundaries and Political Divisions Red lines indicate boundaries and political divisions. Dotted red lines indicate disputed or uncertain boundaries.

Political Maps

Political maps portray features such as international boundaries, the locations of cities, road networks, and other important elements of the world's human geography. Most index entries are keyed to the political maps, listing the page numbers and then the specific locations on those pages. (See page 230 for details on how to use the index.) Boundaries and political divisions are defined with both lines and colored bands.

Physical Features Gray shaded relief depicts surface features such as mountains, hills, and valleys.

Water Features Shown in blue, solid lines indicate perrenial water features; dashed lines and patterns indicate intermittent features.

Boundaries and Political Divisions Defined with both lines and color, they vary according to whether a boundary is internal or international.

Cities Four categories of labels are depicted, based on population size. Red tints around cities indicate built-up areas. See map key, on next page, for city symbols.

World Thematic Maps

Thematic maps reveal the rich patchwork and infinite interrelationships of our changing planet. The thematic section at the beginning of this atlas covers physical and natural topics such as tectonics, land cover, and climate. It also charts human patterns, with information on recent trends in urbanization, religion, economy, globalization, and digital connectivity. Two-page spreads on energy and minerals illustrate how people have learned to use Earth's resources, while spreads devoted to environmental stress and protected lands focus on the far-reaching effects of human activities and the need for resource conservation. Throughout this section of the atlas, maps are coupled with satellite imagery, charts, diagrams, photographs, and tabular information; together, they create a very useful framework for studying geographic patterns.

Land Cover
(see page 28)

Globalization
(see page 76)

Regional Maps

This atlas divides the continents into several subregions, each displayed on a two-page spread. Large-scale maps capture the political divisions and major surface features, whereas accompanying regional physical maps lend insight into the natural factors that give character to a region. Fact boxes, which include flag designs and information on populations, languages, religions, and economies, appear alongside the maps as practical reference tools.

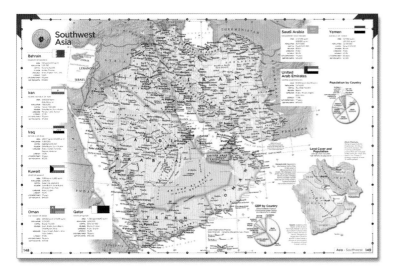

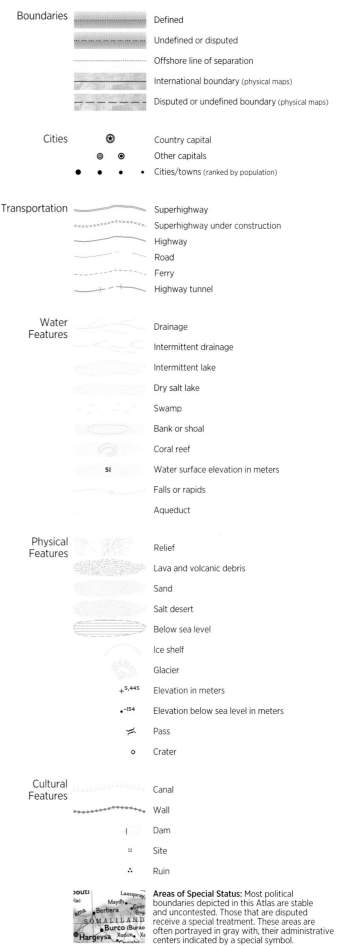

Map Symbols

Boundaries

- Defined
- Undefined or disputed
- Offshore line of separation
- International boundary (physical maps)
- Disputed or undefined boundary (physical maps)

Cities

- ✪ Country capital
- ◎ ◉ Other capitals
- ● ● ● ● Cities/towns (ranked by population)

Transportation

- Superhighway
- Superhighway under construction
- Highway
- Road
- Ferry
- Highway tunnel

Water Features

- Drainage
- Intermittent drainage
- Intermittent lake
- Dry salt lake
- Swamp
- Bank or shoal
- Coral reef
- 51 Water surface elevation in meters
- Falls or rapids
- Aqueduct

Physical Features

- Relief
- Lava and volcanic debris
- Sand
- Salt desert
- Below sea level
- Ice shelf
- Glacier
- +5,445 Elevation in meters
- •-154 Elevation below sea level in meters
- ⤺ Pass
- ⊙ Crater

Cultural Features

- Canal
- Wall
- ⊢ Dam
- ⊠ Site
- ∴ Ruin

Areas of Special Status: Most political boundaries depicted in this Atlas are stable and uncontested. Those that are disputed receive a special treatment. These areas are often portrayed in gray with their administrative centers indicated by a special symbol.

Using This Atlas continued on following pages ▶

Using This Atlas

Non-Subject Areas
Countries immediately surrounding the region of interest are shown in a neutral color. A feathered edge surrounds both land and ocean areas, gradually fading to white.

Sample Regional Map Plate

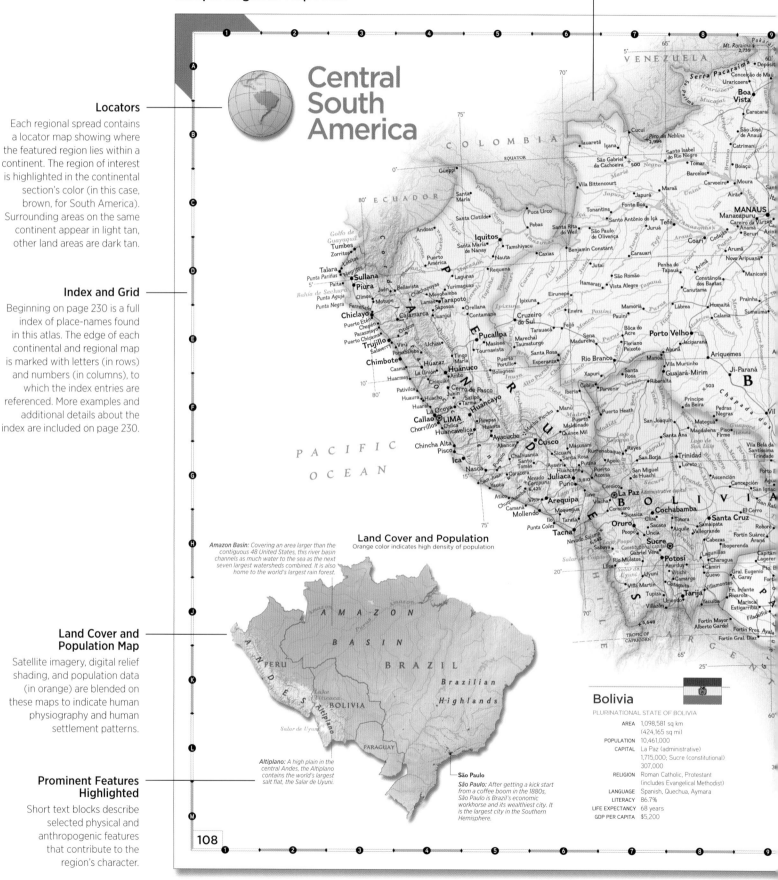

Locators

Each regional spread contains a locator map showing where the featured region lies within a continent. The region of interest is highlighted in the continental section's color (in this case, brown, for South America). Surrounding areas on the same continent appear in light tan, other land areas are dark tan.

Index and Grid

Beginning on page 230 is a full index of place-names found in this atlas. The edge of each continental and regional map is marked with letters (in rows) and numbers (in columns), to which the index entries are referenced. More examples and additional details about the index are included on page 230.

Land Cover and Population Map

Satellite imagery, digital relief shading, and population data (in orange) are blended on these maps to indicate human physiography and human settlement patterns.

Prominent Features Highlighted

Short text blocks describe selected physical and anthropogenic features that contribute to the region's character.

Central South America

Amazon Basin: Covering an area larger than the contiguous 48 United States, this river basin channels as much water to the sea as the next seven largest watersheds combined. It is also home to the world's largest rain forest.

Land Cover and Population
Orange color indicates high density of population

Altiplano: A high plain in the central Andes, the Altiplano contains the world's largest salt flat, the Salar de Uyuni.

São Paulo: After getting a kick start from a coffee boom in the 1880s, São Paulo is Brazil's economic workhorse and its wealthiest city. It is the largest city in the Southern Hemisphere.

Bolivia
PLURINATIONAL STATE OF BOLIVIA

AREA	1,098,581 sq km
	(424,165 sq mi)
POPULATION	10,461,000
CAPITAL	La Paz (administrative)
	1,715,000; Sucre (constitutional)
	307,000
RELIGION	Roman Catholic, Protestant
	(includes Evangelical Methodist)
LANGUAGE	Spanish, Quechua, Aymara
LITERACY	86.7%
LIFE EXPECTANCY	68 years
GDP PER CAPITA	$5,200

◀ Using This Atlas continued on previous pages

Map Projection

Map projections determine how land shapes are distorted when transferred from a sphere (Earth) to a flat piece of paper. Many different projections are used in this atlas—each carefully chosen for a map's particular coverage area and purpose.

Map Scales

Scale information indicates the distance on Earth represented by a given length on the map. Here, map scale is expressed in three ways: 1) As a representative fraction where scale is shown as a fraction or ratio, as in 1:15,016,000. This means that one unit on the map represents 15,016,000 units on Earth's surface. 2) As a verbal statement: one centimeter equals 150 kilometers or one inch equals 237 miles. 3) As a bar scale: a linear graph symbol subdivided to show map lengths in kilometers and miles in the real world.

Pie Charts

Pie charts include data for the featured countries in each region. The values are given in descending order (clockwise), in colors corresponding to the country colors on the map. At the continent scale, only the top ten values are individually labeled, with the others grouped together due to space constraints.

Gross Domestic Product (GDP) Pie Charts

The figures shown for the latest available GDP (gross domestic product) values reflect PPP (purchasing power parity) estimates, in U.S. dollars.

Population Pie Charts

These are the latest available figures for total population by country. The population of the region's largest city is shown in a darker shade.

Flags and Facts

This atlas recognizes 195 independent nations. All of these countries are profiled in the regional sections of this atlas. Accompanying each entry are highlights of geographic, demographic, and economic data. These details provide a brief overview of each country; they are not intended to be comprehensive.

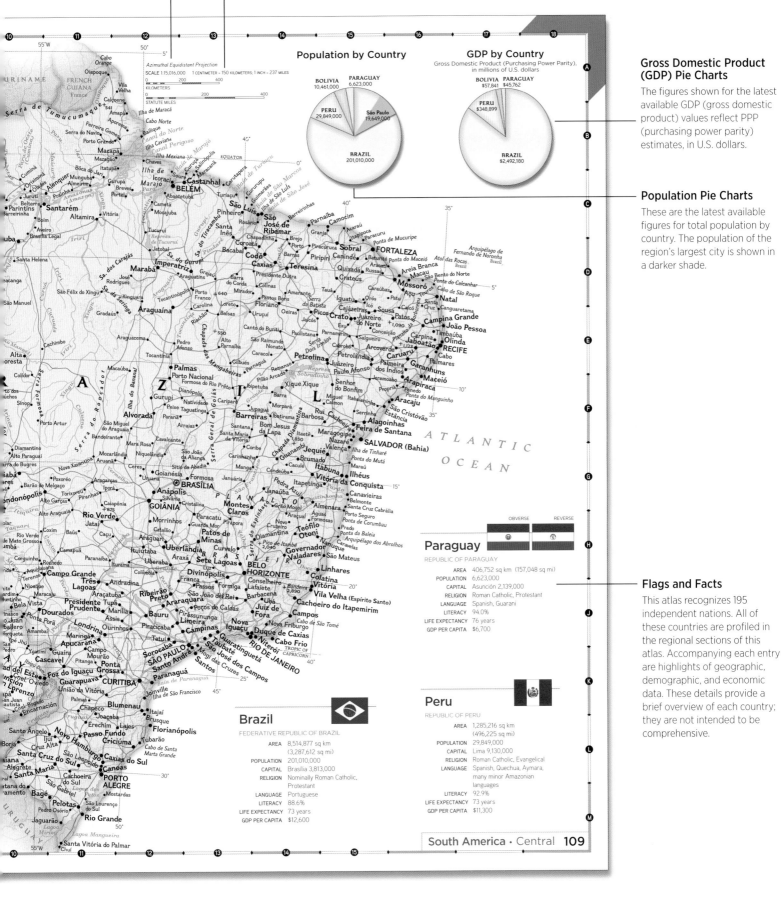

Population by Country

BOLIVIA 10,461,000
PARAGUAY 6,623,000
PERU 29,849,000
São Paulo 19,649,000
BRAZIL 201,010,000

GDP by Country
Gross Domestic Product (Purchasing Power Parity), in millions of U.S. dollars

BOLIVIA $57,841
PARAGUAY $45,762
PERU $348,899
BRAZIL $2,492,180

Azimuthal Equidistant Projection
SCALE 1:15,016,000   1 CENTIMETER = 150 KILOMETERS; 1 INCH = 237 MILES

Paraguay
REPUBLIC OF PARAGUAY

AREA	406,752 sq km (157,048 sq mi)
POPULATION	6,623,000
CAPITAL	Asunción 2,139,000
RELIGION	Roman Catholic, Protestant
LANGUAGE	Spanish, Guarani
LITERACY	94.0%
LIFE EXPECTANCY	76 years
GDP PER CAPITA	$6,700

Brazil
FEDERATIVE REPUBLIC OF BRAZIL

AREA	8,514,877 sq km (3,287,612 sq mi)
POPULATION	201,010,000
CAPITAL	Brasilia 3,813,000
RELIGION	Nominally Roman Catholic, Protestant
LANGUAGE	Portuguese
LITERACY	88.6%
LIFE EXPECTANCY	73 years
GDP PER CAPITA	$12,600

Peru
REPUBLIC OF PERU

AREA	1,285,216 sq km (496,225 sq mi)
POPULATION	29,849,000
CAPITAL	Lima 9,130,000
RELIGION	Roman Catholic, Evangelical
LANGUAGE	Spanish, Quechua, Aymara, many minor Amazonian languages
LITERACY	92.9%
LIFE EXPECTANCY	73 years
GDP PER CAPITA	$11,300

OBVERSE   REVERSE

South America · Central **109**

Physical World

O C E A N

30° 45° 60° 75° 90° 105° 120° 135° 150° 165° 90° 180°

North East Land

George Land

Graham Bell Island

Komsomolets Island

October Revolution Island

Bol'shevik Island

New Siberian Islands

EAST SIBERIAN SEA

Franz Josef Land
+606
North Land
Cape Chelyuskin
Wrangel I.

Edge Island
+12,111
Vize I.
1,146
Chukchi Range

r Island

BARENTS
SEA

Novaya Zemlya

KARA SEA

Taymyr Peninsula
Lake Taymyr

LAPTEV SEA

Koryak Range

North Cape

Gyda Peninsula

North Siberian Lowland

Lena

Verkhoyansk Range

Cherskiy Range

ARCTIC CIRCLE

Kolyma

Kolguyev I.

Yamal Pen.

Gulf of Ob

1,701

656

Central

Gora Mus Khaya +2,959

1,830

Central Range
4,750

BERING SEA

Narodnaya
1,895
Ob
Yenisey

S I B E R I A

Siberian

Stanovoy Range

2,412

Kamchatka Peninsula

SEA OF OKHOTSK

Aleutian Is.
Attu

Timan Ridge
Ural Mountains
West Siberian Plain
Plateau
Angara

Sakhalin

Hokkaido

45°

Lake Onega
Lake Ladoga

Volga

Irtysh

Siberian Plain

Sikhote Alin Range

Source of the Volga

Central Russian Upland
Highest point in Europe

The Steppes
Kazakh Uplands

Belukha 4,506

Eastern Sayan Mts.

Lake Baikal

Yablonovyy Range

Greater Khingan Range

Amur

Manchurian Plain

Tatar Strait

SEA OF JAPAN (EAST SEA)

Kuril Islands

Honshu

Fuji
3,776

Pinsk Marshes

Carpathian Mts.

Ural

Aral Sea

Syr Darya

Lake Balkhash

Altay Mountains
3,957 Mongolian

Plateau

GOBI

Korea

North China Plain

Yellow Sea

Kyushu

Shikoku

NORTH

PACIFIC

30°

Crimea

Caspian Depression

Elbrus 5,642 m (18,510 ft)

Turan Lowland

Qizilqum

Dzungarian Basin
5,445

Tian Shan

Turpan Depression
2,584

Qinghai Hu

Nampo Shoto

OCEAN

Balkan Peninsula

Black Sea
Bosporus

Caucasus Mts.

Ustyurt Plateau

Turan Lowland

Ysyk Köl
Pobedy Peak +7,439
7,495 +7,649

Taklimakan Desert

Altun Shan

Muztag
6,973

Qin Ling

EAST CHINA SEA

Olympus +
2,917

ANATOLIA (ASIA MINOR)

Mt. Ararat
5,137

Garagum

Kara Kum

-28

Kunlun Mountains

Plateau of Tibet

Brahmaputra

Taiwan

Ryukyu Islands

TROPIC OF CANCER

15°

Crete

Cyprus

Syrian Desert

Zagros Mountains

Elburz Mts.

Hindu Kush
8,611

Source of the Yangtze

HIMALAYA

Yangtze

Taiwan Str.

PHILIPPINE SEA

Wake I.

MEDITERRANEAN SEA

Nile R. Delta

Mesopotamia

Kuh-e Taftan
4,042

Mount Everest
8,850 m (29,035 ft)
Highest point in the world

Luzon Strait

Mariana Islands

Taongi Atoll

Qattara Depression -133

Sinai

Mt. Sinai 2,285

An Nafud
Lowest point in Asia
-412 m (-1,385 ft)

Persian G.

Great Indian Desert

Luzon
Mount Pulog
2,934

Bikini Atoll

Western Desert

Eastern Desert

Libyan Desert

ARABIAN PENINSULA

G. of Oman

Deccan Plateau

INDIA

BAY

Indochina Peninsula

Mount Pinatubo
1,486

Enewetak Atoll

Marshall Islands

Tibesti Mts.
1,893

Emi Koussi
3,415

Nubian Desert

RED SEA

Rub al Khali (Empty Quarter)

Western Ghats

Eastern Ghats

OF

BENGAL

SOUTH

CHINA

Guam

Kwajalein Atoll

Air Massif
+872

Marra Mts. 3,088

Ras Dejen
4,533

Lake Tana
Dallol -156 m
Lowest point in Africa

Gulf of Aden

Socotra

ARABIAN SEA

Andaman Islands

Andaman Sea

Hainan

Gulf of Tonkin

SEA

Kinabalu
4,101

Mindanao

Chuuk (Ponape) Pohnpei

Caroline Islands

MICRONESIA

ke Chad

H

E

L

L

Ethiopian Highlands

Somali Peninsula

Sri Lanka (Ceylon)

Nicobar Islands

Malay Pen.

Strait of Malacca

Borneo
2,987

Celebes

Buru

Molucca

15°

ko

A

F

R

Congo

Lake Albert

Lake Turkana (L. Rudolf)

Maldive Islands

Sumatra

Kerinci
3,800

Greater Sunda

INDONESIA

New Guinea
4,509

Admiralty Is.

Bismarck Archipelago
2,334

EQUATOR

Nauru

Banaba

Gilbert Islands

Beru

0°

Congo Basin

I

C

A

Mount Kenya
5,199

Lake Victoria

Seychelles

Chagos Archipelago

Java Sea

Islands

Java

Banda Sea

Flores

Arafura Sea

Solomon Sea

New Ireland

New Britain
Bougainville

Guadalcanal

Solomon Islands

MELANESIA

Nanumea

Tuvalu

Mitumba Mts.

Kilimanjaro
5,895 m (19,340 ft)
Highest point in Africa

Diego Garcia

Zanzibar I.

Amirante Isles

Aldabra Is.

Comoro Is.

Lesser Sunda Is.

Timor

Timor Sea

Cape York Pen.

Lake Tanganyika

Lake Malawi (L. Nyasa)

Maromokotro
2,876

Namuli
2,419

Gulf of Carpentaria

Great Barrier Reef

CORAL SEA

Vanuatu

Fiji Islands

15°

Lower Guinea

Katanga Plateau

+1,340

Lake Kariba

Mozambique Channel

Madagascar

Mascarene Islands

Rodrigues

INDIAN

Mount Ord
937
Kimberley Plateau

Great Sandy Desert

Great Dividing Range

New Caledonia
1,628

Brandberg
2,573

Namib Desert

Kalahari Desert

Groot Karasberge
2,202

Drakensberg

Mauritius

Réunion

North West Cape

OCEAN

Mount Meharry
1,253

Cape Inscription

WESTERN

Macdonnell Ranges

AUSTRALIA

Great Artesian Basin

Lord Howe I.

TROPIC OF CAPRICORN

SOUTH

PACIFIC

Great Karroo

Cape of Good Hope

Cape Agulhas

Cape Naturaliste

Plateau

Central Lowlands

Lowest point in Australia
Lake Eyre (-52 ft) -16 m

Great Victoria Desert

Nullarbor Plain

Great Australian Bight

Murray

Darling

OCEAN

North Island

30°

Amsterdam
St. Paul

Highest point in Australia
Mt. Kosciuszko +2,228 m (7,310 ft)

Bass's Strait

TASMAN SEA

NEW

ZEALAND
3,797

Crozet Islands

Prince Edward Islands

Kerguelen Islands
1,850

Heard Island

Tasmania

Aoraki/Mt. Cook
3,754

South Island

Stewart Island (Rakiura)

45°

Macquarie I.

Auckland Is.

ARCTIC CIRCLE

Cosmonaut Sea

Riiser-Larsen Peninsula

Cape Ann

Enderby Land

Prydz Bay

Cape Poinsett

South Magnetic Pole
2013

Balleny Is.

60°

een Maud Land

Wilkes Land

T I C A

TRANSANTARCTIC MOUNTAINS

Victoria Land

Ross Ice Shelf

Mt. Erebus
3,794

Ross Sea

30° 45° 60° 75° 90° 105° 120° 135° 150° 165° 90° 180° 75°

Winkel Tripel Projection

SCALE 1:89,822,700   1 CENTIMETER = 898 KILOMETERS; 1 INCH = 1,418 MILES AT THE EQUATOR

0   500   1000   1500   2000   2500
KILOMETERS

0   500   1000   1500   2000   2500
STATUTE MILES

Physical World   **15**

Political World

Political Poles

North Pole

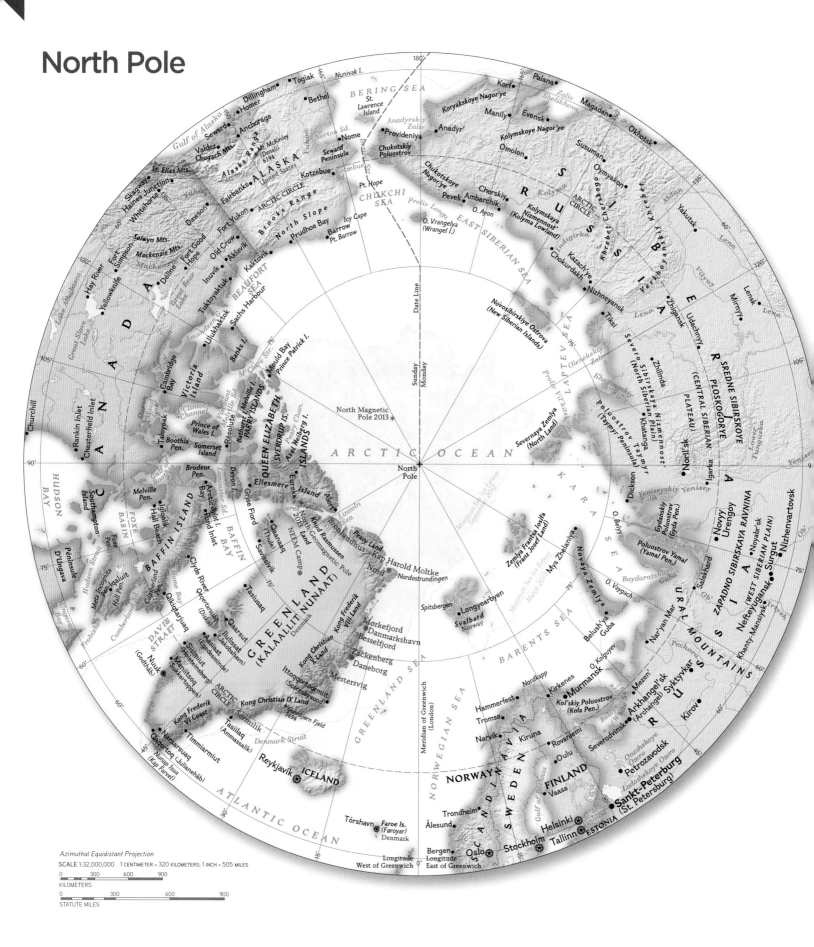

Azimuthal Equidistant Projection

SCALE 1:32,000,000   1 CENTIMETER = 320 KILOMETERS; 1 INCH = 505 MILES

```
0        300       600       900
KILOMETERS

0        300       600       900
STATUTE MILES
```

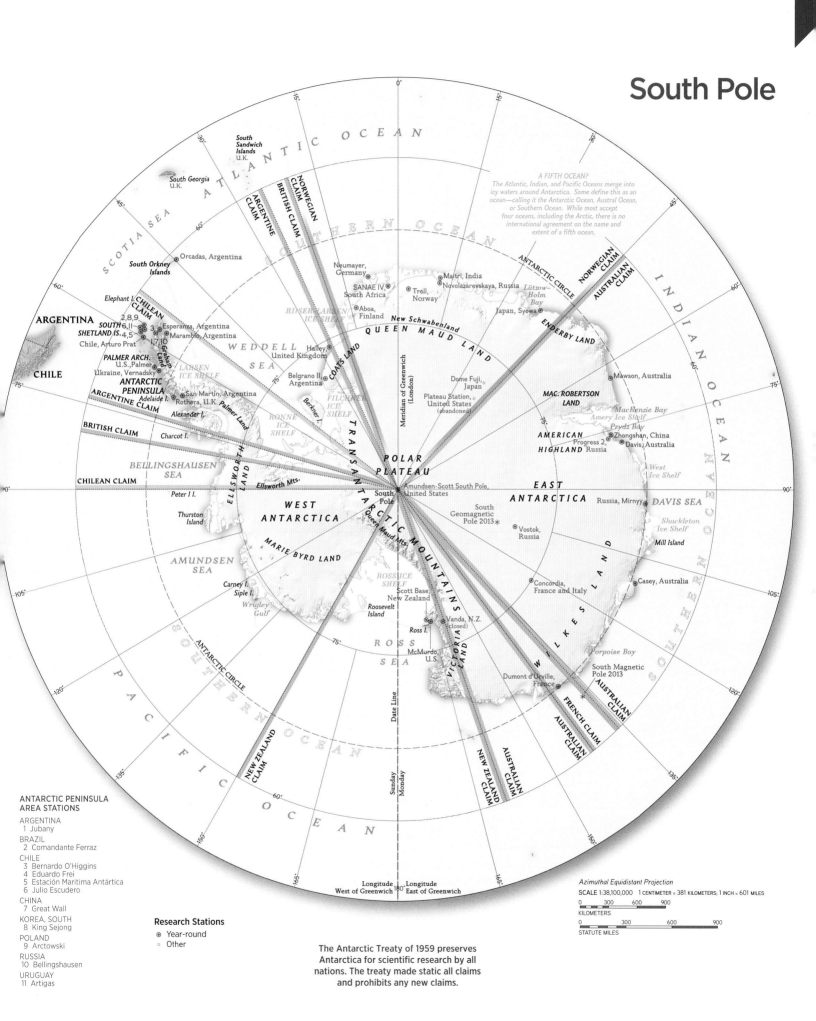

0°

15°

30°

SOUTH SANDWICH Islands U.K.

A T L A N T I C   O C E A N

South Georgia U.K.

S C O T I A   S E A

S O U T H E R N   O C E A N

A FIFTH OCEAN?
The Atlantic, Indian, and Pacific Oceans merge into icy waters around Antarctica. Some define this as an ocean—calling it the Antarctic Ocean, Austral Ocean, or Southern Ocean. While most accept four oceans, including the Arctic, there is no international agreement on the name and extent of a fifth ocean.

I N D I A N   O C E A N

ANTARCTIC CIRCLE

NORWEGIAN CLAIM

AUSTRALIAN CLAIM

Orcadas, Argentina

South Orkney Islands

ARGENTINE CLAIM

BRITISH CLAIM

NORWEGIAN CLAIM

Neumayer, Germany

SANAE IV, South Africa

Troll, Norway

Maitri, India

Novolazarevskaya, Russia

Lützow-Holm Bay

Japan, Syowa

ENDERBY LAND

Elephant I. CHILEAN CLAIM

ARGENTINA

2,8,9 SOUTH 6,11 SHETLAND IS. 4,5 Chile, Arturo Prat 3 1,7,10

CHILE

PALMER ARCH. U.S., Palmer
Ukraine, Vernadsky

ANTARCTIC PENINSULA

ARGENTINE CLAIM

Esperanza, Argentina
Marambio, Argentina

RIISER-LARSEN ICE SHELF

New Schwabenland

QUEEN MAUD LAND

Aboa, Finland

W E D D E L L   S E A

Halley, United Kingdom

LARSEN ICE SHELF

Adelaide I.
Rothera, U.K.

San Martin, Argentina

Belgrano II, Argentina

FILCHNER ICE SHELF

Berkner I.

COATS LAND

Dome Fuji, Japan

MAC. ROBERTSON LAND

Mawson, Australia

MacKenzie Bay

Amery Ice Shelf

Prydz Bay

Zhongshan, China
Progress 2, Russia
Davis, Australia

BRITISH CLAIM

Alexander I.

RONNE ICE SHELF

Palmer Land

Charcot I.

CHILEAN CLAIM

ELLSWORTH LAND

Ellsworth Mts.

Plateau Station, United States (abandoned)

AMERICAN HIGHLAND

West Ice Shelf

BELLINGSHAUSEN SEA

Peter I I.

Thurston Island

Meridian of Greenwich (London)

POLAR PLATEAU

South Pole

Amundsen-Scott South Pole, United States

South Geomagnetic Pole 2013 ✳

EAST ANTARCTICA

Russia, Mirnyy

DAVIS SEA

Shackleton Ice Shelf

Vostok, Russia

Mill Island

TRANSANTARCTIC MOUNTAINS

WEST ANTARCTICA

Queen Maud Mts.

AMUNDSEN SEA

MARIE BYRD LAND

Carney I.
Siple I.

Wrigley Gulf

ROSS ICE SHELF

Roosevelt Island

Concordia, France and Italy

Casey, Australia

Porpoise Bay

WILKES LAND

ANTARCTIC CIRCLE

R O S S   S E A

Vanda, N.Z. (closed)
Ross I.
Scott Base, New Zealand

McMurdo, U.S.

VICTORIA LAND

South Magnetic Pole 2013 ✳

AUSTRALIAN CLAIM

Dumont d'Urville, France

FRENCH CLAIM

AUSTRALIAN CLAIM

NEW ZEALAND CLAIM

NEW ZEALAND CLAIM

AUSTRALIAN CLAIM

P A C I F I C   O C E A N

S O U T H E R N   O C E A N

Date Line

Sunday Monday

Longitude West of Greenwich | Longitude East of Greenwich

180°

ANTARCTIC PENINSULA AREA STATIONS

ARGENTINA
1 Jubany

BRAZIL
2 Comandante Ferraz

CHILE
3 Bernardo O'Higgins
4 Eduardo Frei
5 Estación Marítima Antártica
6 Julio Escudero

CHINA
7 Great Wall

KOREA, SOUTH
8 King Sejong

POLAND
9 Arctowski

RUSSIA
10 Bellingshausen

URUGUAY
11 Artigas

Research Stations
⊙ Year-round
○ Other

The Antarctic Treaty of 1959 preserves Antarctica for scientific research by all nations. The treaty made static all claims and prohibits any new claims.

Azimuthal Equidistant Projection

SCALE 1:38,100,000   1 CENTIMETER = 381 KILOMETERS; 1 INCH = 601 MILES

0   300   600   900
KILOMETERS

0   300   600   900
STATUTE MILES

World
Thematics

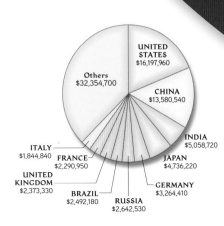

UNITED
STATES
$16,197,960

Others
$32,354,700

CHINA
$13,580,540

INDIA
$5,058,720

ITALY
$1,844,840

FRANCE
$2,290,950

JAPAN
$4,736,220

UNITED
KINGDOM
$2,373,330

GERMANY
$3,264,410

BRAZIL
$2,492,180

RUSSIA
$2,642,530

GDP by Country
Gross Domestic Product
(Purchasing Power Parity),
in millions of U.S. dollars

Mapping the human presence on the planet
over millennia, this impressionistic image delineates the
anthroposphere—the footprint left by cities, agriculture, industry,
communication webs, and transportation—from the Roman
roads to today's undersea data highways. Europe, the
Indian subcontinent, eastern Asia, and vast swaths
of North and South America glow with human
endeavor, while Amazonia, North Africa,
Arabia, and the Arctic remain far
closer to their natural states.

Population by Country

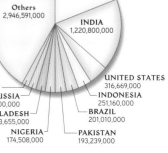

CHINA
1,349,586,000

Others
2,946,591,000

INDIA
1,220,800,000

JAPAN
127,253,000

RUSSIA
142,500,000

BANGLADESH
163,655,000

NIGERIA
174,508,000

UNITED STATES
316,669,000

INDONESIA
251,160,000

BRAZIL
201,010,000

PAKISTAN
193,239,000

Paleogeography

Paleogeography is the field of geology that deals with how Earth's geography—its distribution of oceans and continents—changes over geologic time. The movement of tectonic plates and the associated rise and fall of sea levels, together with changes in climate (paleoclimate), are the dominant forces in paleogeography.

The unceasing but generally incremental movement of tectonic plates causes continents to "drift" over geologic time—breaking apart, reassembling, and again fragmenting to repeat the process. The theory of continental drift was championed in the early 20th century by German scientist Alfred Wegener, who was intrigued by the way the coastlines of Africa and South America seemed to fit together like the pieces of a puzzle, and by the fact that fossils of the same prehistoric species were found on different continents. At the time, accepted scientific belief held that land bridges had once linked continents, but Wegener's studies revolutionized that thinking.

Now paleogeographers can trace three times in the past billion years when Earth's drifting landmasses merged to form supercontinents. Rodinia, a supercontinent in the late Precambrian eon, began breaking apart about 750 million years ago. In time, its pieces reassembled to form another supercontinent that later split into smaller landmasses during the Paleozoic era. The largest two—Euramerica (ancestral Europe and North America) and Gondwana (ancestral Africa, Antarctica, Arabia, India, and Australia)—recombined into Pangaea more than 250 million years ago. In the Mesozoic era, Pangaea split and the Atlantic and Indian Oceans began forming. The Atlantic is still widening, but scientists predict that it will close as the seafloor recycles back into Earth's mantle and that a new supercontinent, Pangaea Ultima, will form.

The **Atlantic Ocean**
is still widening,
at a rate of about
2.5 cm (1 in) per year.

Key to Paleogeographic Maps

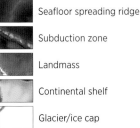

- Seafloor spreading ridge
- Subduction zone
- Landmass
- Continental shelf
- Glacier/ice cap

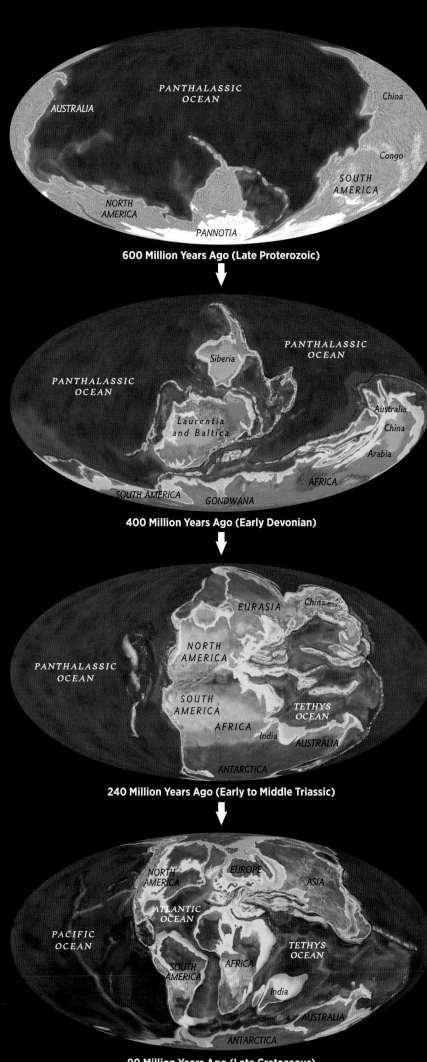

600 Million Years Ago (Late Proterozoic)

400 Million Years Ago (Early Devonian)

240 Million Years Ago (Early to Middle Triassic)

90 Million Years Ago (Late Cretaceous)

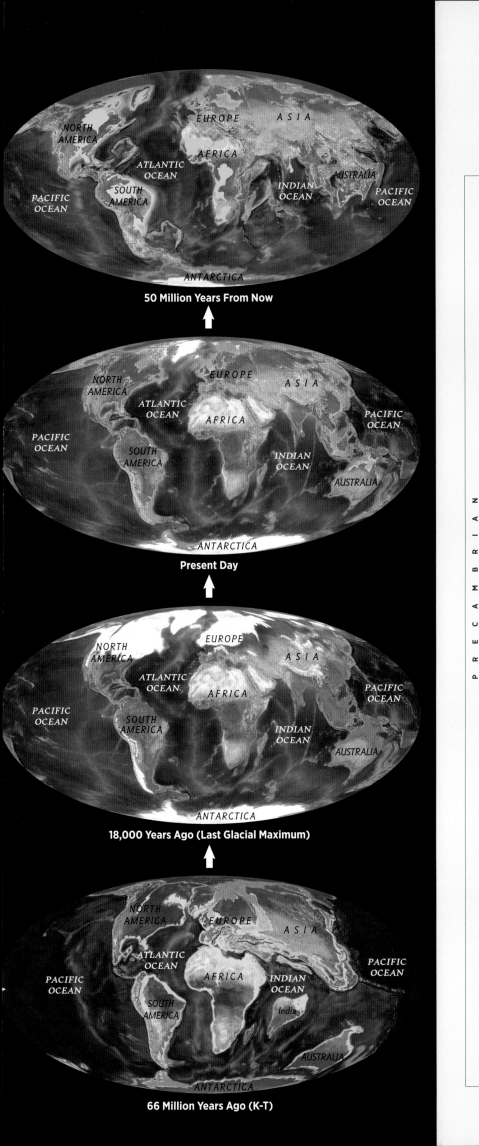

50 Million Years From Now

Present Day

18,000 Years Ago (Last Glacial Maximum)

66 Million Years Ago (K-T)

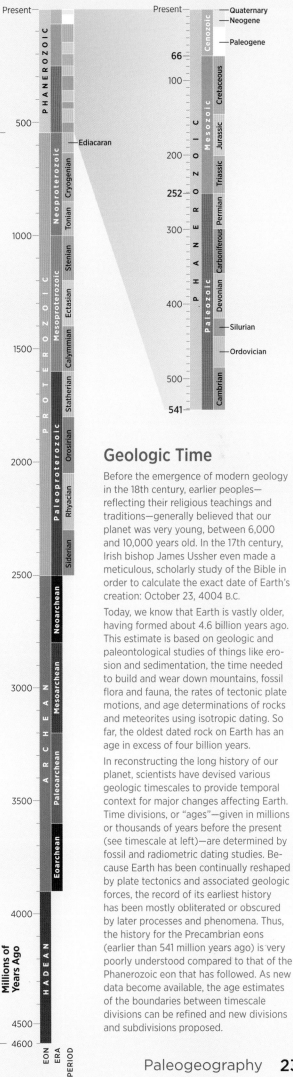

Geologic Time

Before the emergence of modern geology in the 18th century, earlier peoples—reflecting their religious teachings and traditions—generally believed that our planet was very young, between 6,000 and 10,000 years old. In the 17th century, Irish bishop James Ussher even made a meticulous, scholarly study of the Bible in order to calculate the exact date of Earth's creation: October 23, 4004 B.C.

Today, we know that Earth is vastly older, having formed about 4.6 billion years ago. This estimate is based on geologic and paleontological studies of things like erosion and sedimentation, the time needed to build and wear down mountains, fossil flora and fauna, the rates of tectonic plate motions, and age determinations of rocks and meteorites using isotropic dating. So far, the oldest dated rock on Earth has an age in excess of four billion years.

In reconstructing the long history of our planet, scientists have devised various geologic timescales to provide temporal context for major changes affecting Earth. Time divisions, or "ages"—given in millions or thousands of years before the present (see timescale at left)—are determined by fossil and radiometric dating studies. Because Earth has been continually reshaped by plate tectonics and associated geologic forces, the record of its earliest history has been mostly obliterated or obscured by later processes and phenomena. Thus, the history for the Precambrian eons (earlier than 541 million years ago) is very poorly understood compared to that of the Phanerozoic eon that has followed. As new data become available, the age estimates of the boundaries between timescale divisions can be refined and new divisions and subdivisions proposed.

Tectonics

Lava spews from the earth on Hawaii's Big Island, where two volcanoes—Mauna Loa and Kilauea—continue to add to the island's girth.

Slicing down 1,300 kilometers (810 mi) of western California, the San Andreas Fault marks the stress point between two major tectonic plates.

Old lava crusts the surface of Santiago Island in the Galápagos. The Pacific archipelago made famous by Darwin was shaped by volcanism.

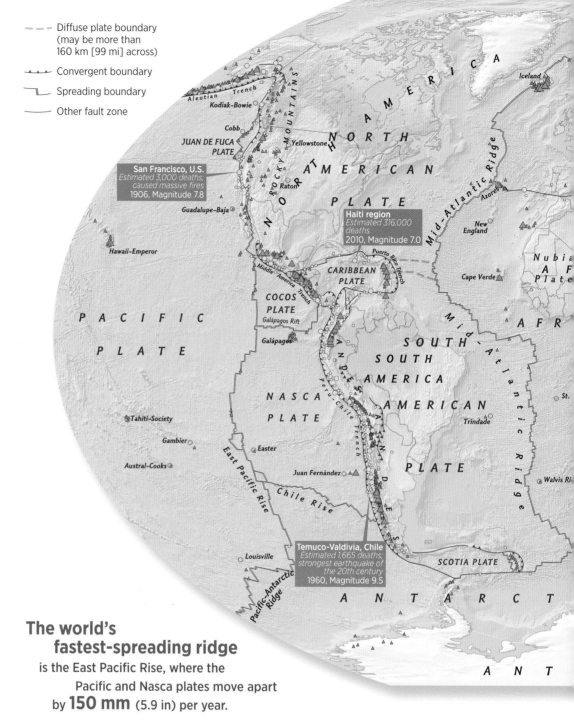

San Francisco, U.S.
*Estimated 3,000 deaths;
caused massive fires*
1906, Magnitude 7.8

Haiti region
*Estimated 316,000
deaths*
2010, Magnitude 7.0

Temuco-Valdivia, Chile
*Estimated 1,665 deaths;
strongest earthquake of
the 20th century*
1960, Magnitude 9.5

The world's fastest-spreading ridge

is the East Pacific Rise, where the Pacific and Nasca plates move apart by **150 mm** (5.9 in) per year.

Like ice on a great lake, Earth's lithosphere—its crust and upper mantle—floats over the planet's molten innards in slow but constant movement. Cracked in many places, it is composed of 16 enormous slabs of rock, called plates, averaging thousands of miles wide and several miles thick. As they perpetually move and grind against each other, the tectonic plates push up mountains, spawn volcanoes, and generate earthquakes and concomitant tsunamis.

Although these often cataclysmic events capture our attention, the movements that cause them are imperceptible—a slow waltz of rafted rock that continues over eons. How slow? The Mid-Atlantic Ridge (see "Spreading" diagram, far right) is being built by magma oozing out between two plates, separating North America and Africa at the speed of a growing human fingernail. The intersections among the plates often mark areas of high volcanic and earthquake activity, caused as plates strain against each other or one dives beneath another. In the Ring of Fire around the Pacific Basin, disastrous earthquakes have impacted Kobe and other more northern cities in Japan as well as Los Angeles and San Francisco in California. In the last several decades, volcanic eruptions with devastating effects have occurred at Mount Pinatubo in the northern Philippines and Mount St. Helens in the state of Washington.

G a k k e l   R i d g e

Location Uncertain A

E U R A S I A N   P L A T E
E U R O P E

At the **Kuril Trench,**
the Pacific Plate is subducting
under the Eurasian Plate at
a rate of **80 mm**
(3.15 in) per year.

Tangshan, China
242,769 deaths
1976, Magnitude 7.5

Sendai, Japan
20,896 deaths;
heavy tsunami damage
2011, Magnitude 9.0

P L A T E

S

A

Plateau of Tibet

H I M A L A Y A

Tibesti
Uplift

ARABIAN
PLATE

I N D I A N
P L A T E

Afar

East Africa

N   P L A T E

Great Rift Valley

Somali

Plate

Comoros

Réunion

PHILIPPINE
PLATE

Kuril Trench

Japan Trench

Ryukyu Trench

Bonin Trench
Izu Trench
Mariana Trench

Philippine Trench

Palau Trench

P A C I F I C

P L A T E

Caroline

Edge of diffuse
plate boundary

Java Trench

CAPRICORN
PLATE

Mid-Indian Ridge

Location Uncertain

A U S T R A L I A N

A U S T R A L I A

P L A T E

East Australia

Tasmantid

Vityaz Trench

N. New Hebrides Trench

Samoa

Tonga Trench

Kermadec Trench

Southwest Indian Ridge

Location Uncertain

Crozet

Kerguelen

Southeast Indian Ridge

P L A T E

A N T A R C T I C A

○ Notable earthquake
since 1900

° Quake since 1900
greater than
magnitude 6

▲ Volcanic eruption
since 1900

▲ Known volcanic
eruption during the
past 10,000 years

○ Selected hot spots

Earth's Interior

By observing how fast the seismic
waves caused by large earthquakes
pass through inner Earth, scientists
have been able to ascertain the composition of the planet's interior. The white-
hot iron core is under pressure so great
that it cannot melt. The next layer,
the outer core, is composed mostly of
liquid iron; it is this layer that creates
Earth's magnetic field. Next comes
the mantle, where viscous rock seeps
like a slow river, its currents created as
hot rock rises and slow rock descends.
The movement of these currents over
eons has caused the rocky outermost
layer of Earth, the lithosphere, to crack,
creating tectonic plates.

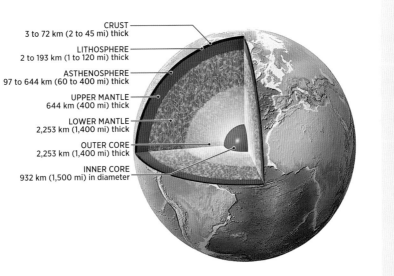

CRUST
3 to 72 km (2 to 45 mi) thick

LITHOSPHERE
2 to 193 km (1 to 120 mi) thick

ASTHENOSPHERE
97 to 644 km (60 to 400 mi) thick

UPPER MANTLE
644 km (400 mi) thick

LOWER MANTLE
2,253 km (1,400 mi) thick

OUTER CORE
2,253 km (1,400 mi) thick

INNER CORE
932 km (1,500 mi) in diameter

Geologic Processes

Accretion

As ocean plates move toward the edges of
continents or island arcs and slide under them,
seamounts are skimmed off and piled up in
submarine trenches. The resulting buildup can
cause continents to grow.

Collision

When two continental plates converge, the
result can be the most dramatic mountain-
building process on Earth. The Himalaya mountain range rose when the Indian subcontinent
collided with Eurasia, driving the land upward.

Faulting

Enormous crustal plates do not slide smoothly.
Strain built up along their edges may release
in a series of small jumps, felt as minor tremors
on land. Extended buildup can cause a sudden
jump, producing an earthquake.

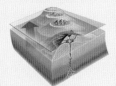

Hot Spots

In the cauldron of inner Earth, some areas
burn hotter than others and periodically blast
through their crustal covering as volcanoes.
Such a "hot spot" built the Hawaiian Islands,
leaving a string of oceanic protuberances.

Spreading

At the divergent boundary known as the Mid-
Atlantic Ridge, oozing magma forces two plates
apart by as much as 20 centimeters (eight
inches) a year. If that rate had been constant,
the ocean could have reached its current width
in 30 million years.

Subduction

When an oceanic plate and a continental
plate converge, the denser sea plate takes a
dive. Plunging back into Earth's interior, it is
transformed into molten material, only to rise
again as magma.

Earth's Surface

Earth's continental surface and ocean floor have evolved over billions of years, producing enormous variations in relief, thanks in large part to the movement of tectonic plates and denudational forces such as weathering and erosion. From Earth's deepest point in the Pacific Ocean's Mariana Trench to its highest, Mount Everest in the Himalaya, the difference in elevation is 19,844 meters (65,105 feet). Beneath the oceans, the variation is greatest—massive volcanoes, near-bottomless trenches, and the great bulk of the tallest mountain, Hawaii's Mauna Kea. On land, vast plateaus create highlands that sweep across South America, Africa, and Asia, while the plains' treeless flats claim their own continental space. Though the forces of nature can alter a landscape over millennia, the forces of man can change the land in the geologic blink of an eye, turning plains to dust bowls and shearing mountaintops for their mineral richness.

Endogenic Landforms

Forces deep within Earth gave rise to mountains and other endogenic landforms. Some mountains were formed when continental plates collided. Others rose as volcanoes when tectonic plates subducted or as plates moved over hot spots in the mantle. Rifting and faulting, which occur near plate boundaries, also generate vertical landforms.

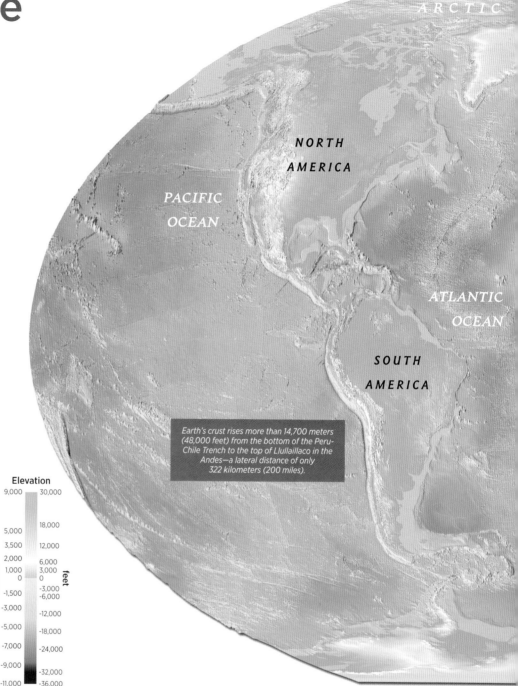

Elevation

meters	feet
9,000	30,000
5,000	18,000
3,500	12,000
2,000	6,000
1,000	3,000
0	0
-1,500	-3,000
	-6,000
-3,000	-12,000
-5,000	-18,000
-7,000	-24,000
-9,000	-32,000
-11,000	-36,000

Depth

Earth's crust rises more than 14,700 meters (48,000 feet) from the bottom of the Peru-Chile Trench to the top of Llullaillaco in the Andes—a lateral distance of only 322 kilometers (200 miles).

Mount Bromo, Indonesia

Dry land covers
only 29%
of the Earth's surface.

A Slice of Earth ▼

A cross section of the oceanic crust includes plains, volcanoes, and ridges. The abyssal plains—large, deep areas of the ocean floor—can reach more than 6,000 meters (19,680 feet) beneath the surface of the ocean, while underwater volcanoes called seamounts rise more than 1,000 meters (3,300 feet) above the seafloor. The 48,000-kilometer (30,000-mile) Mid-Atlantic Ridge, a submarine mountain range, is the longest mountain range in the world. Surrounding most continents is a continental shelf—a shallow, submerged plain. In many places, continental slopes connect the shelf with the oceanic crust in the form of giant escarpments that can descend some 2,000 meters (6,600 feet).

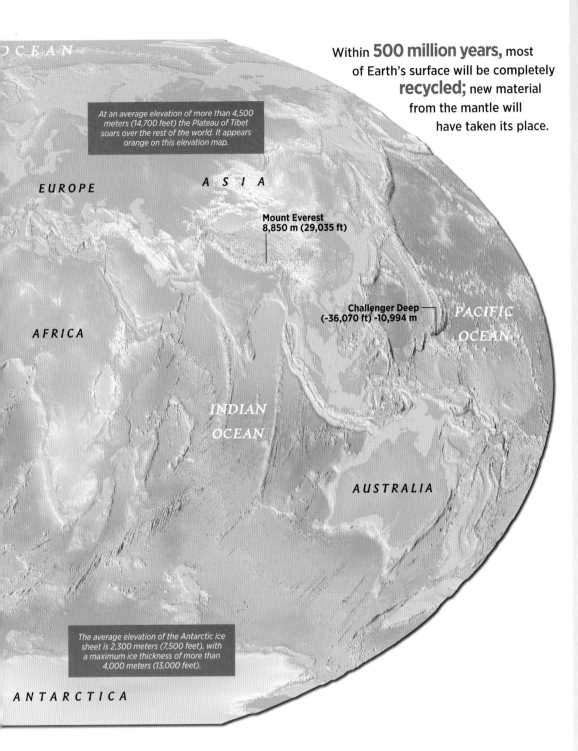

Within 500 million years, most of Earth's surface will be completely **recycled;** new material from the mantle will have taken its place.

At an average elevation of more than 4,500 meters (14,700 feet) the Plateau of Tibet soars over the rest of the world. It appears orange on this elevation map.

EUROPE

ASIA

Mount Everest
8,850 m (29,035 ft)

Challenger Deep
(-36,070 ft) -10,994 m

PACIFIC OCEAN

AFRICA

INDIAN OCEAN

AUSTRALIA

The average elevation of the Antarctic ice sheet is 2,300 meters (7,500 feet), with a maximum ice thickness of more than 4,000 meters (13,000 feet).

ANTARCTICA

Exogenic Landforms

These landforms are created by external agents—weathering by wind, rain, groundwater, ice, and other natural elements—that slowly break down rock. Erosion removes weathered material and transports it from place to place. It continues to shape landforms such as the spires of Bryce Canyon, dramatic coastal cliffs, glaciated regions, and sand dunes, along with many others.

Bryce Canyon Amphitheater, United States

The Twelve Apostles, Australia

Perito Moreno Glacier, Argentina

Namib Desert, Namibia

Earth's Highs and Lows ▲

This computer-generated image of Earth is a digital elevation model—color-coded to show elevation differences. The image was derived from satellite altimetry and shipboard echo-sounding measurements. Earth's deepest point, Challenger Deep at 10,994 meters (36,070 feet) below sea level, is dark blue, while the highest point, Mount Everest at 8,850 meters (29,035 feet) above sea level, is orange. Antarctica, the world's highest continent thanks to its thick ice sheet, shows up in shades of orange, with an average elevation of 2,300 meters (7,500 feet). Green expanses highlight lowland areas, and the adjacent light blue regions reveal underwater continental shelves.

tlas untains | Alps | Mediterranean Ridge | The Steppes | Himalaya | Mount Everest 8,850 m (29,035 ft) | Challenger Deep (-36,070 ft) -10,994 m | Kamchatka Peninsula

EUROPE

ASIA

AFRICA

Arabian Sea

Bay of Bengal

PACIFIC OCEAN

Land Cover

Satellite data provide the most reliable picture of global vegetative cover over time. The map at right is based on imagery from the Moderate Resolution Imaging Spectroradiometer (MODIS), at a spatial resolution of 500 m (1,640 ft).

By recording how different wavelengths of the electromagnetic spectrum reflect from the surface, scientists can derive land cover types through the variation of these reflectances over time. Vast areas of Earth have been altered by humans over millennia, and such changes are captured in the satellite record, contributing to a rich data bank for conservation, biodiversity assessments, and land resource management.

NORTH AMERICA

ATLANTIC OCEAN

PACIFIC OCEAN

SOUTH AMERICA

Urban and **built-up** areas cover **less than 1%** of Earth's total land area.

EVERGREEN NEEDLELEAF FOREST

More than 60 percent of this land is covered by a forest canopy; tree height exceeds 2 m (7 ft). These forests are common in temperate regions of the U.S., Europe, and Asia. In many of them, trees are grown on plantations and logged for the making of paper and building products.

EVERGREEN BROADLEAF FOREST

More than 60 percent of this land is covered by a forest canopy; tree height exceeds 2 m (7 ft). These include rain forests and dominate in the tropics; they have the greatest concentrations of biodiversity. In many areas, farms, ranches, and tree plantations are replacing this land cover.

DECIDUOUS NEEDLELEAF FOREST

More than 60 percent of this land is covered by a forest canopy; tree height exceeds 2 m (7 ft). Trees respond to cold seasons by shedding their leaves simultaneously. This land cover class is dominant only in Siberia, taking the form of larch forests with a short June to August growing season.

DECIDUOUS BROADLEAF FOREST

More than 60 percent of this land is covered by a forest canopy; tree height exceeds 2 m (7 ft). In dry or cold seasons, trees shed their leaves simultaneously. Much of this forest has been converted to cropland in temperate regions, with large remnants found only on steep and remote slopes.

MIXED FOREST

More than 60 percent of this land is covered by a forest canopy; tree height exceeds 2 m (7 ft). Both evergreen and deciduous types appear, with neither having coverage of less than 25 percent or more than 75 percent. This type is largely found between temperate deciduous and boreal evergreen forests.

WOODY SAVANNA

Land has herbaceous or woody understories, and a tree canopy cover of 30 to 60 percent; trees exceed 2 m (7 ft) and may be evergreen or deciduous. This type is common in the tropics and is most highly degraded in areas with long histories of human habitation, such as West Africa.

SAVANNA

Land has herbaceous or woody understories, and a tree canopy cover of 10 to 30 percent; trees exceed 2 m (7 ft) and may be evergreen or deciduous. This type includes classic African savanna as well as open boreal woodlands that demarcate tree lines and the beginning of tundra ecosystems.

CLOSED SHRUBLAND

Bushes or shrubs dominate, with a canopy cover of more than 60 percent. Bushes do not exceed 2 m (7 ft) in height; shrubs or bushes can be evergreen or deciduous. Tree canopy is less than 10 percent. This land cover can be found where prolonged cold or dry seasons limit plant growth.

OPEN SHRUBLAND

Shrubs are dominant, with a canopy cover of between 10 and 60 percent; they do not exceed 2 m (7 ft) in height and can be evergreen or deciduous. The remaining land is either barren or characterized by annual herbaceous cover. This land cover occurs in semiarid or severely cold regions.

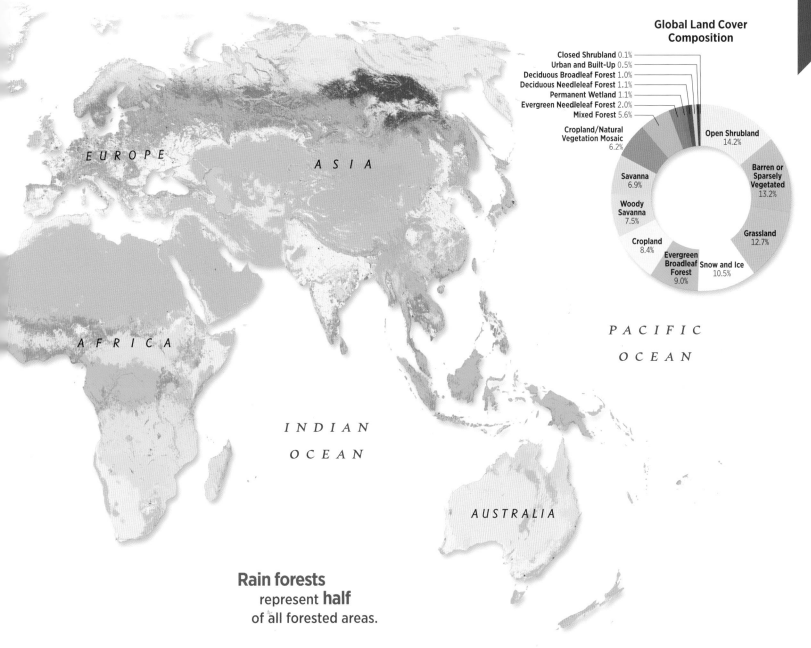

ARCTIC OCEAN

EUROPE

ASIA

AFRICA

PACIFIC OCEAN

INDIAN OCEAN

AUSTRALIA

Rain forests represent **half** of all forested areas.

ANTARCTICA

Global Land Cover Composition

Closed Shrubland 0.1%
Urban and Built-Up 0.5%
Deciduous Broadleaf Forest 1.0%
Deciduous Needleleaf Forest 1.1%
Permanent Wetland 1.1%
Evergreen Needleleaf Forest 2.0%
Mixed Forest 5.6%
Cropland/Natural Vegetation Mosaic 6.2%
Savanna 6.9%
Woody Savanna 7.5%
Cropland 8.4%
Evergreen Broadleaf Forest 9.0%
Snow and Ice 10.5%
Grassland 12.7%
Barren or Sparsely Vegetated 13.2%
Open Shrubland 14.2%

WATER

GRASSLAND

This land has continuous herbaceous cover and less than 10 percent tree or shrub canopy cover. This type occurs in a wide range of habitats. Perennial grasslands in the central United States and Russia, for example, are the most extensive and mark a line of decreased precipitation that limits agriculture.

PERMANENT WETLAND

This permanent mixture of water and herbaceous or woody vegetation can be present in either salt, brackish, or fresh water. The Everglades (pictured) are one of the world's largest permanent wetlands. Other wetlands include the Hudson Bay lowlands and the Sundarbans of India and Bangladesh.

CROPLAND

Crop-producing fields make up more than 60 percent of the landscape. Areas of high-intensity agriculture, including mechanized farming, stretch across temperate regions. Much agriculture in the developing world is fragmented, however, and occurs frequently on small plots of land.

CROPLAND/NATURAL VEGETATION MOSAIC

Lands with a mosaic of croplands, forests, shrubland, and grasslands in which no one component makes up more than 60 percent of the landscape. This land cover class can be seen in much of the U.S.; examples include southwestern Wisconsin and the Susquehanna River Valley (pictured).

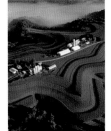

URBAN AND BUILT-UP

Land cover includes buildings, roads, and other manufactured structures. This class was mapped as an independent layer from MODIS 500-meter-resolution imagery (Schneider et al., 2010). Urban and built-up cover represents the most densely developed areas of human habitation.

BARREN OR SPARSELY VEGETATED

Exposed soil, sand, or rocks are typical; the land never has more than 10 percent vegetated cover during any time of year. This includes true deserts, such as the Sahara (Africa) and Gobi (Asia). Desertification, the expansion of deserts due to land degradation or climate change, is a problem in these areas.

SNOW AND ICE

Land has permanent snow and ice; it never has more than 10 percent vegetated cover at any time of year. The greatest expanses of this class can be seen in Greenland, on other Arctic islands, and in Antarctica. Glaciers at high elevations form significant examples in Alaska, the Himalaya, Chile, and Scandinavia.

Oceans

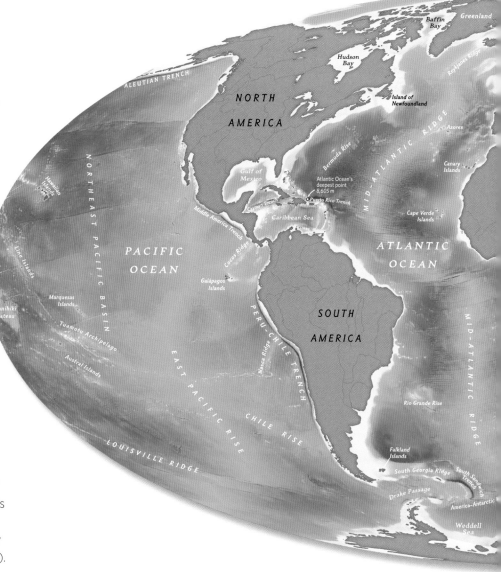

The only planet in our solar system with liquid water at the surface, Earth is known as the blue planet. The majority of Earth's surface (71 percent) is submerged beneath about 1.35 billion cubic kilometers (324 million cubic miles) of saline water; the remaining 29 percent is covered by a less dense continental crust that rises above sea level. Of the total amount of water on Earth's surface, 97.5 percent is saline; approximately 3.5 percent of the total ocean mass is composed of salt.

The global ocean is subdivided into five major basins. The vast Pacific comprises roughly half of the oceans' footprint, followed by—in descending order of size—the Atlantic, Indian, "Southern" (around Antarctica), and Arctic Oceans. The salt water that fills these ocean basins is slowly mixed by a giant density-driven current known as the global conveyor belt, which starts in the northern Atlantic and flows southward into the southern ocean basin and then onward to the Indian and Pacific, taking approximately a thousand years for the entire water exchange. Earth's immense quantity of ocean water plays a critical role in regulating the planet's surface temperature and climate (below, at right) and supports a diverse ecological system that is increasingly being impacted through human activities (below, at left).

Lying below an average ocean depth of more than 3,800 meters (12,400 feet) are towering mountains and the deepest valleys on the planet. The lithospheric plates that make up Earth's surface crust are being continuously created along the vast chain of undersea mountains known as mid-ocean ridges and pulled into the mantle at subduction zones in deep-sea trenches through the process of continental drift. New oceanic crust is formed along the Mid-Atlantic Ridge at a rate of approximately 10 to 30 millimeters (0.4 to 1.2 inches) per year, causing a progressive expansion of the Atlantic. In contrast, oceanic crust is destroyed at subduction zones located around the perimeter of the Pacific Ocean—resulting in numerous island and continental arc volcanoes—known as the Ring of Fire.

The **Pacific Ocean Basin** is **shrinking** as it is subsumed under surrounding continents.

Human Impact on the Oceans

Human activities affect the ocean in many ways, and this map charts how different human drivers of change, from commercial fisheries to land-based pollution, are impacting various marine ecosystems worldwide. The places with the most severe human impact are adjacent to densely populated areas in the North Sea and the South and East China Seas. Today, more than 40 percent of the ocean surface is heavily affected by human activity, and even the remote marine ecosystems of the poles are showing signs of stress.

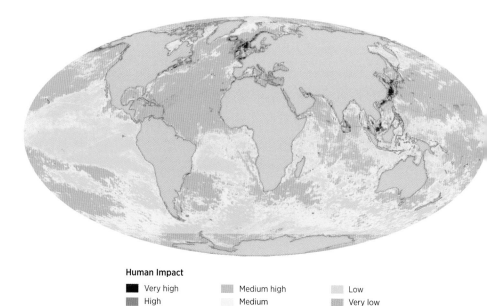

Human Impact

- ■ Very high
- ■ High
- ■ Medium high
- ■ Medium
- ■ Low
- ■ Very low

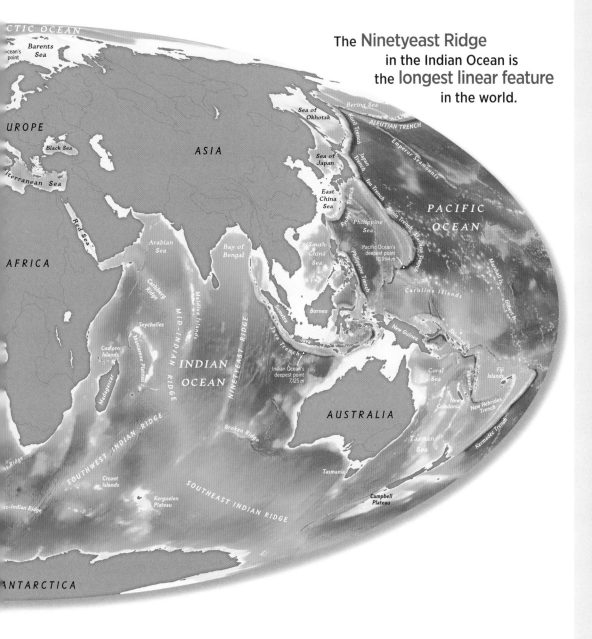

The **Ninetyeast Ridge**
in the Indian Ocean is
the **longest linear feature**
in the world.

Incubator for Earth's first life-forms, the ocean has always been self-regulating and unassailable—that is, until very recently, when one species, the human, has begun to disturb its majesty. But awareness that the ocean can be overexploited and made unhealthy by our activities has grown in the past 50 years, and international efforts to protect its life and waters are now ongoing.

Killer whales *(Orcinus orca)* swim past an oil tanker near the San Juan Islands.

Blackfin barracudas form a spiraling school at 21 meters (70 ft) deep, Solomon Islands.

A dolphin surfs a large wave. Dolphins are found in nearly all of the oceans and seas.

Breaking wave at Le Four Lighthouse, built on a rock near the Brittany coast, France.

Sea Surface Temperatures

A composite of satellite images shows sea surface temperatures in the anticipated lateral bands—the coldest at the poles, the warmest at the Equator. Prevailing winds and ocean currents distort these patterns somewhat through clockwise fluid motion in the Northern Hemisphere and counterclockwise in the Southern. This motion and the high heat capacity of water keep ocean temperatures within a far narrower range than land temperatures. Thus, the oceans act as a giant heat pump modulating Earth's climate.

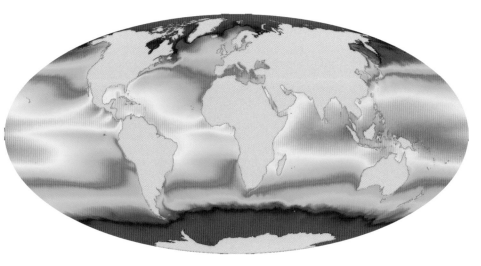

Sea Surface Temperature (°C)

-2   4   10   16   22   28   34   40   44

Fresh Water

With 82,100 square kilometers (31,700 square miles) of surface area, Lake Superior is the largest freshwater lake in the world by surface area.

Europe

North America

Oceania

The Amazon River discharges around 17 trillion liters (4.5 trillion gallons) of water each day—some 15% of all the water that rivers send to the sea.

Africa

South America

Partly due to its remote location in arid southern Africa, the Okavango Delta creates critical wetland habitat for hundreds of thousands of animals.

World of Rivers

Perennial River
Average discharge 1961–1990, hectoliters per second (gallons per second)
— More than 4,921 (130,000)
— 284–4,921 (7,500–130,000)
— 47–283 (1,250–7,499)
— 9–46 (250–1,249)
— Fewer than 9 (250)

Intermittent River
Average discharge 1961–1990, hectoliters per second (gallons per second)
— More than 284 (7,500)
— 47–284 (1,250–7,500)
— 9–46 (250–1,249)
— Fewer than 9 (250)

▱ Glacier or ice cap

Baikal, Earth's oldest and deepest lake, holds vast fresh water reserves but is now threatened by industrial contaminants.

A majority of America's winter produce is grown in California's Imperial Valley, where waters from the embattled Colorado River feed irrigation.

Salmon leap upstream at Brooks Falls, on Alaska's Katmai Peninsula. Its complex water system takes In lakes, wetlands, glaciers, and streams.

Human water use
has been growing at
more than double the rate
of population increase in the
last 100 years.

On average, human beings use 38 liters (10 gallons) or more of fresh water a day for drinking, cooking, and cleaning. It seems like so little, and yet roughly 1.1 billion people lack easy access to fresh water and use far less, spending valuable hours every day hauling and husbanding water. And as the population grows, the demand for water does as well, taxing already strained freshwater resources and making clean water as precious as gold.

In the Middle East, North America, Asia, and elsewhere, fresh water is being diverted for farming or urban use or bought outright by those who can afford it—be they nations, individuals, or businesses. This leaves poor nations and peoples facing an even greater water shortage. While bottom-up solutions like small pumps and drip lines for irrigation may go a long way to alleviate human-caused water problems in the developing world, the worldwide effects of freshwater diversion and depletion have catastrophic effects on the natural world. Rivers deliver essential nutrients downstream, and floodplains and wetlands act as natural filters, but they've been altered in recent decades by dams and other human interventions that have disrupted natural systems. Half of the planet's wetlands disappeared in the past century, and more than 20 percent of the world's known freshwater fish species have become extinct or imperiled in just the past half century. With supplies of fresh water expected to reach crisis levels in the coming century, governments and organizations are working hard to find solutions to the dilemma of sharing what is surely Earth's greatest resource.

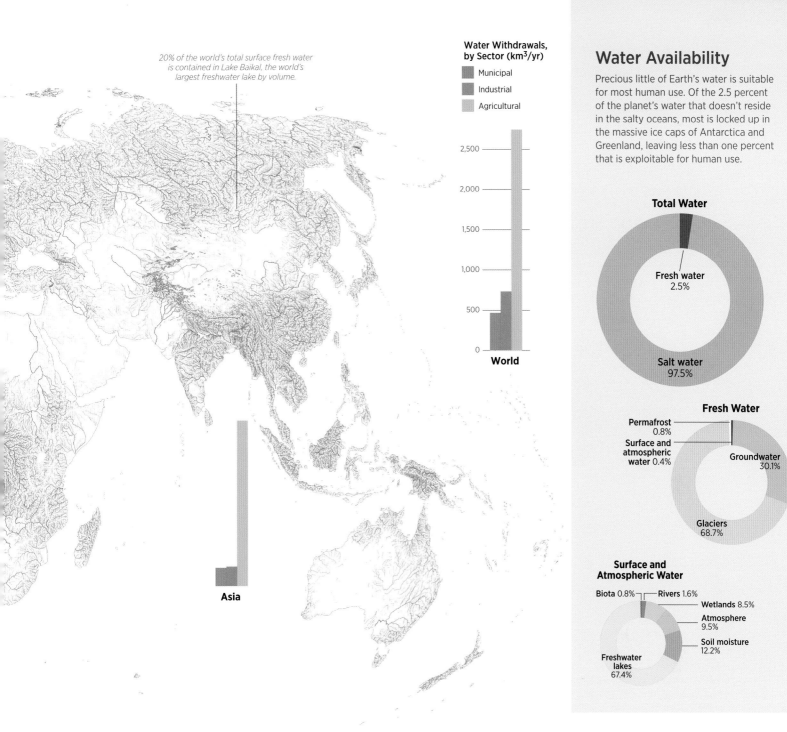

20% of the world's total surface fresh water is contained in Lake Baikal, the world's largest freshwater lake by volume.

Water Withdrawals, by Sector (km³/yr)

- Municipal
- Industrial
- Agricultural

2,500
2,000
1,500
1,000
500
0

World

Asia

Water Availability

Precious little of Earth's water is suitable for most human use. Of the 2.5 percent of the planet's water that doesn't reside in the salty oceans, most is locked up in the massive ice caps of Antarctica and Greenland, leaving less than one percent that is exploitable for human use.

Total Water

Fresh water
2.5%

Salt water
97.5%

Fresh Water

Permafrost
0.8%

Surface and
atmospheric
water 0.4%

Groundwater
30.1%

Glaciers
68.7%

**Surface and
Atmospheric Water**

Biota 0.8% — Rivers 1.6%

Wetlands 8.5%

Atmosphere
9.5%

Soil moisture
12.2%

Freshwater
lakes
67.4%

Mapping Irrigation

In many parts of the world, agriculture is impossible without irrigation. While irrigation needs and methods vary regionally, the need for water to grow food does not. From California's Central Valley to India's Ganges River Valley to the rice paddies of China, irrigation means food for billions of mouths.

Percent Irrigated Area

- 60%–100%
- 30%–59%
- 5%–29%
- Less than 5%
- No data

Safe Drinking Water

The 1.1 billion people lacking clean drinking water must often resort to using water contaminated with pathogens, disease vectors, and chemicals. Water-borne diseases—from cholera to dysentery to salmonella-caused illnesses—claim an estimated 2.2 million lives a year, with young children being the most vulnerable.

Proportion of Population Using Improved Drinking Water Sources, 2010

- More than 90%
- 76%–90%
- 50%–75%
- Less than 50%
- No data

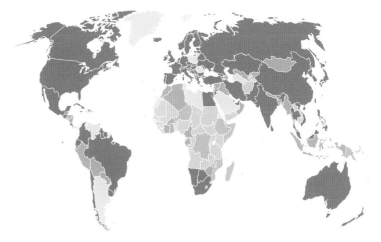

Climate

One of Earth's oldest deserts, the Namib hugs the Atlantic coast of Namibia and receives more moisture from ocean fog than from rain.

Geese in the Canadian Rockies will migrate south when lakes and rivers begin their winter freeze and make it hard for the geese to find food.

Crowded onto a motorbike, three people brave the seasonal monsoon rains that keep Cambodia's rice fields a lush green.

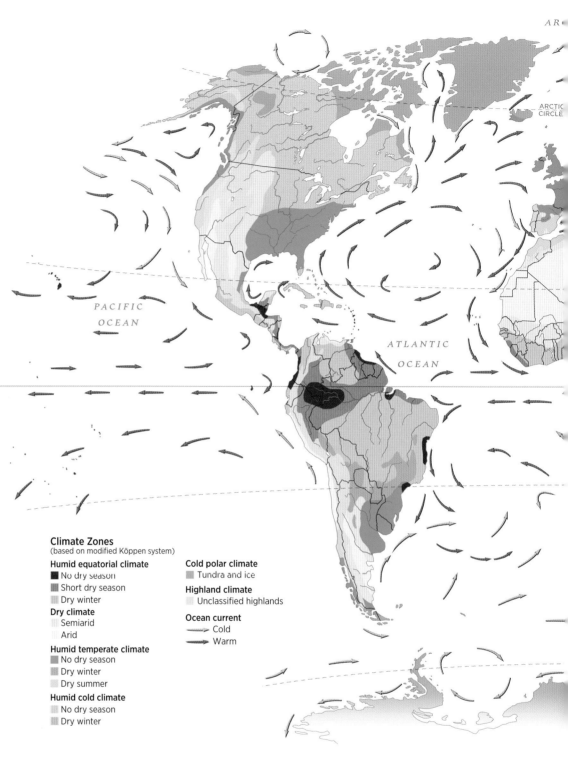

PACIFIC OCEAN

ATLANTIC OCEAN

ARCTIC CIRCLE

Climate Zones
(based on modified Köppen system)

Humid equatorial climate
- No dry season
- Short dry season
- Dry winter

Dry climate
- Semiarid
- Arid

Humid temperate climate
- No dry season
- Dry winter
- Dry summer

Humid cold climate
- No dry season
- Dry winter

Cold polar climate
- Tundra and ice

Highland climate
- Unclassified highlands

Ocean current
- Cold
- Warm

The term *climate* describes the average weather conditions, as measured over many years, that prevail at any given point around the world at a given time of the year. Daily weather may differ dramatically from the norm based on climatic statistics.

Climate zones are primarily controlled by latitude—which governs the prevailing winds, the angle of the sun's rays, and the length of day throughout the year—and by geographical location with respect to mountains and oceans. Elevation, surface attributes, and other variables modify the primary controlling factors.

Comparing global trends shows that latitudinal banding of climate zones is most pronounced over Africa and Asia, where fewer north-south mountain ranges mean less disruption of prevailing winds. In the Western Hemisphere, the high, almost continuous mountain range that extends from western Canada to southern South America helps create dry regions on its leeward slopes. Over the United States, where westerly winds prevail, areas to the east of the range lie in a "rain shadow" and are therefore drier. In northern parts of South America, where easterly trade winds prevail, the rain shadow lies west of the mountains. Ocean effects dominate much of Western Europe and southern parts of Australia.

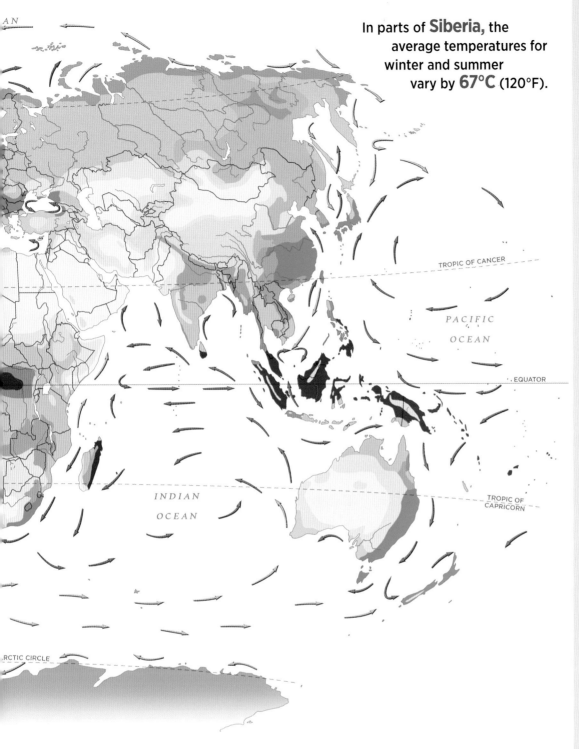

In parts of **Siberia**, the average temperatures for winter and summer vary by **67°C** (120°F).

TROPIC OF CANCER

PACIFIC OCEAN

EQUATOR

INDIAN OCEAN

TROPIC OF CAPRICORN

RCTIC CIRCLE

Temperature and Precipitation Patterns

Temperatures vary seasonally and with latitude as Earth offers first one and then the other hemisphere to more direct sunlight. Temperatures are modified by ocean currents and vegetation, and are depressed by altitude.

Rainfall hugs the Equator but alternates between the Northern and Southern Hemispheres as they experience summer, when the land is warmer than surrounding seas and rising hot air draws in moisture.

Average Temperatures

January

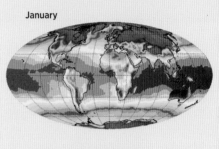

July

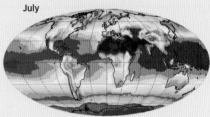

	°Fahrenheit	
-40	32	104
-40	0	40
	°Celsius	

Average Precipitation

January

July

	Inches			
0	4.9	9.8	14.8	19.7
0	125	250	375	500
		Millimeters		

Changing of the Seasons

As Earth circles the sun, the tilt of Earth's axis causes changes in the angle of the sun's rays and in the periods of daylight. Summer arrives when the rays become more direct and their heat is more concentrated. Winter's cold comes as the sun's rays slant at a steeper angle and cover a larger area. Polar areas see the greatest variation, with periods of limited sunlight in the winter and sometimes 24 hours of daylight in the summer.

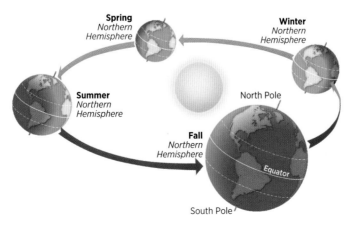

Spring *Northern Hemisphere*

Winter *Northern Hemisphere*

Summer *Northern Hemisphere*

North Pole

Fall *Northern Hemisphere*

Equator

South Pole

Climate **35**

Climate Change

The scientific evidence is clear: Earth is warming at a pace that signals an unprecedented shift in the global climate. Such epochal changes have occurred in the past, but they were set in motion by the natural variations in Earth's orbit that affect the amount of sunlight warming the planet. Those cycles of cooling and warming unfolded slowly, over the course of millennia. In fact, only recently did the 10,000-year period of climate stability that helped human civilization flourish come to an end. Now, though, the climate is changing more rapidly than it has for 650,000 years, and human activity—and the attendant rise in greenhouse gases—is the main cause.

The industrial revolution that created the modern lifestyle has been sustained by burning ever-increasing amounts of fossil fuels—oil, gas, coal. This has flooded the atmosphere with heat-trapping carbon dioxide (CO_2) and triggered a 1°F (0.6°C) spike in average global temperature in the past century, largely in the past 30 years. Scientists now believe that unless greenhouse gas emissions peak in 2015 and are reduced by 50 percent by 2050, the damage to Earth will be irreversible. Already impacts include altered precipitation patterns, melting glaciers and permafrost, more intense weather events, and a rise in sea level.

Particularly hard hit will be people in the tropics and poorer countries without the resources to adapt. Even now they, and others worldwide, are experiencing more extreme weather, water scarcity and food insecurity, more flooding and disease, and population displacement.

Scientists calculate that **Greenland** is losing **five times** as much ice now as in 1992.

In the past 40 years, the number of people **requiring assistance, evacuation, or relocation** due to climate-related events has **doubled every decade.**

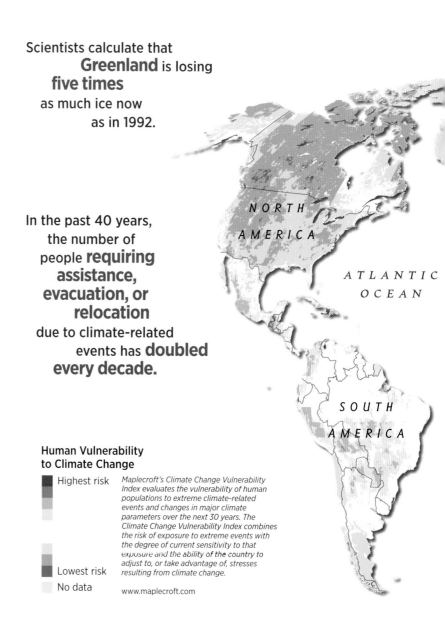

Human Vulnerability to Climate Change

Highest risk

Lowest risk

No data

Maplecroft's Climate Change Vulnerability Index evaluates the vulnerability of human populations to extreme climate-related events and changes in major climate parameters over the next 30 years. The Climate Change Vulnerability Index combines the risk of exposure to extreme events with the degree of current sensitivity to that exposure and the ability of the country to adjust to, or take advantage of, stresses resulting from climate change.

www.maplecroft.com

Rising Temperatures and CO_2

When graphed together, the rise in the global average temperature—an increase of about 1.4°F (0.8°C) since the early 20th century—and the exponential rise in CO_2 concentrations track each other closely over the past half-century. And the trend is only getting more severe: The ten warmest years on record have all occurred since 1998.

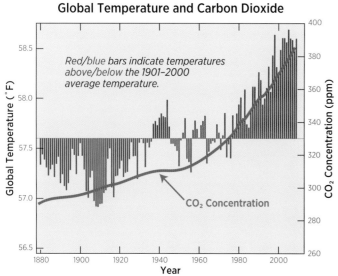

Global Temperature and Carbon Dioxide

Red/blue bars indicate temperatures above/below the 1901–2000 average temperature.

CO₂ Concentration

Global Temperature (°F) — 56.5, 57.0, 57.5, 58.0, 58.5
CO₂ Concentration (ppm) — 260, 280, 300, 320, 340, 360, 380, 400
Year — 1880, 1900, 1920, 1940, 1960, 1980, 2000

Diminishing Ice and Sea Level Rise

Earth is rapidly losing ice. In September 2012, the Arctic ice cap reached a record-breaking minimum, smaller by 777,000 square kilometers (300,000 square miles) than its previous low in 2007. The Greenland ice sheet is shrinking rapidly too, as are Antarctic ice shelves and glaciers. Scientists worry that ice melt could reach a "tipping point" in Earth's climate, and they're sure meltwater will impact sea levels, inundating coasts and islands worldwide.

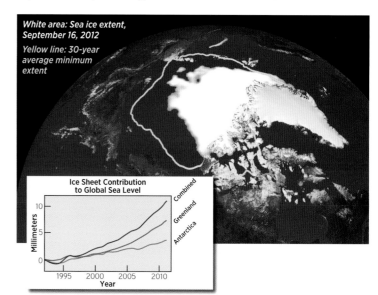

White area: Sea ice extent, September 16, 2012

Yellow line: 30-year average minimum extent

Ice Sheet Contribution to Global Sea Level

Combined
Greenland
Antarctica

Millimeters — 0, 5, 10
Year — 1995, 2000, 2005, 2010

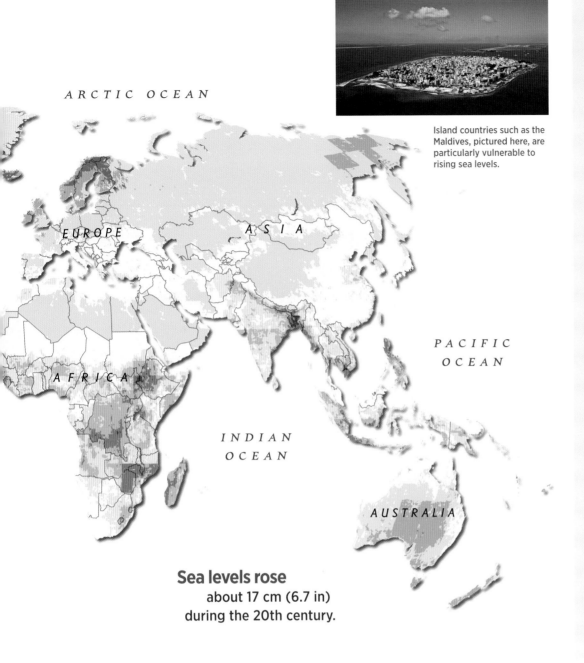

Island countries such as the Maldives, pictured here, are particularly vulnerable to rising sea levels.

Sea levels rose
about 17 cm (6.7 in)
during the 20th century.

Environmental Impacts

No region of the world is immune to the effects of climate change. The effects are seen everywhere, from glacial mountaintops to inland lakes to low-lying islands in the middle of the ocean. Plants and animals whose existence depends on natural cues—such as the timing of spring, the presence of ice, or the number of days below freezing—have been the first to feel the change. Some are migrating to cooler latitudes, but others, especially polar species, can't. Shrinking sea ice in particular spells trouble for polar bears and Pacific walruses, which depend on it to hunt, rest, and travel. The UN estimates that some 20 to 30 percent of Earth's plant and animal species could face extinction if temperatures rise another 2.7°F to 3.7°F (1.5°C to 2°C). No longer an abstraction studied by experts, climate change is a reality impacting the daily lives of all Earth's inhabitants.

Climate change paradox: melting and flooding in some areas; drought and desertification in others.

Ethical Considerations

Since the mid-20th century, there has been a distinct increase across the globe in the frequency of extreme weather events, with succeeding decades seeing more and more devastating hurricanes, typhoons, localized storms, droughts, and flooding—each causing extensive human suffering and taking an ever-higher economic toll. Although wealthy countries, particularly the U.S. and China, produce the most carbon emissions, the poorest countries, including much of Africa, are enduring the greatest impact as age-old systems break down. Glacial meltwater is no longer a reliable source of fresh water in remote mountains or is out of sync with the growing season; rain-fed farming is no longer viable; and malaria spreads as mosquitoes extend their range. And with it all, mortality rates increase.

More than 98%
of **climate change–
related mortality**
occurs in developing
countries.

Countries With the Highest Levels of Greenhouse Gas Emissions

Carbon Dioxide (CO₂) Emissions, Thousand Metric Tons of CO₂, 2009
- 1,000,000–7,700,000
- 100,000–1,000,000
- 10,000–100,000
- 1,000–10,000
- 0–1,000
- No data

Countries That Will Suffer the Most Due to Climate Change

Vulnerability to Climate Health Impact, 2010*
- Acute
- Severe
- High
- Moderate
- Low
- No data

*Based on DARA Climate Vulnerability Monitor, 2012

Natural Hazards

Torrential rains flooded Seoul's streets and caused deadly mudslides throughout South Korea in 2011. Such extreme weather has become more the norm than the exception.

Ruins of a cathedral in Port-au-Prince create a stunning but tragic symbol of the earthquake that devastated southern Haiti in 2010, taking up to 300,000 lives and leaving 1.5 million homeless.

Lightning rakes the desert near Phoenix, Arizona, where extreme heat and moisture moving up from Mexico collide to create spectacular and often violent thunderstorms during the summer.

Roughly **64%** of the world's population has been directly **affected by natural disasters** during the past 20 years.

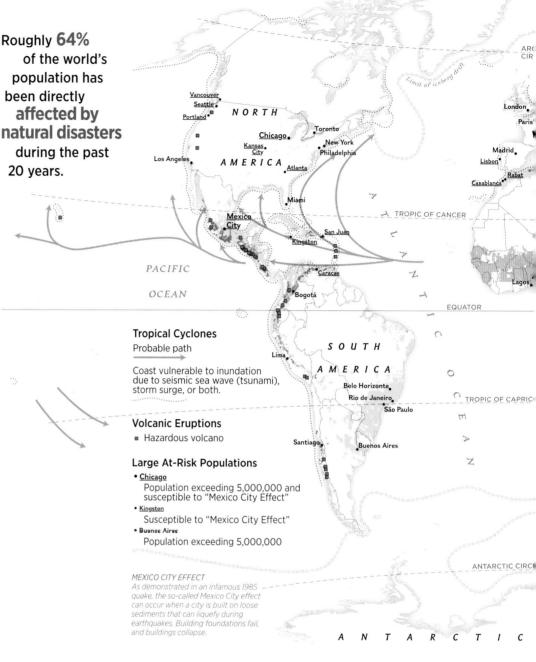

Tropical Cyclones

Probable path

Coast vulnerable to inundation due to seismic sea wave (tsunami), storm surge, or both.

Volcanic Eruptions

▪ Hazardous volcano

Large At-Risk Populations

• Chicago
Population exceeding 5,000,000 and susceptible to "Mexico City Effect"

• Kingston
Susceptible to "Mexico City Effect"

• Buenos Aires
Population exceeding 5,000,000

MEXICO CITY EFFECT
As demonstrated in an infamous 1985 quake, the so-called Mexico City effect can occur when a city is built on loose sediments that can liquefy during earthquakes. Building foundations fail, and buildings collapse.

Earth may be humanity's safe harbor in the vast universe, but our planet is hardly benign. Its ever-dynamic environment—which is subject to earthquakes, tornadoes, and volcanic eruptions as well as to devastating wind, rain, cold, and drought—is far from predictably hospitable. In some ways, we deal with natural disasters better than ever before. Thanks to improved transportation, weather forecasting, and post-disaster interventions, many fewer people are killed by these events today than just a century ago. On the other hand, a natural disaster is more devastating when it occurs in an area already compromised by human activity. The destruction of wetlands and coastal forests allows the full force of waves to reach shorelines that used to be protected. And buildings that cannot withstand Earth's shaking tragically exacerbate human death and suffering when earthquakes hit, as they did in China's Sichuan province in 2008, in Haiti in 2010, and again in 2011 when an earthquake and tsunami in northern Japan seriously compromised three nuclear reactors, threatening fallout as far away as Tokyo.

The trend toward urbanization, which concentrates humans in densely packed areas, only increases the suffering when disasters like Hurricane Sandy, which struck the New York metropolitan area in 2012, occur. In poor countries, such catastrophes are often followed by outbreaks of disease and by permanent displacement. Living is most dangerous where natural hazard, human habitation, and debilitating poverty collide. From Indonesia to India to South America, those precariously perched on fault lines, flood plains, and storm-wracked coasts watch and wait for the next disaster to strike.

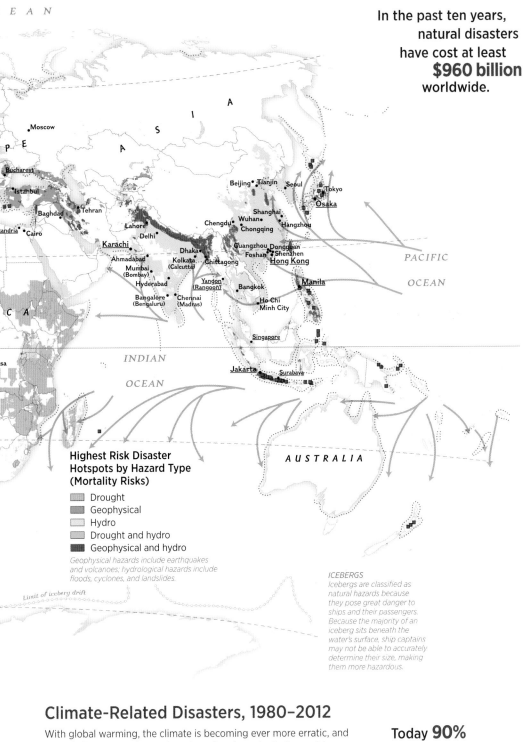

O C E A N

In the past ten years, natural disasters have cost at least **$960 billion** worldwide.

Highest Risk Disaster Hotspots by Hazard Type (Mortality Risks)

- Drought
- Geophysical
- Hydro
- Drought and hydro
- Geophysical and hydro

Geophysical hazards include earthquakes and volcanoes; hydrological hazards include floods, cyclones, and landslides.

Limit of iceberg drift

ICEBERGS
Icebergs are classified as natural hazards because they pose great danger to ships and their passengers. Because the majority of an iceberg sits beneath the water's surface, ship captains may not be able to accurately determine their size, making them more hazardous.

PACIFIC OCEAN

INDIAN OCEAN

AUSTRALIA

Impacts

Floods, droughts, and earthquakes are the natural disasters that most impact humanity, and many vulnerable people live in poverty in Asia, where a single devastating event can spell doom. In the past few years, though, North America has ranked as the continent with the most volatile weather and the largest increase in weather-related devastation, with tornadoes, hurricanes, thunderstorms, floods, drought, and extreme heat impacting millions of people and costing billions of dollars.

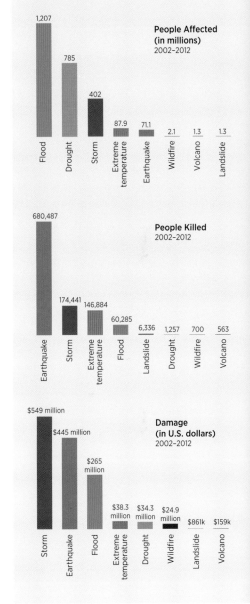

People Affected (in millions) 2002-2012

- Flood: 1,207
- Drought: 785
- Storm: 402
- Extreme temperature: 87.9
- Earthquake: 71.1
- Wildfire: 2.1
- Volcano: 1.3
- Landslide: 1.3

People Killed 2002-2012

- Earthquake: 680,487
- Storm: 174,441
- Extreme temperature: 146,884
- Flood: 60,285
- Landslide: 6,336
- Drought: 1,257
- Wildfire: 700
- Volcano: 563

Damage (in U.S. dollars) 2002-2012

- Storm: $549 million
- Earthquake: $445 million
- Flood: $265 million
- Extreme temperature: $38.3 million
- Drought: $34.3 million
- Wildfire: $24.9 million
- Landslide: $861k
- Volcano: $159k

Climate-Related Disasters, 1980–2012

With global warming, the climate is becoming ever more erratic, and natural disasters are increasing at an alarming rate. In the past two decades, they have doubled, from some 200 a year to more than 400, with nine out of ten being climate related. Droughts, extreme temperatures (2012 had the tenth highest on record), violent storms (2010 and 2011 were the wettest on record), and other weather events wreak havoc and uproot millions of people a year.

Today **90%** of natural disasters are **climate related.**

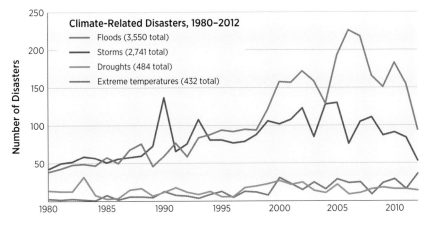

Climate-Related Disasters, 1980–2012

- Floods (3,550 total)
- Storms (2,741 total)
- Droughts (484 total)
- Extreme temperatures (432 total)

Number of Disasters — 250, 200, 150, 100, 50

1980 1985 1990 1995 2000 2005 2010

The three largest cities likely to be affected by various types of hazards:

Cyclones
Tokyo, Shanghai, Manila

Floods
Tokyo, Delhi, Mexico City

Droughts
Kolkata, Karachi, Los Angeles

Landslides
Taipei, Bandung, Quito

Earthquakes
Los Angeles, Manila, Istanbul

Volcanoes
Naples, Quito, Bogor

Human Impact

Earth's 4.5-billion-year history has been characterized by epochs—arenas of time that leave a clear record in the planet's rock layers. These geologic epochs last from a few million to tens of millions of years, but the most recent one, the Holocene, which began when the last ice age ended, may have come to a sudden end after only 11,500 years. Some scientists now believe a new and entirely different phase in Earth's history has begun, and they're calling it the Anthropocene— or "new man" epoch—an age in which humans are radically changing the planet.

The Anthropocene's origins have been dated back to 1700 and the industrial revolution, when humans suddenly acquired an unprecedented ability to exploit energy, especially fossil fuels, and thereby manipulate the environment. As technologies have advanced since then, so has this manipulation. Now human impacts—habitat conversion for land use, environmental pollution, and plant and animal extinctions—are leaving a record in the rock, the very definition of an epoch.

At the beginning of the industrial revolution, almost half of Earth's land was still without significant human populations or use of land; most of the other half, too, was seminatural, with only the light footprint of agriculture or small settlements. But with industrialization, human influences on the biosphere began to change dramatically. As urban centers attracted more and more workers, intensive agricultural and forestry techniques altered more and more of the terrestrial biosphere, from its rock layers to its ocean waters to its atmosphere—changing the very nature of planet Earth.

In the year 1700,
only 5% of ice-free land
was used intensively
by humans.
By the year 2000,
that had increased to
more than 39%.

Anthromes

Dense Settlements
- Urban
- Mixed settlements

Villages
- Rice villages
- Irrigated villages
- Rainfed villages
- Pastoral villages

Croplands
- Residential irrigated croplands
- Residential rainfed croplands
- Populated croplands
- Remote croplands

Rangelands
- Residential rangelands
- Populated rangelands
- Remote rangelands

Seminatural
- Residential woodlands
- Populated woodlands
- Remote woodlands
- Inhabited treeless and barren lands

Wildlands
- Wild woodlands
- Wild treeless and barren lands

The towers of a large housing complex in Shanghai speak to the astonishing growth of Chinese cities in recent years.

A lavender field in Hokkaido, Japan, scents the air and colors the view, but the human footprint rarely lies so gently on the land.

Earth's largest salt flat offers a route across Bolivia's Altiplano and a breeding ground for flamingoes.

Wildlands now persist on **less than 25%** of Earth's ice-free land, mostly in the colder and drier reaches of the biosphere.

Human Influences Over Time

Early in the 20th century, Earth passed a milestone: its terrestrial biosphere passed from the mostly wild and lightly used lands that had characterized the planet for eons to land under the influence of intense human development and use. That milestone heralds what scientists believe is an irreversible transformation of Earth's ecology. From now on humans, not natural influences, will define the world's biomes, creating anthropogenic biomes—"anthromes."

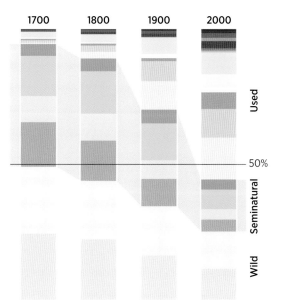

1700   1800   1900   2000

Used

50%

Seminatural

Wild

Anthromes

Dense Settlements
- ▉ Urban
- ▉ Mixed settlements

Villages
- ▉ Rice villages
- ▒ Irrigated villages
- ▉ Rainfed villages
- ▓ Pastoral villages

Croplands
- ▢ Residential irrigated croplands
- ▢ Residential rainfed croplands
- ▢ Populated croplands
- ▢ Remote croplands

Rangelands
- ▓ Residential rangelands
- ▒ Populated rangelands
- ▢ Remote rangelands

Seminatural
- ▓ Residential woodlands
- ▒ Populated woodlands
- ▢ Remote woodlands
- ▓ Inhabited treeless and barren lands

Wildlands
- ▢ Wild woodlands
- ▢ Wild treeless and barren lands

Population: Density and Growth

In the past millennium, world population inched up only slightly from century to century—until the last 150 years. Since then, advances in technology and health care have decreased infant mortality and increased general longevity, spurring an exponential fivefold growth in worldwide population. That swift swell of humanity has put profound stresses on natural resources and systems, the overall effects of which are only now beginning to be observed in the planet's atmosphere, oceans, and biosphere.

In recent decades, though, Japan and Europe's rich industrialized nations have shown almost no growth or even a downturn in population, as birthrates have dropped. Many of these countries have had to rely on immigrant workers to keep their economies thriving, while China's young work population has helped fuel its stupendous economic rise on the world stage. Meanwhile, in many poorer countries in the Middle East and Africa, where sometimes half the population is below the age of 20, lack of jobs and lack of educational opportunities create a continuing cycle of poverty and often civil unrest.

Today, some 360,000 humans are born daily, most in poor African, Asian, and South American countries. The world population topped seven billion in 2011, and by 2025, that figure is expected to reach eight billion, after which UN projections show population growth slowing substantially.

Shoppers crowd Shanghai's popular Nanjing Road, one of the world's busiest commercial districts.

The eastern half of the United States is much more densely populated than the west. The difference in density closely corresponds to the area receiving at least 50 cm (20 in) of precipitation per year.

In South America, the population forms two wide bands, one along each coast. The Amazon rainforest, impenetrable for so long, is now being encroached upon as Brazilian ranchers and farmers move into the area.

Chicago 9,676,400
New York 20,351,700
Los Angeles 13,395,000
Mexico City 20,445,790
Lima 9,129,790
Rio de Janeiro 11,959,730
São Paulo 19,924,458
Buenos Aires 13,527,850

Population Density

People per Square Kilometer	People per Square Mile
More than 195	More than 500
40–195	101–500
10–39	25–100
1–9	1–24
Less than 1	Less than 1

Tokyo 37,217,390 — Urban agglomeration population (2012)

By **2025,** the world population is expected to reach **8 billion.**

A.D. 1 50 100 150 200 250 300 350 400 450 500 550 600 650 700 750
Year

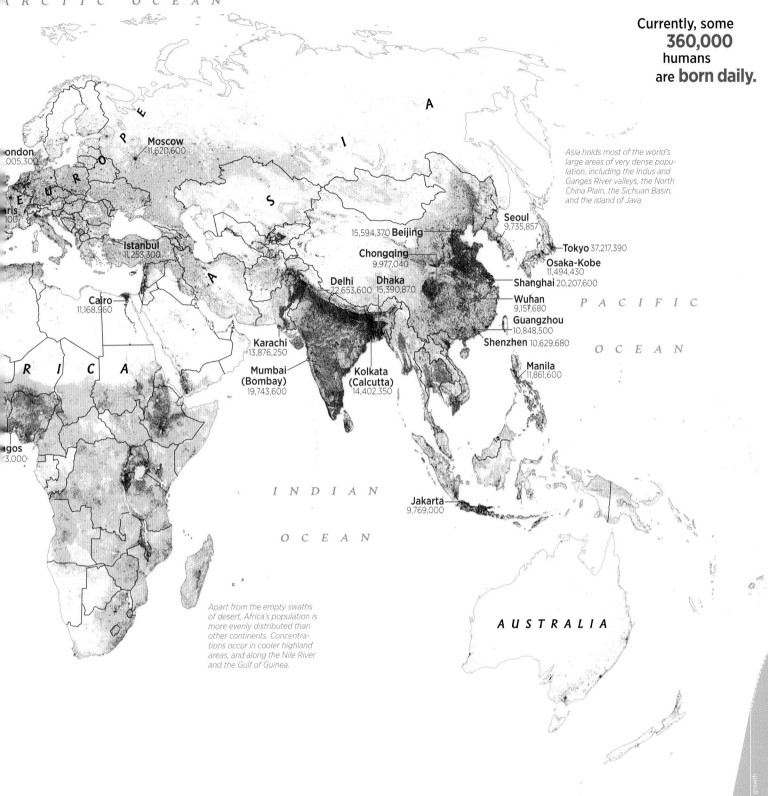

Currently, some
360,000
humans
are **born daily.**

A
S
I
A

Asia holds most of the world's large areas of very dense population, including the Indus and Ganges River valleys, the North China Plain, the Sichuan Basin, and the island of Java.

EUROPE

London
005,300

Moscow
11,620,600

ris
100

Istanbul
11,253,300

Cairo
11,168,960

A S A

Delhi
22,653,600

Dhaka
15,390,870

15,594,370 Beijing

Chongqing
9,977,040

Seoul
9,735,857

Tokyo 37,217,390

Osaka-Kobe
11,494,430

Shanghai 20,207,600

Wuhan
9,157,680

Guangzhou
10,848,500

Shenzhen 10,629,680

PACIFIC

OCEAN

Karachi
13,876,250

Mumbai
(Bombay)
19,743,600

Kolkata
(Calcutta)
14,402,350

Manila
11,861,600

RICA

gos
3,000

INDIAN

OCEAN

Jakarta
9,769,000

Apart from the empty swaths of desert, Africa's population is more evenly distributed than other continents. Concentrations occur in cooler highland areas, and along the Nile River and the Gulf of Guinea.

AUSTRALIA

Regional Population Growth Disparities

Two centuries ago, with the industrial revolution, world population began to arc up, eventually making an almost vertical climb. Today, Asia and Africa top the population growth chart; China and India now have more than a billion people each, though Africa has the fastest growth rate overall. Despite continued growth, the populations of North America and Australia fall at the bottom of the chart, below Latin America and Europe. Much of this is owing to fertility rates, which vary wildly: A 2012 study estimates more than seven children per woman in Niger to fewer than one child per woman in Singapore and Macau. Western Europe has the most pronounced regional decline.

Asia
Africa
Latin America
Europe
North America
Australia & Oceania

Number of people (in billions)

Projected growth

9
8
7
6
5
4
3
2
1
0

900 950 1000 1050 1100 1150 1200 1250 1300 1350 1400 1450 1500 1550 1600 1650 1700 1750 1800 1850 1900 1950 2000 2050
Year

Population: Demographics

Extrapolating what is to come by evaluating current trends is central to demographics. Current census figures (compiled by most developed countries), fertility rates, and life-expectancy projections all factor into predictions for what the coming decades will hold. Several trends seem likely to continue and define how and where humans will live on the planet. Chief among them is the "demographic divide"—the widening gulf between the developed world and the developing world. In general, the wealthier nations are expected to see far slower population growth. Even now their fertility rates are decreasing and are expected to continue that way, a trend that has taken demographers by surprise. At the same time, older people in these countries are living longer, with an average life expectancy of 75 years. In developing countries, younger people still outnumber older ones, but by 2050, demographers expect that the number of people worldwide who are 60 and older will be about 3.5 times more than the number of children 4 and under.

The trend toward urbanization and the growth of cities is also expected to change the pace and character of life, particularly in Asia and Africa, where megacities of 10 million people will be home to more and more of the population. By 2050, two-thirds of humanity is expected to live in cities.

Fertility

The year 2003 marked the first time in human history that more than half of all women lived in areas where the rate of reproduction was lower than the rate of replacement. That downward trend in fertility rates is expected to continue, but for now Central Africa is untouched by it, with rates far higher than other regions.

Total Fertility Rate, 2012
- More than 5.9
- 4.0–5.9
- 2.2–3.9
- 1.6–2.1
- Less than 1.6

Migration

International migration has reached its highest level, with foreign workers now dominating the labor force in several Middle Eastern countries and with immigrant workers proving essential to rich countries with low birthrates. Political instability, religious persecution, and disasters both environmental and natural contribute large numbers of refugees to the migrant mix worldwide.

Net Migration Rate, 2012
(per 1,000 people)
- 3 or greater immigration
- .01–2.9 immigration
- No net migration
- .01–2.9 emigration
- 3 or greater emigration
- No data

Disparities in Population Growth

A bar graph depicting a population's age and gender distribution (males in blue, females in light red) provides a snapshot of the present from which we can deduce future trends. Graphs of countries with high birthrates and high percentages of young, such as Nigeria, look like pyramids. Those for countries such as Italy, whose birthrate is below the replacement fertility level of 2.1 children per couple, have bulges in the higher age brackets, showing a situation that strains the economy. The United States' graph clearly shows the baby boom—a sharp increase in the birthrate—in the years after World War II. As nations develop and access to medical care improves, their graphs show pyramids with narrower bases.

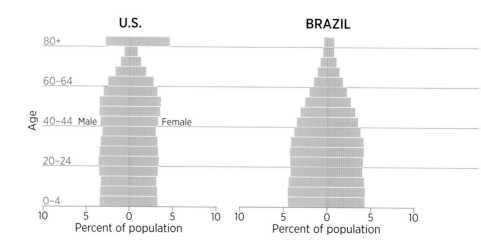

Life Expectancy

An **Afghani male** can expect to live only **44 years,** whereas the average **Japanese male** ages to **80.**

The gap in life expectancy between developed and developing nations has narrowed as better medical care and education have lowered the infant mortality rate. Yet in some countries, including many in Africa, people still die early. In Asia, an Afghani male can expect to live only 44 years, whereas the average Japanese male ages to 80.

Life Expectancy at Birth, 2012
(in years, both sexes)
- 80 or older
- 75–79
- 65–74
- 55–64
- 54 or younger
- No data

Projected Population

By 2050, the world population is projected to pass nine billion, with virtually all of that growth in the developing countries of Africa, Asia, Latin America, and Oceania. If current trends continue, the global population balance will continue to shift dramatically from today's wealthier countries to today's poorer countries.

Percentage of Population Change
(2012–2050, projected)
- More than 100
- 76–100
- 26–75
- 0–25
- Population decline

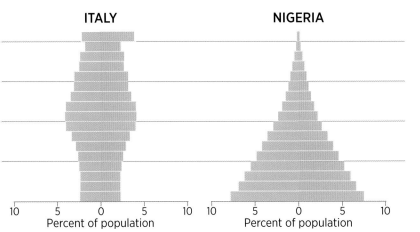

ITALY

NIGERIA

Percent of population

Percent of population

By **2050,** demographers expect the number of people worldwide who are **60 or older** will be about **3.5 times more** than the number of children **four and under.**

Highest Fertility
(number of children born per woman)

Country	Rate
Niger	7.1
Somalia	6.4
Burundi	6.4
Mali	6.3
Angola	6.3

Lowest Fertility
(number of children born per woman)

Country	Rate
Taiwan (China)	1.1
Latvia	1.1
Macao (China)	1.2
Singapore	1.2
Andorra	1.2

Highest Net Immigration
(migrants per 1,000 people)

Country	Rate
Qatar	40.6
United Arab Emirates	16.8
Singapore	15.6
Bahrain	14.7
Cyprus	10.8

Highest Net Emigration
(migrants per 1,000 people)

Country	Rate
Jordan	33.4
Syria	27.8
Federated States of Micronesia	21.0
Tonga	17.9
Nauru	15.0

Highest Life Expectancy
(both sexes)

Country	Number of Years
Hong Kong (China)	83
Japan	83
San Marino	83
Australia	82
Spain	82

Lowest Life Expectancy
(both sexes)

Country	Number of Years
Afghanistan	44
Zimbabwe	46
Guinea-Bissau	48
Swaziland	49
Zambia	49

Greatest % Population Change
(2012–2050)

Country	% Change
Niger	233%
Zambia	224%
Malawi	213%
Angola	202%
Tanzania	190%

Greatest % Population Decline
(2012–2050)

Country	% Change
Moldova	-36%
Georgia	-26%
Japan	-25%
Bulgaria	-22%
Bosnia and Herzegovina	-21%

Urbanization: Megacities

In 1950, New York and Tokyo were the only cities that had more than ten million inhabitants. By 2025, the UN predicts there will be 37 such megacities around the world, home to roughly 13.6 percent of the human population. Only very recently, in 2008, did city dwellers outnumber Earth's rural population, but by 2050, 67 percent of the planet's people are expected to live in urban areas.

Throughout the world, urbanization is picking up speed, but this change is happening far more rapidly in less developed regions, where the race is on to urbanize. Cities in countries like China are swollen with new residents seeking jobs and a better life for themselves and their children. While cities in the developing world continue to grow at a feverish pace, the growth of megacities in the developed world has lost some momentum, as natural population growth and rural-to-urban migration rates have fallen. Some cities are also experiencing counterurbanization, with residents escaping to smaller cities or rural areas in search of lower population density, pollution, and crime.

Centers of power, wealth, ideas, and culture, cities act as magnets for underemployed populations living elsewhere. Yet new urbanites, often unskilled, may settle into worse poverty than they knew before. Where urban growth is at its fastest, vast, overcrowded slums sometimes encircle entire cities; other slums spring up alongside modern luxury buildings, highlighting the great gulf between rich and poor. Many cities are unable to keep pace with growth, forcing slum dwellers to live without clean water, sewage disposal, or electricity, only exacerbating the spread of diseases. With their dense concentrations of humans—and in the less developed world, also animals—cities hold the potential for catastrophic and quickly spreading outbreaks of historic proportions.

Approximately one in 20 people worldwide live in megacities today. That number will be one in 7 by the year 2025.

NORTH AMERICA

Los Angeles 13,400,000

New York 20,350,000

New York was the world's first megacity, reaching 10 million people by 1930. Its population did not change significantly between 1970 and 1990.

Mexico City 20,450,000

Mexico City is the largest urban agglomeration in the Western Hemisphere, with a population of 20,450,000.

Paris 10,620,000

Lagos 11,220,000

SOUTH AMERICA

Rio de Janeiro 11,960,000

São Paulo 19,920,000

São Paulo is the Southe[rn] Hemisphere's largest me[tro]politan area, with a pop[ulation] of 19,920,000.

Buenos Aires 13,530,000

Megacities (over 10 million)
- population in 2011
- population in 1990
- population in 1970

Circle sizes are based on population.

Other cities (4 million–9.9 million)
- ● 8 million–9.9 million
- ● 6 million–7.9 million
- • 4 million–5.9 million

Average Annual Growth Rate of the Urban Population, 2005–2010
- 3% or more
- 2–2.99%
- 1–1.99%
- 0–0.99%
- Population reduction

Growth in More Developed vs. Less Developed Regions

From the mid-20th to the mid-21st century, prospects for urbanization have increased sharply in the developing world while declining in developed regions. And throughout the globe, rural areas, which were the bulwarks of population until the past century, have lost ground. By 2020, half of Asia is expected to live in urban areas, and by 2035, the same will be true for Africa. B[y] 2050, half of the world's projected 9.3 billion people will concentrate in urban areas of these now-developing regions, while the more developed countries wil[l] be 86 percent urban.

Population in Billions

1950 1960 1970 1980 1990 2000 2010 2020 2030 2040 2050

Urban Population   Rural Population

More developed regions

Less developed regions

The world's **urban population** is expected to **increase** from **3.6 billion** in 2011 to **6.3 billion** in 2050.

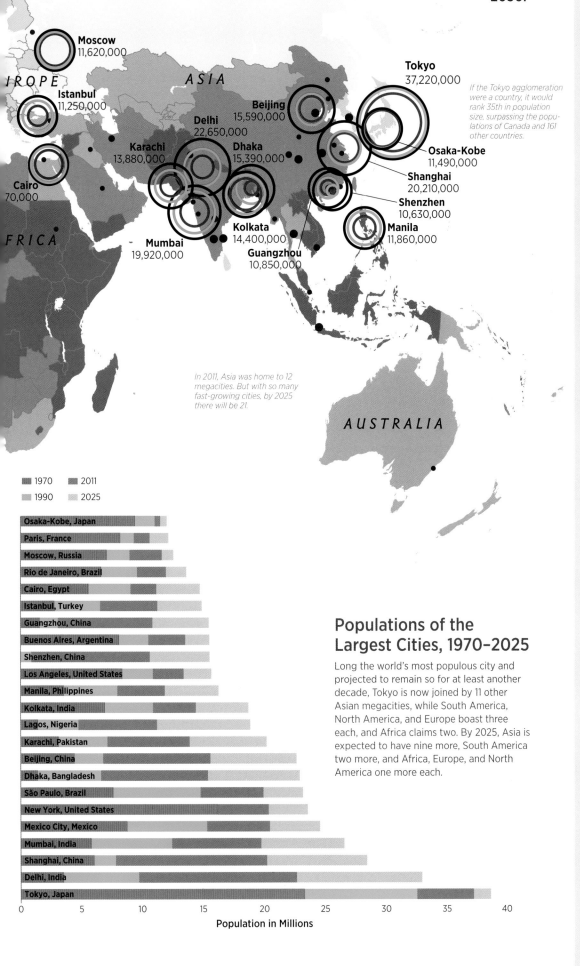

Moscow
11,620,000

IROPE

Istanbul
11,250,000

ASIA

Cairo
70,000

FRICA

Delhi
22,650,000

Karachi
13,880,000

Beijing
15,590,000

Dhaka
15,390,000

Mumbai
19,920,000

Kolkata
14,400,000

Guangzhou
10,850,000

Tokyo
37,220,000

If the Tokyo agglomeration were a country, it would rank 35th in population size, surpassing the populations of Canada and 161 other countries.

Osaka-Kobe
11,490,000

Shanghai
20,210,000

Shenzhen
10,630,000

Manila
11,860,000

In 2011, Asia was home to 12 megacities. But with so many fast-growing cities, by 2025 there will be 21.

AUSTRALIA

■ 1970   ■ 2011
■ 1990   ■ 2025

Populations of the Largest Cities, 1970–2025

Long the world's most populous city and projected to remain so for at least another decade, Tokyo is now joined by 11 other Asian megacities, while South America, North America, and Europe boast three each, and Africa claims two. By 2025, Asia is expected to have nine more, South America two more, and Africa, Europe, and North America one more each.

Osaka-Kobe, Japan
Paris, France
Moscow, Russia
Rio de Janeiro, Brazil
Cairo, Egypt
Istanbul, Turkey
Guangzhou, China
Buenos Aires, Argentina
Shenzhen, China
Los Angeles, United States
Manila, Philippines
Kolkata, India
Lagos, Nigeria
Karachi, Pakistan
Beijing, China
Dhaka, Bangladesh
São Paulo, Brazil
New York, United States
Mexico City, Mexico
Mumbai, India
Shanghai, China
Delhi, India
Tokyo, Japan

0   5   10   15   20   25   30   35   40
Population in Millions

City Living

A riot of styles, cultures, histories, colors, and cravings, the world's cities differ vastly in character and geography—some at the edge of mountains or deserts, others occupying valleys or coastlines. They also vary widely in what they give to their citizenry, and what they take. From the comforts of New York, Tokyo, and Paris to the favelas of Rio and the slums of Mumbai, cities are both challenging and rewarding, often pushing humankind to the limits of its creativity—and endurance.

São Paulo, Brazil

New York City, United States

Delhi, India

Tokyo, Japan

Urbanization: Other Cities

Cities can come in many forms and sizes. The UN tracks urban areas with populations in excess of half a million people, and by that standard, there are now almost a thousand such cities worldwide. The majority, 525 of them, have populations ranging from half a million to a million, but a few claim 20 and even 30 million inhabitants. In between these extremes lay medium-size cities with a million to just under 5 million residents (394 of them) and large cities with populations ranging from 5 million to just under 10 million (40 of them). Demographers consider these "megacities in waiting"—cities whose populations will at some point in the future top 10 million; more than 75 percent of them are located in developing countries, where the ongoing trend of urbanization is altering age-old patterns of life.

Currently three in every five urbanites live in cities of fewer than a million people, but the UN projects that in just a dozen years this figure will change to two in every five, as cities grow ever larger. By 2025, 47 percent of the urban population will probably live in cities of more than a million.

In human history, widespread urbanization is an extremely new phenomenon. Even as recently as 1930 only some 400 million people, or a fifth of the total population, lived in cities, while the rest lived in small rural communities and relied on the same subsistence patterns that had existed almost since the dawn of civilization. Yet as early as 1810, London had topped a million people, setting a trend that was about to explode. In the subsequent two centuries—as technological innovations and the availability and use of fossil fuels increased the means and methods of manufacturing, transportation, and global trade—cities became magnets for an ever-swelling flood of humanity. Today, urban centers are the loci of life, affecting everything and everyone on the planet.

Over half of the world's 3.6 billion urban dwellers live in cities or towns with fewer than 500,000 inhabitants.

China, India, and the United States account for 37% of the world's urban population.

Although 73% of Europe's population lives in urban areas, only 9% lives in cities with more than 5 million inhabitants.

North America—along with Australia and New Zealand—has a relatively high level of urbanization, at over 80%.

At 79%, the level of urbanization in Latin America and the Caribbean is exceptionally high among the less developed regions.

Cities by Population
- 10 million or more
- 5 million–10 million
- 1 million–5 million
- 750,000–1 million
- More developed regions
- Less developed regions

Distribution of Cities by Population and Area

By 2025, an anticipated half billion people will live in megacities, and most of them will be in the less developed regions of the world, reversing historical trends in which the Western, industrialized world was far more urbanized and the less developed world much more rural. Even in 2011, 78 percent of the more developed world's population lived in urban settings, compared to 47 percent in the less developed world. In Europe and Africa, the majority of these urbanites live in small cities of fewer than 500,000, and only some nine percent live in cities of more than five million people. In Asia, Latin America, and North America, by contrast, urbanites live in large cities, which are getting ever larger.

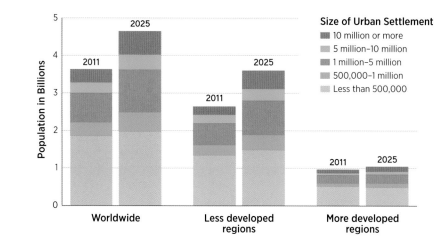

Size of Urban Settlement
- 10 million or more
- 5 million–10 million
- 1 million–5 million
- 500,000–1 million
- Less than 500,000

Population in Billions (y-axis)

Worldwide: 2011, 2025
Less developed regions: 2011, 2025
More developed regions: 2011, 2025

ASIA

AUSTRALIA

Despite being home to some of the largest cities, Asia and Africa are mostly rural, with only 45% and 40%, respectively, of their populations living in urban areas.

The Timeless City

Climate, geography, and history are the features that most frequently define cities, giving them their raison d'être. The past can meld into the present or disappear into the future, as cities are repurposed and reimagined from decade to decade and century to century. The coming age of urbanization could be a force for positive change worldwide, resulting in dynamic solutions to challenges now facing humankind and the planet.

Vancouver, Canada: Population 2,235,000

Valparaíso, Chile: Population 874,000

Hamburg, Germany: Population 1,786,000

Perth, Australia: Population 1,617,000

Contributions to Urbanization, by Country

As urban populations swell in the next half century, the greatest growth will come in the developing nations of Africa and Asia—along with the powerhouses India and China. Demographers predict the increase will come from a growth in cities in particular, rather than echoing an overall population rise. The U.S. is an exception to the rule, both because it's not in those regions and because its urban gain will be attributable to a countrywide increase in population, rather than being specific to city growth.

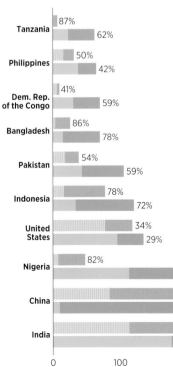

Tanzania: 87%, 62%
Philippines: 50%, 42%
Dem. Rep. of the Congo: 41%, 59%
Bangladesh: 86%, 78%
Pakistan: 54%, 59%
Indonesia: 78%, 72%
United States: 34%, 29%
Nigeria: 82%, 50%
China: 78%, 98%
India: 49%, 70%

■ 1950–2000 non-urban population growth   ■ 1950–2000 urban growth
■ 2000–2050 non-urban population growth   ■ 2000–2050 urban growth

0   100   200   300   400   500   600
Urban Population Change (in millions)

Health and Education

In the past half-century, health conditions for humans have improved dramatically. With better economic and living conditions and access to immunization and other basic health services, global life expectancy has risen to an average of roughly 68 years, and diseases that once killed and disabled millions have been eradicated, eliminated, or greatly reduced in impact. Worldwide, the death rate for children under five years old has fallen by more than 70 percent, thanks in large part to vaccines and other medical interventions. Yet seven million children under five die annually, about 60 percent from infectious diseases. And about half of those seven million are in only five countries—India, Nigeria, Democratic Republic of the Congo, Pakistan, and China. The story is similar for life expectancy: In poorer African countries, for example, life expectancy is in the low 50s (in some, it's even less than 50 years), while in the smallest wealthy countries, it's in the mid- to upper 80s.

Still, the developing world has benefited overwhelmingly from HIV/AIDS prevention and treatment protocols, with a 20 percent drop in new infections worldwide between 2001 and 2011 and a more than 50 percent decline in some countries in hard-hit sub-Saharan Africa. By contrast, in many high- and middle-income countries, chronic, lifestyle-related diseases such as cardiovascular conditions, diabetes, and cancer are becoming the predominant causes of disability and death, taxing the already stressed health-care system. Worldwide, tobacco-related illnesses are epidemic, taking the lives of half of all smokers and a total of six million smokers and nonsmokers annually.

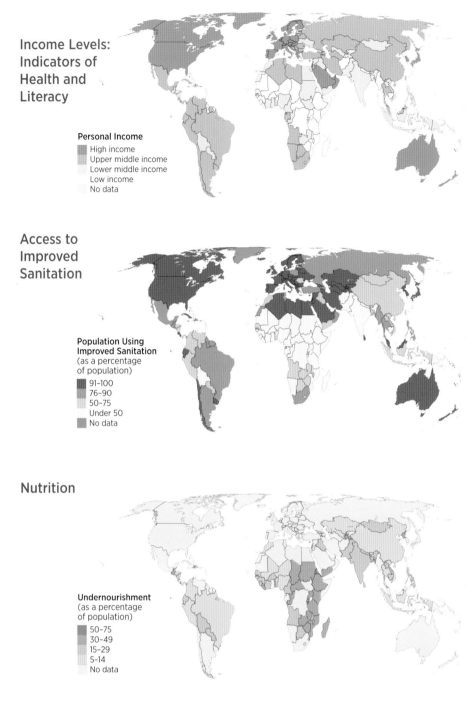

Income Levels: Indicators of Health and Literacy

Personal Income
- High income
- Upper middle income
- Lower middle income
- Low income
- No data

Access to Improved Sanitation

Population Using Improved Sanitation (as a percentage of population)
- 91–100
- 76–90
- 50–75
- Under 50
- No data

Nutrition

Undernourishment (as a percentage of population)
- 50–75
- 30–49
- 15–29
- 5–14
- No data

Education

Basic education is an investment in the long-term prosperity of a country, generating individual, household, and social benefits. Countries in Europe, North America, Australia, and New Zealand have long traditions of high educational attainment for both genders and well-educated populations of all ages. In contrast, many low-income countries have only recently expanded access to primary education, and girls, particularly in rural areas where household labor takes precedence, still lag behind boys in enrollment and completion of primary school and in transitioning to secondary school.

The expansion of secondary schooling tends to lag even further behind, so countries with low educational attainment will likely be at a disadvantage for at least a generation. Many poor countries face the tremendous challenge of paying for schools and teachers today but having to wait 20 years for an economic return on that investment.

Adult Literacy

Adult Literacy (as a percentage of population)
- More than 94
- 80–94
- 60–79
- 40–59
- 0–39
- No data

HIV/AIDS

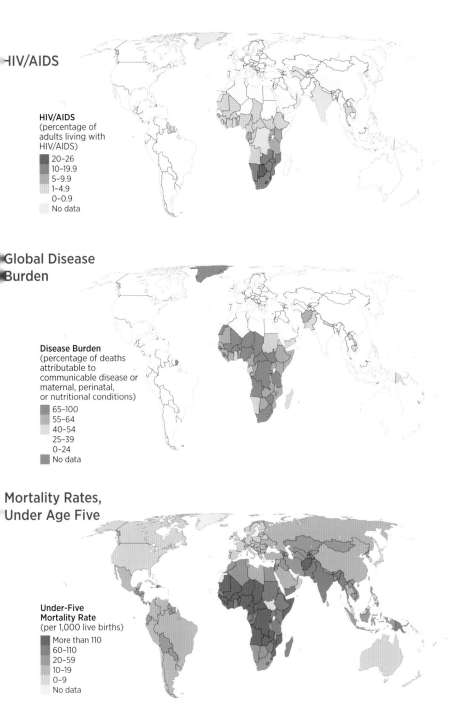

HIV/AIDS
(percentage of adults living with HIV/AIDS)
- 20–26
- 10–19.9
- 5–9.9
- 1–4.9
- 0–0.9
- No data

Global **child mortality has fallen** by one-third since 1990.

More than half of all out-of-school children are in **sub-Saharan Africa.**

Global Disease Burden

Disease Burden
(percentage of deaths attributable to communicable disease or maternal, perinatal, or nutritional conditions)
- 65–100
- 55–64
- 40–54
- 25–39
- 0–24
- No data

Causes of Death
- Infectious & parasitic diseases
- Cardiovascular diseases
- Respiratory infections
- Perinatal conditions
- Unintentional injuries
- Cancers
- Respiratory diseases
- Digestive diseases
- Intentional injuries
- Maternal conditions
- Neuropsychiatric disorders
- Other

High-income Countries

Low-income Countries

Mortality Rates, Under Age Five

Under-Five Mortality Rate
(per 1,000 live births)
- More than 110
- 60–110
- 20–59
- 10–19
- 0–9
- No data

Maternal Mortality Ratio per 100,000 Live Births*

Countries With the Highest Maternal Mortality Rates		Countries With the Lowest Maternal Mortality Rates	
Chad	1,100	Estonia	2
Somalia	1,000	Greece and Singapore	3
Central African Republic, Sierra Leone	890	Austria, Belarus, Italy, Sweden	4
Burundi	800	Czech Republic, Finland, Iceland, Japan, Poland	5
Guinea-Bissau	790	Ireland, Netherlands,	
Liberia	770	Australia, Germany, Israel, Norway, Qatar	7
Sudan	730	Belgium, Bosnia and Herzegovina, France, Lithuania, Malta, Montenegro, Portugal, Switzerland	8
Cameroon	690		
Nigeria	630	Cyprus, Macedonia	10
Lesotho	620	Bulgaria	11
		Canada, Denmark, Serbia, Slovenia, United Arab Emirates, United Kingdom	12

Adjusted for underreporting and misclassification

School Enrollment for Girls

Primary Education Enrollment of Girls
(as a percentage of primary-school-aged girls)
- More than 95
- 91–95
- 86–90
- 61–85
- 0–60
- No data

Developing Human Capital

Burkina Faso and Sri Lanka are similar in population size, but their human capital measures are significantly different. In these graphs, more red and blue in the bars indicates a higher level of educational attainment, which contributes greatly to a country's potential for future economic growth.

Education Level
- Secondary
- Primary
- No schooling

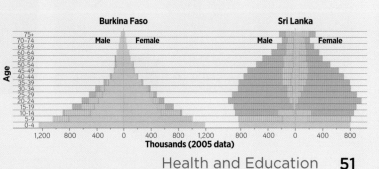

Human Development

What constitutes, or detracts from, a healthy and fulfilling life? Most people would probably agree with the UN assertion that fairness, social justice, and access to a reasonable quality of life are key factors. With this in mind, that world body compiles an annual Human Development Report that provides an alternative to GDP (gross domestic product) as a way of assessing quality of life. Based on certain indices, the report generally measures "the expansion of people's freedoms and capabilities to lead lives that they value and have reason to value."

While there has been great improvement in the Human Development Index (HDI) in recent decades—particularly in healthcare and education—three areas have not improved: Income growth has become closely associated with environmental degradation; the distribution of income has become less even on a national level; and a rise in the HDI has not always signaled more empowerment of all the citizenry of a country.

Many governments and NGOs are working to improve access to the simple tools that enhance daily life—energy, clean water, sanitation facilities, reproductive healthcare—along with more gender equality and opportunities for economic betterment. But increasingly, planetary degradation has become an issue of critical concern for current and future human development, and the 2011 Human Development Report closely links environmental sustainability to human equity. In poorer countries particularly, where life is already hard, people are ever more adversely impacted by environmental deterioration, extreme weather events, air and water pollution, and the lack of natural resources they rely on for a living.

Human Development Index (HDI) Value (2012)
- Very high
- High
- Medium
- Low
- No data

HDI Progress over the past decade was especially strong in developing countries.

At a regional launch of the "Because I am a Girl" international campaign, Yingluck Shinawatra, Thailand's first female prime minister, admires a Thai schoolgirl's painting on the theme of gender equality.

A small lake in Switzerland displays the healthy conditions that—along with policy leadership—have led to the country's high environmental performance rankings.

Children in Copenhagen turn a city square into a celebration of dance, making a point to passersby about the importance of health and fitness practice

The world's average
HDI increased 18%
between 1990 and 2010.

In many countries,
development is **internally
uneven** across regions
and social groups.

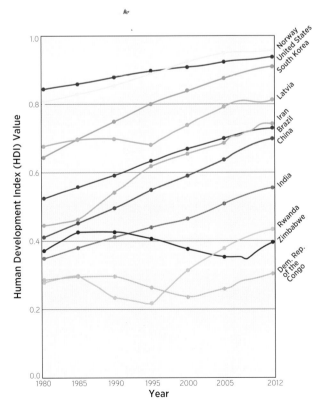

Human Development Index (HDI) Value

Norway
United States
South Korea

Latvia

Iran
Brazil
China

India

Rwanda
Zimbabwe

Dem. Rep.
of the
Congo

Year

HDI Rankings Over Time

Since 1970, when the UN created its first
Human Development Index, quality of life
has increased across the globe. Most of the
gains have been in health, education, and
income per capita, which has doubled in the
past four decades. But for some countries,
especially those in sub-Saharan Africa, the
national HDI has been a roller-coaster ride
of ups and downs.

The current aggregated HDI is influenced
by China and India: As the most populous
nations, their improvements have skewed
the overall results upward. In the past 20
years, both countries have doubled their
output per capita, creating an economic
maelstrom impacting more humans than
did the industrial revolution. Economists
predict that by 2050, these two giants,
along with Brazil, will be responsible for
40 percent of global purchasing power.

Gender Inequality

This index is closely tied to access to
reproductive choices and healthcare for
women as well as to their participation in
political decision-making, which still lags
far beyond men worldwide.

Highest Equality (2012)	Lowest Equality
Netherlands	Yemen
Sweden	Afghanistan
Switzerland	Niger
Denmark	Saudi Arabia
Norway	Dem. Rep. of the Congo
Germany	Liberia
Finland	Central African Republic
Slovenia	Mali
France	Mauritania

Educational Attainment

This is determined by the years of schooling a person in each country measured
is expected to receive. Although New
Zealand and Australia topped the list,
European countries in aggregate made
the strongest showing.

Highest Values (2012)	Lowest Values
New Zealand	Somalia
Australia	Sudan
Ireland	Eritrea
Iceland	Niger
Norway	Djibouti
South Korea	Papua New Guinea
Netherlands	Côte d'Ivoire
Slovenia	Central African Republic
Finland	Burkina Faso

Poverty

The Multidimensional Poverty Index tracks
deficiencies in health, education, standards of
living, and environmental deprivations (e.g.,
lack of modern cooking fuel, drinking water,
and sanitation). Globally, 40 percent of the
population experiences two or more of these.

Highest Values (latest avail.)	Next Highest
Niger	Sierra Leone
Ethiopia	Senegal
Mali	Benin
Burkina Faso	Dem. Rep. of the Congo
Burundi	Uganda
Somalia	Timor-Leste
Mozambique	Madagascar
Guinea	Côte d'Ivoire
Liberia	Mauritania

Overall Life Satisfaction

Rankings are based on responses to a
Gallup World Poll asking how people would
rate their lives on a scale from zero to ten,
with ten representing "the best possible
life," and zero, "the worst possible life."

Highest Values (2007–2011)	Lowest Values
Denmark (7.8)	Togo (2.8)
Norway (7.6)	Central African Rep. (3.6)
Netherlands (7.6)	Botswana (3.6)
Sweden (7.5)	Chad (3.7)
Switzerland (7.5)	Benin (3.7)
Austria (7.5)	Yemen (3.7)
Venezuela (7.5)	Senegal, Nepal (3.8)
Australia (7.5)	Mali, Haiti, Burundi (3.8)
Canada, Israel, Finland (7.4)	Afghan. (3.8)

Human Migration

Migration has been a human impulse since time immemorial. Our proto-ancestors migrated out of Africa and gradually spread across the globe. Presumably, they were inspired to move for the same essential reasons that have motivated emigrants in centuries since: They sought to escape harsh, even deadly conditions or to pursue a more promising future. Although humans have often been forced to move to escape natural disasters, wars, or persecution, many of the great migrations of history have been inspired by a yearning for more economic opportunities, greater freedoms, and other ingredients of human flourishing. Whatever the reasons for migration, the movement and melding of peoples have given a richness to human experience and have frequently led to cultural and material innovations.

Today, some 200 million people live outside their country of birth, and more than 60 million have relocated from the developing world to developed countries. Yet that long-time trend is changing, as a rising anti-refugee sentiment in industrialized countries is curtailing the number of asylum seekers from poorer nations. At the same time, the developing world is experiencing more civil unrest and climate-related disasters, prompting people either to flee to another region within their own country or to cross the border into a neighboring country. The UN estimates that more than seven million humans are trapped in "protracted exile," without any foreseeable solution for permanent resettlement.

With extreme weather events related to climate change and political turmoil expected to persist, it is likely that the number of refugees will grow and the plight of the displaced will worsen.

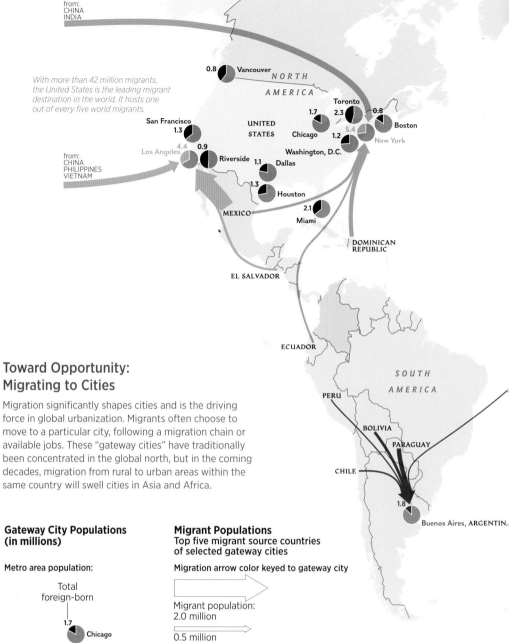

With more than 42 million migrants, the United States is the leading migrant destination in the world. It hosts one out of every five world migrants.

Toward Opportunity: Migrating to Cities

Migration significantly shapes cities and is the driving force in global urbanization. Migrants often choose to move to a particular city, following a migration chain or available jobs. These "gateway cities" have traditionally been concentrated in the global north, but in the coming decades, migration from rural to urban areas within the same country will swell cities in Asia and Africa.

Gateway City Populations (in millions)

Metro area population:

Total foreign-born

1.7 Chicago

Total native-born

Migrant Populations
Top five migrant source countries of selected gateway cities

Migration arrow color keyed to gateway city

Migrant population: 2.0 million

0.5 million

0.1 million

City data includes greater metropolitan area; most current census data used.

Migrant workers browse the job postings at an employment center in Zhejiang Province. The cheaper labor migrants provide fuels China's growing urban service industry.

At a UNHCR refugee camp, displaced people took shelter in tents after Cyclone Nargis created Myanmar's worst natural disaster in 2008, displacing some 2.4 million people.

The civil war that began in 2003 in the Darfur regio of western Sudan left millions of people—like thes women—displaced, and hundreds of thousands de

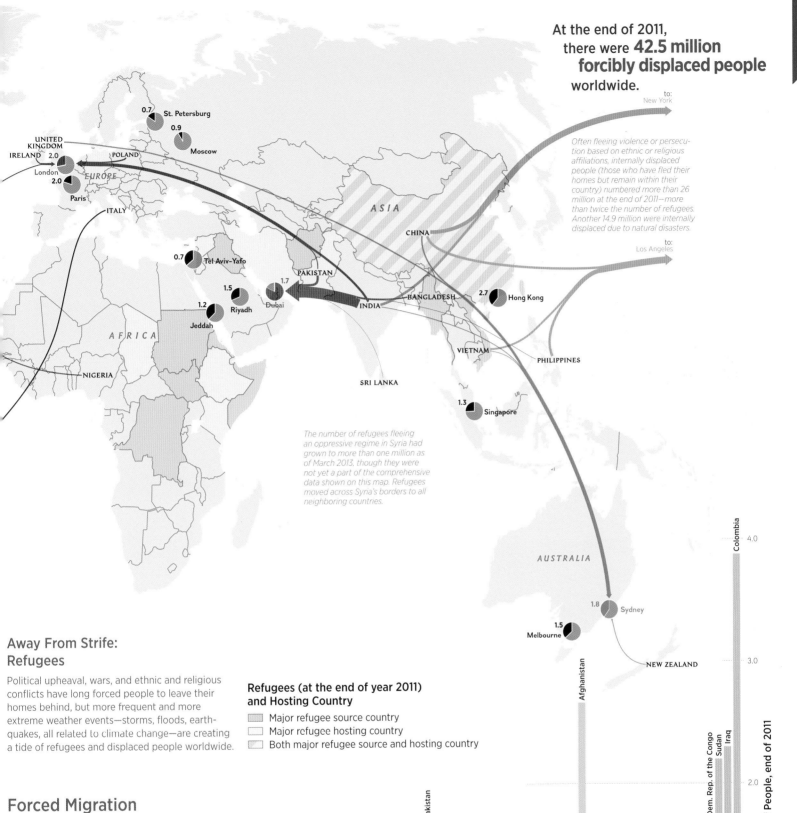

At the end of 2011, there were **42.5 million forcibly displaced people** worldwide.

to:
New York

Often fleeing violence or persecution based on ethnic or religious affiliations, internally displaced people (those who have fled their homes but remain within their country) numbered more than 26 million at the end of 2011—more than twice the number of refugees. Another 14.9 million were internally displaced due to natural disasters.

to:
Los Angeles

The number of refugees fleeing an oppressive regime in Syria had grown to more than one million as of March 2013, though they were not yet a part of the comprehensive data shown on this map. Refugees moved across Syria's borders to all neighboring countries.

Away From Strife: Refugees

Political upheaval, wars, and ethnic and religious conflicts have long forced people to leave their homes behind, but more frequent and more extreme weather events—storms, floods, earthquakes, all related to climate change—are creating a tide of refugees and displaced people worldwide.

Forced Migration

The number of displaced people has been on the rise in recent decades, and in 2011, about 43 million people found themselves uprooted. Roughly 80 percent of them were being hosted by developing countries, further straining already limited resources. Forty-four percent of refugees are under the age of 18, and some—but not all—lack access to education. Refugee camps organized by the UN and other relief organizations can actually open horizons, offering opportunities that would have been unavailable in the rural villages from which refugees were forced to flee. Classes in reading and other traditional subjects are frequently offered, as is training in better healthcare practices, hygiene, nutrition, human rights, and community rebuilding.

Refugees (at the end of year 2011) and Hosting Country

- Major refugee source country
- Major refugee hosting country
- Both major refugee source and hosting country

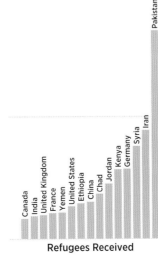

Refugees Received

Refugees (by place of origin)

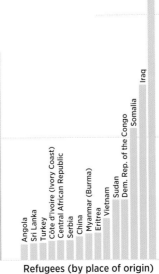

Internally Displaced Persons

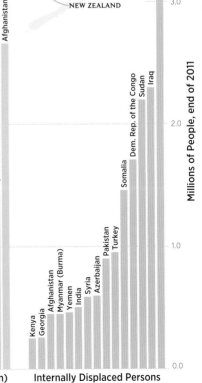

Languages

Neon signs in Mandarin, and occasionally English, beckon strollers and shoppers on the popular Nanjing Road in Shanghai, once a British settlement.

A polyglot collection of newspapers reflects the sweep of languages that are spoken and read throughout the world today.

A Seri woman in Mexico keeps alive an ancient language and culture that has persisted in the face of conquest and modernity.

A variety of indigenous languages exist in the Americas, but because their distribution is fairly sparse, many are not shown on this generalized map.

Language Families

- Afro-Asiatic
- Altaic
- American Indian (Meso-)
- American Indian (North)
- American Indian (South)
- Australian families
- Austro-Asiatic
- Austronesian
- Caucasian families
- Dravidian
- Eskimo-Aleut
- Hmong-Mien
- Indo-European
- Japanese/Korean
- Khoisan
- Niger-Congo
- Nilo-Saharan
- Papuan families
- Sino-Tibetan
- Tai-Kadai
- Uralic
- Other
- No major family

Classifying and Grouping Languages

Linguists classify languages in a number of ways, based broadly on where they are spoken and what their particular features are. These classifications include somewhat controversial higher-level family groupings (map above), determined by shared linguistic origins that can be traced back at least 10,000 years.

Language may easily be ranked as one of humankind's most distinctive and versatile adaptations. Though its exact origins are lost in the recesses of prehistory, spoken language has allowed humans to communicate and develop in ways inconceivable without it. Written language came much later, and even in recent history, many languages had no written component. Yet today, the written word has a profound impact on daily life, global communications, and human development. It's virtually impossible to imagine a world without it.

Living, organic entities, languages easily morph over time and place to fit cultural and geographical circumstances. In an often-cited example of this, Arctic peoples have many different words for snow—words that reflect different qualities, because those qualities can be critical to human survival in a harsh environment. By studying subtle variations in sounds and concepts embedded in languages, linguists have devised systems to classify them into broad families.

Today Earth's seven billion people speak some 7,000 languages. Figures can be misleading and are vastly skewed to only a few of the languages. Roughly 80 percent of the world's population speaks only 85 of the largest languages, while some 3,500 of the smallest languages have only 8.25 million speakers in all. Often speakers of these smaller languages are the elder members of cultural groups that have been marginalized over time by a more dominant culture. As they die out, so too do the languages only they kept alive. Globalization has only exacerbated this trend, but some small cultures, aware of the fragility of their own languages, are working hard to preserve linguistic traditions.

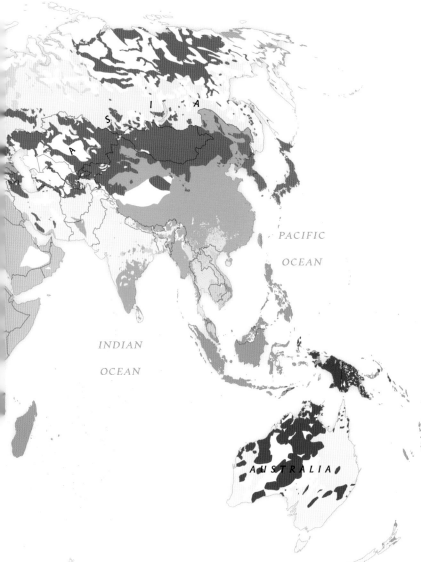

RCTIC OCEAN

A S I A

PACIFIC OCEAN

INDIAN OCEAN

AUSTRALIA

80% of the world's population **speaks 1%** of its languages.

How Many Speak What?

Languages can paint vivid historical pictures of migration and colonization. English, Spanish, and Portuguese, for example, originated in parts of Europe with only a tenth of China's population and area, yet they rival Mandarin Chinese in total number of speakers. Their reach expanded because England, Spain, and Portugal built widespread overseas colonies. India, which has been a part of several empires, currently has a population of 1.2 billion and 22 official languages (in addition to English) spoken in different states and by different ethnic or tribal groups. Only a fifth of India's population speaks the official national language, Hindi.

Australia and Oceania, a vast constellation of isolated islands scattered across the Pacific, account for only a bare sliver of the world's total population (0.5 percent), yet they hold a treasure trove of languages, claiming 19 percent of the global total. In Indonesia alone, some 700 languages are spoken by 237 million inhabitants representing a myriad of ethnic groups and backgrounds.

World Population and Languages by Region

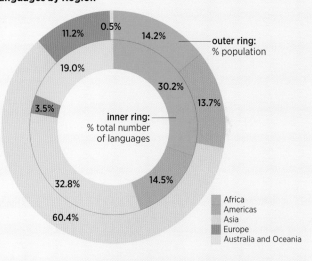

outer ring: % population

inner ring: % total number of languages

0.5% — 14.2% — 30.2% — 13.7% — 14.5% — 32.8% — 60.4% — 3.5% — 19.0% — 11.2%

Africa
Americas
Asia
Europe
Australia and Oceania

Small Languages Get Smaller

The trend seems irreversible—smaller languages near extinction as dominant ones spread. Hoping to preserve their endangered languages, various indigenous groups are using audio and video recordings to create archives and dictionaries for future generations.

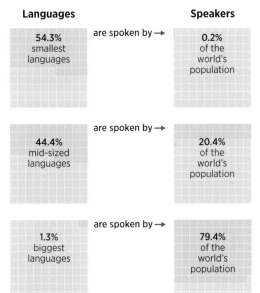

Languages		Speakers
54.3% smallest languages	are spoken by →	**0.2%** of the world's population
44.4% mid-sized languages	are spoken by →	**20.4%** of the world's population
1.3% biggest languages	are spoken by →	**79.4%** of the world's population

Vanishing Languages

Every 14 days, another endangered language somewhere in the world dies with its last speaker. These endangered languages tend to be concentrated in hot spots scattered through the world. Linguists fear that by 2100, over half of the 7,000 languages now spoken (many of them with no recordings for posterity) will be lost forever.

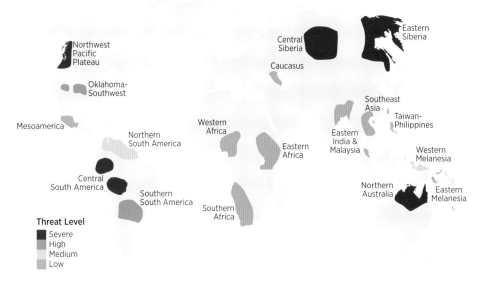

Northwest Pacific Plateau

Oklahoma-Southwest

Mesoamerica

Northern South America

Central South America

Southern South America

Central Siberia

Caucasus

Eastern Siberia

Western Africa

Eastern Africa

Southern Africa

Southeast Asia

Eastern India & Malaysia

Taiwan-Philippines

Western Melanesia

Northern Australia

Eastern Melanesia

Threat Level
Severe
High
Medium
Low

Religion

At a Buddhist temple in central Thailand, tens of thousands of novice monks gather for ordination.

St. Peter's Dome in Vatican City rises above Rome but beckons to Catholics worldwide.

Hindus in Ahmedabad, India, celebrate the birth of one of their gods with lamps and prayers.

Every year more than 1.5 million Muslims make the pilgrimage to Mecca and Islam's sacred Kaaba.

For Jews, the Western Wall in Jerusalem is a place of prayer and a powerful symbol of Israel.

One in six people in the world are **unaffiliated with any religion.**

Sacred Places

BUDDHISM
1. **Bodhgaya:** Where Buddha attained awakening
2. **Kusinagara:** Where Buddha entered nirvana
3. **Lumbini:** Place of Buddha's last human birth
4. **Sarnath:** Place where Buddha delivered his first sermon
5. **Sanchi:** Location of famous stupa containing relics of Buddha

CHRISTIANITY
1. **Jerusalem:** Church of the Holy Sepulchre, Jesus's crucifixion
2. **Bethlehem:** Jesus's birthplace
3. **Nazareth:** Hometown of Jesus Christ
4. **Shore of the Sea of Galilee:** Where Jesus gave the Sermon on the Mount
5. **Rome and the Vatican:** Tombs of St. Peter and St. Paul
6. **Wittenberg:** Martin Luther nailed his Ninety-Five Theses to the door of All Saints' Church, a watershed of the Protestant Reformation

HINDUISM
1. **Varanasi (Benares):** Most holy Hindu site, home of Shiva
2. **Vrindavan:** Krishna's birthplace
3. **Allahabad:** At confluence of Ganges and Yamuna Rivers, purest place to bathe
4. **Madurai:** Temple of Minakshi, great goddess of the south
5. **Badrinath:** Vishnu's shrine

ISLAM
1. **Mecca:** The Prophet Muhammad's birthplace; destination of the pilgrimage, or hajj; houses the Kaaba (shrine that Muslims face when praying)
2. **Medina:** Burial place of the Prophet Muhammad; contains the tombs of the 2nd, 4th, 5th, and 6th Shiite imams
3. **Jerusalem:** The first Qibla (direction of the prayers) before being replaced by Mecca; site of nightlong ascension of the Prophet Muhammad to the heavens
4. **Najaf (Shiite):** Tomb of the first imam, Ali; ancient center of Shiite learning; known as the "Vatican City" of Shiism
5. **Karbala (Shiite):** Tomb of the 3rd imam and martyr, Hussein

JUDAISM
1. **Jerusalem:** Location of the Western Wall and First and Second Temples; City of David; the ancient and modern capital of Israel
2. **Hebron:** Burial spot of patriarchs and matriarchs
3. **Safed:** Where Kabbalah (Jewish mysticism) flourished
4. **Tiberias:** Where Talmud (source of Jewish law) first composed
5. **Bethlehem:** Site of Rachel's tomb
6. **Mount Sinai:** Site of God's revelation, where God appeared to Moses and gave him the Ten Commandments

There are nearly as many Jews living in the United States as there are in Israel. The United States also has almost as many Muslims as Jews, approximately five million each.

ATLANTIC

OCEAN

Christianity dominates in the Americas as a result of large-scale European colonization.

The great power of religion comes from its ability to speak to the yearning people have for a greater understanding of and connection among themselves and something more universal. Since earliest human times, honoring nature spirits or the belief in a supreme being has brought comfort and security in the face of fundamental questions of life and death.

Billions of people are now adherents of the world's major faiths—Judaism, Christianity, and Islam, all of whose roots are found in the Middle East; and Hinduism and Buddhism, whose origins are in Asia. Each of these five religions blossomed from the teachings and revelations of individuals who transmitted the voice of God or discovered a way to salvation that could be understood by others—Abraham and Moses for Jews, the Buddha for Buddhists, Jesus Christ for Christians, and Muhammad for Muslims. In addition to these five worldwide faiths, Chinese traditional religions (especially Daoism and Confucianism), Shintoism and the New Religions of Japan, and Native American belief systems have shaped millions of people.

Expressions of faith can take many forms: collective beliefs about the spiritual realm; sacred sites; saints, martyrs, prophets, and sages; ritual clothing; dietary laws and fasting; festivals and holy days; special ceremonies for life's major moments; and moral guidelines for daily life. The tenets and ceremonies of faith are taught not only in churches, synagogues, mosques, kivas, and temples but also at schools and around dinner tables. Sadly, despite the tolerance generally inherent in these teachings, religious differences have too often been the catalyst for political conflict and violence.

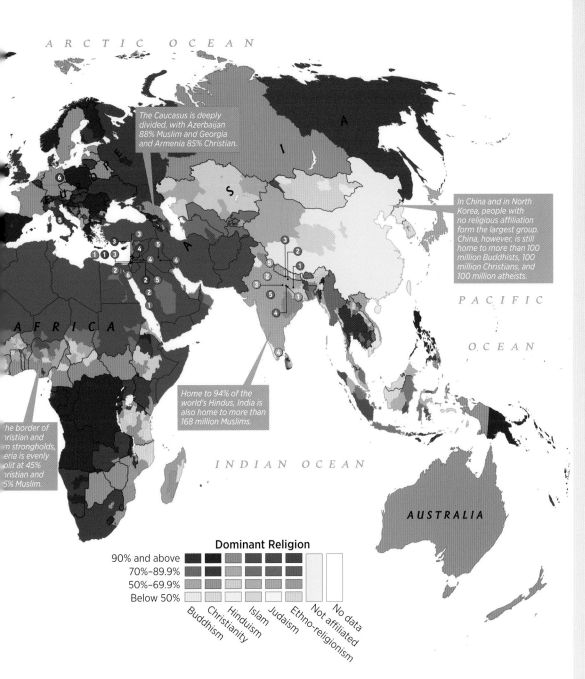

The Caucasus is deeply divided, with Azerbaijan 88% Muslim and Georgia and Armenia 85% Christian.

In China and in North Korea, people with no religious affiliation form the largest group. China, however, is still home to more than 100 million Buddhists, 100 million Christians, and 100 million atheists.

Home to 94% of the world's Hindus, India is also home to more than 168 million Muslims.

...he border of ...ristian and ...n strongholds, ...eria is evenly ...plit at 45% ...ristian and ...5% Muslim.

Dominant Religion

	Buddhism	Christianity	Hinduism	Islam	Judaism	Ethno-religionism	Not affiliated	No data
90% and above								
70%–89.9%								
50%–69.9%								
Below 50%								

Adherents Worldwide

The growth of Islam and the decline of Chinese traditional religion stand out as significant changes over the past century. The number of adherents of Christianity, the largest of the world's main faiths, has remained fairly stable. Today more than one in six people are either nonreligious or otherwise unaffiliated with any specific religion.

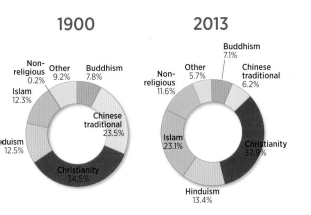

1900

- Non-religious 0.2%
- Other 9.2%
- Buddhism 7.8%
- Islam 12.3%
- ...duism 12.5%
- Christianity 34.5%
- Chinese traditional 23.5%

2013

- Other 5.7%
- Buddhism 7.1%
- Non-religious 11.6%
- Chinese traditional 6.2%
- Islam 23.1%
- Christianity 32.9%
- Hinduism 13.4%

Adherents by Continent

Asia ranks first in total number of religious adherents, not only because half the world's people live there but also because three of the five major faiths are practiced there: Hinduism in South Asia; Buddhism in East and Southeast Asia; and Islam in Indonesia, Central Asia, and Turkey. Islam, Christianity, and traditional animism are found throughout Africa, while Christianity is dominant in Europe, Oceania, and the Americas.

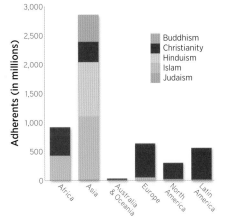

Adherents (in millions) — Africa, Asia, Australia & Oceania, Europe, North America, Latin America

- Buddhism
- Christianity
- Hinduism
- Islam
- Judaism

Adherents by Country

Countries with the Most Buddhists

Country	Buddhists
1. China	208,182,000
2. Japan	71,711,000
3. Thailand	58,838,000
4. Vietnam	45,489,000
5. Myanmar (Burma)	41,204,000
6. Sri Lanka	14,940,000
7. Cambodia	12,145,000
8. India	8,743,000
9. South Korea	7,325,000
10. Taiwan (China)	6,167,000

Countries with the Most Christians

Country	Christians
1. United States	253,576,000
2. Brazil	182,852,000
3. Russia	115,753,000
4. Mexico	111,512,000
5. China	107,140,000
6. Philippines	96,064,000
7. Nigeria	81,059,000
8. Dem. Rep. of the Congo	71,738,000
9. India	57,092,000
10. Germany	56,895,000

Countries with the Most Hindus

Country	Hindus
1. India	890,789,000
2. Nepal	20,601,000
3. Bangladesh	15,514,000
4. Indonesia	4,074,000
5. Sri Lanka	2,828,000
6. Pakistan	2,549,000
7. Malaysia	1,857,000
8. United States	1,474,000
9. South Africa	1,159,000
10. Myanmar (Burma)	941,000

Countries with the Most Muslims

Country	Muslims
1. Indonesia	198,775,000
2. Pakistan	185,818,000
3. India	172,826,000
4. Bangladesh	145,406,000
5. Nigeria	79,461,000
6. Turkey	79,319,000
7. Iran	78,888,000
8. Egypt	76,162,000
9. Algeria	37,517,000
10. Morocco	32,535,000

Countries with the Most Jews

Country	Jews
1. Israel	5,589,000
2. United States	5,225,000
3. France	508,000
4. Canada	369,000
5. United Kingdom	297,000
6. Russia	205,000
7. Argentina	190,000
8. Germany	117,000
9. Brazil	116,000
10. Australia	111,000

All figures are estimates for the year 2013. Countries with the highest reported nonreligious populations include China, United States, Germany, North Korea, Vietnam, Japan, India, France, the United Kingdom, and Russia.

Economy

Combines harvest soybeans in east-central Brazil. Brazilian and Argentine exports of the sought-after crop have risen dramatically in recent years.

Production lines for the upscale Maserati opened in Turin in 2013, after Italian-based Fiat bought the Maserati's former maker.

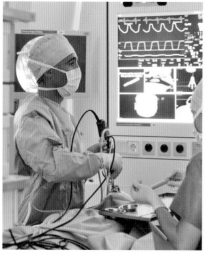

In Leipzig, Germany, a state-of-the-art operating room speaks to the importance health care now plays as an economic driver in many countries.

The world's combined **gross domestic product** (GDP) is more than $70 trillion.

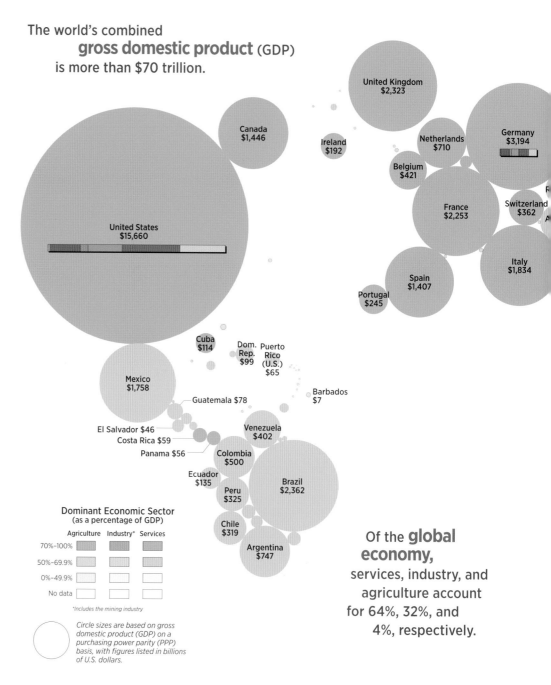

United Kingdom $2,323

Canada $1,446

Ireland $192

Netherlands $710

Germany $3,194

Belgium $421

France $2,253

Switzerland $362

United States $15,660

Italy $1,834

Spain $1,407

Portugal $245

Cuba $114

Dom. Rep. $99

Puerto Rico (U.S.) $65

Mexico $1,758

Guatemala $78

Barbados $7

El Salvador $46

Venezuela $402

Costa Rica $59

Panama $56

Colombia $500

Ecuador $135

Peru $325

Brazil $2,362

Chile $319

Argentina $747

Dominant Economic Sector
(as a percentage of GDP)

	Agriculture	Industry*	Services
70%–100%			
50%–69.9%			
0%–49.9%			
No data			

*Includes the mining industry

Circle sizes are based on gross domestic product (GDP) on a purchasing power parity (PPP) basis, with figures listed in billions of U.S. dollars.

Of the **global economy,** services, industry, and agriculture account for 64%, 32%, and 4%, respectively.

In the Dorling cartogram above, the size of a country's circle represents the size of its economy relative to that of other countries throughout the world. The U.S. remains the clear global powerhouse, with China a strong second, but old patterns are shifting, with India far ahead of Germany and Brazil just behind Russia. Despite recent economic downturns, western Europe overall, along with Japan, places high in the GDP rankings.

Colors on the cartogram indicate which economic sector dominates the country shown. Like much of the Western world, the U.S. economy is service driven. The lavender shading of China, Vietnam, Thailand, and Indonesia indicates the rise of industry in Asia, but China's multicolored bar—which breaks down its GDP into sectors—shows that agriculture still plays a healthy role in its economy. That's unusual given the shrinking role agriculture is playing in GDP across the globe; those countries still relying on it rank among the least robust economies.

The phenomenal growth in China's economy over the past several decades has relied on a young workforce and average wages far below those in Europe and the U.S. And while most Chinese workers take home only a fraction of the cash pocketed each week by their economic rivals in the West, the Chinese middle class is growing rapidly, as is a taste for cars, cell phones, and other consumer products. India too, another new giant on the world economic stage, has a growing middle class, while across much of the Western world the middle class is shrinking.

The United States and China account for one-third of the **entire world economy.**

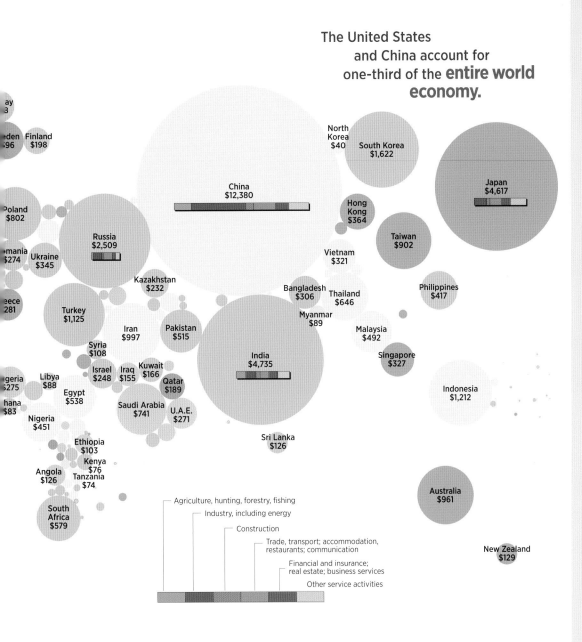

Country bubble labels (GDP, billions):
- Finland $198
- North Korea $40
- South Korea $1,622
- China $12,380
- Japan $4,617
- Poland $802
- Hong Kong $364
- Russia $2,509
- Taiwan $902
- Ukraine $345
- Vietnam $321
- Kazakhstan $232
- Bangladesh $306
- Thailand $646
- Myanmar $89
- Philippines $417
- Turkey $1,125
- Iran $997
- Pakistan $515
- Syria $108
- India $4,735
- Malaysia $492
- Israel $248
- Iraq $155
- Kuwait $166
- Singapore $327
- Libya $88
- Qatar $189
- Egypt $538
- Saudi Arabia $741
- U.A.E. $271
- Indonesia $1,212
- Nigeria $451
- Ethiopia $103
- Sri Lanka $126
- Kenya $76
- Angola $126
- Tanzania $74
- South Africa $579
- Australia $961
- New Zealand $129

Legend:
- Agriculture, hunting, forestry, fishing
- Industry, including energy
- Construction
- Trade, transport; accommodation, restaurants; communication
- Financial and insurance; real estate; business services
- Other service activities

Value Added, by Sector

"Value added" describes the amount a sector contributes to the overall economy. The graph at right shows the global shifts in those sectors in recent decades: Agriculture and manufacturing have shrunk; the trade and transportation/communications sectors have generally held steady; and the "other activities" sector, which includes financial services as well as health care and other personal services, has grown.

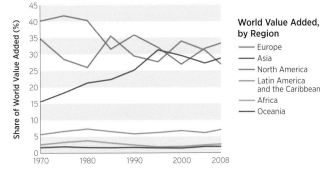

World Value Added, by Sector (percent of total, worldwide)

1970, 1980, 1990, 2000, 2008
0% 10 20 30 40 50 60 70 80 90 100

Legend:
- Agriculture
- Mining and utilities
- Manufacturing
- Construction
- Wholesale and retail trade, restaurant and hotels
- Transports, storage, and communications
- Other activities

Value Added, by Region

In the past four decades, Asia has made a meteoric climb in its global economic strength, whereas Europe and North America have experienced a roller coaster of ups and downs that have ultimately left them below 1970 levels. Meanwhile, the developing regions of Africa, Oceania, and Latin America and the Caribbean show little change in their negligible contribution to the world economy.

Share of World Value Added (%)
45 40 35 30 25 20 15 10 5 0
1970 1980 1990 2000 2008

World Value Added, by Region
- Europe
- Asia
- North America
- Latin America and the Caribbean
- Africa
- Oceania

Richest Countries

When national GDP is divided per capita—per person—among a country's population, a new picture emerges, with smaller countries ranking as the richest. While Qatar and Brunei are fueled by petrodollars, Luxembourg, Liechtenstein, and Singapore thrive on the service sector.

Country	GDP per Capita, 2012
Qatar	$102,800
Liechtenstein	$89,400
Luxembourg	$80,700
Singapore	$60,900
Norway	$55,300
Brunei	$50,500
United States	$49,800
United Arab Emirates	$49,000
Switzerland	$45,300

Poorest Countries

Applying the same criterion (GDP per person) for the poorest countries results in a list of African nations, particularly those in the central belt, where poverty is endemic.

Country	GDP per Capita, 2012
Dem. Rep. of the Congo	$400
Zimbabwe	$500
Burundi	$600
Somalia	$600
Liberia	$700
Eritrea	$800
Central African Republic	$800
Niger	$900
Malawi	$900

Fastest Growing Economies

Less burdened by financial turmoil and debt than larger nations, developing countries are the fastest growing, especially when recently liberated from tyrannical leaders. Amazingly, behemoth China places fifteenth on the list.

Country	GDP Growth Rate, 2012
Libya	121.9%
Sierra Leone	21.3%
Niger	14.5%
Mongolia	12.7%
Afghanistan	11.0%
Iraq	10.2%
Timor-Leste	10.0%
Bhutan	9.9%
Liberia	9.0%

Leaders in Innovation

The Global Innovation Index weighs a country's institutions and infrastructure, human capital and research, and business and market sophistication against its knowledge, technology, and creative outputs to determine world leaders in innovation.

Country	Index Score, 2012
Switzerland	68.2
Sweden	64.8
Singapore	63.5
Finland	61.8
United Kingdom	61.2
Netherlands	60.5
Denmark	59.9
Ireland	58.7
United States	57.7

Trade

Stacked containers filled with cargo await shipping at Tianjin, China. Once offloaded, the containers move overland by truck or train.

An electronic board in Tokyo tracks the Nikkei stock index. Tokyo, London, Singapore, and New York are home to the largest stock exchanges.

Headquartered in Brussels, the European Union was founded in 1945 and is now an uneasy economic alliance among 27 countries.

Values listed on main map are in billions of U.S. dollars.

Of the **world's total volume of trade,** the top ten countries account for half.

United States
China
Germany
Japan
France
Netherlands
United Kingdom
Italy
South Korea
Belgium

Volume indices: 2005 = 100

Value of World Merchandise Exports (logarithmic scale)

Fuels & mining products

Agricultural products

Manufactures

100

10

1

1950 1960 1970 1980 1990 2000 2011

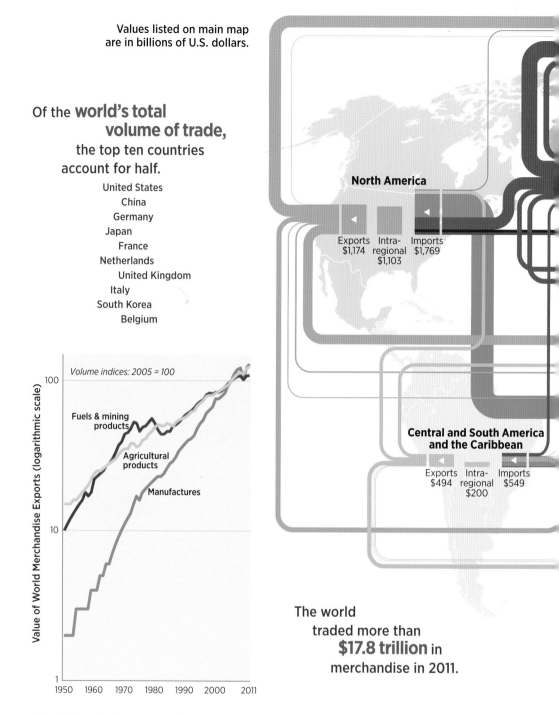

North America

Exports $1,174   Intra-regional $1,103   Imports $1,769

Central and South America and the Caribbean

Exports $494   Intra-regional $200   Imports $549

The world traded more than **$17.8 trillion** in merchandise in 2011.

World trade has expanded at a dizzying pace in the decades since World War II. The dollar value of global merchandise exports rose from $61 billion in 1950 to $17.8 trillion in 2011. Adjusted for price changes, world trade grew 30 times over the last 55 years, much faster than world output. Trade in manufactures far outpaced mining products, including fuels, and agricultural products. In recent decades China, Russia, Mexico, and other developing countries have become important exporters of manufactured goods. However, there are still many less developed countries—primarily in Africa and the Middle East—that are dependent on a few primary commodities for their export earnings. Given the interconnectivity of global markets, local events, such as earthquakes or wars, can have far-ranging economic ripples: In 2011, world trade growth decelerated as a result of natural disasters, general financial uncertainty, and civil conflicts.

Yet even in 2011, exports of commercial services remained robust, rising by 11 percent, in keeping with their almost exponential expansion in the past two decades. While developed countries currently account for more than two-thirds of commercial services trade, developing countries are rapidly expanding their services exports. Earnings from tourism in the Caribbean and from IT (information technology) and outsourced business processing in India are prominent examples of developing countries with dynamic service exports. Capital flows and worker remittances have gained in importance worldwide and are another important aspect of globalization. Still, capital markets in many developing countries remain small, fragile, and underdeveloped, which hampers household savings and the funding of local enterprises.

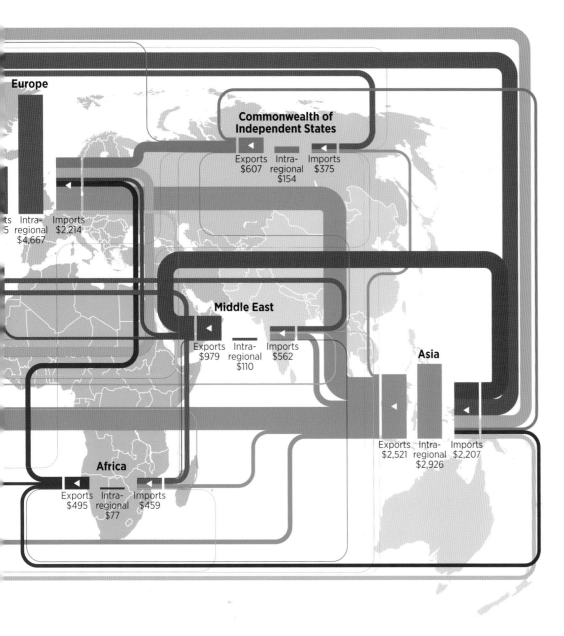

Europe

**Commonwealth of
Independent States**

Exports $607   Intra-regional $154   Imports $375

ts Intra-regional Imports $2,214
5 $4,667

Middle East

Exports $979   Intra-regional $110   Imports $562

Asia

Exports $2,521   Intra-regional $2,926   Imports $2,207

Africa

Exports $495   Intra-regional $77   Imports $459

NORTH
AMERICA

EUROPE

ASIA

AFRICA

SOUTH
AMERICA

AUSTRALIA

Trade Blocs

Regional trade is on the rise. Agreements among neighboring countries to offer one another trade benefits can create larger markets and improve the economy as a whole. But they can also lead to discrimination, especially when more-efficient suppliers excluded by the regional agreements are prevented from supplying their goods and services.

Major Regional Trade Agreements

- APEC: Asia-Pacific Economic Cooperation
- ASEAN: Association of Southeast Asian Nations
- CACM: Central American Common Market
- CEMAC: Economic and Monetary Community of Central Africa
- COMESA: Common Market for Eastern and Southern Africa
- ECOWAS: Economic Community of West African States
- EU: European Union
- GCC: Gulf Cooperation Council
- MERCOSUR: Southern Common Market
- SAPTA: South Asian Preferential Trade Arrangement
- NAFTA: North American Free Trade Agreement; and APEC
- APEC and ASEAN

Top Merchandise Importers

The U.S. is the biggest global importer, with a trade deficit in 2011 of 5.2 percent of GDP. The next largest importers, China and Germany, both ran trade surpluses in 2011.

Country	Value (billions of U.S. dollars)
United States	$2,266
China	$1,743
Germany	$1,254
Japan	$855
France	$714
United Kingdom	$638
Netherlands	$599
Italy	$557
South Korea	$524
Hong Kong (China)	$511

Top Merchandise Exporters

The same three countries lead the way as merchandise exporters, though China takes the top slot. In both imports and exports, Japan is in fourth place.

Country	Value (billions of U.S. dollars)
China	$1,898
United States	$1,480
Germany	$1,472
Japan	$823
Netherlands	$661
France	$596
South Korea	$555
Italy	$523
Russia	$522
Belgium	$477

Top Services Importers

In service imports, the same four countries again lead the way, along with the United Kingdom—though China and Japan both ran services deficits in 2011.

Country	Value (billions of U.S. dollars)
United States	$395
Germany	$289
China	$237
United Kingdom	$170
Japan	$166
France	$143
India	$124
Netherlands	$118
Ireland	$114
Italy	$114

Top Services Exporters

Owing to their strong exports, both the U.S. and the U.K. have run surpluses in their trade services since the 1980s.

Country	Value (billions of U.S. dollars)
United States	$581
United Kingdom	$274
Germany	$253
China	$182
France	$167
Japan	$142
Spain	$140
India	$137
Netherlands	$134
Singapore	$129

Food

The most intense **fishing** occurs in northern Europe, China, and Southeast Asia.

Cereals provide **80%** of the human **calorie supply.**

Wheat from a winter harvest in Kansas can find its way to countries throughout the world in an increasingly globalized food chain.

Some 50% of city dwellers in Latin America and the Caribbean engage in **urban agricultural activity.**

A worker in Manila climbs a wall of rice sacks stockpiled by the National Food Authority of the Philippines.

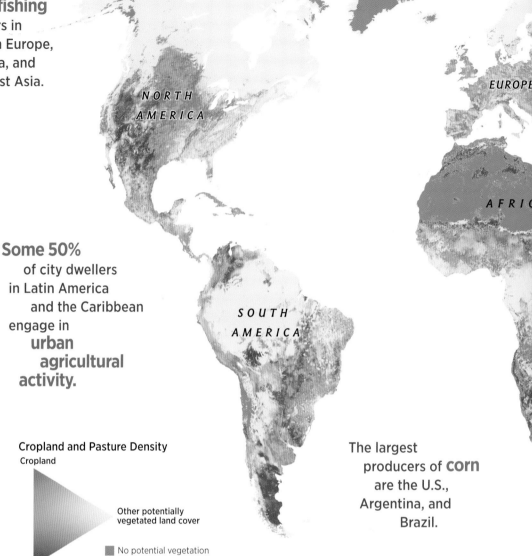

NORTH AMERICA

EUROPE

AFRICA

SOUTH AMERICA

The largest producers of **corn** are the U.S., Argentina, and Brazil.

Cropland and Pasture Density

Cropland

Other potentially vegetated land cover

■ No potential vegetation

Pasture

Saturated greens and browns represent the land areas most degraded because of extensive agriculture and overgrazing.

Fish pens dot the Norwegian fjords and coastline, where salmon and cod farming has become a lucrative business.

For at least 10,000 years, agriculture and animal husbandry have been transforming the terrestrial biosphere, and now roughly 35 percent of Earth's ice-free surface is in agricultural use. The sea, too, adds to the harvest. Local fishermen have long provided sustenance to their families and communities, but in recent centuries, advances in technology and a growing appetite for seafood have spawned a rapacious, worldwide fisheries industry. Aquaculture is adding significantly to the marine bounty, but fish and shellfish farms can have serious, negative environmental consequences.

The world produces moderately more food than its inhabitants need; undernourishment and starvation are results of poor distribution rather than underproduction. Yet the exuberant success of humankind, made possible in large part by the productiveness of modern agriculture, has meant that more people are demanding more, and richer, foods. As large areas of existing farmland become too dry, salty, or eroded to produce, newly cleared land is being pressed into service—at the cost of unfathomable loss of wild species and habitats. Trying to coax more food per acre from the land will mean an intensification of irrigation, fertilization, chemical pest control, genetic modification, ecosystem management, and urban agriculture. From New York to Nairobi, there is expanding focus and activity on ways cities can contribute to their own food needs. In an increasingly urbanized world, this may prove critical to stability and survival.

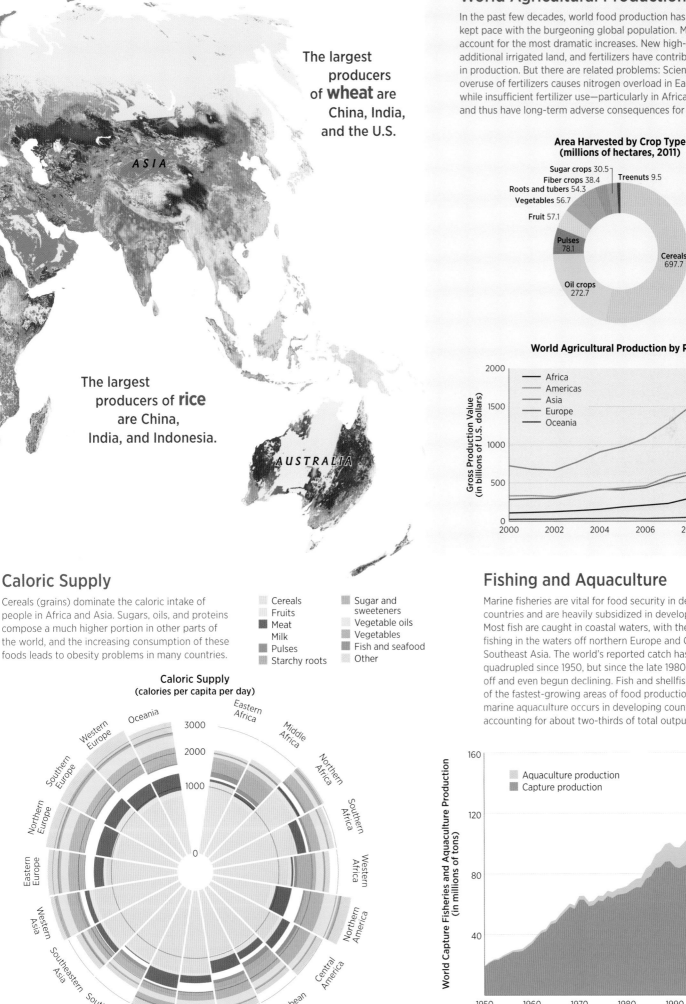

The largest producers of **wheat** are China, India, and the U.S.

ASIA

The largest producers of **rice** are China, India, and Indonesia.

AUSTRALIA

World Agricultural Production

In the past few decades, world food production has more than kept pace with the burgeoning global population. Meat and cereals account for the most dramatic increases. New high-yield crops, additional irrigated land, and fertilizers have contributed to the rise in production. But there are related problems: Scientists warn that overuse of fertilizers causes nitrogen overload in Earth's waters, while insufficient fertilizer use—particularly in Africa—can harm soils and thus have long-term adverse consequences for food security.

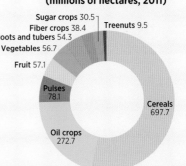

Area Harvested by Crop Type
(millions of hectares, 2011)

Sugar crops 30.5
Fiber crops 38.4
Treenuts 9.5
Roots and tubers 54.3
Vegetables 56.7
Fruit 57.1
Pulses 78.1
Cereals 697.7
Oil crops 272.7

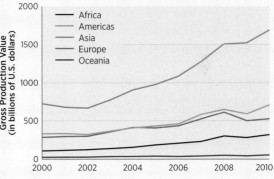

World Agricultural Production by Region

- Africa
- Americas
- Asia
- Europe
- Oceania

Gross Production Value (in billions of U.S. dollars)

Caloric Supply

Cereals (grains) dominate the caloric intake of people in Africa and Asia. Sugars, oils, and proteins compose a much higher portion in other parts of the world, and the increasing consumption of these foods leads to obesity problems in many countries.

- Cereals
- Fruits
- Meat
- Milk
- Pulses
- Starchy roots
- Sugar and sweeteners
- Vegetable oils
- Vegetables
- Fish and seafood
- Other

Caloric Supply
(calories per capita per day)

Fishing and Aquaculture

Marine fisheries are vital for food security in developing countries and are heavily subsidized in developed countries. Most fish are caught in coastal waters, with the most intense fishing in the waters off northern Europe and China and Southeast Asia. The world's reported catch has more than quadrupled since 1950, but since the late 1980s it has leveled off and even begun declining. Fish and shellfish farming is one of the fastest-growing areas of food production. The bulk of marine aquaculture occurs in developing countries, with China accounting for about two-thirds of total output.

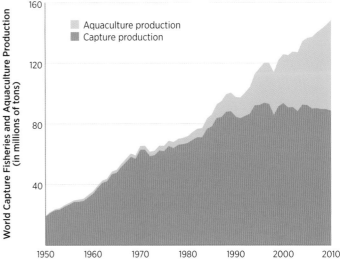

- Aquaculture production
- Capture production

World Capture Fisheries and Aquaculture Production (in millions of tons)

Energy

The world runs on energy, and in the industrialized world that typically means burning oil, natural gas, or coal. Our modern life is built on the idea that energy is cheap and plentiful, powering heavy industry and our homes, our global transportation networks, and even the billions of electronic devices vital to business and communications in the 21st century. Access to fuel is more than a luxury: It can mean the difference between edible food or indigestible grain; and it makes it possible to survive frigid nights and sweltering days. Most energy is consumed in the wealthiest nations or in recently industrialized China and India, while in the poorer nations, the fuel likely to be available for everyday life may still be animal dung or gathered firewood. North America, with less than one-tenth of the world's population, consumes about one-quarter of the energy used; Africa, with twice the population, uses five times less than that.

Worldwide, oil accounts for more than 40 percent of energy usage. But as oil supplies dwindle and prices rise, new energy sources are being explored and exploited—from natural gas (obtained by "fracking") to renewable energy from the sun, wind, and tides. Not only are these renewable sources inexhaustible, but they are also environmentally neutral, unlike fossil fuels—such as natural gas, petroleum, and coal—whose burning releases greenhouse gases. Those gases, particularly CO_2, are a major cause of the climate change that is now proving so damaging to life and the future of the planet.

Oil accounts for more than **40%** of **energy usage** worldwide.

23% of global energy is consumed by the United States, even though it has only 5% of the world's population.

Energy Consumption, by Leading Source, 2011
Percent of total world consumption by source

Petroleum products
- More than 10%
- 1%–10%
- Less than 1%

Natural gas
- More than 10%
- 1%–10%
- Less than 1%

Coal
- More than 10%
- 1%–10%
- Less than 1%

No data

Global Production, by Fuel Type

The production of energy grows yearly to meet the demands of an ever more populous, affluent, and industrialized world. Even the demand for coal, the least-clean-burning fuel, has climbed in recent years, but like all fossil fuels, coal's reserves are limited and nonrenewable.

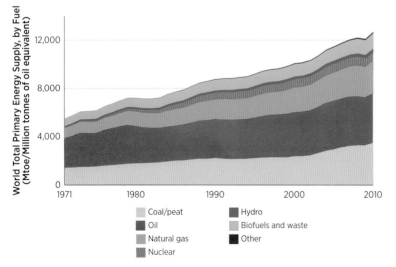

World Total Primary Energy Supply, by Fuel (Mtoe/Million tonnes of oil equivalent)

- Coal/peat
- Oil
- Natural gas
- Nuclear
- Hydro
- Biofuels and waste
- Other

Global Production, by Region

The global energy market both influences economic conditions and is influenced by them. For example, the energy crises of the 1970s led to a general downturn in oil consumption in the 1980s, and Asian producers (specifically those in the Middle East) reacted with a drop in production.

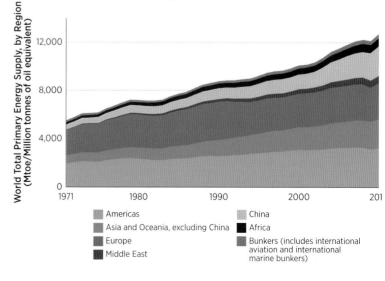

World Total Primary Energy Supply, by Region (Mtoe/Million tonnes of oil equivalent)

- Americas
- Asia and Oceania, excluding China
- Europe
- Middle East
- China
- Africa
- Bunkers (includes international aviation and international marine bunkers)

France currently gets 76% of its electricity from nuclear power, but it plans to reduce its use of nuclear energy for future needs.

Renewables will make up roughly **30%** of **total electricity output** by 2035.

1.3 billion people, mostly in the developing world, do not have **access to electricity.**

In the race to find renewable alternatives to oil, coal, and gas, some energy sources are gaining—and some are losing—ground. Enthusiasm for nuclear energy, a leading renewable in the 20th century, is waning in light of increasing public concern about nuclear waste disposal and the safety of nuclear plants. And despite an anticipated rise in wind, hydroelectric, and solar power usage in the coming three decades, the International Energy Agency expects fossil fuels to remain dominant.

Nuclear power plant, Germany

Three Gorges Dam hydropower, China

Solar power plant, Provence, France

Renewable Leaders

Not surprisingly, the big energy users—Germany, the U.S., Brazil, and China—are among the innovators searching for alternatives to fossil fuels. But smaller countries are searching as well, all of them committed to developing ever more effective ways to harness solar, wind, geothermal, and water power. Brazil has been a leader in pioneering innovations in an age-old energy source, biomass (plant and animal material), particularly in its use of sugarcane ethanol for automotive fuel.

5 ICELAND

CANADA **4 3**

3 1 2 GERMANY

UNITED STATES **2 4 1 1 1**

4 2 ITALY

4 5 SPAIN

RUSSIA **5 5**

CHINA **1 1 2 5 3**

JAPAN **4 5**

MEXICO **2**

INDIA **5**

Renewable energy, 2011
Countries ranked by capacity

1 Total renewable power
1 Hydroelectric
1 Geothermal
1 Wind
1 Solar, tidal, and wave
1 Biomass and waste

BRAZIL **3 2 4**

3 NEW ZEALAND

Wind farm near Palm Springs, California, U.S.

Mineral Resources

The world's second largest iron ore exporter, Rio Tinto, will replace trucks with trains to move ore from Western Australia mines to port cities.

Demand for Chinese steel slowed in late 2012 and early 2013, affecting the Chinese economy and workers like this man in Zhejiang Province.

A metals plant in Siberia produces ingots of almost pure gold. Such bars are one of the oldest forms of metal currency.

Major industries that consume processed mineral materials make up 15% of the U.S. economy.

Latin America's mineral giant, Brazil is a leading producer of iron and aluminum ores. Chile is the world's leading producer and exporter of copper.

Exports in Non-Fuel Mining Products, 2011
(in millions of U.S. dollars)
- 50,000–92,000
- 20,000–50,000
- 10,000–20,000
- 2,500–10,000
- 1,000–2,500
- 0–1,000
- No data

Currently, only about
50% of metal is recycled.

The map above traces more than 90 percent of the total tonnage of mined metallic minerals—generally those with high unit value, measured in dollars to hundreds of dollars per ton—but many other metals are also required to manufacture the products of our modern world. These less glamorous commodities command low unit values but are nonetheless invaluable. Cement, sand and gravel, sulfur, potash, and phosphates all play essential roles, the last two as critical components in the fertilizers the world relies on to feed an ever expanding population.

Geology, climate, economic systems, and social preferences are among the factors that create the global patterns of mineral production. Valuable concentrations of minerals form through the processes of plate movements, volcanism, and sedimentation. The same forces that formed the Andes, for example, are responsible for the porphyry copper deposits along South America's Pacific coast. Other geologic processes concentrate copper in sedimentary basins and in volcanic arcs, while climatic conditions contribute to the formation of bauxite, nickel, and other minerals.

Mineral consumption is generally tied to GDP. Developed countries use larger volumes of materials and, consequently, a wider variety of mineral commodities than are used by less developed countries. Recent economic growth in some parts of the developing world, though, has led to greater demand for many mineral resources. Meeting that need without causing harm to the environment will be one of the major challenges of the 21st century.

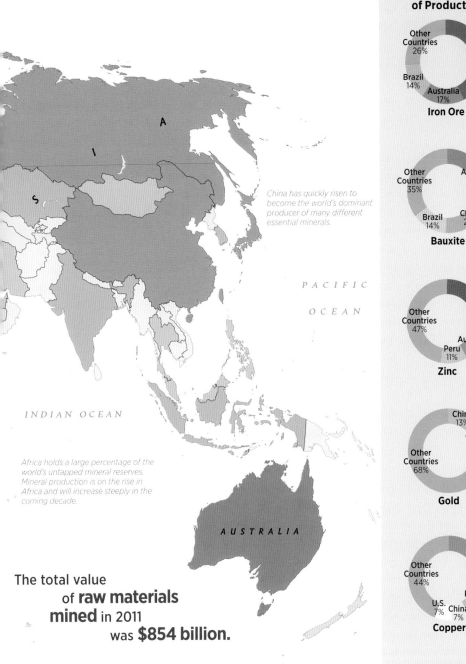

China has quickly risen to become the world's dominant producer of many different essential minerals.

PACIFIC OCEAN

INDIAN OCEAN

Africa holds a large percentage of the world's untapped mineral reserves. Mineral production is on the rise in Africa and will increase steeply in the coming decade.

AUSTRALIA

The total value of **raw materials mined** in 2011 was **$854 billion.**

World Mineral Production

As the chart below indicates, steel vastly outranks all other minerals in production, accounting for more than 83 percent; its closest competitor, precious metals, accounts for only 4 percent. Steel's economic importance is so pervasive that the health of steelmaking and manufacturing is linked to GDP. Composed of iron, carbon, and various other elements, steel is classified into hundreds of different grades.

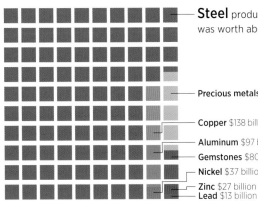

Steel produced in 2012 was worth about **$4 trillion.**

Precious metals $192 billion

Copper $138 billion

Aluminum $97 billion

Gemstones $80 billion

Nickel $37 billion

Zinc $27 billion
Lead $13 billion

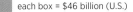 each box = $46 billion (U.S.)

World Share of Production

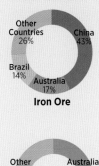

Other Countries 26%
China 43%
Brazil 14%
Australia 17%
Iron Ore

Iron ore: Primary iron oxide ores range from 35 to 70 percent iron content. The richer ores, those from Australia, Brazil, and South Africa, can be shipped directly to smelters, whereas the rest require on-site grinding, separation, and concentration. Iron is critical to the production of steel, but the annual 1.5 billion tons of raw steel produced worldwide require large quantities of many other metals as well. In the past few years alone, global steel consumption has increased by about 6 percent annually.

Other Countries 35%
Australia 30%
Brazil 14%
China 21%
Bauxite

Bauxite (aluminum ore): Bauxite, critical to aluminum production, comes from aluminous rocks that have spent millions of years near Earth's surface in tropical or subtropical climates. Deep, prolonged weathering leaches most elements from the parent rock, leaving aluminum and iron oxides. Despite this natural pretreatment, large amounts of energy are still required to convert the ore to aluminum metal. Today, however, a significant percentage of the world's aluminum production comes from recycled products.

China 31%
Other Countries 47%
Australia 11%
Peru 11%
Zinc

Zinc: Currently, more than 50 percent of zinc is used in the production of galvanized steel, while nearly 40 percent is consumed as zinc-based alloys, including brass, an alloy of zinc and copper. Zinc sulfide is commonly found in ores with copper sulfide minerals, and thus the original brass was certainly an accidental product. Nearly all the primary cadmium (for nickel-cadmium batteries) and germanium (for fiber-optic cables) come as by-products from zinc mining.

China 13%
Australia 10%
Other Countries 68%
U.S. 9%
Gold

Precious metals: Gold prices have nearly tripled in the past five years, resulting in the breadth of production indicated on the map. Twenty years ago, South Africa generated nearly 33 percent of the world's annual gold production (falling to 21 percent ten years ago) from the world's deepest mines, but those mines are now nearing technological exhaustion. Two-thirds of silver production comes from three countries—Mexico, China, and Peru. South Africa accounts for almost 80 percent of platinum.

Chile 34%
Other Countries 44%
Peru 8%
U.S. 7%
China 7%
Copper

Copper: Humans have used copper for at least 10,000 years, and it ranks third after iron and aluminum in annual consumption. A soft metal, copper was alloyed with zinc to create brass and with tin to create the bronze tools and weapons that ended the Stone Age. Most copper is recovered from sulfide minerals, and historically open-hearth smelting led to severe acid rain. Copper and its alloys are used in building construction (45 percent), electric and electronic products (23 percent), and transportation equipment (12 percent).

Russia 16%
Other Countries 58%
Philippines 13%
Indonesia 13%
Nickel

Nickel: Globally, stainless steel and non-iron-based alloys and superalloys account for nearly 90 percent of nickel consumption. China's dramatic expansion of its stainless steel industry is certainly the major cause of the nearly threefold price increase in nickel since 2005. Newly discovered sources of nickel in Canada should help counter what could have been a prolonged global shortage of the mineral, but for now Russia remains the leader in nickel production.

Other Countries 31%
China 49%
U.S. 8%
Australia 12%
Lead

Lead: Lead-acid automotive batteries continue to be the major end-product for lead sales, accounting for 86 percent of U.S. consumption. Lead is also the recycling king—83 percent of U.S. consumption is recycled (mostly postconsumer) lead. Dramatic expansion of the transportation sector in China in recent years has led to a volatile lead market, with demand and stockpiling causing fluctuations in price. China far outranks all other nations in lead production.

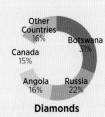

Other Countries 16%
Botswana 31%
Canada 15%
Angola 16%
Russia 22%
Diamonds

Gemstones: Diamonds dominate the world gemstone trade, accounting for 95 percent of gem imports. Canadian diamonds from the Northwest Territories have been mined since 1999, and new deposits continue to be found, spurring further exploration across North America. Most diamonds are several billion years old and have been brought to the surface relatively recently as accidental inclusions in unusual volcanic rocks. Other gemstones such as rubies, sapphires, and emeralds occur in different geological settings and thus in different countries.

Protected Areas

A UNESCO World Heritage site, Australia's Great Barrier Reef holds the world's largest array of coral reefs—some 400 different kinds.

America's largest national park, Wrangell-St. Elias, encompasses 13.2 million acres of Alaskan ice fields, glaciers, and mountains.

Kenya's Lake Nakuru National Park, a rhino sanctuary since 1983, offers critically endangered black rhinos a haven from poachers.

The World Database on Protected Areas classifies some reserves as marine protected areas, even though they may also include terrestrial regions. One example is Northeast Greenland National Park.

NORTH AMERICA

EUROP

PACIFIC OCEAN

A T L A N T I C   O C E A N

SOUTH AMERICA

AFRIC

20% of Latin America is protected land and marine areas—it is by far the world's leader in this category.

As defined by the International Union for Conservation of Natur (IUCN), a protected area is "a clearly defined geographical space, recognized, dedicated and managed, through legal or other effective means, to achieve the long-term conservation of nature with associated ecosyste services and cultural values."

A N T A R C T I C A

There are more than 150,000 protected areas around the globe—on every continent and in every ocean. Some preserve exotic landscapes with rare and imperiled plants and animals; some protect whole ecosystems; some supply natural resources; some offer valuable spiritual, scientific, educational, or recreational opportunities; and some serve as buffer zones for neighboring ecosystems or provide migration corridors for wildlife. Together, these areas are thought to store at least 15 percent of the planet's terrestrial carbon in their soils and plant life. The largest protected area on Earth is the 972,000-square-kilometer (375,300-square-mile) Northeast Greenland National Park.

The International Union for Conservation of Nature (IUCN) evaluates the world's protected areas and places them in seven categories, based on how they are managed and what limits they set on human encroachment. Most restricted are the strict nature reserves, followed by wilderness areas, national parks, national monuments, habitat- and species-management areas, protected landscape/seascapes, and managed resource protection areas.

Local, national, and international governments collaborate with a wide range of environmental agencies to provide protection to these areas. Agencies like WWF (World Wildlife Fund), the Nature Conservancy, and Conservation International work with one another, local shareholders and officials, national agencies, and international organizations like the United Nations to ensure the preservation of environmental and cultural treasures as well as the livelihoods and traditions of local peoples.

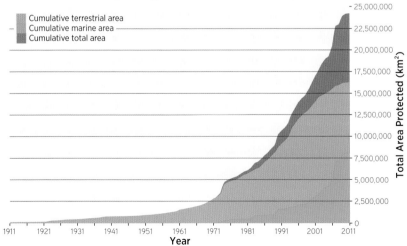

There are now more than **157,000** **protected areas** in the world.

A
S
I
A

PACIFIC OCEAN

INDIAN OCEAN

AUSTRALIA

The World Protected Areas Database is used to report progress relating to the UN Millennium Development Goals and the Convention on Biological Diversity, and is also used in partnership with many other conservation organizations.

Protected Areas and Biodiversity Hot Spots
- Marine
- Terrestrial
- Both
- Biodiversity hot spots (outer limits)

Biodiversity Hot Spots The concept of a biodiversity hot spot was identified and adopted by the conservation community in 1988. Since that time, hot spots have been identified around the world. To qualify as a hot spot, an area must contain at least 1,500 species of endemic vascular plants and have lost at least 70 percent of its original habitat. Currently there are 43 hot spots. Such areas once covered 15.7 percent of Earth's surface but have now been reduced to only 2.3 percent.

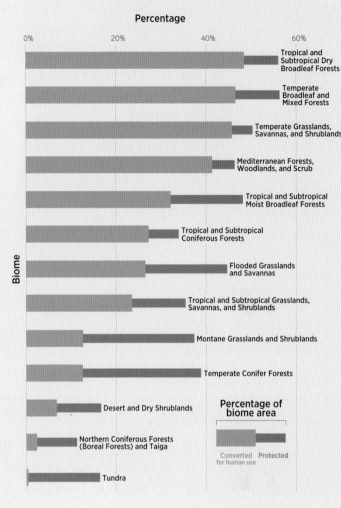

Biome Protection

The extent of human disruption and conversion—as well as conservation—varies across the planet, but almost every biome is threatened to some degree. Temperate grasslands, such as those in North America and Asia, are the least protected. Tundra regions are unique as they have a much greater percentage of land conserved than converted. Mediterranean forests, such as those found in Chile, California, and Italy, are highly converted—only a very small share are protected.

Percentage

0%   20%   40%   60%

Biome:
- Tropical and Subtropical Dry Broadleaf Forests
- Temperate Broadleaf and Mixed Forests
- Temperate Grasslands, Savannas, and Shrublands
- Mediterranean Forests, Woodlands, and Scrub
- Tropical and Subtropical Moist Broadleaf Forests
- Tropical and Subtropical Coniferous Forests
- Flooded Grasslands and Savannas
- Tropical and Subtropical Grasslands, Savannas, and Shrublands
- Montane Grasslands and Shrublands
- Temperate Conifer Forests
- Desert and Dry Shrublands
- Northern Coniferous Forests (Boreal Forests) and Taiga
- Tundra

Percentage of biome area

Converted for human use   Protected

Tracking Conservation ▼

Ocean conservation is growing even as land conservation appears to be reaching a plateau. Still, the gap between the two categories remains large, and many ocean conservationists continue to push for greater protection of our marine resources.

Growth in Nationally Designated Protected Areas (1911–2011)

- Cumulative terrestrial area
- Cumulative marine area
- Cumulative total area

Total Area Protected (km²)

25,000,000
22,500,000
20,000,000
17,500,000
15,000,000
12,500,000
10,000,000
7,500,000
5,000,000
2,500,000
0

1911 1921 1931 1941 1951 1961 1971 1981 1991 2001 2011

Year

Charting Threatened Species ▶

Globally, the number of imperiled animal species continues to rise. This growth can be partially attributed to a greater understanding and tracking of endangered species. Although a species may be recognized internationally as threatened or endangered, the responsibility of protecting that species falls to the individual countries where it is found. The Endangered Species Act of 1973 protects recognized endangered species within U.S. borders. The Convention on International Trade in Endangered Species of Wild Fauna and Flora (CITES) is an international agreement that regulates the global trade and sale of endangered plants and animals and their products.

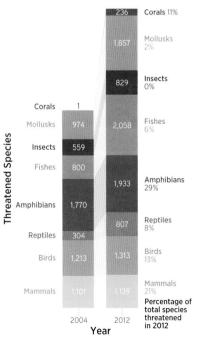

Threatened Species

	2004	2012	Percentage of total species threatened in 2012
Corals	1	236	Corals 11%
Mollusks	974	1,857	Mollusks 2%
Insects	559	829	Insects 0%
Fishes	800	2,058	Fishes 6%
Amphibians	1,770	1,933	Amphibians 29%
Reptiles	304	807	Reptiles 8%
Birds	1,213	1,313	Birds 13%
Mammals	1,101	1,139	Mammals 21%

Year

Environmental Stress

Like all life-forms on Earth, humans need natural systems—from deserts to forests to riverine biosystems to oceans—to thrive. Yet through human-caused pollution and exploitation, these systems have been degraded and compromised. The negative consequences of this are already playing out and will continue to do so into the future.

Many types of environmental stresses are interrelated and have far-reaching consequences. For example, the thinning of the protective ozone layer, resulting from the release of chlorofluorocarbons (CFCs) into the atmosphere through aerosol sprays and refrigeration equipment, has already led to more ultraviolet light penetrating the atmosphere, which affects plant growth on land and in the sea and the health of humans. And in the coming decades, global warming caused by the burning of fossil fuels will likely increase water scarcity, desertification, deforestation, and sea level increase, all of which will create significant problems for humans in both the developed and developing world.

Although socioeconomic indicators can reveal a great deal about long-term trends in human impact on the environment, this kind of data is not collected routinely in many countries. But the rapid conversion of countryside to built-up areas is one indicator that change is occurring at a fast pace. While scientists work to develop products and technologies with few or no adverse effects on the environment, their efforts will be nullified if humans' population and consumption of resources continue to increase worldwide.

Desertification

When land has been degraded by such human activities as overgrazing, farming, and deforestation, an exceptionally prolonged drought can trigger desertification. Global warming is expected to increase droughts worldwide, and thus desertification will claim more of Earth's surface.

Desertification and Land Degradation
- Dryland systems
- Land degradation in drylands

Deforestation

Forests have gained moderate ground in temperate zones in recent decades, although widespread deforestation of tropical rain forests, due to short-term exploitation and unsustainable practices, has been cataclysmic. Since forests act as "carbon sinks" (absorbing more carbon than they release), this loss only exacerbates the atmospheric buildup of carbon dioxide.

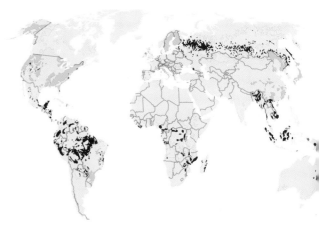

Deforestation Hot Spots
- Net loss of forest
- Current forest cover
- Net gain of forest

Drought parched the North American plains in 2012, ruining the largest corn crop planted since 1937. Canada's Red River Valley (above) was particularly hard hit.

A key player in the environmental health of the planet, Brazil's vast forests have fallen to human hands in recent decades, but new laws are now slowing deforestation.

Visitors to Tiananmen Square wear protective face masks to guard against the hazardous smog that blankets Beijing, a result of growing industrial and auto pollution.

Precious water drips from a tap in Shilin in China's Yunnan Province, where four years of severe drought has left some 600,000 people facing a shortage of drinking water.

The Kyoto Protocol to cut greenhouse gas emissions lists **190 countries** as parties to the treaty, but not the U.S. or Canada.

Air Pollution

Fine particulate matter ($PM_{2.5}$) is harmful to human health and affects climate. In some regions, $PM_{2.5}$ is dominated by natural sources from fires and deserts. However, in many populated regions—such as North America, Europe, and Asia—it is mostly caused by human emissions.

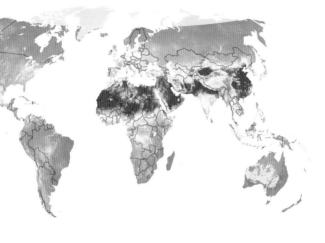

Abundance of Fine Particulate Matter ($PM_{2.5}$), 2001–2006

High

Low

No data

Water Scarcity

Many areas of the world are suffering shortages of clean drinking water. The UN predicts that if that trend continues, by 2025, 1.8 billion people will be dealing with absolute water scarcity, and two-thirds of the entire human population could be subject to water stress.

Water Scarcity
- Physical water scarcity
- Approaching physical water scarcity
- Economic water scarcity
- Little or no water scarcity
- Not estimated

Physical water scarcity: Available resources are insufficient to meet all demands, including minimum environmental flow requirements.

Economic water scarcity: A lack of investment or human capacity is available to keep up with growing water demands.

Carbon Emissions

The energy that propels modern industrial society generally comes from burning fossil fuels, and that in turn accounts for 80 percent of the extra CO_2 now in the atmosphere. Some 18 percent of the rest comes from land-use changes, primarily the cutting of tropical forests for farmland or timber. As vast tracts of the Amazon and Indonesia have been felled, their vital role in carbon storage has been lost.

CO_2 Emissions by Region (millions of metric tons)

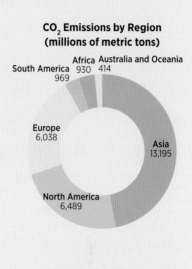

- South America 969
- Africa 930
- Australia and Oceania 414
- Europe 6,038
- Asia 13,195
- North America 6,489

CO_2 Emissions by Sector (millions of metric tons)

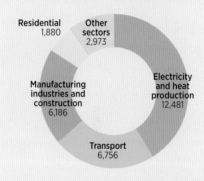

- Residential 1,880
- Other sectors 2,973
- Manufacturing industries and construction 6,186
- Electricity and heat production 12,481
- Transport 6,756

Environmental Performance Rankings

The top ten countries evaluated in Yale University's 2012 Environmental Performance Index (EPI) were all European, with the exception of Costa Rica; the U.S. ranking was 49, while Iraq held the lowest spot at 132.

Based on national policies aimed at both environmental public health and ecosystem vitality, the EPI takes into account present performance and trends in performance over the past ten years.

Environmental Performance Index Rankings, 2012
- Strongest performers
- Strong performers
- Modest performers
- Weaker performers
- Weakest performers
- No data

Smokestacks of a coal-fired power plant in Kentucky belch CO_2 into the atmosphere. Such emissions are a major cause of global warming, acid rain, and smog.

Transportation

Each day,
more than **230,000**
automobiles are
manufactured.

Glowing arteries of U.S. Interstate 45 link Texas' largest cities, Dallas and Houston, before continuing on to the Gulf of Mexico.

Europe's busiest port, the Netherlands' Rotterdam, handles cargo moving between Europe, the Americas, and South Africa.

The original "jumbo jets," the wide-bodied Boeing 747s revolutionized transport and travel when they began regular flights in the 1970s.

The Global Transportation System

 Roads

 Shipping routes

Air networks

We may be living in the digital age, but we still inhabit a physical world. And for all that has been said about the knowledge economy and virtual connections, the global economy continues to rely to a large degree on the physical movement of goods and people. By all measures, more material is shipped throughout the globe today than ever before. And whether for business or pleasure, people continue to travel cross-country or around the world at speeds and frequencies that would have astounded their ancestors.

Over the past century, flying has gone from near miracle to commonplace—and for many people, a too-frequent inconvenience. But access to air travel is anything but universal: While commercial flights reach most corners of the populated world, their frequency is skewed dramatically toward the Northern Hemisphere. That's not just because the bulk of landmass and population lies north of the Equator; it's also because air travel is expensive, and the wealthier nations are concentrated in the north as well.

The age-old method of transport—by sea—still moves 90 percent of international freight by volume, but from perishable foods and flowers to pharmaceuticals, from pricey microelectronics to thousands of just-in-time components for manufacturing, items transported by air make up 40 percent of international freight by value. Even with recent increases in the cost of air transport, it is still 10 percent less costly to move goods by air today than it was in 1955.

Today's **largest ocean liners** can each hold more than **14,000 shipping containers.**

Comparing Travel

A trip from London to Paris can be taken by plane, car, or train, but the travel time and carbon dioxide emissions will vary greatly among these modes of transportation. Traveling by air creates the most emissions but is also the fastest option. A train trip produces the fewest emissions and is faster than traveling by car.

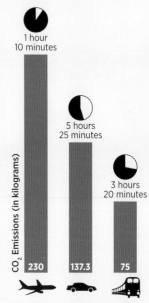

London to Paris

1 hour 10 minutes — 230

5 hours 25 minutes — 137.3

3 hours 20 minutes — 75

CO_2 Emissions (in kilograms)

World's Busiest Airports

Airport	Total Passengers, 2010
1. Atlanta (ATL), U.S.	89,332,000
2. Beijing (PEK), China	73,948,000
3. Chicago O'Hare (ORD), U.S.	66,775,000
4. London Heathrow (LHR), U.K.	65,884,000
5. Tokyo Haneda (HND), Japan	64,211,000
6. Los Angeles (LAX), U.S.	59,070,000
7. Paris Charles de Gaulle (CDG), France	58,167,000
8. Dallas/Fort Worth (DFW), U.S.	56,907,000
9. Frankfurt (FRA), Germany	53,009,000
10. Denver (DEN), U.S.	52,209,000

Shipping the World's Goods

The leading ports are clustered in East Asia, where enormous quantities of goods are produced and then shipped to foreign markets. Cheaper than air transport, maritime transport continues to be the preferred option for many manufactured goods. Major straits (Hormuz, Malacca) and canals (Suez, Panama) are critical to sea commerce and as choke points are vulnerable to conflict and natural disaster.

⑩ Rotterdam 11.88 million

Strait of Hormuz

Suez Canal

Panama Canal

⑧ Qingdao 13.02 million
⑤ Busan 16.17 million
⑦ Guangzhou 14.26 million
❶ Shanghai 31.74 million
❻ Ningbo 14.72 million
⑨ Dubai 13.00 million
❹ Shenzhen 22.51 million
Strait of Malacca
❷ Singapore 29.94 million
❸ Hong Kong 24.38 million

Top 30 ports, 2011
Total cargo ranked by volume in TEUs*

◯ 1-10   ◯ 11-30

The Twenty-foot Equivalent Unit (TEU) is a measure of cargo capacity roughly equivalent to the volume of a standard 20-foot-long metal shipping container.

Charting International Tourism

International tourism suffered a decline in 2009 because of a slow global economy, but it rebounded to reach a record one billion arrivals in 2012. Just over half of all tourists travel for recreation and the same percentage arrive by air, while road trips account for 41 percent. Europe is the top destination for international tourists, and France the top country.

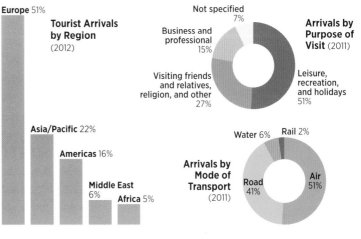

Tourist Arrivals by Region (2012)

Europe 51%
Asia/Pacific 22%
Americas 16%
Middle East 6%
Africa 5%

Arrivals by Purpose of Visit (2011)

Not specified 7%
Business and professional 15%
Visiting friends and relatives, religion, and other 27%
Leisure, recreation, and holidays 51%

Arrivals by Mode of Transport (2011)

Water 6%
Rail 2%
Road 41%
Air 51%

Globalization

Transglobal companies like McDonald's reach into many countries and cultures, including predominantly Muslim Bangladesh.

In Brussels's Grand Place, a lighted art installation replaces the traditional, more Christian-centric Christmas tree.

In recent years, the Philippines has joined India as a major player in the burgeoning offshore call-center industry.

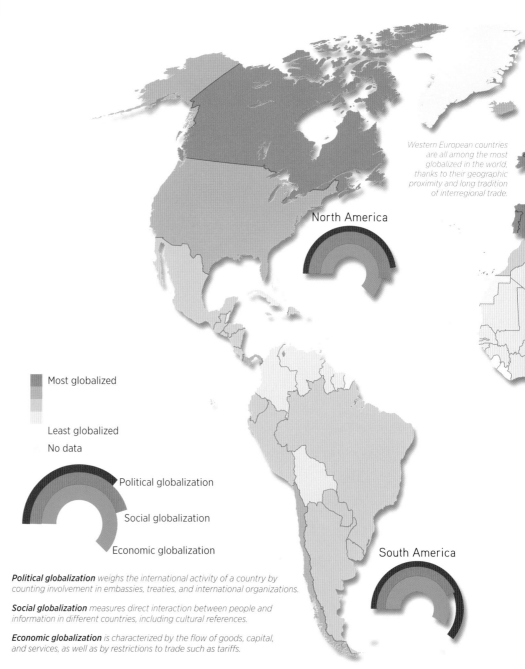

Western European countries are all among the most globalized in the world, thanks to their geographic proximity and long tradition of interregional trade.

North America

Most globalized

Least globalized

No data

Political globalization

Social globalization

Economic globalization

Political globalization *weighs the international activity of a country by counting involvement in embassies, treaties, and international organizations.*

Social globalization *measures direct interaction between people and information in different countries, including cultural references.*

Economic globalization *is characterized by the flow of goods, capital, and services, as well as by restrictions to trade such as tariffs.*

South America

On some level, globalization, like migration, has been a perpetual human trend, historically accomplished through trade. But in the postmodern world, interdependence among humans and cultures over vast distances has accelerated—not just in the economic realm, but through person-to-person contact, technological connectivity, and political ties. Globalization indexes, like the Swiss-based KOF index reflected in the map data above, measure the dimensions of globalization by looking at it country by country and also worldwide through three lenses—political, social, and economic. In the political sphere, the level of cooperation among countries drives the index results; in the economic, real trade and investment volumes are measured, as are trade restrictions; and in the social, the free flow of information and ideas is tracked.

Not surprisingly, the worldwide economic downturn that began in 2009 has slowed the pace of globalization in that sector and somewhat in the social sector. As in the past, Belgium tops the KOF list of most globalized countries, with Ireland at number two, while Lesotho and the Dominican Republic are making the most rapid progress in globalization; Cyprus proves to be the most socially globalized, followed by Singapore. In recent years, Eastern Europe and South and Central Asia have been the regions with the strongest upward trends in globalization.

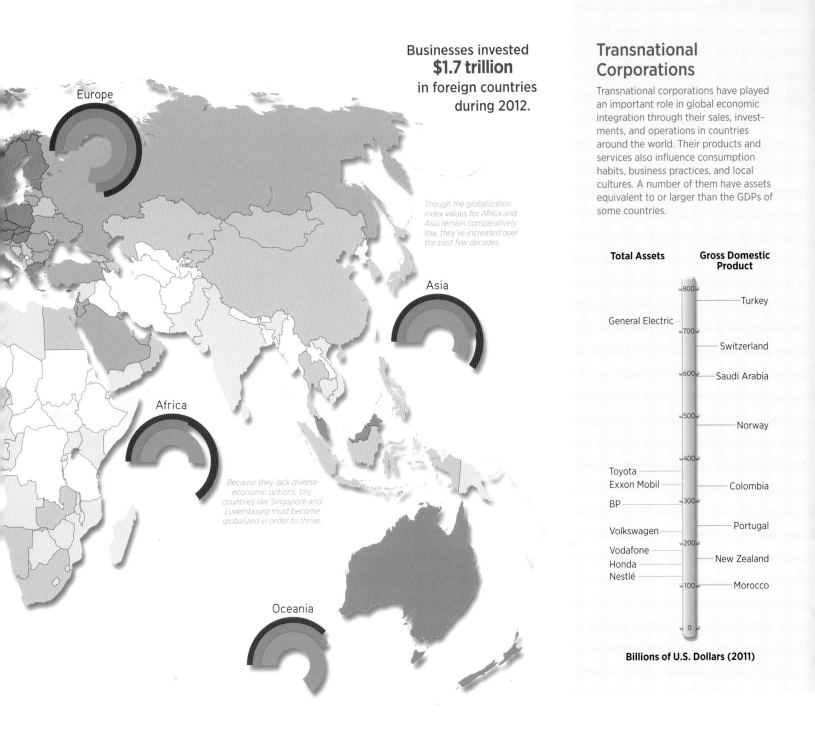

Businesses invested
$1.7 trillion
in foreign countries
during 2012.

Europe

Though the globalization index values for Africa and Asia remain comparatively low, they've increased over the past few decades.

Asia

Africa

Because they lack diverse economic options, tiny countries like Singapore and Luxembourg must become globalized in order to thrive.

Oceania

Transnational Corporations

Transnational corporations have played an important role in global economic integration through their sales, investments, and operations in countries around the world. Their products and services also influence consumption habits, business practices, and local cultures. A number of them have assets equivalent to or larger than the GDPs of some countries.

Total Assets		Gross Domestic Product
	800	
General Electric		Turkey
	700	
		Switzerland
	600	Saudi Arabia
	500	Norway
	400	
Toyota		
Exxon Mobil		Colombia
BP	300	
Volkswagen		Portugal
Vodafone	200	
Honda		New Zealand
Nestlé		
	100	Morocco
	0	

Billions of U.S. Dollars (2011)

Offshore Services

Since the 1990s, the meteoric transformation of information and communication technologies has allowed transglobal companies to outsource some of their services from the industrialized world to the developing world, where lower paid, skilled workers provide an eager, educated, and less expensive workforce. The fields of information technology and business processing have been particularly susceptible to outsourcing, greatly benefiting the economies of outsourcing leaders like India. The financial and manufacturing industries have led the way in offshoring, and in recent years, even small- and medium-size firms have joined in the enthusiasm for offshoring jobs and facilities. The latest studies, however, point to the offshore trend's slowing or even reversing in the coming decade.

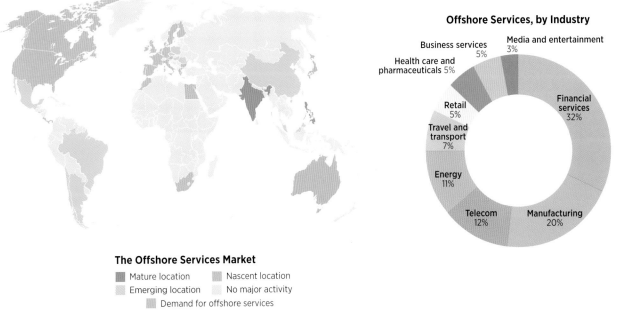

The Offshore Services Market

■ Mature location   ■ Nascent location
■ Emerging location   ■ No major activity
■ Demand for offshore services

Offshore Services, by Industry

Business services 5%
Media and entertainment 3%
Health care and pharmaceuticals 5%
Retail 5%
Travel and transport 7%
Energy 11%
Telecom 12%
Financial services 32%
Manufacturing 20%

Digital Connectivity

A specially designed pipe system facilitates the laying of fiber-optic cable in Germany.

In rural Kenya, as elsewhere, mobile devices are tools of connectivity and empowerment.

A Vietnamese couple reflects the growing reliance on cell phones among young people.

Use of digital technology is surging in classrooms worldwide, including this one in Libya.

At the end of 2011,
2.3 billion people,
one in three,
were **using the Internet.**

The Five Regions

The diameter of each region's circle depicts total international Internet bandwidth connected to cities within that region. The ring around the circle is divided into sections to illustrate the percentage of total bandwidth used to connect that region to other regions. The light gray part of the ring represents bandwidth connections within the region. Internet hub cities within each region, noted with yellow circles, are numbered to indicate the top ten cities' rank in terms of total international Internet bandwidth. (Africa has nine cities, not ten.)

The Full Spectrum of Bandwidth

Disparities in Internet capacity across the regions depicted make it necessary to have a separate cutoff for each region. Without these very different cutoffs, it would be impossible to show the largest route in the world between New York and London (1.5 terabits per second [Tbps]) alongside lower-capacity routes in Africa. "Gbps" stands for billions of bits per second.

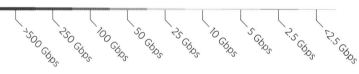

>500 Gbps   250 Gbps   100 Gbps   50 Gbps   25 Gbps   10 Gbps   5 Gbps   2.5 Gbps   <2.5 Gbps

www.telegeography.com

In the past decade, technological advances have changed the face of communication—and with it everything from geopolitics to finance to health care. For the first time in human history, enormous amounts of data can be shared almost instantaneously across the planet, connecting people and cultures in ways that would have been unimaginable less than a quarter century ago. Voice and Internet communications penetrate virtually every corner of the globe, thanks in large part to the fiber-optic cables, cell-phone towers, and satellites that link humans in ways that copper wire connectivity never could have. And with increasingly less reliance on infrastructure—poles or cable lines—the latest technologies allow residents in remote areas and developing countries access to global information and the global dialogue in unprecedented ways, fueling business, educational opportunities, and political change.

The speed of these new modes of interacting is at least metaphorically matched by the speed of innovations in the field of global communications and by a new kind of "war"—cyber war. Nations, businesses, and individuals who lead much of their lives online grapple with their vulnerability to hackers, as well as to weather-related interruptions and system breakdowns. Still, from international stock traders to microbusiness owners to citizen journalists broadcasting breaking news from their cell phones, most people will accept these risks in order to be part of the Internet-created global village—a virtual world where distance and time no longer limit human potential.

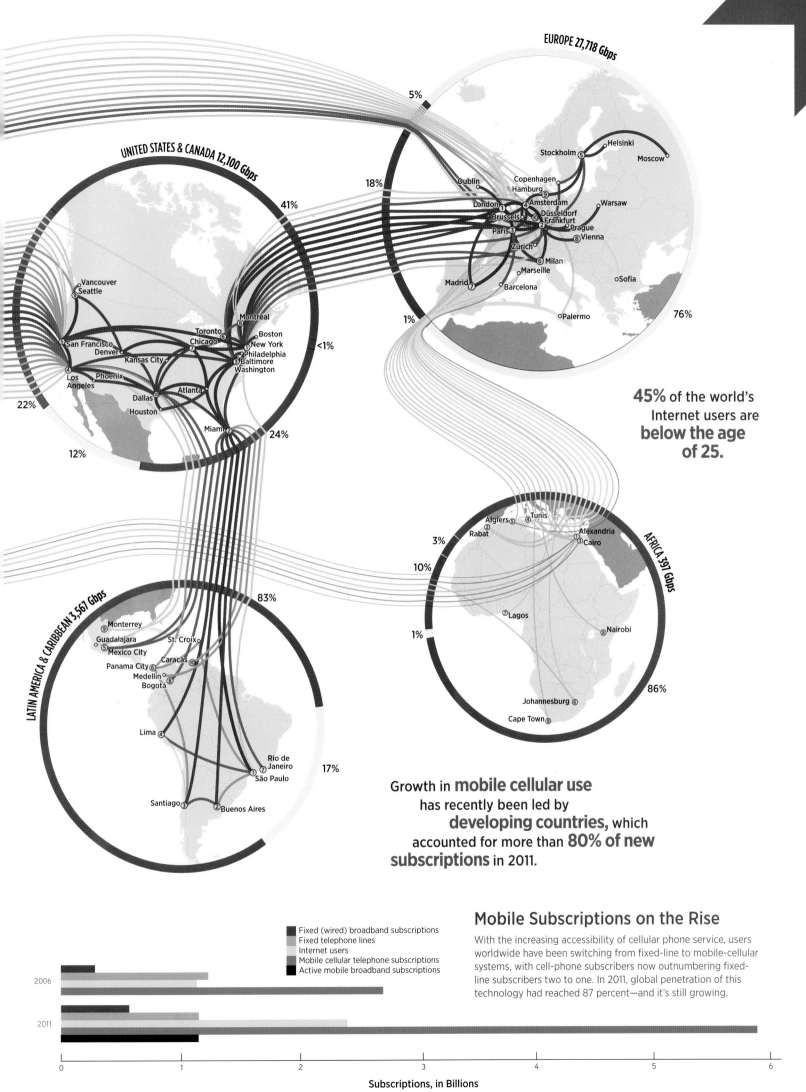

EUROPE 27,718 Gbps

5%

Stockholm ⑤ Helsinki

Moscow

Copenhagen
Hamburg
Dublin
London ①   Amsterdam ⑨
      Brussels ④ Düsseldorf
      Paris ③ ⑩ Frankfurt ②   Warsaw
      Zürich ⑧ Vienna
            ⑥ Milan   Prague
18%   Marseille
Madrid ⑦   Barcelona   ° Sofia

1%   ° Palermo   76%

UNITED STATES & CANADA 12,100 Gbps

41%

Vancouver
Seattle ⑨
                  Montréal ⑧
            Toronto   Boston
      Chicago ⑥ New York
San Francisco ⑤   ⑦ Philadelphia
      Denver   ① Baltimore
Kansas City   ③ Washington
④
Los   Phoenix
Angeles   Dallas ⑩ Atlanta
      Houston

22%   Miami ②

<1%

24%

12%

45% of the world's Internet users are below the age of 25.

AFRICA 397 Gbps

      Tunis
Algiers ⑤ ④
Rabat ②   Alexandria ①
      ③ Cairo

3%

10%

⑦ Lagos   ° Nairobi ⑧

1%

            Johannesburg ⑥

86%

Cape Town ⑨

LATIN AMERICA & CARIBBEAN 3,567 Gbps

83%

Monterrey ⑨
Guadalajara °
⑤ Mexico City   St. Croix °
Panama City ⑥   Caracas ⑩
Medellín °   ⑧
Bogotá °

Lima ④

            Rio de
            Janeiro ⑦
            São Paulo ①
17%
Santiago ③   ② Buenos Aires

Growth in mobile cellular use has recently been led by **developing countries,** which accounted for more than **80% of new subscriptions** in 2011.

Mobile Subscriptions on the Rise

With the increasing accessibility of cellular phone service, users worldwide have been switching from fixed-line to mobile-cellular systems, with cell-phone subscribers now outnumbering fixed-line subscribers two to one. In 2011, global penetration of this technology had reached 87 percent—and it's still growing.

Fixed (wired) broadband subscriptions
Fixed telephone lines
Internet users
Mobile cellular telephone subscriptions
Active mobile broadband subscriptions

2006

2011

0   1   2   3   4   5   6

Subscriptions, in Billions

Time Zones

1:00 A.M.	2:00 A.M.	3:00 A.M.	4:00 A.M.	5:00 A.M.	6:00 A.M.	7:00 A.M.	8:00 A.M.	9:00 A.M.	10:00 A.M.	11:00 A.M.
-12	-11	-10	-9	-8	-7	-6	-5	-4	-3	-2	-1
X	W	V	U	T	S	R	Q	P		N

ARCTIC OCEAN

QUEEN ELIZABETH ISLANDS

PARRY ISLANDS

GREENLAND (KALAALLIT NUNAAT)
Denmark
75°

Z

Banks I.

Victoria Island

Baffin Bay

Ellesmere Island

N

Greenland Jan Mayen Norway

Chukchi Sea

Beaufort Sea

Great Bear Lake

Baffin Island

ARCTIC CIRCLE

RUSSIA

V

ALASKA U.S.

Great Slave Lake

Hudson Bay

S

Labrador Sea

Nuuk (Godthåb)

Q

60°

O

ICELAND
Reykjavík

Z

BERING SEA

Gulf of Alaska

U

T

CANADA

S

R

IRELAND
Dublin

NORTH ATLANTIC

KIN

W

Aleutian Islands

All of Alaska, except the western Aleutian Islands and St. Lawrence Island, use "V" zone time. The exceptions use "W" zone.

Calgary

Lake Winnipeg
Winnipeg

Montréal

Ottawa

Toronto
Detroit

Chicago

New York

Q+30
P

Island of Newfoundland

St.-Pierre and Miquelon France

45°

FR

Vancouver

NORTH PACIFIC OCEAN

Halifax

San Francisco

Denver

UNITED STATES

St. Louis
Washington

Philadelphia

Azores Portugal

PORT.
Lisbon

Los Angeles
San Diego

Phoenix

Memphis

Dallas

Bermuda U.K.

Q

P

O

N

Rabat

HAWAI'I U.S.

Houston

New Orleans

Jacksonville

30°

Madeira Is. Portugal
Canary Is. Sp.

MORO

Hawai'i

San Antonio
Monterrey

Gulf of Mexico

Miami

Nassau

BAHAMAS

TROPIC OF CANCER

WESTERN SAHARA Mor.

Z

MEXICO

S

Havana
CUBA
Port-au-Prince

DOMINICAN REPUBLIC

PUERTO RICO U.S.

ST. KITTS AND NEVIS
ANTIGUA AND BARBUDA

Nouakchott

CAPE VERDE
Praia

Dakar

MAURITANIA

Ouagad

X

W

V

U

T

Mexico City

Guatemala City

BELIZE
HONDURAS
Tegucigalpa

JAMAICA

HAITI

Santo Domingo

DOMINICA
ST. LUCIA
BARBADOS

15° N

GAMBIA
GUINEA-BISSAU

Bamako

SENEGAL

GUATEMALA
San Salvador
EL SALVADOR

NICARAGUA
Managua
San José

ST. VINCENT AND THE GRENADINES
GRENADA

TRINIDAD AND TOBAGO

GUINEA

CO
D'IVO
(IVO
COA

COSTA RICA

PANAMA

Caracas

Georgetown

Freetown

SIERRA LEONE

Monrovia
LIBERIA

M+60

Line Islands

KIRIBATI

M+120

Marquesas Is. France
W+30

Panama City
Bogotá

VENEZUELA
R+30

COLOMBIA

Paramaribo
Cayenne
FRENCH GUIANA Fr.

SURINAME

GUYANA

0°
EQUATOR

Ascension U.K.

TOKELAU N.Z.

Quito
ECUADOR

Manaus

Fortaleza

SAMOA

M+60

AMERICAN SAMOA U.S.

Papeete

FRENCH POLYNESIA France

S

Galápagos Islands
Ecuador

PERU

Q

BRAZIL

Recife

M+60

Nuku'alofa
TONGA

Lima

R

La Paz
BOLIVIA
Sucre

Salvador

Brasília

15° S

Belo Horizonte

Pitcairn I. U.K.

Easter I. Sala y Gómez I. Chile

San Ambrosio I. Chile

PARAGUAY

Rio de Janeiro
São Paulo

SOUTH ATLANTIC

TROPIC OF CAPRICORN

INTERNATIONAL DATE LINE
The position of the date line is based on international acceptance, but it has no legal status. The island nations of Kiribati and Samoa, along with Tokelau (a territory of New Zealand) have advanced their time zones. They are now the first to start a new day and the first to celebrate a new year.

M

Date Line
Monday
Sunday

CHILE

Chile Juan Fernández Is.

Asunción

Porto Alegre

30°

Santiago

URUGUAY

Buenos Aires
Montevideo

P

Q

ARGENTINA

Chatham Is. N.Z.
M+45

SOUTH PACIFIC OCEAN

Falkland Islands (Islas Malvinas) U.K.

Tristan da Cunha Gro

P

O

N

45°

South Georgia U.K.

Longitude West of Greenwich

165°	150°	135°	120°	105°	90°	75°	60°	45°	30°	15°
X	W	V	U	T	S	R	Q	P	O	N
-12	-11	-10	-9	-8	-7	-6	-5	-4	-3	-2	-1

The numeral in each tab directly above shows the number of hours to be added to, or subtracted from, Coordinated Universal Time (UTC), formerly Greenwich Mean Time (GMT).

North America

This most northerly of continents—the tips of its Arctic islands lie less than 1,000 kilometers (620 miles) from the North Pole—has been marked dramatically by the forces of ice and snow. Vast stretches of North America were covered by kilometers-thick sheets of ice during the most recent ice age, ending some 10,000 years ago, and that force still shows across the continent's North, from the bare bedrock of the broad Canadian Shield to the North American Great Lakes, the world's largest freshwater lake system. Millennia after the greater-still glacial Lake Agassiz emptied to the sea, much of the continent's interior still drains along similar routes, north to Hudson Bay, east through the St. Lawrence Seaway and through the Mississippi, to the Gulf of Mexico in the South.

   North America's West is dominated by the Rocky Mountains and other relatively new mountain chains. At the continent's southern extreme, the narrow Isthmus of Panama makes a tenuous connection to South America. The gap between these sister continents was closed just three million years ago, separating the Pacific Ocean from the Atlantic. Thick forests and unfinished roadways have kept that land bridge closed to human passage for generations, but millions of birds still make the annual migration from the tundra and boreal forest of the North to the wetlands forests of South America.

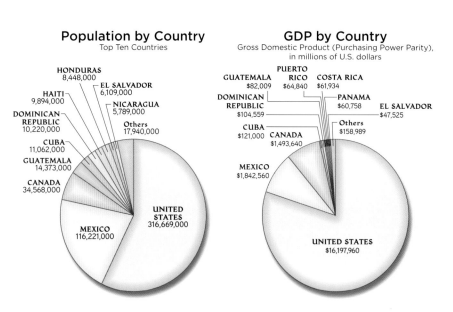

Population by Country
Top Ten Countries

HONDURAS
8,448,000
EL SALVADOR
6,109,000
HAITI
9,894,000
NICARAGUA
5,789,000
DOMINICAN
REPUBLIC
10,220,000
Others
17,940,000
CUBA
11,062,000
GUATEMALA
14,373,000
CANADA
34,568,000
UNITED
STATES
316,669,000
MEXICO
116,221,000

GDP by Country
Gross Domestic Product (Purchasing Power Parity),
in millions of U.S. dollars

PUERTO
RICO
$64,840
GUATEMALA
$82,009
COSTA RICA
$61,934
DOMINICAN
REPUBLIC
$104,559
PANAMA
$60,758
EL SALVADOR
$47,525
CUBA
$121,000
Others
$158,989
CANADA
$1,493,640
MEXICO
$1,842,560
UNITED STATES
$16,197,960

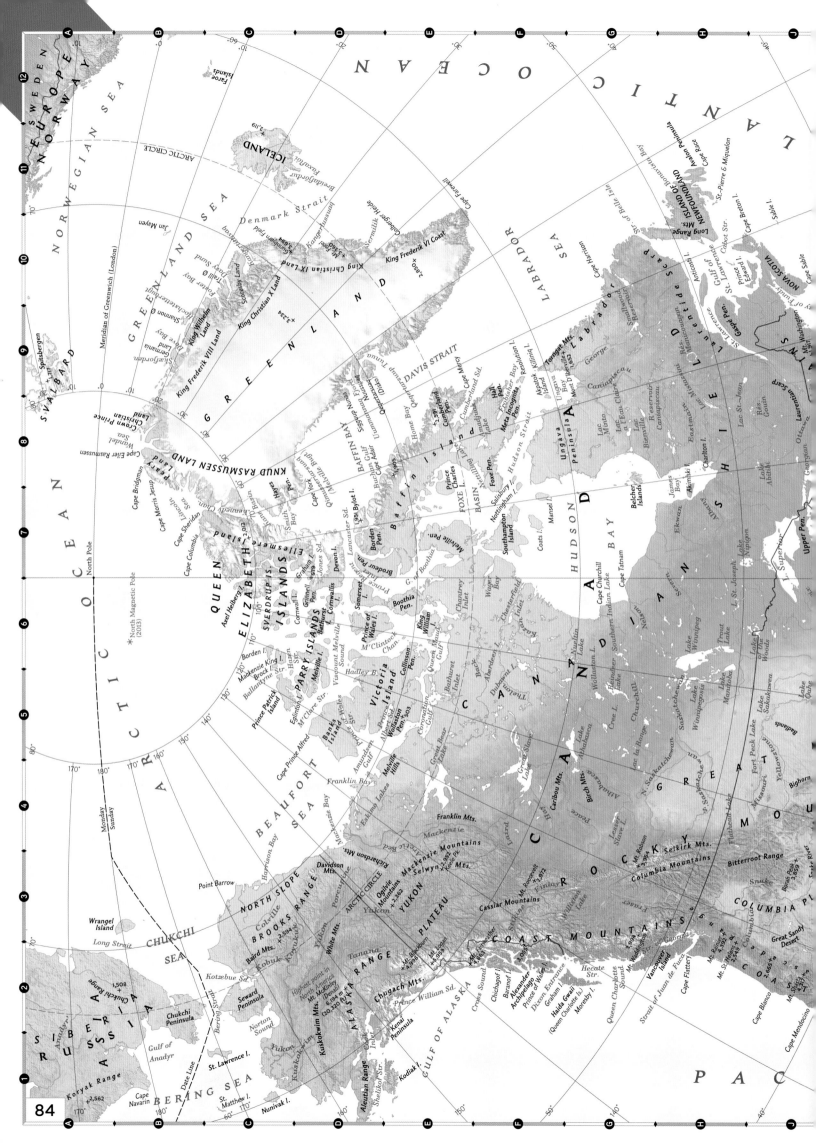

Physical North America

Azimuthal Equidistant Projection
SCALE 1:25,000,000   1 CENTIMETER = 250 KILOMETERS   1 INCH = 395 MILES

KILOMETERS
0   300   600   900

STATUTE MILES
0   300   600   900

Bermuda Is.

TROPIC OF CANCER

WEST INDIES

ST. KITTS AND NEVIS ANTIGUA AND BARBUDA
Anguilla
Virgin Is.
St. Thomas St. Croix
Barbuda Antigua
Guadeloupe
Montserrat
Dominica
Martinique
ST. LUCIA DOMINICA
ST. VINCENT AND THE GRENADINES
BARBADOS
GRENADA
Tobago TRINIDAD AND TOBAGO
Trinidad

LESSER ANTILLES
Windward Islands
Leeward Islands
LESSER ANTILLES

PUERTO RICO
Mona Pass.
DOMINICAN REPUBLIC
HAITI HISPANIOLA
W. of Guadeloupe
Windward Pass.
G. of Gonâve

BAHAMAS
Great Abaco I.
Eleuthera I.
Cat I.
Rum Cay
Long I.
Crooked I.
Acklins I.
Andros I.
Great Exuma I.
Exuma Is.
Turks Is.
Mayaguana I.
Great Inagua I.
Caicos Is.

CUBA
Isle of Youth
G. of Batabanó
Cape San Antonio
Yucatan Channel
Cayman Is.
Grand Cayman
JAMAICA
+2,974

GREATER ANTILLES

CARIBBEAN SEA

Bonaire
Curaçao
Aruba
Guajira Peninsula
Gulf of Venezuela
Lake Maracaibo

SOUTH AMERICA

VENEZUELA
COLOMBIA
GUYANA

Orinoco
Caura
Negro
Branco

Pico da Neblina
+2,994
Cerro Marahuaca
+2,579

BRAZIL
Amazon
Japurá
Purus
Juruá
Madeira

ECUADOR
PERU
Quito
+6,267
Guaviare
Caquetá
Putumayo
Napo
Marañón
Huascarán
6,768
Ucayali
Gulf of Guayaquil

EQUATOR

Galápagos Islands
Pinta Marchena
Genovesa
Santiago San Salvador San Cristóbal
Fernandina Santa Cruz
Isabela Santa María Española
Darwin Wolf

Cocos I.
Malpelo I.

PANAMA
PANAMA CANAL
Gulf of Panama
Isthmus of Panama
Azuero Peninsula
Coiba I.
Gulf of Chiriquí
Chiriquí Volcano
+3,432

COSTA RICA
Chirripó +3,819
Coronado Bay
Os Peninsula
Dulce Gulf
Punta Burica
Nicoya Peninsula
Coco I.

NICARAGUA
Lake Managua
Lake Nicaragua
Mosquito Coast
Caratasca Lagoon
Mosquito Cays
Roncador Cay
Providencia I.
Corn I. San Andrés I.
Mono Point (Monkey Point)

HONDURAS
Cape Gracias a Dios
Cape Camarón
Gulf of Honduras
Bay Islands

BELIZE
Chetumal Bay
Ascension Bay

GUATEMALA
+3,537

EL SALVADOR
Gulf of Fonseca

CENTRAL AMERICA

MEXICO

Yucatan Peninsula
Cape Catoche
Cozumel Island

GULF OF MEXICO

Isthmus of Tehuantepec
Gulf of Tehuantepec
Terminos Lagoon
Usumacinta
Grijalva

SIERRA MADRE ORIENTAL
SIERRA MADRE OCCIDENTAL
SIERRA MADRE DEL SUR

Popocatépetl +5,426
Pico de Orizaba +5,747
+3,540
Balsas
Lerma
Chihuahuan Desert
Bolsón de Mapimí +3,348
Cape Rojo
Laguna Madre
Rio Grande
Conchos
Pecos

Baja California
Marías Is.
Revillagigedo Islands
Clarión I.
Socorro I.
San Benedicto I.
Banderas Bay
Cape Corrientes
Manzanillo Bay
Lake Chapala
San Telmo Point
Petacalco Bay

Gulf of California
Cedros I.
Eugenia Point
Vizcaíno Bay
Sebastián Vizcaíno Bay
Magdalena Bay
Magdalena I.
Cape Colonet
Piacho del Diablo +3,096
Guadalupe I.
False Cape

TROPIC OF CANCER

UNITED STATES

CENTRAL LOWLAND
APPALACHIAN MTS.
APPALACHIAN PLATEAU
ALLEGHENY Mts.
Allegheny Plateau
+2,037

Chesapeake Bay
C. Charles
Great Dismal Swamp
Albemarle Sound
Cape Hatteras
Pamlico Sound
Cape Lookout
Cape Fear
Long Island
Delaware
Sea Islands
Port Royal Sound
Savannah
Okefenokee Swamp
Chattahoochee
Apalachicola
Florida
Cape Canaveral (Cape Kennedy)
Lake Okeechobee
The Everglades
Straits of Florida
Florida Keys
Tampa Bay

Ohio
Mississippi
Missouri
Des Moines
Republican
Platte
Arkansas
Red
Ouachita Mts.
Ozark Plateau
Sabine
Brazos
Colorado
Pecos
Edwards Plateau
Llano Estacado (Staked Plain)
Canadian
Rio Grande
Gila

GREAT BASIN
COLORADO PLATEAU
Painted Desert
Grand Canyon
Lake Mead
Lake Powell
Mojave Desert
Sonoran Desert
Altar Desert
Colorado
Green
San Juan Mts.
Sangre de Cristo Mountains
Pikes Peak +4,301
Wheeler Peak +4,011
Mt. Whitney +4,418
Lowest point in North America -86
Death Valley -86
San Joaquin Valley
Monterey Bay
Point Conception
Channel Islands
Nevada

Front Range
Gunnison
Humboldt

RANGES

PACIFIC OCEAN

BERING SEA AND THE ALEUTIAN ISLANDS

RUSSIA
Chukchi Peninsula
Gulf of Anadyr
C. Navarin
St. Lawrence Island
St. Matthew I.
Koryak Range +2,562
Kamchatka Pen.
Cape Olyutorskiy
Olyutorskiy Gulf
Karaginskiy I.
Karaginskiy
Shelikhov Gulf
Commander Is.
Bering I.
Medinyy I.
Cape Dezhnev
Dezhnev Bay
Bering Strait

ALASKA U.S.
Seward Peninsula
Norton Sound
Nunivak I.
St. Paul I.
St. George I.
Pribilof Is.
Cape Newenham
Kuskokwim Bay
Kuskokwim
Bristol Bay
Nushagak Bay
Cape Romanzof
Yukon
Illiamna Lake
Cook Inlet
Kodiak I.
Trinity Is.
Chirikof I.
Sutwik I.
Shumagin Islands
Shishaldin Volcano +2,857
Sanak Is.
Unimak
Stefania Str.
Shelikof Str.
GULF OF ALASKA

ALEUTIAN Range
BERING SEA

ALEUTIAN ISLANDS
Fox Islands
Unalaska
Umnak
Chuginadak
Yunaska
Amukta
Amukta Passage
Seguam
Atka
Adak
Andreanof Islands
Kanaga
Tanaga
Ulak
Amlia
Amatignak
Rat Is.
Amchitka
Kiska
Little Sitkin
Near Is.
Attu Agattu
Semisopochnoi

Date Line
Sunday Monday

ARCTIC CIRCLE

Longitude West 170° of Greenwich
Longitude West 180°
Long. East 170° of Greenwich

Same scale as main map

Longitude West 80° of Greenwich
Longitude West 90° of Greenwich

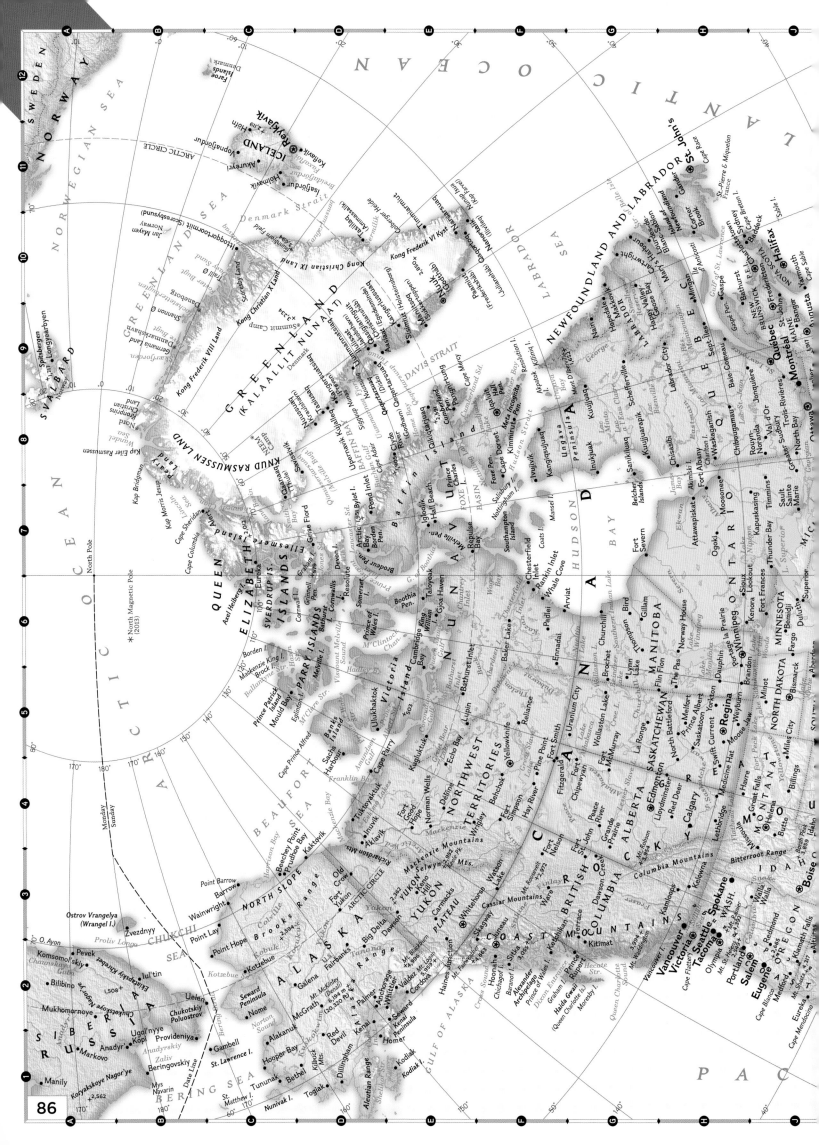

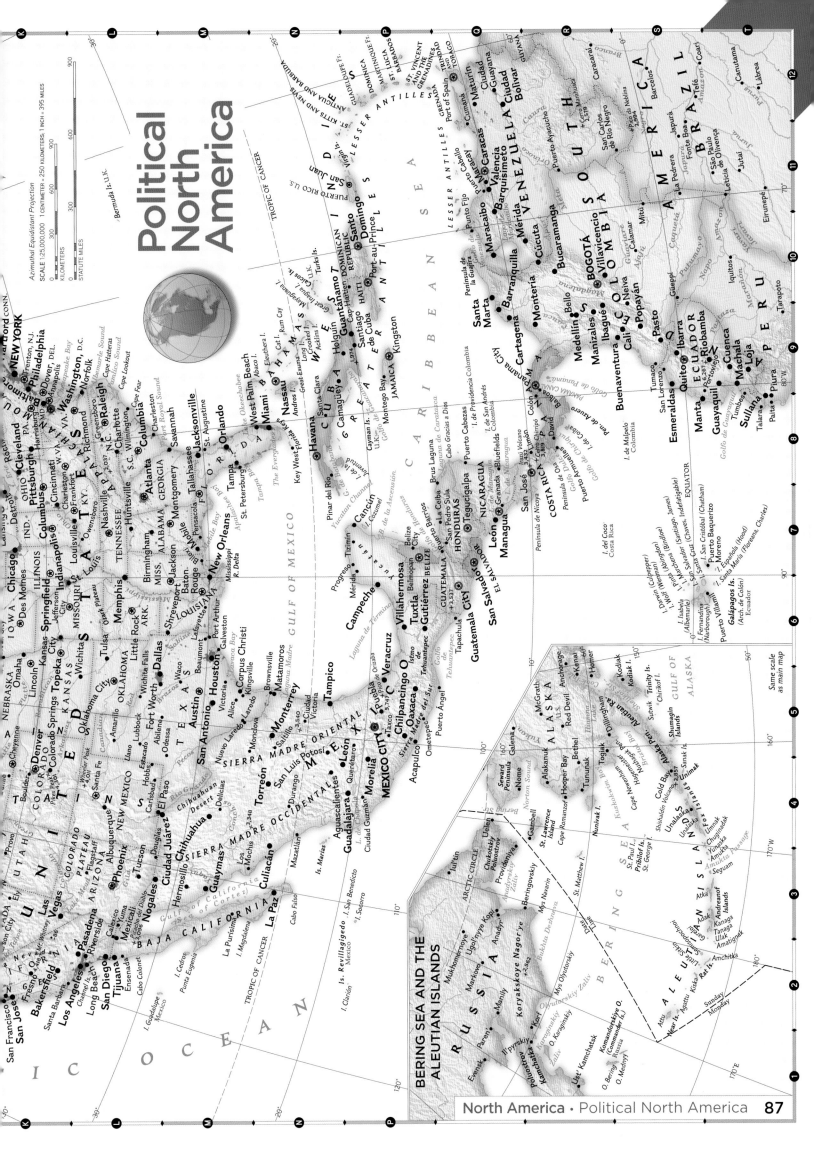

Canada

Population by Country

GREENLAND
57,700

ST.-PIERRE AND
MIQUELON
5,800

Toronto
5,485,000

CANADA
34,568,000

GREENLAND
$2,133

ST.-PIERRE AND
MIQUELON
$215

CANADA
$1,493,640

GDP by Country

Gross Domestic Product (Purchasing Power Parity),
in millions of U.S. dollars

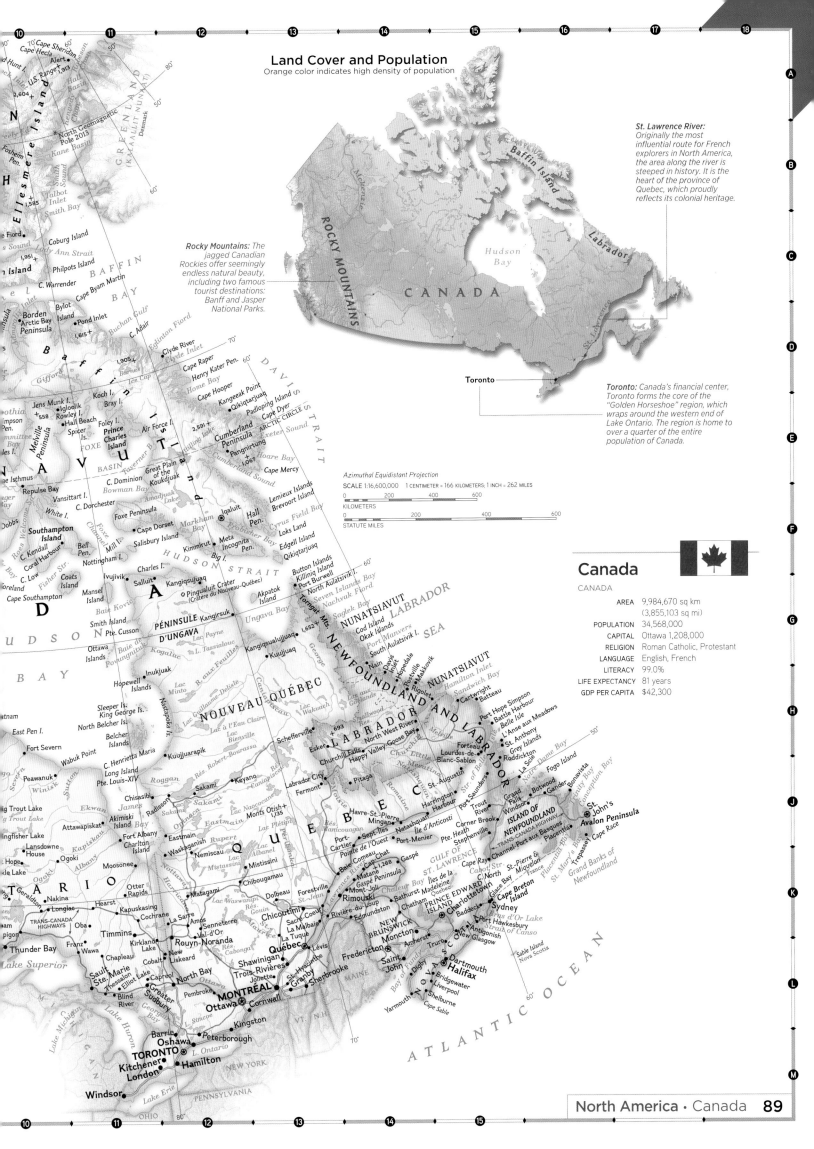

Land Cover and Population
Orange color indicates high density of population

St. Lawrence River: Originally the most influential route for French explorers in North America, the area along the river is steeped in history. It is the heart of the province of Quebec, which proudly reflects its colonial heritage.

Rocky Mountains: The jagged Canadian Rockies offer seemingly endless natural beauty, including two famous tourist destinations: Banff and Jasper National Parks.

Toronto: Canada's financial center, Toronto forms the core of the "Golden Horseshoe" region, which wraps around the western end of Lake Ontario. The region is home to over a quarter of the entire population of Canada.

Azimuthal Equidistant Projection

SCALE 1:16,600,000   1 CENTIMETER = 166 KILOMETERS; 1 INCH = 262 MILES

KILOMETERS

STATUTE MILES

Canada
CANADA

AREA	9,984,670 sq km (3,855,103 sq mi)
POPULATION	34,568,000
CAPITAL	Ottawa 1,208,000
RELIGION	Roman Catholic, Protestant
LANGUAGE	English, French
LITERACY	99.0%
LIFE EXPECTANCY	81 years
GDP PER CAPITA	$42,300

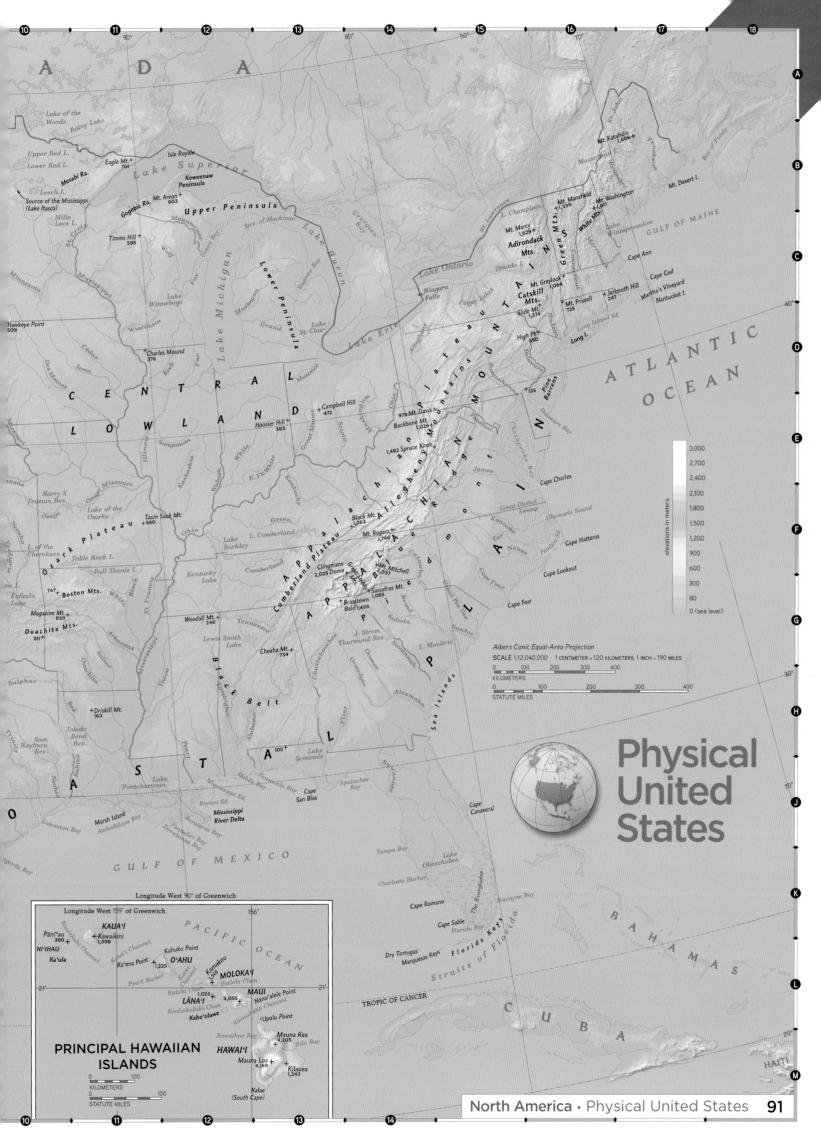

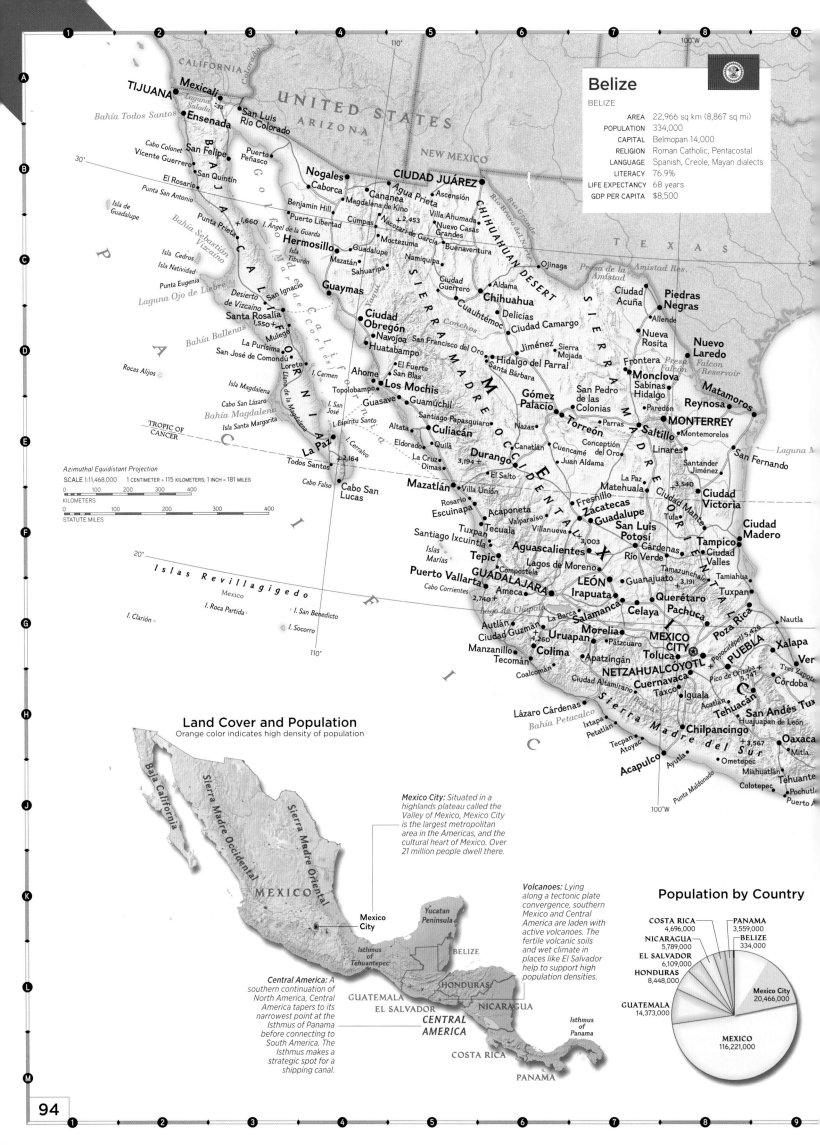

Belize

BELIZE

AREA	22,966 sq km (8,867 sq mi)
POPULATION	334,000
CAPITAL	Belmopan 14,000
RELIGION	Roman Catholic, Pentacostal
LANGUAGE	Spanish, Creole, Mayan dialects
LITERACY	76.9%
LIFE EXPECTANCY	68 years
GDP PER CAPITA	$8,500

Land Cover and Population
Orange color indicates high density of population

Azimuthal Equidistant Projection

SCALE 1:11,468,000   1 CENTIMETER = 115 KILOMETERS; 1 INCH = 181 MILES

0 100 200 300 400
KILOMETERS

0 100 200 300 400
STATUTE MILES

Mexico City: Situated in a highlands plateau called the Valley of Mexico, Mexico City is the largest metropolitan area in the Americas, and the cultural heart of Mexico. Over 21 million people dwell there.

Volcanoes: Lying along a tectonic plate convergence, southern Mexico and Central America are laden with active volcanoes. The fertile volcanic soils and wet climate in places like El Salvador help to support high population densities.

Central America: A southern continuation of North America, Central America tapers to its narrowest point at the Isthmus of Panama before connecting to South America. The Isthmus makes a strategic spot for a shipping canal.

Population by Country

- COSTA RICA 4,696,000
- PANAMA 3,559,000
- NICARAGUA 5,789,000
- BELIZE 334,000
- EL SALVADOR 6,109,000
- HONDURAS 8,448,000
- GUATEMALA 14,373,000
- Mexico City 20,466,000
- MEXICO 116,221,000

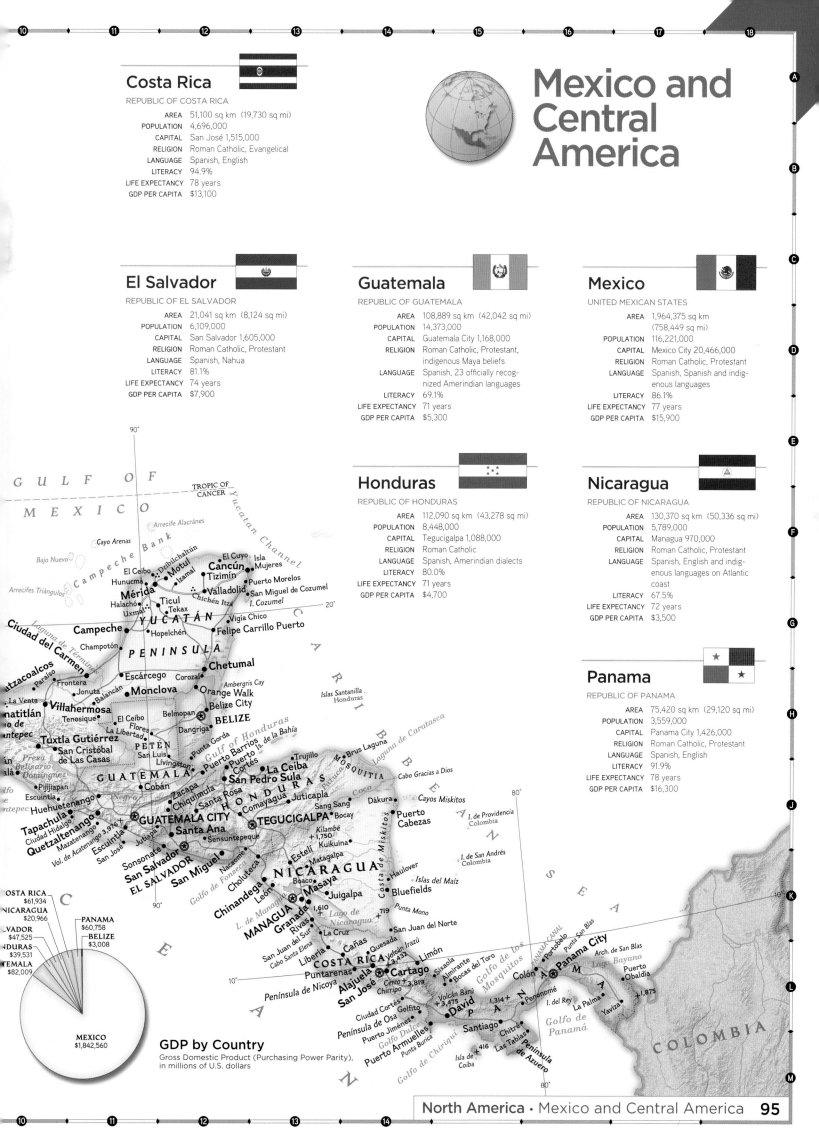

Mexico and Central America

Costa Rica
REPUBLIC OF COSTA RICA

AREA	51,100 sq km (19,730 sq mi)
POPULATION	4,696,000
CAPITAL	San José 1,515,000
RELIGION	Roman Catholic, Evangelical
LANGUAGE	Spanish, English
LITERACY	94.9%
LIFE EXPECTANCY	78 years
GDP PER CAPITA	$13,100

El Salvador
REPUBLIC OF EL SALVADOR

AREA	21,041 sq km (8,124 sq mi)
POPULATION	6,109,000
CAPITAL	San Salvador 1,605,000
RELIGION	Roman Catholic, Protestant
LANGUAGE	Spanish, Nahua
LITERACY	81.1%
LIFE EXPECTANCY	74 years
GDP PER CAPITA	$7,900

Guatemala
REPUBLIC OF GUATEMALA

AREA	108,889 sq km (42,042 sq mi)
POPULATION	14,373,000
CAPITAL	Guatemala City 1,168,000
RELIGION	Roman Catholic, Protestant, indigenous Maya beliefs
LANGUAGE	Spanish, 23 officially recognized Amerindian languages
LITERACY	69.1%
LIFE EXPECTANCY	71 years
GDP PER CAPITA	$5,300

Mexico
UNITED MEXICAN STATES

AREA	1,964,375 sq km (758,449 sq mi)
POPULATION	116,221,000
CAPITAL	Mexico City 20,466,000
RELIGION	Roman Catholic, Protestant
LANGUAGE	Spanish, Spanish and indigenous languages
LITERACY	86.1%
LIFE EXPECTANCY	77 years
GDP PER CAPITA	$15,900

Honduras
REPUBLIC OF HONDURAS

AREA	112,090 sq km (43,278 sq mi)
POPULATION	8,448,000
CAPITAL	Tegucigalpa 1,088,000
RELIGION	Roman Catholic
LANGUAGE	Spanish, Amerindian dialects
LITERACY	80.0%
LIFE EXPECTANCY	71 years
GDP PER CAPITA	$4,700

Nicaragua
REPUBLIC OF NICARAGUA

AREA	130,370 sq km (50,336 sq mi)
POPULATION	5,789,000
CAPITAL	Managua 970,000
RELIGION	Roman Catholic, Protestant
LANGUAGE	Spanish, English and indigenous languages on Atlantic coast
LITERACY	67.5%
LIFE EXPECTANCY	72 years
GDP PER CAPITA	$3,500

Panama
REPUBLIC OF PANAMA

AREA	75,420 sq km (29,120 sq mi)
POPULATION	3,559,000
CAPITAL	Panama City 1,426,000
RELIGION	Roman Catholic, Protestant
LANGUAGE	Spanish, English
LITERACY	91.9%
LIFE EXPECTANCY	78 years
GDP PER CAPITA	$16,300

GDP by Country
Gross Domestic Product (Purchasing Power Parity), in millions of U.S. dollars

- COSTA RICA $61,934
- NICARAGUA $20,966
- EL SALVADOR $47,525
- HONDURAS $39,531
- GUATEMALA $82,009
- PANAMA $60,758
- BELIZE $3,008
- MEXICO $1,842,560

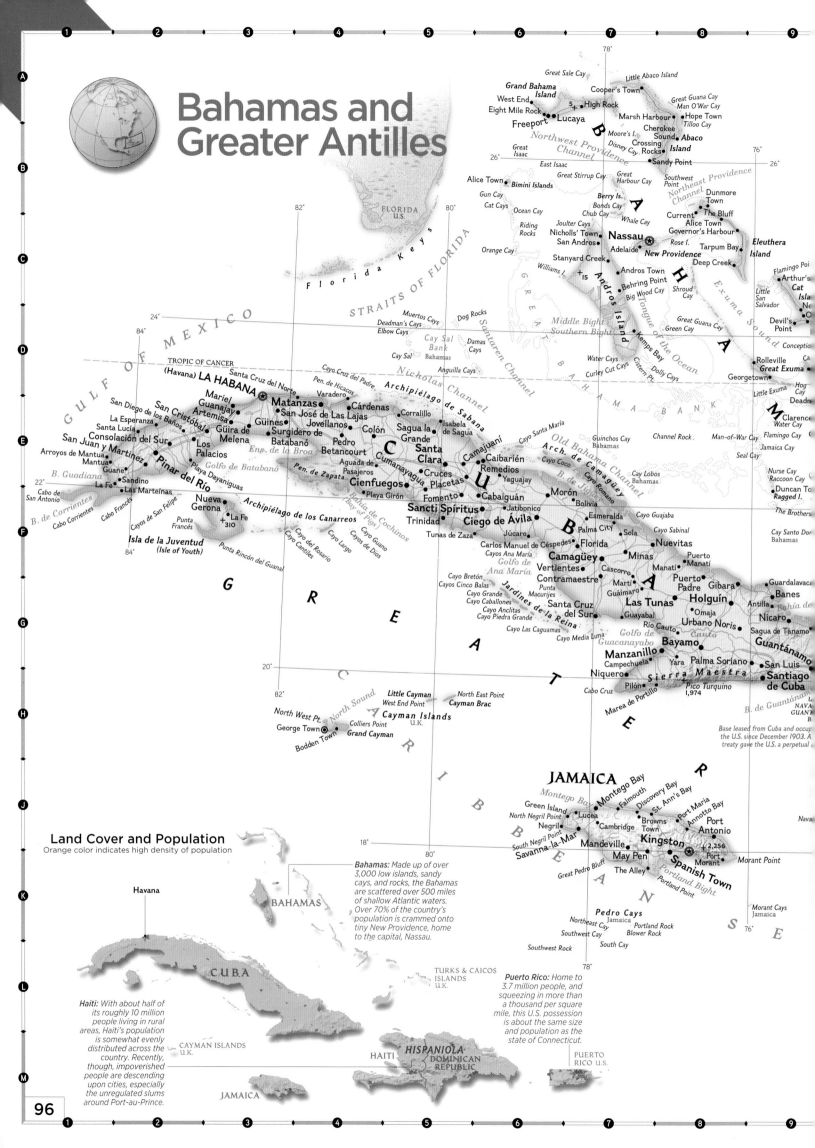

Bahamas and Greater Antilles

Land Cover and Population
Orange color indicates high density of population

Bahamas: Made up of over 3,000 low islands, sandy cays, and rocks, the Bahamas are scattered over 500 miles of shallow Atlantic waters. Over 70% of the country's population is crammed onto tiny New Providence, home to the capital, Nassau.

Haiti: With about half of its roughly 10 million people living in rural areas, Haiti's population is somewhat evenly distributed across the country. Recently, though, impoverished people are descending upon cities, especially the unregulated slums around Port-au-Prince.

Puerto Rico: Home to 3.7 million people, and squeezing in more than a thousand per square mile, this U.S. possession is about the same size and population as the state of Connecticut.

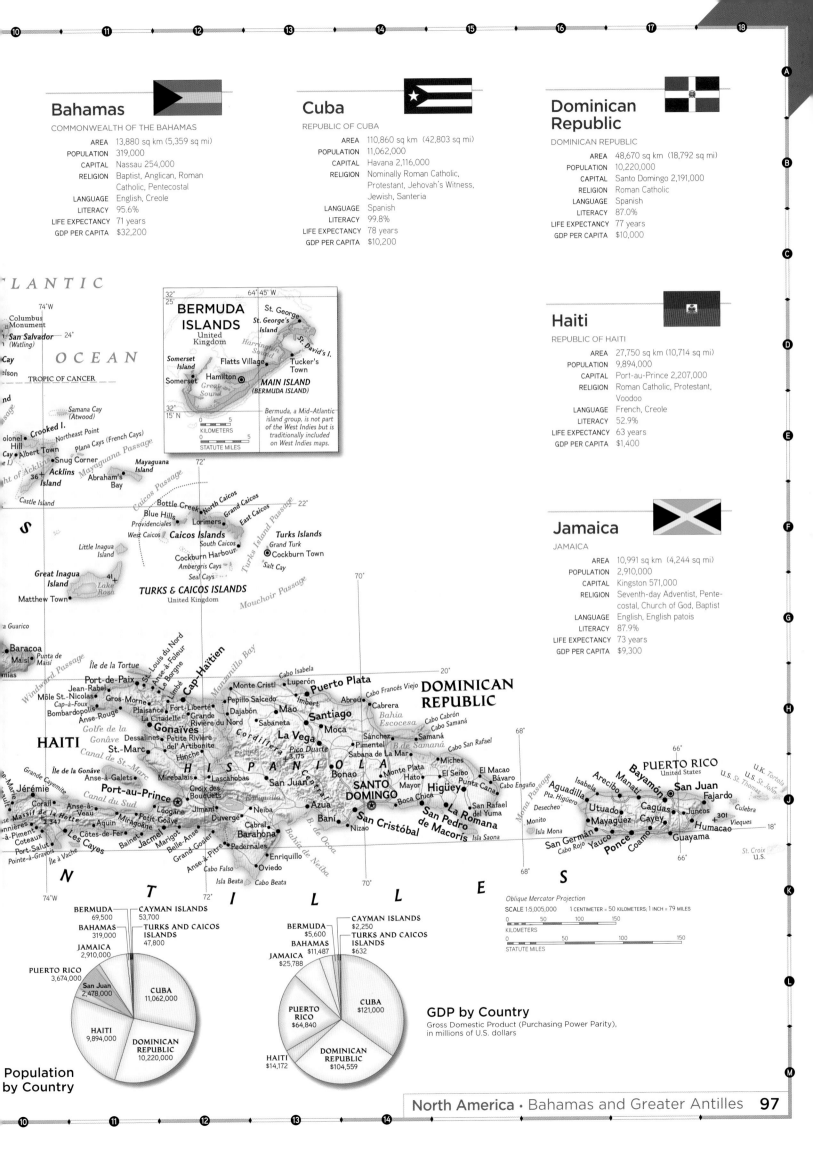

Bahamas
COMMONWEALTH OF THE BAHAMAS

AREA	13,880 sq km (5,359 sq mi)
POPULATION	319,000
CAPITAL	Nassau 254,000
RELIGION	Baptist, Anglican, Roman Catholic, Pentecostal
LANGUAGE	English, Creole
LITERACY	95.6%
LIFE EXPECTANCY	71 years
GDP PER CAPITA	$32,200

Cuba
REPUBLIC OF CUBA

AREA	110,860 sq km (42,803 sq mi)
POPULATION	11,062,000
CAPITAL	Havana 2,116,000
RELIGION	Nominally Roman Catholic, Protestant, Jehovah's Witness, Jewish, Santeria
LANGUAGE	Spanish
LITERACY	99.8%
LIFE EXPECTANCY	78 years
GDP PER CAPITA	$10,200

Dominican Republic
DOMINICAN REPUBLIC

AREA	48,670 sq km (18,792 sq mi)
POPULATION	10,220,000
CAPITAL	Santo Domingo 2,191,000
RELIGION	Roman Catholic
LANGUAGE	Spanish
LITERACY	87.0%
LIFE EXPECTANCY	77 years
GDP PER CAPITA	$10,000

Haiti
REPUBLIC OF HAITI

AREA	27,750 sq km (10,714 sq mi)
POPULATION	9,894,000
CAPITAL	Port-au-Prince 2,207,000
RELIGION	Roman Catholic, Protestant, Voodoo
LANGUAGE	French, Creole
LITERACY	52.9%
LIFE EXPECTANCY	63 years
GDP PER CAPITA	$1,400

Jamaica
JAMAICA

AREA	10,991 sq km (4,244 sq mi)
POPULATION	2,910,000
CAPITAL	Kingston 571,000
RELIGION	Seventh-day Adventist, Pentecostal, Church of God, Baptist
LANGUAGE	English, English patois
LITERACY	87.9%
LIFE EXPECTANCY	73 years
GDP PER CAPITA	$9,300

BERMUDA ISLANDS
United Kingdom

St. George
St. George's Island
St. David's I.
Somerset Island
Flatts Village
Tucker's Town
Somerset
Hamilton
MAIN ISLAND (BERMUDA ISLAND)
Great Sound
Harrington Sound

Bermuda, a Mid-Atlantic island group, is not part of the West Indies but is traditionally included on West Indies maps.

KILOMETERS 0 5
STATUTE MILES 0 5

64° 45' W
32° 25'
32° 15' N
72°

ATLANTIC OCEAN

Columbus Monument
San Salvador (Watling)
Cay
elson
TROPIC OF CANCER

Samana Cay (Atwood)
Crooked I.
olonel Hill
Cay • Albert Town
Northeast Point
Plana Cays (French Cays)
Snug Corner
Acklins Island
Abraham's Bay
Castle Island
Little Inagua Island
Great Inagua Island
Lake Rosa
Matthew Town
36
41

Bottle Creek North Caicos
Blue Hills
Providenciales
West Caicos
Caicos Islands
Lorimers
Grand Caicos
East Caicos
South Caicos
Cockburn Harbour
Ambergris Cays
Seal Cays
Turks Islands
Grand Turk
Cockburn Town
Salt Cay
TURKS & CAICOS ISLANDS
United Kingdom

Mayaguana Island
Mayaguana Passage
Caicos Passage
Turks Island Passage
Mouchoir Passage

HAITI
St-Louis du Nord
St-à-Foleur
Île de la Tortue
Port-de-Paix
Le Borgne
Cap-Haïtien
Jean-Rabel
Môle St-Nicolas
Gros-Morne
Cap-à-Foux
Bombardopolis
Plaisance
Anse-Rouge
Fort-Liberté
Grande Rivière du Nord
La Citadelle
Gonaïves
Dessalines
Petite Rivière del' Artibonite
St-Marc
Hinche
Golfe de la Gonâve
Canal de St-Marc
Île de la Gonâve
Anse-à-Galets
Mirebalais
Lascahobas
Port-au-Prince
Croix des Bouquets
Léogâne
Jimani
Duvergé
Grande Cayemite
Jérémie
Anse-à-Veau
Corail
Petit-Goâve
Massif de la Hotte
Aquin
Miragoâne
Anse-d'Hainault
Côtes-de-Fer
Les Cayes
Bainet
Jacmel
Port-Salut
Pointe-à-Gravois
Île à Vache
Belle-Anse
Marigot
Grand-Gosier
Anse-à-Pitre

Monte Cristi
Pepillo Salcedo
Dajabón
Sabaneta
Mao
Santiago
Moca
La Vega
Pimentel
Pico Duarte
Sabana de La Mar
San Juan
HISPANIOLA
Cordillera Central
Neiba
Azua
Bani
San Cristóbal
Nizao
San Pedro de Macorís
Barahona
Pedernales
Oviedo
Enriquillo
Cabral
Cabo Falso
Isla Beata
Cabo Beata
Bahía de Ocoa
B. de Neiba

Cabo Isabela
Luperón
Puerto Plata
Imbert
Abreu
Cabo Francés Viejo
Cabrera
DOMINICAN REPUBLIC
Bahía Escocesa
Cabo Cabrón
Cabo Samaná
Sánchez
Samaná
B. de Samaná
Cabo San Rafael
Miches
Monte Plata
Hato Mayor
El Seibo
El Macao
Bávaro
Punta Cana
Cabo Engaño
SANTO DOMINGO
Bonao
Boca Chica
Higüey
La Romana
San Rafael del Yuma
San Pedro de Macorís
Isla Saona

Mona Passage
Pta. Higüero
Desecheo
Monito
Isla Mona

PUERTO RICO
United States
Aguadilla
Isabela
Arecibo
Manatí
Bayamón
San Juan
Utuado
Caguas
Fajardo
Mayagüez
Cayey
Juncos
Humacao
San Germán
Yauco
Ponce
Coamo
Guayama
Cabo Rojo
Culebra
Vieques
301
U.S. St. Thomas
U.S. St. John
U.K. Tortola
St. Croix U.S.

Windward Passage
Baracoa
Maisí
Punta de Maisí
mías

20°
70°
68°
66°
18°

Oblique Mercator Projection
SCALE 1:5,005,000   1 CENTIMETER = 50 KILOMETERS; 1 INCH = 79 MILES
KILOMETERS 0 50 100 150
STATUTE MILES 0 50 100 150

Population by Country

BERMUDA 69,500
CAYMAN ISLANDS 53,700
BAHAMAS 319,000
TURKS AND CAICOS ISLANDS 47,800
JAMAICA 2,910,000
PUERTO RICO 3,674,000
San Juan 2,478,000
CUBA 11,062,000
HAITI 9,894,000
DOMINICAN REPUBLIC 10,220,000

GDP by Country
Gross Domestic Product (Purchasing Power Parity), in millions of U.S. dollars

BERMUDA $5,600
CAYMAN ISLANDS $2,250
TURKS AND CAICOS ISLANDS $632
BAHAMAS $11,487
JAMAICA $25,788
PUERTO RICO $64,840
CUBA $121,000
HAITI $14,172
DOMINICAN REPUBLIC $104,559

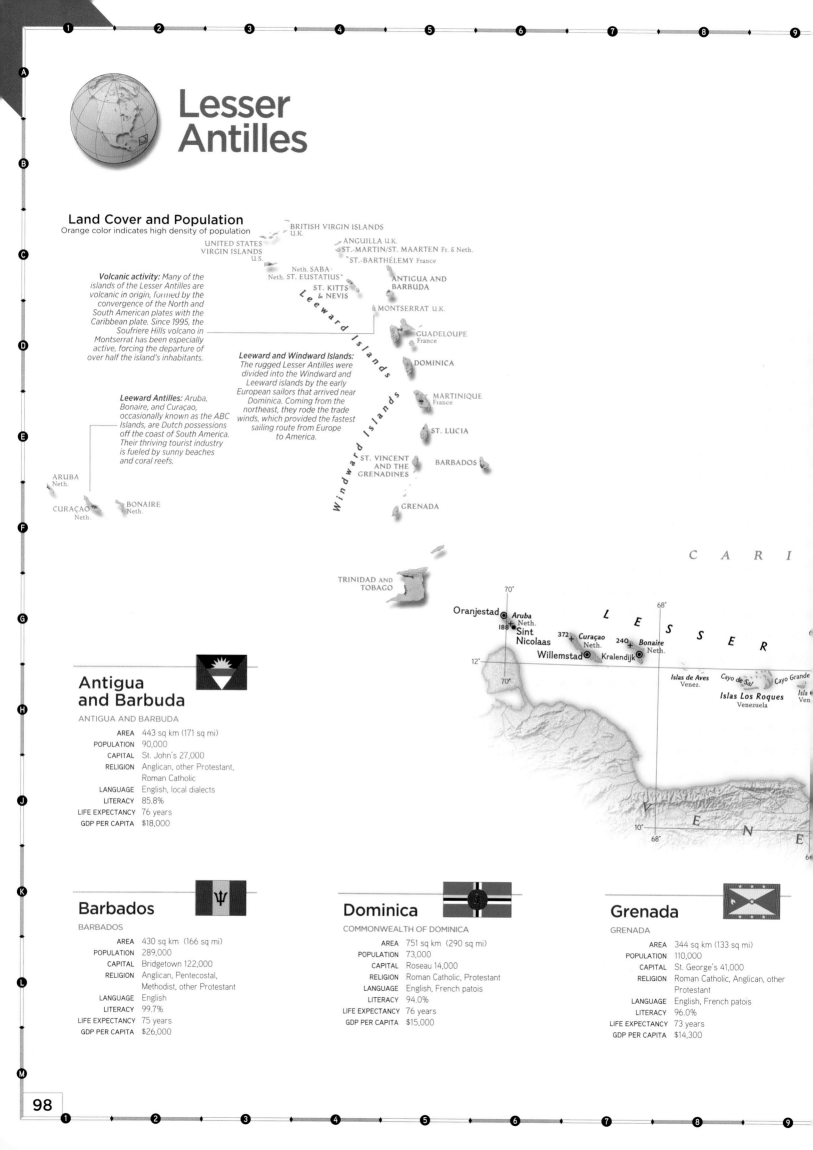

Lesser Antilles

Land Cover and Population
Orange color indicates high density of population

Volcanic activity: Many of the islands of the Lesser Antilles are volcanic in origin, formed by the convergence of the North and South American plates with the Caribbean plate. Since 1995, the Soufriere Hills volcano in Montserrat has been especially active, forcing the departure of over half the island's inhabitants.

Leeward Antilles: Aruba, Bonaire, and Curaçao, occasionally known as the ABC Islands, are Dutch possessions off the coast of South America. Their thriving tourist industry is fueled by sunny beaches and coral reefs.

Leeward and Windward Islands: The rugged Lesser Antilles were divided into the Windward and Leeward islands by the early European sailors that arrived near Dominica. Coming from the northeast, they rode the trade winds, which provided the fastest sailing route from Europe to America.

BRITISH VIRGIN ISLANDS U.K.
UNITED STATES VIRGIN ISLANDS U.S.
ANGUILLA U.K.
ST.-MARTIN/ST. MAARTEN Fr. & Neth.
ST.-BARTHÉLEMY France
Neth. SABA
Neth. ST. EUSTATIUS
ST. KITTS & NEVIS
ANTIGUA AND BARBUDA
MONTSERRAT U.K.
GUADELOUPE France
DOMINICA
MARTINIQUE France
ST. LUCIA
BARBADOS
ST. VINCENT AND THE GRENADINES
GRENADA

Leeward Islands
Windward Islands

ARUBA Neth.
CURAÇAO Neth.
BONAIRE Neth.

TRINIDAD AND TOBAGO

C A R I

Oranjestad ◎ Aruba Neth.
188 ● Sint Nicolaas
372 + Curaçao Neth.
240 + Bonaire Neth.
Willemstad ◎ Kralendijk ◎

L E S S E R

Islas de Aves Venez.
Cayo de Sal
Cayo Grande
Islas Los Roques Venezuela
Isla Ven

V E N E

70°
68°
12°
10°

Antigua and Barbuda

ANTIGUA AND BARBUDA

AREA	443 sq km (171 sq mi)
POPULATION	90,000
CAPITAL	St. John's 27,000
RELIGION	Anglican, other Protestant, Roman Catholic
LANGUAGE	English, local dialects
LITERACY	85.8%
LIFE EXPECTANCY	76 years
GDP PER CAPITA	$18,000

Barbados

BARBADOS

AREA	430 sq km (166 sq mi)
POPULATION	289,000
CAPITAL	Bridgetown 122,000
RELIGION	Anglican, Pentecostal, Methodist, other Protestant
LANGUAGE	English
LITERACY	99.7%
LIFE EXPECTANCY	75 years
GDP PER CAPITA	$26,000

Dominica

COMMONWEALTH OF DOMINICA

AREA	751 sq km (290 sq mi)
POPULATION	73,000
CAPITAL	Roseau 14,000
RELIGION	Roman Catholic, Protestant
LANGUAGE	English, French patois
LITERACY	94.0%
LIFE EXPECTANCY	76 years
GDP PER CAPITA	$15,000

Grenada

GRENADA

AREA	344 sq km (133 sq mi)
POPULATION	110,000
CAPITAL	St. George's 41,000
RELIGION	Roman Catholic, Anglican, other Protestant
LANGUAGE	English, French patois
LITERACY	96.0%
LIFE EXPECTANCY	73 years
GDP PER CAPITA	$14,300

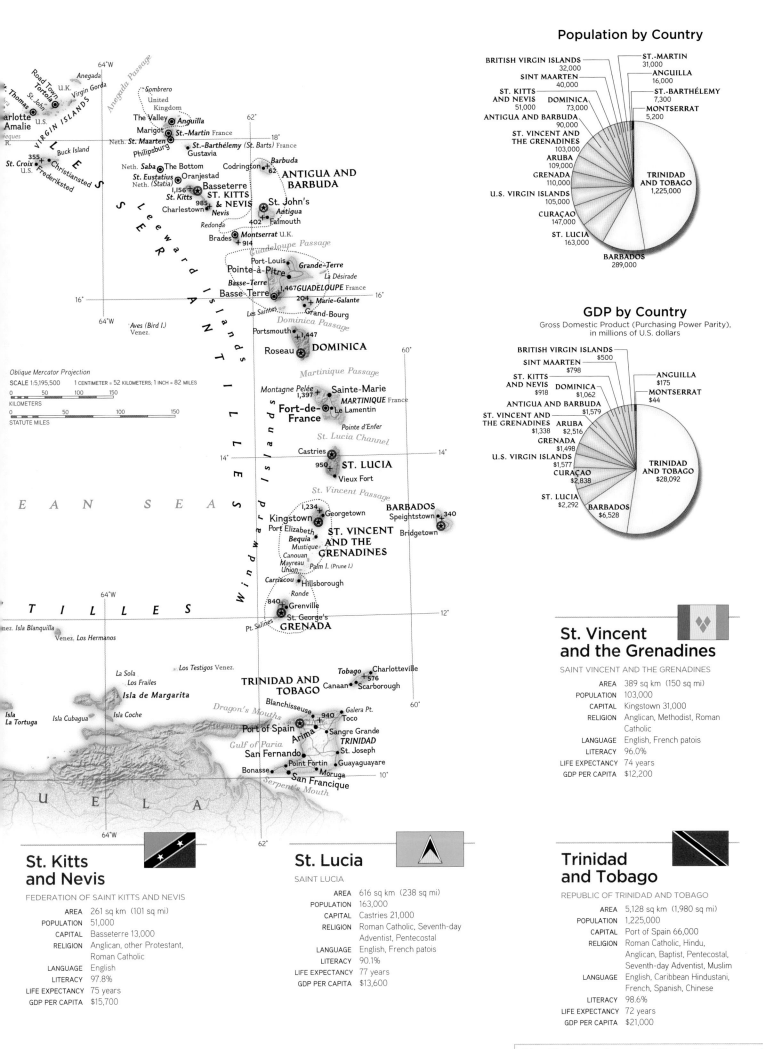

Population by Country

Country	Population
BRITISH VIRGIN ISLANDS	32,000
ST.-MARTIN	31,000
SINT MAARTEN	40,000
ANGUILLA	16,000
ST. KITTS AND NEVIS	51,000
DOMINICA	73,000
ST.-BARTHÉLEMY	7,300
ANTIGUA AND BARBUDA	90,000
MONTSERRAT	5,200
ST. VINCENT AND THE GRENADINES	103,000
ARUBA	109,000
GRENADA	110,000
U.S. VIRGIN ISLANDS	105,000
CURAÇAO	147,000
ST. LUCIA	163,000
BARBADOS	289,000
TRINIDAD AND TOBAGO	1,225,000

GDP by Country

Gross Domestic Product (Purchasing Power Parity), in millions of U.S. dollars

Country	GDP
BRITISH VIRGIN ISLANDS	$500
SINT MAARTEN	$798
ANGUILLA	$175
ST. KITTS AND NEVIS	$918
DOMINICA	$1,062
MONTSERRAT	$44
ANTIGUA AND BARBUDA	$1,579
ST. VINCENT AND THE GRENADINES	$1,338
ARUBA	$2,516
GRENADA	$1,498
U.S. VIRGIN ISLANDS	$1,577
CURAÇAO	$2,838
ST. LUCIA	$2,292
TRINIDAD AND TOBAGO	$28,092
BARBADOS	$6,528

St. Vincent and the Grenadines

SAINT VINCENT AND THE GRENADINES

AREA	389 sq km (150 sq mi)
POPULATION	103,000
CAPITAL	Kingstown 31,000
RELIGION	Anglican, Methodist, Roman Catholic
LANGUAGE	English, French patois
LITERACY	96.0%
LIFE EXPECTANCY	74 years
GDP PER CAPITA	$12,200

St. Kitts and Nevis

FEDERATION OF SAINT KITTS AND NEVIS

AREA	261 sq km (101 sq mi)
POPULATION	51,000
CAPITAL	Basseterre 13,000
RELIGION	Anglican, other Protestant, Roman Catholic
LANGUAGE	English
LITERACY	97.8%
LIFE EXPECTANCY	75 years
GDP PER CAPITA	$15,700

St. Lucia

SAINT LUCIA

AREA	616 sq km (238 sq mi)
POPULATION	163,000
CAPITAL	Castries 21,000
RELIGION	Roman Catholic, Seventh-day Adventist, Pentecostal
LANGUAGE	English, French patois
LITERACY	90.1%
LIFE EXPECTANCY	77 years
GDP PER CAPITA	$13,600

Trinidad and Tobago

REPUBLIC OF TRINIDAD AND TOBAGO

AREA	5,128 sq km (1,980 sq mi)
POPULATION	1,225,000
CAPITAL	Port of Spain 66,000
RELIGION	Roman Catholic, Hindu, Anglican, Baptist, Pentecostal, Seventh-day Adventist, Muslim
LANGUAGE	English, Caribbean Hindustani, French, Spanish, Chinese
LITERACY	98.6%
LIFE EXPECTANCY	72 years
GDP PER CAPITA	$21,000

South America

The Amazon's great bulk dominates the map of South America, and deservedly so. The largest rain forest and the largest river system on Earth cover some 7 million square kilometers (2.7 million square miles), nearly the size of mainland Australia, and may account for a third or more of all the world's plant and animal species. But South America extends from warm Caribbean shores southward toward the outstretched tip of the Antarctic Peninsula, and it, too, is a continent of great diversity.

Although it ranks only fourth in total size, South America accounts for the largest single landmass in the Southern Hemisphere, which is dominated by vast stretches of open ocean.

South America's coastlines are variously draped in dense forest and exposed by some of the world's driest deserts, while the interior shades from dense forest, to the mixed woodland and savanna of the Cerrado region woodland, to seasonally flooded wetlands of the Pantanal. At the continent's western margin, the Andes thrust upward to an average of 4,000 meters (13,000 feet), creating Earth's longest terrestrial mountain chain and one of the most dramatic. The shift in elevation from Pacific shores to Andean peaks can support a sweep of ecosystems ranging from desert to shrub to evergreen forest in just a few tens of kilometers. In the mountains' eastern lee, the dry scrub of the Gran Chaco and the wide Pampas grasslands stretches out uninterrupted across almost 30 degrees of latitude.

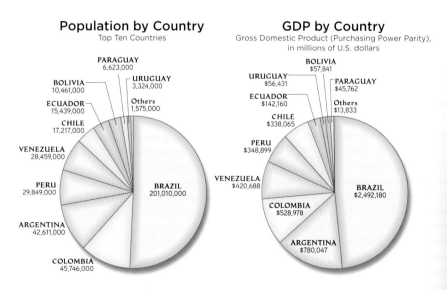

Population by Country
Top Ten Countries

PARAGUAY 6,623,000
URUGUAY 3,324,000
BOLIVIA 10,461,000
Others 1,575,000
ECUADOR 15,439,000
CHILE 17,217,000
VENEZUELA 28,459,000
PERU 29,849,000
BRAZIL 201,010,000
ARGENTINA 42,611,000
COLOMBIA 45,746,000

GDP by Country
Gross Domestic Product (Purchasing Power Parity), in millions of U.S. dollars

BOLIVIA $57,841
URUGUAY $56,431
PARAGUAY $45,762
ECUADOR $142,160
Others $13,833
CHILE $338,065
PERU $348,899
VENEZUELA $420,688
BRAZIL $2,492,180
COLOMBIA $528,978
ARGENTINA $780,047

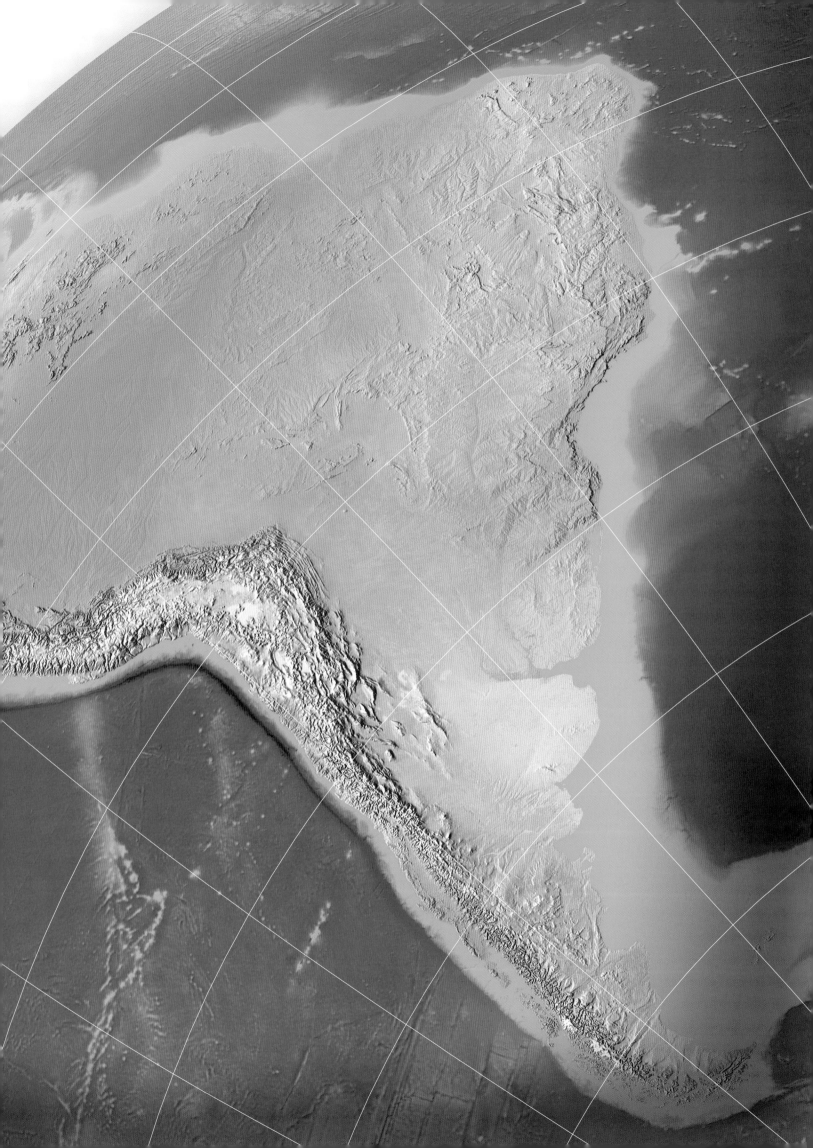

Physical South America

ATLANTIC OCEAN

EQUATOR

Longitude West 50° of Greenwich

CARIBBEAN SEA

LESSER ANTILLES
Leeward Is.
Guadeloupe
DOMINICA
Martinique
ST. LUCIA
BARBADOS
ST. VINCENT
& THE GRENADINES
Windward Is.
GRENADA
Tortuga I.
Margarita I.
TRINIDAD AND TOBAGO
Tobago
Trinidad
Paria Pen.
Boca Grande
Serpent's Mouth
Dragon's Mouth
Shell Beach

Aruba
Curaçao
Bonaire

Espada Pt.
Guajira Peninsula
Paraguaná Pen.
Gulf of Venezuela
Gulf of Morrosquillo
Gulf of Urabá
Sa. Nevada de Sta. Marta 5,775
Lake Maracaibo
Maracaibo Basin
Cordillera de Mérida
L. Valencia
Coast Range

VENEZUELA
Orinoco
Apure
Meta
Orinoco River Delta
Sa. de Imataca

COLOMBIA
Magdalena
Cauca
Cordillera Occidental
Cordillera Central 4,080
Cordillera Oriental
Guaviare
Guainía
Vaupés
Caquetá

Serranía de Baudó
Gulf of Tribugá
Cape Corrientes
Buenaventura Bay
Ancón de Sardinas Bay
Ensenada de Tumaco
Cape Posado
Monta Cape
San Lorenzo
Galera Point
Santa Elena Peninsula
Gulf of Guayaquil
Parifias Point
Aguja Point
Sechura Bay
Sechura Desert

ECUADOR
Napo
Pastaza
Pongo de Manseriche
Marañón

PANAMA
Isthmus of Panama
Gulf of Panama
Rey I.
Pearl Is.
Coiba I.
Malpelo Island
Azuero Pen.

FRENCH GUIANA
SURINAME
GUYANA
Wilhelmina Mts.
+1,230
GUIANA HIGHLANDS
Serra de Tumucumaque
Kanuku Mts.
1,009
Pakaraima Mts.
Mt. Roraima 2,739
Sierra Pacaraima
World's highest waterfall
Angel Falls
Total drop 979 meters
Cerro Marahuaca 2,579
2,994 Pico da Neblina
Essequibo
Wakenam Island
Point Isère
Cape Orange
Cape Cassiporé
Maracá Island
Cape North
Maroni
635
Jari
Araguari
Anbana

Cerro Orinoco
Branco
Negro
Maicuru
Trombetas
Guaviare

Marajó Bay
Marajó Island
Pará
North Channel the Amazon
Mouths of the Amazon
Perigoso Channel
Cape Gurupi
Cape Gurupí
Gurupá I.
Xingu
Iriri

AMAZON
BRASIL
Amazon (Solimões)
Japurá
Purus
Madeira
Madre de Dios
Beni
Mamoré
Guaporé
San Miguel
Juruá
Jutaí
Coari
Purus
Javari
Ucayali
Huallaga
Amazon
Marañón

PERU
LA MONTAÑA
Cordillera Oriental
Cordillera Central
Nevado Huascarán 6,768
Nevado Coropuna 6,425
Paracas Peninsula
Parada Point
Point Coles
Madrid Point

BOLIVIA
Altiplano
Cord. Oriental
Cordillera Central
Lake Poopó
6,542
Salar de Coipasa
Chiquimata Point
ATACAMA

Theodore Roosevelt
Jiparaná
Aripuanã
Xingu
Teles Pires
Juruena
Serra do Tombador
Chapada dos Parecis
1,995
Serra do Roncador
Serra do Rio das Mortes
Bananal Island
Araguaia
Tocantins
Tucuruí Reservoir
Balbina Reservoir

MATO GROSSO PLATEAU
Paraguay
Taquari
Pantanal
Bañados del Izozog
Grande
Cerros de Bala

BRAZILIAN HIGHLANDS
Campos
Espigão Mestre
Sa. do Tiracambu
Gurupi
Grajaú
Parnaíba
Piauí
Sa. da Ibiapaba
São Francisco
Sobradinho Reservoir
Chapada Diamantina
Chapada do Araripe
Borborema Plateau
Serra do Espinhaço
Jequitinhonha
Corumbá
Paranaíba
Velhas
Doce
Três Marias Reservoir
Serra da Canastra
Grande
Contas
Verde
São Francisco
Sa. do Urucuí

Point Tubarão
Pt. Calcanhar
C. Branco
Murcuripe Point
Pt. Jericoacoara
Mucuripe Point
Manguinho Point
Todos os Santos Bay
Corumbau Point
Baleia Point
Regência Pt.
Cape São Roque
São Marcos Bay
São José Bay

102

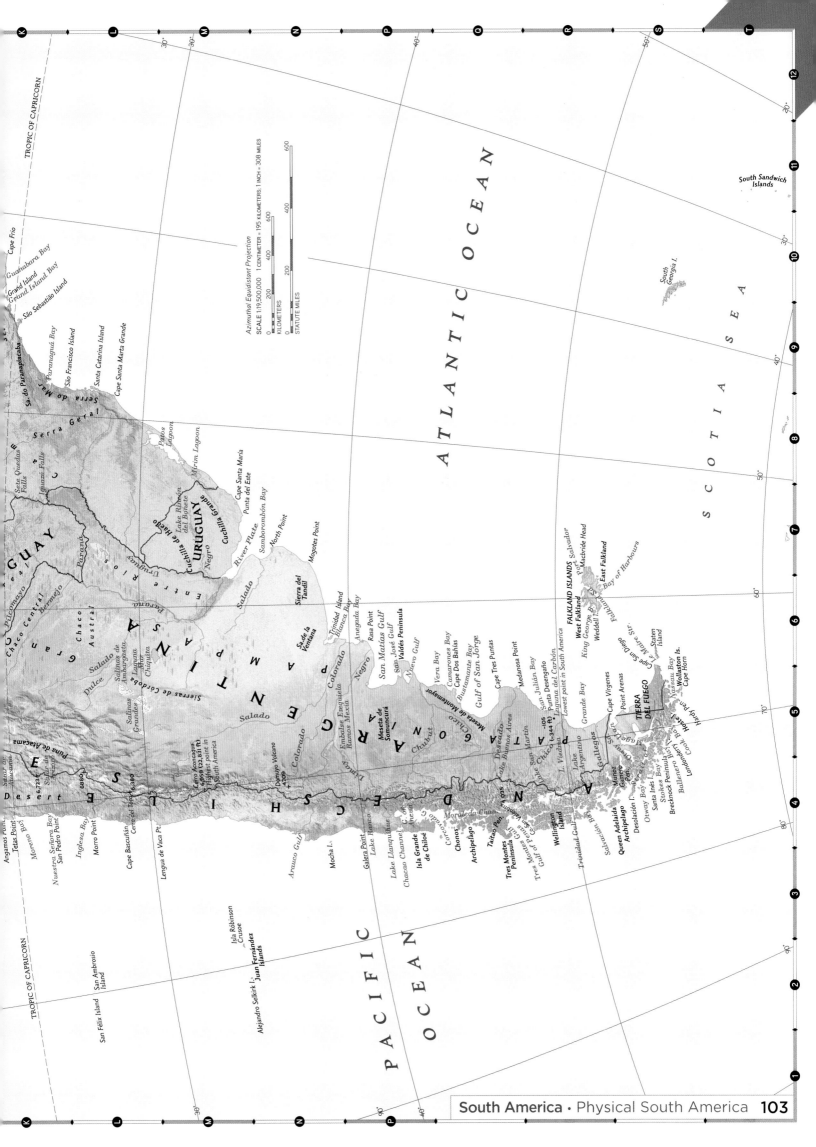

ATLANTIC OCEAN

PACIFIC

OCEAN

SCOTIA SEA

TROPIC OF CAPRICORN

TROPIC OF CAPRICORN

Azimuthal Equidistant Projection
SCALE 1:19,500,000 1 CENTIMETER = 195 KILOMETERS; 1 INCH = 308 MILES
KILOMETERS
STATUTE MILES

South Sandwich
Islands

South
Georgia I.

Cape Frio
Guanabara Bay
Grand Island
Grand Island Bay
São Sebastião Island
Paranaguá Bay
São do Paranapiacaba
São Francisco Island
Santa Catarina Island
Cape Santa Marta Grande
Serra do Mar
Serra Geral
Sete Quedas Falls
Iguaçu Falls
Serra Geral
Patos Lagoon
Mirim Lagoon

URUGUAY
URUGUAY
Lake Rincón del Bonete
Cuchilla de Haedo
Cuchilla Grande
Negro
Cape Santa María
Punta del Este
River Plate
Samborombón Bay
North Point
Mogotes Point
Sierra del Tandil

PARAGUAY
Paraná
Pilcomayo
Bermejo
Chaco Central
Gran Chaco
Chaco Austral
Entre Ríos
Uruguay
Paraná

Salado
Salado de Ambargasta
Laguna Mar Chiquita
Salinas Grandes
Salado Dulce
Salinas de Córdoba
Sierras de Córdoba
Salado

ARGENTINA

Trinidad Island
Sa de la Ventana
Blanca Bay
Rasa Point
Anegada Bay
San Matías Gulf
San José Gulf
Valdés Peninsula
Nuevo Gulf
Vera Bay
Camarones Bay
Cape Dos Bahías
Bustamante Bay
Gulf of San Jorge
Cape Tres Puntas
Medanosa Point

Negro
Colorado
Colorado
Embalse Ezequiela Ramos Mexía
Meseta de Somuncurá
Chubut
Chico
Meseta de Montemayor
Deseado
San Julián Bay
Punta del Carbón
Punta Desengaño
Lowest point in South America (-105)
Lowest point in South America (-344 ft)
Chico
Santa Cruz
Gallegos
Lake Buenos Aires
Lake San Martín
Lake Viedma
Lake Argentino
Grande Bay
Cape Vírgenes
Point Arenas

PATAGONIA

FALKLAND ISLANDS
Port Salvador
P. Macbride Head
West Falkland
East Falkland
King George B.
Weddell I.
Falkland Sound
Bay of Harbours

Cerro Aconcagua 6,959 (22,831 ft) Highest point in South America
Cerro del Toro 6,380
Domuyo Volcano 4109
6890
6723
Salar de Atacama
Puna de Atacama
Atacama Desert

ANDES

Cabo de Hornos
TIERRA DEL FUEGO
Cape San Diego
Staten Island
Nassau Bay
Wollaston Is.
Cape Horn
Hardy Pen.
Londonderry I.
Cook I.
Stokes Peninsula
Santa Inés I.
Ballenero Bay
Brecknock Peninsula
Desolación I.
Otway Bay
Queen Adelaida Archipelago
Muñoz Gamero Pen.
Sarmiento Gulf
Salvación Bay
Trinidad Gulf
Wellington Island
Tres Montes Peninsula
Tres Montes Gulf
Gulf of Penas
Taitao Pen.
Chonos Archipelago
Moraleda Channel
Corcovado Gulf
Isla Grande de Chiloé
Chacao Channel
C. of Chiloé
Corcovado Volcano
Lake Ranco
Lake Llanquihue
Galera Point
Mocha I.
Arauco Gulf
Lengua de Vaca Pt.
Cape Bascuñán
Cerro del Toro 6,380
Morro Point
San Pedro Point
Nuestra Señora Bay
Inglesa Bay
Moreno Bay
Tetas Point
Angamos Point
Salar de Atacama

CHILE
Desert

San Félix Island
San Ambrosio Island
Isla Róbinson Crusoe
Alejandro Selkirk I.
Juan Fernández Islands

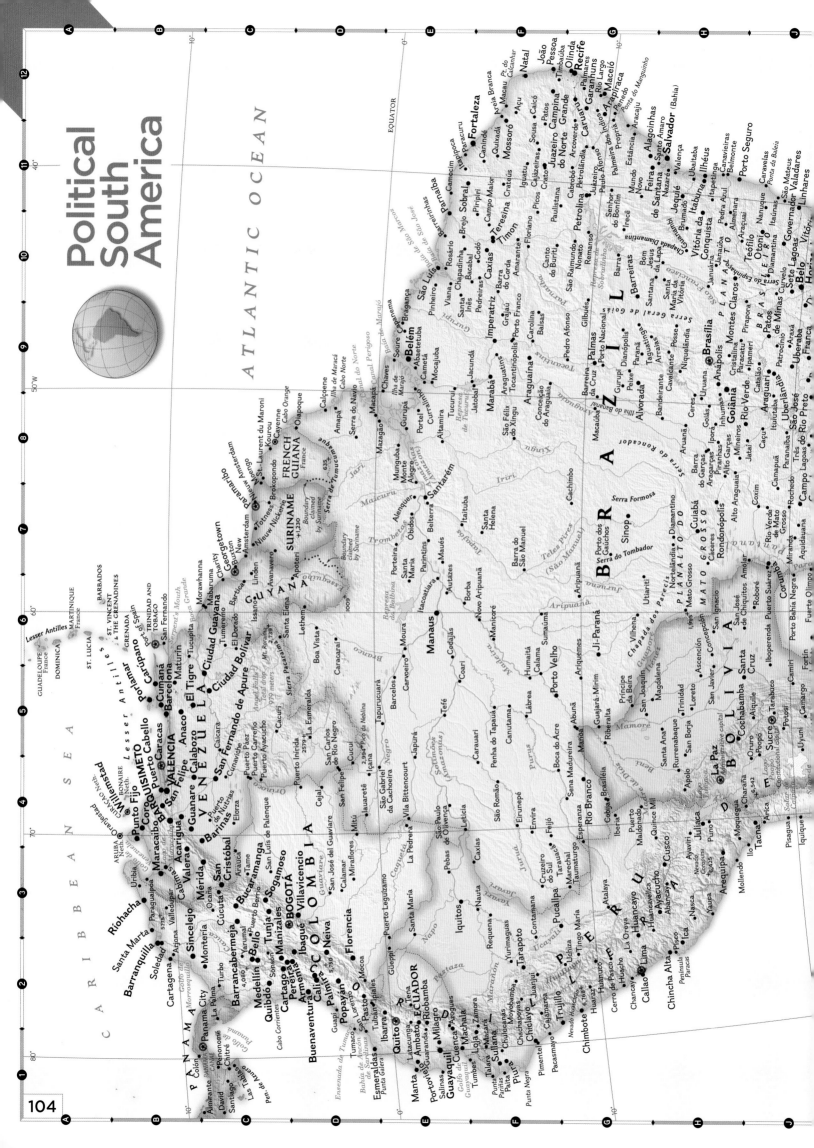

Political South America

ATLANTIC OCEAN

CARIBBEAN SEA

EQUATOR

BRAZIL

VENEZUELA

COLOMBIA

PERU

BOLIVIA

ECUADOR

GUYANA

SURINAME

FRENCH GUIANA
France

PANAMA

Fortaleza
Recife
Salvador (Bahia)
Belém
Brasília
Goiânia
Manaus
BOGOTÁ
Caracas
Quito
Lima
La Paz
Sucre
National capital
Constitutional capital

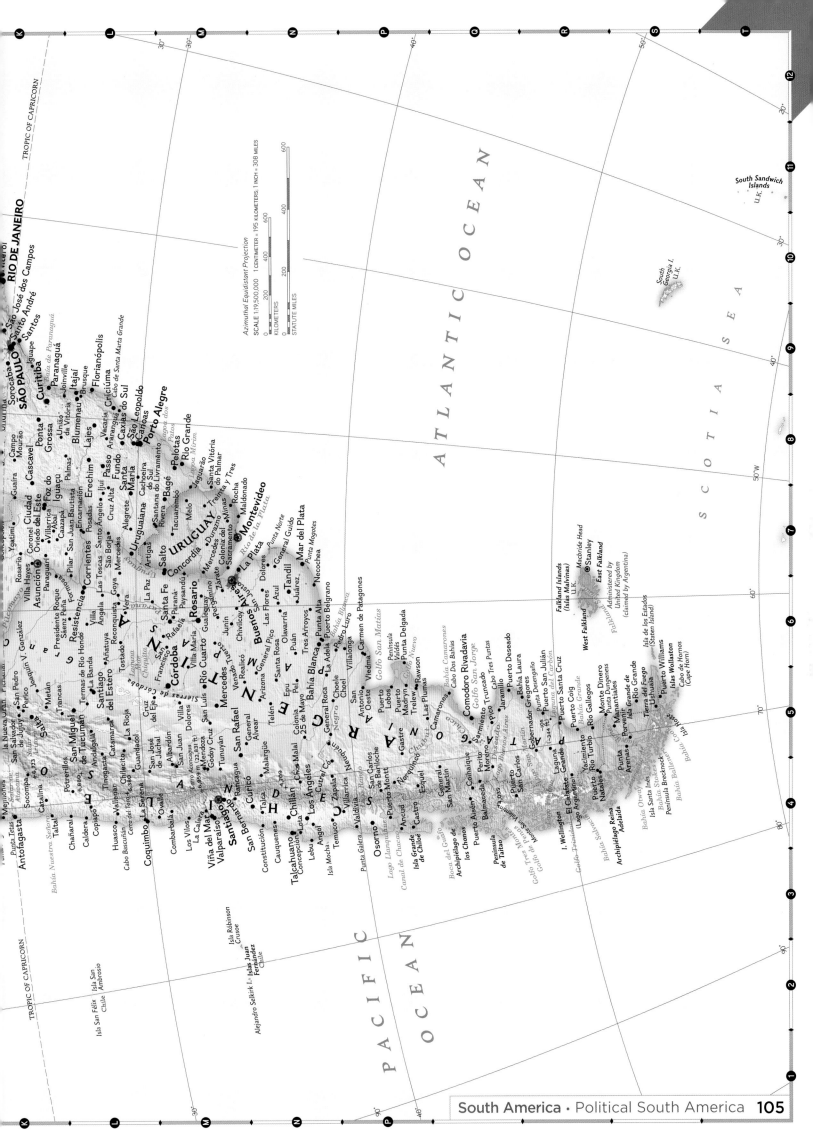

South America · Political South America 105

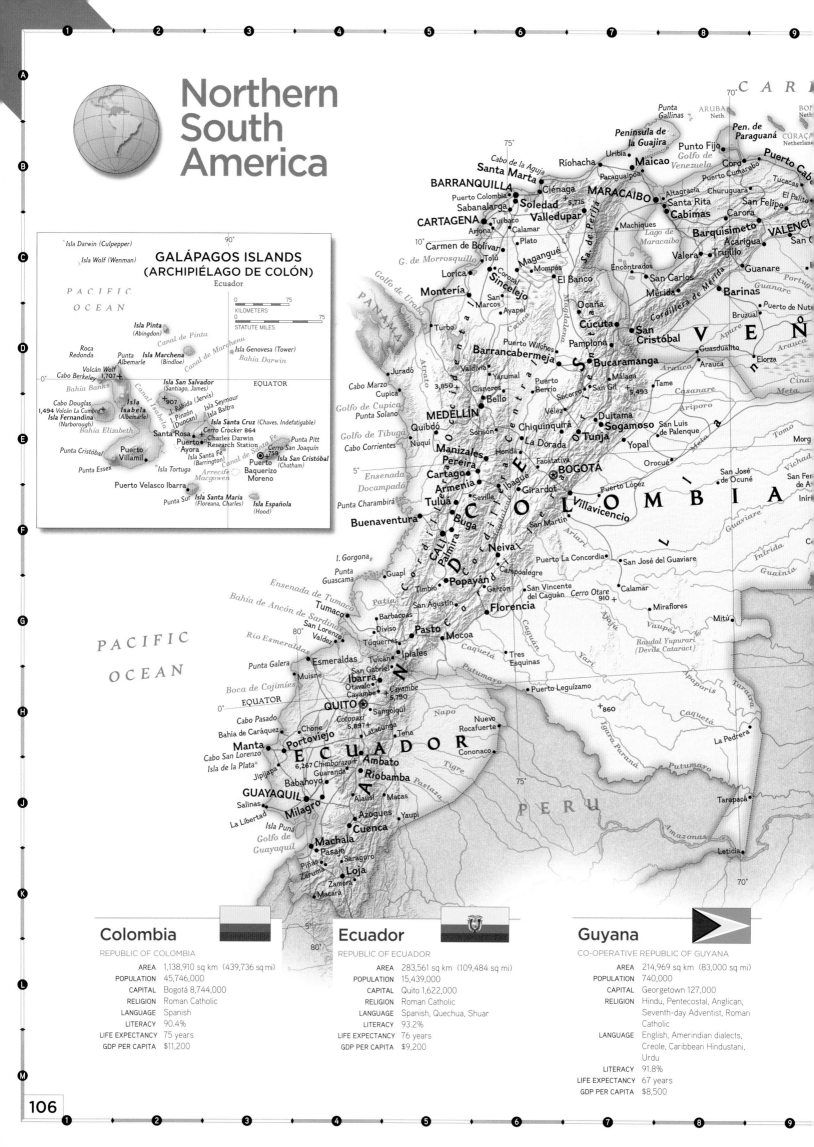

Northern South America

GALÁPAGOS ISLANDS
(ARCHIPIÉLAGO DE COLÓN)
Ecuador

KILOMETERS
0   75

STATUTE MILES
0   75

`Isla Darwin (Culpepper)`

`Isla Wolf (Wenman)`

PACIFIC OCEAN

Roca Redonda
Isla Pinta (Abingdon)
Punta Albemarle
Isla Marchena (Bindloe)
Isla Genovesa (Tower)
Bahía Darwin
Canal de Pinta
Canal de Marchena
Volcán Wolf 1,707
Cabo Berkeley
Bahía Banks
Cabo Douglas 1,494 Volcán La Cumbre
Isla Fernandina (Narborough)
Isla Isabela (Albemarle)
Isla San Salvador (Santiago, James)
907
J. Rábida (Jervis)
J. Pinzón (Duncan)
Isla Seymour
Isla Baltra
Isla Santa Cruz (Chaves, Indefatigable)
Santa Rosa
Cerro Crocker 864
Puerto Ayora
Charles Darwin Research Station
Isla Santa Fe (Barrington)
Cerro San Joaquín 759
Punta Pitt
Isla San Cristóbal (Chatham)
Puerto Baquerizo Moreno
Bahía Elizabeth
Punta Cristóbal
Puerto Villamil
Punta Essex
Isla Tortuga
Arrecife Macgowen
Punta Sur
Isla Santa María (Floreana, Charles)
Isla Española (Hood)
Puerto Velasco Ibarra
EQUATOR

PACIFIC OCEAN

COLOMBIA · ECUADOR · VENEZUELA cities and features:

Punta Gallinas
Peninsula de la Guajira
ARUBA Neth.
CURAÇAO Netherlands
Pen. de Paraguaná
Punta Fijo
Golfo de Venezuela
Puerto Cumarebo
Cabo de la Aguja
Ríohacha
Maicao
Coro
Tucacas
Puerto Colombia
Santa Marta
Uribia
Paraguaipoa
Puerto Cabello
Santa Rita
Churuguara
El Felipe
BARRANQUILLA
Ciénaga
MARACAIBO
Cabimas
Carora
Sabanalarga
Soledad
5,775
Altagracia
Barquisimeto
VALENCI
CARTAGENA
Turbaco
Valledupar
Machiques
Acarigua
San
Arjona
Calamar
Lago de Maracaibo
Valera
Trujillo
Carmen de Bolívar
Plato
Encontrados
Guanare
Magangué
San Carlos
G. de Morrosquillo
Tolú
Mompós
El Banco
Mérida
Barinas
Lorica
Corozal
Sincelejo
Ocaña
Cordillera de Mérida
Puerto de Nutr
Montería
San Marcos
Cúcuta
Bruzual
Ayapel
Pamplona
San Cristóbal
Guasdualito
Elorza
Túrbo
Puerto Wilches
Barrancabermeja
Bucaramanga
Arauca
Jurado
Valdivia
Yarumal
Málaga
Tame
Casanare
3,850
Cisneros
Puerto Berrío
San Gil
5,493
Cabo Marzo
Cupica
Bello
Socorro
Ariporo
MEDELLÍN
Vélez
Duitama
San Luis de Palenque
Golfo de Cupica
Quibdó
Chiquinquirá
Sogamoso
Tomo
Punta Solano
Sonsón
La Dorada
Tunja
Yopal
Golfo de Tibugá
Manizales
Honda
Cabo Corrientes
Pereira
Facatativá
Orocué
Nuquí
Cartago
BOGOTÁ
San José de Ocuné
Armenia
Ibagué
Girardot
Puerto López
Tuluá
Seville
Puerto La Concordia
San José del Guaviare
Buga
Villavicencio
Buenaventura
CALI
Palmira
San Martín
Ariari
I. Gorgona
Neiva
Inírida
Punta Guascama
Campoalegre
Guaviare
Guapí
Timbío
Popayán
Garzón
San Vicente del Caguán
Calamar
Cerro Otare 910
Miraflores
Ensenada de Tumaco
Patía
Tumaco
Barbacoas
San Agustín
Florencia
Mitú
Bahía de Ancón de Sardinas
Diviso
Pasto
Mocoa
Río Esmeraldas
San Lorenzo
Túquerres
Vaupés
Valdez
Ipiales
Tres Esquinas
Raudal Yupurari (Devils Cataract)
Esmeraldas
Tulcán
Punta Galera
Muisne
San Gabriel
Caquetá
Boca de Cojimíes
Ibarra
Otavalo
Putumayo
EQUATOR
Cayambe
Cayambe 5,790
Puerto Leguízamo
Cabo Pasado
QUITO
Sangolquí
Napo
Nuevo Rocafuerte
860
Bahía de Caráquez
Chone
Cotopaxi 5,897
Latacunga
Tena
La Pedrera
Manta
Portoviejo
Cononaco
Cabo San Lorenzo
6,267 Chimborazo
Ambato
Isla de la Plata
Guaranda
Riobamba
Jipijapa
Babahoyo
Pastaza
Tigre
Alausí
Macas
GUAYAQUIL
Salinas
Azogues
Yaupi
Milagro
Cuenca
La Libertad
Isla Puná
Machala
Golfo de Guayaquil
Pasaje
Saraguro
Amazonas
Piñas
Loja
Leticia
Zaruma
Zamora
Macará
Tarapacá
PERU
70°

Colombia
REPUBLIC OF COLOMBIA

AREA	1,138,910 sq km (439,736 sq mi)
POPULATION	45,746,000
CAPITAL	Bogotá 8,744,000
RELIGION	Roman Catholic
LANGUAGE	Spanish
LITERACY	90.4%
LIFE EXPECTANCY	75 years
GDP PER CAPITA	$11,200

Ecuador
REPUBLIC OF ECUADOR

AREA	283,561 sq km (109,484 sq mi)
POPULATION	15,439,000
CAPITAL	Quito 1,622,000
RELIGION	Roman Catholic
LANGUAGE	Spanish, Quechua, Shuar
LITERACY	93.2%
LIFE EXPECTANCY	76 years
GDP PER CAPITA	$9,200

Guyana
CO-OPERATIVE REPUBLIC OF GUYANA

AREA	214,969 sq km (83,000 sq mi)
POPULATION	740,000
CAPITAL	Georgetown 127,000
RELIGION	Hindu, Pentecostal, Anglican, Seventh-day Adventist, Roman Catholic
LANGUAGE	English, Amerindian dialects, Creole, Caribbean Hindustani, Urdu
LITERACY	91.8%
LIFE EXPECTANCY	67 years
GDP PER CAPITA	$8,500

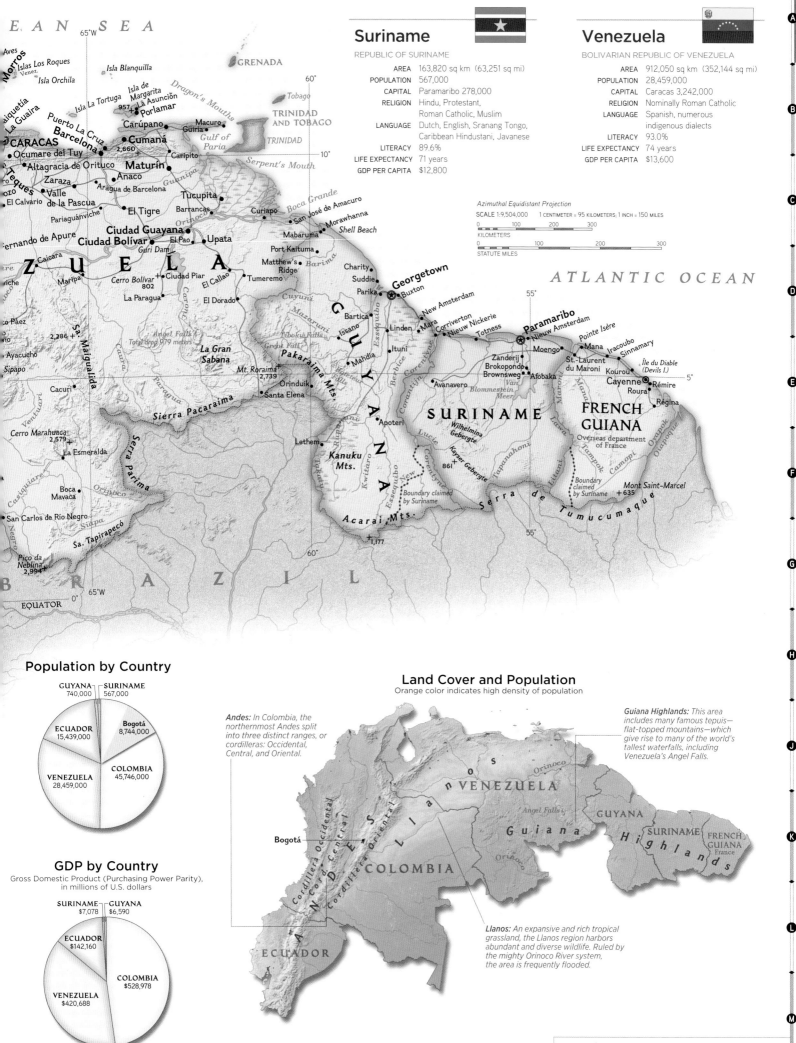

E A N   S E A

65°W

Aves
Morros
Islas Los Roques
Venez.
Isla Orchila
Isla Blanquilla

GRENADA

60°

Tobago

Isla La Tortuga
Isla de Margarita
957 La Asunción
Porlamar

aiquetía
La Guaira
Puerto La Cruz
Barcelona
CARACAS
Cumaná
Carúpano
Macuro
Güiria
Dragon's Mouths

TRINIDAD AND TOBAGO

TRINIDAD

Gulf of Paria

10°

Ocumare del Tuy
Altagracia de Orituco
Maturín
Caripito
2,660

Teques
Zaraza
Anaco
Aragua de Barcelona
Tucupita
Serpent's Mouth

ozo
Valle de la Pascua
El Tigre
Barrancas
Guanipa

El Calvario
Paraguanviche
Curiapo
San José de Amacuro

Altagracia de Orituco
Ciudad Guayana
El Pao
Upata
Mabaruma
Morawhanna

rnando de Apure
Ciudad Bolívar
Guri Dam
Shell Beach

Caicara
Port Kaituma

Z U E L A
Cerro Bolívar
Ciudad Piar
Matthew's Ridge
Barima

Páez
La Paragua
El Callao
Tumeremo
Charity
Suddie
Georgetown

iche
2,286
Ayacucho
Cerro Bolívar
802
El Dorado
Parika
Buxton

Sipapo
La Gran Sabana
Cuyuni
Bartica
Linden
New Amsterdam

Cacuri
Mazaruni
Issano
Mara
Corriverton
Nieuw Nickerie
Totness

Cerro Marahuaca
2,579
Angel Falls
Total drop 979 meters
Tibokuri Falls
Ituni
Berbice
Paramaribo
Nieuw Amsterdam

La Esmeralda
Pakaraima Mts.
Mahdia
Pointe Isère

Mt. Roraima
2,739
Orinduik
Santa Elena
Zanderij
Brokopondo
Brownsweg
Mana
Iracoubo
Sinnamary

Boca Mavaca
Sierra Pacaraima
Avanavero
Afobaka
St.-Laurent du Maroni
Kourou
Île du Diable
(Devils I.)

San Carlos de Río Negro
Apoteri
Wilhelmina Gebergte
Cayenne
Rémire

G U Y A N A
Kanuku Mts.
Lethem
Kayser Gebergte
861
SURINAME
FRENCH GUIANA
Overseas department of France
Régina
Roura

Pico da Neblina
2,994
Sa. Tapirapecó
Boundary claimed by Suriname
Acarai Mts.
1,177
Boundary claimed by Suriname
Mont Saint-Marcel
635

B R A Z I L

Serra de Tumucumaque

65°W
EQUATOR
0°
60°

ATLANTIC OCEAN

Suriname
REPUBLIC OF SURINAME

AREA	163,820 sq km (63,251 sq mi)
POPULATION	567,000
CAPITAL	Paramaribo 278,000
RELIGION	Hindu, Protestant, Roman Catholic, Muslim
LANGUAGE	Dutch, English, Sranang Tongo, Caribbean Hindustani, Javanese
LITERACY	89.6%
LIFE EXPECTANCY	71 years
GDP PER CAPITA	$12,800

Venezuela
BOLIVARIAN REPUBLIC OF VENEZUELA

AREA	912,050 sq km (352,144 sq mi)
POPULATION	28,459,000
CAPITAL	Caracas 3,242,000
RELIGION	Nominally Roman Catholic
LANGUAGE	Spanish, numerous indigenous dialects
LITERACY	93.0%
LIFE EXPECTANCY	74 years
GDP PER CAPITA	$13,600

Azimuthal Equidistant Projection

SCALE 1:9,504,000   1 CENTIMETER = 95 KILOMETERS; 1 INCH = 150 MILES

KILOMETERS
0   100   200   300

STATUTE MILES
0   100   200   300

Population by Country

GUYANA
740,000
SURINAME
567,000
ECUADOR
15,439,000
Bogotá
8,744,000
VENEZUELA
28,459,000
COLOMBIA
45,746,000

Land Cover and Population
Orange color indicates high density of population

Andes: In Colombia, the northernmost Andes split into three distinct ranges, or cordilleras: Occidental, Central, and Oriental.

Guiana Highlands: This area includes many famous tepuis—flat-topped mountains—which give rise to many of the world's tallest waterfalls, including Venezuela's Angel Falls.

VENEZUELA
Llanos
Orinoco
Angel Falls
Guiana
GUYANA
SURINAME
FRENCH GUIANA
France
Highlands
A N D E S
Cordillera Occidental
Cord. Central
Cordillera Oriental
Bogotá
COLOMBIA
Orinoco
ECUADOR

Llanos: An expansive and rich tropical grassland, the Llanos region harbors abundant and diverse wildlife. Ruled by the mighty Orinoco River system, the area is frequently flooded.

GDP by Country
Gross Domestic Product (Purchasing Power Parity), in millions of U.S. dollars

SURINAME
$7,078
GUYANA
$6,590
ECUADOR
$142,160
COLOMBIA
$528,978
VENEZUELA
$420,688

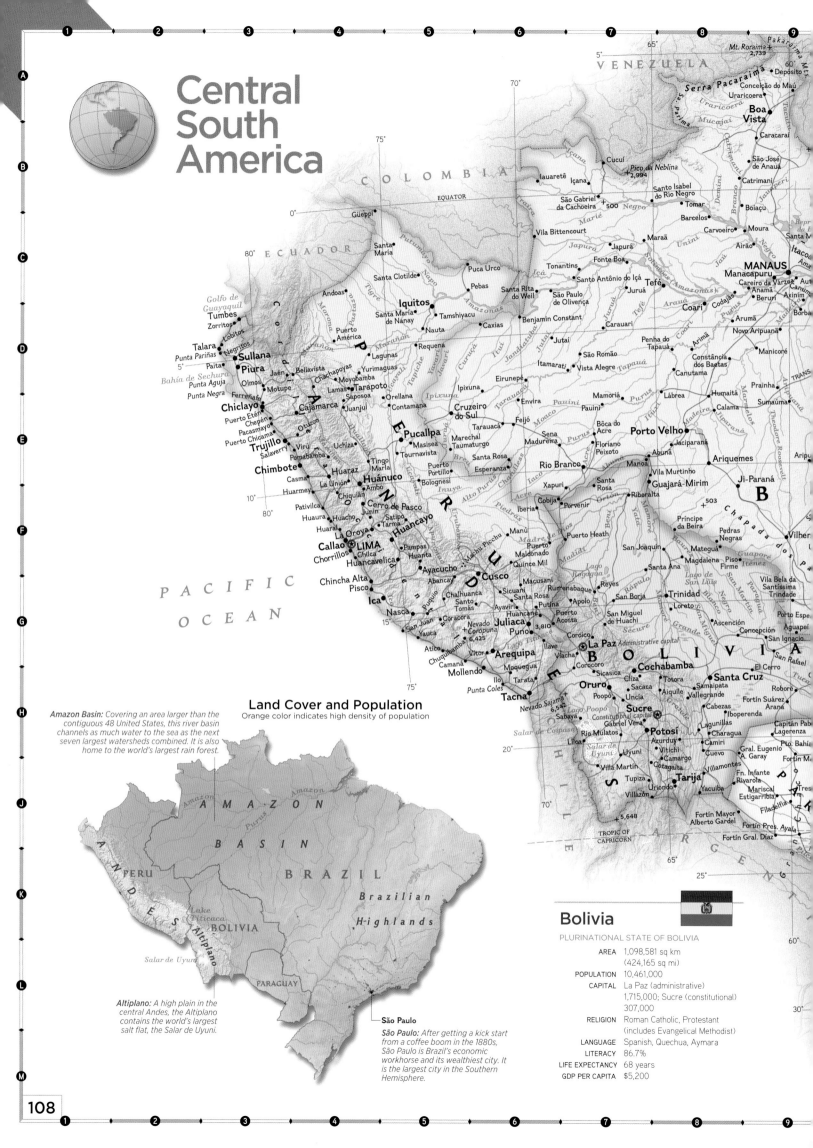

Central South America

VENEZUELA
Mt. Roraima +2,739
Pakaraima Mts.
Depósito
Conceção do Maú
Uraricoera
Serra Pacaraima
Boa Vista
Caracaraí
Cucuí
Pico da Neblina +2,994
Santo Isabel do Rio Negro
São Gabriel da Cachoeira +500
Tomar
Catrimani
São José de Anauá
Boiaçú

COLOMBIA
Iauaretê
Içana
Vila Bittencourt
Barcelos
Carvoeiro
Moura
Güeppi
EQUATOR

ECUADOR
Santa María
Santa Clotilde
Puca Urco
Pebas
Andoas
Tonantins
Fonte Boa
Maraã
Airão
Santo Antônio do Içá
Tefé
Juruá
MANAUS
Manacapuru
Careiro da Várzea
Anamã
Coari
Codajás
Beruri
Novo Aripuanã
Manicoré

Iquitos
Santa María de Nanay
Tamshiyacu
Nauta
Santa Rita do Weil
São Paulo de Olivença
Benjamin Constant
Caxias
Carauari
Jutaí
São Romão
Constância dos Baetas
Canutama
Prainha
Humaitá

Puerto América
Requena
Lagunas
Yurimaguas
Ipixuna
Eirunepé
Mamoriá
Lábrea
Calama
Sumaúma

Tumbes
Zorritos
Golfo de Guayaquil
Contamana
Cruzeiro do Sul
Envira
Pauini
Bôca do Acre
Porto Velho
Sena Madureira
Floriano Peixoto
Jaciparaná
Ariquemes
Ji-Paraná

Talara
Punta Pariñas
Negritos
Paita
Bahía de Sechura
Punta Aguja
Punta Negra
Sullana
Piura
Jaén
Bellavista
Chachapoyas
Moyobamba
Lamas
Tarapoto
Saposoa
Orellana
Juanjuí
Pucallpa
Masisea
Tournavista
Marechal Taumaturgo
Tarauacá
Feijó
Moaco
Santa Rosa
Esperanza
Rio Branco
Xapuri
Manoa
Vila Murtinho
Guajará-Mirim

Olmos
Motupe
Ferreñafe
Chiclayo
Puerto Etén
Chepén
Pacasmayo
Puerto Chicama
Trujillo
Salaverry
Virú
Pomabamba
Uchiza
Tingo María
Puerto Portillo
Bolognesi
Iberia
Cobija
Porvenir
Riberalta
Príncipe da Beira
Pedras Negras

Chimbote
Casma
Huaraz
La Unión
Chiquián
Huánuco
Ambo
Cerro de Pasco
Pativilca
Huarmey
Huaura
Huacho
Junín
Satipo
Manú
Puerto Maldonado
Quince Mil
Rurrenabaque
Reyes
Magdalena
Piso Firme
San Joaquín

Huaral
La Oroya
Tarma
Huancayo
Pampas
Huanta
Machu Picchu
Puerto Heath
San Borja
Trinidad
Loreto
Vila Bela da Santissima Trindade
Callao
LIMA
Chorrillos
Chilca
Huancavelica
Ayacucho
Abancay
Cusco
Macusani
Santa Ana
Lago de San Luís

Chincha Alta
Pisco
Ica
Chalhuanca
Santo Tomás
Sicuani
Santa Rosa
Putina
Apolo
San Miguel de Huachi
Ascención
Concepción
Aguapeí
San Ignacio

Nasca
San Juan
Coracora
Ayaviri
Huancané
Puerto Acosta
Coroico
Porto Espe.
Yauca
Nevado Coropuna +6,425
Juliaca
Puno 3,810
Llave
La Paz *Administrative capital*
Atico
Chuquibamba
Vitor
Arequipa
Viacha
Corocoro
B O L I V I A
San Rafael
Camaná
Mollendo
Moquegua
Ilo
Tarata
Coipasa
Sicasica
Totora
Cochabamba
Samaipata
Santa Cruz
El Cerro
Roboré
Fortín Suárez
Arana

Tacna
Punta Coles
Nevado Sajama +6,542
Oruro
Poopó
Uncía
Aiquile
Vallegrande
Cabezas
Iboperenda
Capitán Pablo Lagerenza

Lago Poopó
Sabaya
Sucre
Constitutional capital
Gabriel Vera
Lagunillas
Río Mulatos
Potosí
Camiri
Gral. Eugenio A. Garay
Pto. Bahía

Salar de Coipasa
Salar de Uyuni
Azurduy
Cuevo
Fn. Infante Rivarola
Fortín M.

Llica
Uyuni
Vitichi
Camargo
Villamontes
Mariscal Estigarribia
Tres...

Villa Martín
Cotagaita
Tarija
Filadelfia

Tupiza
Uriondo
Yacuiba
Fortín Mayor Alberto Gardel

Villazón
+5,648
Fortín Gral. Díaz
Fortín Pres. Ayala

TROPIC OF CAPRICORN

ARGENTINA
CHILE
PARAGUAY

PACIFIC OCEAN

Land Cover and Population

Orange color indicates high density of population

Amazon Basin: *Covering an area larger than the contiguous 48 United States, this river basin channels as much water to the sea as the next seven largest watersheds combined. It is also home to the world's largest rain forest.*

A M A Z O N   B A S I N

B R A Z I L

Brazilian Highlands

PERU

A N D E S

Lake Titicaca
BOLIVIA
Altiplano
Salar de Uyuni

PARAGUAY

São Paulo

Altiplano: *A high plain in the central Andes, the Altiplano contains the world's largest salt flat, the Salar de Uyuni.*

São Paulo: *After getting a kick start from a coffee boom in the 1880s, São Paulo is Brazil's economic workhorse and its wealthiest city. It is the largest city in the Southern Hemisphere.*

Bolivia

PLURINATIONAL STATE OF BOLIVIA

AREA	1,098,581 sq km (424,165 sq mi)
POPULATION	10,461,000
CAPITAL	La Paz (administrative) 1,715,000; Sucre (constitutional) 307,000
RELIGION	Roman Catholic, Protestant (includes Evangelical Methodist)
LANGUAGE	Spanish, Quechua, Aymara
LITERACY	86.7%
LIFE EXPECTANCY	68 years
GDP PER CAPITA	$5,200

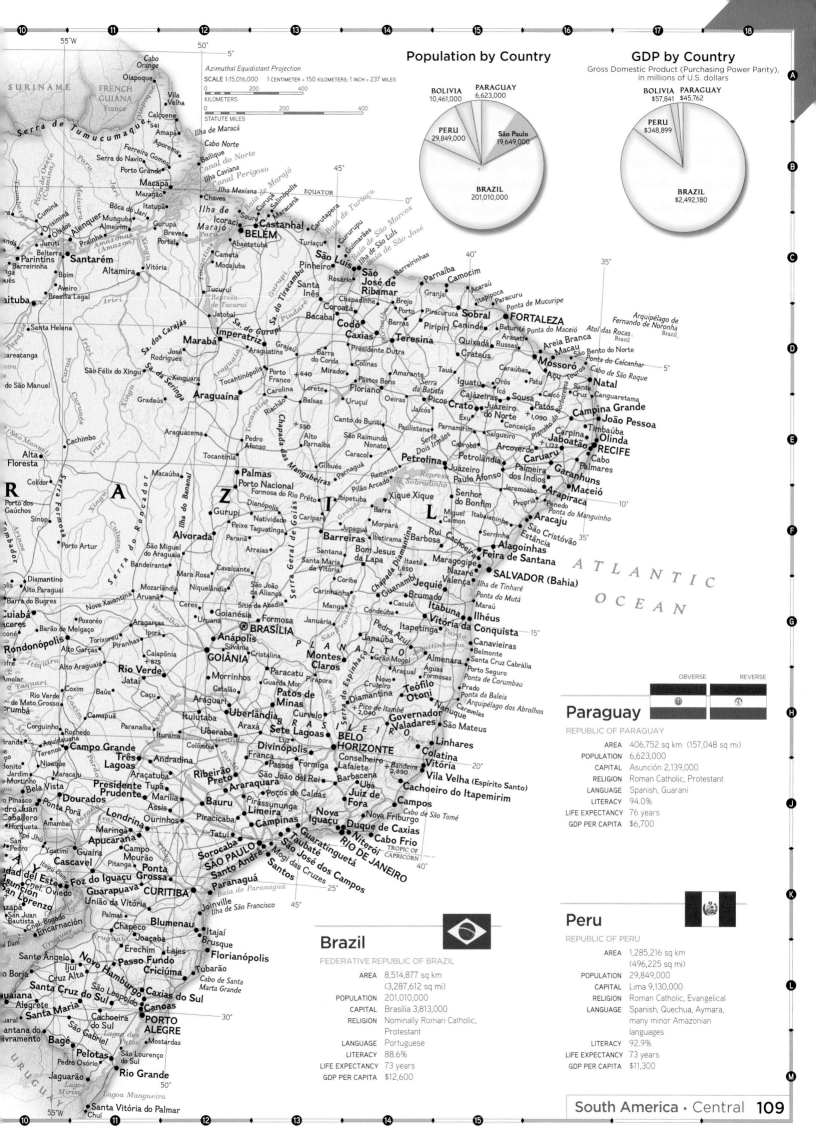

Population by Country

BOLIVIA 10,461,000
PARAGUAY 6,623,000
PERU 29,849,000
São Paulo 19,649,000
BRAZIL 201,010,000

GDP by Country
Gross Domestic Product (Purchasing Power Parity), in millions of U.S. dollars

BOLIVIA $57,841
PARAGUAY $45,762
PERU $348,899
BRAZIL $2,492,180

Paraguay
REPUBLIC OF PARAGUAY

OBVERSE   REVERSE

AREA	406,752 sq km (157,048 sq mi)
POPULATION	6,623,000
CAPITAL	Asunción 2,139,000
RELIGION	Roman Catholic, Protestant
LANGUAGE	Spanish, Guarani
LITERACY	94.0%
LIFE EXPECTANCY	76 years
GDP PER CAPITA	$6,700

Brazil
FEDERATIVE REPUBLIC OF BRAZIL

AREA	8,514,877 sq km (3,287,612 sq mi)
POPULATION	201,010,000
CAPITAL	Brasília 3,813,000
RELIGION	Nominally Roman Catholic, Protestant
LANGUAGE	Portuguese
LITERACY	88.6%
LIFE EXPECTANCY	73 years
GDP PER CAPITA	$12,600

Peru
REPUBLIC OF PERU

AREA	1,285,216 sq km (496,225 sq mi)
POPULATION	29,849,000
CAPITAL	Lima 9,130,000
RELIGION	Roman Catholic, Evangelical
LANGUAGE	Spanish, Quechua, Aymara, many minor Amazonian languages
LITERACY	92.9%
LIFE EXPECTANCY	73 years
GDP PER CAPITA	$11,300

Azimuthal Equidistant Projection
SCALE 1:15,016,000   1 CENTIMETER = 150 KILOMETERS; 1 INCH = 237 MILES

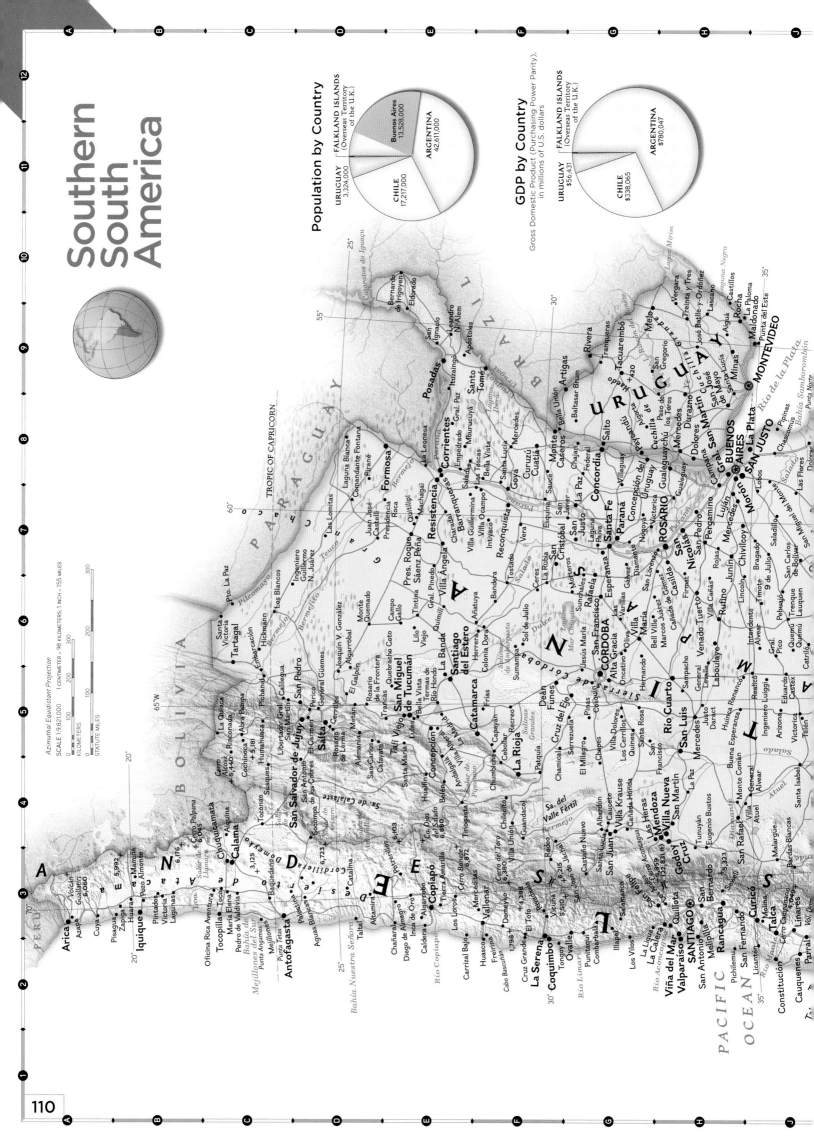

Southern South America

Population by Country

FALKLAND ISLANDS (Overseas Territory of the U.K.)
URUGUAY 3,324,000
CHILE 17,217,000
ARGENTINA 42,611,000
Buenos Aires 13,528,000

GDP by Country
Gross Domestic Product (Purchasing Power Parity), in millions of U.S. dollars

FALKLAND ISLANDS (Overseas Territory of the U.K.)
URUGUAY $56,431
CHILE $338,065
ARGENTINA $780,047

Azimuthal Equidistant Projection
SCALE 1:9,821,000   1 CENTIMETER = 98 KILOMETERS; 1 INCH = 155 MILES
KILOMETERS
STATUTE MILES

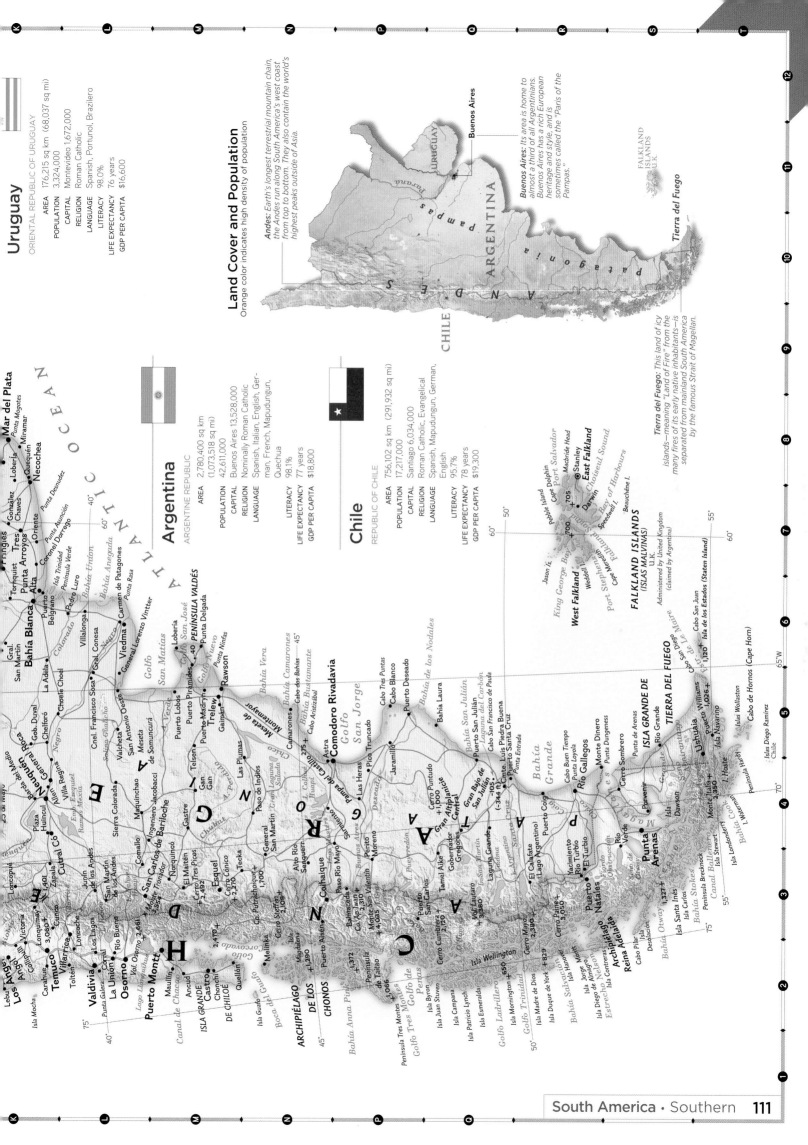

Uruguay

ORIENTAL REPUBLIC OF URUGUAY

AREA	176,215 sq km (68,037 sq mi)
POPULATION	3,324,000
CAPITAL	Montevideo 1,672,000
RELIGION	Roman Catholic
LANGUAGE	Spanish, Portunol, Braziliero
LITERACY	98.0%
LIFE EXPECTANCY	76 years
GDP PER CAPITA	$16,600

Land Cover and Population
Orange color indicates high density of population

Andes: Earth's longest terrestrial mountain chain, the Andes run along South America's west coast, from top to bottom. They also contain the world's highest peaks outside of Asia.

Buenos Aires: Its area is home to almost a third of all Argentinians. Buenos Aires has a rich European heritage and style, and is sometimes called the "Paris of the Pampas."

Tierra del Fuego: This land of icy islands—meaning "Land of Fire" from the many fires of its early native inhabitants—is separated from mainland South America by the famous Strait of Magellan.

Argentina

ARGENTINE REPUBLIC

AREA	2,780,400 sq km (1,073,518 sq mi)
POPULATION	42,611,000
CAPITAL	Buenos Aires 13,528,000
RELIGION	Nominally Roman Catholic
LANGUAGE	Spanish, Italian, English, German, French, Mapudungun, Quechua
LITERACY	98.1%
LIFE EXPECTANCY	77 years
GDP PER CAPITA	$18,800

Chile

REPUBLIC OF CHILE

AREA	756,102 sq km (291,932 sq mi)
POPULATION	17,217,000
CAPITAL	Santiago 6,034,000
RELIGION	Roman Catholic, Evangelical
LANGUAGE	Spanish, Mapudungun, German, English
LITERACY	95.7%
LIFE EXPECTANCY	78 years
GDP PER CAPITA	$19,300

Europe

Measuring in at nearly 10 million square kilometers (3.8 million square miles) by the most common definition—from the Ural Mountains west—Europe is officially the world's second smallest continent. In geologic terms, it is a western peninsula of the massive Eurasian supercontinent, and absent eastern Russia, it becomes smaller even than Australia. But small size notwithstanding, Europe has at times played a disproportionate role in human affairs—one reason that it is generally considered a distinct continent today.

Despite its northern placement, Europe benefits from a relatively benign geography. For millennia, its landmass has been warmed by currents and winds from the south and west, raising its average temperatures significantly above those equivalent areas of North America and Asia. Its land is relatively free from ice and desert, while a network of rivers flowing down from central mountain chains allows for agriculture over a greater proportion of the landscape than that of any other continent. The inland waterways of navigable rivers and the Mediterranean, Adriatic, and Aegean Seas, along with proximity to Africa and the Middle East, helped nurture early empires and their trade—and wars—with far-flung areas of the globe.

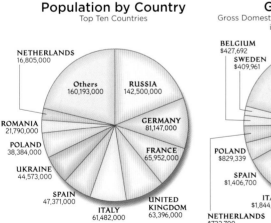

Population by Country
Top Ten Countries

NETHERLANDS 16,805,000
Others 160,193,000
RUSSIA 142,500,000
ROMANIA 21,790,000
POLAND 38,384,000
UKRAINE 44,573,000
SPAIN 47,371,000
ITALY 61,482,000
UNITED KINGDOM 63,396,000
GERMANY 81,147,000
FRANCE 65,952,000

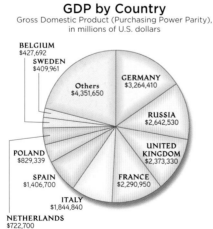

GDP by Country
Gross Domestic Product (Purchasing Power Parity), in millions of U.S. dollars

BELGIUM $427,692
SWEDEN $409,961
Others $4,351,650
GERMANY $3,264,410
RUSSIA $2,642,530
UNITED KINGDOM $2,373,330
FRANCE $2,290,950
ITALY $1,844,840
SPAIN $1,406,700
POLAND $829,339
NETHERLANDS $722,700

Physical Europe

Azimuthal Equidistant Projection
SCALE 1:14,500,000   1 CENTIMETER = 145 KILOMETERS; 1 INCH = 229 MILES

0   100   200   300   400   500
KILOMETERS

0   100   200   300   400   500
STATUTE MILES

A commonly accepted division between Asia and
Europe—here marked by an orange line—is
formed by the Ural Mountains, Ural River, Caspian
Sea, Caucasus Mountains, and the Black Sea with
its outlets, the Bosporus and Dardanelles.

BARENTS SEA

FINLAND · Oulu · Helsinki · Tampere · Pori · Lahti · Kotka · Vaasa · Kuopio · Joensuu · Rovaniemi · Kemi · Kajaani

Murmansk · Kirkenes · Nikel · Vardø · Vadsø · Pechenga · Hammerfest · Alta · Ivalo · Muonio · Monchegorsk · Kirovsk · Kandalaksha · Kola · Ponoy

Kol'skiy Poluostrov · Kem' · Belomorsk · Segezha · Medvezh'yegorsk · Kondopoga · Petrozavodsk · Sortavala

BELOYE MORE (WHITE SEA) · Archangel (Arkhangel'sk) · Severodvinsk · Novodvinsk · Onega

ESTONIA · Tallinn · Tartu · Pärnu · Narva · Saaremaa

LATVIA · Riga · Daugavpils · Rēzekne · Ventspils · Valmiera

LITHUANIA · Vilnius · Kaunas · Klaipėda · Panevėžys · Šiauliai

Kaliningrad · Chernyakhovsk

BELARUS · Minsk · Homyel' · Babruysk · Barysaw · Orsha · Mahilyow · Hrodna · Baranavichy · Pinsk · Brest · Mazyr

Sankt Peterburg (St. Petersburg) · Vyborg · Velikiy Novgorod · Pskov · Luga · Chudovo · Borovichi · Staraya Russa

MOSKVA (Moscow) · Tver' · Dubna · Vladimir · Ryazan' · Tula · Kaluga · Smolensk · Bryansk · Orel · Kursk · Voronezh · Lipetsk · Tambov · Penza · Saransk

Nizhniy Novgorod · Dzerzhinsk · Cheboksary · Kazan' · Kirov · Izhevsk · Perm' · Yekaterinburg · Chelyabinsk · Ufa · Magnitogorsk · Orenburg · Samara · Syzran' · Ul'yanovsk · Saratov · Engels · Volgograd (Stalingrad) · Astrakhan' · Kamyshin

Nizhniy Tagil · Kurgan · Zlatoust · Troitsk · Kopeysk · Sterlitamak · Orsk · Novotroitsk

URAL MOUNTAINS · ZAPADNO SIBIRSKAYA RAVNINA

Surgut · Nizhnevartovsk · Tyumen' · Tobol'sk · Omsk · Nazyvayevsk · Khanty-Mansiysk · Ob'

KAZAKHSTAN · Atyraū · Oral

UKRAINE · Kyyiv (Kiev) · Kharkiv · Dnipropetrovs'k · Zaporizhzhya · Donets'k · Makiyivka · Mariupol' · Odesa · Lviv · Vinnytsya · Poltava · Luhans'k · Lysychans'k · Kryvyy Rih · Melitopol' · Kherson · Simferopol' · Sevastopol' · Yalta · Kerch · Feodosiya

CRIMEA · Sea of Azov

MOLDOVA · Chişinău · Bălţi · Tiraspol · Iaşi · TRANSDNIESTRIA

ROMANIA · Bucharest · Braşov · Sibiu · Timişoara · Cluj-Napoca · Oradea · Craiova · Ploieşti · Brăila · Galaţi · Constanţa · Bacău · Focşani · Giurgiu

BULGARIA · Sofia (Sofiya) · Plovdiv · Varna · Burgas · Ruse · Pleven · Stara Zagora · Shumen

SERBIA · Beograd (Belgrade)

MACEDONIA · Skopje · Bitola · Prilep

GREECE · Athina (Athens) · Thessaloníki · Lárissa · Vólos · Pátra · Pireás · Iráklio · Kríti (Crete)

Warszawa (Warsaw) · Lublin · Kielce · Rzeszów · Debrecen · Košice

ROSTOV NA DONU · Taganrog · Shakhty · Volgodonsk · Krasnodar · Stavropol' · Armavir · Maykop · Novorossiysk · Sochi · Elista

CAUCASUS MOUNTAINS · GEORGIA · T'bilisi (Tbilisi) · Sukhumi · ABKHAZIA · S. OSSETIA

AZERBAIJAN · Baki (Baku) · NAGORNO KARABAKH

ARMENIA · Yerevan

Nal'chik · Groznyy · Vladikavkaz · Nazran' · Makhachkala · Derbent · Cherkessk · Kizlyar

CASPIAN SEA · Caspian Sea: Surface elevation (-92 ft) -28

UZBEKISTAN · USTYURT PLATEAU · Aral Sea · North Aral Sea

TURKMENISTAN · Garagum

TURKEY · Istanbul (Constantinople) · Ankara · ANATOLIA (ASIA MINOR) · Kuzey Anadolu Daglari · Toros Daglari

NORTHERN CYPRUS · Lefkosia (Lefkoşa, Nicosia) · CYPRUS · Lemesos (Limassol) · Ammochostos (Famagusta)

SYRIA · Dimashq (Damascus) · SYRIAN DESERT · LEBANON · Beyrouth (Beirut)

IRAQ · Baghdad (Baghdād) · Euphrates · Tigris

IRAN · TEHRĀN (Tehran) · Kūhhā-ye Zāgros (Zagros Mountains)

BLACK SEA · SEA OF CRETE · AEGEAN SEA

GULF OF FINLAND · GULF OF BOTHNIA

ARCTIC CIRCLE

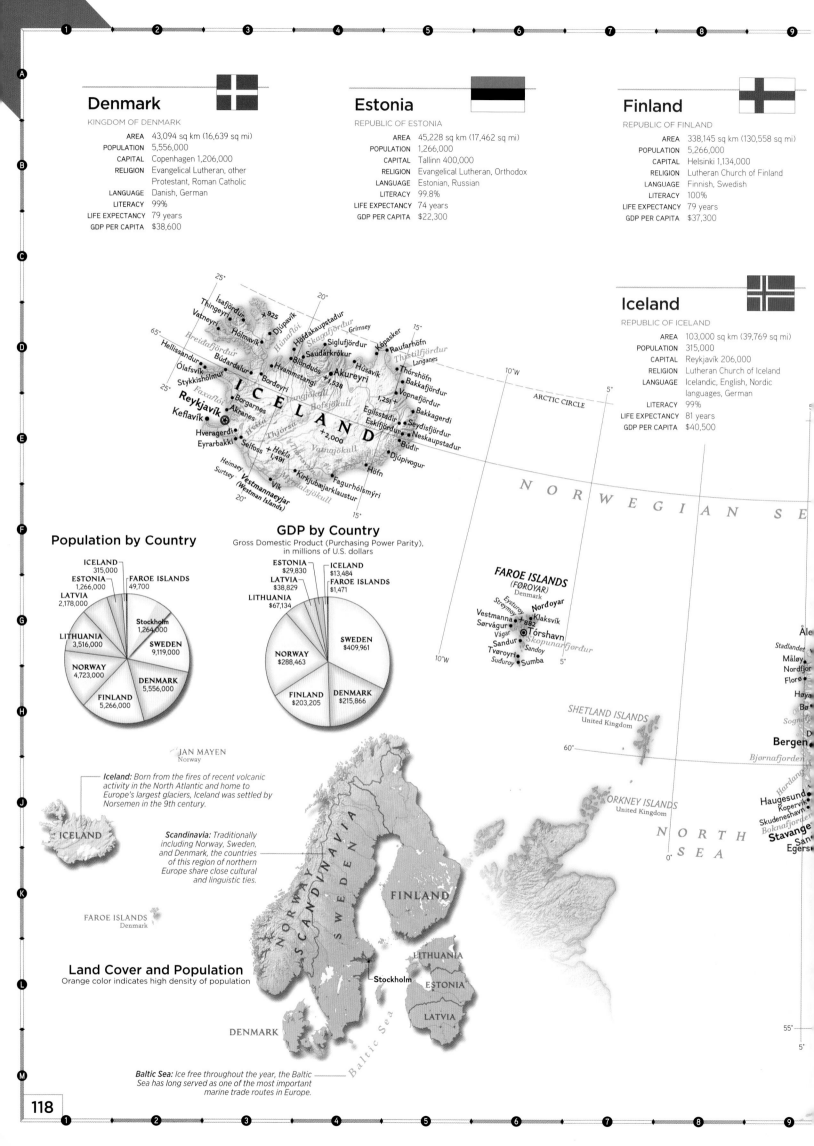

Denmark

KINGDOM OF DENMARK

AREA	43,094 sq km (16,639 sq mi)
POPULATION	5,556,000
CAPITAL	Copenhagen 1,206,000
RELIGION	Evangelical Lutheran, other Protestant, Roman Catholic
LANGUAGE	Danish, German
LITERACY	99%
LIFE EXPECTANCY	79 years
GDP PER CAPITA	$38,600

Estonia

REPUBLIC OF ESTONIA

AREA	45,228 sq km (17,462 sq mi)
POPULATION	1,266,000
CAPITAL	Tallinn 400,000
RELIGION	Evangelical Lutheran, Orthodox
LANGUAGE	Estonian, Russian
LITERACY	99.8%
LIFE EXPECTANCY	74 years
GDP PER CAPITA	$22,300

Finland

REPUBLIC OF FINLAND

AREA	338,145 sq km (130,558 sq mi)
POPULATION	5,266,000
CAPITAL	Helsinki 1,134,000
RELIGION	Lutheran Church of Finland
LANGUAGE	Finnish, Swedish
LITERACY	100%
LIFE EXPECTANCY	79 years
GDP PER CAPITA	$37,300

Iceland

REPUBLIC OF ICELAND

AREA	103,000 sq km (39,769 sq mi)
POPULATION	315,000
CAPITAL	Reykjavík 206,000
RELIGION	Lutheran Church of Iceland
LANGUAGE	Icelandic, English, Nordic languages, German
LITERACY	99%
LIFE EXPECTANCY	81 years
GDP PER CAPITA	$40,500

ICELAND

NORWEGIAN SEA

FAROE ISLANDS
(FØROYAR)
Denmark

SHETLAND ISLANDS
United Kingdom

Population by Country

ICELAND 315,000
ESTONIA 1,266,000
FAROE ISLANDS 49,700
LATVIA 2,178,000
LITHUANIA 3,516,000
NORWAY 4,723,000
FINLAND 5,266,000
DENMARK 5,556,000
SWEDEN 9,119,000
Stockholm 1,264,000

GDP by Country

Gross Domestic Product (Purchasing Power Parity), in millions of U.S. dollars

ESTONIA $29,830
ICELAND $13,484
LATVIA $38,829
FAROE ISLANDS $1,471
LITHUANIA $67,134
SWEDEN $409,961
NORWAY $288,463
FINLAND $203,205
DENMARK $215,866

JAN MAYEN
Norway

Iceland: Born from the fires of recent volcanic activity in the North Atlantic and home to Europe's largest glaciers, Iceland was settled by Norsemen in the 9th century.

ICELAND

Scandinavia: Traditionally including Norway, Sweden, and Denmark, the countries of this region of northern Europe share close cultural and linguistic ties.

FAROE ISLANDS
Denmark

ORKNEY ISLANDS
United Kingdom

NORTH SEA

Bergen

Haugesund
Kopervik
Skudeneshavn
Stavanger
Egers

Land Cover and Population

Orange color indicates high density of population

Stockholm

NORWAY
SCANDINAVIA
SWEDEN
FINLAND
LITHUANIA
ESTONIA
LATVIA
Baltic Sea
DENMARK

Baltic Sea: Ice free throughout the year, the Baltic Sea has long served as one of the most important marine trade routes in Europe.

Northern Europe

Latvia
REPUBLIC OF LATVIA

AREA	64,589 sq km (24,938 sq mi)
POPULATION	2,178,000
CAPITAL	Riga 701,000
RELIGION	Lutheran, Orthodox
LANGUAGE	Latvian, Russian, Lithuanian
LITERACY	99.8%
LIFE EXPECTANCY	73 years
GDP PER CAPITA	$19,100

Lithuania
REPUBLIC OF LITHUANIA

AREA	65,300 sq km (25,212 sq mi)
POPULATION	3,516,000
CAPITAL	Vilnius 546,000
RELIGION	Roman Catholic, Russian Orthodox
LANGUAGE	Lithuanian, Russian, Polish
LITERACY	99.7%
LIFE EXPECTANCY	76 years
GDP PER CAPITA	$21,100

Norway
KINGDOM OF NORWAY

AREA	323,802 sq km (125,021 sq mi)
POPULATION	4,723,000
CAPITAL	Oslo 915,000
RELIGION	Church of Norway (Lutheran)
LANGUAGE	Norwegian, Sami
LITERACY	100%
LIFE EXPECTANCY	80 years
GDP PER CAPITA	$56,700

Sweden
KINGDOM OF SWEDEN

AREA	450,295 sq km (173,860 sq mi)
POPULATION	9,119,000
CAPITAL	Stockholm 1,264,000
RELIGION	Lutheran
LANGUAGE	Swedish, Sami, Finnish
LITERACY	99%
LIFE EXPECTANCY	81 years
GDP PER CAPITA	$43,000

Azimuthal Equidistant Projection

SCALE 1:8,047,000   1 CENTIMETER = 80 KILOMETERS; 1 INCH = 127 MILES

STATUTE MILES

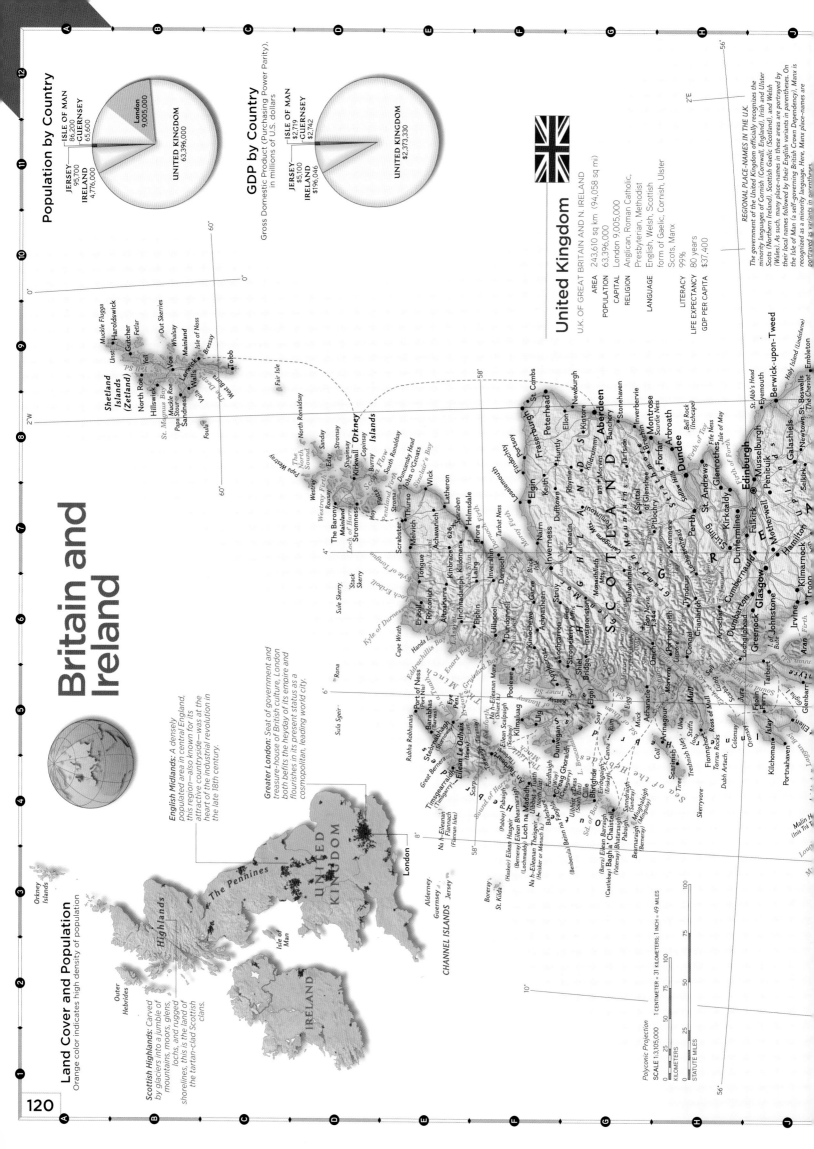

Britain and Ireland

Population by Country

ISLE OF MAN 86,200
GUERNSEY 65,600
JERSEY 95,700
IRELAND 4,776,000
London 9,005,000
UNITED KINGDOM 63,396,000

GDP by Country

Gross Domestic Product (Purchasing Power Parity), in millions of U.S. dollars

ISLE OF MAN $2,779
GUERNSEY $2,742
JERSEY $5,100
IRELAND $196,046
UNITED KINGDOM $2,373,330

United Kingdom

U.K. OF GREAT BRITAIN AND N. IRELAND

AREA 243,610 sq km (94,058 sq mi)
POPULATION 63,396,000
CAPITAL London 9,005,000
RELIGION Anglican, Roman Catholic, Presbyterian, Methodist
LANGUAGE English, Welsh, Scottish form of Gaelic, Cornish, Ulster Scots, Manx
LITERACY 99%
LIFE EXPECTANCY 80 years
GDP PER CAPITA $37,400

REGIONAL PLACE-NAMES IN THE U.K.
The government of the United Kingdom officially recognizes the minority languages of Cornish (Cornwall, England), Irish and Ulster Scots (Northern Ireland), Scottish Gaelic (Scotland), and Welsh (Wales). As such, many place-names in these areas are portrayed by their local names followed by their English variants in parentheses. On the Isle of Man (a self-governing British Crown Dependency), Manx is recognized as a minority language. Here, Manx place-names are portrayed as variants in parentheses.

Land Cover and Population

Orange color indicates high density of population

Scottish Highlands: Carved by glaciers into a jumble of mountains, moors, glens, lochs, and rugged shorelines, this is the land of the tartan-clad Scottish clans.

English Midlands: A densely populated area in central England, this region—also known for its attractive countryside—was at the heart of the industrial revolution in the late 18th century.

Greater London: Seat of government and treasure-house of British culture, London both befits the heyday of its empire and flourishes in its present status as a cosmopolitan, leading world city.

Polyconic Projection
SCALE 1:3,105,000
1 CENTIMETER = 31 KILOMETERS; 1 INCH = 49 MILES

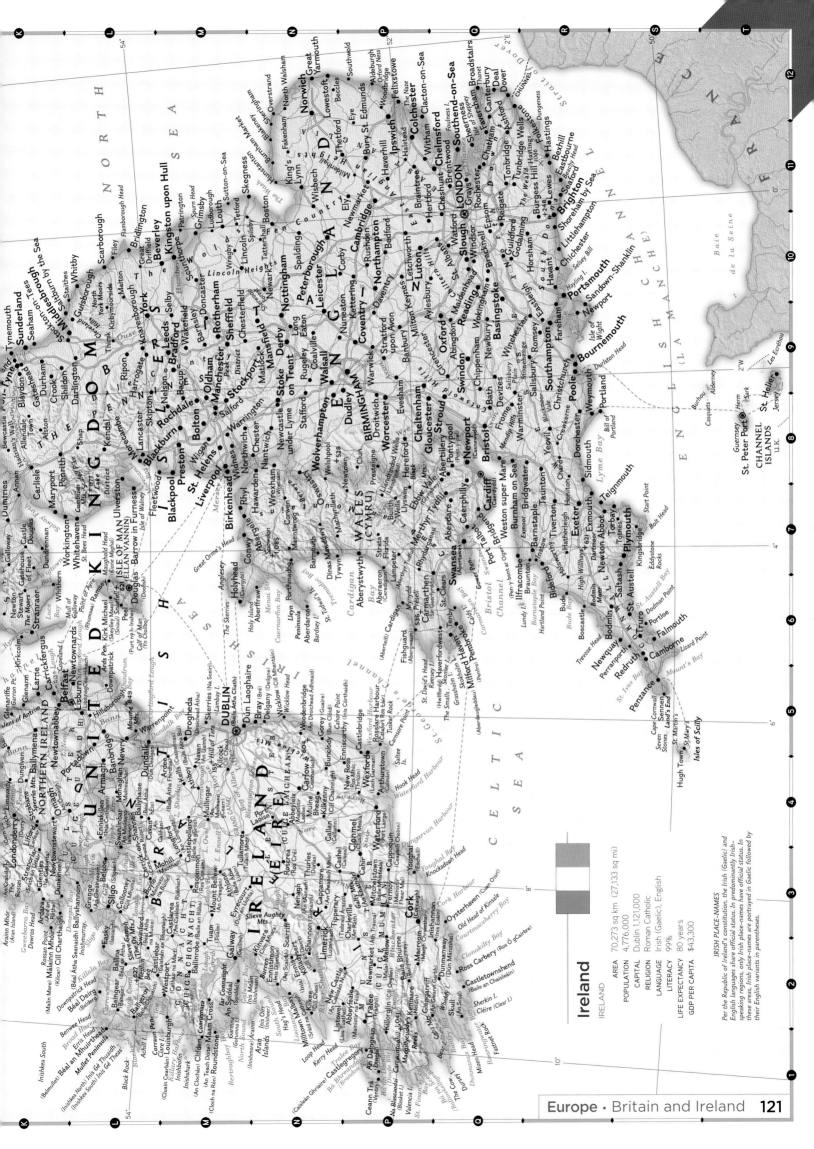

Ireland

IRELAND

AREA	70,273 sq km (27,133 sq mi)
POPULATION	4,776,000
CAPITAL	Dublin 1,121,000
RELIGION	Roman Catholic
LANGUAGE	Irish (Gaelic), English
LITERACY	99%
LIFE EXPECTANCY	80 years
GDP PER CAPITA	$43,300

IRISH PLACE-NAMES

Per the Republic of Ireland's constitution, the Irish (Gaelic) and English languages share official status. In predominantly Irish-speaking regions, only Irish place-names have official status. In these areas, Irish place-names are portrayed in Gaelic followed by their English variants in parentheses.

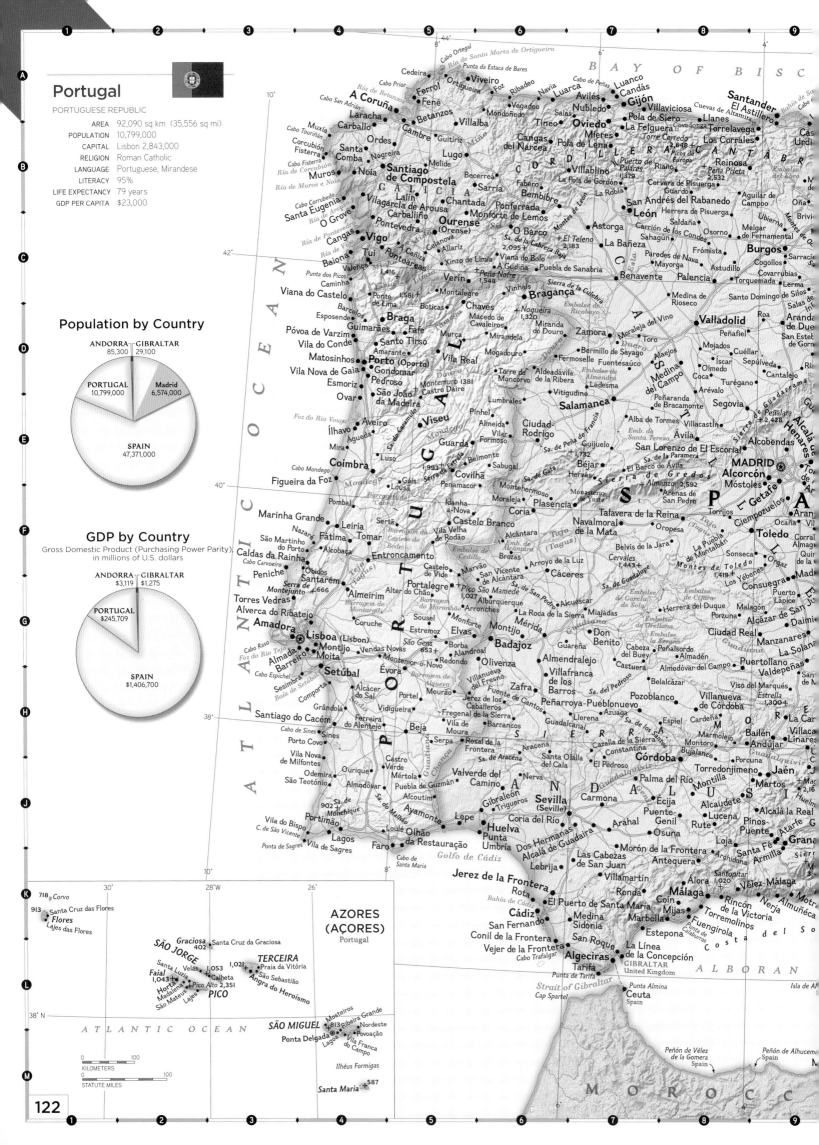

Portugal

PORTUGUESE REPUBLIC

AREA	92,090 sq km (35,556 sq mi)
POPULATION	10,799,000
CAPITAL	Lisbon 2,843,000
RELIGION	Roman Catholic
LANGUAGE	Portuguese, Mirandese
LITERACY	95%
LIFE EXPECTANCY	79 years
GDP PER CAPITA	$23,000

Population by Country

ANDORRA 85,300 — GIBRALTAR 29,100
PORTUGAL 10,799,000
Madrid 6,574,000
SPAIN 47,371,000

GDP by Country

Gross Domestic Product (Purchasing Power Parity), in millions of U.S. dollars

ANDORRA $3,119 — GIBRALTAR $1,275
PORTUGAL $245,709
SPAIN $1,406,700

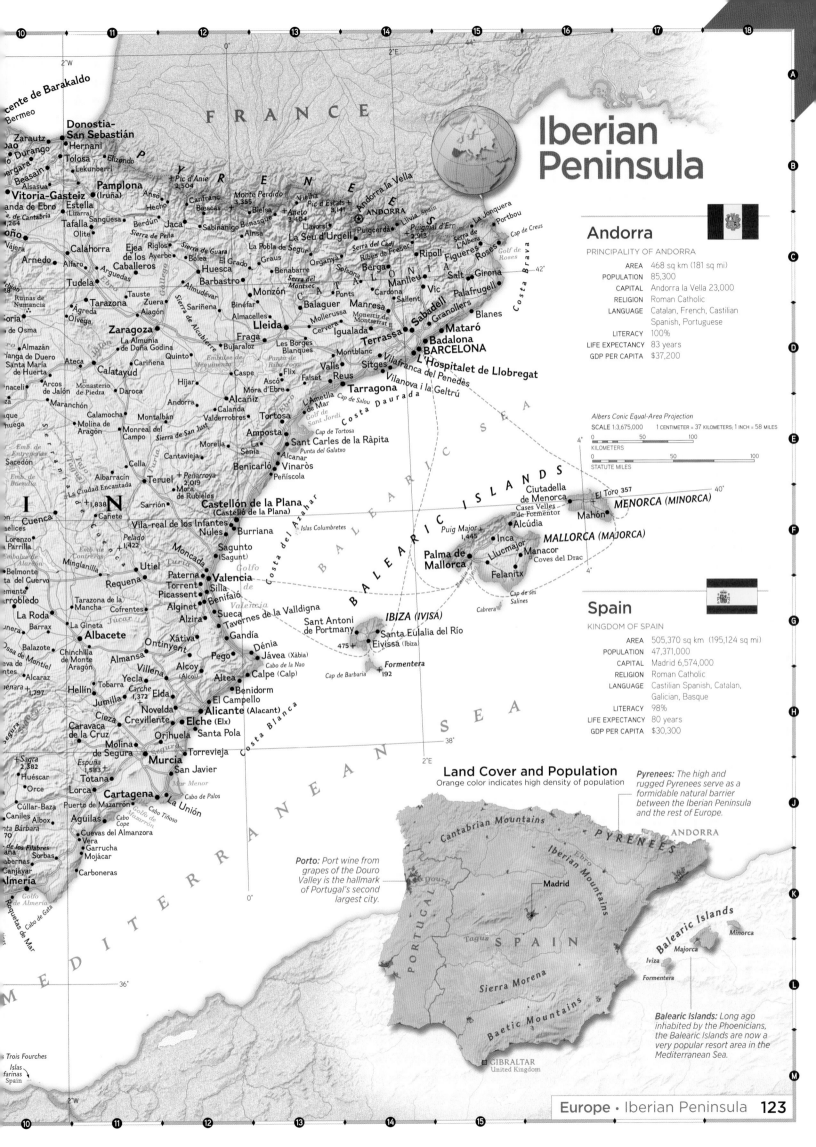

Iberian Peninsula

Andorra
PRINCIPALITY OF ANDORRA
AREA	468 sq km (181 sq mi)
POPULATION	85,300
CAPITAL	Andorra la Vella 23,000
RELIGION	Roman Catholic
LANGUAGE	Catalan, French, Castilian Spanish, Portuguese
LITERACY	100%
LIFE EXPECTANCY	83 years
GDP PER CAPITA	$37,200

Albers Conic Equal-Area Projection

SCALE 1:3,675,000   1 CENTIMETER = 37 KILOMETERS; 1 INCH = 58 MILES

KILOMETERS
0   50   100

STATUTE MILES
0   50   100

Spain
KINGDOM OF SPAIN
AREA	505,370 sq km (195,124 sq mi)
POPULATION	47,371,000
CAPITAL	Madrid 6,574,000
RELIGION	Roman Catholic
LANGUAGE	Castilian Spanish, Catalan, Galician, Basque
LITERACY	98%
LIFE EXPECTANCY	80 years
GDP PER CAPITA	$30,300

Land Cover and Population
Orange color indicates high density of population

Pyrenees: The high and rugged Pyrenees serve as a formidable natural barrier between the Iberian Peninsula and the rest of Europe.

Porto: Port wine from grapes of the Douro Valley is the hallmark of Portugal's second largest city.

Balearic Islands: Long ago inhabited by the Phoenicians, the Balearic Islands are now a very popular resort area in the Mediterranean Sea.

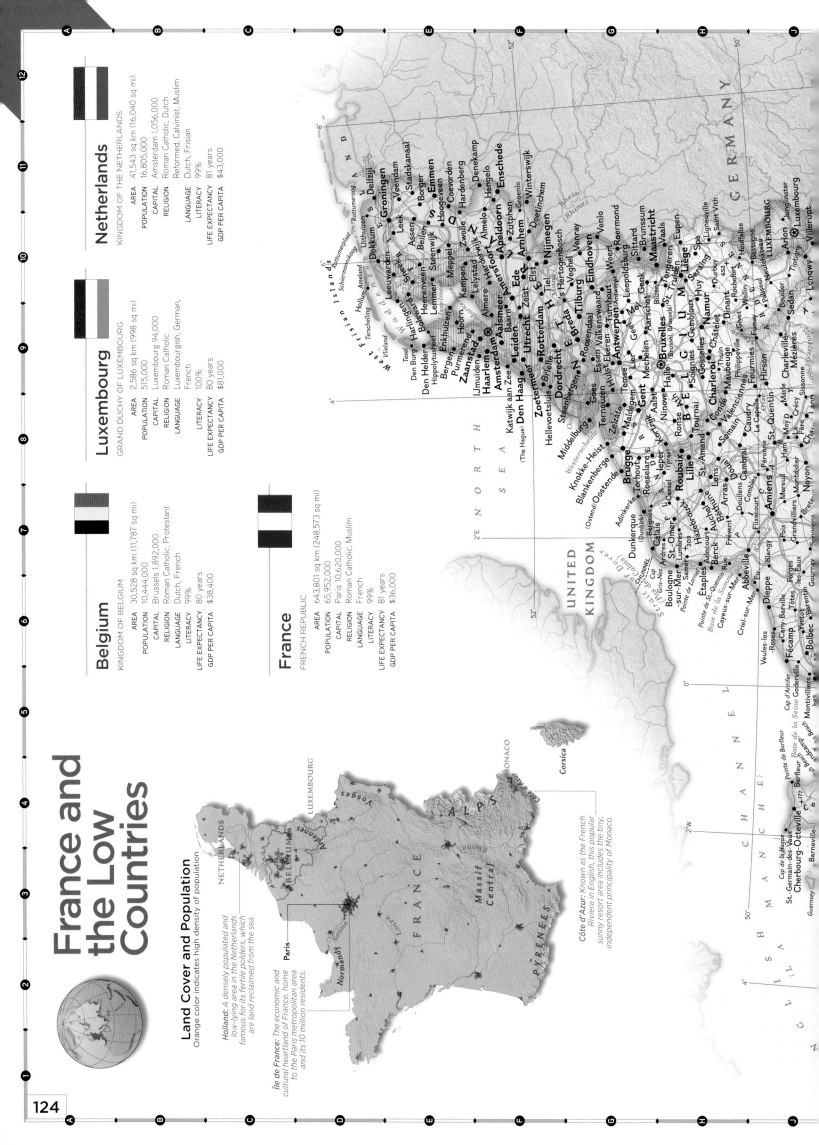

France and the Low Countries

Netherlands
KINGDOM OF THE NETHERLANDS

AREA	41,543 sq km (16,040 sq mi)
POPULATION	16,805,000
CAPITAL	Amsterdam 1,056,000
RELIGION	Roman Catholic, Dutch Reformed, Calvinist, Muslim
LANGUAGE	Dutch, Frisian
LITERACY	99%
LIFE EXPECTANCY	81 years
GDP PER CAPITA	$43,000

Luxembourg
GRAND DUCHY OF LUXEMBOURG

AREA	2,586 sq km (998 sq mi)
POPULATION	515,000
CAPITAL	Luxembourg 94,000
RELIGION	Roman Catholic
LANGUAGE	Luxembourgish, German, French
LITERACY	100%
LIFE EXPECTANCY	80 years
GDP PER CAPITA	$81,000

Belgium
KINGDOM OF BELGIUM

AREA	30,528 sq km (11,787 sq mi)
POPULATION	10,444,000
CAPITAL	Brussels 1,892,000
RELIGION	Roman Catholic, Protestant
LANGUAGE	Dutch, French
LITERACY	99%
LIFE EXPECTANCY	80 years
GDP PER CAPITA	$38,400

France
FRENCH REPUBLIC

AREA	643,801 sq km (248,573 sq mi)
POPULATION	65,952,000
CAPITAL	Paris 10,620,000
RELIGION	Roman Catholic, Muslim
LANGUAGE	French
LITERACY	99%
LIFE EXPECTANCY	81 years
GDP PER CAPITA	$36,000

Land Cover and Population
Orange color indicates high density of population

Holland: A densely populated and low-lying area in the Netherlands famous for its fertile polders, which are land reclaimed from the sea.

Île de France: The economic and cultural heartland of France, home to the Paris metropolitan area and its 10 million residents.

Côte d'Azur: Known as the French Riviera in English, this popular sunny resort area includes the tiny, independent principality of Monaco.

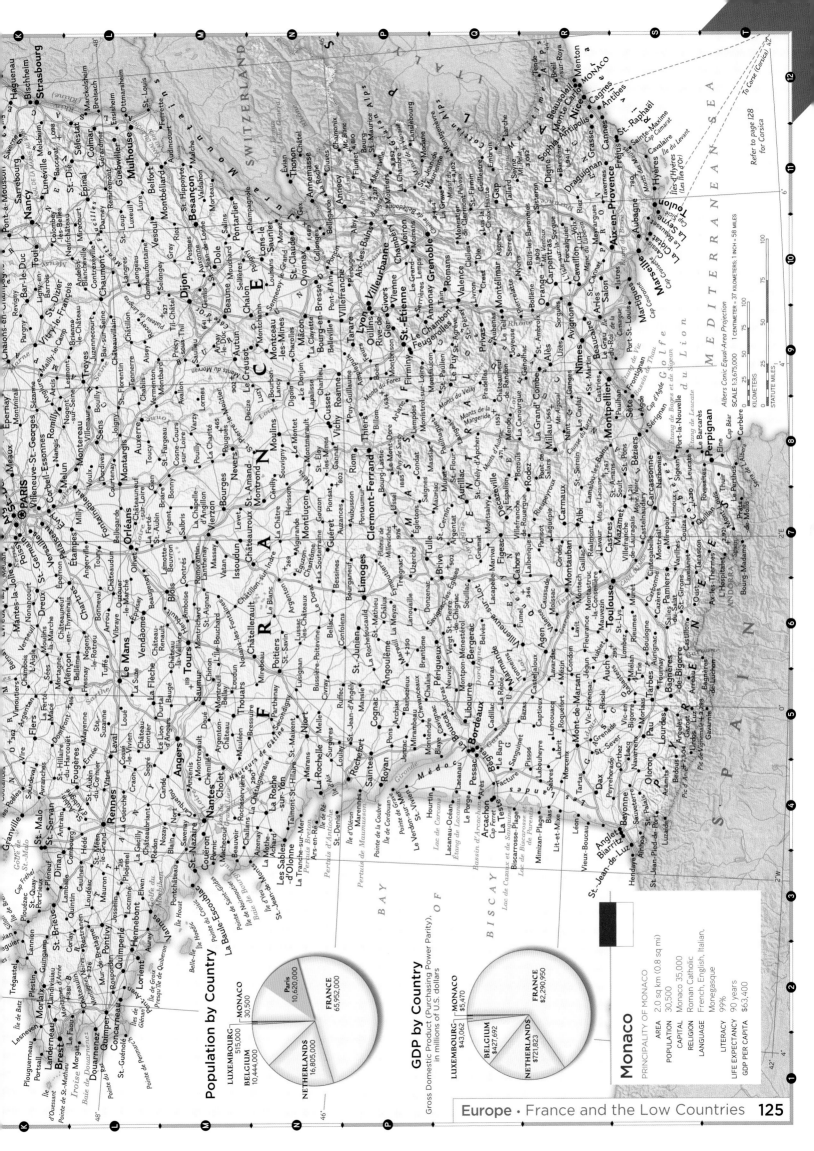

Population by Country

- MONACO 30,500
- LUXEMBOURG 515,000
- BELGIUM 10,444,000
- FRANCE 65,952,000
- Paris 10,620,000
- NETHERLANDS 16,805,000

GDP by Country

Gross Domestic Product (Purchasing Power Parity), in millions of U.S. dollars

- MONACO $5,470
- LUXEMBOURG $43,062
- BELGIUM $427,692
- FRANCE $2,290,950
- NETHERLANDS $721,823

Monaco

PRINCIPALITY OF MONACO

AREA	2.0 sq km (0.8 sq mi)
POPULATION	30,500
CAPITAL	Monaco 35,000
RELIGION	Roman Catholic
LANGUAGE	French, English, Italian, Monegasque
LITERACY	99%
LIFE EXPECTANCY	90 years
GDP PER CAPITA	$63,400

Refer to page 128 for Corsica

Central Europe

Austria
REPUBLIC OF AUSTRIA

AREA	83,871 sq km (32,383 sq mi)
POPULATION	8,222,000
CAPITAL	Vienna 1,720,000
RELIGION	Roman Catholic, Protestant, Muslim
LANGUAGE	German
LITERACY	98%
LIFE EXPECTANCY	80 years
GDP PER CAPITA	$43,300

Czech Republic
CZECH REPUBLIC

AREA	78,867 sq km (30,451 sq mi)
POPULATION	10,163,000
CAPITAL	Prague 1,276,000
RELIGION	Roman Catholic
LANGUAGE	Czech
LITERACY	99%
LIFE EXPECTANCY	77 years
GDP PER CAPITA	$27,700

Germany
FEDERAL REPUBLIC OF GERMANY

AREA	357,022 sq km (137,847 sq mi)
POPULATION	81,147,000
CAPITAL	Berlin 3,462,000
RELIGION	Protestant, Roman Catholic
LANGUAGE	German
LITERACY	99%
LIFE EXPECTANCY	80 years
GDP PER CAPITA	$40,000

Ruhr Valley: The largest greater metropolitan area in Germany, the Ruhr Valley is a former industrial area comprising the cities of Dortmund, Essen, Duisburg, Bochum, Gelsenkirchen, and many others.

Land Cover and Population
Orange color indicates high density of population

Carpathian Mountains: Extending for nearly a thousand miles in a long, curving arc into Ukraine and Romania, the Carpathians reach their highest points in the Tatra Mountains along the border of Poland and Slovakia.

Alps: Central Europe's highest and most formidable mountains, the Alps form a natural barrier to transportation while also providing inspiration and recreation for millions of Europeans.

Hungary
HUNGARY

AREA	93,028 sq km (35,918 sq mi)
POPULATION	9,939,000
CAPITAL	Budapest 1,737,000
RELIGION	Roman Catholic, Calvinist
LANGUAGE	Hungarian
LITERACY	99%
LIFE EXPECTANCY	75 years
GDP PER CAPITA	$20,200

Liechtenstein

PRINCIPALITY OF LIECHTENSTEIN

AREA	160 sq km (62 sq mi)
POPULATION	37,000
CAPITAL	Vaduz 5,000
RELIGION	Roman Catholic, Protestant
LANGUAGE	German, Alemannic dialect
LITERACY	100%
LIFE EXPECTANCY	82 years
GDP PER CAPITA	$89,400

Poland

REPUBLIC OF POLAND

AREA	312,685 sq km (120,728 sq mi)
POPULATION	38,384,000
CAPITAL	Warsaw 1,723,000
RELIGION	Roman Catholic
LANGUAGE	Polish
LITERACY	99.5%
LIFE EXPECTANCY	76 years
GDP PER CAPITA	$21,700

Slovakia

SLOVAK REPUBLIC

AREA	49,035 sq km (18,932 sq mi)
POPULATION	5,448,000
CAPITAL	Bratislava 434,000
RELIGION	Roman Catholic, Protestant
LANGUAGE	Slovak, Hungarian
LITERACY	99.6%
LIFE EXPECTANCY	76 years
GDP PER CAPITA	$25,300

Population by Country

SLOVAKIA 5,488,000
LIECHTENSTEIN 37,000
AUSTRIA 8,222,000
HUNGARY 9,939,000
CZECH REPUBLIC 10,163,000
Berlin 3,462,000
GERMANY 81,147,000
POLAND 38,384,000

GDP by Country

Gross Domestic Product (Purchasing Power Parity), in millions of U.S. dollars

SLOVAKIA $137,907
LIECHTENSTEIN $3,200
AUSTRIA $367,553
HUNGARY $201,005
CZECH REPUBLIC $292,782
POLAND $829,339
GERMANY $3,264,410

Albers Conic Equal-Area Projection

SCALE 1:4,309,000   1 CENTIMETER = 43 KILOMETERS; 1 INCH = 68 MILES

KILOMETERS 0 25 50 75 100 125 150

STATUTE MILES 0 25 50 75 100 125 150

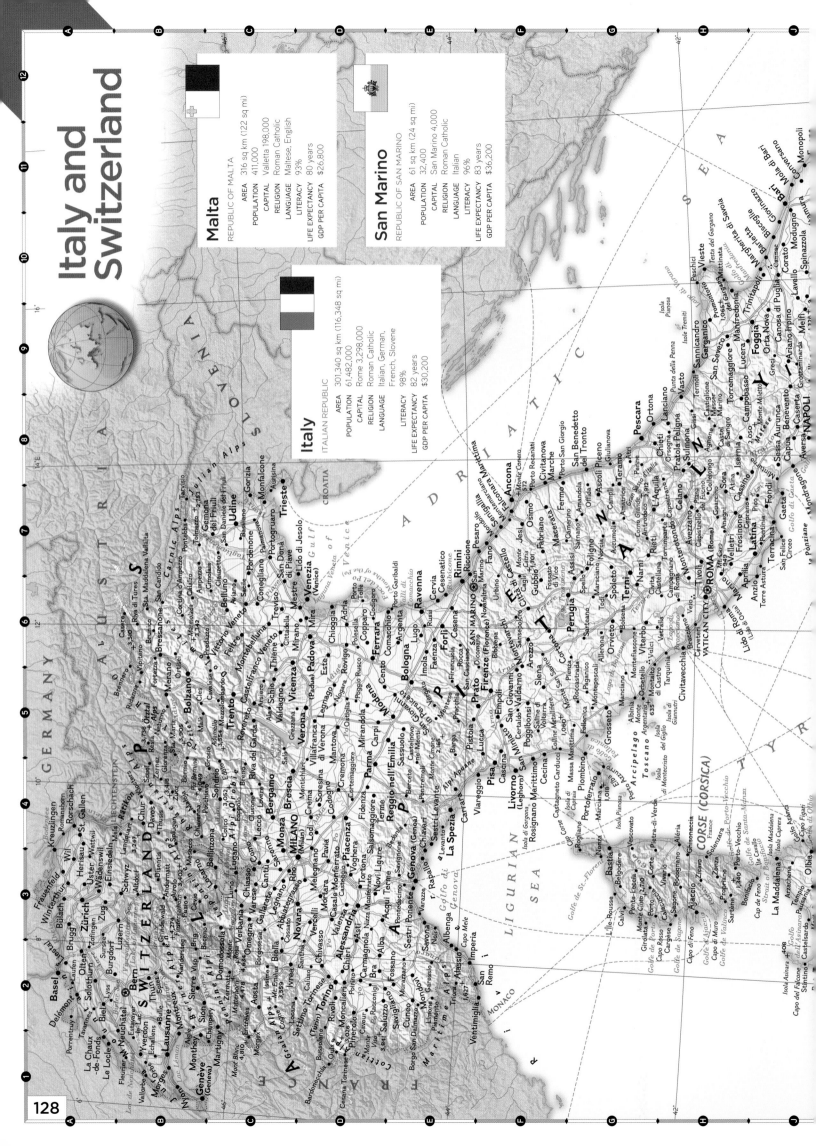

Italy and Switzerland

Malta
REPUBLIC OF MALTA

AREA	316 sq km (122 sq mi)
POPULATION	411,000
CAPITAL	Valletta 198,000
RELIGION	Roman Catholic
LANGUAGE	Maltese, English
LITERACY	93%
LIFE EXPECTANCY	80 years
GDP PER CAPITA	$26,800

San Marino
REPUBLIC OF SAN MARINO

AREA	61 sq km (24 sq mi)
POPULATION	32,400
CAPITAL	San Marino 4,000
RELIGION	Roman Catholic
LANGUAGE	Italian
LITERACY	96%
LIFE EXPECTANCY	83 years
GDP PER CAPITA	$36,200

Italy
ITALIAN REPUBLIC

AREA	301,340 sq km (116,348 sq mi)
POPULATION	61,482,000
CAPITAL	Rome 3,298,000
RELIGION	Roman Catholic
LANGUAGE	Italian, German, French, Slovene
LITERACY	98%
LIFE EXPECTANCY	82 years
GDP PER CAPITA	$30,200

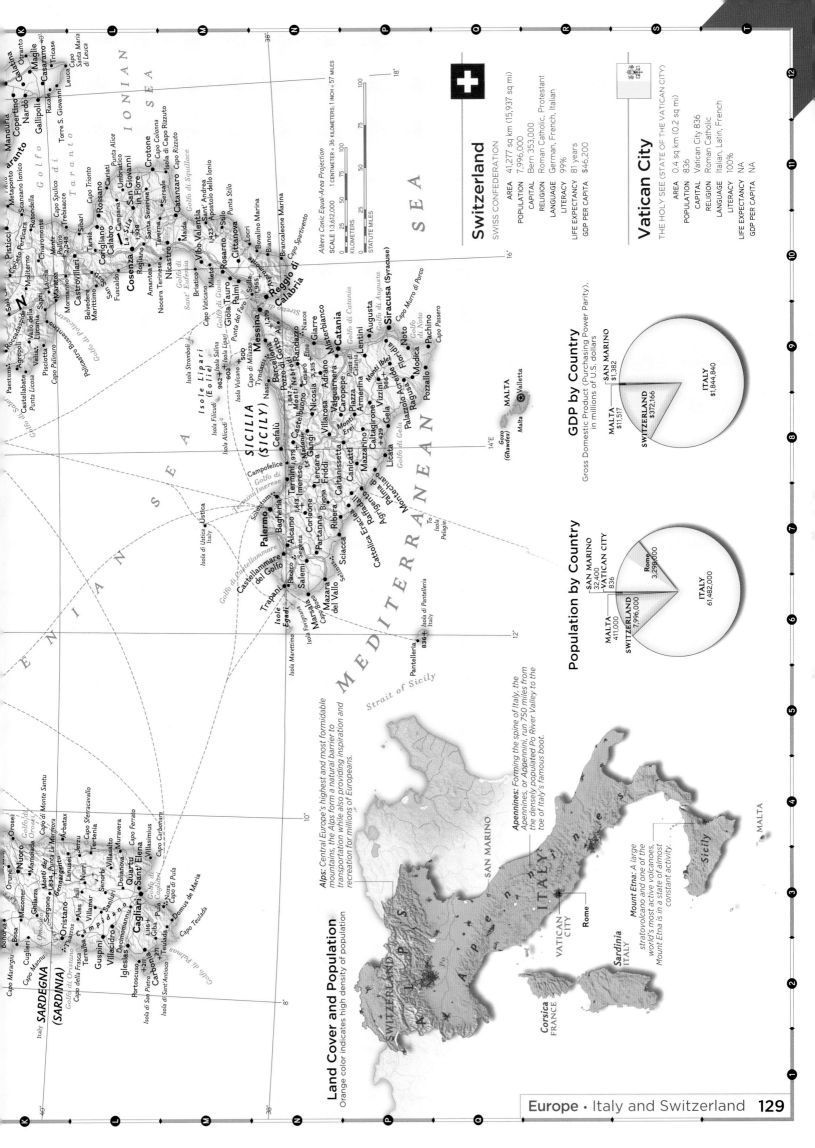

Switzerland
SWISS CONFEDERATION

AREA 41,277 sq km (15,937 sq mi)
POPULATION 7,996,000
CAPITAL Bern 353,000
RELIGION Roman Catholic, Protestant
LANGUAGE German, French, Italian
LITERACY 99%
LIFE EXPECTANCY 81 years
GDP PER CAPITA $46,200

Vatican City
THE HOLY SEE (STATE OF THE VATICAN CITY)

AREA 0.4 sq km (0.2 sq mi)
POPULATION 836
CAPITAL Vatican City 836
RELIGION Roman Catholic
LANGUAGE Italian, Latin, French
LITERACY 100%
LIFE EXPECTANCY NA
GDP PER CAPITA NA

Albers Conic Equal-Area Projection

1 CENTIMETER = 36 KILOMETERS; 1 INCH = 57 MILES
SCALE 1:3,612,000

GDP by Country
Gross Domestic Product (Purchasing Power Parity), in millions of U.S. dollars

ITALY $1,844,840
SWITZERLAND $372,166
MALTA $11,517
SAN MARINO $1,382

Population by Country

ITALY 61,482,000
SWITZERLAND 7,996,000
MALTA 411,000
Rome 3,298,000
SAN MARINO 32,400
VATICAN CITY 836

Land Cover and Population
Orange color indicates high density of population

Alps: Central Europe's highest and most formidable mountains, the Alps form a natural barrier to transportation while also providing inspiration and recreation for millions of Europeans.

Apennines: Forming the spine of Italy, the Apennines, or Appennini, run 750 miles from the densely populated Po River Valley to the toe of Italy's famous boot.

Mount Etna: A large stratovolcano and one of the world's most active volcanoes, Mount Etna is in a state of almost constant activity.

Sardinia
ITALY

Corsica
FRANCE

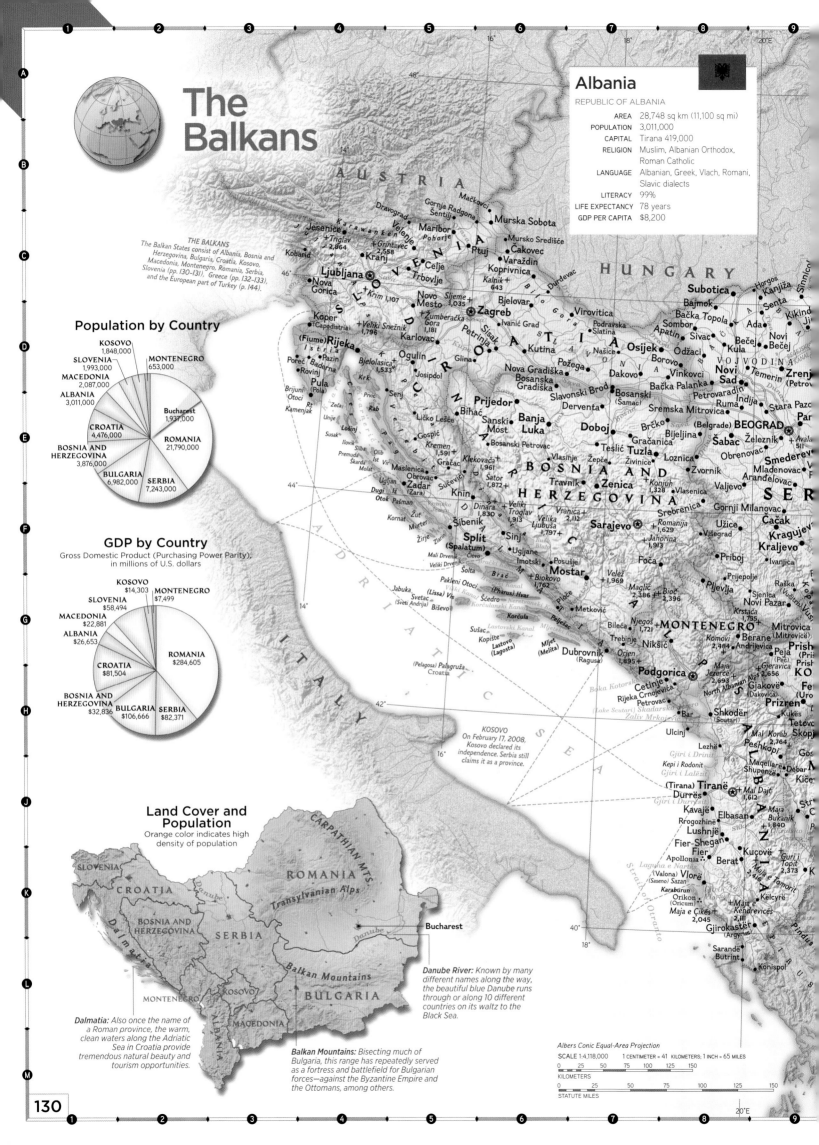

The Balkans

THE BALKANS
The Balkan States consist of Albania, Bosnia and Herzegovina, Bulgaria, Croatia, Kosovo, Macedonia, Montenegro, Romania, Serbia, Slovenia (pp. 130-131), Greece (pp. 132-133), and the European part of Turkey (p. 144).

Albania
REPUBLIC OF ALBANIA

AREA	28,748 sq km (11,100 sq mi)
POPULATION	3,011,000
CAPITAL	Tirana 419,000
RELIGION	Muslim, Albanian Orthodox, Roman Catholic
LANGUAGE	Albanian, Greek, Vlach, Romani, Slavic dialects
LITERACY	99%
LIFE EXPECTANCY	78 years
GDP PER CAPITA	$8,200

Population by Country

- KOSOVO 1,848,000
- SLOVENIA 1,993,000
- MACEDONIA 2,087,000
- ALBANIA 3,011,000
- MONTENEGRO 653,000
- CROATIA 4,476,000
- BOSNIA AND HERZEGOVINA 3,876,000
- BULGARIA 6,982,000
- SERBIA 7,243,000
- Bucharest 1,937,000
- ROMANIA 21,790,000

GDP by Country
Gross Domestic Product (Purchasing Power Parity), in millions of U.S. dollars

- KOSOVO $14,303
- SLOVENIA $58,494
- MACEDONIA $22,881
- ALBANIA $26,653
- MONTENEGRO $7,499
- CROATIA $81,504
- BOSNIA AND HERZEGOVINA $32,836
- BULGARIA $106,666
- SERBIA $82,371
- ROMANIA $284,605

Land Cover and Population
Orange color indicates high density of population

KOSOVO
On February 17, 2008, Kosovo declared its independence. Serbia still claims it as a province.

Dalmatia: Also once the name of a Roman province, the warm, clean waters along the Adriatic Sea in Croatia provide tremendous natural beauty and tourism opportunities.

Danube River: Known by many different names along the way, the beautiful blue Danube runs through or along 10 different countries on its waltz to the Black Sea.

Balkan Mountains: Bisecting much of Bulgaria, this range has repeatedly served as a fortress and battlefield for Bulgarian forces—against the Byzantine Empire and the Ottomans, among others.

Albers Conic Equal-Area Projection
SCALE 1:4,118,000   1 CENTIMETER = 41 KILOMETERS; 1 INCH = 65 MILES
KILOMETERS
STATUTE MILES

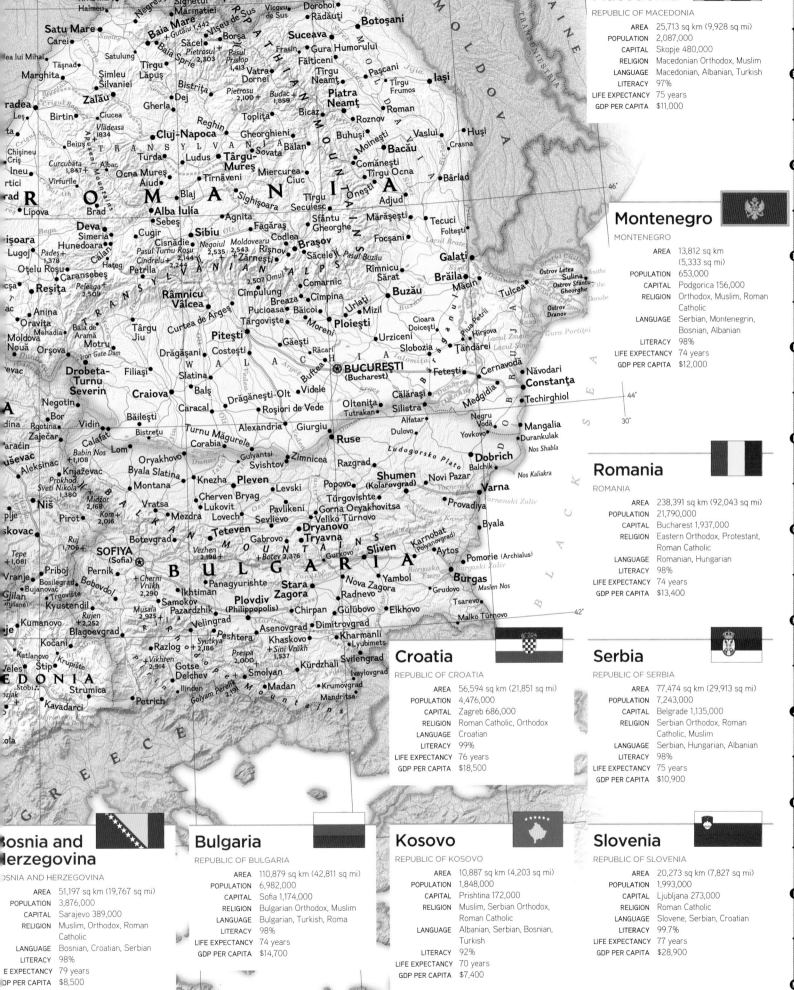

Macedonia

REPUBLIC OF MACEDONIA

AREA	25,713 sq km (9,928 sq mi)
POPULATION	2,087,000
CAPITAL	Skopje 480,000
RELIGION	Macedonian Orthodox, Muslim
LANGUAGE	Macedonian, Albanian, Turkish
LITERACY	97%
LIFE EXPECTANCY	75 years
GDP PER CAPITA	$11,000

Montenegro

MONTENEGRO

AREA	13,812 sq km (5,333 sq mi)
POPULATION	653,000
CAPITAL	Podgorica 156,000
RELIGION	Orthodox, Muslim, Roman Catholic
LANGUAGE	Serbian, Montenegrin, Bosnian, Albanian
LITERACY	98%
LIFE EXPECTANCY	74 years
GDP PER CAPITA	$12,000

Romania

ROMANIA

AREA	238,391 sq km (92,043 sq mi)
POPULATION	21,790,000
CAPITAL	Bucharest 1,937,000
RELIGION	Eastern Orthodox, Protestant, Roman Catholic
LANGUAGE	Romanian, Hungarian
LITERACY	98%
LIFE EXPECTANCY	74 years
GDP PER CAPITA	$13,400

Croatia

REPUBLIC OF CROATIA

AREA	56,594 sq km (21,851 sq mi)
POPULATION	4,476,000
CAPITAL	Zagreb 686,000
RELIGION	Roman Catholic, Orthodox
LANGUAGE	Croatian
LITERACY	99%
LIFE EXPECTANCY	76 years
GDP PER CAPITA	$18,500

Serbia

REPUBLIC OF SERBIA

AREA	77,474 sq km (29,913 sq mi)
POPULATION	7,243,000
CAPITAL	Belgrade 1,135,000
RELIGION	Serbian Orthodox, Roman Catholic, Muslim
LANGUAGE	Serbian, Hungarian, Albanian
LITERACY	98%
LIFE EXPECTANCY	75 years
GDP PER CAPITA	$10,900

Bosnia and Herzegovina

BOSNIA AND HERZEGOVINA

AREA	51,197 sq km (19,767 sq mi)
POPULATION	3,876,000
CAPITAL	Sarajevo 389,000
RELIGION	Muslim, Orthodox, Roman Catholic
LANGUAGE	Bosnian, Croatian, Serbian
LITERACY	98%
LIFE EXPECTANCY	79 years
GDP PER CAPITA	$8,500

Bulgaria

REPUBLIC OF BULGARIA

AREA	110,879 sq km (42,811 sq mi)
POPULATION	6,982,000
CAPITAL	Sofia 1,174,000
RELIGION	Bulgarian Orthodox, Muslim
LANGUAGE	Bulgarian, Turkish, Roma
LITERACY	98%
LIFE EXPECTANCY	74 years
GDP PER CAPITA	$14,700

Kosovo

REPUBLIC OF KOSOVO

AREA	10,887 sq km (4,203 sq mi)
POPULATION	1,848,000
CAPITAL	Prishtina 172,000
RELIGION	Muslim, Serbian Orthodox, Roman Catholic
LANGUAGE	Albanian, Serbian, Bosnian, Turkish
LITERACY	92%
LIFE EXPECTANCY	70 years
GDP PER CAPITA	$7,400

Slovenia

REPUBLIC OF SLOVENIA

AREA	20,273 sq km (7,827 sq mi)
POPULATION	1,993,000
CAPITAL	Ljubljana 273,000
RELIGION	Roman Catholic
LANGUAGE	Slovene, Serbian, Croatian
LITERACY	99.7%
LIFE EXPECTANCY	77 years
GDP PER CAPITA	$28,900

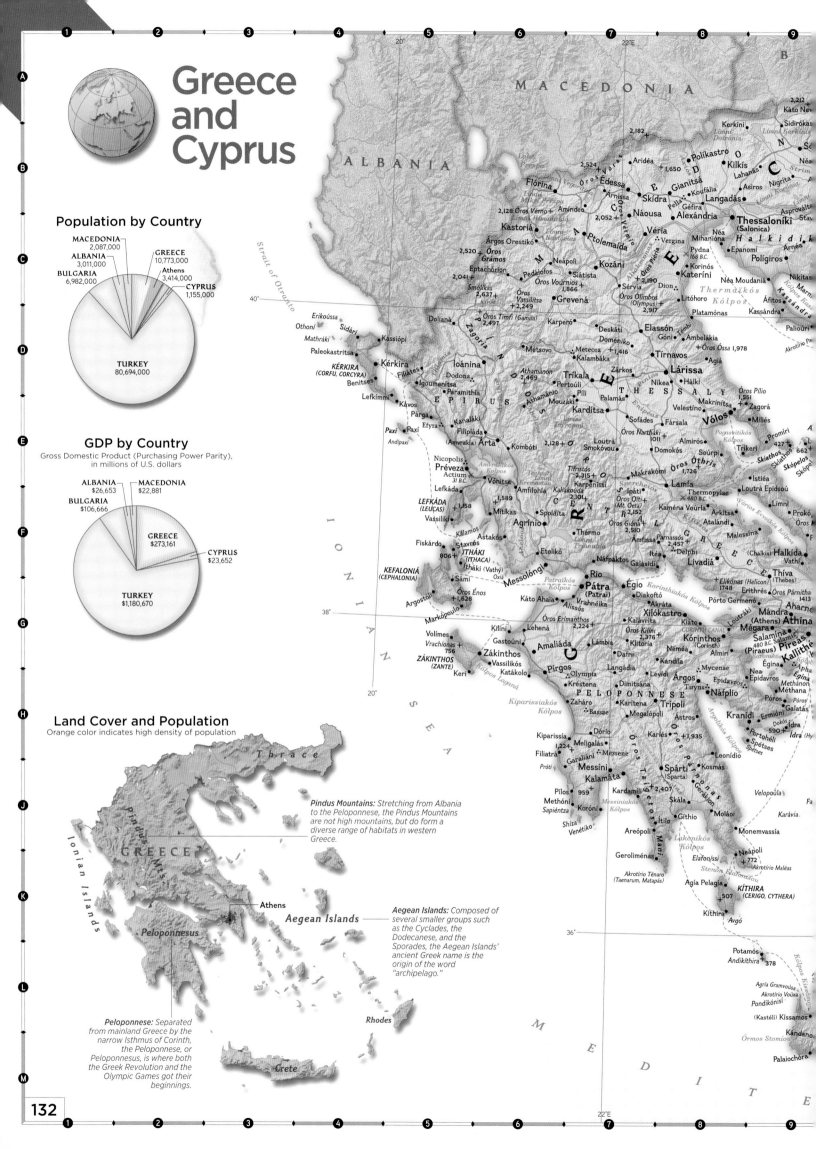

Greece and Cyprus

Population by Country

- MACEDONIA 2,087,000
- ALBANIA 3,011,000
- BULGARIA 6,982,000
- GREECE 10,773,000
- Athens 3,414,000
- CYPRUS 1,155,000
- TURKEY 80,694,000

GDP by Country

Gross Domestic Product (Purchasing Power Parity), in millions of U.S. dollars

- ALBANIA $26,653
- MACEDONIA $22,881
- BULGARIA $106,666
- GREECE $273,161
- CYPRUS $23,652
- TURKEY $1,180,670

Land Cover and Population

Orange color indicates high density of population

Pindus Mountains: Stretching from Albania to the Peloponnese, the Pindus Mountains are not high mountains, but do form a diverse range of habitats in western Greece.

Aegean Islands: Composed of several smaller groups such as the Cyclades, the Dodecanese, and the Sporades, the Aegean Islands' ancient Greek name is the origin of the word "archipelago."

Peloponnese: Separated from mainland Greece by the narrow Isthmus of Corinth, the Peloponnese, or Peloponnesus, is where both the Greek Revolution and the Olympic Games got their beginnings.

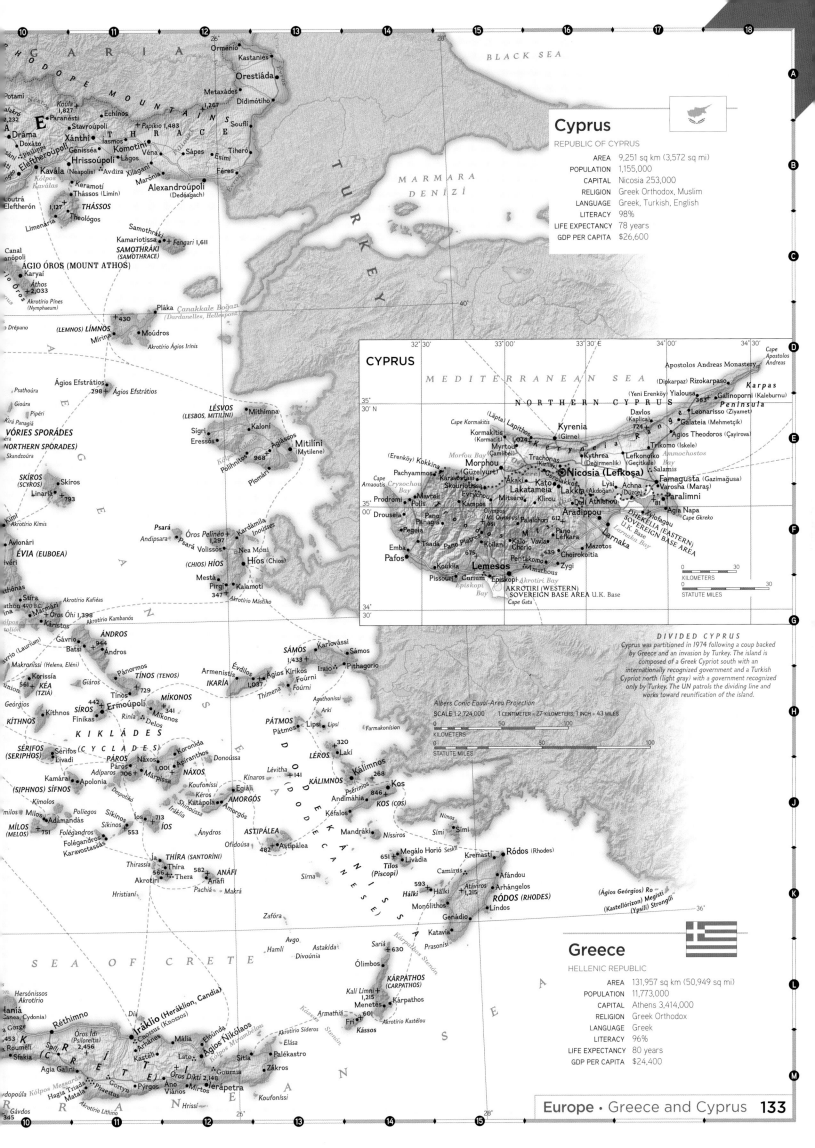

Cyprus
REPUBLIC OF CYPRUS

AREA	9,251 sq km (3,572 sq mi)
POPULATION	1,155,000
CAPITAL	Nicosia 253,000
RELIGION	Greek Orthodox, Muslim
LANGUAGE	Greek, Turkish, English
LITERACY	98%
LIFE EXPECTANCY	78 years
GDP PER CAPITA	$26,600

DIVIDED CYPRUS
Cyprus was partitioned in 1974 following a coup backed by Greece and an invasion by Turkey. The island is composed of a Greek Cypriot south with an internationally recognized government and a Turkish Cypriot north (light gray) with a government recognized only by Turkey. The UN patrols the dividing line and works toward reunification of the island.

Albers Conic Equal-Area Projection
SCALE 1:2,724,000   1 CENTIMETER = 27 KILOMETERS; 1 INCH = 43 MILES

Greece
HELLENIC REPUBLIC

AREA	131,957 sq km (50,949 sq mi)
POPULATION	11,773,000
CAPITAL	Athens 3,414,000
RELIGION	Greek Orthodox
LANGUAGE	Greek
LITERACY	96%
LIFE EXPECTANCY	80 years
GDP PER CAPITA	$24,400

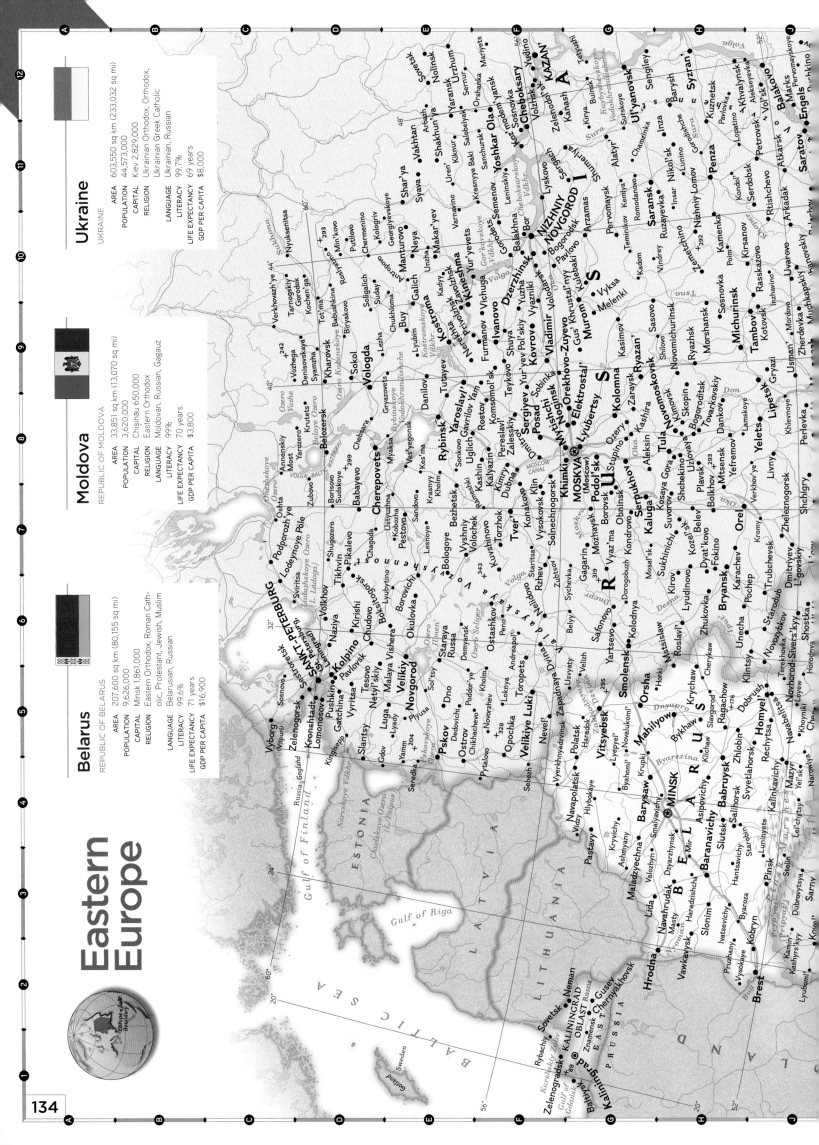

Eastern Europe

Ukraine
UKRAINE

AREA	603,550 sq km (233,032 sq mi)
POPULATION	44,573,000
CAPITAL	Kiev 2,829,000
RELIGION	Ukrainian Orthodox, Orthodox, Ukrainian Greek Catholic
LANGUAGE	Ukrainian, Russian
LITERACY	99.7%
LIFE EXPECTANCY	69 years
GDP PER CAPITA	$8,000

Moldova
REPUBLIC OF MOLDOVA

AREA	33,851 sq km (13,070 sq mi)
POPULATION	3,620,000
CAPITAL	Chişinău 650,000
RELIGION	Eastern Orthodox
LANGUAGE	Moldovan, Russian, Gagauz
LITERACY	99%
LIFE EXPECTANCY	70 years
GDP PER CAPITA	$3,800

Belarus
REPUBLIC OF BELARUS

AREA	207,600 sq km (80,155 sq mi)
POPULATION	9,626,000
CAPITAL	Minsk 1,861,000
RELIGION	Eastern Orthodox, Roman Catholic, Protestant, Jewish, Muslim
LANGUAGE	Belarusian, Russian
LITERACY	99.6%
LIFE EXPECTANCY	71 years
GDP PER CAPITA	$16,900

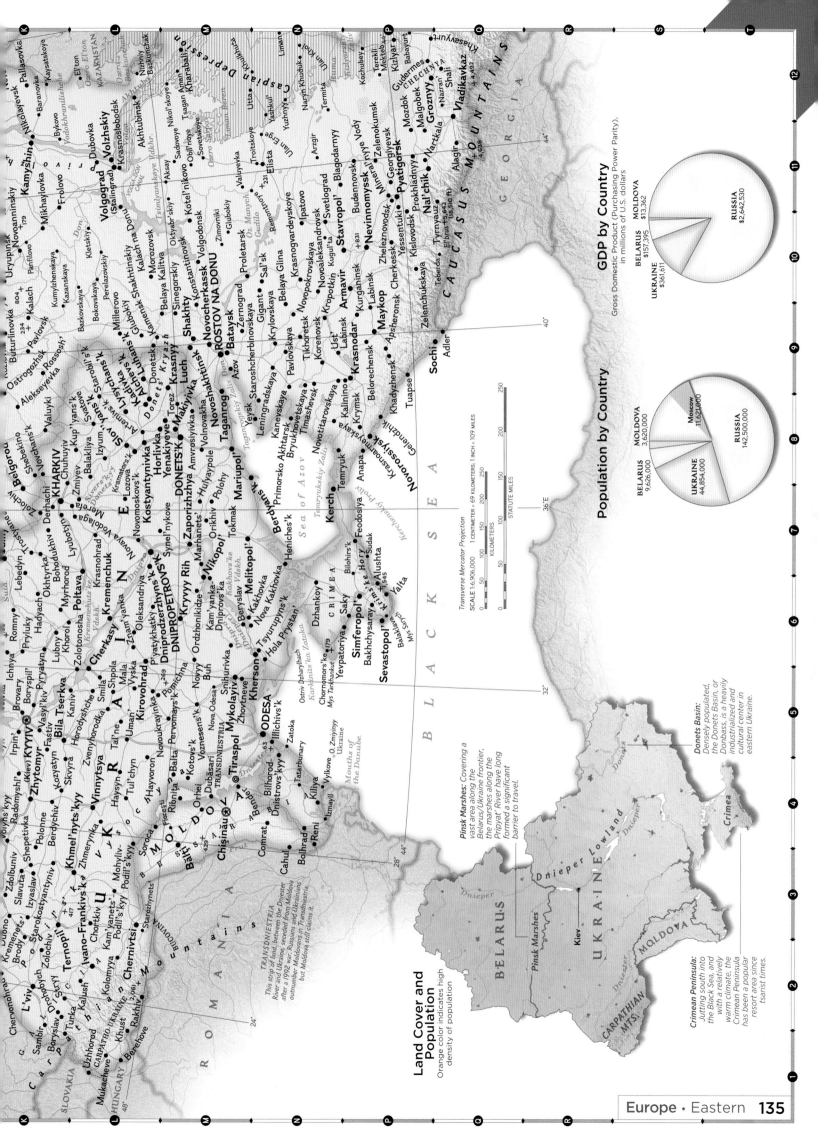

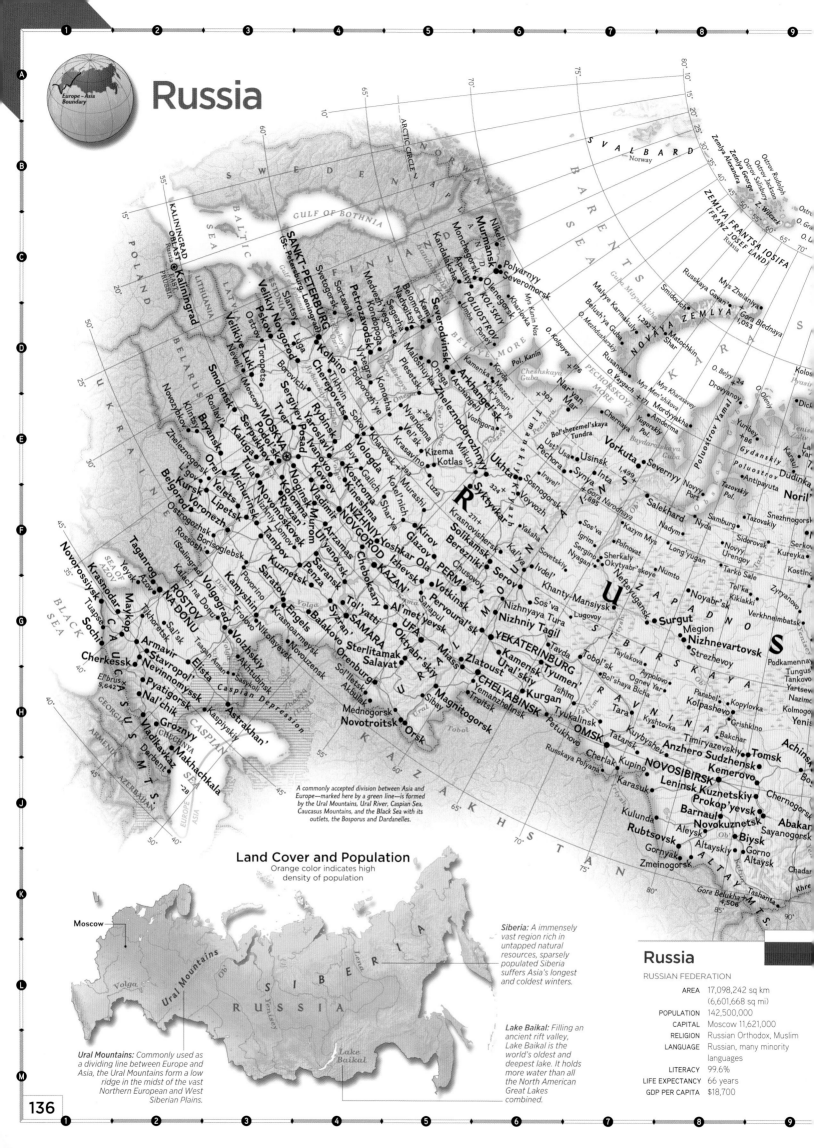

Russia

Europe–Asia Boundary

A commonly accepted division between Asia and Europe—marked here by a green line—is formed by the Ural Mountains, Ural River, Caspian Sea, Caucasus Mountains, and the Black Sea with its outlets, the Bosporus and Dardanelles.

Land Cover and Population

Orange color indicates high density of population

Moscow

Siberia: A immensely vast region rich in untapped natural resources, sparsely populated Siberia suffers Asia's longest and coldest winters.

Lake Baikal: Filling an ancient rift valley, Lake Baikal is the world's oldest and deepest lake. It holds more water than all the North American Great Lakes combined.

Ural Mountains: Commonly used as a dividing line between Europe and Asia, the Ural Mountains form a low ridge in the midst of the vast Northern European and West Siberian Plains.

Russia

RUSSIAN FEDERATION

AREA	17,098,242 sq km (6,601,668 sq mi)
POPULATION	142,500,000
CAPITAL	Moscow 11,621,000
RELIGION	Russian Orthodox, Muslim
LANGUAGE	Russian, many minority languages
LITERACY	99.6%
LIFE EXPECTANCY	66 years
GDP PER CAPITA	$18,700

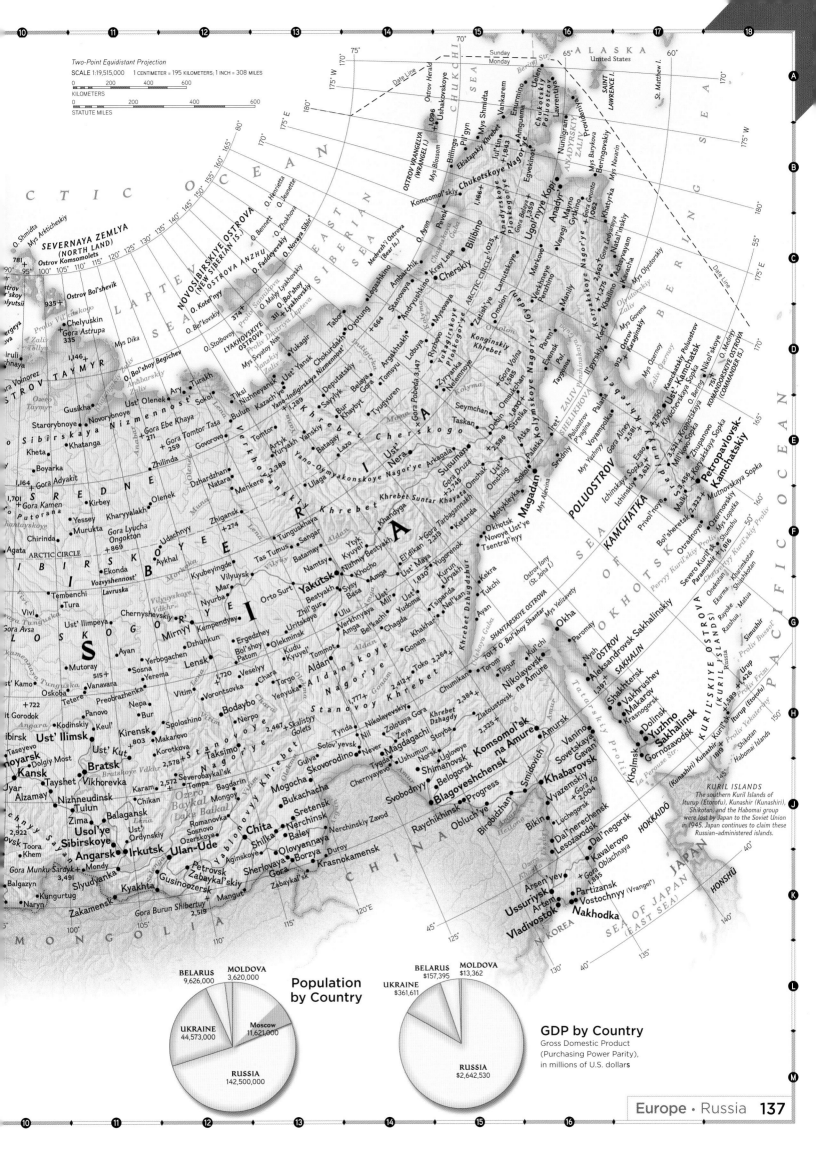

Asia

To call Asia the largest continent is almost an understatement. At more than 44.5 million square kilometers (17 million square miles), Asia makes up nearly one-third of Earth's total landmass. From the West Siberian Plain to the Malay Archipelago, and from the Arctic Ocean to the Indian Ocean, three out of every five humans call Asia home. The continent's current population more than doubles the global total just a century ago. At its eastern, western, and southern edges, Asia gave birth to some of Earth's earliest civilizations. Today, the continent is home to some of humanity's most enduring and unique cultures.

The subcontinent of India, a mere appendage in geological terms, adds some 4.4 million square kilometers (1.7 million square miles)—and well more than a billion people—to what would still be the largest continent without it. The tectonic shifting that thrust India into Asia some 50 million years ago also threw up Earth's highest mountains, including Everest at 8,850 meters (29,035 feet) and K2 at 8,611 meters (28,251 feet). In turn the Himalaya and the broad Tibetan Plateau continue to influence vast swaths of Asia to this day. The landmass helps drive the monsoon rains that sweep back and forth from Africa to Oceania each year, and the many great rivers washing down from its heights carry water to nearly half of the world's people.

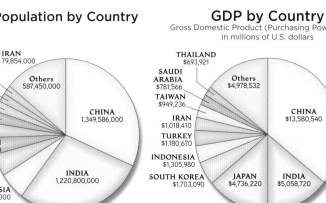

Population by Country

- IRAN 79,854,000
- TURKEY 80,694,000
- VIETNAM 92,478,000
- PHILIPPINES 105,721,000
- JAPAN 127,253,000
- BANGLADESH 163,655,000
- PAKISTAN 193,239,000
- INDONESIA 251,160,000
- Others 587,450,000
- CHINA 1,349,586,000
- INDIA 1,220,800,000

GDP by Country
Gross Domestic Product (Purchasing Power Parity), in millions of U.S. dollars

- THAILAND $693,921
- SAUDI ARABIA $781,566
- TAIWAN $949,236
- IRAN $1,018,410
- TURKEY $1,180,670
- INDONESIA $1,305,980
- SOUTH KOREA $1,703,090
- Others $4,978,532
- CHINA $13,580,540
- JAPAN $4,736,220
- INDIA $5,058,720

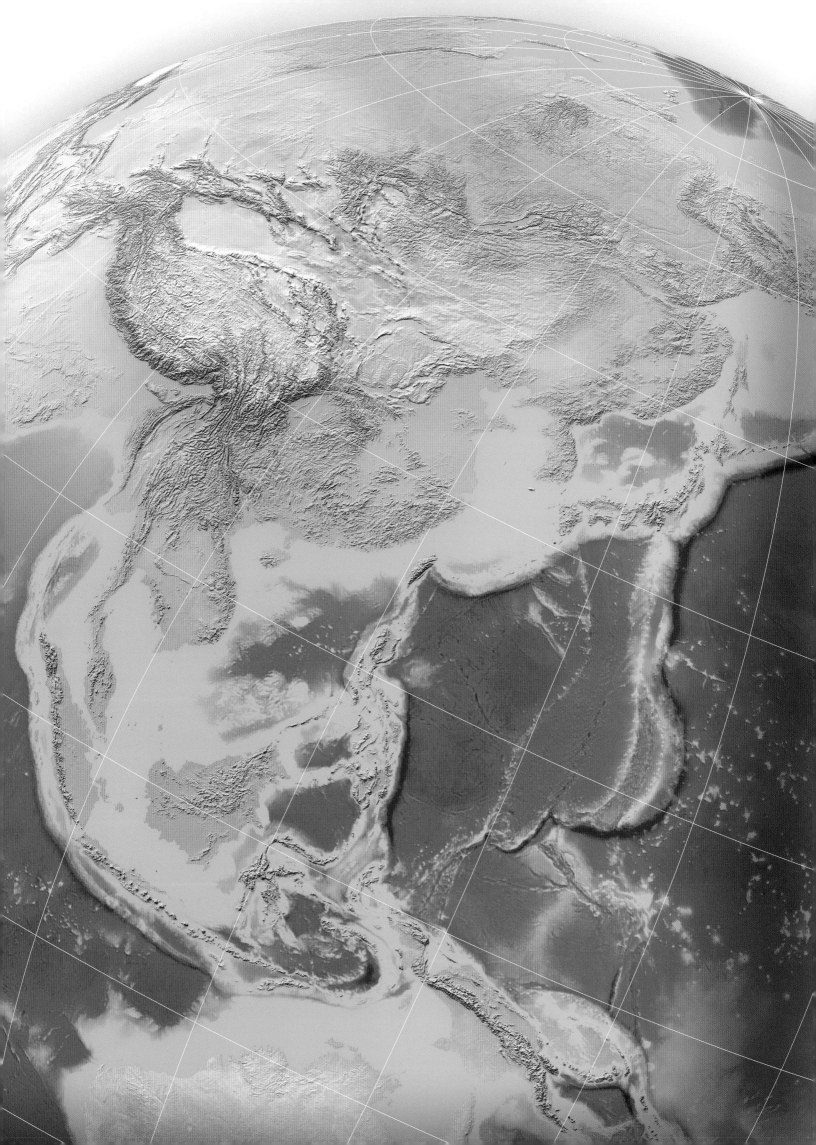

ATLANTIC OCEAN

ICELAND

GREENLAND SEA

GREENLAND

Jan Mayen

NORWEGIAN SEA

ARC

Spitsbergen +1,717
North East Land

SVALBARD

George Land

FRANZ JOSEF LAND

BARENTS SEA

NOVAYA ZEMLYA

KARA SEA

Canary Islands

WESTERN SAHARA

MAURITANIA

MALI

MOROCCO

ATLAS MOUNTAINS

Cape St. Vincent
Strait of Gibraltar
Cape Finisterre

PORTUGAL

IBERIAN PENINSULA

SPAIN

ANDORRA

Balearic Is.

Cape Nao

Sardinia

Corsica

MONACO

Cape Breton
Bay of Biscay

Ireland
IRE.

CELTIC SEA

BRITISH ISLES

U.K.

Great Britain

Hebrides

Orkney Is.
Shetland Islands

Faroe Islands

NORTH SEA

NETH.
BELG.

FRANCE

LUX.

GERMANY

NORTHERN EUROPEAN PLAIN

POLAND

Faroe Islands

NORWAY

SCANDINAVIA

SWEDEN

FINLAND

Gulf of Bothnia

BALTIC SEA

EST.
LATV.
LITH.

RUSSIA

BELARUS

Spitsbergen

North Cape

Kola Peninsula

White Sea

Timan Ridge

Pechora Basin

Northern Urals

URAL MOUNTAINS

WEST SIBERIAN PLAIN

R U S S I

ALGERIA

Great Western Erg

Great Eastern Erg

TUNISIA

TRIPOLITANIA

SAHARA

NIGER

CHAD

SUDAN

CENTRAL AFRICAN REPUBLIC

SOUTH SUDAN

DEMOCRATIC REPUBLIC OF THE CONGO

UGANDA

RWANDA

BURUNDI

TANZANIA

ZAMBIA

MALAWI

ZIMBABWE

MOZAMBIQUE

MEDITERRANEAN SEA

LIBYA

EGYPT

FEZZAN

CYRENAICA

TROPIC OF CANCER

ITALY

SICILY

MALTA

ALBANIA

GREECE

BULGARIA

ROMANIA

MACED.

SERBIA

MONT.

BOSN.

HERZ.

CROATIA

SLOVENIA

HUNGARY

SLOVAKIA

CZECH REP.

AUSTRIA

SWITZ.

UKRAINE

MOLD.

Crimea

BLACK SEA

Bosporus

TURKEY

ANATOLIA (ASIA MINOR)

CYPRUS

LEB.

ISRAEL

JORDAN

SYRIA

IRAQ

SAUDI ARABIA

KUWAIT

BAHRAIN

QATAR

U.A.E.

OMAN

YEMEN

ERITREA

DJIBOUTI

ETHIOPIA

ETHIOPIAN HIGHLANDS

SOMALIA

KENYA

GULF OF ADEN

Socotra

ARABIAN SEA

GEORGIA

ARMENIA

AZERBAIJAN

Caucasus Mountains

CASPIAN SEA

IRAN

AFGHANISTAN

PAKISTAN

TURKM.

UZBEKISTAN

KAZAKHSTAN

THE STEPPES

KYRGYZSTAN

TAJIKISTAN

TAKLIMAKAN DESERT

KUNLUN MOU

KASHMIR

NEPAL

INDIA

HIMALAYA

DECCAN PLATEAU

Western Ghats

Eastern Ghats

Coromandel Coast

SRI LANKA

MALDIVES

Maldive Islands

Lakshadweep

LACCADIVE SEA

BAY OF

INDIAN OCEAN

SEYCHELLES

Seychelles

EQUATOR

MADAGASCAR

Longitude East 60° of Greenwich

Two-Point Equidistant Projection

SCALE 1:36,000,000   1 CENTIMETER = 360 KILOMETERS; 1 INCH = 568 MILES

0   400   800   1200
KILOMETERS

0   400   800   1200
STATUTE MILES

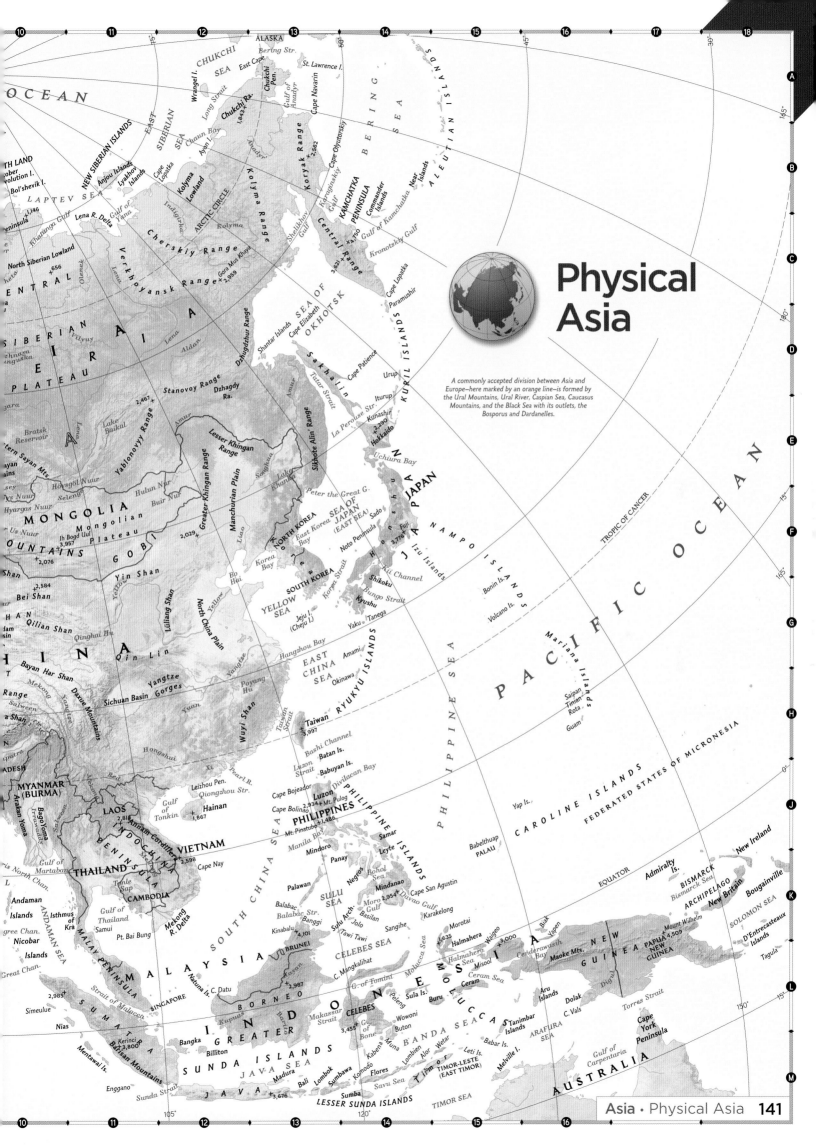

Physical Asia

A commonly accepted division between Asia and Europe—here marked by an orange line—is formed by the Ural Mountains, Ural River, Caspian Sea, Caucasus Mountains, and the Black Sea with its outlets, the Bosporus and Dardanelles.

Map labels

ARCTIC OCEAN
CHUKCHI SEA
ALASKA
Bering Str.
East Cape
St. Lawrence I.
Chukchi Pen.
Gulf of Anadyr
Cape Navarin
BERING SEA
Wrangel I.
Long Strait
1,843 +
Chukchi Ra.
Cape Oyatorsky
Karaginskiy Gulf
Koryak Range × 2,562
KAMCHATKA PENINSULA
ALEUTIAN ISLANDS
Near Islands
Commander Islands
Gulf of Kamchatka
NEW SIBERIAN ISLANDS
Anjou Islands
Lyakhov Islands
Cape Lopatka
Kolyma Lowland
Kolyma Range
Central Range × 4,750
Karaginskiy Gulf
Gulf of Kamchatka
NORTH LAND
October Revolution I.
Bol'shevik I.
LAPTEV SEA
EAST SIBERIAN SEA
Chaun Bay
Ayon I.
Anadyr
Anadyr'
Cape Lopatka
Paramushir
+1,146
Lena R. Delta
Gulf of Yana
Indigirka
ARCTIC CIRCLE
Kolyma
Shelikhov Gulf
Kronotskiy Gulf
Peninsula
Khatanga Gulf
North Siberian Lowland
Olenek
Cherskiy Range
Gora Mus Khaya + 2,959
SEA OF OKHOTSK
Cape Elizabeth
Shantar Islands
Cape Patience
Cape Lopatka
CENTRAL
+656
Lena
Verkhoyansk Range
3,621 + × 2,959
Dzhugdzhur Range
Urup
KURIL ISLANDS
SIBERIAN PLATEAU
Vilyuy
Aldan
Sakhalin
Iturup
Cape Patience
zhnaya unguska
Lena
Stanovoy Range
Dzhagdy Ra.
Tatar Strait
Kunashir
La Perouse Str.
Amur
2,467 +
Amur
Lesser Khingan Range
Sakhalin
Hokkaido + 2,290
Lake Baikal
Yablonovyy Range
Greater Khingan Range
Sikhote Alin' Range
Uchiura Bay
Bratsk Reservoir
Hulun Nur
Manchurian Plain
Lake Khanka
JAPAN
stern Sayan Mts
Hövsgöl Nuur
Mongolian Plateau
2,029 +
Liao
Peter the Great G.
Honshu
Nampo Islands
rey Nys Nuur
Selenge
Buir Nur
Amur
East Korea Bay
SEA OF JAPAN (EAST SEA)
Fuji 3,776 +
Sado
Izu Islands
Hyargas Nuur
MONGOLIA
Yin Shan
Yellow
Bo Hai
NORTH KOREA
Noto Peninsula
Kii Channel
Bonin Is.
Us Nuur
Ih Bogd Uul 3,957
GOBI
Korea Bay
Korea
Shikoku
Bungo Strait
Volcano Is.
OUNTAINS + 2,076
Liuliang Shan
Korea Strait
Kyushu
Shan
+2,584
Bei Shan
Yellow
SOUTH KOREA
Jeju (Cheju I.)
Yaku Tanega
Volcano Is.
HAN
Qilian Shan
Qin Lin
North China Plain
YELLOW SEA
Amami
RYUKYU ISLANDS
Mariana Islands
lam
Bayan Har Shan
Yangtze
Hangzhou Bay
EAST CHINA SEA
Saipan Tinian Rota
Range
Mekong
Daxue Mountains
Sichuan Basin
Gorges
Yangtze
Poyang Hu.
Okinawa
Guam
a Shan
Salween
Yangtze
Wuyi Shan
Taiwan + 3,997
Taiwan Strait
PACIFIC OCEAN
Hongshui
Bashi Channel
Batan Is.
aputra
Xi
Pearl R.
Luzon Strait
Babuyan Is.
PHILIPPINE SEA
ADESH
MYANMAR (BURMA)
Red
Leizhou Pen.
Qiongzhou Str.
Cape Bojeador
Divilacan Bay
Yap Is.
CAROLINE ISLANDS
Arakan Yoma
Gulf of Tonkin
Hainan
Cape Bolinao
Luzon 2,934 + Mt. Pulog
PHILIPPINE ISLANDS
FEDERATED STATES OF MICRONESIA
Bago Yoma Irrawaddy
LAOS
2,819
+ 1,867
Mt. Pinatubo + 1,486
PHILIPPINES
Babelthuap PALAU
Arakan Yoma
Annam Cordillera
VIETNAM + 2,598
Manila Bay
Samar
New Ireland
's North Chan.
THAILAND
INDOCHINA PENINSULA
Cape Nay
Mindoro
LEYTE ISLANDS
Admiralty Is.
BISMARCK ARCHIPELAGO
New Britain
L
Gulf of Martaban
Tonle Sap
CAMBODIA
Panay
Negros
Bohol Sea
Mindanao
EQUATOR
Bismarck Sea
Bougainville
Andaman Islands
Isthmus of Kra
Samui
Mekong R. Delta
Palawan
SULU SEA
Moro Gulf 2,954 +
Davao Gulf
Cape San Agustin
SOLOMON SEA
gree Chan.
Nicobar Islands
Gulf of Thailand
Pt. Bai Bung
Balabac
Balabac Str.
Banggi
Basilan
Jolo
Sangihe
Karakelong
D'Entrecasteaux Islands
Great Chan.
MALAY PENINSULA
Kinabalu + 4,101
Tawi Tawi
Morotai
Tagula
Andaman Sea
2,985 +
Strait of Malacca
SINGAPORE
Natuna Is. C. Datu
BRUNEI
CELEBES SEA
C. Mangkalihat
+ 1,635
Halmahera
Waigeo
+ 3,000
Maoke Mts.
Mount Wilhelm 4,509
NEW GUINEA
Simeulue
MALAYSIA
BORNEO
Kayan + 2,987
MOLUCCA
Halmahera Sea
Misool
Cenderawasih Bay
PAPUA NEW GUINEA
Nias
Kerinci + 3,800
Barisan Mountains
Kapuas
Barito
Makassar Strait
CELEBES
3,455 +
G. of Tomini
Peleng
Sula Is.
Buru
Ceram
Ceram Sea
Dolak
C. Vals
Digul
SUMATRA
INDONESIA
GREATER SUNDA ISLANDS
G. of Bone
Wowoni
Buton
BANDA SEA
Tanimbar Islands
Aru Islands
Cape York Peninsula
Mentawai Is.
Bangka
Billiton
Muna
Kabena
ARAFURA SEA
Gulf of Carpentaria
Enggano
Sunda Strait
JAVA + 3,676
JAVA SEA
Madura
Bali
Lombok
Sumbawa
Flores
Savu Sea
Komodo
Alor
Wetar
Babar Is.
Leti Is.
Melville I.
TIMOR SEA
AUSTRALIA
Sumba
LESSER SUNDA ISLANDS
Timor
TIMOR-LESTE (EAST TIMOR)
Torres Strait

TROPIC OF CANCER
EQUATOR

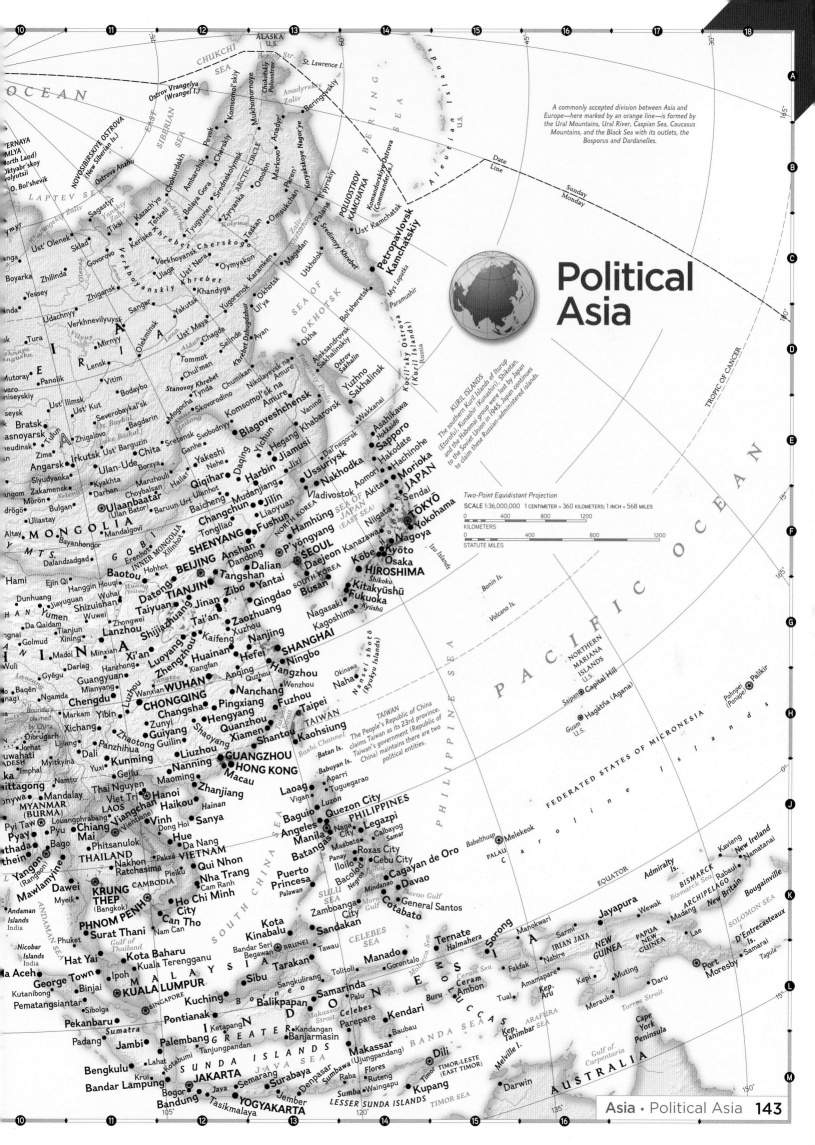

Political Asia

A commonly accepted division between Asia and Europe—here marked by an orange line—is formed by the Ural Mountains, Ural River, Caspian Sea, Caucasus Mountains, and the Black Sea with its outlets, the Bosporus and Dardanelles.

KURIL ISLANDS
The southern Kuril Islands of Iturup (Etorofu) Kunashir (Kunashiri), Shikotan, and the Habomai group were lost by Japan to the Soviet Union in 1945. Japan continues to claim these Russian-administered islands.

TAIWAN
The People's Republic of China claims Taiwan as its 23rd province. Taiwan's government (Republic of China) maintains there are two political entities.

Two-Point Equidistant Projection
SCALE 1:36,000,000   1 CENTIMETER = 360 KILOMETERS; 1 INCH = 568 MILES

0   400   800   1200
KILOMETERS

0   400   800   1200
STATUTE MILES

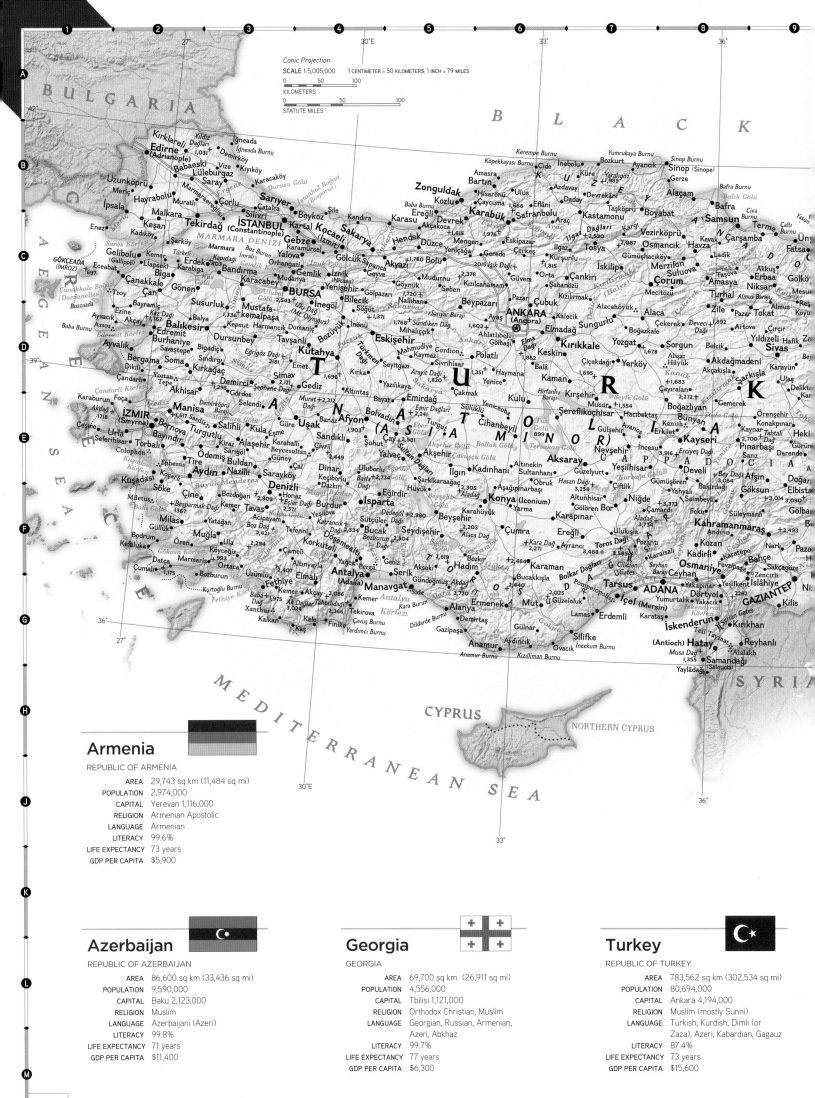

Armenia

REPUBLIC OF ARMENIA

AREA	29,743 sq km (11,484 sq mi)
POPULATION	2,974,000
CAPITAL	Yerevan 1,116,000
RELIGION	Armenian Apostolic
LANGUAGE	Armenian
LITERACY	99.6%
LIFE EXPECTANCY	73 years
GDP PER CAPITA	$5,900

Azerbaijan

REPUBLIC OF AZERBAIJAN

AREA	86,600 sq km (33,436 sq mi)
POPULATION	9,590,000
CAPITAL	Baku 2,123,000
RELIGION	Muslim
LANGUAGE	Azerbaijani (Azeri)
LITERACY	99.8%
LIFE EXPECTANCY	71 years
GDP PER CAPITA	$11,400

Georgia

GEORGIA

AREA	69,700 sq km (26,911 sq mi)
POPULATION	4,556,000
CAPITAL	Tbilisi 1,121,000
RELIGION	Orthodox Christian, Muslim
LANGUAGE	Georgian, Russian, Armenian, Azeri, Abkhaz
LITERACY	99.7%
LIFE EXPECTANCY	77 years
GDP PER CAPITA	$6,300

Turkey

REPUBLIC OF TURKEY

AREA	783,562 sq km (302,534 sq mi)
POPULATION	80,694,000
CAPITAL	Ankara 4,194,000
RELIGION	Muslim (mostly Sunni)
LANGUAGE	Turkish, Kurdish, Dimli (or Zaza), Azeri, Kabardian, Gagauz
LITERACY	87.4%
LIFE EXPECTANCY	73 years
GDP PER CAPITA	$15,600

Caucasus Mountains: Traditionally viewed as a boundary between Europe and Asia, the snow-capped range tops out at 5,642 meters (18,510 feet) at El'brus. The mountains were formed by the collision of the African and Eurasian plates.

KURDISTAN
Kurds, the largest ethnic minority in Turkey at some 12 million, live in the southeastern highlands—Turkey's poorest region. Clashes between militants of the Kurdistan Workers' Party (PKK) and Turkish armed forces have left villages in ruins and thousands dead.

NAGORNO-KARABAKH
This southwestern Azerbaijan region, largely populated by ethnic Armenians, declared independence in 1991. A Russian-brokered cease-fire in 1994 left Karabakh Armenians controlling—but Azerbaijan still claiming—Nagorno-Karabakh.

Asia Minor and Transcaucasia

Istanbul: The strategic location and historic importance of this city is without parallel. Situated on the narrow Bosporus strait, it has been the capital of four famous empires and a constant center of trade. It is the only city in the world to straddle two continents, and its metropolitan area has grown to over 10 million people.

Baku: One of the world's largest cities situated below sea level, the capital of Azerbaijan has been an oil industry leader since the early 1900s. A recent petroleum resurgence has made Baku a wealthy city; it maintains a busy port on the Caspian Sea.

Population by Country

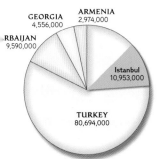

GEORGIA 4,556,000
ARMENIA 2,974,000
RBAIJAN 9,590,000
Istanbul 10,953,000
TURKEY 80,694,000

GDP by Country

oss Domestic Product (Purchasing Power Parity), in millions of U.S. dollars

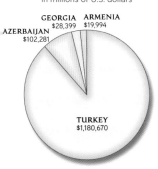

GEORGIA $28,399
ARMENIA $19,994
AZERBAIJAN $102,281
TURKEY $1,180,670

Land Cover and Population
Orange color indicates high density of population

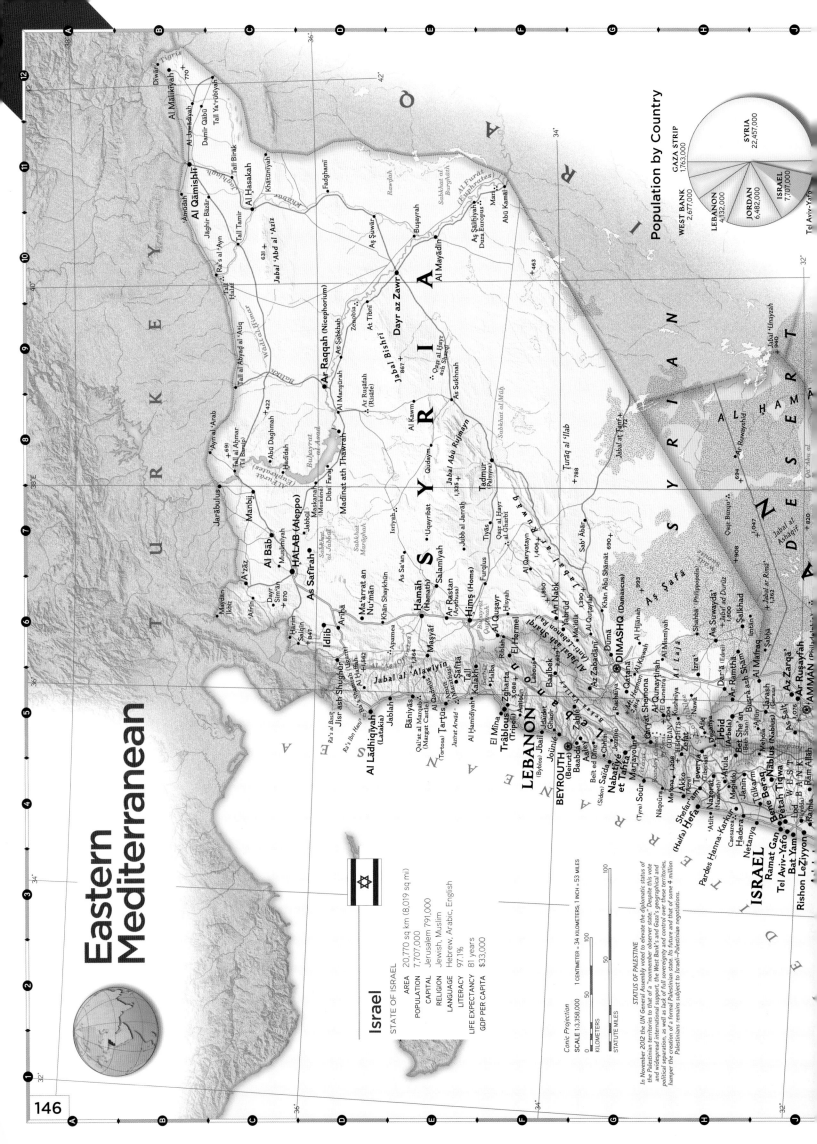

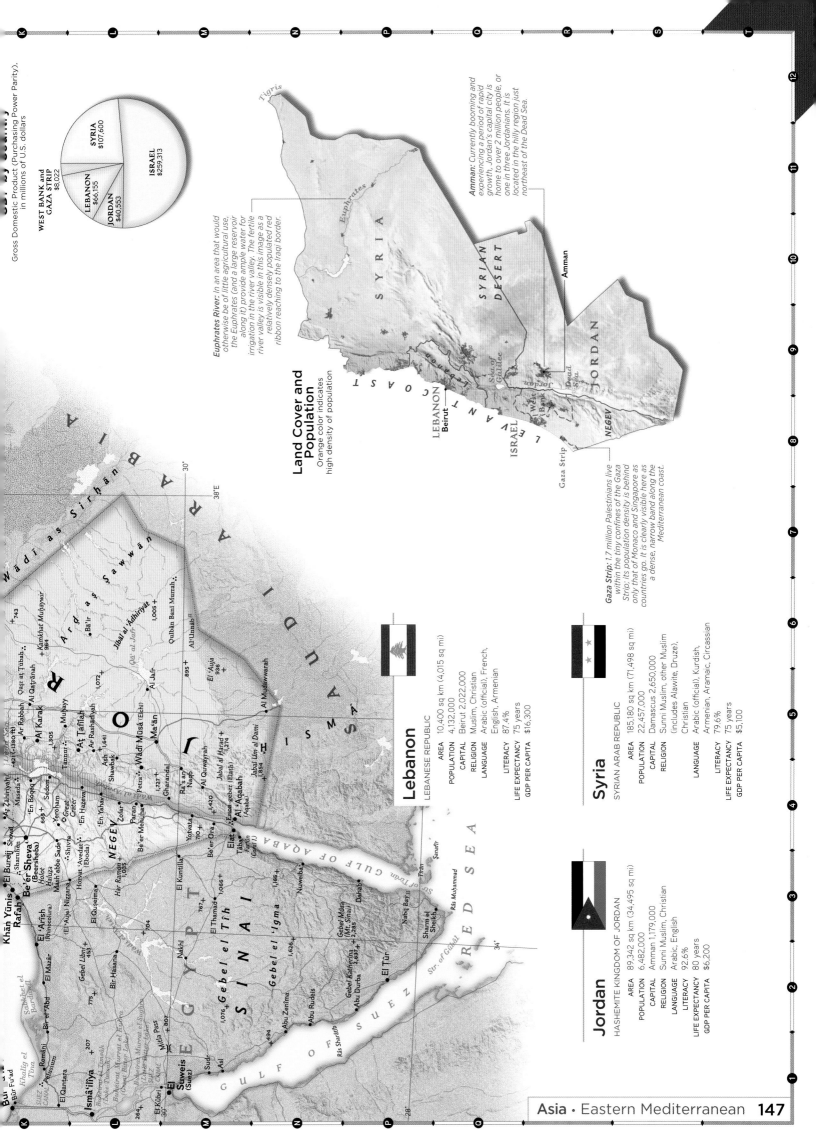

Gross Domestic Product (Purchasing Power Parity), in millions of U.S. dollars

SYRIA $107,600

WEST BANK and GAZA STRIP $8,022

LEBANON $66,155

JORDAN $40,553

ISRAEL $259,313

Euphrates River: In an area that would otherwise be of little agricultural use, the Euphrates (and a large reservoir along it) provide ample water for irrigation in the river valley. The fertile river valley is visible in this image as a relatively densely populated red ribbon reaching to the Iraqi border.

Amman: Currently booming and experiencing a period of rapid growth, Jordan's capital city is home to over 2 million people, or one in three Jordanians. It is located in the hilly region just northeast of the Dead Sea.

Land Cover and Population

Orange color indicates high density of population

Gaza Strip: 1.7 million Palestinians live within the tiny confines of the Gaza Strip; its population density is behind only that of Monaco and Singapore as countries go. It is clearly visible here as a dense, narrow band along the Mediterranean coast.

Lebanon

LEBANESE REPUBLIC

AREA	10,400 sq km (4,015 sq mi)
POPULATION	4,132,000
CAPITAL	Beirut 2,022,000
RELIGION	Muslim, Christian
LANGUAGE	Arabic (official), French, English, Armenian
LITERACY	87.4%
LIFE EXPECTANCY	75 years
GDP PER CAPITA	$16,300

Syria

SYRIAN ARAB REPUBLIC

AREA	185,180 sq km (71,498 sq mi)
POPULATION	22,457,000
CAPITAL	Damascus 2,650,000
RELIGION	Sunni Muslim, other Muslim (includes Alawite, Druze), Christian
LANGUAGE	Arabic (official), Kurdish, Armenian, Aramaic, Circassian
LITERACY	79.6%
LIFE EXPECTANCY	75 years
GDP PER CAPITA	$5,100

Jordan

HASHEMITE KINGDOM OF JORDAN

AREA	89,342 sq km (34,495 sq mi)
POPULATION	6,482,000
CAPITAL	Amman 1,179,000
RELIGION	Sunni Muslim, Christian
LANGUAGE	Arabic, English
LITERACY	92.6%
LIFE EXPECTANCY	80 years
GDP PER CAPITA	$6,200

Southwest Asia

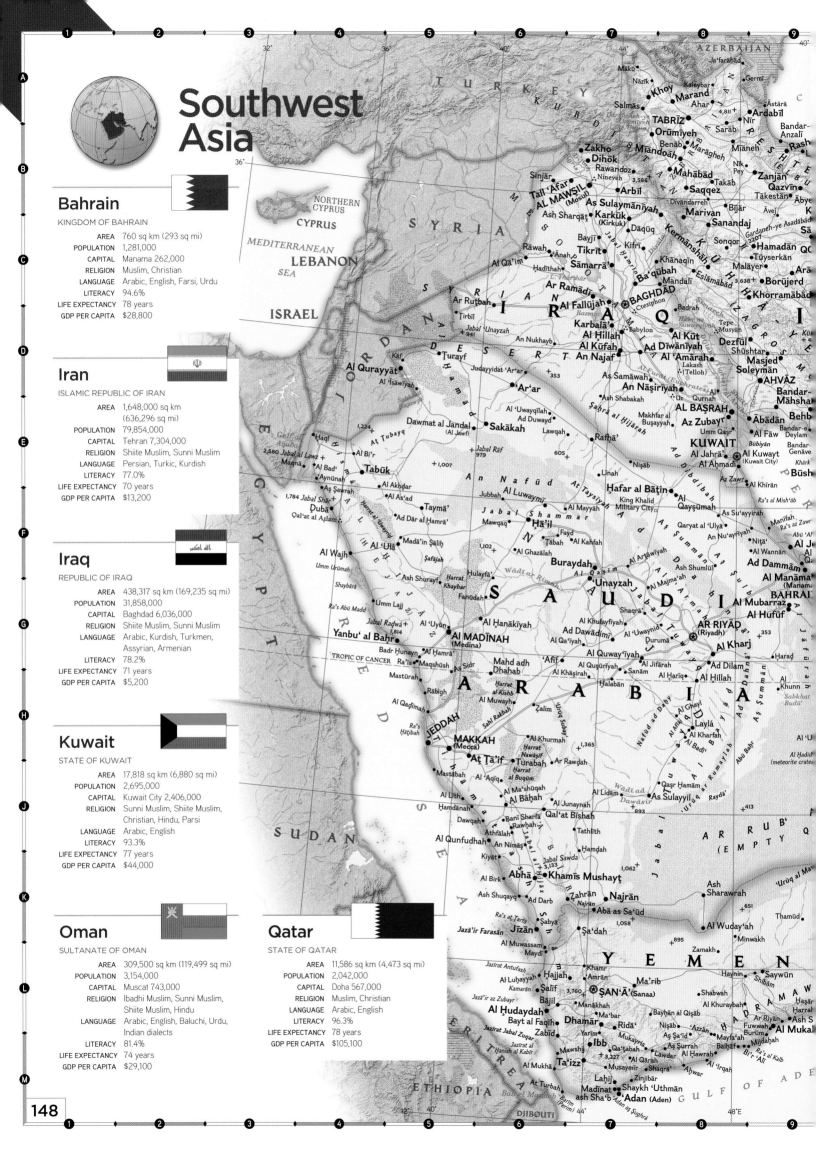

Bahrain

KINGDOM OF BAHRAIN

AREA	760 sq km (293 sq mi)
POPULATION	1,281,000
CAPITAL	Manama 262,000
RELIGION	Muslim, Christian
LANGUAGE	Arabic, English, Farsi, Urdu
LITERACY	94.6%
LIFE EXPECTANCY	78 years
GDP PER CAPITA	$28,800

Iran

ISLAMIC REPUBLIC OF IRAN

AREA	1,648,000 sq km (636,296 sq mi)
POPULATION	79,854,000
CAPITAL	Tehran 7,304,000
RELIGION	Shiite Muslim, Sunni Muslim
LANGUAGE	Persian, Turkic, Kurdish
LITERACY	77.0%
LIFE EXPECTANCY	70 years
GDP PER CAPITA	$13,200

Iraq

REPUBLIC OF IRAQ

AREA	438,317 sq km (169,235 sq mi)
POPULATION	31,858,000
CAPITAL	Baghdad 6,036,000
RELIGION	Shiite Muslim, Sunni Muslim
LANGUAGE	Arabic, Kurdish, Turkmen, Assyrian, Armenian
LITERACY	78.2%
LIFE EXPECTANCY	71 years
GDP PER CAPITA	$5,200

Kuwait

STATE OF KUWAIT

AREA	17,818 sq km (6,880 sq mi)
POPULATION	2,695,000
CAPITAL	Kuwait City 2,406,000
RELIGION	Sunni Muslim, Shiite Muslim, Christian, Hindu, Parsi
LANGUAGE	Arabic, English
LITERACY	93.3%
LIFE EXPECTANCY	77 years
GDP PER CAPITA	$44,000

Oman

SULTANATE OF OMAN

AREA	309,500 sq km (119,499 sq mi)
POPULATION	3,154,000
CAPITAL	Muscat 743,000
RELIGION	Ibadhi Muslim, Sunni Muslim, Shiite Muslim, Hindu
LANGUAGE	Arabic, English, Baluchi, Urdu, Indian dialects
LITERACY	81.4%
LIFE EXPECTANCY	74 years
GDP PER CAPITA	$29,100

Qatar

STATE OF QATAR

AREA	11,586 sq km (4,473 sq mi)
POPULATION	2,042,000
CAPITAL	Doha 567,000
RELIGION	Muslim, Christian
LANGUAGE	Arabic, English
LITERACY	96.3%
LIFE EXPECTANCY	78 years
GDP PER CAPITA	$105,100

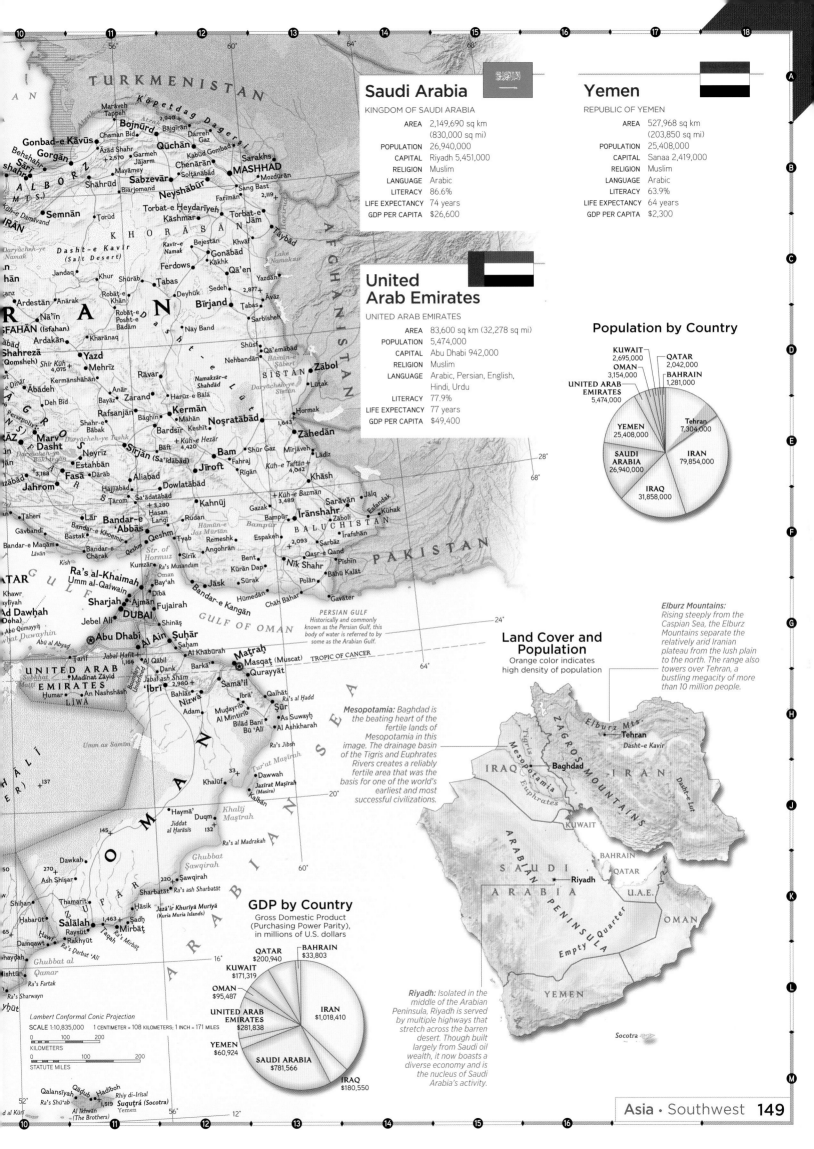

Saudi Arabia

KINGDOM OF SAUDI ARABIA

AREA	2,149,690 sq km (830,000 sq mi)
POPULATION	26,940,000
CAPITAL	Riyadh 5,451,000
RELIGION	Muslim
LANGUAGE	Arabic
LITERACY	86.6%
LIFE EXPECTANCY	74 years
GDP PER CAPITA	$26,600

Yemen

REPUBLIC OF YEMEN

AREA	527,968 sq km (203,850 sq mi)
POPULATION	25,408,000
CAPITAL	Sanaa 2,419,000
RELIGION	Muslim
LANGUAGE	Arabic
LITERACY	63.9%
LIFE EXPECTANCY	64 years
GDP PER CAPITA	$2,300

United Arab Emirates

UNITED ARAB EMIRATES

AREA	83,600 sq km (32,278 sq mi)
POPULATION	5,474,000
CAPITAL	Abu Dhabi 942,000
RELIGION	Muslim
LANGUAGE	Arabic, Persian, English, Hindi, Urdu
LITERACY	77.9%
LIFE EXPECTANCY	77 years
GDP PER CAPITA	$49,400

Population by Country

- KUWAIT 2,695,000
- QATAR 2,042,000
- OMAN 3,154,000
- BAHRAIN 1,281,000
- UNITED ARAB EMIRATES 5,474,000
- YEMEN 25,408,000
- SAUDI ARABIA 26,940,000
- Tehran 7,304,000
- IRAN 79,854,000
- IRAQ 31,858,000

Land Cover and Population
Orange color indicates high density of population

Elburz Mountains: Rising steeply from the Caspian Sea, the Elburz Mountains separate the relatively arid Iranian plateau from the lush plain to the north. The range also towers over Tehran, a bustling megacity of more than 10 million people.

Mesopotamia: Baghdad is the beating heart of the fertile lands of Mesopotamia in this image. The drainage basin of the Tigris and Euphrates Rivers creates a reliably fertile area that was the basis for one of the world's earliest and most successful civilizations.

Riyadh: Isolated in the middle of the Arabian Peninsula, Riyadh is served by multiple highways that stretch across the barren desert. Though built largely from Saudi oil wealth, it now boasts a diverse economy and is the nucleus of Saudi Arabia's activity.

PERSIAN GULF Historically and commonly known as the Persian Gulf, this body of water is referred to by some as the Arabian Gulf.

GDP by Country
Gross Domestic Product (Purchasing Power Parity), in millions of U.S. dollars

- QATAR $200,940
- BAHRAIN $33,803
- KUWAIT $171,319
- OMAN $95,487
- UNITED ARAB EMIRATES $281,838
- YEMEN $60,924
- SAUDI ARABIA $781,566
- IRAN $1,018,410
- IRAQ $180,550

Lambert Conformal Conic Projection
SCALE 1:10,835,000   1 CENTIMETER = 108 KILOMETERS; 1 INCH = 171 MILES
KILOMETERS 0 — 200
STATUTE MILES 0 — 200

Central Asia

Kazakhstan

REPUBLIC OF KAZAKHSTAN

AREA	2,724,900 sq km (1,052,089 sq mi)
POPULATION	17,737,000
CAPITAL	Astana 664,000
RELIGION	Muslim, Russian Orthodox
LANGUAGE	Kazakh (Qazaq), Russian
LITERACY	99.8%
LIFE EXPECTANCY	70 years
GDP PER CAPITA	$14,900

Turkmenistan

TURKMENISTAN

AREA	488,100 sq km (188,456 sq mi)
POPULATION	5,113,000
CAPITAL	Ashgabat 683,000
RELIGION	Muslim, Eastern Orthodox
LANGUAGE	Turkmen, Russian, Uzbek
LITERACY	98.8%
LIFE EXPECTANCY	69 years
GDP PER CAPITA	$9,100

Uzbekistan

REPUBLIC OF UZBEKISTAN

AREA	447,400 sq km (172,742 sq mi)
POPULATION	28,662,000
CAPITAL	Tashkent 2,227,000
RELIGION	Muslim, Eastern Orthodox
LANGUAGE	Uzbek, Russian, Tajik
LITERACY	99.3%
LIFE EXPECTANCY	73 years
GDP PER CAPITA	$3,800

ARAL SEA
Once the world's fourth largest lake, the Aral Sea today is less than half its 1960 extent. Soviet-era irrigation canals divert river water—causing the sea to shrink and changing the former lake bed into desert. A UN study predicts the Aral Sea could disappear by 2016.

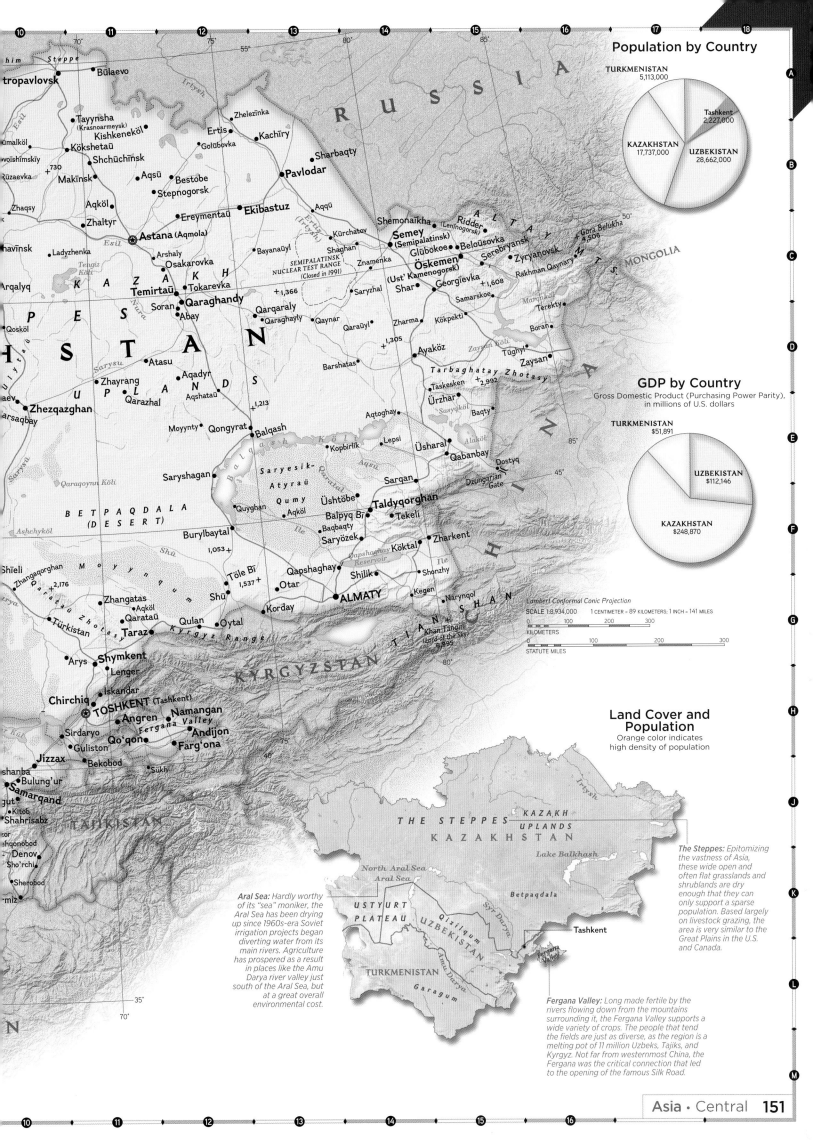

Population by Country

TURKMENISTAN 5,113,000

Tashkent 2,227,000

KAZAKHSTAN 17,737,000

UZBEKISTAN 28,662,000

GDP by Country

Gross Domestic Product (Purchasing Power Parity), in millions of U.S. dollars

TURKMENISTAN $51,891

UZBEKISTAN $112,146

KAZAKHSTAN $248,870

Lambert Conformal Conic Projection

SCALE 1:8,934,000   1 CENTIMETER = 89 KILOMETERS; 1 INCH = 141 MILES

KILOMETERS
0   100   200   300

STATUTE MILES
0   100   200   300

Land Cover and Population

Orange color indicates high density of population

The Steppes: Epitomizing the vastness of Asia, these wide open and often flat grasslands and shrublands are dry enough that they can only support a sparse population. Based largely on livestock grazing, the area is very similar to the Great Plains in the U.S. and Canada.

Aral Sea: Hardly worthy of its "sea" moniker, the Aral Sea has been drying up since 1960s-era Soviet irrigation projects began diverting water from its main rivers. Agriculture has prospered as a result in places like the Amu Darya river valley just south of the Aral Sea, but at a great overall environmental cost.

Fergana Valley: Long made fertile by the rivers flowing down from the mountains surrounding it, the Fergana Valley supports a wide variety of crops. The people that tend the fields are just as diverse, as the region is a melting pot of 11 million Uzbeks, Tajiks, and Kyrgyz. Not far from westernmost China, the Fergana was the critical connection that led to the opening of the famous Silk Road.

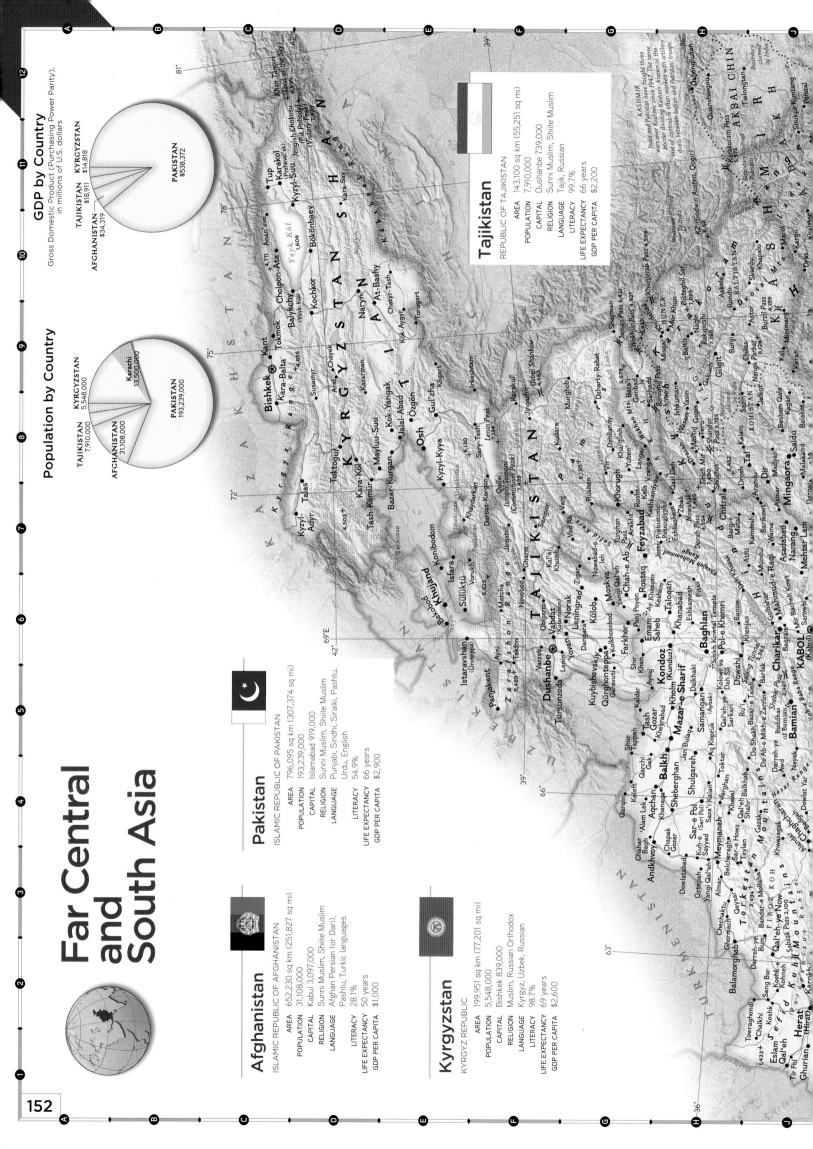

Far Central and South Asia

Afghanistan

ISLAMIC REPUBLIC OF AFGHANISTAN

AREA	652,230 sq km (251,827 sq mi)
POPULATION	31,108,000
CAPITAL	Kabul 3,097,000
RELIGION	Sunni Muslim, Shiite Muslim
LANGUAGE	Afghan Persian (or Dari), Pashtu, Turkic languages
LITERACY	28.1%
LIFE EXPECTANCY	50 years
GDP PER CAPITA	$1,000

Kyrgyzstan

KYRGYZ REPUBLIC

AREA	199,951 sq km (77,201 sq mi)
POPULATION	5,548,000
CAPITAL	Bishkek 839,000
RELIGION	Muslim, Russian Orthodox
LANGUAGE	Kyrgyz, Uzbek, Russian
LITERACY	98.7%
LIFE EXPECTANCY	69 years
GDP PER CAPITA	$2,600

Pakistan

ISLAMIC REPUBLIC OF PAKISTAN

AREA	796,095 sq km (307,374 sq mi)
POPULATION	193,239,000
CAPITAL	Islamabad 919,000
RELIGION	Sunni Muslim, Shiite Muslim
LANGUAGE	Punjabi, Sindhi, Siraiki, Pashtu, Urdu, English
LITERACY	54.9%
LIFE EXPECTANCY	66 years
GDP PER CAPITA	$2,900

Tajikistan

REPUBLIC OF TAJIKISTAN

AREA	143,100 sq km (55,251 sq mi)
POPULATION	7,910,000
CAPITAL	Dushanbe 739,000
RELIGION	Sunni Muslim, Shiite Muslim
LANGUAGE	Tajik, Russian
LITERACY	99.7%
LIFE EXPECTANCY	66 years
GDP PER CAPITA	$2,200

Population by Country

- PAKISTAN 193,239,000
  - Karachi 13,500,000
- AFGHANISTAN 31,108,000
- TAJIKISTAN 7,910,000
- KYRGYZSTAN 5,548,000

GDP by Country

Gross Domestic Product (Purchasing Power Parity), in millions of U.S. dollars

- PAKISTAN $538,372
- AFGHANISTAN $34,319
- TAJIKISTAN $18,911
- KYRGYZSTAN $14,818

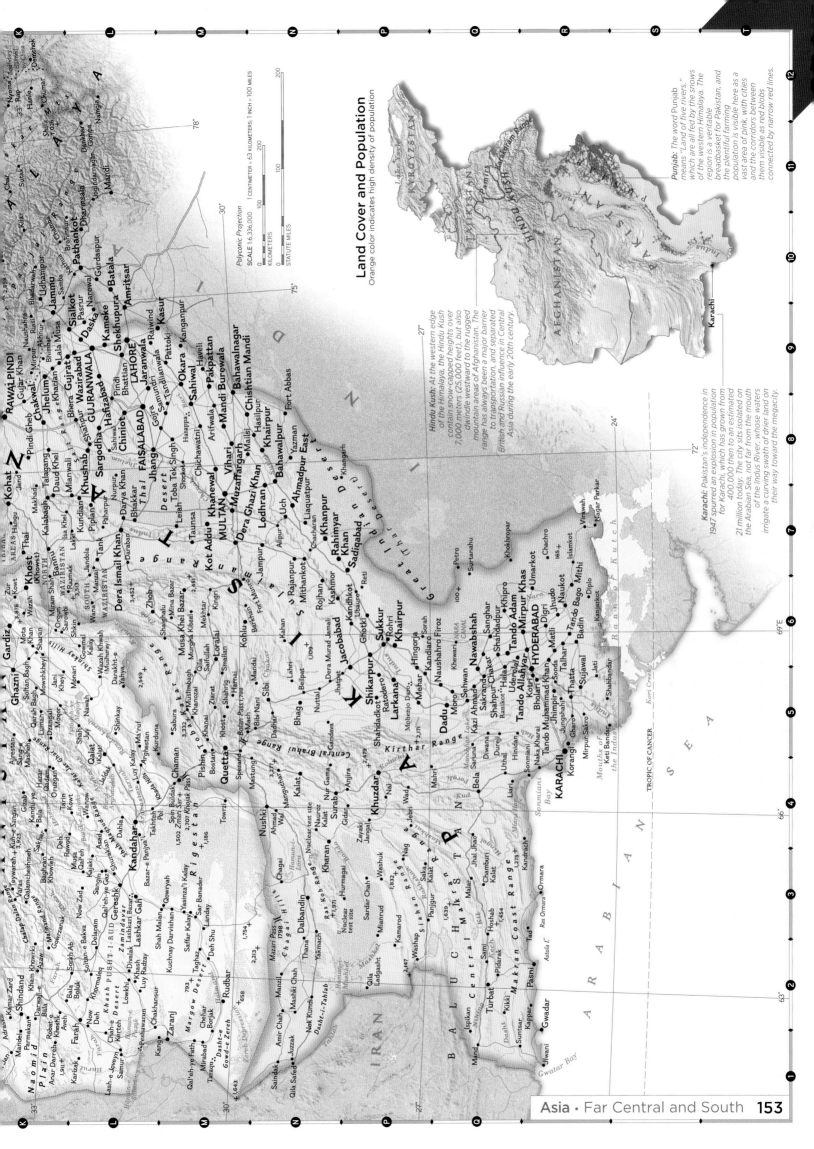

Land Cover and Population
Orange color indicates high density of population

Polyconic Projection
SCALE 1:6,336,000
1 CENTIMETER = 63 KILOMETERS; 1 INCH = 100 MILES

Punjab: The word Punjab means "Land of five rivers," which are all fed by the snows of the western Himalaya. The region is a veritable breadbasket for Pakistan, and the plentiful farming population is visible here as a vast area of pink, with cities and the corridors between them visible as red blobs connected by narrow red lines.

Hindu Kush: At the western edge of the Himalaya, the Hindu Kush contain snow-capped heights over 7,000 meters (25,000 feet), but also dwindle westward to the rugged mountain areas of Afghanistan. The range has always been a major barrier to transportation, and separated British and Russian influence in Central Asia during the early 20th century.

Karachi: Pakistan's independence in 1947 spurred an explosion in population for Karachi, which has grown from 400,000 then to an estimated 21 million today. The city sits isolated on the Arabian Sea, not far from the mouth of the Indus River, whose waters irrigate a curving swath of drier land on their way toward the megacity.

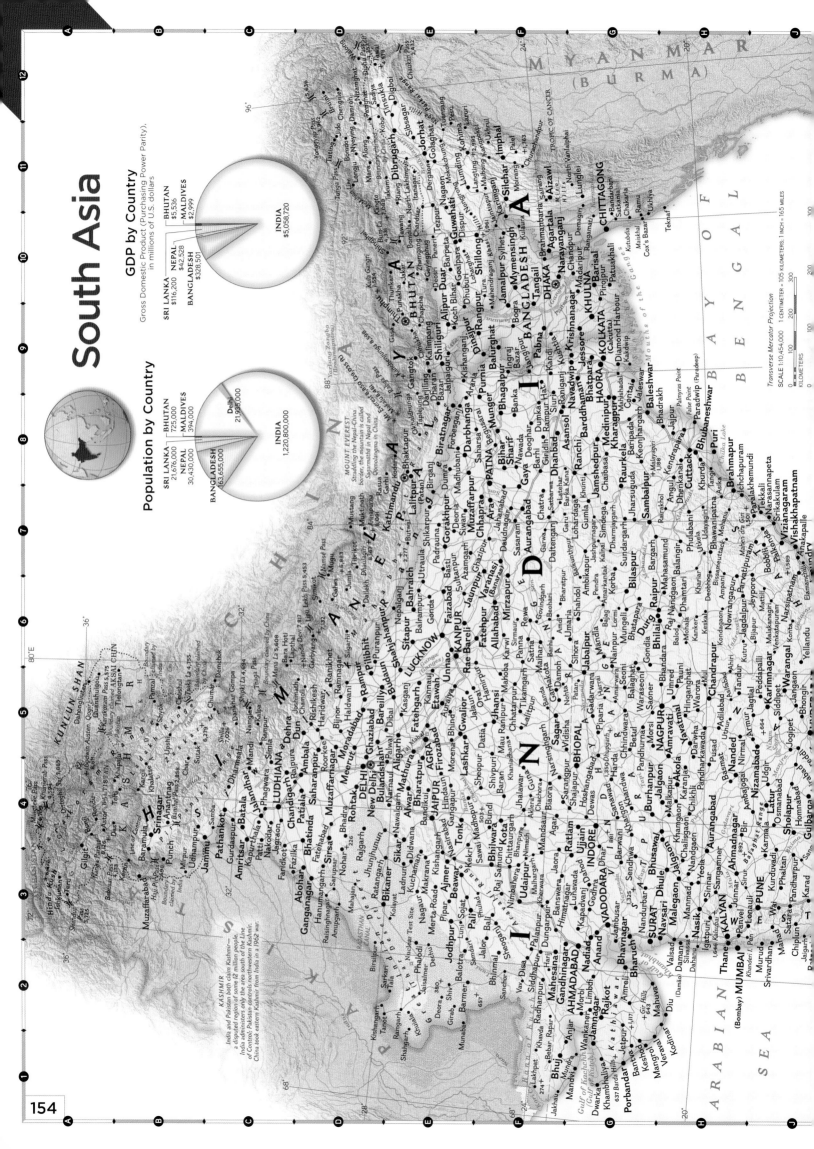

South Asia

GDP by Country

Gross Domestic Product (Purchasing Power Parity), in millions of U.S. dollars

Population by Country

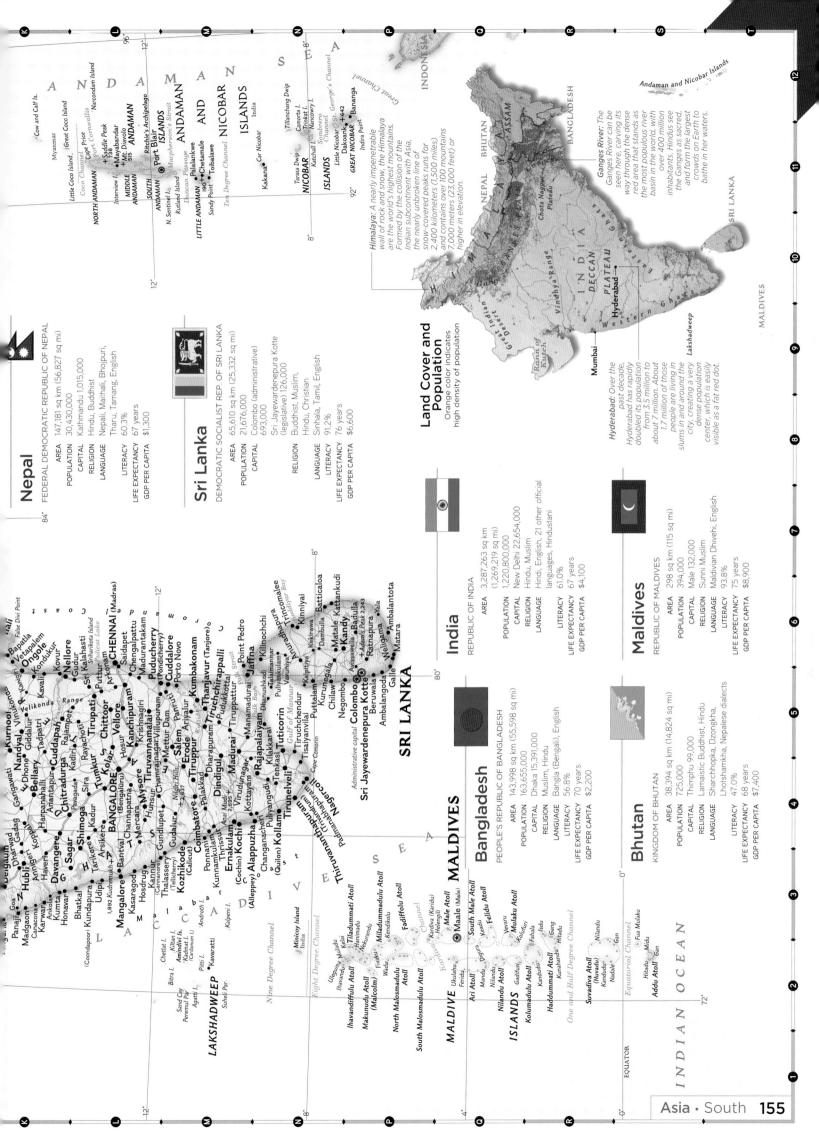

Nepal

FEDERAL DEMOCRATIC REPUBLIC OF NEPAL

AREA	147,181 sq km (56,827 sq mi)
POPULATION	30,430,000
CAPITAL	Kathmandu 1,015,000
RELIGION	Hindu, Buddhist
LANGUAGE	Nepali, Maithali, Bhojpuri, Tharu, Tamang, English
LITERACY	60.3%
LIFE EXPECTANCY	67 years
GDP PER CAPITA	$1,300

Sri Lanka

DEMOCRATIC SOCIALIST REP. OF SRI LANKA

AREA	65,610 sq km (25,332 sq mi)
POPULATION	21,676,000
CAPITAL	Colombo (administrative) 693,000 Sri Jayewardenepura Kotte (legislative) 126,000
RELIGION	Buddhist, Muslim, Hindu, Christian
LANGUAGE	Sinhala, Tamil, English
LITERACY	91.2%
LIFE EXPECTANCY	76 years
GDP PER CAPITA	$6,600

India

REPUBLIC OF INDIA

AREA	3,287,263 sq km (1,269,219 sq mi)
POPULATION	1,220,800,000
CAPITAL	New Delhi 22,654,000
RELIGION	Hindu, Muslim
LANGUAGE	Hindi, English, 21 other official languages, Hindustani
LITERACY	61.0%
LIFE EXPECTANCY	67 years
GDP PER CAPITA	$4,100

Bangladesh

PEOPLE'S REPUBLIC OF BANGLADESH

AREA	143,998 sq km (55,598 sq mi)
POPULATION	163,655,000
CAPITAL	Dhaka 15,391,000
RELIGION	Muslim, Hindu
LANGUAGE	Bangla (Bengali), English
LITERACY	56.8%
LIFE EXPECTANCY	70 years
GDP PER CAPITA	$2,200

Bhutan

KINGDOM OF BHUTAN

AREA	38,394 sq km (14,824 sq mi)
POPULATION	725,000
CAPITAL	Thimphu 99,000
RELIGION	Lamaistic Buddhist, Hindu
LANGUAGE	Sharchhopka, Dzongkha, Lhotshamkha, Nepalese dialects
LITERACY	47.0%
LIFE EXPECTANCY	68 years
GDP PER CAPITA	$7,400

Maldives

REPUBLIC OF MALDIVES

AREA	298 sq km (115 sq mi)
POPULATION	394,000
CAPITAL	Male 132,000
RELIGION	Sunni Muslim
LANGUAGE	Maldivian Dhivehi, English
LITERACY	93.8%
LIFE EXPECTANCY	75 years
GDP PER CAPITA	$8,900

Land Cover and Population
Orange color indicates high density of population

Himalaya: A nearly impenetrable wall of rock and snow, the Himalaya are the world's highest mountains. Formed by the collision of the Indian subcontinent with Asia, the nearly unbroken line of snow-covered peaks runs for 2,400 kilometers (1,500 miles) and contains over 100 mountains 7,000 meters (23,000 feet) or higher in elevation.

Ganges River: The Ganges River can be seen here, carving its way through the dense red area that stands as the most populous river basin in the world, with over 400 million inhabitants. Hindus see the Ganges as sacred, and form the largest crowds on Earth to bathe in her waters.

Hyderabad: Over the past decade, Hyderabad has rapidly doubled its population from 3.5 million to about 7 million. About 1.7 million of those people are living in slums in and around the city, creating a very dense population center, which is easily visible as a fat red dot.

China and Mongolia

China

![flag]

PEOPLE'S REPUBLIC OF CHINA

AREA	9,596,961 sq km (3,705,407 sq mi)
POPULATION	1,349,586,000
CAPITAL	Beijing 15,594,000
RELIGION	Daoist (Taoist), Buddhist
LANGUAGE	Standard Chinese or Mandarin, Yue, Wu, Minbei, local dialects and languages
LITERACY	92.2%
LIFE EXPECTANCY	75 years
GDP PER CAPITA	$10,000

Mongolia

![flag]

MONGOLIA

AREA	1,564,116 sq km (603,909 sq mi)
POPULATION	3,227,000
CAPITAL	Ulaanbaatar 1,184,000
RELIGION	Buddhist Lamaist, Shamanist, Christian, Muslim
LANGUAGE	Khalkha Mongol, Turkic, Russian
LITERACY	97.4%
LIFE EXPECTANCY	69 years
GDP PER CAPITA	$6,200

Western China: The western half of China is very sparsely populated. The Plateau of Tibet is a lake-speckled area in southwestern China, and averages 4,500 meters (15,000 feet) in elevation over an area more than three times the size of Texas. The Kunlun Mountains form the crisp boundary between the plateau and the Tarim Basin to the north, which is filled by the low-lying sands of the Taklimakan Desert. The basin is framed on the north by the snow-covered Tian Shan.

Land Cover and Population
Orange color indicates high density of population

North China Plain: The Yellow River carves a barely detectable sliver out of an otherwise solid backdrop of population in the North China Plain. With a climate too cool to produce much rice, this low-lying flat area instead provides much of China's wheat, corn, and vegetables. The dense area is anchored by Beijing in the north, and Shanghai in the southeast.

Sichuan Basin: Surrounded by mountains on all sides and visible here as a distinct island of red, the Sichuan Basin is a broad, flat area in central China that is home to over 100 million people, many of whom cultivate rice in the fertile farmlands. The two largest cities in the area, visible as darker red dots in the dense area, are Chengdu (in the west) and Chongqing (in the east).

Pearl River Delta: This low-lying region including Hong Kong, Macau, Shenzhen, and Guangzhou has been at the forefront of China's rapidly expanding economy since the 1980s. The area's population has been growing rapidly, as people migrate from inland provinces to seek manufacturing jobs making goods for export.

Taiwan: About 23 million people live on the island of Taiwan, though most of them along the flat western plain which faces mainland China. The central and eastern parts of the island are covered by high, rugged mountains, topping out at nearly 3,950 meters (13,000 feet).

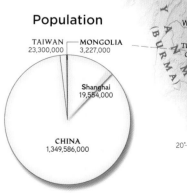

Population

TAIWAN 23,300,000
MONGOLIA 3,227,000
Shanghai 19,554,000
CHINA 1,349,586,000

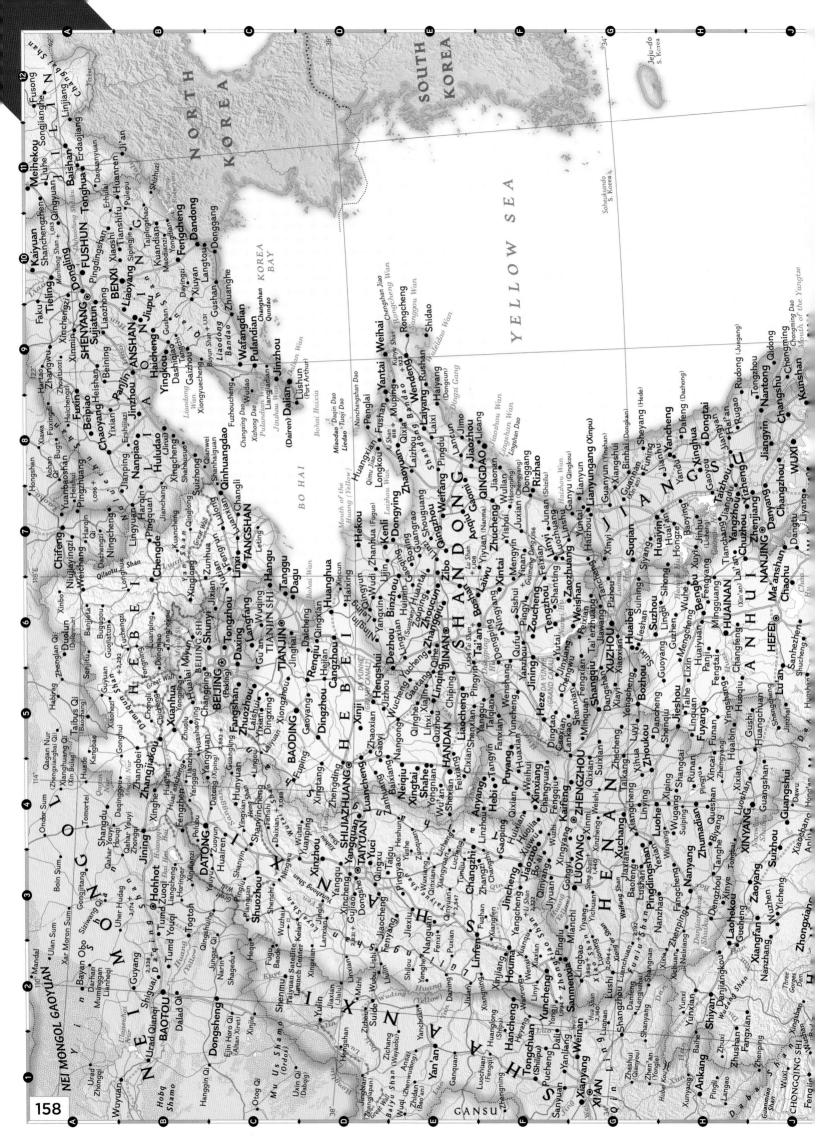

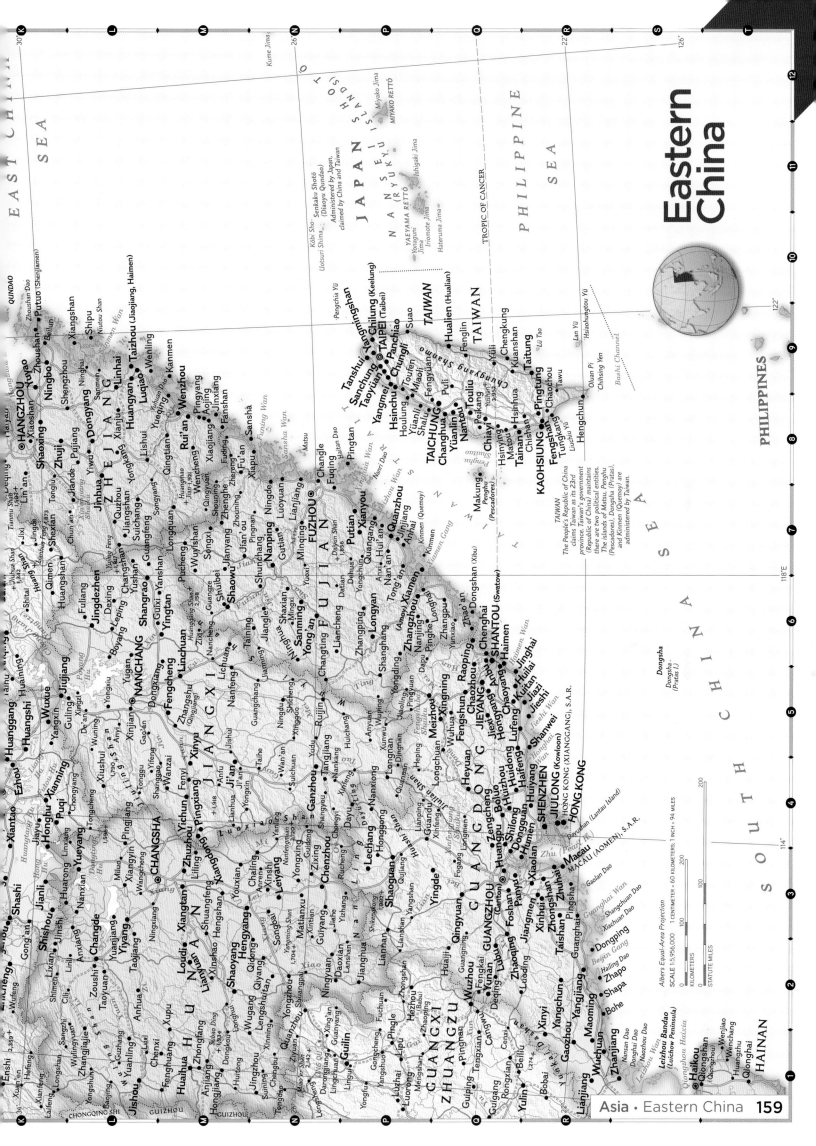

Eastern China

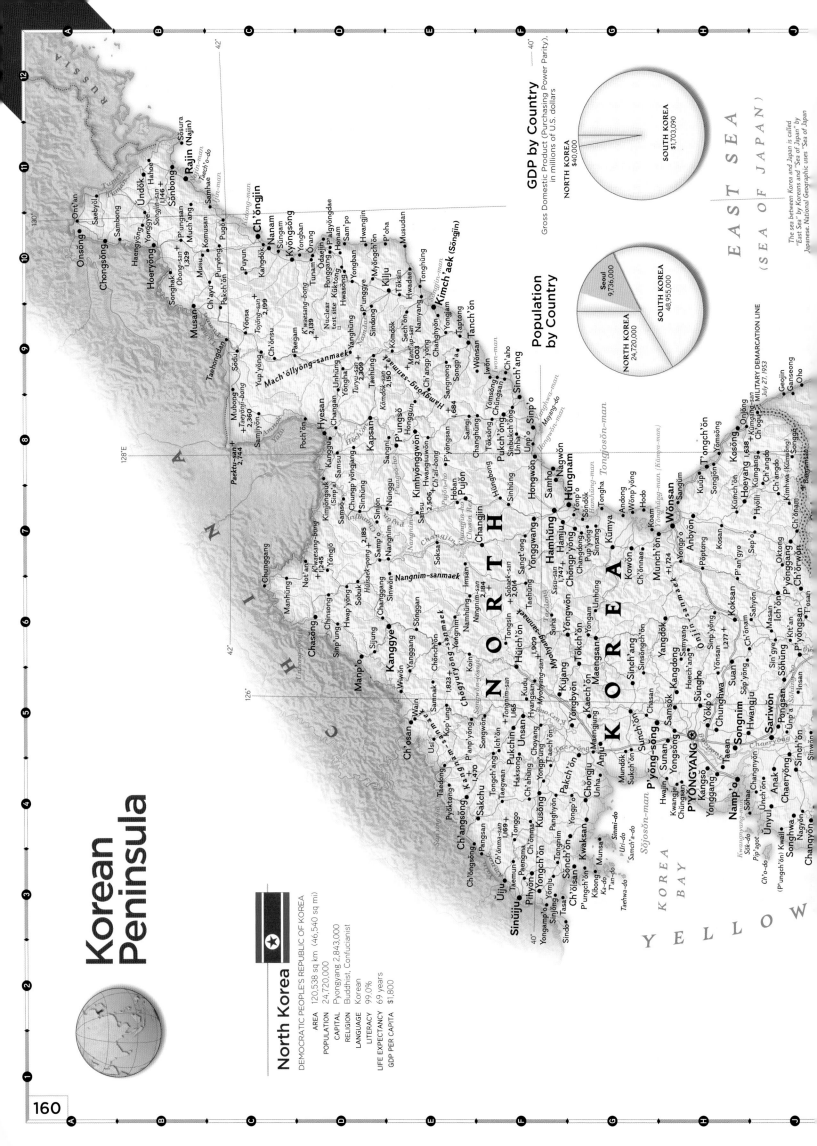

Korean Peninsula

North Korea

DEMOCRATIC PEOPLE'S REPUBLIC OF KOREA

AREA	120,538 sq km (46,540 sq mi)
POPULATION	24,720,000
CAPITAL	Pyongyang 2,843,000
RELIGION	Buddhist, Confucianist
LANGUAGE	Korean
LITERACY	99.0%
LIFE EXPECTANCY	69 years
GDP PER CAPITA	$1,800

GDP by Country

Gross Domestic Product (Purchasing Power Parity), in millions of U.S. dollars

NORTH KOREA $40,000

SOUTH KOREA $1,703,090

Population by Country

NORTH KOREA 24,720,000

SOUTH KOREA 48,955,000

Seoul 9,736,000

The sea between Korea and Japan is called "East Sea" by Koreans and "Sea of Japan" by Japanese. National Geographic uses "Sea of Japan."

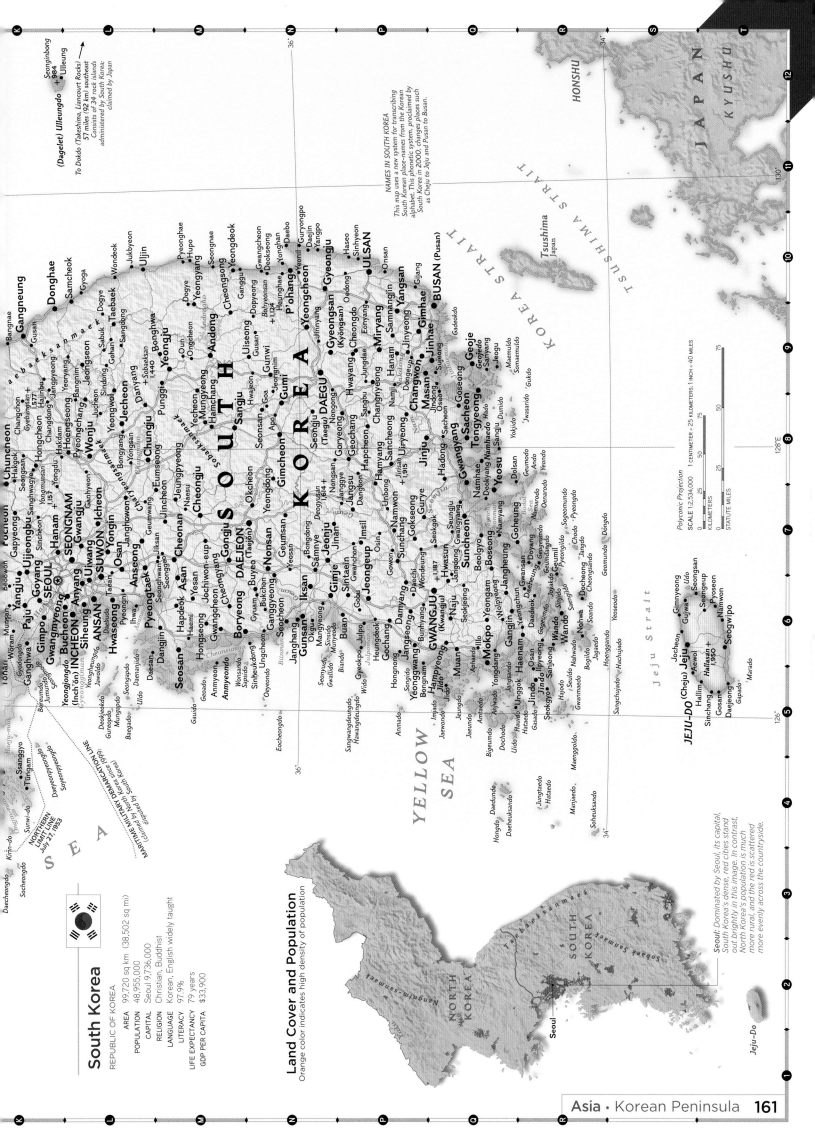

South Korea

REPUBLIC OF KOREA

AREA	99,720 sq km (38,502 sq mi)
POPULATION	48,955,000
CAPITAL	Seoul 9,736,000
RELIGION	Christian, Buddhist
LANGUAGE	Korean, English widely taught
LITERACY	97.9%
LIFE EXPECTANCY	79 years
GDP PER CAPITA	$33,900

Land Cover and Population
Orange color indicates high density of population

Seoul: Dominated by Seoul, its capital, South Korea's dense, red cities stand out brightly in this image. In contrast, North Korea's population is much more rural, and the red is scattered more evenly across the countryside.

NAMES IN SOUTH KOREA
This map uses a new system for transcribing South Korean place-names from the Korean alphabet. This phonetic system, proclaimed by South Korea in 2000, changes places such as Cheju to Jeju and Pusan to Busan.

(Dagelet) **Ulleungdo**
To Dokdo (Takeshima, Liancourt Rocks)
57 miles (92 km) southeast
Consists of 34 rock islands
administered by South Korea;
claimed by Japan

Seonginbong
▲ 984
+ Ulleung

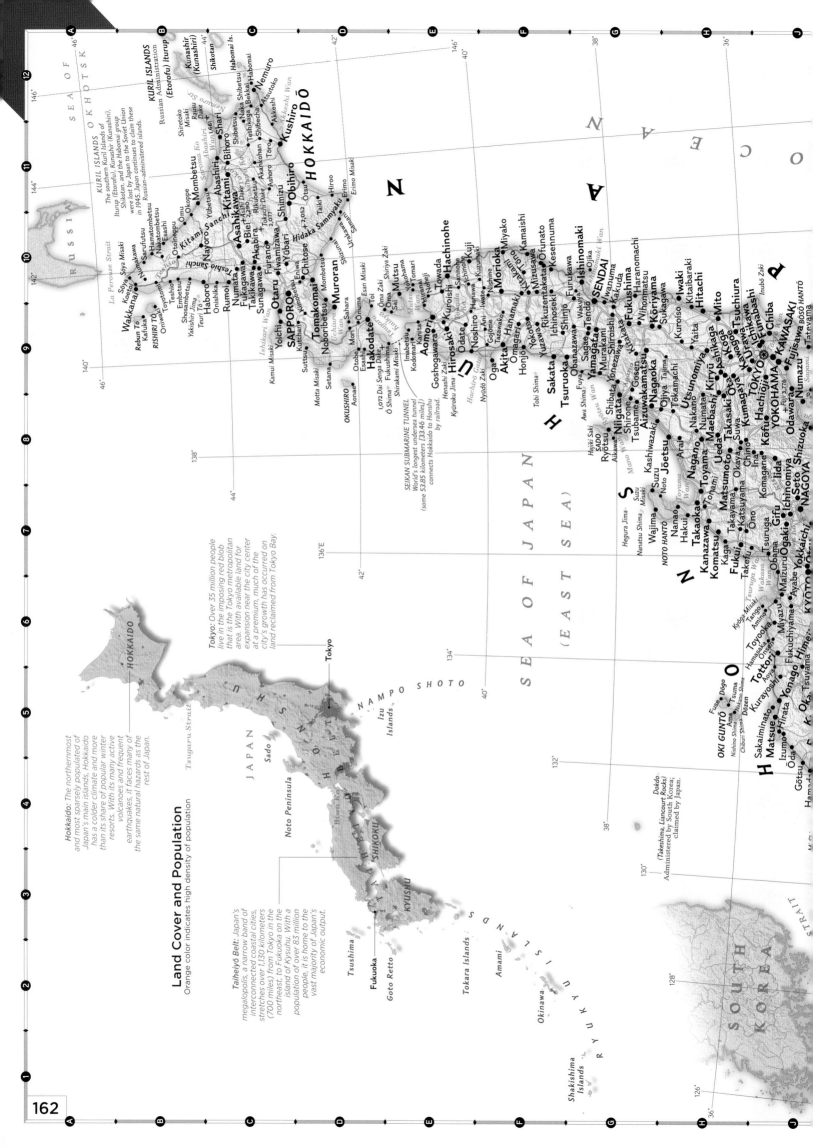

Land Cover and Population
Orange color indicates high density of population

Hokkaido: The northernmost and most sparsely populated of Japan's main islands, Hokkaido has a colder climate and more than its share of popular winter resorts. With its many active volcanoes and frequent earthquakes, it faces many of the same natural hazards as the rest of Japan.

Taiheiyō Belt: Japan's megalopolis, a narrow band of interconnected coastal cities, stretches over 1,130 kilometers (700 miles) from Tokyo in the northeast, to Fukuoka on the island of Kyushu. With a population of over 83 million people, it is home to the vast majority of Japan's economic output.

Tokyo: Over 35 million people live in the imposing red blob that is the Tokyo metropolitan area. With available land for expansion near the city center at a premium, much of the city's growth has occurred on land reclaimed from Tokyo Bay.

SEIKAN SUBMARINE TUNNEL World's longest undersea tunnel (some 53.85 kilometers (33.46 miles)) connects Hokkaido to Honshu by railroad.

KURIL ISLANDS The southern Kuril Islands of Iturup (Etorofu), Kunashir (Kunashiri), Shikotan, and the Habomai group were lost by Japan to the Soviet Union in 1945. Japan continues to claim these Russian-administered islands.

Dokdo (Takeshima, Liancourt Rocks) Administered by South Korea; claimed by Japan.

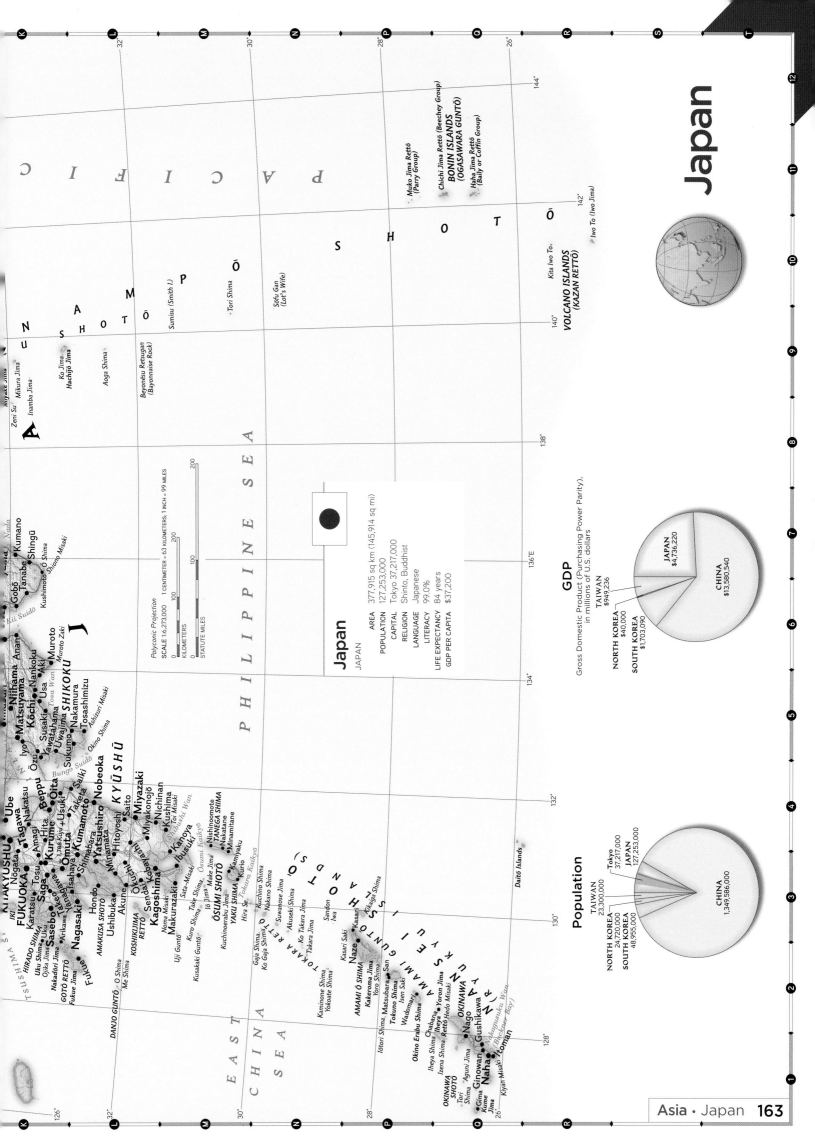

Japan

Japan

JAPAN

AREA	377,915 sq km (145,914 sq mi)
POPULATION	127,253,000
CAPITAL	Tokyo 37,217,000
RELIGION	Shinto, Buddhist
LANGUAGE	Japanese
LITERACY	99.0%
LIFE EXPECTANCY	84 years
GDP PER CAPITA	$37,200

Polyconic Projection   SCALE 1:6,273,000   1 CENTIMETER = 63 KILOMETERS; 1 INCH = 99 MILES

KILOMETERS   0   100   200

STATUTE MILES   0   100   200

Population

TAIWAN 23,300,000
NORTH KOREA 24,720,000
SOUTH KOREA 48,955,000
Tokyo 37,217,000
JAPAN 127,253,000
CHINA 1,349,586,000

GDP

Gross Domestic Product (Purchasing Power Parity), in millions of U.S. dollars

TAIWAN $949,236
NORTH KOREA $40,000
SOUTH KOREA $1,703,090
JAPAN $4,736,220
CHINA $13,580,540

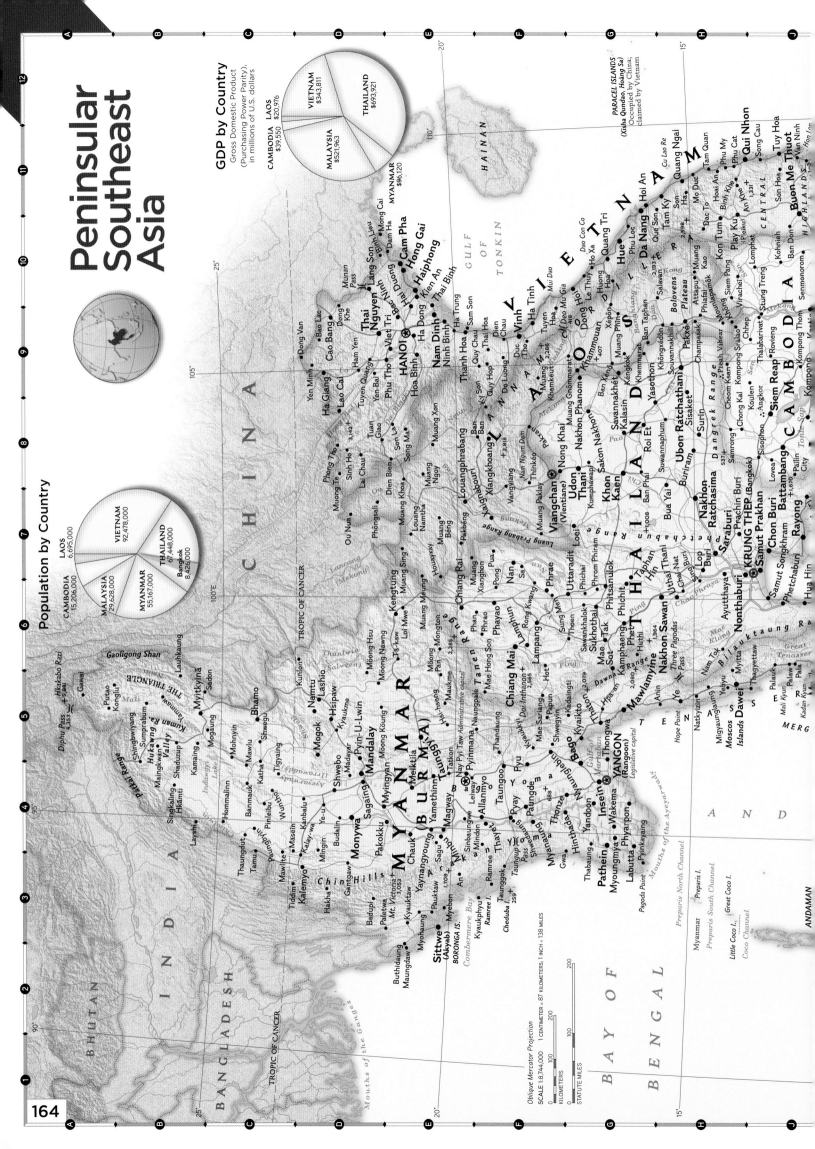

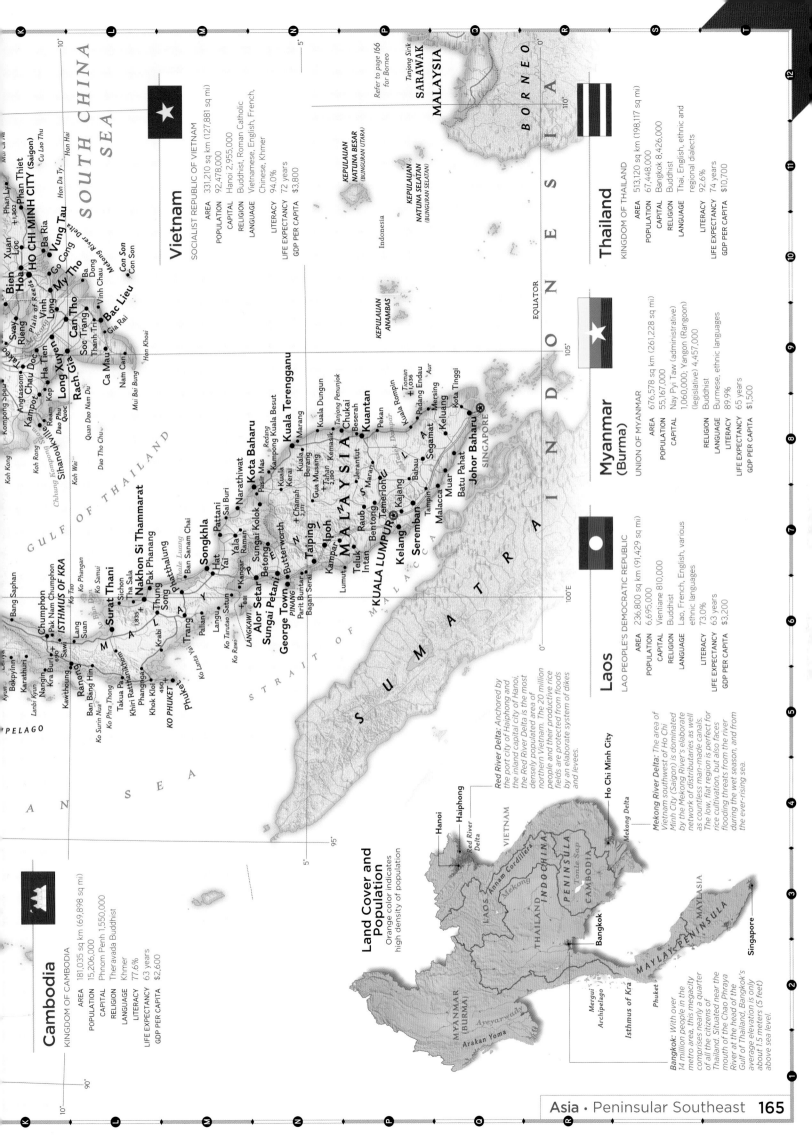

Vietnam

SOCIALIST REPUBLIC OF VIETNAM

AREA	331,210 sq km (127,881 sq mi)
POPULATION	92,478,000
CAPITAL	Hanoi 2,955,000
RELIGION	Buddhist, Roman Catholic
LANGUAGE	Vietnamese, English, French, Chinese, Khmer
LITERACY	94.0%
LIFE EXPECTANCY	72 years
GDP PER CAPITA	$3,800

Thailand

KINGDOM OF THAILAND

AREA	513,120 sq km (198,117 sq mi)
POPULATION	67,448,000
CAPITAL	Bangkok 8,426,000
RELIGION	Buddhist
LANGUAGE	Thai, English, ethnic and regional dialects
LITERACY	92.6%
LIFE EXPECTANCY	74 years
GDP PER CAPITA	$10,700

Myanmar (Burma)

UNION OF MYANMAR

AREA	676,578 sq km (261,228 sq mi)
POPULATION	55,167,000
CAPITAL	Nay Pyi Taw (administrative) 1,060,000; Yangon (Rangoon) (legislative) 4,457,000
RELIGION	Buddhist
LANGUAGE	Burmese, ethnic languages
LITERACY	89.9%
LIFE EXPECTANCY	65 years
GDP PER CAPITA	$1,500

Laos

LAO PEOPLE'S DEMOCRATIC REPUBLIC

AREA	236,800 sq km (91,429 sq mi)
POPULATION	6,695,000
CAPITAL	Vientiane 810,000
RELIGION	Buddhist
LANGUAGE	Lao, French, English, various ethnic languages
LITERACY	73.0%
LIFE EXPECTANCY	63 years
GDP PER CAPITA	$3,200

Cambodia

KINGDOM OF CAMBODIA

AREA	181,035 sq km (69,898 sq mi)
POPULATION	15,206,000
CAPITAL	Phnom Penh 1,550,000
RELIGION	Theravada Buddhist
LANGUAGE	Khmer
LITERACY	77.6%
LIFE EXPECTANCY	63 years
GDP PER CAPITA	$2,600

Land Cover and Population

Orange color indicates high density of population

Red River Delta: Anchored by the port city of Haiphong and the inland capital city of Hanoi, the Red River Delta is the most densely populated area of northern Vietnam. The 20 million people and their productive rice fields are protected from floods by an elaborate system of dikes and levees.

Mekong River Delta: The area of Vietnam southwest of Ho Chi Minh City (Saigon) is dominated by the Mekong River's elaborate network of distributaries as well as countless man-made canals. The low, flat region is perfect for rice cultivation, but also faces flooding threats from the river during the wet season, and from the ever-rising sea.

Bangkok: With over 14 million people in the metro area, this megacity comprises nearly a quarter of all the citizens of Thailand. Situated near the mouth of the Chao Phraya River at the head of the Gulf of Thailand, Bangkok's average elevation is only about 1.5 meters (5 feet) above sea level.

Refer to page 166 for Borneo

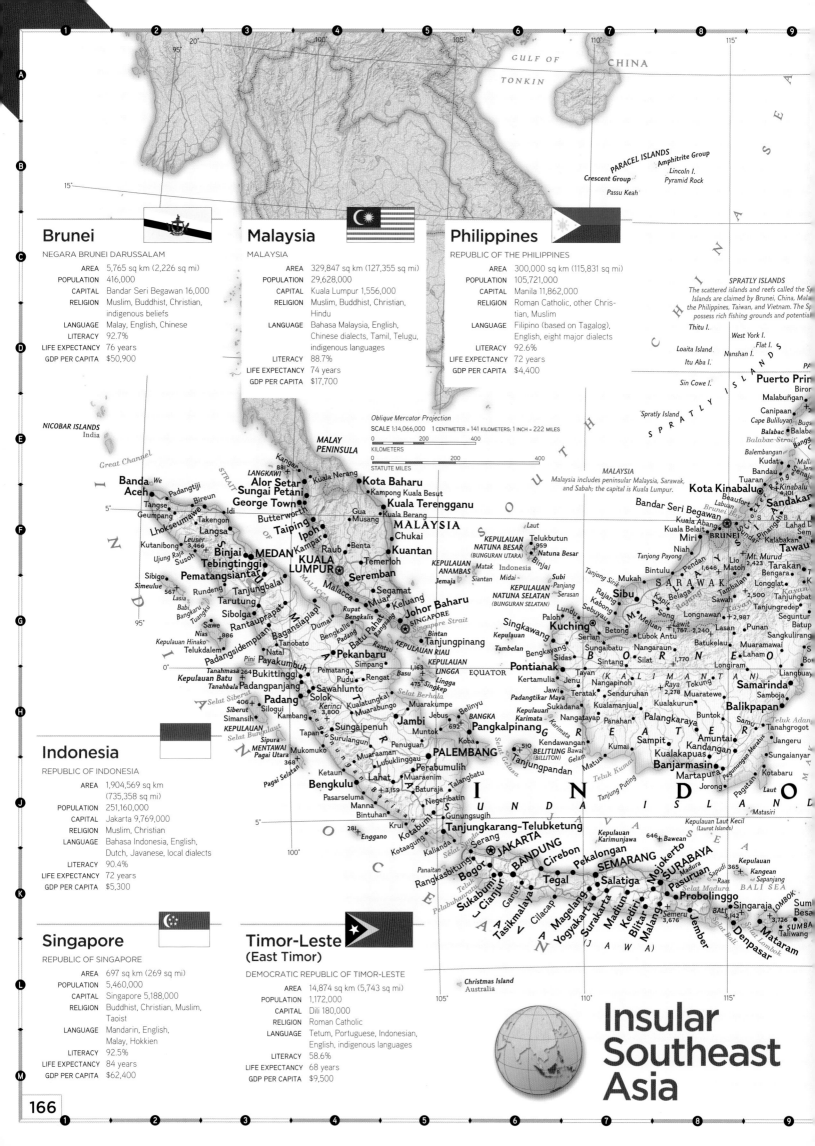

Brunei
NEGARA BRUNEI DARUSSALAM

AREA	5,765 sq km (2,226 sq mi)
POPULATION	416,000
CAPITAL	Bandar Seri Begawan 16,000
RELIGION	Muslim, Buddhist, Christian, indigenous beliefs
LANGUAGE	Malay, English, Chinese
LITERACY	92.7%
LIFE EXPECTANCY	76 years
GDP PER CAPITA	$50,900

Malaysia
MALAYSIA

AREA	329,847 sq km (127,355 sq mi)
POPULATION	29,628,000
CAPITAL	Kuala Lumpur 1,556,000
RELIGION	Muslim, Buddhist, Christian, Hindu
LANGUAGE	Bahasa Malaysia, English, Chinese dialects, Tamil, Telugu, indigenous languages
LITERACY	88.7%
LIFE EXPECTANCY	74 years
GDP PER CAPITA	$17,700

Philippines
REPUBLIC OF THE PHILIPPINES

AREA	300,000 sq km (115,831 sq mi)
POPULATION	105,721,000
CAPITAL	Manila 11,862,000
RELIGION	Roman Catholic, other Christian, Muslim
LANGUAGE	Filipino (based on Tagalog), English, eight major dialects
LITERACY	92.6%
LIFE EXPECTANCY	72 years
GDP PER CAPITA	$4,400

Indonesia
REPUBLIC OF INDONESIA

AREA	1,904,569 sq km (735,358 sq mi)
POPULATION	251,160,000
CAPITAL	Jakarta 9,769,000
RELIGION	Muslim, Christian
LANGUAGE	Bahasa Indonesia, English, Dutch, Javanese, local dialects
LITERACY	90.4%
LIFE EXPECTANCY	72 years
GDP PER CAPITA	$5,300

Singapore
REPUBLIC OF SINGAPORE

AREA	697 sq km (269 sq mi)
POPULATION	5,460,000
CAPITAL	Singapore 5,188,000
RELIGION	Buddhist, Christian, Muslim, Taoist
LANGUAGE	Mandarin, English, Malay, Hokkien
LITERACY	92.5%
LIFE EXPECTANCY	84 years
GDP PER CAPITA	$62,400

Timor-Leste
(East Timor)
DEMOCRATIC REPUBLIC OF TIMOR-LESTE

AREA	14,874 sq km (5,743 sq mi)
POPULATION	1,172,000
CAPITAL	Dili 180,000
RELIGION	Roman Catholic
LANGUAGE	Tetum, Portuguese, Indonesian, English, indigenous languages
LITERACY	58.6%
LIFE EXPECTANCY	68 years
GDP PER CAPITA	$9,500

Oblique Mercator Projection
SCALE 1:14,066,000 1 CENTIMETER = 141 KILOMETERS; 1 INCH = 222 MILES

MALAYSIA
Malaysia includes peninsular Malaysia, Sarawak, and Sabah; the capital is Kuala Lumpur.

SPRATLY ISLANDS
The scattered islands and reefs called the Spratly Islands are claimed by Brunei, China, Malaysia, the Philippines, Taiwan, and Vietnam. The Spratlys possess rich fishing grounds and potential...

Insular Southeast Asia

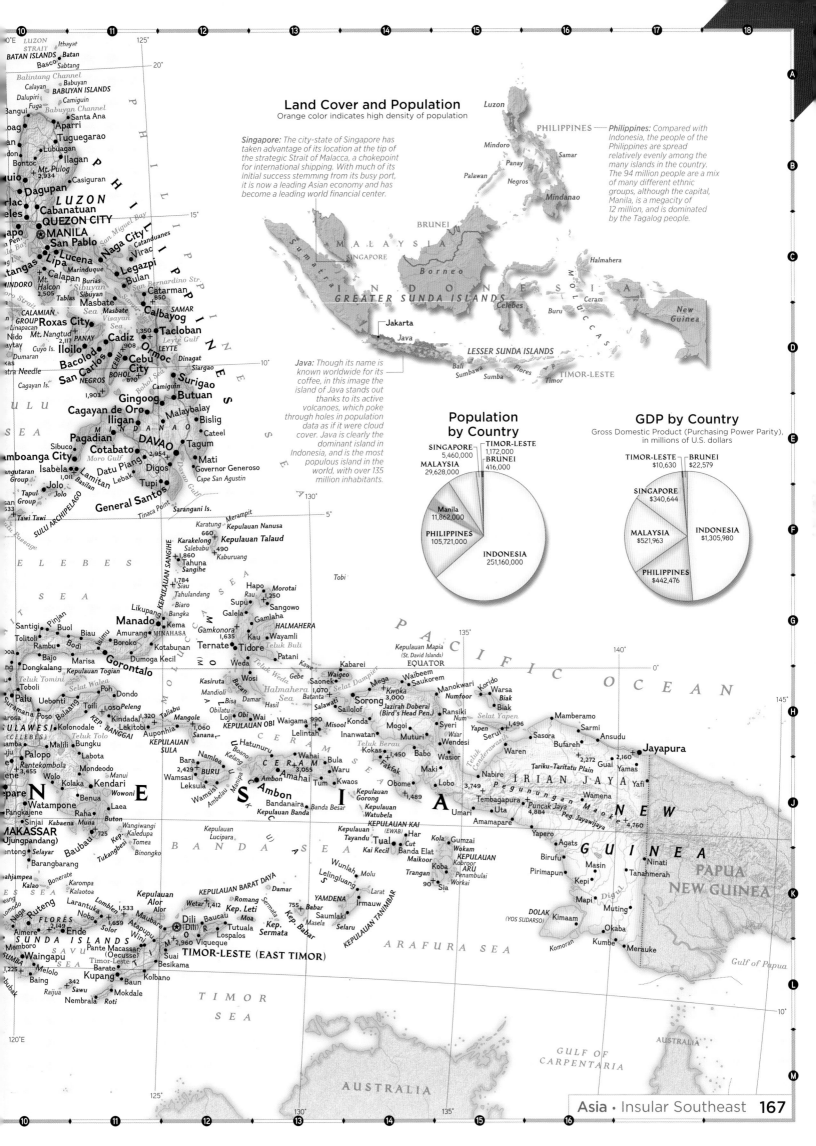

Land Cover and Population

Orange color indicates high density of population

Singapore: *The city-state of Singapore has taken advantage of its location at the tip of the strategic Strait of Malacca, a chokepoint for international shipping. With much of its initial success stemming from its busy port, it is now a leading Asian economy and has become a leading world financial center.*

Philippines: *Compared with Indonesia, the people of the Philippines are spread relatively evenly among the many islands in the country. The 94 million people are a mix of many different ethnic groups, although the capital, Manila, is a megacity of 12 million, and is dominated by the Tagalog people.*

Java: *Though its name is known worldwide for its coffee, in this image the island of Java stands out thanks to its active volcanoes, which poke through holes in population data as if it were cloud cover. Java is clearly the dominant island in Indonesia, and is the most populous island in the world, with over 135 million inhabitants.*

Population by Country

- SINGAPORE 5,460,000
- TIMOR-LESTE 1,172,000
- MALAYSIA 29,628,000
- BRUNEI 416,000
- Manila 11,862,000
- PHILIPPINES 105,721,000
- INDONESIA 251,160,000

GDP by Country

Gross Domestic Product (Purchasing Power Parity), in millions of U.S. dollars

- TIMOR-LESTE $10,630
- BRUNEI $22,579
- SINGAPORE $340,644
- MALAYSIA $521,963
- INDONESIA $1,305,980
- PHILIPPINES $442,476

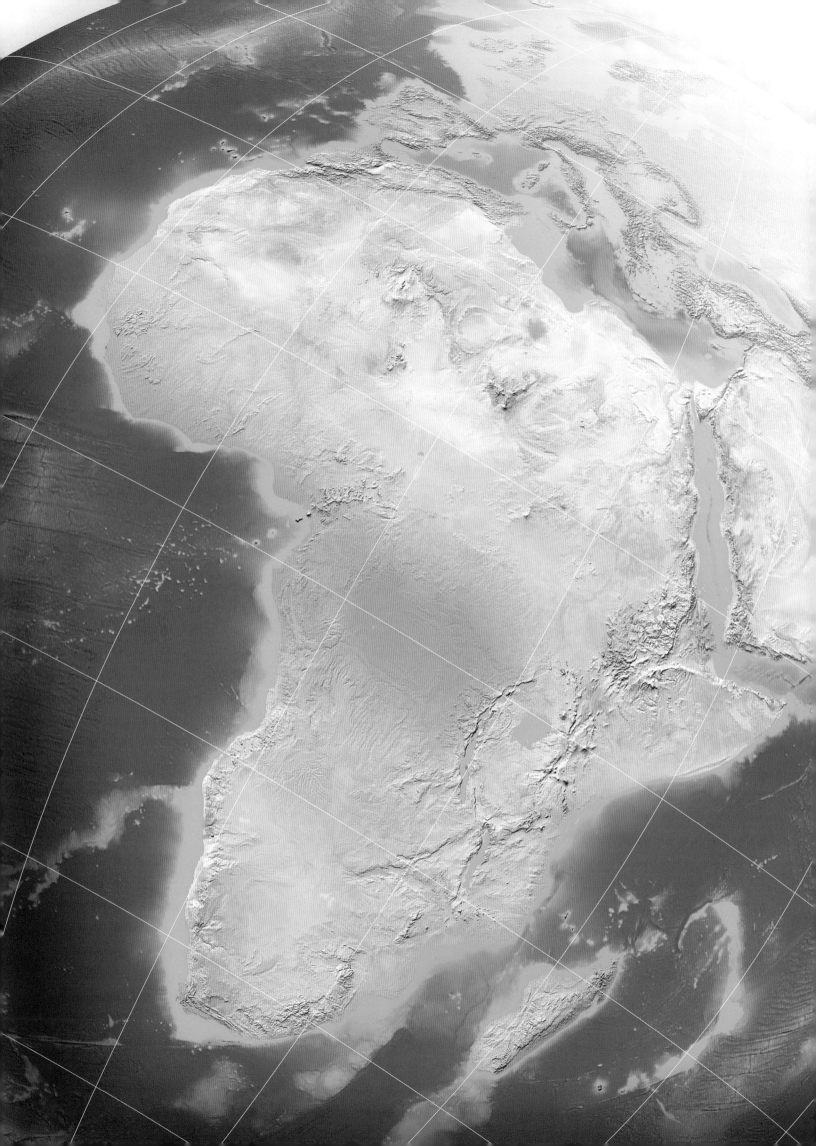

Africa

Sitting firmly astride the Equator, Africa may be the most diverse of Earth's seven continents. In the north, the world's longest river wends its way through the eastern extreme of its largest hot desert, as the Nile flows north through the Sahara, fed from the wet, densely forested Ethiopian Highlands and the massive lakes of the Great Rift Valley. Between Alexandria, in the great river's Mediterranean delta, and far-distant Cape Town, where the continent's southern tip is bathed by warm waters to the east and frigid Antarctic currents to the west, lie vast savannas, daunting mountain ranges, dramatic floodplains, and, in the Congo Basin, perhaps the densest remaining tropical rain forest on Earth.

Africa also holds a special place in human history, as the site of our emergence as a species some 200,000 years ago. From that Rift Valley origin, in Africa's northeast, we have spread to every corner of the planet. But Africa remains the ancestral home of us all, and is as rich in cultures and human history as it is in biological diversity and mineral wealth. Recent history in much of the continent has been marred by colonialism, poverty, disease, and war. But to focus only on Africa's problems is to miss its great strengths, beauty, and potential. Humans have lived longer in Africa than on any other continent. In many ways, it is still the land of the future.

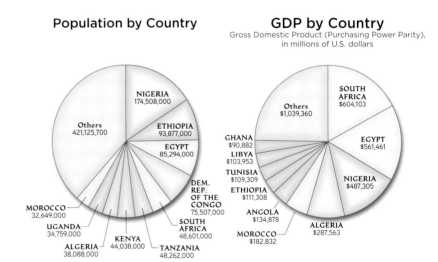

Population by Country

NIGERIA 174,508,000
ETHIOPIA 93,877,000
EGYPT 85,294,000
DEM. REP. OF THE CONGO 75,507,000
SOUTH AFRICA 48,601,000
TANZANIA 48,262,000
KENYA 44,038,000
ALGERIA 38,088,000
UGANDA 34,759,000
MOROCCO 32,649,000
Others 421,125,700

GDP by Country
Gross Domestic Product (Purchasing Power Parity), in millions of U.S. dollars

SOUTH AFRICA $604,103
EGYPT $561,461
NIGERIA $487,305
ALGERIA $287,563
MOROCCO $182,832
ANGOLA $134,878
ETHIOPIA $111,308
TUNISIA $109,309
LIBYA $103,953
GHANA $90,882
Others $1,039,360

INDIAN

OCEAN

MOZAMBIQUE CHANNEL

ATLANTIC

OCEAN

SOMALIA

SUDAN

KENYA

UGANDA

RWANDA

BURUNDI

TANZANIA

DEMOCRATIC

REPUBLIC

OF THE CONGO

CENTRAL AFRICAN

REPUBLIC

CAMEROON

GABON

CONGO

EQ. GUINEA

RÍO MUNI

SAO TOME
AND PRINCIPE

GULF OF GUINEA

ANGOLA

GUINEA

CABINDA

ZAMBIA

MALAWI

MOZAMBIQUE

ZIMBABWE

BOTSWANA

NAMIBIA

SOUTH AFRICA

LESOTHO

SWAZILAND

MADAGASCAR

COMOROS

SEYCHELLES

KALAHARI

DESERT

NAMIB

DESERT

KAROO

Great Rift Valley

Katanga Plateau

Bié Plateau

Highest point in Africa

Kilimanjaro 5,895 (19,340 ft)

Mt. Kenya 5,199

Ruwenzori 5,109

Lake Victoria

Lake Tanganyika

Lake Nyasa (L. Malawi)

Lake Turkana (L. Rudolf)

Lake Albert

Lake Edward

Lake Kivu

Lake Mweru

Lake Eyasi

Lake Rukwa

Lake Natron

Lake Kariba

Lake Nasser

Lake Abaya

Congo

Nile

Zambezi

Limpopo

Orange

Okavango Delta

Victoria Falls

Lake Chad

Niger R. Delta

Tristan da
Cunha Group

Saint Helena

Ascension

EQUATOR

TROPIC OF CAPRICORN

Meridain of Greenwich (London)

Azimuthal Equidistant Projection

SCALE 1:27,000,000   1 CENTIMETER = 270 KILOMETERS; 1 INCH = 426 MILES

KILOMETERS

STATUTE MILES

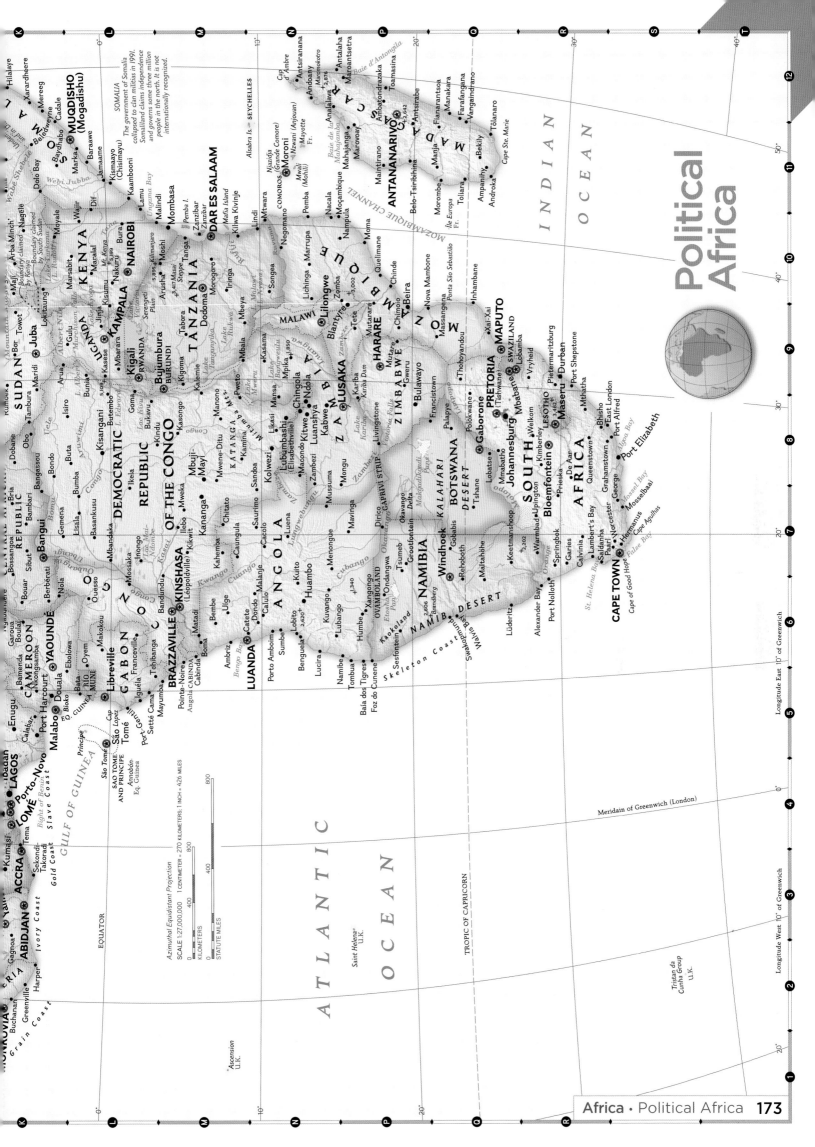

Political
Africa

INDIAN

OCEAN

MOZAMBIQUE CHANNEL

ATLANTIC

OCEAN

GULF OF GUINEA

Azimuthal Equidistant Projection
SCALE 1:27,000,000 1 CENTIMETER = 270 KILOMETERS; 1 INCH = 426 MILES

KILOMETERS
0   400   800
STATUTE MILES
0   400   800

EQUATOR

TROPIC OF CAPRICORN

Meridain of Greenwich (London)

Longitude West 10° of Greenwich

Longitude East 10° of Greenwich

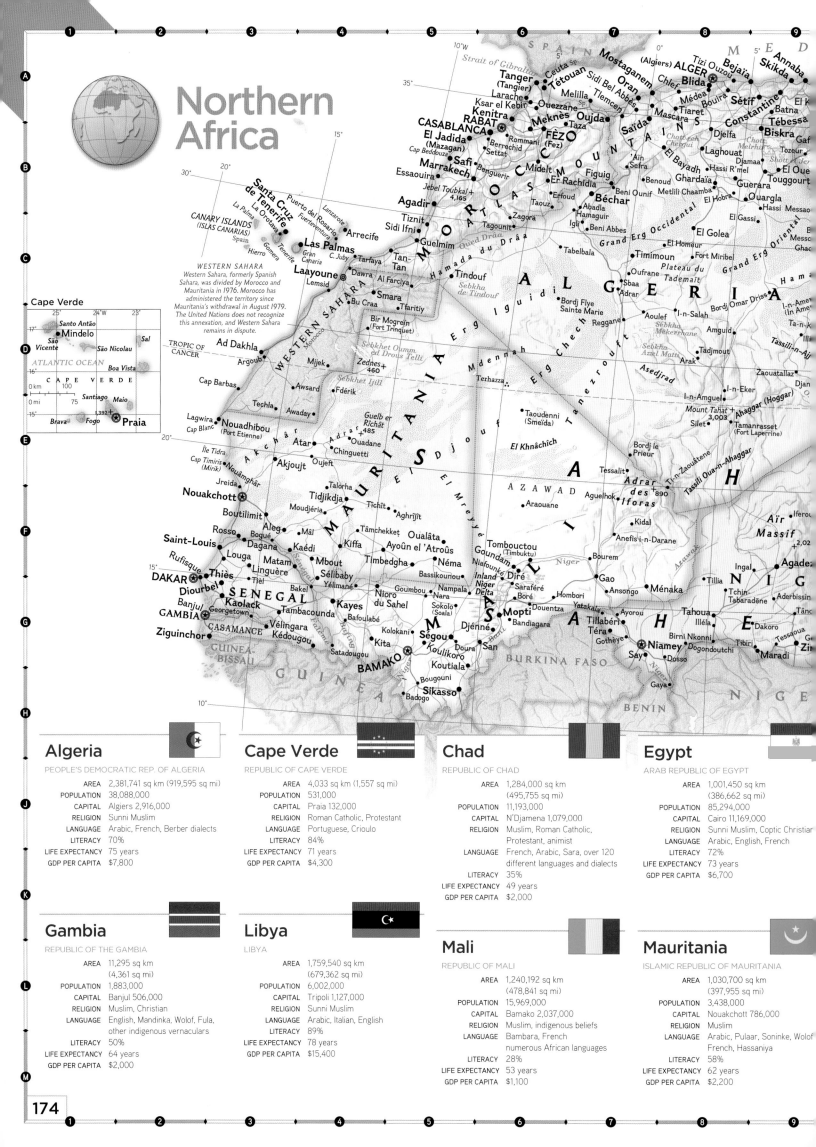

Northern Africa

CANARY ISLANDS (ISLAS CANARIAS) Spain

WESTERN SAHARA
Western Sahara, formerly Spanish Sahara, was divided by Morocco and Mauritania in 1976. Morocco has administered the territory since Mauritania's withdrawal in August 1979. The United Nations does not recognize this annexation, and Western Sahara remains in dispute.

Cape Verde

ATLANTIC OCEAN

CAPE VERDE

Algeria
PEOPLE'S DEMOCRATIC REP. OF ALGERIA
AREA	2,381,741 sq km (919,595 sq mi)
POPULATION	38,088,000
CAPITAL	Algiers 2,916,000
RELIGION	Sunni Muslim
LANGUAGE	Arabic, French, Berber dialects
LITERACY	70%
LIFE EXPECTANCY	75 years
GDP PER CAPITA	$7,800

Cape Verde
REPUBLIC OF CAPE VERDE
AREA	4,033 sq km (1,557 sq mi)
POPULATION	531,000
CAPITAL	Praia 132,000
RELIGION	Roman Catholic, Protestant
LANGUAGE	Portuguese, Crioulo
LITERACY	84%
LIFE EXPECTANCY	71 years
GDP PER CAPITA	$4,300

Chad
REPUBLIC OF CHAD
AREA	1,284,000 sq km (495,755 sq mi)
POPULATION	11,193,000
CAPITAL	N'Djamena 1,079,000
RELIGION	Muslim, Roman Catholic, Protestant, animist
LANGUAGE	French, Arabic, Sara, over 120 different languages and dialects
LITERACY	35%
LIFE EXPECTANCY	49 years
GDP PER CAPITA	$2,000

Egypt
ARAB REPUBLIC OF EGYPT
AREA	1,001,450 sq km (386,662 sq mi)
POPULATION	85,294,000
CAPITAL	Cairo 11,169,000
RELIGION	Sunni Muslim, Coptic Christian
LANGUAGE	Arabic, English, French
LITERACY	72%
LIFE EXPECTANCY	73 years
GDP PER CAPITA	$6,700

Gambia
REPUBLIC OF THE GAMBIA
AREA	11,295 sq km (4,361 sq mi)
POPULATION	1,883,000
CAPITAL	Banjul 506,000
RELIGION	Muslim, Christian
LANGUAGE	English, Mandinka, Wolof, Fula, other indigenous vernaculars
LITERACY	50%
LIFE EXPECTANCY	64 years
GDP PER CAPITA	$2,000

Libya
LIBYA
AREA	1,759,540 sq km (679,362 sq mi)
POPULATION	6,002,000
CAPITAL	Tripoli 1,127,000
RELIGION	Sunni Muslim
LANGUAGE	Arabic, Italian, English
LITERACY	89%
LIFE EXPECTANCY	78 years
GDP PER CAPITA	$15,400

Mali
REPUBLIC OF MALI
AREA	1,240,192 sq km (478,841 sq mi)
POPULATION	15,969,000
CAPITAL	Bamako 2,037,000
RELIGION	Muslim, indigenous beliefs
LANGUAGE	Bambara, French numerous African languages
LITERACY	28%
LIFE EXPECTANCY	53 years
GDP PER CAPITA	$1,100

Mauritania
ISLAMIC REPUBLIC OF MAURITANIA
AREA	1,030,700 sq km (397,955 sq mi)
POPULATION	3,438,000
CAPITAL	Nouakchott 786,000
RELIGION	Muslim
LANGUAGE	Arabic, Pulaar, Soninke, Wolof, French, Hassaniya
LITERACY	58%
LIFE EXPECTANCY	62 years
GDP PER CAPITA	$2,200

Population by Country

- MAURITANIA 3,438,000
- LIBYA 6,002,000
- TUNISIA 10,836,000
- CHAD 11,193,000
- SENEGAL 13,300,000
- MALI 15,969,000
- NIGER 16,899,000
- MOROCCO 32,649,000
- ALGERIA 38,088,000
- GAMBIA 1,883,000
- CAPE VERDE 531,000
- WESTERN SAHARA 539,000
- Cairo 11,169,000
- EGYPT 85,294,000

GDP by Country

Gross Domestic Product (Purchasing Power Parity), in millions of U.S. dollars

- MAURITANIA $8,247
- SENEGAL $28,021
- MALI $18,109
- NIGER $14,616
- MOROCCO $182,832
- ALGERIA $287,563
- GAMBIA $3,884
- LIBYA $103,953
- CHAD $22,144
- TUNISIA $109,309
- CAPE VERDE $2,301
- WESTERN SAHARA $907
- EGYPT $561,461

Land Cover and Population

Orange color indicates high density of population

Sahara: The world's largest hot desert, it dominates North Africa, rendering most of the land economically useless.

Sahel: The semi-arid transition zone between the desert to the north and the more fertile and heavily populated savanna region to the south, the Sahel is hit hard by droughts.

Nile River Valley and Delta: Today home to 98% of Egypt's population, the agricultural area along the world's longest river and its delta supported one of the world's first civilizations.

Morocco

KINGDOM OF MOROCCO

- AREA 446,550 sq km (172,413 sq mi)
- POPULATION 32,649,000
- CAPITAL Rabat 1,843,000
- RELIGION Muslim
- LANGUAGE Arabic, Berber dialects, French
- LITERACY 56%
- LIFE EXPECTANCY 76 years
- GDP PER CAPITA $5,600

Niger

REPUBLIC OF NIGER

- AREA 1,267,000 sq km (489,191 sq mi)
- POPULATION 16,899,000
- CAPITAL Niamey 1,297,000
- RELIGION Muslim, indigenous beliefs, Christian
- LANGUAGE French, Hausa, Djerma
- LITERACY 29%
- LIFE EXPECTANCY 54 years
- GDP PER CAPITA $900

Senegal

REPUBLIC OF SENEGAL

- AREA 196,722 sq km (75,955 sq mi)
- POPULATION 13,300,000
- CAPITAL Dakar 3,035,000
- RELIGION Muslim, Christian
- LANGUAGE French, Wolof, Pulaar, Jola, Mandinka
- LITERACY 39%
- LIFE EXPECTANCY 60 years
- GDP PER CAPITA $2,000

Tunisia

TUNISIAN REPUBLIC

- AREA 163,610 sq km (63,170 sq mi)
- POPULATION 10,836,000
- CAPITAL Tunis 790,000
- RELIGION Muslim
- LANGUAGE Arabic, French
- LITERACY 74%
- LIFE EXPECTANCY 75 years
- GDP PER CAPITA $10,000

Azimuthal Equidistant Projection
SCALE 1:17,361,000 1 CENTIMETER = 174 KILOMETERS; 1 INCH = 274 MILES

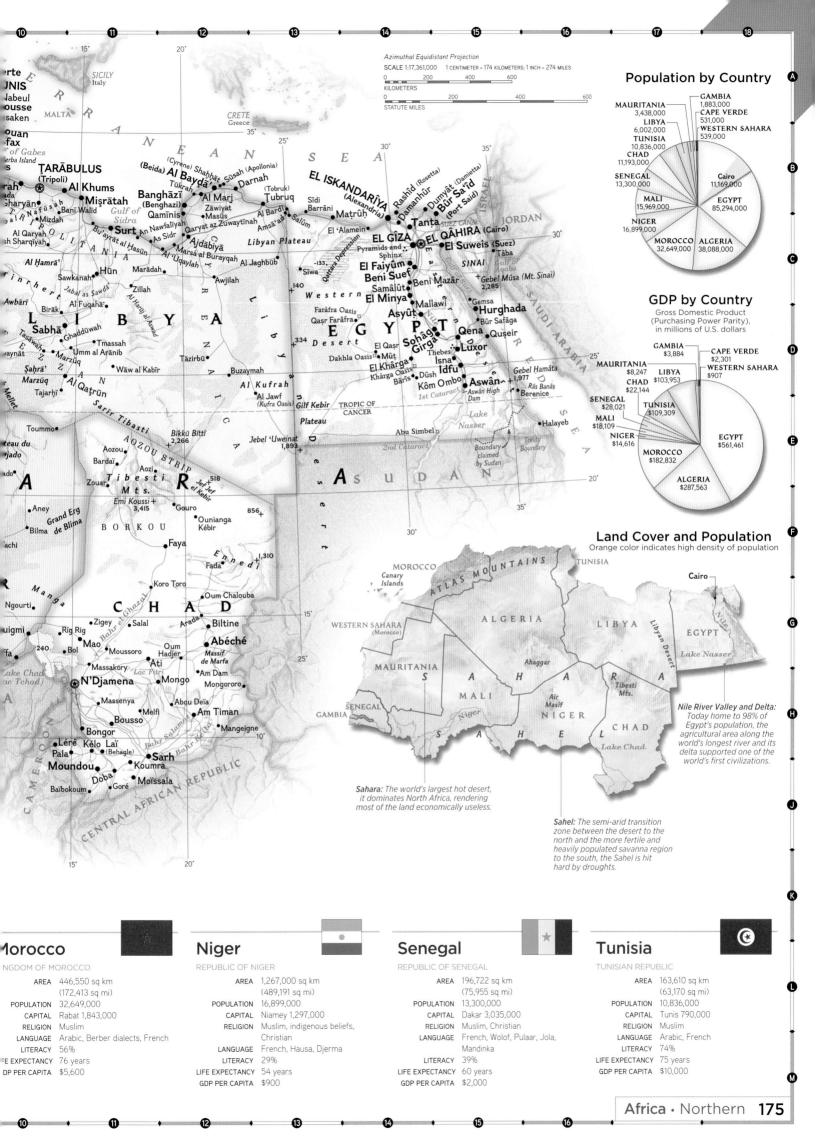

Eastern Africa

Burundi

REPUBLIC OF BURUNDI

AREA	27,830 sq km (10,745 sq mi)
POPULATION	10,888,000
CAPITAL	Bujumbura 393,000
RELIGION	Roman Catholic, indigenous beliefs, Muslim, Protestant
LANGUAGE	Kirundi, French, Swahili
LITERACY	67%
LIFE EXPECTANCY	59 years
GDP PER CAPITA	$600

Central African Republic

CENTRAL AFRICAN REPUBLIC

AREA	622,984 sq km (240,535 sq mi)
POPULATION	5,167,000
CAPITAL	Bangui 740,000
RELIGION	indigenous beliefs, Protestant, Roman Catholic, Muslim
LANGUAGE	French, Sangho, tribal languages
LITERACY	56%
LIFE EXPECTANCY	50 years
GDP PER CAPITA	$800

Congo, Democratic Republic of the

DEMOCRATIC REPUBLIC OF THE CONGO

AREA	2,344,885 sq km (905,365 sq mi)
POPULATION	75,507,000
CAPITAL	Kinshasa 8,798,000
RELIGION	Roman Catholic, Protestant, Kimbanguist, Muslim
LANGUAGE	French, Lingala, Kingwana, Kikongo, Tshiluba
LITERACY	67%
LIFE EXPECTANCY	56 years
GDP PER CAPITA	$400

Djibouti

REPUBLIC OF DJIBOUTI

AREA	23,200 sq km (8,958 sq mi)
POPULATION	792,000
CAPITAL	Djibouti 496,000
RELIGION	Muslim, Christian
LANGUAGE	French, Arabic, Somali, Afar
LITERACY	68%
LIFE EXPECTANCY	62 years
GDP PER CAPITA	$2,800

Eritrea

STATE OF ERITREA

AREA	117,600 sq km (45,406 sq mi)
POPULATION	6,234,000
CAPITAL	Asmara 712,000
RELIGION	Muslim, Coptic Christian, Roman Catholic, Protestant
LANGUAGE	Afar, Arabic, Tigre, Kunama, Tigrinya, other Cushitic languages
LITERACY	68%
LIFE EXPECTANCY	63 years
GDP PER CAPITA	$800

Ethiopia

FEDERAL DEMOCRATIC REP. OF ETHIOPIA

AREA	1,104,300 sq km (426,373 sq mi)
POPULATION	93,877,000
CAPITAL	Addis Ababa 2,979,000
RELIGION	Christian (Orthodox, Protestant), Muslim
LANGUAGE	Amharic, Oromigna, Tigrinya, Guaragigna, Somali
LITERACY	43%
LIFE EXPECTANCY	57 years
GDP PER CAPITA	$1,200

Kenya

REPUBLIC OF KENYA

AREA	580,367 sq km (224,081 sq mi)
POPULATION	44,038,000
CAPITAL	Nairobi 3,363,000
RELIGION	Protestant, Roman Catholic, Muslim, indigenous beliefs
LANGUAGE	English, Kiswahili, many indigenous languages
LITERACY	87%
LIFE EXPECTANCY	63 years
GDP PER CAPITA	$1,900

Rwanda

REPUBLIC OF RWANDA

AREA	26,338 sq km (10,169 sq mi)
POPULATION	12,013,000
CAPITAL	Kigali 1,004,000
RELIGION	Roman Catholic, Protestant, Adventist
LANGUAGE	Kinyarwanda, French, English, Kiswahili
LITERACY	71%
LIFE EXPECTANCY	58 years
GDP PER CAPITA	$1,500

Somalia

SOMALIA

AREA	637,657 sq km (246,201 sq mi)
POPULATION	10,252,000
CAPITAL	Mogadishu 1,554,000
RELIGION	Sunni Muslim
LANGUAGE	Somali, Arabic, Italian, English
LITERACY	38%
LIFE EXPECTANCY	51 years
GDP PER CAPITA	$600

"HORN" OF DARFUR
Southern South Darfur, an area referred to by some as the "Horn" of Darfur, is marginally administered by both Sudan and South Sudan. The future of this resource-rich area is subject to further Sudanese and South Sudanese negotiations.

Population by Country

ERITREA 6,234,000
SOMALIA 10,252,000
CENTRAL AFRICAN REPUBLIC 5,167,000
BURUNDI 10,888,000
DJIBOUTI 792,000
SOUTH SUDAN 11,090,000
RWANDA 12,013,000
SUDAN 26,587,000
ETHIOPIA 93,877,000
UGANDA 34,759,000
DEMOCRATIC REPUBLIC OF THE CONGO 75,507,000
KENYA 44,038,000
TANZANIA 48,262,000
Kinshasa 8,798,000

GDP by Country

Gross Domestic Product (Purchasing Power Parity), in millions of U.S. dollars

ERITREA $4,625
SOMALIA $5,896
CENTRAL AFRICAN REPUBLIC $4,062
BURUNDI $5,820
DJIBOUTI $2,528
RWANDA $16,240
SOUTH SUDAN $16,612
ETHIOPIA $111,308
SUDAN $81,492
DEMOCRATIC REPUBLIC OF THE CONGO $30,182
UGANDA $54,209
TANZANIA $79,552
KENYA $81,425

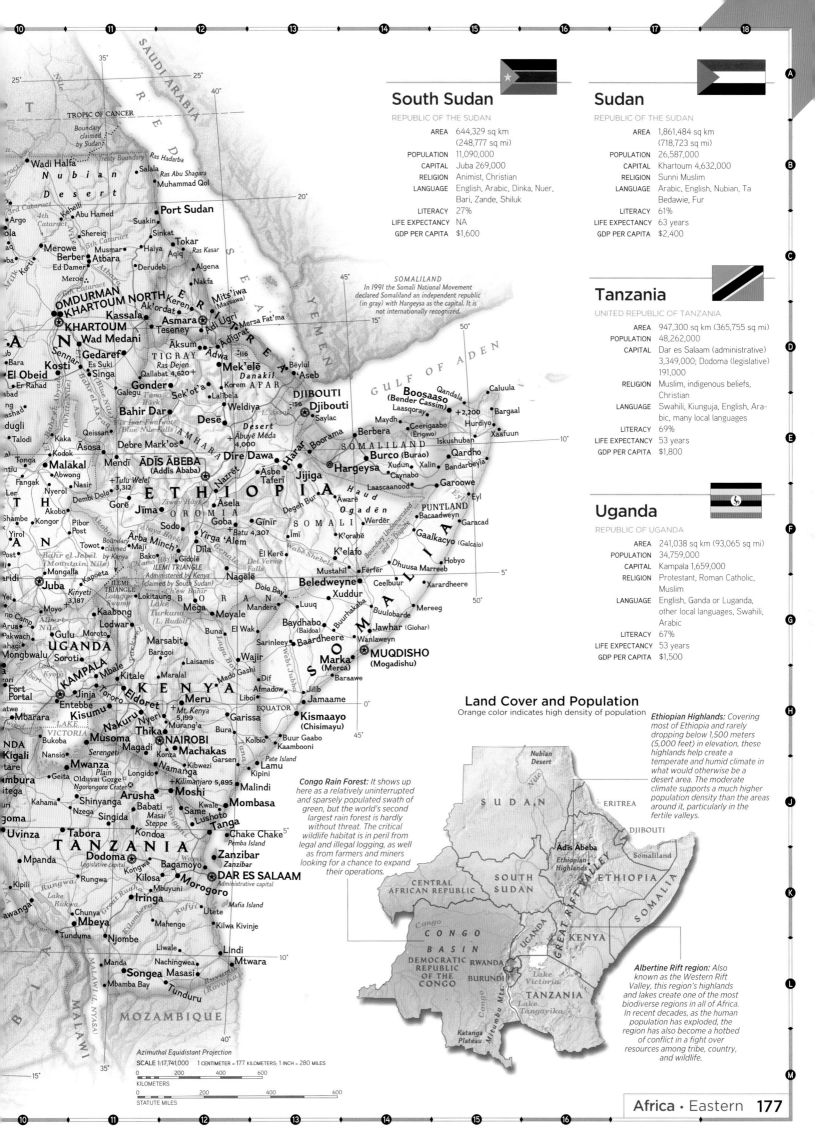

South Sudan
REPUBLIC OF THE SUDAN

AREA	644,329 sq km (248,777 sq mi)
POPULATION	11,090,000
CAPITAL	Juba 269,000
RELIGION	Animist, Christian
LANGUAGE	English, Arabic, Dinka, Nuer, Bari, Zande, Shiluk
LITERACY	27%
LIFE EXPECTANCY	NA
GDP PER CAPITA	$1,600

Sudan
REPUBLIC OF THE SUDAN

AREA	1,861,484 sq km (718,723 sq mi)
POPULATION	26,587,000
CAPITAL	Khartoum 4,632,000
RELIGION	Sunni Muslim
LANGUAGE	Arabic, English, Nubian, Ta Bedawie, Fur
LITERACY	61%
LIFE EXPECTANCY	63 years
GDP PER CAPITA	$2,400

Tanzania
UNITED REPUBLIC OF TANZANIA

AREA	947,300 sq km (365,755 sq mi)
POPULATION	48,262,000
CAPITAL	Dar es Salaam (administrative) 3,349,000; Dodoma (legislative) 191,000
RELIGION	Muslim, indigenous beliefs, Christian
LANGUAGE	Swahili, Kiunguja, English, Arabic, many local languages
LITERACY	69%
LIFE EXPECTANCY	53 years
GDP PER CAPITA	$1,800

Uganda
REPUBLIC OF UGANDA

AREA	241,038 sq km (93,065 sq mi)
POPULATION	34,759,000
CAPITAL	Kampala 1,659,000
RELIGION	Protestant, Roman Catholic, Muslim
LANGUAGE	English, Ganda or Luganda, other local languages, Swahili, Arabic
LITERACY	67%
LIFE EXPECTANCY	53 years
GDP PER CAPITA	$1,500

SOMALILAND
In 1991 the Somali National Movement declared Somaliland an independent republic (in gray) with Hargeysa as the capital. It is not internationally recognized.

Land Cover and Population
Orange color indicates high density of population

Congo Rain Forest: It shows up here as a relatively uninterrupted and sparsely populated swath of green, but the world's second largest rain forest is hardly without threat. The critical wildlife habitat is in peril from legal and illegal logging, as well as from farmers and miners looking for a chance to expand their operations.

Ethiopian Highlands: Covering most of Ethiopia and rarely dropping below 1,500 meters (5,000 feet) in elevation, these highlands help create a temperate and humid climate in what would otherwise be a desert area. The moderate climate supports a much higher population density than the areas around it, particularly in the fertile valleys.

Albertine Rift region: Also known as the Western Rift Valley, this region's highlands and lakes create one of the most biodiverse regions in all of Africa. In recent decades, as the human population has exploded, the region has also become a hotbot of conflict in a fight over resources among tribe, country, and wildlife.

Azimuthal Equidistant Projection

SCALE 1:17,741,000   1 CENTIMETER = 177 KILOMETERS; 1 INCH = 280 MILES

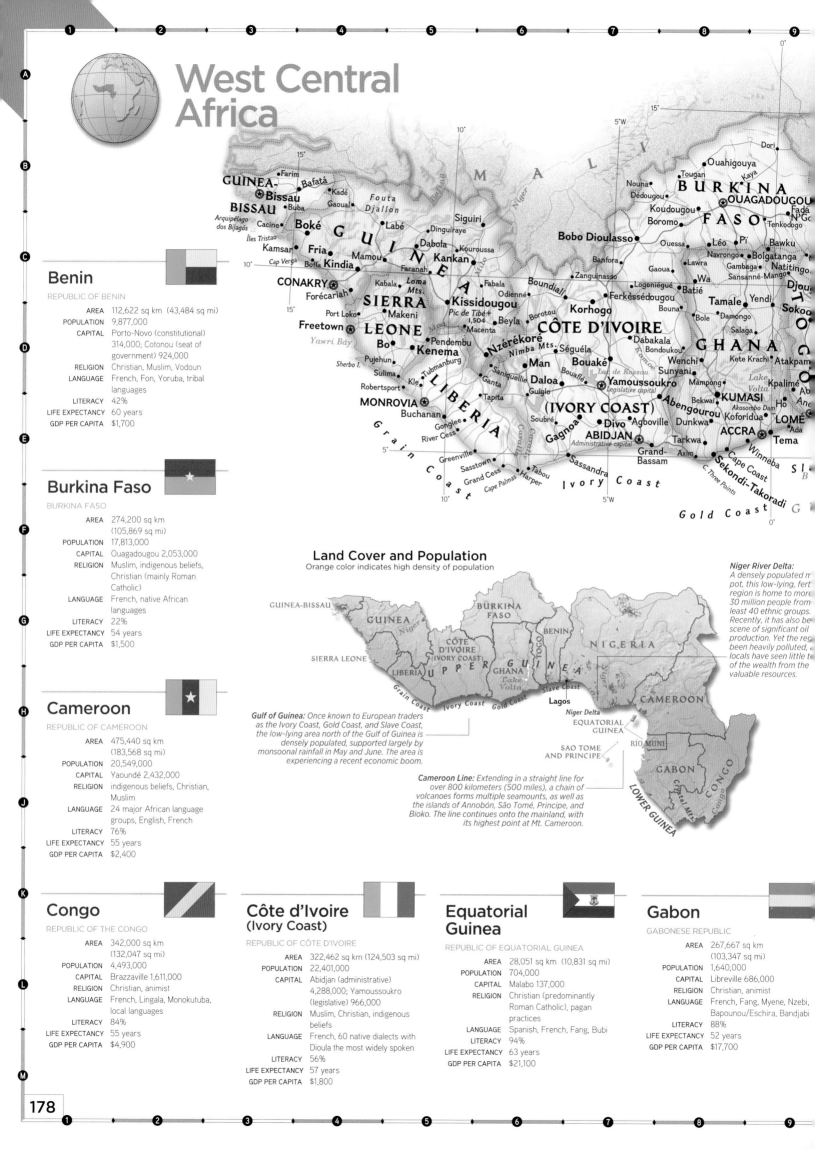

West Central Africa

Benin

REPUBLIC OF BENIN

AREA	112,622 sq km (43,484 sq mi)
POPULATION	9,877,000
CAPITAL	Porto-Novo (constitutional) 314,000; Cotonou (seat of government) 924,000
RELIGION	Christian, Muslim, Vodoun
LANGUAGE	French, Fon, Yoruba, tribal languages
LITERACY	42%
LIFE EXPECTANCY	60 years
GDP PER CAPITA	$1,700

Burkina Faso

BURKINA FASO

AREA	274,200 sq km (105,869 sq mi)
POPULATION	17,813,000
CAPITAL	Ouagadougou 2,053,000
RELIGION	Muslim, indigenous beliefs, Christian (mainly Roman Catholic)
LANGUAGE	French, native African languages
LITERACY	22%
LIFE EXPECTANCY	54 years
GDP PER CAPITA	$1,500

Cameroon

REPUBLIC OF CAMEROON

AREA	475,440 sq km (183,568 sq mi)
POPULATION	20,549,000
CAPITAL	Yaoundé 2,432,000
RELIGION	indigenous beliefs, Christian, Muslim
LANGUAGE	24 major African language groups, English, French
LITERACY	76%
LIFE EXPECTANCY	55 years
GDP PER CAPITA	$2,400

Congo

REPUBLIC OF THE CONGO

AREA	342,000 sq km (132,047 sq mi)
POPULATION	4,493,000
CAPITAL	Brazzaville 1,611,000
RELIGION	Christian, animist
LANGUAGE	French, Lingala, Monokutuba, local languages
LITERACY	84%
LIFE EXPECTANCY	55 years
GDP PER CAPITA	$4,900

Côte d'Ivoire (Ivory Coast)

REPUBLIC OF CÔTE D'IVOIRE

AREA	322,462 sq km (124,503 sq mi)
POPULATION	22,401,000
CAPITAL	Abidjan (administrative) 4,288,000; Yamoussoukro (legislative) 966,000
RELIGION	Muslim, Christian, indigenous beliefs
LANGUAGE	French, 60 native dialects with Dioula the most widely spoken
LITERACY	56%
LIFE EXPECTANCY	57 years
GDP PER CAPITA	$1,800

Equatorial Guinea

REPUBLIC OF EQUATORIAL GUINEA

AREA	28,051 sq km (10,831 sq mi)
POPULATION	704,000
CAPITAL	Malabo 137,000
RELIGION	Christian (predominantly Roman Catholic), pagan practices
LANGUAGE	Spanish, French, Fang, Bubi
LITERACY	94%
LIFE EXPECTANCY	63 years
GDP PER CAPITA	$21,100

Gabon

GABONESE REPUBLIC

AREA	267,667 sq km (103,347 sq mi)
POPULATION	1,640,000
CAPITAL	Libreville 686,000
RELIGION	Christian, animist
LANGUAGE	French, Fang, Myene, Nzebi, Bapounou/Eschira, Bandjabi
LITERACY	88%
LIFE EXPECTANCY	52 years
GDP PER CAPITA	$17,700

Land Cover and Population

Orange color indicates high density of population

Gulf of Guinea: Once known to European traders as the Ivory Coast, Gold Coast, and Slave Coast, the low-lying area north of the Gulf of Guinea is densely populated, supported largely by monsoonal rainfall in May and June. The area is experiencing a recent economic boom.

Niger River Delta: A densely populated m[...] pot, this low-lying, fert[...] region is home to more [...] 30 million people from [...] least 40 ethnic groups. [...] Recently, it has also be[...] scene of significant oil [...] production. Yet the reg[...] been heavily polluted, [...] locals have seen little t[...] of the wealth from the [...] valuable resources.

Cameroon Line: Extending in a straight line for over 800 kilometers (500 miles), a chain of volcanoes forms multiple seamounts, as well as the islands of Annobón, São Tomé, Príncipe, and Bioko. The line continues onto the mainland, with its highest point at Mt. Cameroon.

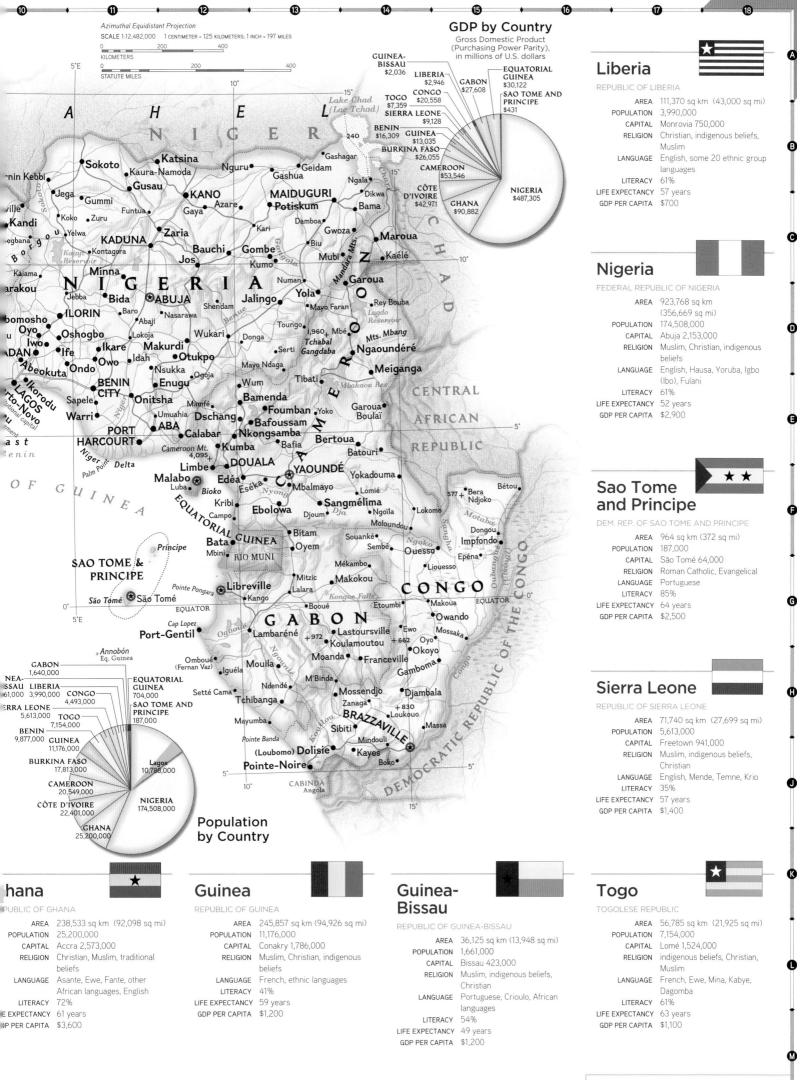

Azimuthal Equidistant Projection
SCALE 1:12,482,000   1 CENTIMETER = 125 KILOMETERS; 1 INCH = 197 MILES
KILOMETERS   0   200   400
STATUTE MILES   0   200   400

GDP by Country

Gross Domestic Product (Purchasing Power Parity), in millions of U.S. dollars

- GUINEA-BISSAU $2,036
- LIBERIA $2,946
- TOGO $7,359
- SIERRA LEONE $9,128
- BENIN $16,309
- BURKINA FASO $26,055
- GABON $27,608
- EQUATORIAL GUINEA $30,122
- SAO TOME AND PRINCIPE $431
- CONGO $20,558
- GUINEA $13,035
- CAMEROON $53,546
- CÔTE D'IVOIRE $42,971
- GHANA $90,882
- NIGERIA $487,305

Population by Country

- GABON 1,640,000
- GUINEA-BISSAU 1,661,000
- LIBERIA 3,990,000
- CONGO 4,493,000
- SIERRA LEONE 5,613,000
- TOGO 7,154,000
- BENIN 9,877,000
- GUINEA 11,176,000
- BURKINA FASO 17,813,000
- CAMEROON 20,549,000
- CÔTE D'IVOIRE 22,401,000
- GHANA 25,200,000
- EQUATORIAL GUINEA 704,000
- SAO TOME AND PRINCIPE 187,000
- Lagos 10,788,000
- NIGERIA 174,508,000

Liberia

REPUBLIC OF LIBERIA

AREA	111,370 sq km (43,000 sq mi)
POPULATION	3,990,000
CAPITAL	Monrovia 750,000
RELIGION	Christian, indigenous beliefs, Muslim
LANGUAGE	English, some 20 ethnic group languages
LITERACY	61%
LIFE EXPECTANCY	57 years
GDP PER CAPITA	$700

Nigeria

FEDERAL REPUBLIC OF NIGERIA

AREA	923,768 sq km (356,669 sq mi)
POPULATION	174,508,000
CAPITAL	Abuja 2,153,000
RELIGION	Muslim, Christian, indigenous beliefs
LANGUAGE	English, Hausa, Yoruba, Igbo (Ibo), Fulani
LITERACY	61%
LIFE EXPECTANCY	52 years
GDP PER CAPITA	$2,900

Sao Tome and Principe

DEM. REP. OF SAO TOME AND PRINCIPE

AREA	964 sq km (372 sq mi)
POPULATION	187,000
CAPITAL	São Tomé 64,000
RELIGION	Roman Catholic, Evangelical
LANGUAGE	Portuguese
LITERACY	85%
LIFE EXPECTANCY	64 years
GDP PER CAPITA	$2,500

Sierra Leone

REPUBLIC OF SIERRA LEONE

AREA	71,740 sq km (27,699 sq mi)
POPULATION	5,613,000
CAPITAL	Freetown 941,000
RELIGION	Muslim, indigenous beliefs, Christian
LANGUAGE	English, Mende, Temne, Krio
LITERACY	35%
LIFE EXPECTANCY	57 years
GDP PER CAPITA	$1,400

Ghana

REPUBLIC OF GHANA

AREA	238,533 sq km (92,098 sq mi)
POPULATION	25,200,000
CAPITAL	Accra 2,573,000
RELIGION	Christian, Muslim, traditional beliefs
LANGUAGE	Asante, Ewe, Fante, other African languages, English
LITERACY	72%
LIFE EXPECTANCY	61 years
GDP PER CAPITA	$3,600

Guinea

REPUBLIC OF GUINEA

AREA	245,857 sq km (94,926 sq mi)
POPULATION	11,176,000
CAPITAL	Conakry 1,786,000
RELIGION	Muslim, Christian, indigenous beliefs
LANGUAGE	French, ethnic languages
LITERACY	41%
LIFE EXPECTANCY	59 years
GDP PER CAPITA	$1,200

Guinea-Bissau

REPUBLIC OF GUINEA-BISSAU

AREA	36,125 sq km (13,948 sq mi)
POPULATION	1,661,000
CAPITAL	Bissau 423,000
RELIGION	Muslim, indigenous beliefs, Christian
LANGUAGE	Portuguese, Crioulo, African languages
LITERACY	54%
LIFE EXPECTANCY	49 years
GDP PER CAPITA	$1,200

Togo

TOGOLESE REPUBLIC

AREA	56,785 sq km (21,925 sq mi)
POPULATION	7,154,000
CAPITAL	Lomé 1,524,000
RELIGION	indigenous beliefs, Christian, Muslim
LANGUAGE	French, Ewe, Mina, Kabye, Dagomba
LITERACY	61%
LIFE EXPECTANCY	63 years
GDP PER CAPITA	$1,100

Angola
REPUBLIC OF ANGOLA

AREA	1,246,700 sq km (481,354 sq mi)
POPULATION	18,565,000
CAPITAL	Luanda 4,790,000
RELIGION	indigenous beliefs, Roman Catholic, Protestant
LANGUAGE	Portuguese, Bantu and other African languages
LITERACY	70%
LIFE EXPECTANCY	55 years
GDP PER CAPITA	$6,500

Botswana
REPUBLIC OF BOTSWANA

AREA	581,730 sq km (224,607 sq mi)
POPULATION	2,128,000
CAPITAL	Gaborone 202,000
RELIGION	Christian, Badimo
LANGUAGE	Setswana, Kalanga
LITERACY	85%
LIFE EXPECTANCY	56 years
GDP PER CAPITA	$17,500

Comoros
UNION OF THE COMOROS

AREA	2,235 sq km (863 sq mi)
POPULATION	752,000
CAPITAL	Moroni 54,000
RELIGION	Sunni Muslim
LANGUAGE	Arabic, French, Shikomoro
LITERACY	75%
LIFE EXPECTANCY	63 years
GDP PER CAPITA	$1,300

Lesotho
KINGDOM OF LESOTHO

AREA	30,355 sq km (11,720 sq mi)
POPULATION	1,936,000
CAPITAL	Maseru 239,000
RELIGION	Christian, indigenous beliefs
LANGUAGE	Sesotho, English, Zulu, Xhosa
LITERACY	90%
LIFE EXPECTANCY	52 years
GDP PER CAPITA	$2,100

Madagascar
REPUBLIC OF MADAGASCAR

AREA	587,041 sq km (226,658 sq mi)
POPULATION	22,599,000
CAPITAL	Antananarivo 1,987,000
RELIGION	indigenous beliefs, Christian, Muslim
LANGUAGE	English, French, Malagasy
LITERACY	65%
LIFE EXPECTANCY	64 years
GDP PER CAPITA	$1,000

Mauritius
REPUBLIC OF MAURITIUS

AREA	2,040 sq km (788 sq mi)
POPULATION	1,322,000
CAPITAL	Port Louis 151,000
RELIGION	Hindu, Roman Catholic, Muslim, other Christian
LANGUAGE	Creole, Bhojpuri, French
LITERACY	89%
LIFE EXPECTANCY	75 years
GDP PER CAPITA	$16,300

Malawi
REPUBLIC OF MALAWI

AREA	118,484 sq km (45,747 sq mi)
POPULATION	16,778,000
CAPITAL	Lilongwe 772,000
RELIGION	Christian, Muslim
LANGUAGE	Chichewa, Chinyanja, Chiyao, Chitumbuka
LITERACY	75%
LIFE EXPECTANCY	52 years
GDP PER CAPITA	$900

Mozambique
REPUBLIC OF MOZAMBIQUE

AREA	799,380 sq km (308,642 sq mi)
POPULATION	24,097,000
CAPITAL	Maputo 1,150,000
RELIGION	Roman Catholic, Muslim, Zionist Christian
LANGUAGE	Emakhuwa, Xichangana, Portuguese, Elomwe, Cisena, Echuwabo, local languages
LITERACY	56%
LIFE EXPECTANCY	52 years
GDP PER CAPITA	$1,300

Population by Country

SWAZILAND 1,403,000
LESOTHO 1,936,000
NAMIBIA 2,183,000
ZAMBIA 14,222,000
MALAWI 16,778,000
ANGOLA 18,565,000
Luanda 4,790,000
MADAGASCAR 22,599,000
MOZAMBIQUE 24,097,000
SOUTH AFRICA 48,601,000
ZIMBABWE 13,183,000
BOTSWANA 2,128,000
COMOROS 752,000
SEYCHELLES 91,000
MAURITIUS 1,322,000

GDP (Cour...)
Gross Domestic Product (PPP), in millions of U.S. dollars

SWAZILAND $6,169
LESOTHO $4,185
NAMIBIA $17,770
ZAMBIA $25,956
MALAWI $15,621
ANGOLA $134,878
MADAGASCAR $22,225
MOZAMBIQUE $28,796
SOUTH AFRICA $604,103
ZIMBABWE $7,423
BOTSWANA $33,233
COMOROS $915
SEYCHELLES $2,528
MAURITIUS $21,297

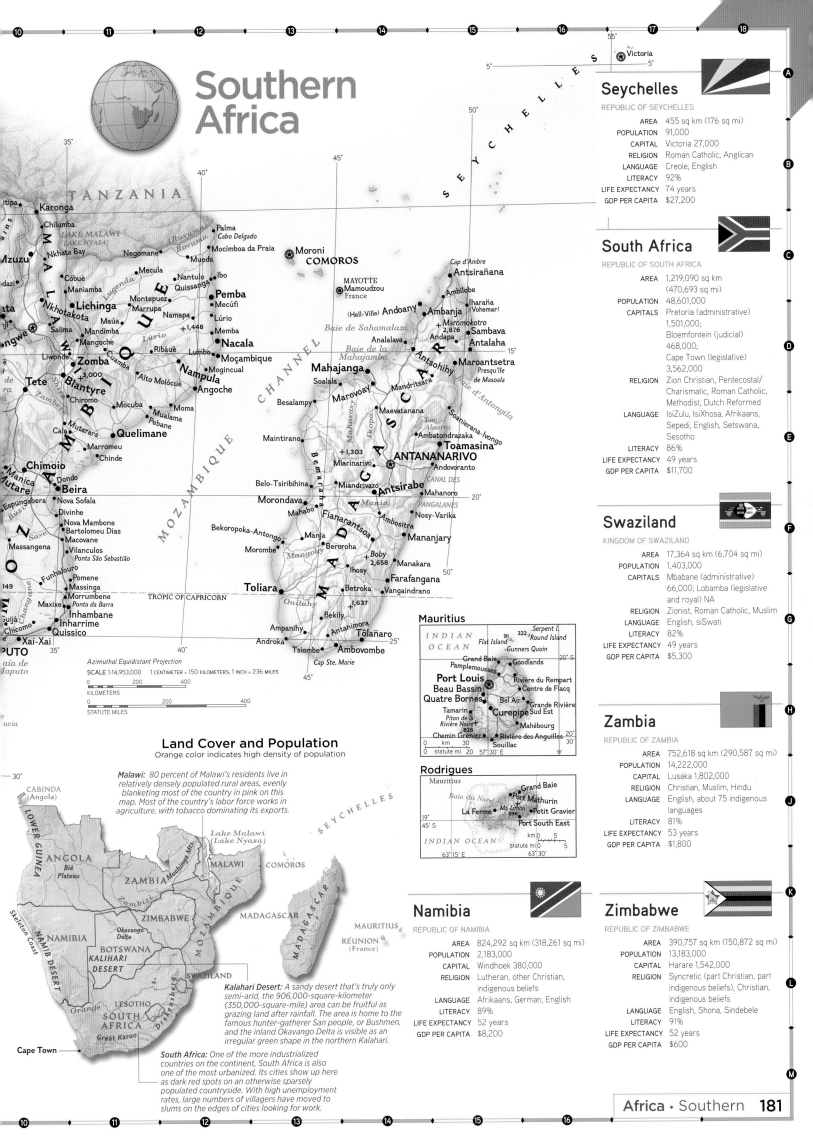

Southern Africa

Seychelles
REPUBLIC OF SEYCHELLES
AREA	455 sq km (176 sq mi)
POPULATION	91,000
CAPITAL	Victoria 27,000
RELIGION	Roman Catholic, Anglican
LANGUAGE	Creole, English
LITERACY	92%
LIFE EXPECTANCY	74 years
GDP PER CAPITA	$27,200

South Africa
REPUBLIC OF SOUTH AFRICA
AREA	1,219,090 sq km (470,693 sq mi)
POPULATION	48,601,000
CAPITALS	Pretoria (administrative) 1,501,000; Bloemfontein (judicial) 468,000; Cape Town (legislative) 3,562,000
RELIGION	Zion Christian, Pentecostal/Charismatic, Roman Catholic, Methodist, Dutch Reformed
LANGUAGE	IsiZulu, IsiXhosa, Afrikaans, Sepedi, English, Setswana, Sesotho
LITERACY	86%
LIFE EXPECTANCY	49 years
GDP PER CAPITA	$11,700

Swaziland
KINGDOM OF SWAZILAND
AREA	17,364 sq km (6,704 sq mi)
POPULATION	1,403,000
CAPITALS	Mbabane (administrative) 66,000; Lobamba (legislative and royal) NA
RELIGION	Zionist, Roman Catholic, Muslim
LANGUAGE	English, siSwati
LITERACY	82%
LIFE EXPECTANCY	49 years
GDP PER CAPITA	$5,300

Zambia
REPUBLIC OF ZAMBIA
AREA	752,618 sq km (290,587 sq mi)
POPULATION	14,222,000
CAPITAL	Lusaka 1,802,000
RELIGION	Christian, Muslim, Hindu
LANGUAGE	English, about 75 indigenous languages
LITERACY	81%
LIFE EXPECTANCY	53 years
GDP PER CAPITA	$1,800

Namibia
REPUBLIC OF NAMIBIA
AREA	824,292 sq km (318,261 sq mi)
POPULATION	2,183,000
CAPITAL	Windhoek 380,000
RELIGION	Lutheran, other Christian, indigenous beliefs
LANGUAGE	Afrikaans, German, English
LITERACY	89%
LIFE EXPECTANCY	52 years
GDP PER CAPITA	$8,200

Zimbabwe
REPUBLIC OF ZIMBABWE
AREA	390,757 sq km (150,872 sq mi)
POPULATION	13,183,000
CAPITAL	Harare 1,542,000
RELIGION	Syncretic (part Christian, part indigenous beliefs), Christian, indigenous beliefs
LANGUAGE	English, Shona, Sindebele
LITERACY	91%
LIFE EXPECTANCY	52 years
GDP PER CAPITA	$600

Azimuthal Equidistant Projection
SCALE 1:14,953,000   1 CENTIMETER = 150 KILOMETERS; 1 INCH = 236 MILES
KILOMETERS
STATUTE MILES

Land Cover and Population
Orange color indicates high density of population

Malawi: 80 percent of Malawi's residents live in relatively densely populated rural areas, evenly blanketing most of the country in pink on this map. Most of the country's labor force works in agriculture, with tobacco dominating its exports.

Kalahari Desert: A sandy desert that's truly only semi-arid, the 906,000-square-kilometer (350,000-square-mile) area can be fruitful as grazing land after rainfall. The area is home to the famous hunter-gatherer San people, or Bushmen, and the inland Okavango Delta is visible as an irregular green shape in the northern Kalahari.

South Africa: One of the more industrialized countries on the continent, South Africa is also one of the most urbanized. Its cities show up here as dark red spots on an otherwise sparsely populated countryside. With high unemployment rates, large numbers of villagers have moved to slums on the edges of cities looking for work.

Mauritius

Rodrigues

Australia
and Oceania

Australia is Earth's smallest continent. Taken together with the myriad islands of Oceania, however, it dominates a vast, watery realm. From the dry bulk of the Australian continent to the scattered atolls of the South Pacific Ocean, not all these islands belong to the same geological structure, though many are united by common formation, and often through links of ecology, culture, and history.

Appropriately for such a watery domain, Australia and Oceania are known as much for their coral reefs and other underwaterscapes as for the islands that define the region. From Australia's Great Barrier Reef, the world's largest, to the Line Islands, possibly the world's most pristine, these underwater ecosystems are among the most exuberant spectacles of life on Earth.

Australia itself is an ancient land in both geological and human terms—the first people arrived here perhaps 50,000 years ago. Farther out, the tiny islands of Micronesia, Melanesia, and beyond look on the map like a mere dusting of sand shaken loose from the shores of Southeast Asia. But seen from below, they are the tips of colossal mountains, rising in great chains and clusters from the sea-bed below. Oceania, built up by eons of volcanic activity, remains one of the most seismically active regions of the world today.

Population by Country
Top Ten Countries

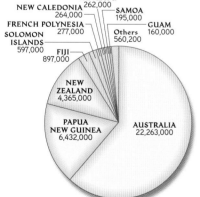

VANUATU 262,000
NEW CALEDONIA 264,000
SAMOA 195,000
FRENCH POLYNESIA 277,000
GUAM 160,000
SOLOMON ISLANDS 597,000
Others 560,200
FIJI 897,000
NEW ZEALAND 4,365,000
PAPUA NEW GUINEA 6,432,000
AUSTRALIA 22,263,000

GDP by Country
Gross Domestic Product (Purchasing Power Parity), in millions of U.S. dollars

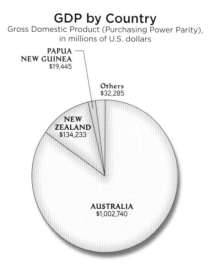

PAPUA NEW GUINEA $19,445
Others $32,285
NEW ZEALAND $134,233
AUSTRALIA $1,002,740

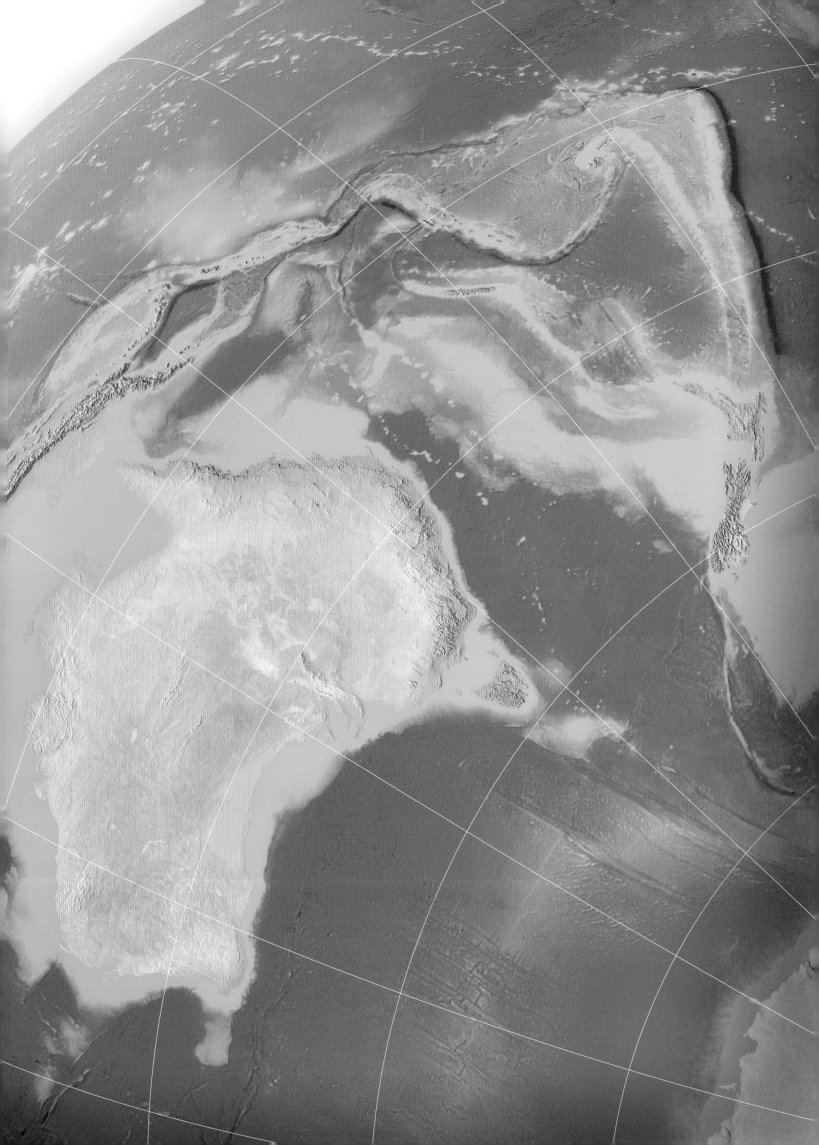

Physical
Australia

Political Australia

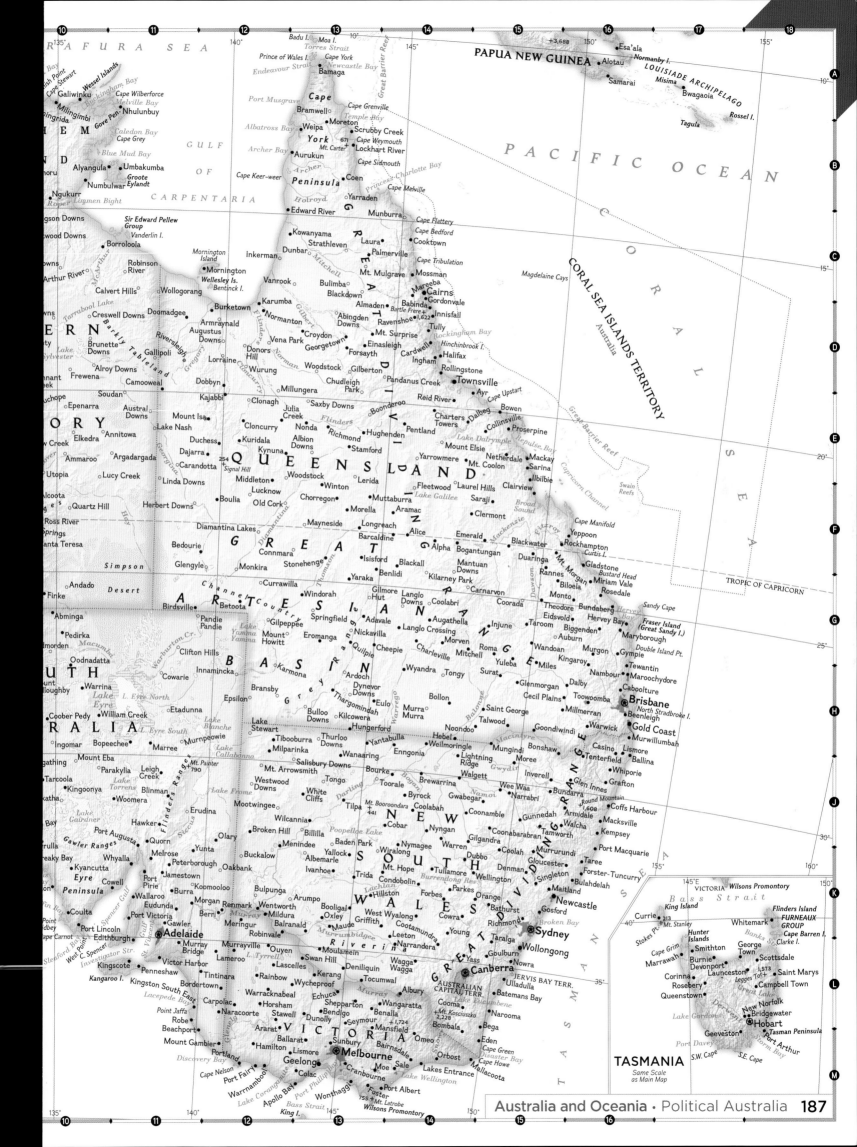

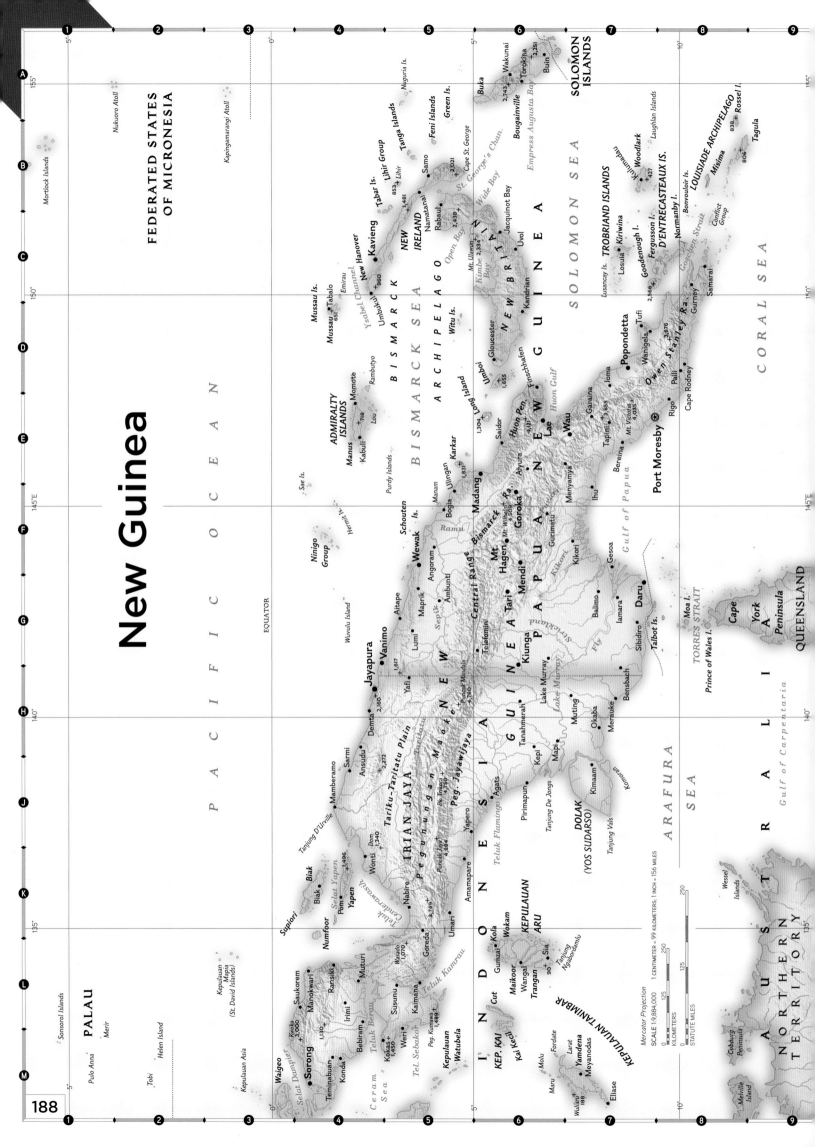

New Guinea

FEDERATED STATES
OF MICRONESIA

PALAU

INDONESIA

PAPUA NEW GUINEA

IRIAN JAYA

SOLOMON
ISLANDS

AUSTRALIA

QUEENSLAND

NORTHERN TERRITORY

PACIFIC OCEAN

BISMARCK SEA

BISMARCK ARCHIPELAGO

SOLOMON SEA

CORAL SEA

ARAFURA SEA

Gulf of Carpentaria

Gulf of Papua

EQUATOR

NEW BRITAIN

NEW IRELAND

ADMIRALTY ISLANDS

TROBRIAND ISLANDS

LOUISIADE ARCHIPELAGO

D'ENTRECASTEAUX IS.

Mortlock Islands
Nukuoro Atoll
Kapingamarangi Atoll

Sonsorol Islands
Pulo Anna
Merir
Tobi
Helen Island
Kepulauan Asia
Kepulauan Mapia
(St. David Islands)

Buka
Wakunai
Torokina 2,251
Buin
Bougainville 2,743
Empress Augusta Bay

Feni Islands
Green Is.
Tanga Islands
Lihir Group 853
Lihir 1,481
Tabar Is.
Samo
2,021
Cape St. George
St. George's Chan.
Namatanai
Rabaul 2,438
Uvol
Jacquinot Bay
Open Bay
Wide Bay
Kimbe 2,334
Mt. Ulawun
Kandrian

Mussau Is.
Mussau 651
Tabalo
Emirau
Ysabel Channel
New Hanover 960
Kavieng

Umboi
Long Island 1,304
Karkar 1,831
Manam
Bogia
Madang
Saidor
Finschhafen 1,655
Huon Pen.
4,121
Lae
Wau
Huon Gulf

Witu Is.
Gloucester
1,655
Ulingan

Monote 718
Manus
Kabuli
Lou
Purdy Islands
Rambutyo
Sae Is.

Wuvulu Island
Ninigo Group
Hermit Is.
Schouten Is.
Wewak
Aitape
Angoram
Maprik
Ambunti
Lumi

Vanimo 1,617
Jayapura
Demta
Yafi
2,160
Sarmi 2,272
Mamberamo
Ansudu

Biak
Supiori
Numfoor
Yapen 1,496
Pom
Wonti
Dom 1,340
Tanjung D'Urville
Selat Yapen
Teluk Cenderawasih

Waigeo
Saukorem
Manokwari
Ransiki
Irimi
Bebiram
Sorong
Teminabuan
Konda
Kwoka 3,000
1,130
Teluk Berau
Selat Dampier
Ceram Sea
Tel. Bintuni

KEP. KAI
Kai Kecil
Kai Besar
Kokas 1,450
Weri 1,489
Kepulauan Watubela
Peg. Kumawa 1,070
Kaimana
Teluk Kamrau
Teluk Sebakor
Peg. Fakfak
Nabire
Umari
Goreda
Wasado 1,070
Muturi
Susunu
3,749

Central Range
Sepik
Ramu
Telefomin
Mt. Hagen
Mendi
Tari
Goroka 4,509
Mt. Wilhelm
Bismarck Ra. 3,676
Gurimatu
Garaina
Toma
Tapini 3,655
Bereina
Mt. Victoria 4,035
Menyamya
Ihu
Kerema

Kikori
Kikori
Gesoa
Balimo
Iamara
Daru
Sibidiro
Bensbach
Talbot Is.

Kiunga
Lake Murray
Lake Murray
Tanahmerah
Kepi
Mapi
Agats
Pirimapun
Tanjung De Jongs
Kimaam
Muting
Okaba
Merauke
Komoran

Pegunungan Maoke
Puncak Jaya 4,884
Pk. Trikora 4,750
Peg. Jayawijaya
Tariku-Taritatu Plain
Taritatu
Mandala 4,760
Oenaka

DOLAK
(YOS SUDARSO)
Tanjung Vals

Amamapare
Yapero

KEPULAUAN ARU
Wokam
Kola
Gumzai
Maikoor
Wangal
Trangan 90
Sia
Tanjung Ngabordamu
Cut

KEPULAUAN TANIMBAR
Larat
Yamdena
Meyanodas
Fordate
Molu
Maru
Wuliaru 183
Selaru
Eilase

Wessel Islands
Melville Island
Cobourg Peninsula
Cape York Peninsula
Moa I.
Prince of Wales I.
TORRES STRAIT

Owen Stanley Ra.
Popondetta
Wanigela
Tufi
Dobu
Port Moresby
Rigo
Pali
Cape Rodney

Woodlark 427
Kulumadau
Laughlan Islands
Lusancay Is.
Kiriwina
Kitava
Losuia
Goodenough I. 2,566
Fergusson I.
Normanby I.
Goschen Strait
Samarai
Gurney
Bonvouloir I.
Conflict Group
Misima 806
Tagula
Rossel I. 838
2,021

Mercator Projection
SCALE 1:9,884,000   1 CENTIMETER = 99 KILOMETERS; 1 INCH = 156 MILES
KILOMETERS   0   125   250
STATUTE MILES   0   125   250

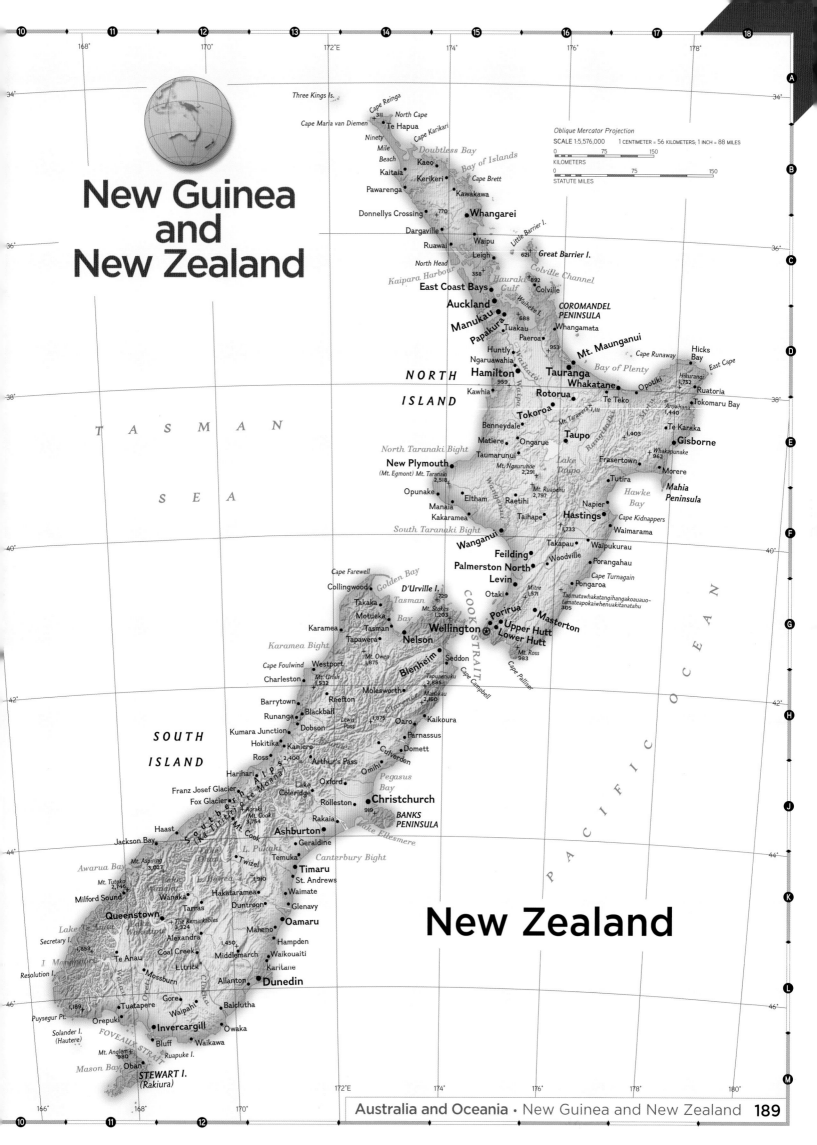

New Guinea and New Zealand

New Zealand

NORTH ISLAND

Three Kings Is.
Cape Reinga
North Cape
Cape Maria van Diemen
Te Hapua
311
Ninety
Mile
Beach
Kaeo
Doubtless Bay
Kaitaia
Kerikeri
Cape Brett
Bay of Islands
Pawarenga
Kawakawa
Cape Karikari
Donnellys Crossing
770
Whangarei
Dargaville
Waipu
Little Barrier I.
Ruawai
Leigh
621
Great Barrier I.
North Head
358
Colville
892
Colville Channel
Kaipara Harbour
Hauraki
Gulf
COROMANDEL
PENINSULA
East Coast Bays
Waiheke I.
Auckland
Whangamata
Manukau
688
Papakura
Tuakau
Paeroa
953
Mt. Maunganui
Huntly
Hicks
Bay
Ngaruawahia
Cape Runaway
Waikato
Tauranga
Hikurangi
Hamilton
959
Whakatane
1,752
East Cape
Kawhia
Rotorua
Opotiki
Ruatoria
Tokoroa
Te Teko
Tokomaru Bay
Mt. Tarawera 1,111
Te Karaka
NORTH
Benneydale
Taupo
1,403
Arowhana
1,440
ISLAND
Matiere
Ongarue
Mt. Tarawera
Gisborne
North Taranaki Bight
Taumarunui
Frasertown
Whakapunake
962
New Plymouth
Mt. Ngauruhoe
2,291
Lake
Taupo
Morere
(Mt. Egmont) Mt. Taranaki
2,518
Tutira
Mahia
Peninsula
Opunake
Mt. Ruapehu
2,797
Napier
Hawke
Bay
Manaia
Eltham
Raetihi
Hastings
Cape Kidnappers
Kakaramea
Taihape
1,733
Waimarama
South Taranaki Bight
Takapau
Waipukurau
Wanganui
Feilding
Woodville
Porangahau
Palmerston North
Cape Turnagain
Levin
Pongaroa
Taumatawhakatangihangakoauauo-
tamateapokaiwhenuakitanatahu
305

SOUTH ISLAND

Cape Farewell
Collingwood
Golden Bay
D'Urville I.
Otaki
Mitre
1,571
Takaka
729
Porirua
Masterton
Motueka
Tasman
Mt. Stokes
1,203
Upper Hutt
Karamea
Tasman
Bay
Wellington
Lower Hutt
Tapawera
Nelson
Mt. Ross
983
Karamea Bight
Mt. Owen
1,875
Seddon
Cape Foulwind
Westport
Blenheim
Cape Campbell
Charleston
Mt. Una
1,532
Tapuaenuku
2,885
Cape Palliser
Barrytown
Reefton
Molesworth
Matakao
2,160
Runanga
Blackball
1,875
Oaro
Dobson
Lewis
Pass
Kaikoura
Kumara Junction
Hokitika
Parnassus
Kaniere
Domett
Ross
2,400
Arthur's Pass
Culverden
Harihari
Omihi
Pegasus
Bay
Franz Josef Glacier
Lake
Oxford
Fox Glacier
Coleridge
Rolleston
Christchurch
Aoraki
(Mt. Cook)
3,754
Rakaia
919
BANKS
PENINSULA
Haast
Mt. Cook
Ashburton
Jackson Bay
Geraldine
L. Pukaki
SOUTH
Awarua Bay
Mt. Aspiring
3,027
Twizel
Temuka
Canterbury Bight
ISLAND
Mt. Tutoko
2,746
1,910
Timaru
St. Andrews
Milford Sound
Wanaka
Hakataramea
Waimate
Southern Alps
Tarras
Duntroon
Glenavy
Queenstown
The Remarkables
2,324
Maheno
Oamaru
Alexandra
Secretary I.
Hampden
1,853
Coal Creek
1,450
Middlemarch
Waikouaiti
Te Anau
Lutrick
Karitane
Resolution I.
Allanton
Dunedin
Mossburn
I Mangnuru
Gore
1,189
Tuatapere
Waipahi
Balclutha
Orepuki
Owaka
Puysegur Pt.
Invercargill
Solander I.
(Hautere)
Bluff
Waikawa
Mt. Anglem
980
Ruapuke I.
FOVEAUX STRAIT
Mason Bay
Oban
STEWART I.
(Rakiura)

TASMAN SEA

PACIFIC OCEAN

COOK STRAIT

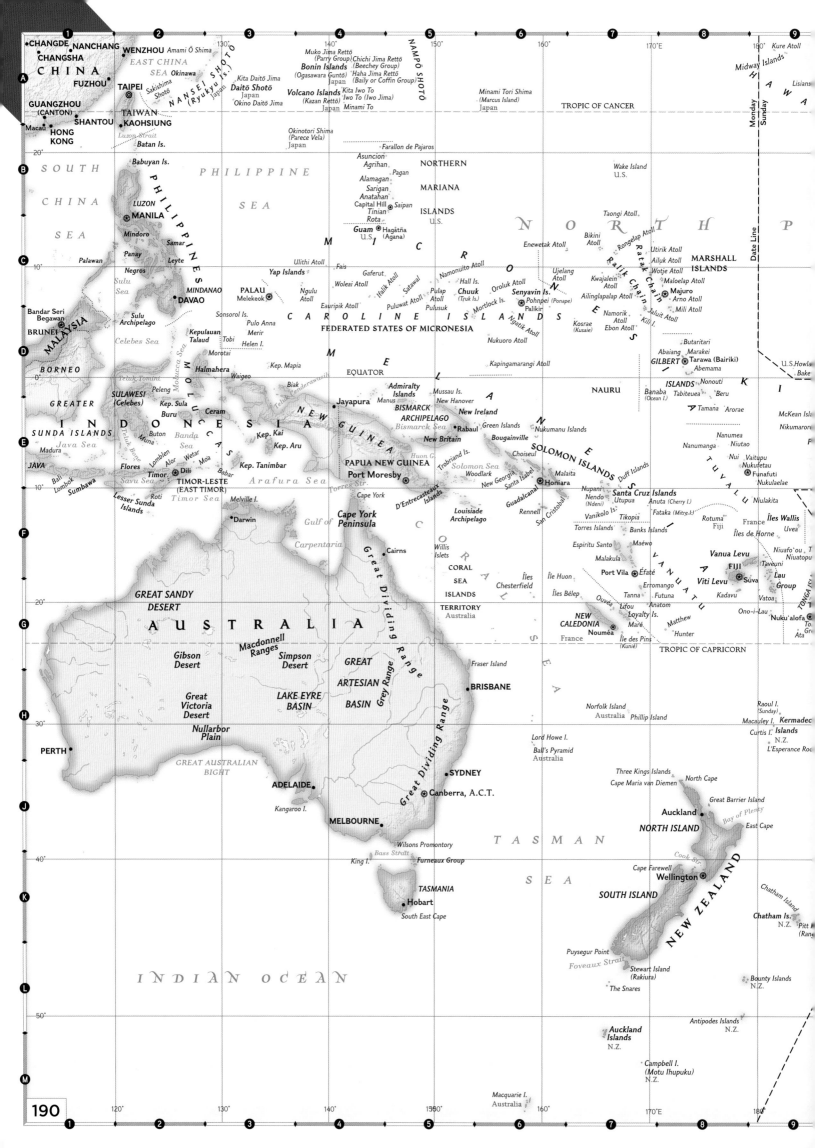

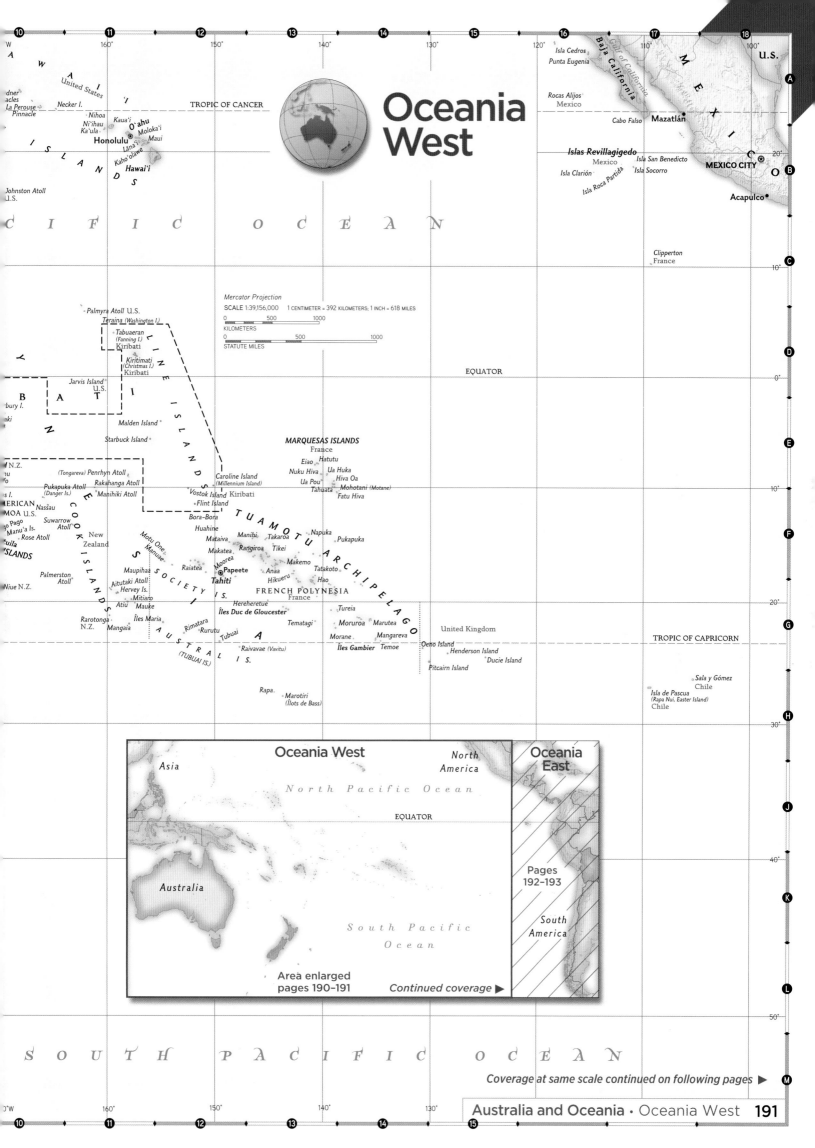

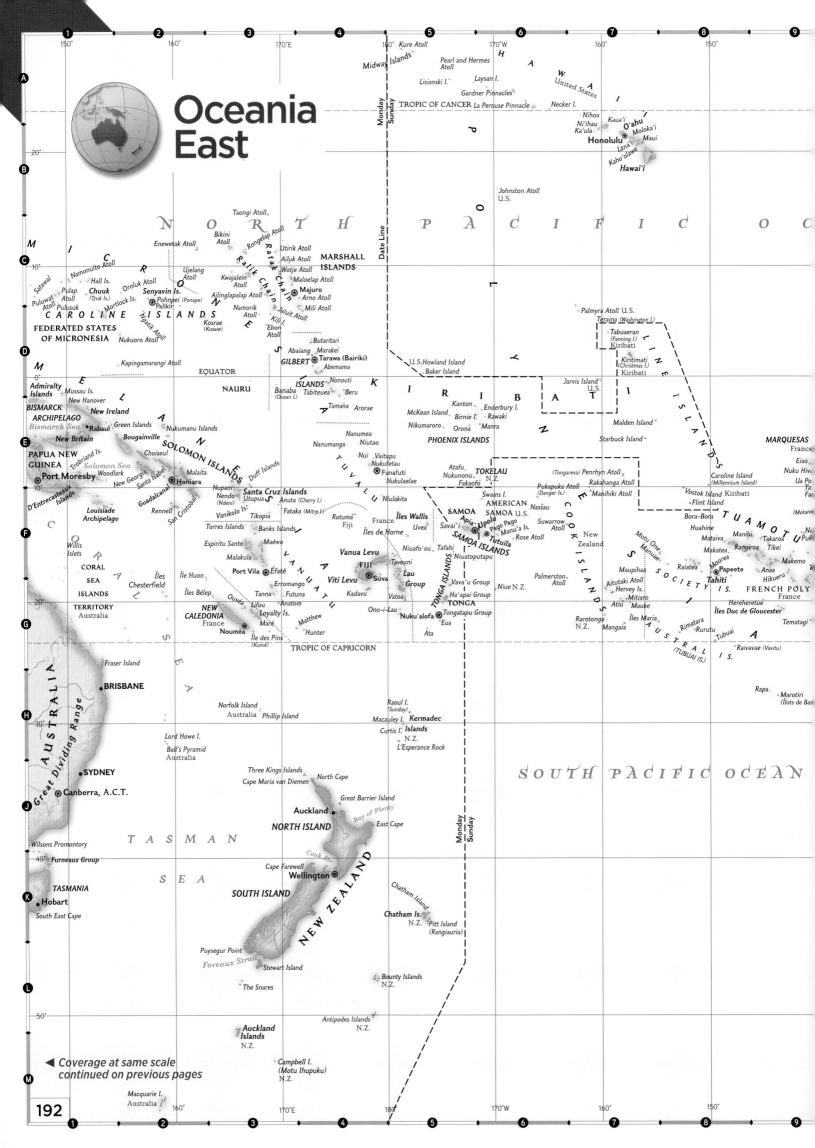

Oceania
East

150°   160°   170°E   180°   170°W   160°   150°

A

Kure Atoll
Midway Islands
Pearl and Hermes Atoll
Lisianski I.
Laysan I.
Gardner Pinnacles
TROPIC OF CANCER   La Perouse Pinnacle
Necker I.
Nihoa
Ni'ihau   Kaua'i
Ka'ula   O'ahu
Honolulu   Moloka'i
Lāna'i   Maui
Kaho'olawe
Hawai'i

United States
H A W A I I

B

Johnston Atoll U.S.

Monday / Sunday
Date Line

C

N O R T H   P A C I F I C   O C

Taongi Atoll
Bikini Atoll
Rongelap Atoll
Enewetak Atoll
Ujelang Atoll
Utirik Atoll
Ailuk Atoll
Wotje Atoll
MARSHALL ISLANDS
Namonuito Atoll
Hall Is.
Oroluk Atoll
Kwajalein Atoll
Maloelap Atoll
Satawal
Pulap Atoll
Chuuk (Truk Is.)
Senyavin Is.
Ailinglapalap Atoll
Majuro
Arno Atoll
Puluwat Atoll
Pulusuk
Mortlock Is.
Pohnpei (Ponape)   Palikir
Namorik Atoll
Mili Atoll
C A R O L I N E   I S L A N D S
Ngatik Atoll
Jaluit Atoll
Kili I.
FEDERATED STATES OF MICRONESIA
Kosrae (Kusaie)
Ebon Atoll
Nukuoro Atoll

Palmyra Atoll U.S.
Teraina (Washington I.)
Tabuaeran (Fanning I.)   **Kiribati**
Kiritimati (Christmas I.)   Kiribati

D

M I C R O N E S I A

Kapingamarangi Atoll

EQUATOR

Butaritari
Abaiang   Marakei
GILBERT   **Tarawa (Bairiki)**
Abemama
Nonouti
ISLANDS   Tabiteuea   Beru
Banaba (Ocean I.)
Tamana   Arorae

U.S.Howland Island
Baker Island

Jarvis Island U.S.

L I N E   I S L A N D S

NAURU

Kanton
McKean Island   Enderbury I.
Birnie I.   Rawaki
Nikumaroro   Orona   Manra

Malden Island

Starbuck Island

E

Admiralty Islands
Mussau Is.
New Hanover
BISMARCK ARCHIPELAGO
New Ireland
Bismarck Sea
Green Islands
Nukumanu Islands
Rabaul
New Britain
Bougainville
SOLOMON ISLANDS
PAPUA NEW GUINEA
Trobriand Is.
Choiseul
Nanumea
Nanumanga   Niutao
Nui   Vaitupu
Nukufetau
Atafu
Nukunonu   **TOKELAU**
Fakaofo   N.Z.
(Tongareva) Penrhyn Atoll
PHOENIX ISLANDS
K I R I B A T I

MARQUESAS
France
Eiao
Nuku Hiva
Ua Huka
Caroline Island
(Millennium Island)

M E L A N E S I A

Solomon Sea
Woodlark
New Georgia
Santa Isabel
Malaita
Honiara
Port Moresby
Guadalcanal
Nupani
Santa Cruz Islands
(Ndeni)
Nendo
Utupua   Anuta (Cherry I.)
TUVALU
Niulakita
Nukulaelae
Funafuti

SAMOA
Apia   **Upolu**
Savai'i
AMERICAN SAMOA U.S.
Nassau
Pago Pago
Manu'a Is.
SAMOA ISLANDS
Tutuila
Rose Atoll
Suwarrow Atoll

P O L Y N E S I A

Caroline Island
Vostok Island   Kiribati
Flint Island

Bora-Bora
Huahine
Maupihaa
Mataiva
Rangiroa   Tikei
Manihi
Makatea   Takaroa
TUAMOTU
Manuae
Motu One
Raiatea
Maupiti
Hervey Is.
Papeete
Moorea
Makemo
Anaa
Hikueru
SOCIETY IS.
Tahiti
FRENCH POLY
France

F

Willis Islets
CORAL SEA ISLANDS
Louisiade Archipelago
D'Entrecasteaux Islands
Rennell
San Cristobal
Vanikolo
Tikopia
Fataka (Mitre I.)
Torres Islands
Banks Islands
Rotuma   **Fiji**
France
Îles Wallis
Uvea
Niuafo'ou
Tafahi
Niuatoputapu

C O R A L   S E A

Îles Chesterfield
Île Huon
Espiritu Santo
Maéwo
Malakula
Vanua Levu
Taveuni
FIJI
Lau Group
Viti Levu   **Suva**
Kadavu
Vatoa
Ono-i-Lau

Île Bélep
VANUATU
Erromango
Port Vila   **Éfaté**
Tanna
Futuna
Vava'u Group
Niue N.Z.
Ha'apai Group
Palmerston Atoll
New Zealand

COOK ISLANDS
Aitutaki Atoll
Mitiaro
Mauke
Atiu
Mangaia
Îles Maria
AUSTRAL IS.
Hereheretue
Îles Duc de Gloucester
Rimatara
Rurutu   Tubuai

G

TERRITORY
Australia
NEW CALEDONIA
France
Ouvéa
Lifou
Loyalty Is.
Maré
Matthew
Hunter
Île des Pins (Kunié)
Nouméa

TROPIC OF CAPRICORN

TONGA ISLANDS
TONGA
Nuku'alofa
Tongatapu Group
Eua
Ata

Rarotonga
N.Z.

A U S T R A L I S.
(TUBUAI IS.)

Rapa
Marotiri (Îlots de Bas
Tematagi

H

Fraser Island
BRISBANE

Norfolk Island
Australia   Phillip Island
Raoul I. (Sunday)
Macauley I.   **Kermadec**
Curtis I.   **Islands**
N.Z.
L'Esperance Rock

S O U T H   P A C I F I C   O C E A N

J

A U S T R A L I A
Great Dividing Range
Lord Howe I.
Ball's Pyramid
Australia
SYDNEY
Canberra, A.C.T.
Three Kings Islands
Cape Maria van Diemen   North Cape
Great Barrier Island
Auckland
Bay of Plenty
NORTH ISLAND
East Cape

Monday / Sunday

T A S M A N
Wilsons Promontory

K

Furneaux Group
Cook Str.
Cape Farewell
Wellington
SOUTH ISLAND
NEW ZEALAND
TASMANIA
Hobart
South East Cape
S E A
Chatham Island
Chatham Is.
N.Z.   Pitt Island
(Rangiauria)

L

Puysegur Point
Foveaux Strait
Stewart Island
The Snares
Bounty Islands
N.Z.

◀ Coverage at same scale continued on previous pages

M

Auckland Islands
N.Z.

Antipodes Islands
N.Z.

Campbell I. (Motu Ihupuku) N.Z.

Macquarie I.
Australia

160°   170°E   180°   170°W   160°   150°

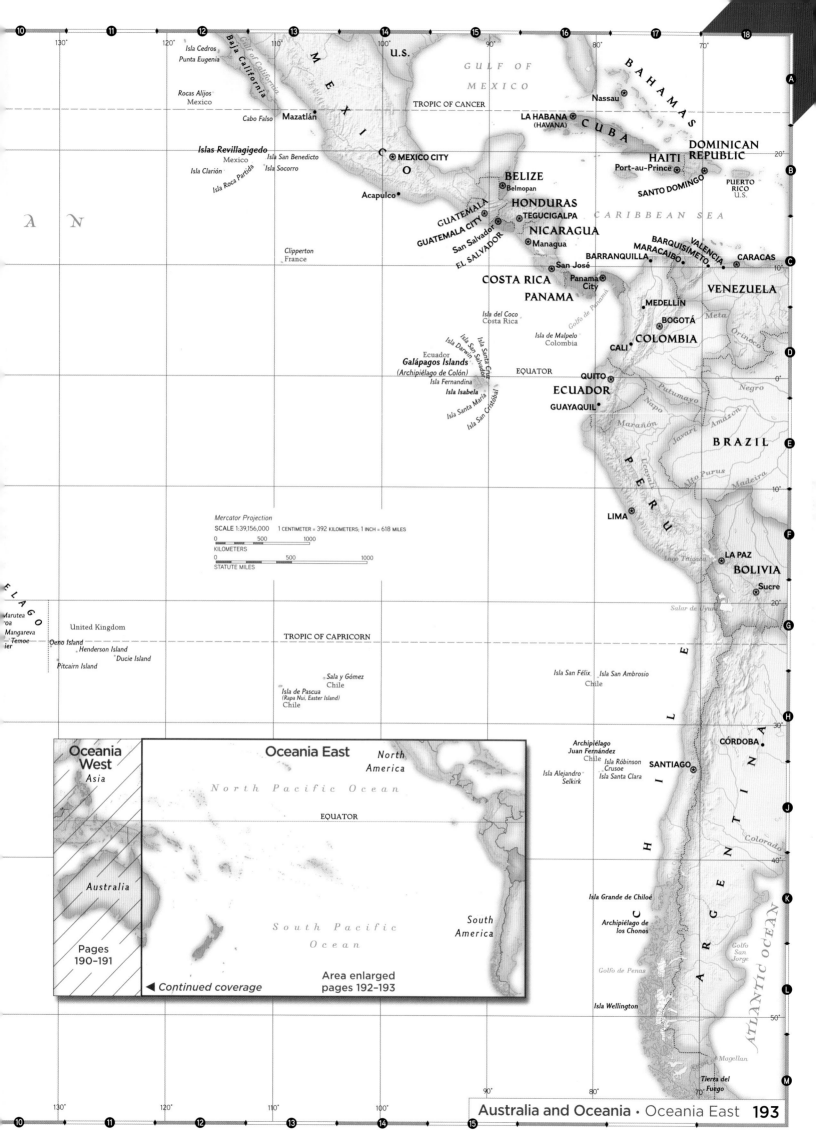

Australia and Oceania Flags and Facts

Australia

COMMONWEALTH OF AUSTRALIA

AREA	7,741,220 sq km (2,988,900 sq mi)
POPULATION	22,263,000
CAPITAL	Canberra 399,000
RELIGION	Roman Catholic, Anglican, other Christian
LANGUAGE	English
LITERACY	99.0%
LIFE EXPECTANCY	82 years
GDP PER CAPITA	$43,700

Micronesia

FEDERATED STATES OF MICRONESIA

AREA	702 sq km (271 sq mi)
POPULATION	106,000
CAPITAL	Palikir 7,000
RELIGION	Roman Catholic, Protestant
LANGUAGE	English, Chuukese, Kosrean, Pohnpeian, other indigenous languages
LITERACY	89.0%
LIFE EXPECTANCY	72 years
GDP PER CAPITA	$3,000

Papua New Guinea

INDEPENDENT STATE OF PAPUA NEW GUINEA

AREA	462,840 sq km (178,703 sq mi)
POPULATION	6,432,000
CAPITAL	Port Moresby 343,000
RELIGION	Roman Catholic, Evangelical Lutheran, United Church, Seventh-day Adventist, other Protestant
LANGUAGE	Melanesian Pidgin, Motu, 820 indigenous languages
LITERACY	57.3%
LIFE EXPECTANCY	66 years
GDP PER CAPITA	$2,800

Fiji

REPUBLIC OF FIJI

AREA	18,274 sq km (7,056 sq mi)
POPULATION	897,000
CAPITAL	Suva 177,000
RELIGION	Christian, Hindu, Muslim
LANGUAGE	English, Fijian, Hindustani
LITERACY	93.7%
LIFE EXPECTANCY	72 years
GDP PER CAPITA	$4,900

Nauru

REPUBLIC OF NAURU

AREA	21 sq km (8 sq mi)
POPULATION	9,500
CAPITAL	Yaren 9,400
RELIGION	Nauru Congregational, Roman Catholic, Nauru Independent Church
LANGUAGE	Nauruan, English
LITERACY	NA
LIFE EXPECTANCY	66 years
GDP PER CAPITA	$5,000

Samoa

INDEPENDENT STATE OF SAMOA

AREA	2,831 sq km (1,093 sq mi)
POPULATION	195,000
CAPITAL	Apia 37,000
RELIGION	Congregationalist, Roman Catholic, Methodist, Latter-day Saints, Assembly of God
LANGUAGE	Samoan (Polynesian), English
LITERACY	99.7%
LIFE EXPECTANCY	73 years
GDP PER CAPITA	$6,300

Kiribati

REPUBLIC OF KIRIBATI

AREA	811 sq km (313 sq mi)
POPULATION	103,000
CAPITAL	Tarawa (Bairiki) 44,000
RELIGION	Roman Catholic, Protestant
LANGUAGE	I-Kiribati, English
LITERACY	NA
LIFE EXPECTANCY	65 years
GDP PER CAPITA	$6,000

New Zealand

NEW ZEALAND

AREA	267,710 sq km (103,363 sq mi)
POPULATION	4,365,000
CAPITAL	Wellington 410,000
RELIGION	Anglican, Roman Catholic, Presbyterian, other Christian
LANGUAGE	English, Maori
LITERACY	99.0%
LIFE EXPECTANCY	81 years
GDP PER CAPITA	$29,800

Solomon Islands

SOLOMON ISLANDS

AREA	28,896 sq km (11,157 sq mi)
POPULATION	597,000
CAPITAL	Honiara 68,000
RELIGION	Church of Melanesia, Roman Catholic, South Seas Evangelical
LANGUAGE	Melanesian pidgin, English, 120 indigenous languages
LITERACY	NA
LIFE EXPECTANCY	74 years
GDP PER CAPITA	$3,500

Marshall Islands

REPUBLIC OF THE MARSHALL ISLANDS

AREA	181 sq km (70 sq mi)
POPULATION	70,000
CAPITAL	Majuro 31,000
RELIGION	Protestant, Assembly of God, Roman Catholic
LANGUAGE	Marshallese, English
LITERACY	93.7%
LIFE EXPECTANCY	72 years
GDP PER CAPITA	$3,200

Palau

REPUBLIC OF PALAU

AREA	459 sq km (177 sq mi)
POPULATION	21,100
CAPITAL	Melekeok 1,000
RELIGION	Roman Catholic, Protestant, Modekngei, Seventh-day Adventist
LANGUAGE	Palauan, Filipino, English, Chinese
LITERACY	92.0%
LIFE EXPECTANCY	72 years
GDP PER CAPITA	$10,500

Tonga

KINGDOM OF TONGA

AREA	747 sq km (289 sq mi)
POPULATION	106,000
CAPITAL	Nuku'alofa 25,000
RELIGION	Free Wesleyan Church, other Christian
LANGUAGE	Tongan, English
LITERACY	98.9%
LIFE EXPECTANCY	75 years
GDP PER CAPITA	$7,700

Tuvalu

TUVALU

AREA	26 sq km (10 sq mi)
POPULATION	11,700
CAPITAL	Funafuti 5,000
RELIGION	Church of Tuvalu (Congregationalist)
LANGUAGE	Tuvaluan, English, Samoan, Kiribati
LITERACY	NA
LIFE EXPECTANCY	65 years
GDP PER CAPITA	$3,400

Vanuatu

REPUBLIC OF VANUATU

AREA	12,189 sq km (4,706 sq mi)
POPULATION	262,000
CAPITAL	Port Vila 47,000
RELIGION	Presbyterian, Anglican, Roman Catholic, Seventh-day Adventist, other Christian, indigenous beliefs
LANGUAGE	over 100 local languages, pidgin (known as Bislama or Bichelama)
LITERACY	74%
LIFE EXPECTANCY	67 years
GDP PER CAPITA	$5,100

Population by Country

NEW ZEALAND 4,365,000
Sydney 4,479,000
PAPUA NEW GUINEA 6,432,000
AUSTRALIA 22,263,000

WALLIS AND FUTUNA 15,500
NORTHERN MARIANA ISLANDS 51,200
PALAU 21,100
COOK ISLANDS 10,400
TUVALU 10,700
AMERICAN SAMOA 54,700
NAURU 9,400
NORFOLK ISLAND 2,200
MARSHALL ISLANDS 70,000
KIRIBATI 103,000
TONGA 106,000
MICRONESIA 106,000
GUAM 160,000
SAMOA 195,000
VANUATU 262,000
NEW CALEDONIA 264,000
FRENCH POLYNESIA 277,000
FIJI 897,000
SOLOMON ISLANDS 597,000

GDP by Country

Gross Domestic Product (Purchasing Power Parity), in millions of U.S. dollars

NEW ZEALAND $134,233
PAPUA NEW GUINEA $19,445
AUSTRALIA $1,002,740

NORTHERN MARIANA ISLANDS $733
PALAU $221
WALLIS AND FUTUNA $60
AMERICAN SAMOA $575
COOK ISLANDS $183
TUVALU $38
MARSHALL ISLANDS $170
KIRIBATI $648
NAURU $60
TONGA $809
MICRONESIA $310
GUAM $4,600
FIJI $4,450
SOLOMON ISLANDS $2,026
SAMOA $1,165
NEW CALEDONIA $9,280
VANUATU $1,307
FRENCH POLYNESIA $5,650

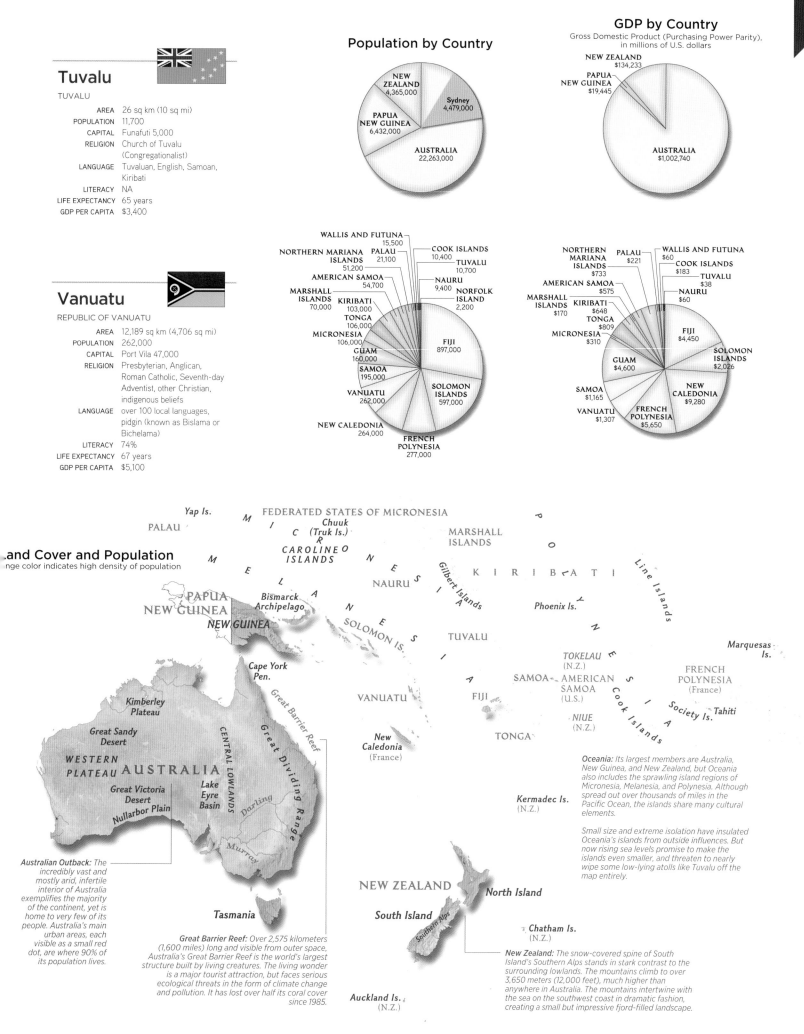

Land Cover and Population
Orange color indicates high density of population

PALAU
Yap Is.
FEDERATED STATES OF MICRONESIA
Chuuk (Truk Is.)
CAROLINE ISLANDS
MARSHALL ISLANDS
NAURU
KIRIBATI
Gilbert Islands
Line Islands
Phoenix Is.
MICRONESIA
MELANESIA
POLYNESIA
PAPUA NEW GUINEA
NEW GUINEA
Bismarck Archipelago
SOLOMON IS.
TUVALU
TOKELAU (N.Z.)
Marquesas Is.
Cape York Pen.
Great Barrier Reef
VANUATU
FIJI
SAMOA
AMERICAN SAMOA (U.S.)
NIUE (N.Z.)
Cook Islands
FRENCH POLYNESIA (France)
Society Is.
Tahiti
Kimberley Plateau
Great Sandy Desert
WESTERN PLATEAU
AUSTRALIA
CENTRAL LOWLANDS
Great Dividing Range
New Caledonia (France)
TONGA
Great Victoria Desert
Nullarbor Plain
Lake Eyre Basin
Darling
Murray
Kermadec Is. (N.Z.)
NEW ZEALAND
North Island
Tasmania
South Island
Southern Alps
Chatham Is. (N.Z.)
Auckland Is. (N.Z.)

Oceania: Its largest members are Australia, New Guinea, and New Zealand, but Oceania also includes the sprawling island regions of Micronesia, Melanesia, and Polynesia. Although spread out over thousands of miles in the Pacific Ocean, the islands share many cultural elements.

Small size and extreme isolation have insulated Oceania's islands from outside influences. But now rising sea levels promise to make the islands even smaller, and threaten to nearly wipe some low-lying atolls like Tuvalu off the map entirely.

Australian Outback: The incredibly vast and mostly arid, infertile interior of Australia exemplifies the majority of the continent, yet is home to very few of its people. Australia's main urban areas, each visible as a small red dot, are where 90% of its population lives.

Great Barrier Reef: Over 2,575 kilometers (1,600 miles) long and visible from outer space, Australia's Great Barrier Reef is the world's largest structure built by living creatures. The living wonder is a major tourist attraction, but faces serious ecological threats in the form of climate change and pollution. It has lost over half its coral cover since 1985.

New Zealand: The snow-covered spine of South Island's Southern Alps stands in stark contrast to the surrounding lowlands. The mountains climb to over 3,650 meters (12,000 feet), much higher than anywhere in Australia. The mountains intertwine with the sea on the southwest coast in dramatic fashion, creating a small but impressive fjord-filled landscape.

The Poles

The polar regions are at once the nexus points for Earth's winds, continents, and oceans and at the same time nearly alien in their landscapes of ice and snow, rock and water. North and South are almost mirror images: the Arctic a broad, shallow sea surrounded by continents, the Antarctic a wide continent surrounded by a constantly circling sea.

Despite the fact that populations remain small, people have lived in the Arctic for thousands of years, clustered mostly in coastal communities along the continental margins and islands, including the southwestern fjords of the world's largest island, Greenland. Increasingly, these northernmost latitudes are also home to itinerant scientists seeking evidence of Earth's climate history in Arctic ice cores and clues to our future in the melting sea ice.

Antarctica remains our planet's one uninhabited continent, free not just of indigenous people but also of terrestrial plants and land mammals. Ice sheets here can measure more than 4 kilometers (2.5 miles) thick, and give rise to the world's strongest winds, sweeping down from the East Antarctic Ice Sheet at 300 kilometers (186 miles) an hour or more.

Appropriately for the ice continent, one of Antarctica's most spectacular events has to do not with life or even geology, but with the vast seasonal sheet of sea ice that spreads out from the continent's fringes each winter, eventually covering more than 18 million square kilometers (7 million square miles) of ocean with a meters-thick layer of sea ice.

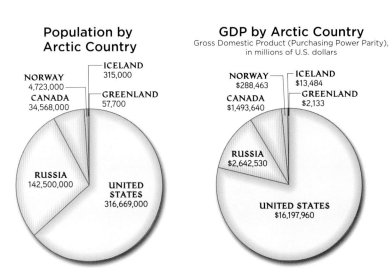

Population by Arctic Country

- ICELAND 315,000
- NORWAY 4,723,000
- CANADA 34,568,000
- GREENLAND 57,700
- RUSSIA 142,500,000
- UNITED STATES 316,669,000

GDP by Arctic Country
Gross Domestic Product (Purchasing Power Parity), in millions of U.S. dollars

- NORWAY $288,463
- ICELAND $13,484
- CANADA $1,493,640
- GREENLAND $2,133
- RUSSIA $2,642,530
- UNITED STATES $16,197,960

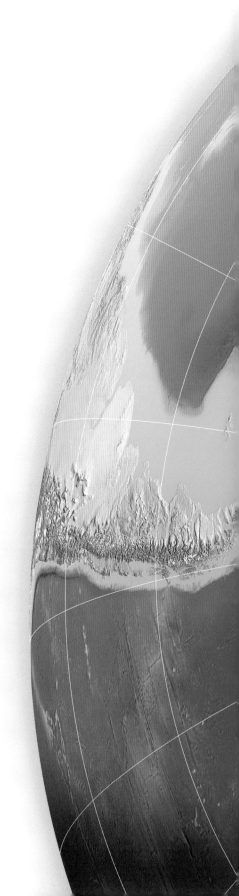

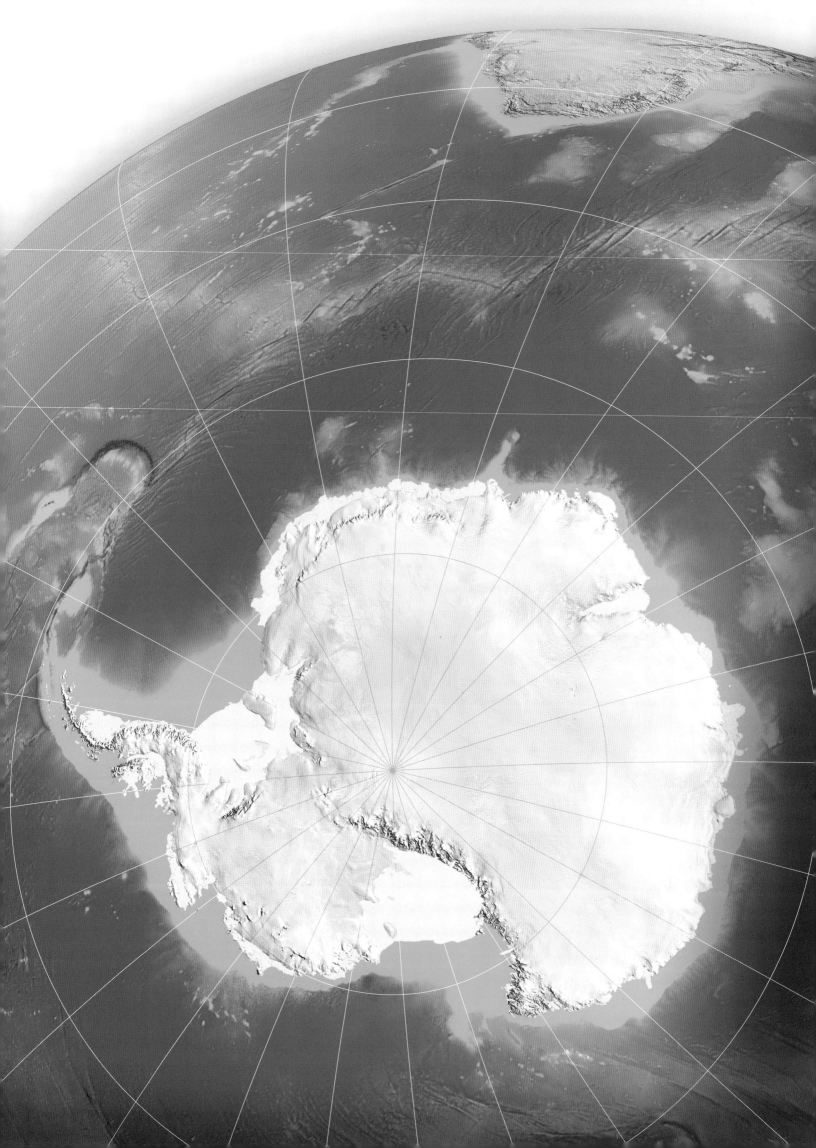

Arctic

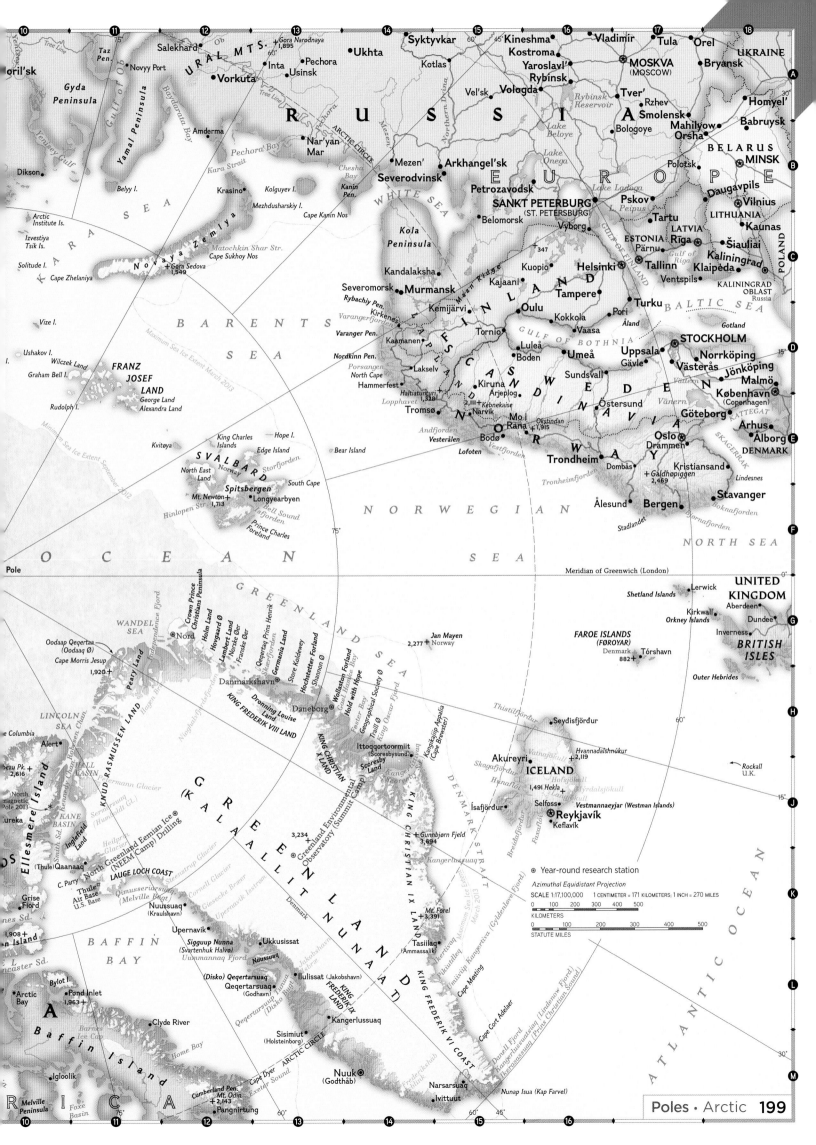

Poles · Arctic 199

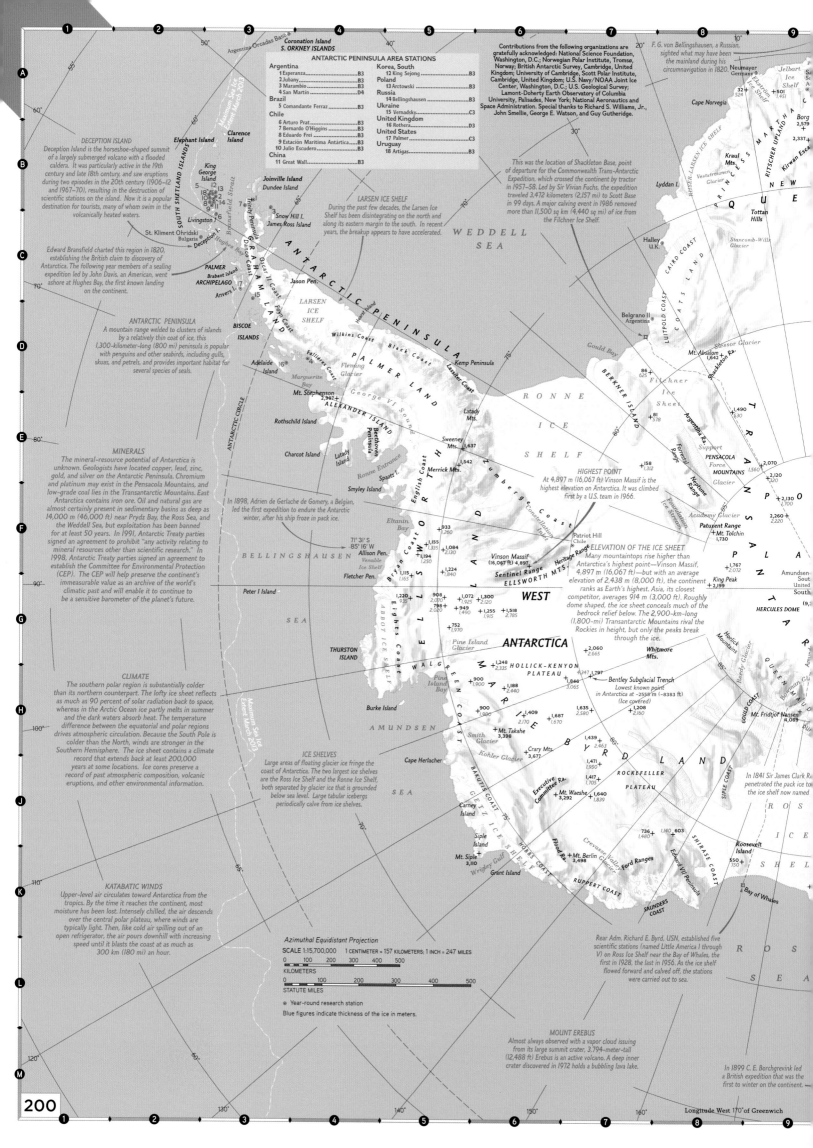

Coronation Island
S. ORKNEY ISLANDS

ANTARCTIC PENINSULA AREA STATIONS

Argentina		Korea, South	
1 Esperanza	B3	12 King Sejong	B3
2 Jubany	B3	**Poland**	
3 Marambio	B3	13 Arctowski	B3
4 San Martín	D4	**Russia**	
Brazil		14 Bellingshausen	B3
5 Comandante Ferraz	B3	**Ukraine**	
Chile		15 Vernadsky	C3
6 Arturo Prat	B3	**United Kingdom**	
7 Bernardo O'Higgins	B3	16 Rothera	C3
8 Eduardo Frei	B3	**United States**	
9 Estación Marítima Antártica	B3	17 Palmer	C3
10 Julio Escudero	B3	**Uruguay**	
11 Great Wall	B3	18 Artigas	B3
China			

Contributions from the following organizations are gratefully acknowledged: National Science Foundation, Washington, D.C.; Norwegian Polar Institute, Tromsø, Norway; British Antarctic Survey, Cambridge, United Kingdom; University of Cambridge, Scott Polar Institute, Cambridge, United Kingdom; U.S. Navy/NOAA Joint Ice Center, Washington, D.C.; U.S. Geological Survey; Lamont-Doherty Earth Observatory of Columbia University, Palisades, New York; National Aeronautics and Space Administration. Special thanks to Richard S. Williams, Jr., John Smellie, George E. Watson, and Guy Gutheridge.

F. G. von Bellingshausen, a Russian, sighted what may have been the mainland during his circumnavigation in 1820.

DECEPTION ISLAND
Deception Island is the horseshoe-shaped summit of a largely submerged volcano with a flooded caldera. It was particularly active in the 19th century and late 18th century, and saw eruptions during two episodes in the 20th century (1906–12 and 1967–70), resulting in the destruction of scientific stations on the island. Now it is a popular destination for tourists, many of whom swim in the volcanically heated waters.

Edward Bransfield charted this region in 1820, establishing the British claim to discovery of Antarctica. The following year members of a sealing expedition led by John Davis, an American, went ashore at Hughes Bay, the first known landing on the continent.

LARSEN ICE SHELF
During the past few decades, the Larsen Ice Shelf has been disintegrating on the north and along its eastern margin to the south. In recent years, the breakup appears to have accelerated.

This was the location of Shackleton Base, point of departure for the Commonwealth Trans-Antarctic Expedition, which crossed the continent by tractor in 1957–58. Led by Sir Vivian Fuchs, the expedition traveled 3,472 kilometers (2,157 mi) to Scott Base in 99 days. A major calving event in 1986 removed more than 11,500 sq km (4,440 sq mi) of ice from the Filchner Ice Shelf.

ANTARCTIC PENINSULA
A mountain range welded to clusters of islands by a relatively thin coat of ice, this 1,300-kilometer-long (800 mi) peninsula is popular with penguins and other seabirds, including gulls, skuas, and petrels, and provides important habitat for several species of seals.

MINERALS
The mineral-resource potential of Antarctica is unknown. Geologists have located copper, lead, zinc, gold, and silver on the Antarctic Peninsula. Chromium and platinum may exist in the Pensacola Mountains, and low-grade coal lies in the Transantarctic Mountains. East Antarctica contains iron ore. Oil and natural gas are almost certainly present in sedimentary basins as deep as 14,000 m (46,000 ft) near Prydz Bay, the Ross Sea, and the Weddell Sea, but exploitation has been banned for at least 50 years. In 1991, Antarctic Treaty parties signed an agreement to prohibit "any activity relating to mineral resources other than scientific research." In 1998, Antarctic Treaty parties signed an agreement to establish the Committee for Environmental Protection (CEP). The CEP will help preserve the continent's immeasurable value as an archive of the world's climatic past and will enable it to continue to be a sensitive barometer of the planet's future.

In 1898, Adrien de Gerlache de Gomery, a Belgian, led the first expedition to endure the Antarctic winter, after his ship froze in pack ice.

HIGHEST POINT
At 4,897 m (16,067 ft) Vinson Massif is the highest elevation on Antarctica. It was climbed first by a U.S. team in 1966.

ELEVATION OF THE ICE SHEET
Many mountaintops rise higher than Antarctica's highest point—Vinson Massif, 4,897 m (16,067 ft)—but with an average elevation of 2,438 m (8,000 ft), the continent ranks as Earth's highest. Asia, its closest competitor, averages 914 m (3,000 ft). Roughly dome shaped, the ice sheet conceals much of the bedrock relief below. The 2,900-km-long (1,800-mi) Transantarctic Mountains rival the Rockies in height, but only the peaks break through the ice.

CLIMATE
The southern polar region is substantially colder than its northern counterpart. The lofty ice sheet reflects as much as 90 percent of solar radiation back to space, whereas in the Arctic Ocean ice partly melts in summer and the dark waters absorb heat. The temperature difference between the equatorial and polar regions drives atmospheric circulation. Because the South Pole is colder than the North, winds are stronger in the Southern Hemisphere. The ice sheet contains a climate record that extends back at least 200,000 years at some locations. Ice cores preserve a record of past atmospheric composition, volcanic eruptions, and other environmental information.

ICE SHELVES
Large areas of floating glacier ice fringe the coast of Antarctica. The two largest ice shelves are the Ross Ice Shelf and the Ronne Ice Shelf, both separated by glacier ice that is grounded below sea level. Large tabular icebergs periodically calve from ice shelves.

KATABATIC WINDS
Upper-level air circulates toward Antarctica from the tropics. By the time it reaches the continent, most moisture has been lost. Intensely chilled, the air descends over the central polar plateau, where winds are typically light. Then, like cold air spilling out of an open refrigerator, the air pours downhill with increasing speed until it blasts the coast at as much as 300 km (180 mi) an hour.

Rear Adm. Richard E. Byrd, USN, established five scientific stations (named Little America I through V) on Ross Ice Shelf near the Bay of Whales, the first in 1928, the last in 1956. As the ice shelf flowed forward and calved off, the stations were carried out to sea.

In 1841 Sir James Clark Ross penetrated the pack ice to the ice shelf now named [...]

In 1899 C. E. Borchgrevink led a British expedition that was the first to winter on the continent.

MOUNT EREBUS
Almost always observed with a vapor cloud issuing from its large summit crater, 3,794-meter-tall (12,488 ft) Erebus is an active volcano. A deep inner crater discovered in 1972 holds a bubbling lava lake.

Azimuthal Equidistant Projection

SCALE 1:15,700,000   1 CENTIMETER = 157 KILOMETERS; 1 INCH = 247 MILES

0 100 200 300 400 500
KILOMETERS

0   100   200   300   400   500
STATUTE MILES

⊛ Year-round research station

Blue figures indicate thickness of the ice in meters.

Longitude West 170° of Greenwich

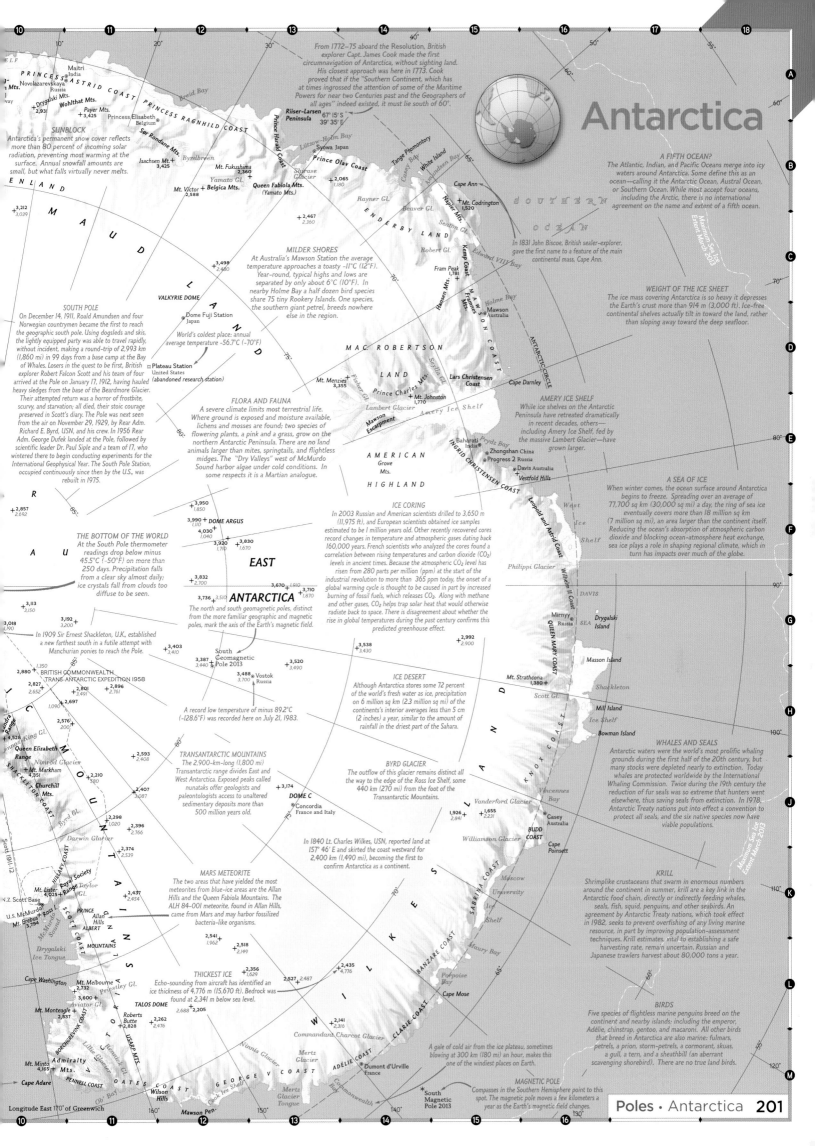

Antarctica

From 1772–75 aboard the Resolution, British explorer Capt. James Cook made the first circumnavigation of Antarctica, without sighting land. His closest approach was here in 1773. Cook proved that if the "Southern Continent," which has at times ingrossed the attention of some of the Maritime Powers for near two Centuries past and the Geographers of all ages" indeed existed, it must lie south of 60°.

A FIFTH OCEAN?
The Atlantic, Indian, and Pacific Oceans merge into icy waters around Antarctica. Some define this as an ocean—calling it the Antarctic Ocean, Austral Ocean, or Southern Ocean. While most accept four oceans, including the Arctic, there is no international agreement on the name and extent of a fifth ocean.

In 1831 John Biscoe, British sealer-explorer, gave the first name to a feature of the main continental mass, Cape Ann.

WEIGHT OF THE ICE SHEET
The ice mass covering Antarctica is so heavy it depresses the Earth's crust more than 914 m (3,000 ft). Ice-free continental shelves actually tilt in toward the land, rather than sloping away toward the deep seafloor.

SUNBLOCK
Antarctica's permanent snow cover reflects more than 80 percent of incoming solar radiation, preventing most warming at the surface. Annual snowfall amounts are small, but what falls virtually never melts.

MILDER SHORES
At Australia's Mawson Station the average temperature approaches a toasty −11°C (12°F). Year-round, typical highs and lows are separated by only about 6°C (10°F). In nearby Holme Bay a half dozen bird species share 75 tiny Rookery Islands. One species, the southern giant petrel, breeds nowhere else in the region.

SOUTH POLE
On December 14, 1911, Roald Amundsen and four Norwegian countrymen became the first to reach the geographic south pole. Using dogsleds and skis, the lightly equipped party was able to travel rapidly, without incident, making a round-trip of 2,993 km (1,860 mi) in 99 days from a base camp at the Bay of Whales. Losers in the quest to be first, British explorer Robert Falcon Scott and his team of four arrived at the Pole on January 17, 1912, having hauled heavy sledges from the base of the Beardmore Glacier. Their attempted return was a horror of frostbite, scurvy, and starvation; all died, their stoic courage preserved in Scott's diary. The Pole was next seen from the air on November 29, 1929, by Rear Adm. Richard E. Byrd, USN, and his crew. In 1956 Rear Adm. George Dufek landed at the Pole, followed by scientific leader Dr. Paul Siple and a team of 17, who wintered there to begin conducting experiments for the International Geophysical Year. The South Pole Station, occupied continuously since then by the U.S., was rebuilt in 1975.

FLORA AND FAUNA
A severe climate limits most terrestrial life. Where ground is exposed and moisture available, lichens and mosses are found; two species of flowering plants, a pink and a grass, grow on the northern Antarctic Peninsula. There are no land animals larger than mites, springtails, and flightless midges. The "Dry Valleys" west of McMurdo Sound harbor algae under cold conditions. In some respects it is a Martian analogue.

World's coldest place: annual average temperature −56.7°C (−70°F)

AMERY ICE SHELF
While ice shelves on the Antarctic Peninsula have retreated dramatically in recent decades, others— including Amery Ice Shelf, fed by the massive Lambert Glacier—have grown larger.

A SEA OF ICE
When winter comes, the ocean surface around Antarctica begins to freeze. Spreading over an average of 77,700 sq km (30,000 sq mi) a day, the ring of sea ice eventually covers more than 18 million sq km (7 million sq mi), an area larger than the continent itself. Reducing the ocean's absorption of atmospheric carbon dioxide and blocking ocean-atmosphere heat exchange, sea ice plays a role in shaping regional climate, which in turn has impacts over much of the globe.

ICE CORING
In 2003 Russian and American scientists drilled to 3,650 m (11,975 ft), and European scientists obtained ice samples estimated to be 1 million years old. Other recently recovered cores record changes in temperature and atmospheric gases dating back 160,000 years. French scientists who analyzed the cores found a correlation between rising temperatures and carbon dioxide (CO_2) levels in ancient times. Because the atmospheric CO_2 level has risen from 280 parts per million (ppm) at the start of the industrial revolution to more than 365 ppm today, the onset of a global warming cycle is thought to be caused in part by increased burning of fossil fuels, which releases CO_2. Along with methane and other gases, CO_2 helps trap solar heat that would otherwise radiate back to space. There is disagreement about whether the rise in global temperatures during the past century confirms this predicted greenhouse effect.

THE BOTTOM OF THE WORLD
At the South Pole thermometer readings drop below minus 45.5°C (−50°F) on more than 250 days. Precipitation falls from a clear sky almost daily; ice crystals fall from clouds too diffuse to be seen.

EAST ANTARCTICA
The north and south geomagnetic poles, distinct from the more familiar geographic and magnetic poles, mark the axis of the Earth's magnetic field.

In 1909 Sir Ernest Shackleton, U.K., established a new farthest south in a futile attempt with Manchurian ponies to reach the Pole.

ICE DESERT
Although Antarctica stores some 72 percent of the world's fresh water as ice, precipitation on 6 million sq km (2.3 million sq mi) of the continent's interior averages less than 5 cm (2 inches) a year, similar to the amount of rainfall in the driest part of the Sahara.

A record low temperature of minus 89.2°C (−128.6°F) was recorded here on July 21, 1983.

TRANSANTARCTIC MOUNTAINS
The 2,900-km-long (1,800 mi) Transantarctic range divides East and West Antarctica. Exposed peaks called nunataks offer geologists and paleontologists access to unaltered sedimentary deposits more than 500 million years old.

BYRD GLACIER
The outflow of this glacier remains distinct all the way to the edge of the Ross Ice Shelf, some 440 km (270 mi) from the foot of the Transantarctic Mountains.

WHALES AND SEALS
Antarctic waters were the world's most prolific whaling grounds during the first half of the 20th century, but many stocks were depleted nearly to extinction. Today whales are protected worldwide by the International Whaling Commission. Twice during the 19th century the reduction of fur seals was so extreme that hunters went elsewhere, thus saving seals from extinction. In 1978, Antarctic Treaty nations put into effect a convention to protect all seals, and the six native species now have viable populations.

MARS METEORITE
The two areas that have yielded the most meteorites from blue-ice areas are the Allan Hills and the Queen Fabiola Mountains. The ALH 84-001 meteorite, found in Allan Hills, came from Mars and may harbor fossilized bacteria-like organisms.

In 1840 Lt. Charles Wilkes, USN, reported land at 157° 46' E and skirted the coast westward for 2,400 km (1,490 mi), becoming the first to confirm Antarctica as a continent.

KRILL
Shrimplike crustaceans that swarm in enormous numbers around the continent in summer, krill are a key link in the Antarctic food chain, directly or indirectly feeding whales, seals, fish, squid, penguins, and other seabirds. An agreement by Antarctic Treaty nations, which took effect in 1982, seeks to prevent overfishing of any living marine resource, in part by improving population-assessment techniques. Krill estimates, vital to establishing a safe harvesting rate, remain uncertain. Russian and Japanese trawlers harvest about 80,000 tons a year.

THICKEST ICE
Echo-sounding from aircraft has identified an ice thickness of 4,776 m (15,670 ft). Bedrock was found at 2,341 m below sea level.

BIRDS
Five species of flightless marine penguins breed on the continent and nearby islands; including the emperor, Adélie, chinstrap, gentoo, and macaroni. All other birds that breed in Antarctica are also marine: fulmars, petrels, a prion, storm-petrels, a cormorant, skuas, a gull, a tern, and a sheathbill (an aberrant scavenging shorebird). There are no true land birds.

A gale of cold air from the ice plateau, sometimes blowing at 300 km (180 mi) an hour, makes this one of the windiest places on Earth.

MAGNETIC POLE
Compasses in the Southern Hemisphere point to this spot. The magnetic pole moves a few kilometers a year as the Earth's magnetic field changes.

Longitude East 170° of Greenwich

Poles · Antarctica 201

Sea Ice Extent

North Pole

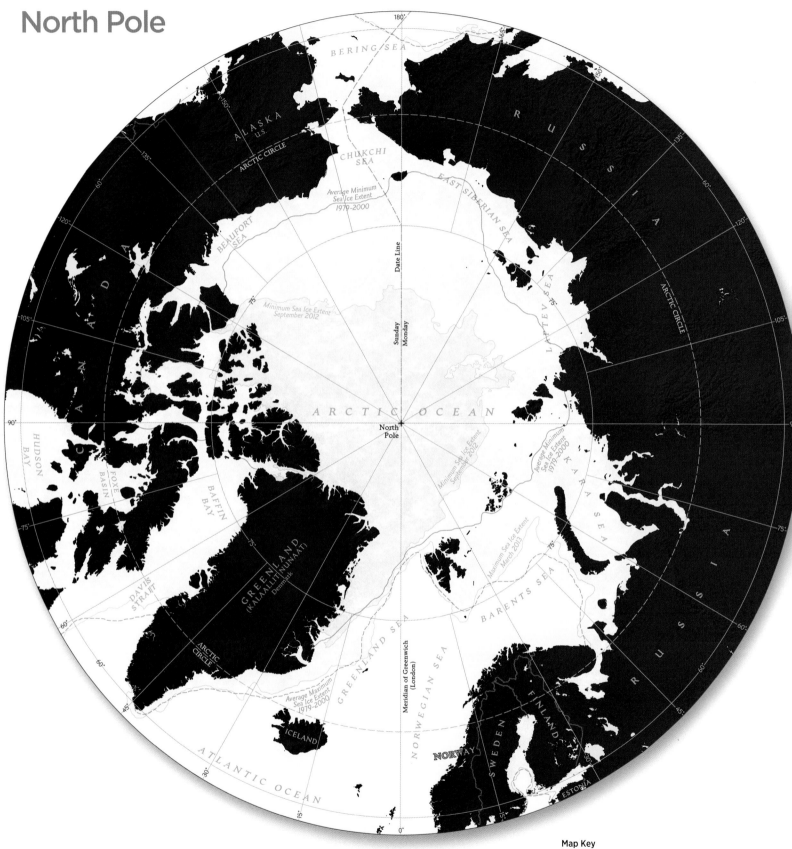

Map Key

Minimum sea ice extent, Sept. 2012

Maximum sea ice extent, March 2013

Average minimum sea ice extent, 1979–2000

Average maximum sea ice extent, 1979–2000

Azimuthal Equidistant Projection

SCALE 1:32,000,000   1 CENTIMETER = 320 KILOMETERS; 1 INCH = 505 MILES

0   300   600   900
KILOMETERS

0   300   600   900
STATUTE MILES

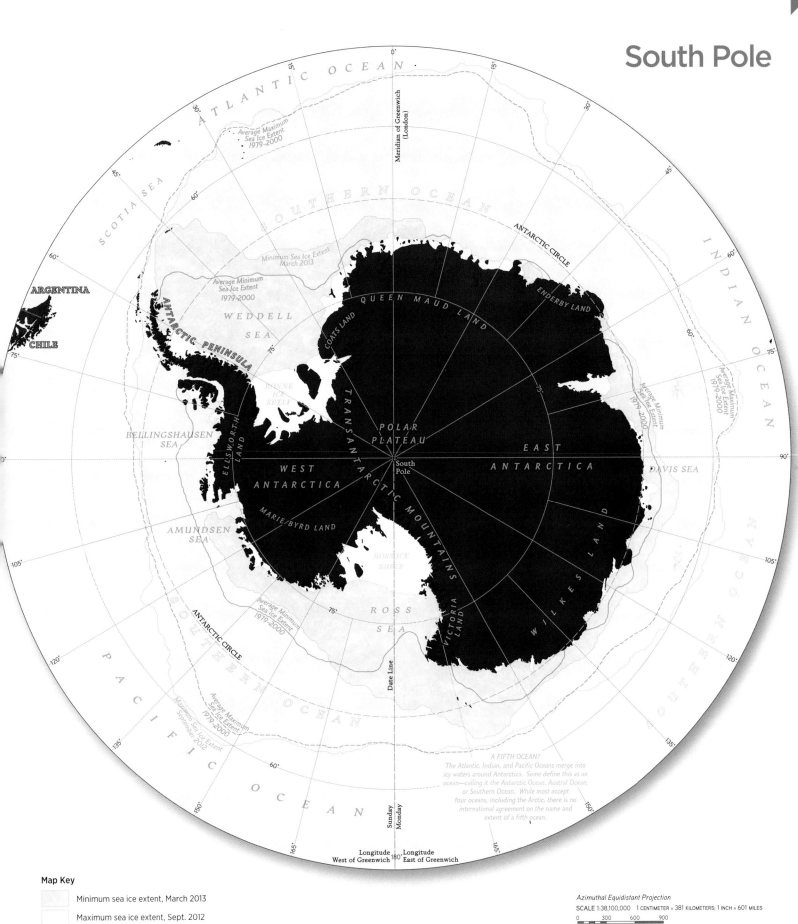

ATLANTIC OCEAN

SOUTHERN OCEAN

INDIAN OCEAN

Meridian of Greenwich (London)

ANTARCTIC CIRCLE

Average Maximum Sea Ice Extent 1979-2000

Minimum Sea Ice Extent March 2013

Average Minimum Sea Ice Extent 1979-2000

SCOTIA SEA

ARGENTINA

CHILE

WEDDELL SEA

COATS LAND

QUEEN MAUD LAND

ENDERBY LAND

ANTARCTIC PENINSULA

RONNE ICE SHELF

BELLINGSHAUSEN SEA

ELLSWORTH LAND

TRANSANTARCTIC MOUNTAINS

POLAR PLATEAU

South Pole

EAST ANTARCTICA

DAVIS SEA

Average Minimum Sea Ice Extent 1979-2000

WEST ANTARCTICA

MARIE BYRD LAND

ROSS ICE SHELF

WILKES LAND

AMUNDSEN SEA

ANTARCTIC CIRCLE

Average Minimum Sea Ice Extent 1979-2000

ROSS SEA

VICTORIA LAND

SOUTHERN OCEAN

Average Maximum Sea Ice Extent 1979-2000

Maximum Sea Ice Extent September 2012

PACIFIC OCEAN

Date Line

A FIFTH OCEAN?
The Atlantic, Indian, and Pacific Oceans merge into
icy waters around Antarctica. Some define this as an
ocean—calling it the Antarctic Ocean, Austral Ocean,
or Southern Ocean. While most accept
four oceans, including the Arctic, there is no
international agreement on the name and
extent of a fifth ocean.

Sunday Monday

Longitude West of Greenwich

Longitude East of Greenwich

Map Key

Minimum sea ice extent, March 2013

Maximum sea ice extent, Sept. 2012

Average minimum sea ice extent, 1979–2000

Average maximum sea ice extent, 1979–2000

Azimuthal Equidistant Projection
SCALE 1:38,100,000   1 CENTIMETER = 381 KILOMETERS; 1 INCH = 601 MILES

| 0 | 300 | 600 | 900 |
KILOMETERS

| 0 | 300 | 600 | 900 |
STATUTE MILES

Appendix

CONTENTS

Geographic Comparisons

Mass: 5,973,600,000,000,000,000,000 (5.9736 sextillion) metric tons

Total Area: 510,066,000 sq km (196,938,000 sq mi)

Land Area: 148,647,000 sq km (57,393,000 sq mi), 29.1% of total

Water Area: 361,419,000 sq km (139,545,000 sq mi), 70.9% of total

Population: 7,095,218,000

THE EARTH'S EXTREMES

Hottest Place: Dalol, Danakil Depression, Ethiopia, annual average temperature 34°C (93°F)

Coldest Place: Ridge A, Antarctica, annual average temperature -74°C (-94°F)

Hottest Recorded Temperature: Furnace Creek Ranch (Death Valley), California, U.S., 56.7°C (134°F), October 7, 1913

Coldest Recorded Temperature: Vostok research station, Antarctica, -89.2°C (-128.6°F), July 21, 1983

Wettest Place: Mawsynram, Meghalaya, India, annual average rainfall 1,187 cm (467 in)

Driest Place: Arica, Atacama Desert, Chile, rainfall barely measurable

Highest Waterfall: Angel Falls, Venezuela, 979 m (3,212 ft)

Largest Hot Desert: Sahara, Africa, 9,000,000 sq km (3,475,000 sq mi)

Largest Ice Desert: Antarctica, 13,209,000 sq km (5,100,000 sq mi)

Largest Canyon: Grand Canyon, Colorado River, Arizona, U.S., 446 km (277 mi) long along river, 180 m (600 ft) to 29 km (18 mi) wide, about 1.6 km (1 mi) deep

Largest Cave Chamber: Sarawak Cave, Gunung Mulu National Park, Malaysia, 16 hectares and 79 meters high (40.2 acres and 260 feet)

Largest Cave System: Mammoth Cave, Kentucky, U.S., over 591 km (367 mi) of passageways mapped

Most Predictable Large Geyser: Old Faithful, Wyoming, U.S., annual average interval 66 to 80 minutes

Longest Reef: Great Barrier Reef, Australia, 2,300 km (1,429 mi)

Greatest Tidal Range: Bay of Fundy, Canadian Atlantic Coast, 16 m (52 ft)

AREA OF EACH CONTINENT

	SQ KM	SQ MI	PERCENT OF EARTH'S LAND
Asia	44,570,000	17,208,000	30.0
Africa	30,065,000	11,608,000	20.2
North America	24,474,000	9,449,000	16.5
South America	17,819,000	6,880,000	12.0
Antarctica	13,209,000	5,100,000	8.9
Europe	9,947,000	3,841,000	6.7
Australia	7,692,000	2,970,000	5.2

HIGHEST POINT ON EACH CONTINENT

	METERS	FEET
Mount Everest, Asia	8,850	29,035
Cerro Aconcagua, South America	6,959	22,831
Mount McKinley (Denali), North America	6,194	20,320
Kilimanjaro, Africa	5,895	19,340
El'brus, Europe	5,642	18,510
Vinson Massif, Antarctica	4,897	16,066
Mount Kosciuszko, Australia	2,228	7,310

LOWEST SURFACE POINT ON EACH CONTINENT

	METERS	FEET
Dead Sea, Asia	-422	-1,385
Lake Assal, Africa	-156	-512
Laguna del Carbón, South America	-105	-344
Death Valley, North America	-86	-282
Caspian Sea, Europe	-28	-92
Lake Eyre, Australia	-16	-52
Bentley Subglacial Trench, Antarctica	-2,555	-8,383

LARGEST ISLANDS

	SQ KM	SQ MI
1 **Greenland**	2,166,000	836,000
2 **New Guinea**	792,500	306,000
3 **Borneo**	725,500	280,100
4 **Madagascar**	587,000	226,600
5 **Baffin Island**	507,500	196,000
6 **Sumatra**	427,300	165,000
7 **Honshu**	227,400	87,800
8 **Great Britain**	218,100	84,200
9 **Victoria Island**	217,300	83,900
10 **Ellesmere Island**	196,200	75,800
11 **Sulawesi (Celebes)**	178,700	69,000
12 **South Island (New Zealand)**	150,400	58,100
13 **Java**	126,700	48,900
14 **North Island (New Zealand)**	113,700	43,900
15 **Luzon**	110,000	42,000

AREA OF EACH OCEAN

	SQ KM	SQ MI	PERCENT OF EARTH'S WATER
Pacific	169,479,000	65,436,200	46.8
Atlantic	91,526,400	35,338,500	25.3
Indian	74,694,800	28,839,800	20.6
Arctic	13,960,100	5,390,000	3.9

DEEPEST POINT IN EACH OCEAN

	METERS	FEET
Challenger Deep, Pacific Ocean	-10,994	-36,070
Puerto Rico Trench, Atlantic Ocean	-8,605	-28,232
Java Trench, Indian Ocean	-7,125	-23,376
Molloy Hole, Arctic Ocean	-5,669	-18,599

LARGEST SEAS BY AREA

	SQ KM	SQ MI	AVERAGE DEPTH METERS	FEET
1 **Coral Sea**	4,183,510	1,615,260	2,471	8,107
2 **South China Sea**	3,596,390	1,388,570	1,180	3,871
3 **Caribbean Sea**	2,834,290	1,094,330	2,596	8,517
4 **Bering Sea**	2,519,580	972,810	1,832	6,010
5 **Mediterranean Sea**	2,469,100	953,320	1,572	5,157
6 **Sea of Okhotsk**	1,625,190	627,490	814	2,671
7 **Gulf of Mexico**	1,531,810	591,430	1,544	5,066

		SQ KM	SQ MI	METERS	FEET
8	Norwegian Sea	1,425,280	550,300	1,768	5,801
9	Greenland Sea	1,157,850	447,050	1,443	4,734
10	Sea of Japan (East Sea)	1,008,260	389,290	1,647	5,404
11	Hudson Bay	1,005,510	388,230	119	390
12	East China Sea	785,990	303,470	374	1,227
13	Andaman Sea	605,760	233,890	1,061	3,481
14	Red Sea	436,280	168,450	494	1,621
15	Black Sea	410,150	158,360	1,336	4,383

LARGEST LAKES BY AREA

		SQ KM	SQ MI	AVERAGE DEPTH METERS	FEET
1	Caspian Sea	371,000	143,200	1,025	3,363
2	Lake Superior	82,100	31,700	406	1,332
3	Lake Victoria	69,500	26,800	82	269
4	Lake Huron	59,600	23,000	229	751
5	Lake Michigan	57,800	22,300	281	922
6	Lake Tanganyika	32,600	12,600	1,470	4,823
7	Lake Baikal	31,500	12,200	1,637	5,371
8	Great Bear Lake	31,300	12,100	446	1,463
9	Lake Malawi (L. Nyasa)	28,900	11,200	695	2,280
10	Great Slave Lake	28,600	11,000	614	2,014

LARGEST DRAINAGE BASINS BY AREA

		SQ KM	SQ MI
1	Amazon, South America	7,050,000	2,722,000
2	Congo, Africa	3,700,000	1,429,000
3	Mississippi-Missouri, N. America	3,250,000	1,255,000
4	Paraná-Río de la Plata, S. America	3,100,000	1,197,000
5	Yenisey-Angara, Asia	2,700,000	1,042,000
6	Ob-Irtysh, Asia	2,430,000	938,000
7	Lena, Asia	2,420,000	934,000
8	Nile, Africa	1,900,000	734,000
9	Amur, Asia	1,840,000	710,000
10	Mackenzie-Peace, North America	1,765,000	681,000
11	Ganges-Brahmaputra, Asia	1,730,000	668,000
12	Volga, Europe	1,380,000	533,000
13	Zambezi, Africa	1,330,000	513,000
14	Niger, Africa	1,200,000	463,000
15	Chang Jiang (Yangtze), Asia	1,175,000	454,000

LONGEST RIVERS

		KM	MI
1	Nile, Africa	6,695	4,160
2	Amazon, South America	6,679	4,150
3	Chang Jiang (Yangtze), Asia	6,244	3,880
4	Mississippi-Missouri, N. America	5,970	3,710
5	Yenisey-Angara, Asia	5,810	3,610
6	Huang (Yellow), Asia	5,778	3,590
7	Ob-Irtysh, Asia	5,410	3,362
8	Congo, Africa	4,700	2,900
9	Paraná-Río de la Plata, S. America	4,695	2,917
10	Amur, Asia	4,416	2,744

11	Lena, Asia	4,400	2,734
12	Mackenzie-Peace, North America	4,241	2,635
13	Mekong, Asia	4,184	2,600
14	Niger, Africa	4,170	2,591
15	Murray-Darling, Australia	3,718	2,310
16	Volga, Europe	3,685	2,290
17	Purus, South America	3,400	2,113
18	Indus, Asia	3,200	2,000
19	Yukon, North America	3,190	1,980
20	Euphrates, Asia	2,800	1,740

GEOPOLITICAL EXTREMES

Largest Country: Russia 17,098,242 sq km (6,601,668 sq mi)

Smallest Country: Vatican City 0.4 sq km (0.2 sq mi)

Most Populous Country: China 1,349,586,000 people

Least Populous Country: Vatican City 836 people

Most Crowded Country: Monaco 15,250 per sq km (38,125 per sq mi)

Least Crowded Country: Mongolia 2.0 per sq km (5.3 per sq mi)

Most Populous Metropolitan Area: Tokyo 37,217,000 people

Country with the Greatest Number of Bordering Countries: China 14, Russia 14

ENGINEERING WONDERS

Tallest Building (Mixed-use): Burj Khalifa, Dubai, United Arab Emirates, 828 m (2,716 ft)

Tallest All-Office Building: Taipei 101, Taipei, Taiwan, 508 m (1,667 ft)

Tallest All-Residential Building: Princess Tower, Dubai, United Arab Emirates, 413 m (1,356 ft)

Tallest All-Hotel Building: JW Marriott Marquis Hotel Dubai Towers 1 & 2, Dubai, United Arab Emirates, 355 m (1,166 ft)

Tallest Tower (Freestanding): Tokyo Skytree, Tokyo, Japan, 634 m (2,080 ft)

Longest Wall: Great Wall of China, approx. 3,460 km (2,150 mi)

Longest Road: Pan American highway (not including gap in Panama and Colombia), more than 24,140 km (15,000 mi)

Longest Railroad: Trans-Siberian Railroad, Russia, 9,288 km (5,772 mi)

Longest Road Tunnel: Laerdal Tunnel, Laerdal, Norway, 24.5 km (15.2 mi)

Longest Rail Tunnel: Seikan submarine rail tunnel, Honshu to Hokkaido, Japan, 53.9 km (33.5 mi)

Tallest Bridge: Millau Viaduct, France, 343 m (1,125 ft)

Longest Highway Bridge: Qingdao-Haiwan Bridge, Shandong, China, 42.6 km (26.4 mi)

Longest Suspension Bridge: Akashi-Kaikyo Bridge, Japan, 3,911 m (12,831 ft)

Longest Boat Canal: Grand Canal, China, more than 1,770 km (1,100 mi)

Longest Irrigation Canal: Garagum Canal, Turkmenistan, nearly 1,400 km (870 mi)

Largest Artificial Lake by Area: Lake Volta, Volta River, Ghana, 9,065 sq km (3,500 sq mi)

Tallest Dam: Nurek Dam, Vakhsh River, Tajikistan, 300 m (984 ft)

Tallest Pyramid: Great Pyramid of Khufu, Egypt, 138 m (455 ft)

Deepest Mine: TauTona Gold Mine, South Africa, 3902 m (12,802 ft) deep

Longest Submarine Cable: Sea-Me-We 3 cable, connects 33 countries on four continents, 39,000 km (24,200 mi) long

See corresponding map ▶ on following pages

Longitude West of Greenwich

ELLESMERE ISLAND

Pan American highway
World's longest road

VICTORIA ISLAND

Molloy Ho
-5,669
(-18,599
*Arctic Ocean
deepest poi*

GREENLAND

ARCTIC CIRCLE

Yukon

BAFFIN ISLAND

Mount McKinley
(Denali),
United States
(20,320 ft) 6,194 m
*North America's
highest point*

Great Bear Lake

GREENLAND
SEA

Mackenzie — *Great Slave Lake*
Peace

HUDSON
BAY

Laerdal Tunnel, No
World's longest road tu

Pan American highway
World's longest road

GREAT BRITAIN

Lake
Superior

N O R T H

Lake
Huron

N O R T H

Old Faithful, United States
World's most predictable large geyser

NORTH
AMERICA
Lake Michigan

Bay of Fundy, Canada
World's greatest tidal range

Sea-Me-We 3 cable
World's longest submarine cable

Furnace Creek Ranch (Death Valley), United States
World's hottest recorded temperature

Grand Canyon,
United States
*World's largest
canyon*

Millau Viaduct, France
World's tallest bridge

Death Valley, United States (-282 ft) -86 m
North America's lowest point

Mississippi-
Missouri

Mammoth Cave, United States
World's largest cave system

A T L A N T I C

P A C I F I C

GULF OF
MEXICO

TROPIC OF CANCER

Puerto Rico Trench
-8,605 m (-28,232 ft)
Atlantic Ocean's deepest point

O C E A N

S   A

Worl

O C E A N

CARIBBEAN
SEA

Angel Falls, Venezuela
World's highest waterfall

Lake Volta, Ghana
*World's largest artificial lake
by area*

Nige

EQUATOR

Amazon

Purus

SOUTH
AMERICA

Meridian of Greenwich
(London)

S O U T H

Arica, Chile
Atacama Desert
World's driest place

Paraná

A T L A N T I C

S O U T H

TROPIC OF CAPRICORN

Pan American highway
World's longest road

Cerro Aconcagua, Chile
(22,831 ft) 6,959 m
South America's highest point

Río de la Plata

O C E A N

P A C I F I C

Laguna del Carbón, Argentina
-105 m (-344 ft)
South America's lowest point

O C E A N

Pan American highway
World's longest road

ANTARCTIC CIRCLE

Vinson Massif
4,897 m (16,066 ft)
Antarctica's highest point

◄ *See lists of "Geographic Comparisons"
on previous pages*

Bentley Subglacial Trench
-2,555 m (-8,383 ft)
Antarctica's lowest known point

A N T

O   C   E   A   N

Longitude East of Greenwich

30° 60° 90° 120° 150° 90° 180°

ARCTIC CIRCLE

BERING
SEA

NORTH

Trans-Siberian
Railroad, Russia
World's longest railroad

Ob   Yenisey   Lena

Volga   Ob   Irtysh   Angara   Lake
Baikal   Amur

SEA OF
OKHOTSK

Trans-Siberian
Railroad, Russia
World's longest railroad

A   S   I   A

OPE

Seikan submarine tunnel, Japan
World's longest rail tunnel

BLACK SEA

El'brus, Russia 5,642 m (18,510 ft)
+ Europe's highest point

Great Wall of China
World's longest wall

SEA OF
JAPAN
(EAST SEA)

PACIFIC

• CASPIAN SEA -28 m (-92 ft)
Europe's lowest point

Huang
(Yellow)

HONSHU

Tokyo Skytree, Japan
World's tallest tower

Nurek Dam, Tajikistan
World's tallest dam

Qingdao-Haiwan
Bridge, China
World's longest
highway bridge

Akashi-Kaikyo Bridge, Japan
World's longest suspension bridge

30°

NEAN SEA

Garagum Canal,
Turkmenistan
World's longest
irrigation canal

Mount Everest,
China, Nepal
(29,035 ft) 8,850 m
World's highest point

Grand Canal, China
World's longest boat canal

EAST
CHINA
SEA

TROPIC OF CANCER

• Dead Sea,
Israel, Jordan
-422 m (-1,385 ft)
World's lowest point

Euphrates

Indus

Brahmaputra

Chang Jiang
(Yangtze)

Taipei 101, Taiwan
World's tallest all-office building

OCEAN

RA

Great Pyramid
of Khufu, Egypt
rld's tallest pyramid

Princess Tower,
United Arab Emirates
World's tallest all-residential
building

Ganges

Mawsynram, Meghalaya, India
World's wettest place

Sea-Me-We 3 cable
World's longest submarine cable

RED SEA

Burj Khalifa,
United Arab Emirates
World's tallest building

JW Marriott Marquis Hotel
Dubai Towers 1 & 2,
United Arab Emirates
World's tallest all-hotel
building

LUZON

Nile

Dalol, Ethiopia
Danakil Depression
World's hottest place

ANDAMAN
SEA

Mekong

Challenger Deep
-10,994 m (-36,070 ft)
World's greatest ocean depth

• Lake Assal, Djibouti
-156 m (-512 ft)
Africa's lowest point

Sea-Me-We 3 cable
World's longest
submarine cable

SOUTH CHINA SEA

Sarawak Cave
Gunung Mulu National Park, Malaysia
World's largest cave chamber

EQUATOR   0°

Congo

Lake Victoria

BORNEO

+ Kilimanjaro, Tanzania
5,895 m (19,340 ft)
Africa's highest point

SUMATRA

SULAWESI

NEW
GUINEA

+ Mt. Wilhelm, Papua New Guinea
4,509 m (14,793 ft)
Oceania's highest point

Lake Tanganyika

Lake Malawi
(Lake Nyasa)

JAVA

Java Trench
-7,125 m (-23,376 ft)
Indian Ocean's deepest point

CORAL SEA

Zambezi

I   N   D   I   A   N

Great Barrier Reef
World's longest reef

MADAGASCAR

SOUTH

TauTona Gold Mine,
South Africa
World's deepest mine

O   C   E   A   N

Sea-Me-We 3 cable
World's longest submarine cable

AUSTRALIA

TROPIC OF CAPRICORN

PACIFIC

Map Key

Drainage basin

☐ Natural extreme point location

■ Human extreme point location

+ Elevation

• Depression

Lake Eyre, Australia
(-52 ft) -16 m
Australia's lowest point

Darling

OCEAN

30°

Mount Kosciuszko, Australia
+ 2,228 m (7,310 ft)
Australia's highest point

Murray

NORTH ISLAND
(New Zealand)

SOUTH ISLAND
(New Zealand)

ANTARCTIC CIRCLE

60°

Winkel Tripel Projection

SCALE 1:89,822,700   1 CENTIMETER = 898 KILOMETERS; 1 INCH = 1,418 MILES AT THE EQUATOR

0   500   1000   1500   2000   2500
KILOMETERS

0   500   1000   1500   2000   2500
STATUTE MILES

Vostok,
Russian research station
World's coldest recorded
temperature ☐

Ridge A,
World's coldest place ☐

C   T   I   C   A

World's largest ice desert

30° 60° 90° 120° 150° 90° 180°

Abbreviations

A.
A.	Arroio, Arroyo
A.C.T.	Australian Capital Territory
A.F.B.	Air Force Base
A.F.S.	Air Force Station
A.R.B.	Air Reserve Base
Adm.	Administrative
Af.	Africa
Afghan.	Afghanistan
Ala.	Alabama
Alas.	Alaska
Alban.	Albania
Alg.	Algeria
Alta.	Alberta
Amer.	America-n
Amzns.	Amazonas
Anch.	Anchorage
And. & Nic.	Andaman and Nicobar Islands
And. Prad.	Andhra Pradesh
Antil.	Antilles
Arch.	Archipelago, Archipiélago
Arg.	Argentina
Ariz.	Arizona
Ark.	Arkansas
Arkh.	Arkhangel'sk
Arm.	Armenia
Arun. Prad.	Arunachal Pradesh
Astrak.	Astrakhan'
Atl. Oc.	Atlantic Ocean
Aust.	Austria
Austral.	Australia
Auton.	Autonomous
Azerb.	Azerbaijan

B.
B.	Baai, Baía, Baie, Bahía, Bay, Bugt-en, Buḥayrat
B. Aires	Buenos Aires
B.C.	British Columbia
B. Qazaq.	Batys Qazaqstan
Bashk.	Bashkortostan
Belg.	Belgium
Bol.	Bolivia
Bol.	Bol'sh-oy, -aya, -oye
Bosn. & Herzg.	Bosnia and Herzegovina
Br.	Branch
Braz.	Brazil
Bulg.	Bulgaria
Burya.	Buryatiya

C.
C.	Cabo, Cap, Cape, Capo
C.H.	Court House
C.P.	Conservation Park
C.R.	Costa Rica
C.S.I. Terr.	Coral Sea Islands Territory
Cach.	Cachoeira
Calif.	California
Can.	Canada
Cap.	Capitán
Catam.	Catamarca
Cd.	Ciudad
Cen. Af. Rep.	Central African Republic
Cga.	Ciénaga
Chan.	Channel
Chand.	Chandigarh
Chap.	Chapada
Chech.	Chechnya
Chely.	Chelyabinsk
Chhat.	Chhattisgarh
Chongq.	Chongqing Shi
Chuk.	Chukotskiy
Chuv.	Chuvashiya
Chyrv.	Chyrvony, -aya, -aye
Cmte.	Comandante
Cnel.	Coronel
Co.-s.	Cerro-s
Col.	Colombia
Colo.	Colorado
Conn.	Connecticut
Cord.	Cordillera
Corr.	Corrientes
Cr.	Creek, Crique

D.
D.	Danau
D. & Diu	Daman and Diu
D. & Nagar	Dadra and Nagar Haveli
D.C.	District of Columbia
D.F.	Distrito Federal
Del.	Delaware
Dem.	Democratic
Den.	Denmark
Dist.	District, Distrito
Dom. Rep.	Dominican Republic
Dr.	Doctor
Dz.	Dzong

E.
E.	East-ern
E. Ríos	Entre Ríos
E. Santo	Espírito Santo
Ea.	Estancia
Ecua.	Ecuador
El Salv.	El Salvador
Emb.	Embalse
Eng.	England
Ens.	Ensenada
Entr.	Entrance
Eq.	Equatorial
Esc.	Escarpment
Est.	Estaci´on
Est.	Estonia
Ét.	Étang
Eth.	Ethiopia
Eur.	Europe
Ez.	Ezers

F.
F.	Fiume
F.S.M.	Federated States of Micronesia
Falk. Is.	Falkland Islands
Fd.	Fiord, Fiordo, Fjord
Fed.	Federal, Federation
Fin.	Finland
Fk.	Fork
Fla.	Florida
Fn.	Fortín
Fr.	France, French
Ft.	Fort
Fy.	Ferry
F.Z.	Fracture zone

G.
G.	Golfe, Golfo, Gulf
G. Altay	Gorno-Altay
G.R.	Game Reserve
Ga.	Georgia
Geb.	Gebergte, Gebirge
Gen.	General
Ger.	Germany
Gez.	Gezîra-t, Gezîret
Gezr.	Gezˆair
Gl.	Glacier, Gletscher
Gob.	Gobernador
Gr.	Greece
Gr.	Gross-er
Gral.	General
Gt.	Great-er
Guang.	Guangdong

H.
H.K.	Hong Kong
Hbr.	Harbor, Harbour
Hdqrs.	Headquarters
Heilong.	Heilongjiang
Hi. Prad.	Himachal Pradesh
Hist.	Historic, -al
Hond.	Honduras
Hts.	Heights
Hung.	Hungary
Hwy.	Highway

I.
I.H.S.	International Historic Site
I.-s.	Île-s, Ilha-s, Isla-s, Island-s, Isle, Isol-a, -e
Ice.	Iceland
Ig.	Igarapé
Igr.	Ingeniero
Ill.	Illinois
Ind.	Indiana
Ind. Oc.	Indian Ocean
Ingush.	Ingushetiya
Intl.	International
Ire.	Ireland
It.	Italy

J.
J.	Järvi, Joki
J. & Kash.	Jammu and Kashmir
J.A.R.	Jewish Autonomous Region
Jab., Jeb.	Jabal, Jebel
Jam.	Jamaica
Jct.	Jonction, Junction
Jez.	Jezero, Jezioro
Jhark.	Jharkhand

K.
K.	Kanal
K. Balka.	Kabardino-Balkariya
K. Cherk.	Karachayevo-Cherkesiya
K. Mansi	Khanty-Mansi
Kalin.	Kaliningrad
Kalmy.	Kalmykiya
Kamchat.	Kamchatka
Kans.	Kansas
Karna.	Karnataka
Kaz.	Kazakhstan
Kemer.	Kemerovo
Kep.	Kepulauan
Kh.	Khor
Khabar.	Khabarovsk
Khak.	Khakasiya
Khr.	Khrebet
Km.	Kilómetro
Kól.	Kólpos
Kör.	Körfez,-i
Kos.	Kosovo
Kr.	Krasn-yy, -aya, -oye
Krasnod.	Krasnodar
Krasnoy.	Krasnoyarsk
Ky.	Kentucky
Kyrg.	Kyrgyzstan

L.
L.	Lac, Lago, Lake, Límni, Loch, Lough
La.	Louisiana
Lag.	Laguna
Lakshad.	Lakshadweep
Latv.	Latvia
Ldg.	Landing
Leb.	Lebanon
Lib.	Libya
Liech.	Liechtenstein
Lith.	Lithuania
Lux.	Luxembourg

M.
Mal.	Mal-y-y, -aya, -aya
M.C.A.S.	Marine Corps Air Station
M. Gerais	Minas Gerais
M. Grosso	Mato Grosso
M. Grosso S.	Mato Grosso do Sul
M. Prad.	Madhya Pradesh
Maced.	Macedonia
Mahar.	Maharashtra
Man.	Manitoba
Mangg.	Mangghystaū
Maran.	Maranhão
Mass.	Massachusetts
Md.	Maryland
Me.	Maine
Medit. Sea	Mediterranean Sea
Meghal.	Meghalaya
Mex.	Mexico
Mgne.	Montagne
Mich.	Michigan
Minn.	Minnesota
Miss.	Mississippi
Mo.	Missouri
Mold.	Moldova
Mon.	Monument

Mont.	Montana	Pac. Oc.	Pacific Ocean	Sta., Sto.	Santa, Station, Santo
Mor.	Morocco	Pak.	Pakistan	Sta. Cata.	Santa Catarina
Mord.	Mordoviya	Pan.	Panama	Sta. Cruz.	Santa Cruz
Mt.-s.	Mont-s, Mount-ain-s	Pant.	Pantano	Stavr.	Stavropol'
Mte.-s.	Monte-s	Parag.	Paraguay	Str.-s.	Straat, Strait-s
Mti., Mtii.	Munţi-i	Parq. Nac.	Parque Nacional	Sv.	Svyat-oy, -aya, -oye
Mun.	Municipal	Pass.	Passage	Sverd.	Sverdlovsk
Murm.	Murmansk	Peg.	Pegunungan	Sw.	Sweden
		Pen.	Peninsula, Péninsule	Switz.	Switzerland
N.	North-ern	Per.	Pereval	Syr.	Syria
N.A.S.	Naval Air Station	Pern.	Pernambuco		
N.B.	National Battlefield	Pivd.	Pivdennyy	**T.** Fuego	Tierra del Fuego
N.B.	New Brunswick	Pk.	Peak	T. Nadu	Tamil Nadu
N.B.P.	National Battlefield Park	Pl.	Planina	Taj.	Tajikistan
N.B.S.	National Battlefield Site	Plat.	Plateau	Tartar.	Tartarstan
N.C.	National Cemetery	Pol.	Poland	Tas.	Tasmania
N.C.	North Carolina	Pol.	Poluostrov	Tel.	Teluk
N.C.A.	National Conservation Area	Por.	Porog	Tenn.	Tennessee
N. Dak.	North Dakota	Port.	Portugal	Terr.	Territory
N.E.	North East	Pres.	Presidente	Tex.	Texas
N.H.	New Hampshire	Prov.	Province, Provincial	Tg.	Tanjung
N.H.P.	National Historic, -al Park	Pt.-e.	Point-e	Thai.	Thailand
N.H.S.	National Historic Site	Pta.	Ponta, Punta	Tmt.-s	Tablemount-s
N. Ire.	Northern Ireland	Pto.	Puerto	Tocant.	Tocantins
N.J.	New Jersey			Trin.	Trinidad
N.L.	National Lakeshore	**Q.**	Quebrada	Tun.	Tunisia
N.M.	National Monument	Qarag.	Qaraghandy	Turk.	Turkey
N.M.P.	National Military Park	Qnsld.	Queensland	Turkm.	Turkmenistan
N. Mem.	National Memorial	Que.	Quebec		
N. Mem. P.	National Memorial Park	Qyzyl.	Qyzylorda	**U.**A.E.	United Arab Emirates
N. Mex.	New Mexico			U.K.	United Kingdom
N. Mongol	Nei Mongol	**R.**	Río, River, Rivière	U. Prad.	Uttar Pradesh
N.P.	National Park	R.R.	Railroad	U.S.	United States
N.R.	Nature Reserve	R. Gr. Norte	Rio Grande do Norte	Udmur.	Udmurtiya
N.R.A.	National Recreation Area	R. Gr. Sul	Rio Grande do Sul	Uj.	Ujung
N.S.	Nova Scotia	R.I.	Rhode Island	Ukr.	Ukraine
N.S.R.	National Scenic Riverway	R. Jan.	Rio de Janeiro	Ulyan.	Ul'yanovsk
N.S.R.A.	National Seashore Recreational Area	R. Negro	Río Negro	Uru.	Uruguay
N.S.T.	National Scenic Trail	Ra.-s.	Range-s	Uttar.	Uttarakhand
N.S.W.	New South Wales	Raja.	Rajasthan	Uzb.	Uzbekistan
N.T.	Northern Territory	Reg.	Region		
N.T.C.	Naval Training Center	Rep.	Republic	**V.**a.	Virginia
N.T.S.	Naval Training Station	Res.	Reservoir, Reserve, Reservatório	Val.	Valle
N.V.M.	National Volcanic Monument	Rk.	Rock	Vdkhr.	Vodokhranil-ishche
N.W.T.	Northwest Territories	Rom.	Romania	Vdskh.	Vodoskhovy-shche
N.Y.	New York	Russ.	Russia	Venez.	Venezuela
N.Z.	New Zealand			Verkh.	Verkhn-iy, -yaya, -eye
Nat. Mem.	National Memorial	**S.**	South-ern	Vic.	Victoria
Nat. Mon.	National Monument	S.A.R.	Special Administrative Region	Vol.	Volcán, Volcano
Nat. Park	National Park	S. Aust.	South Australia	Volg.	Volgograd
Nebr.	Nebraska	S.C.	South Carolina	Voz.	Vozyera, -yero, -yera
Neth.	Netherlands	S. Dak.	South Dakota	Vozv.	Vozvyshennost'
Nev.	Nevada, Nevado	S. Estero	Santiago del Estero	Vr.	Vester
Nfld. & Lab.	Newfoundland and Labrador	S. Ossetia	South Ossetia	Vt.	Vermont
Nicar.	Nicaragua	S. Paulo	São Paulo	Vyal.	Vyaliki, -ikaya,-ikaye
Niz. Nov.	Nizhniy Novgorod	S.W.	Southwest		
Nizh.	Nizhn-iy, -yaya, -eye	Sa.-s.	Serra, Sierra-s	**W.**	Wadi, Wâdi, Wādī, Webi
Nor.	Norway	Sal.	Salar, Salina	W.	West-ern
Nov.	Nov-yy, -aya, -aye, -oye	Sask.	Saskatchewan	W. Aust.	Western Australia
Novg.	Novgorod	Scot.	Scotland	W. Bengal	West Bengal
Novo.	Novosibirsk	Sd.	Sound, Sund	W.H.	Water Hole
Nr.	Nørre	Sel.	Selat	W. Va.	West Virginia
		Ser.	Serranía	Wash.	Washington
O.	Ostrov, Oued	Serb.	Serbia	Wis.	Wisconsin
Oc.	Ocean	Sev.	Severn-yy, -aya, -oye	Wyo.	Wyoming
Of.	Oficina	Sev. Oset.	Severnaya Osetiya-Alaniya		
Okla.	Oklahoma	Sgt.	Sargento	**Y.** Nenets	Yamal-Nenets
Ong. Qazaq.	Ongtüstik Qazaqstan	Shand.	Shandong	Yar.	Yarymadasy
Ont.	Ontario	Shy. Qazaq.	Shyghys Qazaqstan	Yaro.	Yaroslavl'
Ør.	Øster	Sk.	Shankou	Yu.	Yuzhn-yy, -aya, -oye
Oreg.	Oregon	Slov.	Slovenia		
Orenb.	Orenburg	Smt.-s	Seamount-s	**Z.**akh.	Zakhod-ni, -nyaya, -nye
Oz.	Ozero	Solt. Qazaq.	Soltüstik Qazaqstan	Zal.	Zaliv
		Sp.	Spain, Spanish	Zap.	Zapadn-yy, -aya, -oye
P.	Paso, Pass, Passo	Spr.-s.	Spring-s	Zimb.	Zimbabwe
P.E.I.	Prince Edward Island	Sq.	Square		
P.N.G.	Papua New Guinea	Sr.	Sønder		
P.R.	Puerto Rico	St.-e.	Saint-e, Sankt, Sint		
Pa.	Pennsylvania	St. Peter.	Saint Petersburg		

Foreign Terms

A aglet _____ well
Aain _____ spring
Aauinat _____ spring
Āb _____ river, water
Ache _____ stream
Açude _____ reservoir
Ada,-si _____ island
Adrar _____ mountain-s, plateau
Aguada _____ dry lake bed
Aguelt _____ water hole, well
'Ain, Aïn _____ spring, well
Aïoun-et _____ spring-s, well
Aivi _____ mountain
Ákra, Akrotírion _____ cape, promontory
Alb _____ mountain, ridge
Alföld _____ plain
Alin' _____ mountain range
Alpe-n _____ mountain-s
Altiplanicie _____ high plain, plateau
Alto _____ hill-s, mountain-s, ridge
Älv-en _____ river
Āmba _____ hill, mountain
Anou _____ well
Anse _____ bay, inlet
Ao _____ bay, cove, estuary
Ap _____ cape, point
Archipel, Archipiélago _____ archipelago
Arcipelago, Arkhipelag _____ archipelago
Arquipélago _____ archipelago
Arrecife-s _____ reef-s
Arroio, Arroyo _____ brook, gully, rivulet, stream
Ås _____ ridge
Ava _____ channel
Aylagy _____ gulf
'Ayn _____ spring, well

B a _____ intermittent stream, river
Baai _____ bay, cove, lagoon
Bāb _____ gate, strait
Badia _____ bay
Bælt _____ strait
Bagh _____ bay
Bahar _____ drainage basin
Bahía _____ bay
Bahr, Baḥr _____ bay, lake, river, sea, wadi
Baía, Baie _____ bay
Bajo-s _____ shoal-s
Ban _____ village
Bañado-s _____ flooded area, swamp-s
Banc, Banco-s _____ bank-s, sandbank-s, shoal-s
Band _____ lake
Bandao _____ peninsula
Baño-s _____ hot spring-s, spa
Baraj-ı _____ dam, reservoir
Barra _____ bar, sandbank
Barrage, Barragem _____ dam, lake, reservoir
Barranca _____ gorge, ravine
Bazar _____ marketplace
Beinn, Ben _____ mountain
Belt _____ strait
Bereg _____ bank, coast, shore
Berg-e _____ mountain-s
Bil _____ lake
Biq'at _____ plain, valley
Bir, Bîr, Bi'r _____ spring, well
Birket _____ lake, pool, swamp
Bjerg-e _____ mountain-s, range

Boca, Bocca _____ channel, river, mouth
Bocht _____ bay
Bodden _____ bay
Boğaz, -ı _____ strait
Bögeni _____ reservoir
Boka _____ gulf, mouth
Bol'sh-oy, -aya, -oye _____ big
Bolsón _____ inland basin
Boubairet _____ lagoon, lake
Bras _____ arm, branch of a stream
Braţ, -ul _____ arm, branch of a stream
Bre, -en _____ glacier, ice cap
Bredning _____ bay, broad water
Bruch _____ marsh
Bucht _____ bay
Bugt-en _____ bay
Buḥayrat, Buheirat _____ lagoon, lake, marsh
Bukhta, Bukta, Bukt-en _____ bay
Bulak, Bulaq _____ spring
Bum _____ hill, mountain
Burnu, Burun _____ cape, point
Busen _____ gulf
Buuraha _____ hill-s, mountain-s
Büyük _____ big, large

C abeza-s _____ head-s, summit-s
Cabo _____ cape
Cachoeira _____ rapids, waterfall
Cal _____ hill, peak
Caleta _____ cove, inlet
Campo-s _____ field-s, flat country
Canal _____ canal, channel, strait
Caño _____ channel, stream
Cao Nguyen _____ mountain, plateau
Cap, Capo _____ cape
Capitán _____ captain
Càrn _____ mountain
Castillo _____ castle, fort
Catarata-s _____ cataract-s, waterfall-s
Causse _____ upland
Çay _____ brook, stream
Cay-s, Cayo-s _____ island-s, key-s, shoal-s
Cerro-s _____ hill-s, peak-s
Chaîne, Chaînons _____ mountain chain, range
Chapada-s _____ plateau, upland-s
Chedo _____ archipelago
Chenal _____ river channel
Chersónisos _____ peninsula
Chhung _____ bay
Chi _____ lake
Chiang _____ bay
Chiao _____ cape, point, rock
Ch'ih _____ lake
Chink _____ escarpment
Chott _____ intermittent salt lake, salt marsh
Chou _____ island
Ch'ü _____ canal
Ch'üntao _____ archipelago, islands
Chute-s _____ cataract-s, waterfall-s
Chyrvony _____ red
Cima _____ mountain, peak, summit
Ciudad _____ city
Co _____ lake
Col _____ pass
Collina, Colline _____ hill, mountains
Con _____ island
Cordillera _____ mountain chain

Corno _____ mountain, peak
Coronel _____ colonel
Corredeira _____ cascade, rapids
Costa _____ coast
Côte _____ coast, slope
Coxilha, Cuchilla _____ range of low hills
Crique _____ creek, stream
Csatorna _____ canal, channel
Cul de Sac _____ bay, inlet

D a _____ great, greater
Daban _____ pass
Dağ, -ı, Dagh _____ mountain
Dağlar, -ı _____ mountains
Dahr _____ cliff, mesa
Dake _____ mountain, peak
Dal-en _____ valley
Dala _____ steppe
Dan _____ cape, point
Danau _____ lake
Dao _____ island
Dar'ya _____ lake, river
Daryācheh _____ lake, marshy lake
Dasht _____ desert, plain
Dawan _____ pass
Dawḩat _____ bay, cove, inlet
Deniz, -i _____ sea
Dent-s _____ peak-s
Deo _____ pass
Desēt _____ hummock, island, land-tied island
Desierto _____ desert
Détroit _____ channel, strait
Dhar _____ hills, ridge, tableland
Ding _____ mountain
Distrito _____ district
Djebel _____ mountain, range
Do _____ island-s, rock-s
Doi _____ hill, mountain
Dome _____ ice dome
Dong _____ village
Dooxo _____ floodplain
Dzong _____ castle, fortress

E iland-en _____ island-s
Eilean _____ island
Ejland _____ island
Elv _____ river
Embalse _____ lake, reservoir
Emi _____ mountain, rock
Enseada, Ensenada _____ bay, cove
Ér _____ rivulet, stream
Erg _____ sand dune region
Est _____ east
Estación _____ railroad station
Estany _____ lagoon, lake
Estero _____ estuary, inlet, lagoon, marsh
Estrecho _____ strait
Étang _____ lake, pond
Eylandt _____ island
Ežeras _____ lake
Ezers _____ lake

F alaise _____ cliff, escarpment
Farvand-et _____ channel, sound
Fell _____ mountain
Feng _____ mount, peak
Fiord-o _____ inlet, sound

Fiume	river
Fjäll-et	mountain
Fjällen	mountains
Fjärd-en	fjord
Fjarđar, Fjörđur	fjord
Fjeld	mountain
Fjell-ene	mountain-s
Fjöll	mountain-s
Fjord-en	inlet, fjord
Fleuve	river
Fljót	large river
Flói	bay, marshland
Foci	river mouths
Főcsatorna	principal canal
Förde	fjord, gulf, inlet
Forsen	rapids, waterfall
Fortaleza	fort, fortress
Fortín	fortified post
Foss-en	waterfall
Foum	pass, passage
Foz	mouth of a river
Fuerte	fort, fortress
Fwafwate	waterfalls

Gacan-ka — hill, peak

Gal	pond, spring, water hole, well
Gang	harbor
Gangri	peak, range
Gaoyuan	plateau
Garaet, Gara'et	lake, lake bed, salt lake
Gardaneh	pass
Garet	hill, mountain
Gat	channel
Gata	bay, inlet, lake
Gattet	channel, strait
Gaud	depression, saline tract
Gave	mountain stream
Gebel	mountain-s, range
Gebergte	mountain range
Gebirge	mountains, range
Geçidi	mountain pass, passage
Geçit	mountain pass, passage
Gezâir	islands
Gezîra-t, Gezîret	island, peninsula
Ghats	mountain range
Ghubb-at, -et	bay, gulf
Giri	mountain
Gkiri	bay
Gletscher	glacier
Gobernador	governor
Gobi	desert
Gol	river, stream
Göl, -ü	lake
Golets	mountain, peak
Golf, -e, -o	gulf
Gor-a, -y, Gór-a, -y	mountain,-s
Got	point
Gowd	depression
Goz	sand ridge
Gran, -de	great, large
Gryada	mountains, ridge
Guan	pass
Guba	bay, gulf
Guelta	well
Guntō	archipelago
Gunung	mountain
Gura	mouth, passage

Guyot	table mount

Hađabat — plateau

Haehyŏp	strait
Haff	lagoon
Hai	lake, sea
Haihsia	strait
Haixia	channel, strait
Hakau	reef, rock
Hakuchi	anchorage
Halvø, Halvøy-a	peninsula
Hama	beach
Hamada, Ḥammādah	rocky desert
Hamn	harbor, port
Hāmūn, Hamun	depression, lake
Hana	cape, point
Hantō	peninsula
Har	hill, mound, mountain
Ḥarrat	lava field
Hasi, Hassi	spring, well
Hauteur	elevation, height
Hav-et	sea
Havn, Havre	harbor, port
Hawr	lake, marsh
Hāyk'	lake, reservoir
He	canal, lake, river
Hegy, -ség	mountain, -s, range
Heiau	temple
Hoek	cape, point
Hög-en	high, hill
Höhe, -n	height, high
Høj	height, hill
Holm, -e, Holmene	island-s, islet-s
Holot	dunes
Hon	island-s
Hor-a, -y	mountain, -s
Horn	peak, summit
Houma	point
Hoved	headland, peninsula, point
Hraun	lava field
Hsü	island
Hu	lake, reservoir
Huk	cape, point
Hüyük	hill, mound

Idehan — sand dunes

Île-s, Ilha-s, Illa-s, Îlot-s	island-s, islet-s
Îlet, Ilhéu-s	islet, -s
Irhil	mountain-s
'Irq	sand dune-s
Isblink	glacier, ice field
Is-en	glacier
Isla-s, Islote	island-s, islet
Isol-a, -e	island, -s
Istmo	isthmus
Iwa	island, islet, rock

Jabal, Jebel — mountain-s, range

Järv, -i, Jaure, Javrre	lake
Jazā'ir, Jazīrat, Jazīreh	island-s
Jehīl	lake
Jezero, Jezioro	lake
Jiang	river, stream
Jiao	cape
Jibāl	hill, mountain, ridge
Jima	island-s, rock-s
Jøkel, Jökull	glacier, ice cap

Joki, Jokka	river
Jökulsá	river from a glacier
Jūn	bay

Kaap — cape

Kafr	village
Kaikyō	channel, strait
Kaise	mountain
Kaiwan	bay, gulf, sea
Kanal	canal, channel
Kangri	mountain, peak
Kap, Kapp	cape
Kavīr	salt desert
Kefar	village
Kënet'	lagoon, lake
Kep	cape, point
Kepulauan	archipelago, islands
Khalîg, Khalīj	bay, gulf
Khirb-at, -et	ancient site, ruins
Khrebet	mountain range
Kinh	canal
Klint	bluff, cliff
Kō	bay, cove, harbor
Ko	island, lake
Koh	island, mountain, range
Köl-i	lake
Kólpos	gulf
Kong	mountain
Körfez, -i	bay, gulf
Kosa	spit of land
Kou	estuary, river mouth
Kowtal-e	pass
Krasn-yy, -aya, -oye	red
Kryazh	mountain range, ridge
Kuala	estuary, river mouth
Kuan	mountain pass
Kūh, Kūhhā	mountain-s, range
Kul', Kuli	lake
Kum	sandy desert
Kundo	archipelago
Kuppe	hill-s, mountain-s
Kust	coast, shore
Kyst	coast
Kyun	island

La — pass

Lac, Lac-ul, -us	lake
Lae	cape, point
Lago, -a	lagoon, lake
Lagoen, Lagune	lagoon
Laguna-s	lagoon-s, lake-s
Laht	bay, gulf, harbor
Laje	reef, rock ledge
Laut	sea
Lednik	glacier
Leida	channel
Lhari	mountain
Li	village
Liedao	archipelago, islands
Liehtao	archipelago, islands
Liman-ı	bay, estuary
Límni	lake
Ling	mountain-s, range
Linn	pool, waterfall
Lintasan	passage
Liqen	lake
Llano-s	plain-s

Loch, Lough	lake, arm of the sea
Loma-s	hill-s, knoll-s

Mal .... mountain, range
Mal-yy, -aya, -oye .... little, small
Mamarr .... pass, path
Man .... bay
Mar, Mare .... large lake, sea
Marsa, Marsá .... bay, inlet
Masabb .... mouth of river
Massif .... mountain-s
Mauna .... mountain
Mēda .... plain
Meer .... lake, sea
Melkosopochnik .... undulating plain
Mesa, Meseta .... plateau, tableland
Mierzeja .... sandspit
Minami .... south
Mios .... island
Misaki .... cape, peninsula, point
Mochun .... passage
Mong .... town, village
Mont-e, -i, -s .... mount, –ain, –s
Montagne, -s .... mount, –ain, –s
Montaña, -s .... mountain, –s
More .... sea
Morne .... hill, peak
Morro .... bluff, headland, hill
Motu, -s .... islands
Mouïet .... well
Mouillage .... anchorage
Muang .... town, village
Mui .... cape, point
Mull .... headland, promontory
Munkhafad .... depression
Munte .... mountain
Munţi-i .... mountains
Muong .... town, village
Mynydd .... mountain
Mys .... cape

Nacional .... national
Nada .... gulf, sea
Næs, Näs .... cape, point
Nafūd .... area of dunes, desert
Nagor'ye .... mountain range, plateau
Nahar, Nahr .... river, stream
Nakhon .... town
Namakzār .... salt waste
Ne .... island, reef, rock-s
Neem .... cape, point, promontory
Nes, Ness .... peninsula, point
Nevado-s .... snow-capped mountain-s
Nez .... cape, promontory
Ni .... village
Nísi, Nísia, Nisís, Nísoi .... island-s, islet-s
Nisídhes .... islets
Nizhn-iy, -yaya, -eye .... lower
Nizmennost' .... low country
Noord .... north
Nord-re .... north-ern
Nørre .... north-ern
Nos .... cape, nose, point
Nosy .... island, reef, rock
Nov-yy, -aya, -oye .... new
Nudo .... mountain
Numa .... lake

Nunatak, -s, -ker .... peak-s surrounded by ice cap
Nur .... lake, salt lake
Nuruu .... mountain range, ridge
Nut-en .... peak
Nuur .... lake

Ö-n, Ø-er .... island-s
Oblast' .... administrative division, province, region
Oceanus .... ocean
Odde-n .... cape, point
Øer-ne .... islands
Oglat .... group of wells
Oguilet .... well
Ór-os, -i .... mountain, -s
Órmos .... bay, port
Ort .... place, point
Øst-er .... east
Ostrov, -a, Ostrv-o, -a .... island, -s
Otoci, Otok .... islands, island
Ouadi, Oued .... river, watercourse
Øy-a .... island
Øyane .... islands
Ozer-o, -a .... lake, -s

Pää .... mountain, point
Palus .... marsh
Pampa-s .... grassy plain-s
Pantà .... lake, reservoir
Pantanal .... marsh, swamp
Pao, P'ao .... lake
Parbat .... mountain
Parque .... park
Pas, -ul .... pass
Paso, Passo .... pass
Passe .... channel, pass
Pedra .... rock
Pegunungan .... mountain range
Pellg .... bay, bight
Peña .... cliff, rock
Pendi .... basin
Penedo-s .... rock-s
Péninsule .... peninsula
Peñón .... point, rock
Pereval .... mountain pass
Pertuis .... strait
Peski .... sands, sandy region
Phnom .... hill, mountain, range
Phou .... mountain range
Phu .... mountain
Piana-o .... plain
Pic, Pik, Piz .... peak
Picacho .... mountain, peak
Pico-s .... peak-s
Pistyll .... waterfall
Piton-s .... peak-s
Pivdennyy .... southern
Plaja, Playa .... beach, inlet, shore
Planalto, Plato .... plateau
Planina .... mountain, plateau
Plassen .... lake
Ploskogor'ye .... plateau, upland
Pointe .... point
Polder .... reclaimed land
Poluostrov .... peninsula
Pongo .... water gap
Ponta, -l .... cape, point

Ponte .... bridge
Poolsaar .... peninsula
Portezuelo .... pass
Porto .... port
Poulo .... island
Praia .... beach, seashore
Presa .... reservoir
Presidente .... president
Presqu'île .... peninsula
Prokhod .... pass
Proliv .... strait
Promontorio .... promontory
Průsmyk .... mountain pass
Przylądek .... cape
Puerto .... bay, pass, port
Pulao .... island-s
Pulau, Pulo .... island
Puncak .... peak, summit, top
Punt, Punta, -n .... point, -s
Pun .... peak
Pu'u .... hill, mountain
Puy .... peak

Qā' .... depression, marsh, mudflat
Qal'at .... fort
Qal'eh .... castle, fort
Qanâ .... canal
Qārat .... hill-s, mountain-s
Qaşr .... castle, fort, hill
Qila .... fort
Qiryat .... settlement, suburb
Qolleh .... peak
Qooriga .... anchorage, bay
Qoz .... dunes, sand ridge
Qu .... canal
Quebrada .... ravine, stream
Qullai .... peak, summit
Qum .... desert, sand
Qundao .... archipelago, islands
Qurayyāt .... hills

Raas .... cape, point
Rabt .... hill
Rada .... roadstead
Rade .... anchorage, roadstead
Rags .... point
Ramat .... hill, mountain
Rand .... ridge of hills
Rann .... swamp
Raqaba .... wadi, watercourse
Ras, Râs, Ra's .... cape
Ravnina .... plain
Récif-s .... reef-s
Regreg .... marsh
Represa .... reservoir
Reservatório .... reservoir
Restinga .... barrier, sand area
Rettō .... chain of islands
Ri .... mountain range, village
Ría .... estuary
Ribeirão .... stream
Río, Rio .... river
Roca-s .... cliff, rock-s
Roche-r, -s .... rock-s
Rosh .... mountain, point
Rt .... cape, point
Rubha .... headland

Rupes	scarp

Saar ... island

Saari, Sari	island
Sabkha-t, Sabkhet	lagoon, marsh, salt lake
Sagar	lake, sea
Sahara, Ṣaḥrā'	desert
Sahl	plain
Saki	cape, point
Salar	salt flat
Salina	salt pan
Salin-as, -es	salt flat-s, salt marsh-es
Salto	waterfall
Sammyaku	mountain range
San	hill, mountain
San, -ta, -to	saint
Sandur	sandy area
Sankt	saint
Sanmaek	mountain range
São	saint
Sarīr	gravel desert
Sasso	mountain, stone
Savane	savanna
Scoglio	reef, rock
Se	reef, rock-s, shoal-s
Sebjet	salt lake, salt marsh
Sebkha	salt lake, salt marsh
Sebkhet	lagoon, salt lake
See	lake, sea
Selat	strait
Selkä	lake, ridge
Semenanjung	peninsula
Sen	mountain
Seno	bay, gulf
Serra, Serranía	range of hills or mountains
Severn-yy, -aya, -oye	northern
Sgùrr	peak
Sha	island, shoal
Sha'ib	ravine, watercourse
Shamo	desert
Shan	island-s, mountain-s, range
Shankou	mountain pass
Shanmo	mountain range
Sharm	cove, creek, harbor
Shaṭṭ	large river
Shi	administrative division, municipality
Shima	island-s, rock-s
Shō	island, reef, rock
Shotō	archipelago
Shott	intermittent salt lake
Shuiku	reservoir
Shuitao	channel
Shyghanaghy	bay, gulf
Sierra	mountain range
Silsilesi	mountain chain, ridge
Sint	saint
Sinus	bay, sea
Sjö-n	lake
Skarv-et	barren mountain
Skerry	rock
Slieve	mountain
Sø	lake
Sønder, Søndre	south-ern
Sopka	conical mountain, volcano
Sor	lake, salt lake
Sør, Sör	south-ern
Sory	salt lake, salt marsh

Spitz-e	peak, point, top
Sredn-iy, -yaya, -eye	central, middle
Stagno	lake, pond
Stantsiya	station
Stausee	reservoir
Stenón	channel, strait
Step'-i	steppe-s
Stor-e	big, great
Straat	strait
Straum-en	current-s
Strelka	spit of land
Stretet, Stretto	strait
Su	reef, river, rock, stream
Sud	south
Sudo	channel, strait
Suidō	channel, strait
Ṣummān	rocky desert
Sund	sound, strait
Sunden	channel, inlet, sound
Svyat-oy, -aya, -oye	holy, saint
Sziget	island

Tagh ... mountain-s

Tall	hill, mound
T'an	lake
Tanezrouft	desert
Tang	plain, steppe
Tangi	peninsula, point
Tanjong, Tanjung	cape, point
Tao	island-s
Tarso	hill-s, mountain-s
Tassili	plateau, upland
Tau	mountain-s, range
Taūy	hills, mountains
Tchabal	mountain-s
Te Ava	tidal flat
Tel-l	hill, mound
Telok, Teluk	bay
Tepe, -si	hill, peak
Tepuí	mesa, mountain
Terara	hill, mountain, peak
Testa	bluff, head
Thale	lake
Thang	plain, steppe
Tien	lake
Tierra	land, region
Ting	hill, mountain
Tir'at	canal
Tó	lake, pool
To, Tō	island-s, rock-s
Tonle	lake
Tope	hill, mountain, peak
Top-pen	peak-s
Träsk	bog, lake
Tso	lake
Tsui	cape, point
Tübegi	peninsula
Tulu	hill, mountain
Tunturi-t	hill-s, mountain-s

Uad ... wadi, watercourse

Udde-m	point
Ujong, Ujung	cape, point
Umi	bay, lagoon, lake
Ura	bay, inlet, lake
'Urūq	dune area
Uul, Uula	mountain, range

'Uyûn	springs

Vaara ... mountain

Vaart	canal
Vær	fishing station
Vaïn	channel, strait
Valle, Vallée	valley, wadi
Vallen	waterfall
Valli	lagoon, lake
Vallis	valley
Vanua	land
Varre	mountain
Vatn, Vatten, Vatnet	lake, water
Veld	grassland, plain
Verkhn-iy, -yaya, -eye	higher, upper
Vesi	lake, water
Vest-er	west
Via	road
Vidda	plateau
Vig, Vík, Vik, -en	bay, cove
Vinh	bay, gulf
Vodokhranilishche	reservoir
Vodoskhovyshche	reservoir
Volcan, Volcán	volcano
Vostochn-yy, -aya, -oye	eastern
Vötn	stream
Vozvyshennost'	plateau, upland
Vozyera	lake-s
Vrchovina	mountains
Vrch-y	mountain-s
Vrh	hill, mountain
Vrŭkh	mountain
Vyaliki	big, large

Wabē ... stream

Wadi, Wâdi, Wādī	valley, watercourse
Wâhât, Wāḥat	oasis
Wald	forest, wood
Wan	bay, gulf
Water	harbor
Webi	stream
Wiek	cove, inlet

Xia ... gorge, strait

Xiao	lesser, little

Yanchi ... salt lake

Yang	ocean
Yarymadasy	peninsula
Yazovir	reservoir
Yŏlto	island group
Yoma	mountain range
Yü	island
Yumco	lake
Yunhe	canal
Yuzhn-yy, -aya, -oye	southern

Zaki ... cape, point

Zaliv	bay, gulf
Zan	mountain, ridge
Zangbo	river, stream
Zapadn-yy, -aya, -oye	western
Zatoka	bay, gulf
Zee	bay, sea
Zemlya	land
Zhotasy	mountains

Major Cities of the World

City	Country	Population
Tokyo	Japan	36,932,780
Delhi	India	21,935,142
Mexico City	Mexico	20,142,334
New York-Newark	United States	20,104,369
São Paulo	Brazil	19,649,366
Shanghai	China	19,554,059
Mumbai	India	19,421,983
Beijing	China	14,999,554
Dhaka	Bangladesh	14,929,647
Kolkata	India	14,283,096
Karachi	Pakistan	13,499,702
Buenos Aires	Argentina	13,369,921
Los Angeles-Long Beach-Santa Ana	United States	13,223,023
Rio de Janeiro	Brazil	11,867,236
Manila	Philippines	11,653,810
Moscow	Russia	11,471,637
Osaka-Kobe	Japan	11,429,912
Cairo	Egypt	11,031,494
Istanbul	Turkey	10,952,950
Lagos	Nigeria	10,788,300
Paris	France	10,516,374
Guangzhou, Guangdong	China	10,485,570
Shenzhen	China	10,222,493
Seoul	South Korea	9,750,693
Chongqing	China	9,732,286
Jakarta	Indonesia	9,629,953
Chicago	United States	9,544,691
Lima	Peru	8,950,481
London	United Kingdom	8,923,000
Wuhan	China	8,904,018
Tianjin	China	8,535,265
Chennai	India	8,522,504
Bogotá	Colombia	8,502,405
Kinshasa	Dem. Rep. of the Congo	8,415,198
Bangalore	India	8,275,032
Bangkok	Thailand	8,213,366
Hyderabad	India	7,577,527
Lahore	Pakistan	7,351,911
Tehran	Iran	7,242,708
Dongguan, Guangdong	China	7,159,504
Hong Kong	China	7,053,189
Madrid	Spain	6,404,626
Chengdu	China	6,397,335
Ahmadabad	India	6,209,893
Foshan	China	6,207,756
Ho Chi Minh City	Vietnam	6,189,423
Miami	United States	5,970,527
Santiago	Chile	5,958,544
Baghdad	Iraq	5,890,677
Philadelphia	United States	5,841,396
Nanjing, Jiangsu	China	5,664,951
Haerbin	China	5,496,375
Barcelona	Spain	5,487,878
Toronto	Canada	5,484,827
Shenyang	China	5,468,771
Belo Horizonte	Brazil	5,406,833
Riyadh	Saudi Arabia	5,227,076
Hangzhou	China	5,189,275
Dallas-Fort Worth	United States	5,142,701
Singapore	Singapore	5,086,418
Chittagong	Bangladesh	5,069,181
Pune	India	4,951,375
Atlanta	United States	4,874,502
Xi'an, Shaanxi	China	4,845,821
St. Petersburg	Russia	4,841,844
Luanda	Angola	4,790,142
Houston	United States	4,784,745
Boston	United States	4,772,358
Washington, D.C.	United States	4,634,045
Khartoum	Sudan	4,515,679
Sydney	Australia	4,478,610
Guadalajara	Mexico	4,441,836
Surat	India	4,438,444
Alexandria	Egypt	4,400,104
Detroit	United States	4,364,429
Yangon	Myanmar	4,355,639
Abidjan	Côte d'Ivoire	4,151,417
Monterrey	Mexico	4,099,598

City	Country	Population
Ankara	Turkey	4,073,828
Shantou	China	4,062,449
Salvador	Brazil	3,946,582
Melbourne	Australia	3,896,074
Pôrto Alegre	Brazil	3,891,719
Phoenix-Mesa	United States	3,830,188
Montréal	Canada	3,808,090
Zhengzhou	China	3,796,482
Johannesburg	South Africa	3,763,095
Brasília	Brazil	3,701,173
Recife	Brazil	3,684,317
San Francisco-Oakland	United States	3,681,072
Qingdao	China	3,679,853
Changchun	China	3,597,815
Medellín	Colombia	3,594,977
Jinan, Shandong	China	3,581,356
Fortaleza	Brazil	3,519,526
Cape Town	South Africa	3,491,778
Jiddah	Saudi Arabia	3,452,470
Berlin	Germany	3,450,076
Dar es Salaam	Tanzania	3,414,656
Busan	South Korea	3,398,435
Taiyuan, Shanxi	China	3,392,059
Kunming	China	3,388,025
Athens	Greece	3,381,828
Tel Aviv-Yafo	Israel	3,319,487
Rome	Italy	3,306,081
Dalian	China	3,305,435
Nagoya	Japan	3,300,082
Seattle	United States	3,297,766
Ekurhuleni (East Rand)	South Africa	3,284,078
Kano	Nigeria	3,270,799
Suzhou, Jiangsu	China	3,248,306
Nairobi	Kenya	3,236,589
Wuxi, Jiangsu	China	3,222,086
Changsha, Hunan	China	3,212,091
Caracas	Venezuela	3,176,446
San Diego	United States	3,119,757
Curitiba	Brazil	3,118,137
Aleppo	Syria	3,067,966
Kabul	Afghanistan	3,052,000
Jaipur	India	3,016,722
Casablanca	Morocco	3,009,217
Ürümqi	China	2,954,226
Durban	South Africa	2,953,589
Faisalabad	Pakistan	2,947,029
Dakar	Senegal	2,925,953
Addis Ababa	Ethiopia	2,918,669
Milan	Italy	2,915,979
Kanpur	India	2,904,192
Ibadan	Nigeria	2,854,984
Lucknow	India	2,854,192
Algiers	Algeria	2,850,907
Fukuoka-Kitakyushu	Japan	2,844,999
Izmir	Turkey	2,841,907
P'yongyang	North Korea	2,834,210
Hefei	China	2,829,545
Lisbon	Portugal	2,824,770
Hà Noi	Vietnam	2,809,164
Kiev	Ukraine	2,804,884
Minneapolis-St. Paul	United States	2,801,553
Fuzhou, Fujian	China	2,799,438
Campinas	Brazil	2,794,150
Surabaya	Indonesia	2,768,199
Shijiazhuang	China	2,740,568
Sapporo	Japan	2,714,289
Xiamen	China	2,701,535
Zhongshan	China	2,694,989
Taipei	China	2,654,039
Mashhad	Iran	2,653,347
Wenzhou	China	2,635,149
Ningbo	China	2,632,375
Incheon	South Korea	2,600,542
Damascus	Syria	2,581,546
Denver-Aurora	United States	2,491,521
Lanzhou	China	2,487,187
Tampa-St. Petersburg	United States	2,484,401
San Juan	Puerto Rico	2,478,159
Nagpur	India	2,470,886

City	Country	Population
Accra	Ghana	2,469,264
Guiyang	China	2,457,594
Zibo	China	2,456,098
Daegu	South Korea	2,449,690
Baltimore	United States	2,414,711
Cali	Colombia	2,401,797
Sendai	Japan	2,401,087
Bandung	Indonesia	2,399,494
St. Louis	United States	2,350,919
Naples	Italy	2,348,100
Douala	Cameroon	2,348,046
Nanchang	China	2,331,101
Changzhou, Jiangsu	China	2,322,650
Yaoundé	Cameroon	2,320,055
Kuwait City	Kuwait	2,317,585
Puebla	Mexico	2,295,503
Sanaa	Yemen	2,293,267
Guayaquil	Ecuador	2,273,133
Birmingham	United Kingdom	2,273,095
Maracaibo	Venezuela	2,254,931
Vancouver	Canada	2,235,465
Manchester	United Kingdom	2,215,719
Tashkent	Uzbekistan	2,212,687
Santo Domingo	Dominican Republic	2,153,779
Xuzhou	China	2,143,975
Port-au-Prince	Haiti	2,143,458
Havana	Cuba	2,127,877
Indore	India	2,127,497
Hiroshima	Japan	2,103,497
Medan	Indonesia	2,100,172
Rawalpindi	Pakistan	2,098,000
Nanning	China	2,095,797
Coimbatore	India	2,095,301
Asunción	Paraguay	2,072,657
Baku	Azerbaijan	2,061,643
Goiânia	Brazil	2,048,878
Belém	Brazil	2,038,227
Portland	United States	2,024,822
Cleveland	United States	2,022,462
Patna	India	2,022,108
Abuja	Nigeria	2,010,282
Las Vegas	United States	1,995,492
Brisbane	Australia	1,993,012
Beirut	Lebanon	1,983,381
Pittsburgh	United States	1,965,129
Kumasi	Ghana	1,935,252
Bucharest	Romania	1,934,641
Brussels	Belgium	1,933,293
Bamako	Mali	1,931,996
Baotou	China	1,931,030
Ouagadougou	Burkina Faso	1,911,188
Antananarivo	Madagascar	1,900,107
Jilin	China	1,888,948
Riverside-San Bernardino	United States	1,881,878
Tangshan, Hebei	China	1,871,118
Barranquilla	Colombia	1,867,337
Bhopal	India	1,851,285
Minsk	Belarus	1,846,994
Dubai	U.A.E.	1,834,882
Valencia	Venezuela	1,820,967
Rabat	Morocco	1,806,721
Port Harcourt	Nigeria	1,806,612
Kyoto	Japan	1,804,361
Manaus	Brazil	1,798,376
Vadodara	India	1,793,525
San Jose	United States	1,789,819
Hamburg	Germany	1,786,468
Huizhou	China	1,760,447
Tijuana	Mexico	1,756,774
Cincinnati	United States	1,756,287
Esfahan	Iran	1,742,597
Budapest	Hungary	1,730,602
Sacramento	United States	1,729,710
Khulna	Bangladesh	1,722,631
Multan	Pakistan	1,719,694
Lusaka	Zambia	1,718,885
Warsaw	Poland	1,717,524
Conakry	Guinea	1,715,207

City	Country	Population
Agra	India	1,714,339
Gujranwala	Pakistan	1,712,483
Vienna	Austria	1,707,648
Toluca	Mexico	1,702,447
Visakhapatnam	India	1,700,228
Weifang	China	1,699,081
La Paz	Bolivia	1,677,859
Grande Vitória	Brazil	1,665,890
Anshan, Liaoning	China	1,662,410
Bursa	Turkey	1,659,420
Montevideo	Uruguay	1,659,414
Baixada Santista	Brazil	1,658,963
Santa Cruz	Bolivia	1,653,073
Hyderabad	Pakistan	1,648,032
Turin	Italy	1,620,111
Perth	Australia	1,617,408
León	Mexico	1,612,858
West Yorkshire	United Kingdom	1,605,203
Virginia Beach	United States	1,598,324
Ludhiana	India	1,598,298
Quito	Ecuador	1,597,586
Kampala	Uganda	1,593,698
Kochi	India	1,592,263
Qiqihaer	China	1,587,629
Haikou	China	1,586,663
San Antonio	United States	1,585,001
Karaj	Iran	1,584,489
Kansas City	United States	1,576,595
San Salvador	El Salvador	1,570,451
Yangzhou	China	1,566,014
Semarang	Indonesia	1,558,270
Brazzaville	Congo	1,557,139
Indianapolis	United States	1,552,364
Nantong	China	1,549,884
Daqing	China	1,547,119
Mecca	Saudi Arabia	1,542,923
Luoyang	China	1,539,403
Córdoba	Argentina	1,532,246
Nashik	India	1,531,365
Xiangyang	China	1,531,037
Yantai	China	1,526,266
Harare	Zimbabwe	1,525,853
Kuala Lumpur	Malaysia	1,523,744
Davao	Philippines	1,522,678
Daejon	South Korea	1,519,783
Kaohsiung	China	1,514,281
Phnom Penh	Cambodia	1,508,875
Milwaukee	United States	1,487,929
Gwangju	South Korea	1,486,014
Lubumbashi	Dem. Rep. of the Congo	1,485,650
Tabriz	Iran	1,483,903
Kaduna	Nigeria	1,476,285
Peshawar	Pakistan	1,475,050
Marseille-Aix-en-Provence	France	1,472,190
Novosibirsk	Russia	1,471,946
Lyon	France	1,471,115
Pretoria	South Africa	1,467,714
San José	Costa Rica	1,466,423
Orlando	United States	1,459,078
Palembang	Indonesia	1,455,227
Lomé	Togo	1,453,256
Vijayawada	India	1,453,128
Kharkiv	Ukraine	1,452,699
Mosul	Iraq	1,446,940
Hohhot	China	1,446,291
Madurai	India	1,442,863
Mbuji-Mayi	Dem. Rep. of the Congo	1,433,256
Linyi, Shandong	China	1,426,466
Mogadishu	Somalia	1,425,660
Adana	Turkey	1,423,161
Varanasi	India	1,419,040
Auckland	New Zealand	1,406,758
Meerut	India	1,406,124
Almaty	Kazakhstan	1,400,451
Huainan	China	1,396,078
Panama City	Panama	1,389,474
Fushun, Liaoning	China	1,377,336
Providence	United States	1,372,826
Columbus, Ohio	United States	1,368,599
Rajkot	India	1,360,905
Stockholm	Sweden	1,359,972
Zhuhai	China	1,359,002
Porto	Portugal	1,355,095
Datong, Shanxi	China	1,354,609
Liuzhou	China	1,352,699
Munich	Germany	1,349,635
Yekaterinburg	Russia	1,348,007
Ujung Pandang	Indonesia	1,345,451
Taizhou, Jiangsu	China	1,337,757
Ciudad Juárez	Mexico	1,332,479
Homs	Syria	1,320,506
Jamshedpur	India	1,320,009
Benin City	Nigeria	1,311,012
Grande São Luís	Brazil	1,303,826
Shiraz	Iran	1,299,805
Yancheng, Jiangsu	China	1,289,682
Austin	United States	1,266,477
Prague	Czech Republic	1,264,835
Rosario	Argentina	1,264,242
Huai'an	China	1,262,097
Jabalpur	India	1,256,953
Nizhniy Novgorod	Russia	1,252,726
Natal	Brazil	1,252,443
Srinagar	India	1,250,571
Handan	China	1,250,308
Taian, Shandong	China	1,239,592
Asansol	India	1,232,198
Niamey	Niger	1,222,066
Torreón	Mexico	1,217,836
Barquisimeto	Venezuela	1,215,001
Jining, Shandong	China	1,206,703
Allahabad	India	1,204,808
Copenhagen	Denmark	1,192,357
Calgary	Canada	1,190,830
Ottawa-Gatineau	Canada	1,190,582
Dhanbad	India	1,186,101
Xining	China	1,184,725
Zürich	Switzerland	1,182,951
Adelaide	Australia	1,181,206
Zaozhuang	China	1,175,487
Sofia	Bulgaria	1,175,262
Vereeniging	South Africa	1,173,941
Wuhu, Anhui	China	1,171,662
Amritsar	India	1,171,367
Aurangabad	India	1,166,797
Memphis	United States	1,165,391
Samara	Russia	1,164,655
Nanyang, Henan	China	1,163,980
Gaziantep	Turkey	1,159,732
Yueyang	China	1,155,469
Maceió	Brazil	1,154,403
Omsk	Russia	1,153,272
Amman	Jordan	1,149,854
Baoding	China	1,148,209
Kazan	Russia	1,142,202
Glasgow	United Kingdom	1,140,326
Suweon	South Korea	1,139,770
Taichung	China	1,139,638
Ulaanbaatar	Mongolia	1,137,840
Belgrade	Serbia	1,133,399
Maputo	Mozambique	1,131,942
Klang	Malaysia	1,131,505
Anyang	China	1,129,385
Chelyabinsk	Russia	1,128,391
Guatemala City	Guatemala	1,128,009
Helsinki	Finland	1,121,945
Edmonton	Canada	1,120,754
Tbilisi	Georgia	1,116,824
Jodhpur	India	1,116,463
Norte/Nordeste Catarinense	Brazil	1,114,002
Yerevan	Armenia	1,113,014
Tripoli	Libya	1,110,929
Ranchi	India	1,106,901
Medina	Saudi Arabia	1,106,293
Jiangmen	China	1,103,252
Dublin	Ireland	1,102,405
Querétaro	Mexico	1,100,622
Bridgeport-Stamford	United States	1,100,202
Hengyang	China	1,099,223
Port Elizabeth	South Africa	1,097,079
Samut Prakan	Thailand	1,092,566
Bucaramanga	Colombia	1,092,197
Buffalo	United States	1,089,978
Rostov Na Donu	Russia	1,089,187
Ulsan	South Korea	1,088,833
Maracay	Venezuela	1,088,795
Charlotte	United States	1,087,977
Raipur	India	1,087,732
Gwalior	India	1,084,426
João Pessoa	Brazil	1,066,628
Jacksonville, Florida	United States	1,066,440
Fès	Morocco	1,064,514
Quanzhou	China	1,062,360
Ufa	Russia	1,061,579
Ahvaz	Iran	1,060,936
Durg-Bhilainagar	India	1,054,091
Yinchuan	China	1,051,836
Tegucigalpa	Honduras	1,051,115
Amsterdam	Netherlands	1,049,258
Haifa	Israel	1,043,860
Zhangjiakou	China	1,043,485
Qom	Iran	1,042,893
Jixi, Heilongjiang	China	1,042,534
San Luis Potosí	Mexico	1,042,028
Salt Lake City	United States	1,040,172
Jingzhou	China	1,039,645
Ogbomosho	Nigeria	1,038,805
Huambo	Angola	1,038,581
N'Djaména	Chad	1,037,509
Mandalay	Myanmar	1,035,163
Lille	France	1,033,942
Putian	China	1,030,025
Nay Pyi Taw	Myanmar	1,025,878
Zhuzhou	China	1,025,254
Pingdingshan, Henan	China	1,024,062
Konya	Turkey	1,022,820
Louisville	United States	1,021,140
Mérida	Mexico	1,020,974
Volgograd	Russia	1,020,897
Xianyang, Shaanxi	China	1,019,278
Xinxiang	China	1,016,141
Zhanjiang	China	1,014,437
Rotterdam	Netherlands	1,010,294
Florianópolis	Brazil	1,010,091
Chandigarh	India	1,009,587
Odesa	Ukraine	1,009,289
Erbil	Iraq	1,009,204
Tiruchirappalli	India	1,009,050
Zhenjiang, Jiangsu	China	1,007,682
Mianyang, Sichuan	China	1,005,791
Maoming	China	1,004,330
Dnipropetrovsk	Ukraine	1,003,320
Johore Bahru	Malaysia	1,001,886
Köln	Germany	1,001,590

Ten Largest Cities

Population (in millions)

	0	5	10	15	20	25	30	35
Tokyo								
Delhi								
Mexico City								
New York-Newark								
São Paulo								
Shanghai								
Mumbai								
Beijing								
Dhaka								
Kolkata								

World Temperature and Rainfall

SELECTED CITIES

KEY

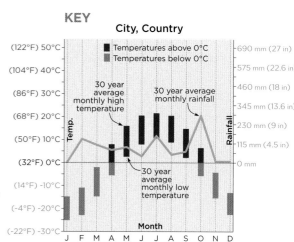

City, Country

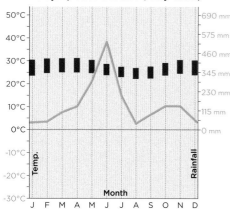

Abidjan, Côte d'Ivoire (Ivory Coast)

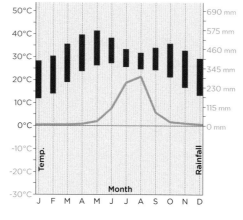

Ahmadabad, India

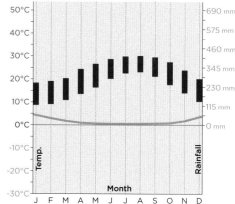

Alexandria, Egypt

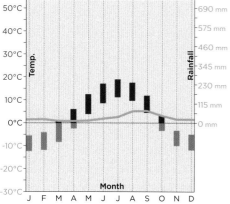

Anchorage, United States

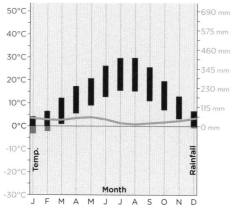

Ankara, Turkey

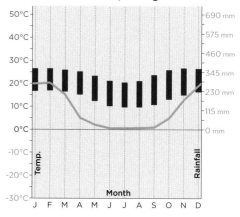

Antananarivo, Madagascar

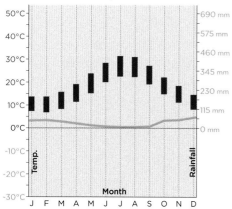

Athens, Greece

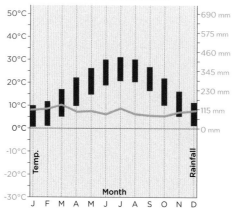

Atlanta, United States

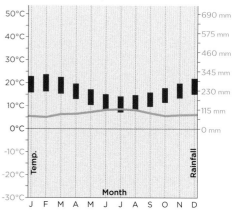

Auckland, New Zealand

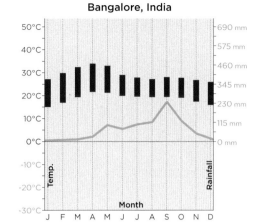

Baghdad, Iraq

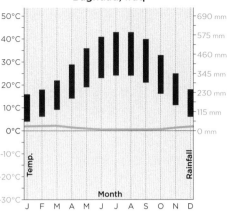

Bangalore, India

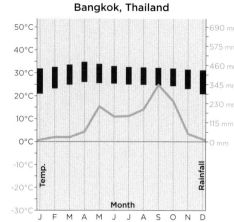

Bangkok, Thailand

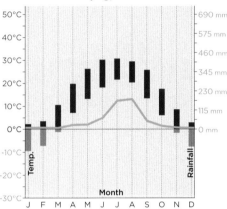

Beijing, China

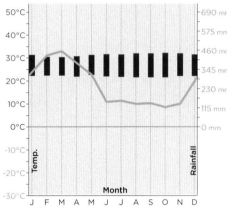

Belem, Brazil

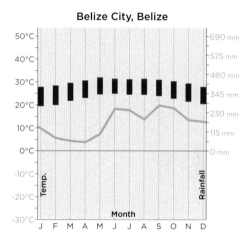

Belize City, Belize

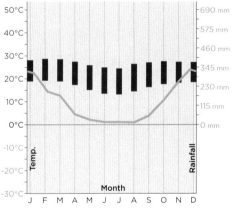

Belo Horizonte, Brazil

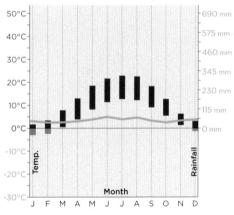

Berlin, Germany

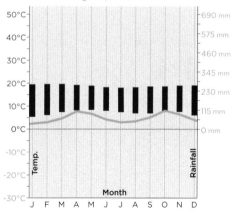

Bogotá, Colombia

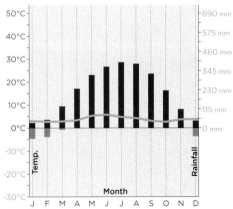

Bucharest, Romania

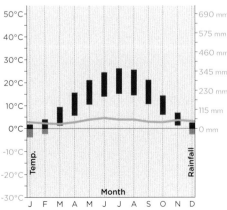

Budapest, Hungary

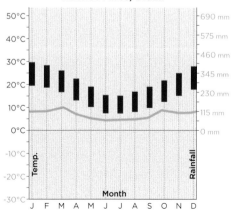

Buenos Aires, Brazil

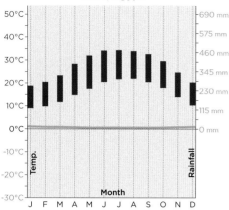

Cairo, Egypt

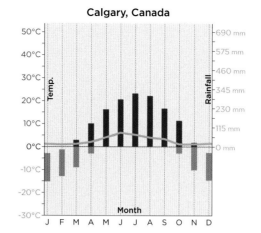

Calgary, Canada

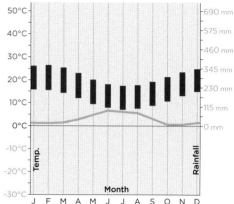

Cape Town, South Africa

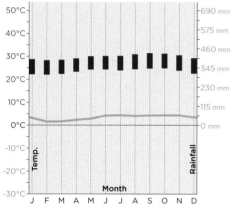

Caracas, Venezuela

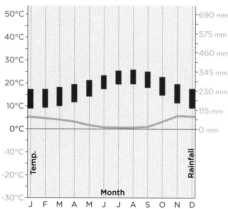

Casablanca, Morroco

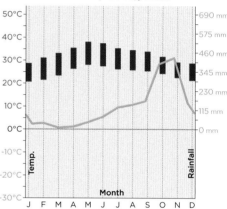

Chennai (Madras), India

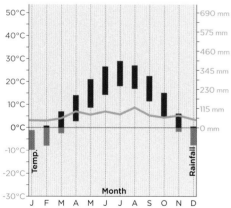

Chicago, United States

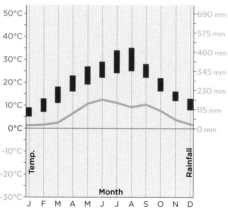

Chongqing, China

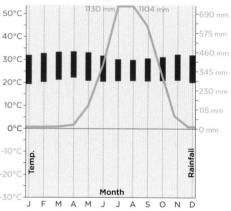

Conkary, Guinea

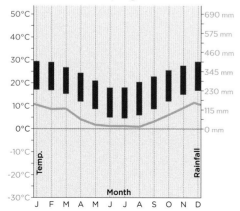

Córboda, Argentina

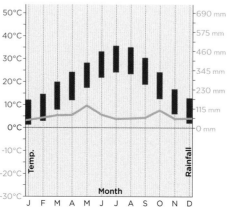

Dallas-Ft. Worth, United States

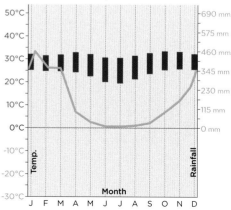

Darwin, Australia

Delhi, India

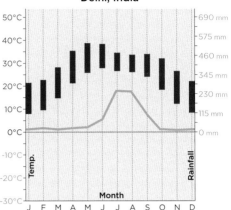

Denver, United States

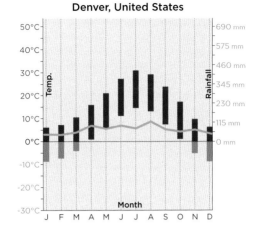

Detroit, United States

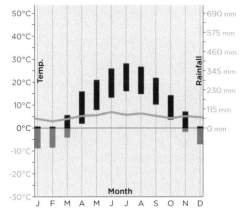

Dhaka, Bangladesh

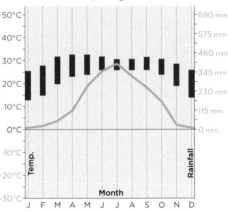

Dubai, United Arab Emirates

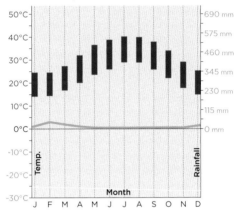

Guangzhou, China

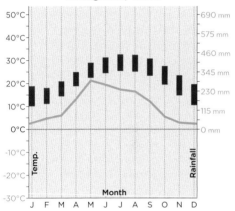

Hagåtña, Guam, United States

Havana, Cuba

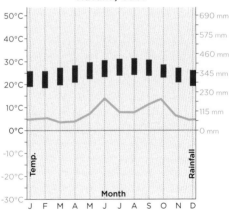

Ho Chi Minh City, Vietnam

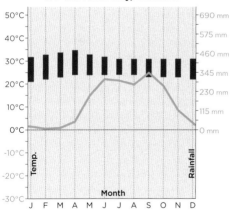

Hong Kong, China

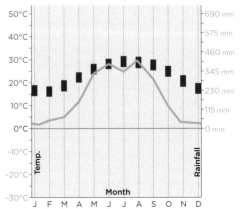

Honolulu, United States

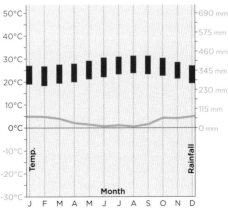

Houston, United States

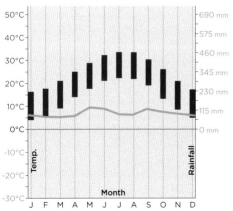

Hyderbad, India

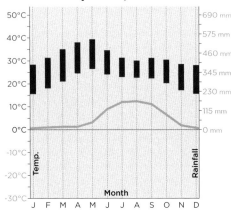

Istanbul, Turkey

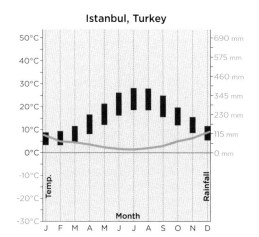

Jacksonville, United States

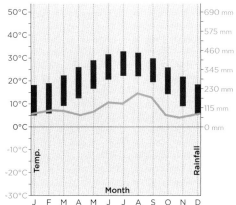

Jakarta, Indonesia

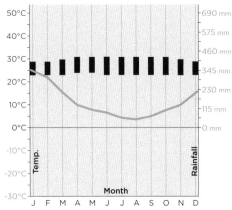

Jeddah, Saudi Arabia

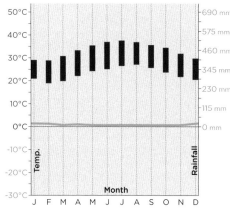

Jerusalem, Israel

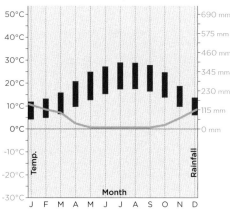

Kabul, Afghanistan

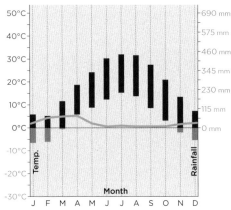

Karachi, Pakistan

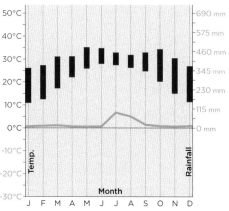

Khartoum, Sudan

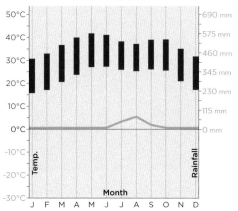

Kinshasa, Dem. Rep. of the Congo

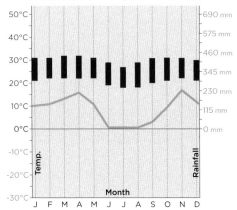

Kolkata (Calcutta), India

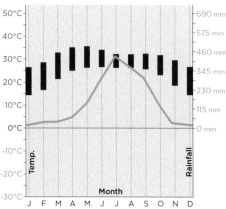

Lagos, Nigeria

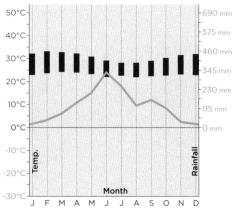

Lahore, Pakistan

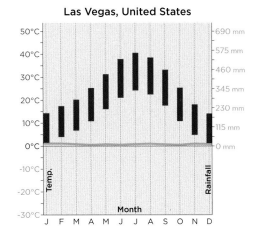

Las Vegas, United States

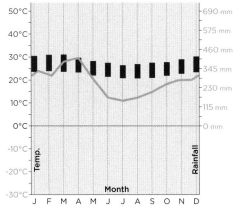

Laucala Bay, Fiji

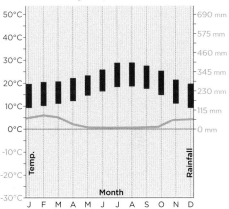

Lima, Peru

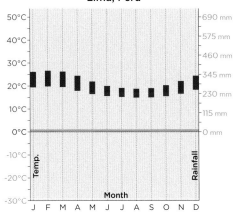

London, United Kingdom

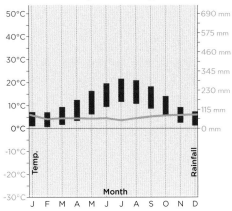

Los Angeles, United States

Lusaka, Zambia

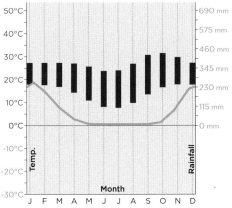

Madrid, Spain

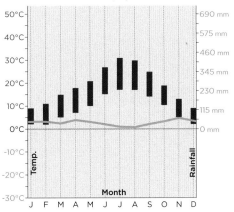

Manaus, Brazil

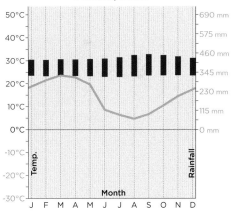

Manila, Philippines

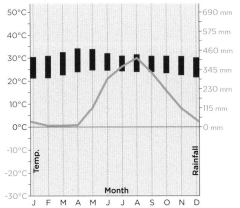

Maracaibo, Venezuela

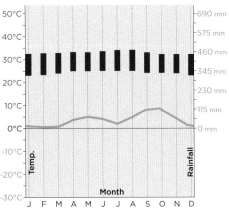

Melbourne, Australia

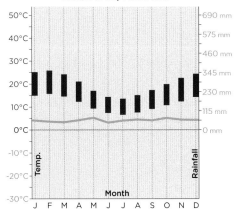

Mexico City, Mexico

Miami, United States

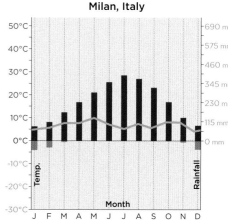

Milan, Italy

Moscow, Russia

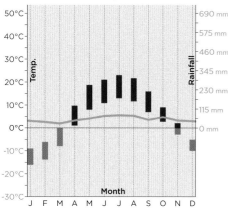

Mumbai (Bombay), India

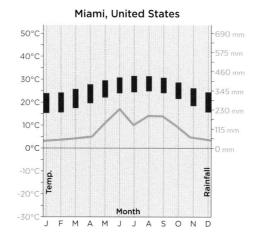

Nairobi, Kenya

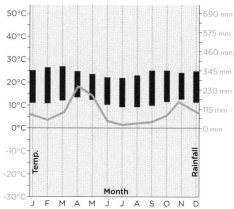

New Orleans, United States

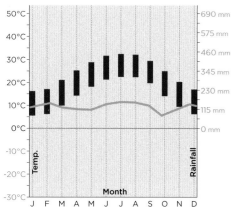

New York, United States

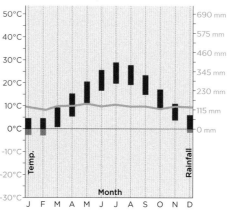

Osaka, Japan

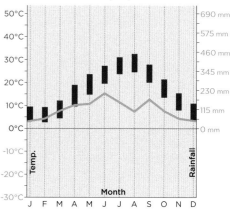

Paris, France

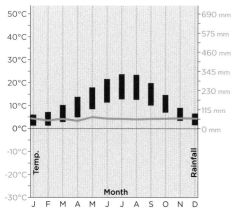

Philadelphia, United States

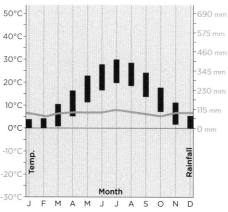

Phoenix, United States

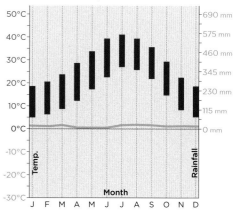

224

Porto Alegre, Brazil

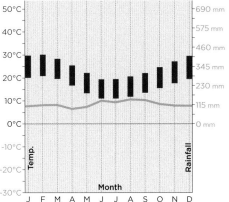

Prague, Czech Republic

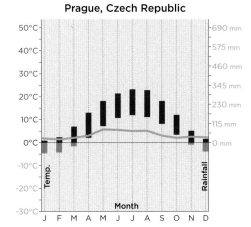

Pretoria (Tshwane), South Africa

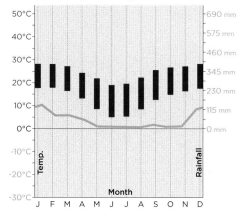

Puntarenas, Costa Rica

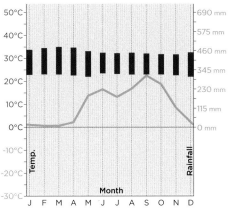

Reykjavik, Iceland

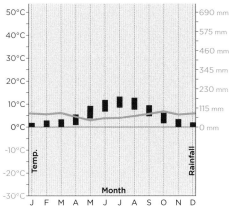

Rio de Janeiro, Brazil

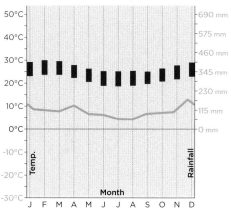

Riyadh, Saudi Arabia

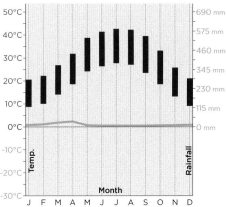

Rome, Italy

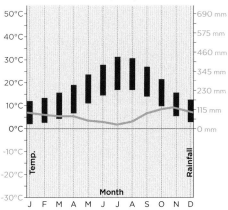

San Francisco, United States

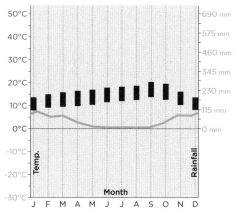

San Juan, United States

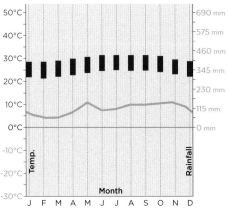

Santiago, Chile

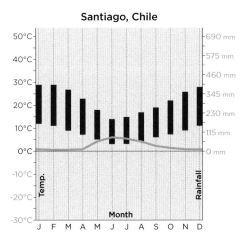

São Paulo, Brazil

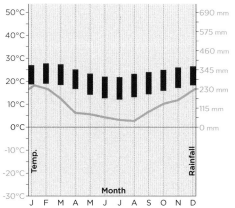

Sapporo, Japan

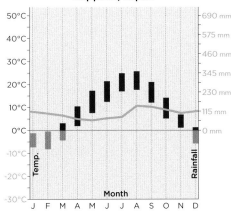

Seattle, United States

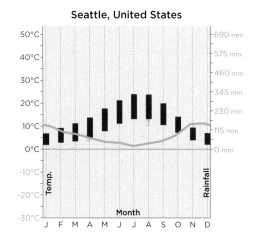

Seoul, South Korea

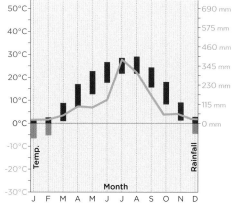

Shanghai, China

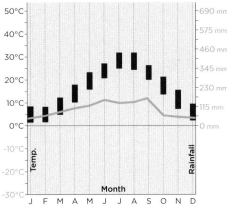

Shenyang, China

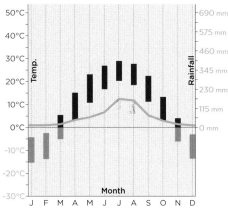

Shiraz, Iran

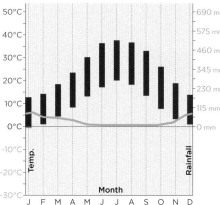

Singapore, Singapore

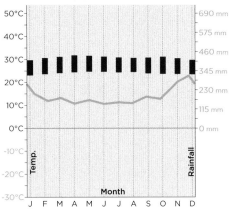

St. Petersburg, Russia

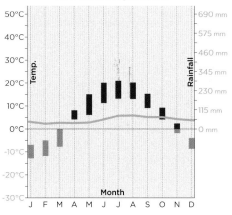

Stockholm, Sweden

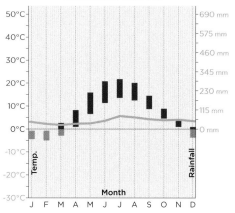

Sydney, Australia

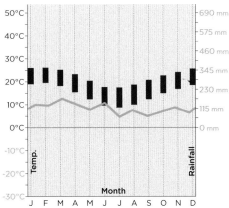

Tashkent, Uzbekistan

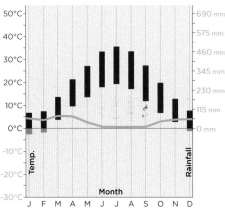

Tehran, Iran

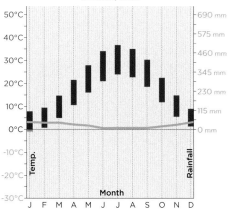

FAHRENHEIT
20°
0°
00°
90°
80°
70°
60
50'
40
30'
20°
10°
0°
-10°
-20
-30
-40
-50
-60
FAHRENHEIT

Timbucktu, Mali
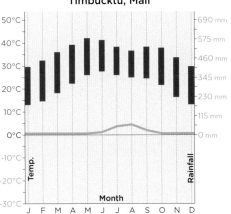

Tokyo, Japan
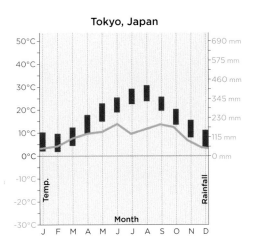

Toronto, Canada
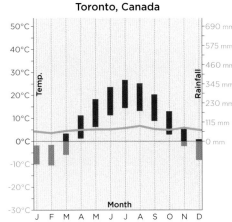

Tunis, Tunisia
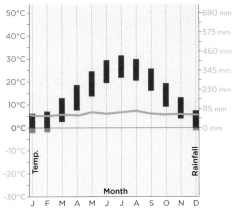

Ulaanbaatar, Mongolia
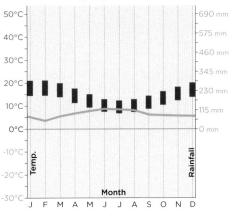

Vientiane, Laos
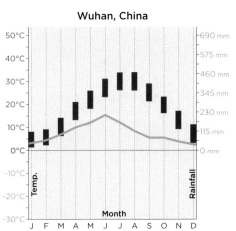

Washington, D.C., United States
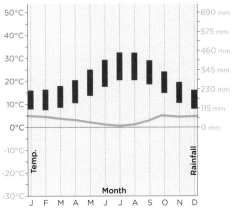

Wellington, New Zealand
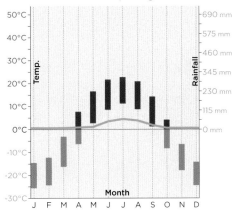

Wuhan, China
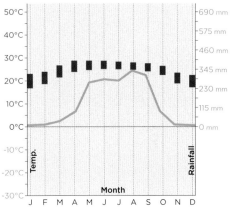

Xi'an, China
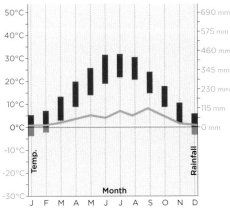

Yangon (Rangoon), Myanmar
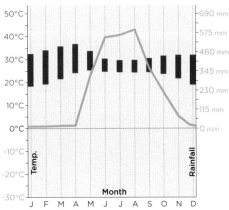

Yellowknife, Canada
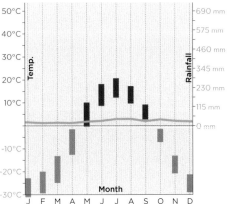

Metric Conversions

CONVERSION FROM METRIC MEASURES

SYMBOL	WHEN YOU KNOW	MULTIPLY BY	TO FIND	SYMBOL
LENGTH				
cm	centimeters	0.39	inches	in
m	meters	3.28	feet	ft
m	meters	1.09	yards	yd
km	kilometers	0.62	miles	mi
AREA				
cm^2	square centimeters	0.16	square inches	in^2
m^2	square meters	10.76	square feet	ft^2
m^2	square meters	1.20	square yards	yd^2
km^2	square kilometers	0.39	square miles	mi^2
ha	hectares	2.47	acres	--
MASS				
g	grams	0.04	ounces	oz
kg	kilograms	2.20	pounds	lb
t	metric tons	1.10	short tons	--
VOLUME				
mL	milliliters	0.06	cubic inches	in^3
mL	milliliters	0.03	liquid ounces	liq oz
L	liters	2.11	pints	pt
L	liters	1.06	quarts	qt
L	liters	0.26	gallons	gal
m^3	cubic meters	35.31	cubic feet	ft^3
m^3	cubic meters	1.31	cubic yards	yd^3
TEMPERATURE				
°C	degrees Celsius (centigrade)	$9/5$ then add 32	degrees Fahrenheit	°F

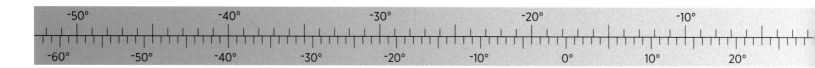

QUICK REFERENCE CHART FOR METRIC TO ENGLISH CONVERSION

1 METER	1 METER = 100 CENTIMETERS
1 FOOT	1 FOOT = 12 INCHES

1 KILOMETER	1 KILOMETER = 1,000 METERS
1 MILE	1 MILE = 5,280 FEET

METERS	1	10	20	50	100	200	500	1,000	2,000	5,000	10,000
FEET	3.28	32.8	65.6	164	328	656	1,640	3,280	6,560	16,400	32,800

KILOMETERS	1	10	20	50	100	200	500	1,000	2,000	5,000	10,000
MILES	0.62	6.2	12.4	31	62	124	310	620	1,240	3,100	6,200

CONVERSION TO METRIC MEASURES

SYMBOL	WHEN YOU KNOW	MULTIPLY BY	TO FIND	SYMBOL
LENGTH				
in	inches	2.54	centimeters	cm
ft	feet	0.30	meters	m
yd	yards	0.91	meters	m
mi	miles	1.61	kilometers	km
AREA				
in^2	square inches	6.45	square centimeters	cm^2
ft^2	square feet	0.09	square meters	m^2
yd^2	square yards	0.84	square meters	m^2
mi^2	square miles	2.59	square kilometers	km^2
ac or A	acres	0.40	hectares	ha
MASS				
oz	ounces	28.35	grams	g
lb	pounds	0.45	kilograms	kg
st or tn	short tons	0.91	metric tons (tonnes)	t
VOLUME				
in^3	cubic inches	16.39	milliliters	mL
liq oz	liquid ounces	29.57	milliliters	mL
pt	pints	0.47	liters	L
qt	quarts	0.95	liters	L
gal	gallons	3.79	liters	L
ft^3	cubic feet	0.03	cubic meters	m^3
yd^3	cubic yards	0.76	cubic meters	m^3
TEMPERATURE				
°F	degrees Fahrenheit	$5/9$ after subtracting 32	degrees Celsius (centigrade)	°C

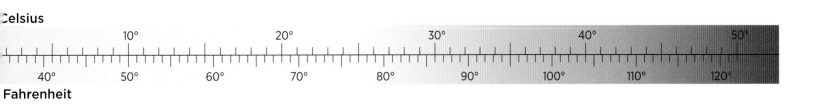

Celsius: 10° 20° 30° 40° 50°
Fahrenheit: 40° 50° 60° 70° 80° 90° 100° 110° 120°

Place-Name Index

Index Diamond

Page

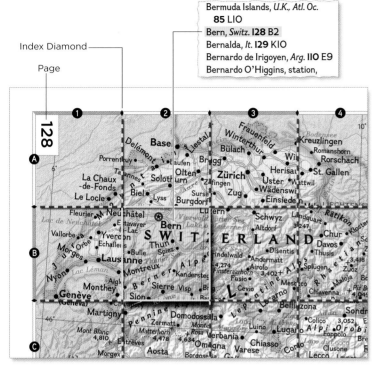

The following system is used to locate a place on a map in the *National Geographic Global Atlas*. The boldface type after an entry refers to the page on which the map is found. The letter-number combination refers to the grid on which the particular place-name is located. The edge of each map is marked horizontally with numbers and vertically with letters. In between, at equally spaced intervals, are index diamonds (♦). If these diamonds were connected with lines, each page would be divided into a grid. Take Bern, Switzerland, for example. The index entry reads "Bern, *Switz.* **128** B2." On page 128, Bern is located within the grid square where row B and column 2 intersect (example at left).

A place-name may appear on several maps, but the index lists only the best presentation. Usually, this means that a feature is indexed to the largest-scale map on which it appears in its entirety. (Note: Rivers are often labeled multiple times even on a single map. In such cases, the rivers are indexed to labels that are closest to their mouths.) The name of the country or continent in which a feature lies is shown in italic type and is usually abbreviated. (A full list of abbreviations appears on pages 210-211.)

The index lists more than proper names. Some entries include a description, as in "Elba, island, *It.* **128** G4" and "Amazon (Solimões), river, *S. Amer.* **102** E5." In languages other than English, the description of a physical feature may be part of the name; e.g., the "Erg" in "Chech, Erg, *Alg., Mali* **174** D7" means "sand dune region." The glossary of Foreign Terms on pages 212-215 translates such terms into English.

When a feature or place can be referred to by more than one name, both may appear in the index with cross-references. For example, the entry for Cairo reads "Cairo *see* El Qâhira, *Egypt* **175** CI4." That entry is "El Qâhira (Cairo), *Egypt* **175** CI4."

Adam, *Oman* **149** HI2
Adámandás, *Gr.* **133** JIO
Adamello, peak, *It.* **128** C5
Adams, Mount, *U.S.* **90** B3
Adam's Peak, *Sri Lanka* **155** P6
'Adan (Aden), *Yemen* **148** M7
Adana, *Turk.* **144** G8
'Adan aş Şughrá, peninsula, *Yemen* **148** M7
Adang, Teluk, *Indonesia* **166** H9
Adare, Cape, *Antarctica* **201** MIO
Adavale, *Qnsld., Austral.* **187** GI3
Adda, river, *It.* **128** D4
Ad Dahnā', desert, *Saudi Arabia* **148** F7
Ad Dakhla, *W. Sahara, Mor.* **174** D3
Ad Dammām, *Saudi Arabia* **148** F9
Ad Dār al Ḥamrā', *Saudi Arabia* **148** F5
Ad Darb, *Saudi Arabia* **148** K6
Ad Dawādimī, *Saudi Arabia* **148** G7
Ad Dawḩah (Doha), *Qatar* **149** GIO
Ad Dibdibah, region, *Iraq, Kuwait, Saudi Arabia* **148** E8
Ad Dilam, *Saudi Arabia* **148** G8
Addis Ababa see Ādīs Ābeba, *Eth.* **177** EI2
Ad Dīwānīyah, *Iraq* **148** D7
Addu Atoll, *Maldives* **155** S2
Ad Duwayd, *Saudi Arabia* **148** E6
Adelaide, *Bahamas* **96** C7
Adelaide, *S. Austral., Austral.* **187** KII
Adelaide Island, *Antarctica* **200** D3
Adelaide Peninsula, *Nunavut, Can.* **88** E9
Adelaide River, *N. Terr., Austral.* **186** B8
Adelfi, island, *Gr.* **133** EIO
Adélie Coast, *Antarctica* **201** MI4
Aden see 'Adan, *Yemen* **148** M7
Aden, Gulf of, *Af., Asia* **140** J4
Aderbissinat, *Niger* **174** G9
'Ādhirīyāt, Jibāl al, *Jordan* **147** L6
Adieu, Cape, *Austral.* **184** J9
Adige, river, *It.* **128** D5
Ādīgrat, *Eth.* **177** DI2
Adilabad, *India* **154** H5
Adímilos, island, *Gr.* **133** JIO
Adinkerke, *Belg.* **124** G7
Adíparos, island, *Gr.* **133** JII
Adirondack Mountains, *U.S.* **91** CI5
Ādīs Ābeba (Addis Ababa), *Eth.* **177** EI2
Adi Ugri, *Eritrea* **177** DI2
Adıyaman, *Turk.* **145** FIO
Adjud, *Rom.* **131** CI4
Adler, *Russ.* **135** Q9
Admiralty Gulf, *Austral.* **184** B6
Admiralty Inlet, *Nunavut, Can.* **89** DIO
Admiralty Island, *U.S.* **90** M6
Admiralty Islands, *P.N.G.* **188** E4
Admiralty Mountains, *Antarctica* **201** MII
Adour, river, *Fr.* **125** R5
Adra, *Sp.* **122** K9
Adrano, *It.* **129** N9
Adrar, *Alg.* **174** C7
Adrar, region, *Mauritania* **174** E4
Adraskan, *Afghan.* **153** K2
Adria, *It.* **128** D6
Adrianople see Edirne, *Turk.* **144** B2
Ādwa, *Eth.* **177** DI2
Adyakit, Gora, *Russ.* **137** FIO
Aegean Sea, *Asia, Europe* **115** LII
Aegina see Égina, island, *Gr.* **132** H9
Aewol, *S. Korea* **161** S5
Afándou, *Gr.* **133** KI5
Afar, region, *Eth.* **177** DI3
Affric, Glen, *Scot., U.K.* **120** G6

Afghanistan, *Asia* **142** G7
Afgonak Island, *U.S.* **90** M3
'Afīf, *Saudi Arabia* **148** G6
Afiq, *Israel* **146** H5
Áfitos, *Gr.* **132** C9
Afmadow, *Somalia* **177** HI3
Afobaka, *Suriname* **107** EI6
'Afrīn, *Syr.* **146** C6
Afşin, *Turk.* **144** E9
'Afula, *Israel* **146** H4
Afyon, *Turk.* **144** E4
Agadez, *Niger* **174** F9
Agadir, *Mor.* **174** B5
Agana see Hagåtña, *Guam, U.S.* **190** C4
Agano, river, *Japan* **162** G9
Agar, *India* **154** F4
Agartala, *India* **154** FIO
Agata, *Russ.* **137** FIO
Agathoníssi, island, *Gr.* **133** HI4
Agats, *Indonesia* **188** J6
Agatti Island, *India* **155** M2
Agattu, island, *U.S.* **85** S2
Agboville, *Côte d'Ivoire* **178** E7
Ağdam see Akna, *Azerb.* **145** DI6
Agde, *Fr.* **125** S8
Agde, Cap d', *Fr.* **125** S8
Agen, *Fr.* **125** R6
Aggtelek, *Hung.* **127** HI3
Aghdash, *Azerb.* **145** CI6
Ağhjabädi, *Azerb.* **145** DI6
Aghrîjît, *Mauritania* **174** F5
Agiá, *Gr.* **132** D8
Agia Galini, *Gr.* **133** MII
Agia Napa, *Cyprus* **133** FI7
Agía Pelagía, *Gr.* **132** K8
Agía Rouméli, *Gr.* **133** MIO
Agiássos, *Gr.* **133** EI3
Ágio Óros, peninsula, *Gr.* **133** CIO
Ágio Óros (Athos, Mount), region, *Gr.* **133** CIO
Ágios Efstrátios, *Gr.* **133** DII
Ágios Irínis, Akrotírio, *Gr.* **133** DII
Ágios Kírikos, *Gr.* **133** HI3
Ágios Nikólaos, *Gr.* **133** MI2
Agios Theodoros (Çayirova), *Cyprus* **133** EI7
Agiou Orous, Kólpos, *Gr.* **132** C9
Agnew, *W. Austral., Austral.* **186** H5
Agnita, *Rom.* **131** DI2
Agnone, *It.* **128** H8
Agra, *India* **154** E5
Ágreda, *Sp.* **123** DII
Agrı, *Turk.* **145** DI3
Agría Gramvoúsa, island, *Gr.* **132** L9
Ağrı Dağı (Ararat, Mount), *Turk.* **145** DI4
Agrigento, *It.* **129** P7
Agrihan, island, *N. Mariana Is., U.S.* **190** B5
Agrínio, *Gr.* **132** F6
Agropoli, *It.* **129** K9
Ağstafa, *Azerb.* **145** CI5
Ağsu, *Azerb.* **145** CI7
Aguada de Pasajeros, *Cuba* **96** E4
Aguadilla, *P.R., U.S.* **97** JI6
Aguapeí, *Braz.* **108** G9
Agua Prieta, *Mex.* **94** B5
Aguas Blancas, *Chile* **110** D3
Aguascalientes, *Mex.* **94** F6
Águas Formosas, *Braz.* **109** HI4
A Gudiña, *Sp.* **122** C6
Águeda, *Port.* **122** E4
Aguelhok, *Mali* **174** F7
Aguilar de Campoo, *Sp.* **122** B8
Aguilas, *Sp.* **123** JII
Aguja, Cabo de la, *Col.* **106** B6
Aguja, Punta, *Peru* **108** D3

Agulhas, Cape, *S. Af.* **180** K6
Aguni Jima, *Japan* **163** QI
Ahaggar (Hoggar), range, *Alg.* **174** E8
Ahar, *Iran* **148** A8
Aharnés, *Gr.* **132** G9
Ahelóos, river, *Gr.* **132** F6
Ahiri, *India* **154** H5
Ahlat, *Turk.* **145** EI3
Ahlatlıbel, ruins, *Turk.* **144** D6
Ahmadabad, *India* **154** G2
Ahmadnagar, *India* **154** H3
Ahmadpur East, *Pak.* **153** N7
Ahmad Wal, *Pak.* **153** N4
Ahome, *Mex.* **94** D4
Ahram, *Iran* **149** EIO
Ahrensburg, *Ger.* **126** B7
Ahtme, *Est.* **119** HI5
Ahvāz, *Iran* **148** D9
Ahvenanmaa see Åland, islands, *Fin.* **119** HI3
Aḩwar, *Yemen* **148** M8
Aigle, *Switz.* **128** B2
Aigoual, Mont, *Fr.* **125** R8
Aiguá, *Uru.* **110** H9
Aigurande, *Fr.* **125** N7
Aţ Ţafīlah, *Jordan* **147** L5
Aikawa, *Japan* **162** G8
Aiken, *S.C., U.S.* **93** GI4
Ailinglapalap Atoll, *Marshall Is.* **190** C7
Ailsa Craig, island, *Scot., U.K.* **121** K6
Ailuk Atoll, *Marshall Is.* **190** C7
Aimere, *Indonesia* **167** KIO
Ainaži, *Latv.* **119** JI5
Aînhoa, *Fr.* **125** S4
Aínsa, *Sp.* **123** CI2
'Aïn Sefra, *Alg.* **174** B7
Ainsworth, *Nebr., U.S.* **92** D9
Aiquile, *Bol.* **108** H8
Aiquina, *Chile* **110** C4
Airão, *Braz.* **108** C9
Air Force Island, *Nunavut, Can.* **89** EII
Aïr Massif, range, *Niger* **174** F9
Airolo, *Switz.* **128** B3
Aisey, *Fr.* **125** L9
Ai Shan, *Shandong, China* **158** E8
Aitape, *P.N.G.* **188** G5
Aitutaki Atoll, *Cook Is., N.Z.* **191** GII
Aiud, *Rom.* **131** CI2
Aix, Île d', *Fr.* **125** N4
Aix-en-Provence, *Fr.* **125** SIO
Aix-les-Bains, *Fr.* **125** PIO
Aiyura, *P.N.G.* **188** E6
Aizawl, *India* **154** FII
Aizenay, *Fr.* **125** N4
Aizpute, *Latv.* **119** KI4
Aizuwakamatsu, *Japan* **162** G9
Ajaccio, *Fr.* **128** H3
Ajaccio, Golfe d', *Fr.* **128** H3
Ajajú, river, *Col.* **106** G7
Aj Bogd Uul, *Mongolia* **156** D9
Ajdābiyā, *Lib.* **175** CI2
Ajjer, Tassili-n-, *Alg.* **174** D9
'Ajlūn, *Jordan* **146** J5
'Ajmān, *U.A.E.* **149** GII
Ajmer, *India* **154** E3
Ajo, *Ariz., U.S.* **92** H4
Ajo, Cabo de, *Sp.* **122** A9
Ajrestan, *Afghan.* **153** K5
Akabira, *Japan* **162** CIO
Akaki, *Cyprus* **133** EI6
Akankohan, *Japan* **162** CII
Akashi, *Japan* **162** J6
Akbulak, *Russ.* **136** H4
Akçaabat, *Turk.* **145** CII
Akçadağ, *Turk.* **144** E9
Akçakale, *Turk.* **145** GIO
Akçakışla, *Turk.* **144** D8
Akçakoca, *Turk.* **144** C5
Akçay, *Turk.* **144** D2

Akçay, *Turk.* **144** G4
Akchâr, region, *Mauritania* **174** E3
Akdağ, peak, *Turk.* **144** EI
Akdağ, peak, *Turk.* **144** G5
Ak Dağlar, *Turk.* **144** G3
Akdağmadeni, *Turk.* **144** D8
Akdoğan see Lysi, *Cyprus* **133** FI7
Akera, river, *Azerb.* **145** DI5
Aketi, *D.R.C.* **176** G8
Akhalts'ikhe, *Ga.* **145** BI3
Akhisar, *Turk.* **144** D2
Akhnur, *India* **153** K9
Akhtuba, river, *Kaz.* **150** D3
Akhtuba, river, *Russ.* **135** LI2
Akhtubinsk, *Russ.* **136** G3
Aki, *Japan* **163** K5
Akimiski Island, *Nunavut, Can.* **89** JII
Akita, *Japan* **162** F9
Akjoujt, *Mauritania* **174** E3
Akkeshi, *Japan* **162** CII
Akkeshi Wan, *Japan* **162** CII
'Akko (Acre), *Israel* **146** H4
Akkuş, *Turk.* **144** C9
Aklavik, *N.W.T., Can.* **88** D5
Aklera, *India* **154** F4
Akna (Ağdam), *Azerb.* **145** DI6
Akobo, *S. Sudan* **177** FII
Ākobo, river, *Eth., S. Sudan* **177** FII
Akola, *India* **154** H4
Ak'ordat, *Eritrea* **177** DI2
Akosombo Dam, *Ghana* **178** E9
Akpatok Island, *Nunavut, Can.* **89** GI3
Akqi, *China* **156** D5
Akranes, *Ice.* **118** E3
Akráta, *Gr.* **132** G7
Akron, *Ohio, U.S.* **93** DI4
Akrotiri, *Gr.* **133** KII
Akrotiri Bay, *Cyprus* **133** GI5
Akrotiri (Western) Sovereign Base Area, *U.K.* **133** GI5
Aksai Chin, region, *China* **156** F5
Aksaray, *Turk.* **144** E7
Aksay, *China* **156** E9
Aksay, *Russ.* **135** MII
Akşehir, *Turk.* **144** E5
Akşehir Gölü, *Turk.* **144** E5
Akseki, *Turk.* **144** F5
Aksu, *China* **156** D6
Aksu, *Kaz.* **150** G5
Aksu, river, *Turk.* **144** F4
Āksum, *Eth.* **177** DI2
Aktag, peak, *China* **156** F7
Akune, *Japan* **163** L3
Akureyri, *Ice.* **118** D4
Akuseki Shima, *Japan* **163** N3
Akyab see Sittwe, *Myanmar* **164** E3
Akyaka, *Turk.* **145** CI3
Akyazı, *Turk.* **144** C5
Ala, *It.* **128** C5
Alà, Monti di, *It.* **128** J3
Alabama, *U.S.* **93** HI3
Alabama, river, *U.S.* **91** HI2
Alaca, *Turk.* **144** D7
Alaca Dağ, *Turk.* **144** F5
Alacahöyük, ruins, *Turk.* **144** D7
Alaçam, *Turk.* **144** B8
Alacant see Alicante, *Sp.* **123** HI2
Alacránes, Arrecife, *Mex.* **95** FII
Aladağ, peak, *Turk.* **144** F5
Aladağ, peak, *Turk.* **144** F7
Alaejos, *Sp.* **122** D7
Al Aflāj, region, *Saudi Arabia* **148** H8
Alagir, *Russ.* **135** QII
Alagoinhas, *Braz.* **109** FI5
Alagón, *Sp.* **123** DII
Al Aḩmadī, *Kuwait* **148** E8
Al Ain, *U.A.E.* **149** GII
Alaja, *Turkm.* **150** J5

Almar, *Afghan.* 152 H3
Al Marj, *Lib.* 175 B12
Al Ma'shūqah, *Saudi Arabia* 148 J6
Almaty, *Kaz.* 151 G13
Al Mawşil (Mosul), *Iraq* 148 B7
Al Mayādīn, *Syr.* 146 E10
Al Mayyāh, *Saudi Arabia* 148 F7
Almazán, *Sp.* 123 D10
Almeida, *Port.* 122 E6
Almeirim, *Braz.* 109 C11
Almeirim, *Port.* 122 G4
Almelo, *Neth.* 124 F11
Almenara, *Braz.* 109 G14
Almenara, peak, *Sp.* 123 H10
Almendra, Embalse de, *Sp.* 122 D7
Almendralejo, *Sp.* 122 G6
Almere, *Neth.* 124 F9
Almería, *Sp.* 123 K10
Almería, Golfo de, *Sp.* 123 K10
Al'met'yevsk, *Russ.* 136 G5
Almina, Punta, *Sp.* 122 L7
Al Mintirib, *Oman* 149 H12
Almirantazgo, Seno, *Chile* 111 S4
Almirante, *Pan.* 95 L15
Almirí, *Gr.* 132 G8
Almirós, *Gr.* 132 E8
Al Mismīyah, *Syr.* 146 H6
Almodôvar, *Port.* 122 J4
Almodóvar del Campo, *Sp.* 122 G8
Al Mubarraz, *Saudi Arabia* 148 G9
Al Mudawwarah, *Jordan* 147 N5
Almudévar, *Sp.* 123 C12
Al Mukallā, *Yemen* 148 L9
Al Mukhā, *Yemen* 148 M6
Almuñécar, *Sp.* 122 K9
Almus, *Turk.* 144 D9
Almus Barajı, *Turk.* 144 C9
Al Muwassam, *Saudi Arabia* 148 L6
Al Muwayh, *Saudi Arabia* 148 H6
Alney, Gora, *Russ.* 137 E17
Alnwick, *Eng., U.K.* 120 J9
Along, *India* 154 D11
Alónissos, *Gr.* 132 E9
Alónissos, island, *Gr.* 132 E9
Alor, island, *Indonesia* 167 K11
Alor, Kepulauan, *Indonesia* 167 K11
Álora, *Sp.* 122 K8
Alor Setar, *Malaysia* 165 N6
Aloysius, Mount, *Austral.* 184 G8
Alpena, *Mich., U.S.* 93 C13
Alpha, *Qnsld., Austral.* 187 F14
Alpine, *Tex., U.S.* 92 J7
Alps, mountains, *Europe* 114 J7
Al Qābil, *Oman* 149 G11
Al Qaḍīmah, *Saudi Arabia* 148 H5
Al Qadmūs, *Syr.* 146 E5
Al Qā'im, *Iraq* 148 C6
Al Qaţrānah, *Jordan* 147 K5
Al Qa'īyah, *Saudi Arabia* 148 G7
Al Qāmishlī, *Syr.* 146 B11
Al Qārah, *Yemen* 148 M7
Al Qaryah ash Sharqīyah, *Lib.* 175 C10
Al Qaryatayn, *Syr.* 146 F7
Al Qaşīm, region, *Saudi Arabia* 148 F7
Al Qaţīf, *Saudi Arabia* 148 F9
Al Qaţrūn, *Lib.* 175 D10
Al Qayşūmah, *Saudi Arabia* 148 F8
Alqueva, Barragem de, *Port.* 122 H5
Al Quţayfah, *Syr.* 146 G6
Al Qunayţirah (El Quneitra), *Syr.* 146 H5
Al Qunfudhah, *Saudi Arabia* 148 J6
Al Qurayyāt, *Saudi Arabia* 148 D5
Al Qurnah, *Iraq* 148 D8
Al Quşayr, *Syr.* 146 F6
Al Quşūrīyah, *Saudi Arabia* 148 G7
Al Quway'īyah, *Saudi Arabia* 148 G7
Al Quwayrah, *Jordan* 147 M4

Alroy Downs, *N. Terr., Austral.* 187 D10
Alsace, region, *Fr.* 125 L12
Alsask, *Sask., Can.* 88 J6
Alsasua, *Sp.* 123 B10
Alston, *Eng., U.K.* 121 K8
Alta, *Nor.* 119 B13
Alta Floresta, *Braz.* 109 E10
Alta Gracia, *Arg.* 110 G5
Altagracia, *Venez.* 106 B8
Altagracia de Orituco, *Venez.* 107 C10
Altamaha, river, *U.S.* 91 H14
Altamira, *Braz.* 109 C11
Altamira, *Chile* 110 D3
Altamira, Cuevas de, site, *Sp.* 122 B9
Altamura, *It.* 128 J10
Altan Xiret *see* Ejin Horo Qi, *Nei Mongol, China* 158 C2
Altar Desert, *Mex.* 85 L3
Altata, *Mex.* 94 E5
Altay, *China* 156 C8
Altay (Yösönbulag), *Mongolia* 157 C10
Altay Mountains, *Russ.* 136 K8
Altayskiy, *Russ.* 136 K8
Altdorf, *Switz.* 128 B3
Altea, *Sp.* 123 H12
Altenburg, *Ger.* 126 E8
Alter do Chão, *Port.* 122 G5
Altıağac, *Azerb.* 145 C17
Altınekin, *Turk.* 144 E6
Altıntaş, *Turk.* 144 D4
Altınyayla, *Turk.* 144 F3
Altmühl, river, *Ger.* 126 G6
Altnaharra, *Scot., U.K.* 120 E6
Alto Araguaia, *Braz.* 109 G11
Alto Garças, *Braz.* 109 G11
Alto Molócuè, *Mozambique* 181 D11
Alton, *Ill., U.S.* 93 E11
Altoona, *Pa., U.S.* 93 D15
Alto, Pico, *Azores, Port.* 122 L2
Alto Paraguai, *Braz.* 109 G10
Alto Parnaíba, *Braz.* 109 E13
Alto Purús, river, *Peru* 108 F5
Alto Río Senguerr, *Arg.* 111 N3
Altunhisar, *Turk.* 144 F7
Altun Shan, mountains, *China* 156 F7
Altun Shan, peak, *China* 156 E9
Al 'Ubaylah, *Saudi Arabia* 148 H9
Alucra, *Turk.* 145 D10
Al 'Ulā, *Saudi Arabia* 148 F5
Al'Unnāb, site, *Jordan* 147 M6
Al 'Uqaylah, *Lib.* 175 C12
Alushta, *Ukr.* 135 P6
Aluta, *D.R.C.* 176 H9
Al 'Uwaynāt, *Lib.* 175 D10
Al 'Uwaynid, *Saudi Arabia* 148 G8
Al 'Uwayqīlah, *Saudi Arabia* 148 E6
Al 'Uyūn, *Saudi Arabia* 148 G5
Älvdalen, *Sweden* 119 H12
Alverca do Ribatejo, *Port.* 122 G4
Alvesta, *Sweden* 119 K12
Älvkarleby, *Sweden* 119 H13
Alvorada, *Braz.* 109 F12
Älvsbyn, *Sweden* 119 E13
Al Wajh, *Saudi Arabia* 148 F4
Al Wannān, *Saudi Arabia* 148 F9
Alwar, *India* 154 E4
Al Wuday'ah, *Saudi Arabia* 148 K8
Alxa Gaoyuan, *China* 157 E10
Alyangula, *N. Terr., Austral.* 187 B11
Alytus, *Lith.* 119 L15
Alzamay, *Russ.* 137 J10
Alzey, *Ger.* 126 G5
Alzira, *Sp.* 123 G12
Ama, *Japan* 162 H5
Amadeus, Lake, *Austral.* 184 F9
Amadeus Depression, *Austral.* 184 F8
Amadi, *S. Sudan* 177 F10

Amadjuak Lake, *Nunavut, Can.* 89 F12
Amadora, *Port.* 122 G3
Amagi, *Japan* 163 K3
Amahai, *Indonesia* 167 J13
Amakusa Shotō, *Japan* 163 L3
Åmål, *Sweden* 119 J11
Amalfi, *It.* 129 K8
Amaliáda, *Gr.* 132 G6
Amamapare, *Indonesia* 188 K5
Amambaí, *Braz.* 109 J10
Amami Guntō, *Japan* 163 P2
Amami Ō Shima, *Japan* 163 P2
Amandola, *It.* 128 G7
Amangeldi, *Kaz.* 150 C9
Amantea, *It.* 129 L10
Amapá, *Braz.* 109 B12
Amarante, *Braz.* 109 D14
Amarante, *Port.* 122 D5
Amarillo, *Tex., U.S.* 92 G8
Amarkantak, *India* 154 G6
Amarwara, *India* 154 G5
Amasra, *Turk.* 144 B6
Amasya, *Turk.* 144 C8
Amata, *S. Austral., Austral.* 186 G9
Amatari, *Braz.* 108 C9
Amathous, ruins, *Cyprus* 133 F16
Amatignak, island, *U.S.* 85 T2
Amatrice, *It.* 128 G7
Amazon *see* Amazonas, river, *S. Amer.* 102 E8
Amazon (Solimões), river, *S. Amer.* 102 E5
Amazon, Mouths of the, *S. Amer.* 102 D9
Amazonas (Amazon), river, *S. Amer.* 102 E8
Amazon Basin, *S. Amer.* 102 E3
Ambajogai, *India* 154 J4
Ambala, *India* 154 D4
Ambalangoda, *Sri Lanka* 155 P5
Ambalantota, *Sri Lanka* 155 P6
Ambanja, *Madag.* 181 D14
Ambarchik, *Russ.* 137 C14
Ambargasta, Salinas de, *Arg.* 110 F5
Ambato, *Ecua.* 106 H4
Ambatondrazaka, *Madag.* 181 E14
Ambelákia, *Gr.* 132 D8
Ambelau, island, *Indonesia* 167 J12
Amberg, *Ger.* 126 G7
Ambergris Cay, *Belize* 95 H12
Ambergris Cays, *Turks & Caicos Is., U.K.* 97 F12
Ambikapur, *India* 154 G7
Ambilobe, *Madag.* 181 C15
Amble, *Eng., U.K.* 120 J9
Ambo, *Peru* 108 F4
Amboise, *Fr.* 125 M6
Ambon, *Indonesia* 167 J13
Ambon, island, *Indonesia* 167 J13
Ambositra, *Madag.* 181 F14
Ambovombe, *Madag.* 181 G13
Ambre, Cap d', *Madag.* 181 C15
Ambriz, *Angola* 180 B4
Ambunti, *P.N.G.* 188 G5
Amburan Burnu, *Azerb.* 145 C18
Amchitka, island, *U.S.* 85 T2
Am Dam, *Chad* 175 H12
Amderma, *Russ.* 136 E7
Amdi, *India* 154 F6
Amdo (Pagnag), *China* 156 H8
Ameca, *Mex.* 94 G6
Ameland, island, *Neth.* 124 D10
American Falls Reservoir, *U.S.* 90 D5
American Highland, *Antarctica* 201 E14
American Samoa, *U.S., Pac. Oc.* 191 F10
Americus, *Ga., U.S.* 93 H13
Amersfoort, *Neth.* 124 F10
Amery Ice Shelf, *Antarctica* 201 E15

Ames, *Iowa, U.S.* 93 D10
Amfilohía, *Gr.* 132 F6
Amfípoli, *Gr.* 132 B9
Ámfissa, *Gr.* 132 F8
Amga, *Russ.* 137 G14
Amga, river, *Russ.* 137 G14
Amguema, *Russ.* 137 B15
Amguid, *Alg.* 174 D8
Amhara, region, *Eth.* 177 E12
Amherst, *N.S., Can.* 89 L14
Amiens, *Fr.* 124 J7
Amíndeo, *Gr.* 132 B7
Amindivi Islands, *India* 155 M2
Amino, *Japan* 162 J6
Aminuis, *Namibia* 180 G6
Amioûn, *Leb.* 146 F5
Amir, river, *Afghan.* 152 H5
Amir Chah, *Pak.* 153 N1
Amistad, Presa de la, *Mex.* 94 C7
Amistad Reservoir, *U.S.* 90 J8
Åmli, *Nor.* 119 J10
'Ammān (Philadelphia), *Jordan* 146 J5
Ammaroo, *N. Terr., Austral.* 187 E10
Ammassalik *see* Tasiilaq, *Greenland, Den.* 199 L15
Ammochostos Bay, *Cyprus* 133 E17
Amnok, river, *N. Korea* 160 F3
Āmol, *Iran* 149 B10
Amolar, *Braz.* 109 H10
Amorgós, island, *Gr.* 133 J12
Amos, *Que., Can.* 89 K12
Amoy *see* Xiamen, *Fujian, China* 159 P7
Ampani, *India* 154 H7
Ampanihy, *Madag.* 181 G13
Ampezzo, *It.* 128 B7
Amphitrite Group, *China* 166 B8
Amplepuis, *Fr.* 125 P9
Amposta, *Sp.* 123 E13
'Amrān, *Yemen* 148 L7
Amravati, *India* 154 H5
Amreli, *India* 154 G2
'Amrīt (Marathus), ruins, *Syr.* 146 E5
Amritsar, *India* 154 C4
Amsā'ad, *Lib.* 175 B13
Amsterdam, *Neth.* 124 F9
Amstetten, *Aust.* 126 J9
Amtaedo, island, *S. Korea* 161 Q5
Am Timan, *Chad* 175 H12
'Āmūdah, *Syr.* 146 B11
Amu Darya (Oxus), river, *Afghan., Turkm.* 150 J9
Amuderýa, *Turkm.* 150 K9
Amukta, island, *U.S.* 85 T3
Amukta Passage, *U.S.* 85 T3
Amund Ringnes Island, *Nunavut, Can.* 88 B9
Amundsen Bay, *Antarctica* 201 B14
Amundsen Gulf, *N.W.T., Can.* 88 D7
Amundsen-Scott South Pole, station, *Antarctica* 200 G9
Amundsen Sea, *Antarctica* 200 H5
Amuntai, *Indonesia* 166 H8
Amur, river, *Asia* 143 G12
Amurang, *Indonesia* 167 G11
Amursk, *Russ.* 137 H16
Amvrakía *see* Árta, *Gr.* 132 E6
Amvrakikós Kólpos, *Gr.* 132 E6
Amvrosiyivka, *Ukr.* 135 M8
An, *Myanmar* 164 E3
Anaa, island, *Fr. Polynesia, Fr.* 191 F13
Anabar, river, *Russ.* 137 E11
Anabarskiy Zaliv, *Russ.* 137 D11
Anaco, *Venez.* 107 C11
Anadyr', *Russ.* 137 B16
Anadyr, Gulf of, *Russ.* 198 G3
Anadyr', river, *Russ.* 198 E3
Anadyrskiy Zaliv, *Russ.* 137 B16

Auponhia, *Indonesia* **167** HI2
Aur, island, *Malaysia* **165** P9
Auraiya, *India* **154** E5
Aurangabad, *India* **154** F7
Aurangabad, *India* **154** H4
Auray, *Fr.* **125** L3
Aurich, *Ger.* **126** B5
Aurignac, *Fr.* **125** S6
Aurillac, *Fr.* **125** Q7
Aurisina, *It.* **128** C7
Aurora, *Colo., U.S.* **92** E7
Aurora, *Ill., U.S.* **93** DI2
Aurukun, *Qnsld., Austral.* **187** BI3
Aus, *Namibia* **180** H5
Auschwitz *see* Oświęcim, *Pol.*
  127 FI2
Austin, *Minn., U.S.* **93** DII
Austin, *Tex., U.S.* **92** J9
Austin, Lake, *Austral.* **184** H4
Austral Downs, *N. Terr., Austral.*
  187 EII
Australian Alps, *Austral.* **185** MI4
Australian Capital Territory, *Austral.*
  187 LI4
Austral Islands (Tubuai Islands), *Fr.*
  Polynesia, Fr. **191** GI2
Austria, *Europe* **116** H8
Austriahütte, site, *Aust.* **126** J9
Austvågøy, island, *Nor.* **119** DII
Autazes, *Braz.* **108** C9
Autlán, *Mex.* **94** G6
Autun, *Fr.* **125** M9
Auxerre, *Fr.* **125** L8
Auxonne, *Fr.* **125** MIO
Auzances, *Fr.* **125** P7
Avala, peak, *Serb.* **130** E9
Avallon, *Fr.* **125** M9
Avalon Peninsula, *Nfld. & Lab., Can.*
  89 JI6
Avanavero, *Suriname* **107** EI5
Avanos, *Turk.* **144** E7
Āvāz, *Iran* **149** CI3
Avdira, ruins, *Gr.* **133** BII
Aveiro, *Braz.* **109** CIO
Aveiro, *Port.* **122** E4
Āvej, *Iran* **148** B9
Avellino, *It.* **128** J9
Aversa, *It.* **128** J8
Aves, Islas de, *Venez.* **107** AIO
Avesta, *Sweden* **119** HI2
Avezzano, *It.* **128** H7
Avgó, island, *Gr.* **132** K8
Avgo, island, *Gr.* **133** LI3
Aviano, *It.* **128** C6
Aviator Glacier, *Antarctica* **201** LII
Avignon, *Fr.* **125** RIO
Ávila, *Sp.* **122** E8
Avilés, *Sp.* **122** A7
Avissawella, *Sri Lanka* **155** P5
Avlonári, *Gr.* **133** FIO
Avon, river, *Eng., U.K.* **121** P9
Avon, river, *Eng., U.K.* **121** Q8
Avranches, *Fr.* **125** K4
Avsa, Gora, *Russ.* **137** GIO
Awaday, *W. Sahara, Mor.* **174** E4
Āwarē, *Eth.* **177** FI3
Awarua Bay, *N.Z.* **189** KII
Awa Shima, *Japan* **162** G9
Awat, *China* **156** D6
Awbārī, Ṣaḥrā', *Lib.* **175** CIO
Awe, Loch, *Scot., U.K.* **120** H6
Aweil, *S. Sudan* **176** E9
Awjilah, *Lib.* **175** CI2
Awsard, *W. Sahara, Mor.* **174** D3
Axel Heiberg Island, *Nunavut, Can.*
  88 B9
Axim, *Ghana* **178** E8
Axinim, *Braz.* **108** C9
Axiós, river, *Gr.* **132** B8
Ax-les-Thermes, *Fr.* **125** T7

Ayabe, *Japan* **162** J6
Ayacucho, *Arg.* **III** K8
Ayacucho, *Peru* **108** F5
Ayakkum Hu, *China* **156** F8
Ayaköz, *Kaz.* **151** DI4
Ayamonte, *Sp.* **122** J5
Ayan, *Russ.* **137** GII
Ayan, *Russ.* **137** GI5
Ayancık, *Turk.* **144** B7
Ayapel, *Col.* **106** D6
Ayaş, *Turk.* **144** D6
Ayat, river, *Kaz.* **150** B8
Ayaviri, *Peru* **108** G6
Aybak *see* Samangan, *Afghan.* **152** H5
Aydar Kŭl, *Uzb.* **151** HIO
Aydere, *Turkm.* **150** J6
Aydın, *Turk.* **144** E2
Aydıncık, *Turk.* **144** G6
Ayerbe, *Sp.* **123** CI2
Ayers Rock *see* Uluṟu, *Austral.* **184** G9
Ayeyarwady (Irrawaddy), river,
  Myanmar **164** D4
Ayeyarwady, Mouths of the, river,
  Myanmar **164** H4
Aykhal, *Russ.* **137** FII
Ay Khanom, ruins, *Afghan.* **152** G6
Aylesbury, *Eng., U.K.* **121** QIO
Ayllón, *Sp.* **122** D9
Aylmer Lake, *N.W.T., Can.* **88** F7
'Ayn al 'Arab, *Syr.* **146** C8
Ayní, *Taj.* **152** F6
'Aynūnah, *Saudi Arabia* **148** E4
Ayon, Ostrov, *Russ.* **137** CI5
Ayorou, *Niger* **174** G7
Ayoûn el 'Atroûs, *Mauritania* **174** F4
Aypolovo, *Russ.* **136** H8
Ayr, *Qnsld., Austral.* **187** DI5
Ayr, *Scot., U.K.* **120** J6
Ayrancı, *Turk.* **144** F6
Ayre, Point of, *Isle of Man, U.K.* **121** L6
Äyteke Bī, *Kaz.* **150** F8
Aytos, *Bulg.* **131** GI5
Ayutla, *Mex.* **94** H8
Ayutthaya, *Thai.* **164** H7
Ayvacık, *Turk.* **144** D2
Ayvaj, *Taj.* **152** G5
Ayvalık, *Turk.* **144** D2
Āzād Shahr, *Iran* **149** BII
Azahar, Costa del, *Sp.* **123** FI3
Azamgarh, *India* **154** E7
Azapa, *Chile* **110** A3
Azare, *Nig.* **179** CI2
Azaw, *Afghan.* **153** K2
Azawad, region, *Mali* **174** F6
Azawak, river, *Mali, Niger* **174** F8
A'zāz, *Syr.* **146** C6
Azdavay, *Turk.* **144** B6
Azerbaijan, *Asia* **142** F6
Azerbaijan, region, *Iran* **148** B8
Azincourt, *Fr.* **124** H7
Azogues, *Ecua.* **106** J4
Azores (Açores), islands, *Port.* **122** L4
Azov, *Russ.* **135** M9
Azov, Sea of, *Russia, Ukr.* **135** N7
Azua, *Dom. Rep.* **97** JI3
Azuaga, *Sp.* **122** H7
Azuero, Península de, *Pan.* **95** MI6
Azul, *Arg.* **110** J7
Azurduy, *Bol.* **108** H8
Az Zabadānī, *Syr.* **146** G5
Aẕ Ẕāhirīyah, *West Bank* **147** K4
'Azzān, *Yemen* **148** M8
Az Zarqā', *Jordan* **146** J5
Az Zawr, *Kuwait* **148** E8
Azzel Matti, Sebkha, *Alg.* **174** D7
Az Zubayr, *Iraq* **148** E8

B

Baabda, *Leb.* **146** G5
Baalbek, *Leb.* **146** F5

Baardheere, *Somalia* **177** GI3
Baarn, *Neth.* **124** F9
Baba Burnu, *Turk.* **144** B5
Baba Burnu, *Turk.* **144** DI
Babadag, peak, *Azerb.* **145** CI7
Baba Dağ, *Turk.* **144** G3
Babaeski, *Turk.* **144** B2
Babahoyo, *Ecua.* **106** J4
Babanūsah, *Sudan* **176** E9
Babar, island, *Indonesia* **167** KI3
Babar, Kepulauan, *Indonesia*
  167 KI3
Babati, *Tanzania* **177** JII
Babayevo, *Russ.* **134** D7
Babayurt, *Russ.* **135** PI2
Babi, island, *Indonesia* **166** G2
Babinda, *Qnsld., Austral.* **187** DI4
Babin Nos, peak, *Bulg., Serb.*
  131 FIO
Babo, *Indonesia* **167** HI4
Babruysk, *Belarus* **134** H4
Babu *see* Hezhou, *Guangxi Zhuangzu,*
  China **159** P2
Babushkina, *Russ.* **134** DIO
Babuyan, island, *Philippines*
  167 AIO
Babuyan Channel, *Philippines*
  167 AIO
Babuyan Islands, *Philippines*
  167 AIO
Babylon, ruins, *Iraq* **148** D7
Bacaadweyn, *Somalia* **177** FI4
Bacabal, *Braz.* **109** DI3
Bacan, island, *Indonesia* **167** HI2
Bacău, *Rom.* **131** CI4
Baccarat, *Fr.* **125** KII
Baceno, *It.* **128** B3
Bachu, *China* **156** E5
Back, river, *Nunavut, Can.* **88** F9
Bačka, region, *Serb.* **130** D8
Bačka Palanka, *Serb.* **130** D8
Bačka Topola, *Serb.* **130** D8
Backbone Mountain, *U.S.* **91** EI4
Bac Lieu, *Viet.* **165** L9
Bac Ninh, *Viet.* **164** E9
Bacolod, *Philippines* **167** DII
Bacup, *Eng., U.K.* **121** M8
Badain Jaran Shamo, *China* **157** EIO
Badajoz, *Sp.* **122** G6
Badalona, *Sp.* **123** DI4
Baddeck, *N.S., Can.* **89** KI5
Baddo, river, *Pak.* **153** P3
Baden, *Aust.* **127** JIO
Baden-Baden, *Ger.* **126** H5
Baden Park, *N.S.W., Austral.* **187** JI3
Baderna, *Croatia* **130** D4
Badgah, *Afghan.* **152** J4
Bad Hersfeld, *Ger.* **126** E6
Bad Homburg, *Ger.* **126** F5
Badin, *Pak.* **153** R6
Bad Ischl, *Aust.* **126** J9
Bad Kissengen, *Ger.* **126** F6
Badlands, region, *U.S.* **90** B8
Bad Mergentheim, *Ger.* **126** G6
Badogo, *Mali* **174** H5
Badong, *Hubei, China* **158** J2
Ba Dong, *Viet.* **165** LIO
Badrah, *Iraq* **148** D8
Bad Reichenhall, *Ger.* **126** J8
Badr Ḩunayn, *Saudi Arabia* **148** G5
Bad Säckingen, *Ger.* **126** J5
Bad Tölz, *Ger.* **126** J7
Badu Island, *Austral.* **185** AI3
Badulla, *Sri Lanka* **155** P6
Badupi, *Myanmar* **164** D3
Baegado, island, *S. Korea* **161** L5
Baegamsan, peak, *N. Korea, S. Korea*
  160 J7
Baengnyeongdo, island, *S. Korea*
  161 K3

Bafa Gölü, *Turk.* **144** F2
Bafatá, *Guinea-Bissau* **178** B4
Baffin Bay, *Nunavut, Can.* **89** CII
Baffin Island, *Nunavut, Can.* **89** DII
Bafia, *Cameroon* **179** EI3
Bafing, river, *Guinea, Mali* **170** J2
Bafoulabé, *Mali* **174** G4
Bafoussam, *Cameroon* **179** EI3
Bafra, *Turk.* **144** B8
Bafra Burnu, *Turk.* **144** B8
Bāft, *Iran* **149** EII
Bagamoyo, *Tanzania* **177** KI2
Bagan Serai, *Malaysia* **165** N7
Bagansiapiapi, *Indonesia* **166** G4
Bagdarin, *Russ.* **137** JI2
Bagé, *Braz.* **109** MII
Bages et de Sigean, Étang de, *Fr.*
  125 S8
Bagh a' Chaisteil (Castlebay), *Scot.,*
  U.K. **120** G4
Baghdād, *Iraq* **148** C7
Bagheria, *It.* **129** N7
Bāghīn, *Iran* **149** EI2
Baghlan, *Afghan.* **152** H6
Baghran Khowleh, *Afghan.* **153** K3
Bağırpaşa Dağı, *Turk.* **145** DII
Bağışlı, *Turk.* **145** FI4
Bagnères-de-Bigorre, *Fr.* **125** S5
Bagnères-de-Luchon, *Fr.* **125** T6
Bago, *Myanmar* **164** G4
Bago Yoma, *Myanmar* **164** F4
Bagram, *Afghan.* **152** J6
Bagrimi, *Afghan.* **152** J6
Baguio, *Philippines* **167** BIO
Bahamas, *N. Amer.* **87** N9
Baharati, station, *Antarctica*
  201 EI5
Bahau, *Malaysia* **165** P8
Bahawalnagar, *Pak.* **153** M9
Bahawalpur, *Pak.* **153** N8
Bahçe, *Turk.* **144** F8
Bahçesaray, *Turk.* **145** FI3
Bäherden, *Turkm.* **150** J6
Bahia *see* Salvador, *Braz.* **109** FI5
Bahía, Isla de la, *Hond.* **95** HI3
Bahía Blanca, *Arg.* **III** K6
Bahía de Caráquez, *Ecua.* **106** H3
Bahía Laura, *Arg.* **III** Q5
Bahías, Cabo dos, *Arg.* **III** N5
Bahir Dar, *Eth.* **177** EI2
Bahlās, *Oman* **149** HI2
Bahraich, *India* **154** E6
Bahrain, *Asia* **142** H5
Bahr el Ghazal, river, *Chad* **175** GII
Bahr el Jebel (Mountain Nile), river,
  S. Sudan **177** FIO
Bahr Kéita, river, *Chad* **175** HI2
Bahr Salamat, river, *Chad* **175** HI2
Bāhū Kalāt, *Iran* **149** FI3
Bai, river, *Henan, China* **158** H3
Baia de Aramă, *Rom.* **131** EII
Baía dos Tigres, *Angola* **180** E4
Baia Mare, *Rom.* **131** BII
Baia Sprie, *Rom.* **131** BII
Baïbokoum, *Chad* **175** JII
Bai Bung, Mui, *Viet.* **165** L9
Baicheng, *China* **156** D6
Baicheng, *China* **157** CI5
Băicoi, *Rom.* **131** EI3
Baidoa *see* Baydhabo, *Somalia*
  177 GI3
Baie-Comeau, *Que., Can.* **89** KI3
Baihe, *Shaanxi, China* **158** HI
Baijiantan, *China* **156** C7
Baikal, Lake *see* Baykal, Ozero, *Russ.*
  137 JI2
Baikha, *Russ.* **136** G9
Baikunthpur, *India* **154** G7
Baile an Chaisleáin *see*
  Castletownshend, *Ire.* **121** Q2

Bazas, *Fr.* 125 R5
Bazhong, *China* 157 H12
Bazkovskaya, *Russ.* 135 LIO
Bazmān, Kūh-e, *Iran* 149 FI3
Beachport, *S. Austral., Austral.*
　187 MII
Beachy Head, *Eng., U.K.* 121 RII
Beagle Bay, *W. Austral., Austral.* 186 C5
Beagle Bay, *Austral.* 184 C5
Beagle Gulf, *Austral.* 184 A8
Béal an Átha *see* Ballina, *Ire.* 121 L2
Béal an Mhuirthead (Belmullet), *Ire.*
　121 L2
Beal Átha hÉis *see* Ballyhaise, *Ire.*
　121 L4
Béal Átha na Muice *see* Swinford, *Ire.*
　121 L2
Béal Átha Seanaidh *see* Ballyshannon,
　Ire. 121 L3
Béal Deirg (Belderg), *Ire.* 121 L2
Béar, Cap, *Fr.* 125 T8
Beardmore Glacier, *Antarctica*
　201 HIO
Bear Island, *Ire.* 121 QI
Bear Islands *see* Medvezh'i Ostrova,
　Russ. 137 CI4
Bearnaraigh (Berneray), island, *Scot.,*
　U.K. 120 G4
Bear Paw Mountains, *U.S.* 90 B6
Bear River Range, *U.S.* 90 D5
Beasain, *Sp.* 123 BIO
Beata, Isla, *Dom. Rep.* 97 K12
Beata, Cabo, *Dom. Rep.* 97 K13
Beatrice, *Nebr., U.S.* 92 E9
Beattock, *Scot., U.K.* 121 K7
Beatton River, *B.C., Can.* 88 G5
Beatty, *Nev., U.S.* 92 F4
Beau Bassin, *Mauritius* 181 HI5
Beaucaire, *Fr.* 125 R9
Beauchêne Island, *Falk. Is., U.K.*
　III S7
Beaufort, *Malaysia* 166 F9
Beaufort, *S.C., U.S.* 93 HI5
Beaufort Sea, *Arctic Ocean* 90 H3
Beaufort West, *S. Af.* 180 J7
Beaugency, *Fr.* 125 L7
Beaumont, *Tex., U.S.* 93 JIO
Beaune, *Fr.* 125 M9
Beausoleil, *Fr.* 125 RI2
Beauvais, *Fr.* 124 J7
Beauvoir, *Fr.* 125 M8
Beaver, *Alas., U.S.* 92 J3
Beaver Glacier, *Antarctica* 201 BI4
Beawar, *India* 154 E3
Bebar, *India* 154 FI
Bebiram, *Indonesia* 188 L4
Beccles, *Eng., U.K.* 121 NI2
Bečej, *Serb.* 130 D9
Becerreá, *Sp.* 122 B6
Béchar, *Alg.* 174 B7
Beckley, *W. Va., U.S.* 93 FI4
Beddouza, Cap, *Mor.* 174 B5
Bedford, *Eng., U.K.* 121 PIO
Bedford, Cape, *Austral.* 185 CI4
Bedford Downs, *W. Austral., Austral.*
　186 C7
Bedonia, *It.* 128 E4
Bedourie, *Qnsld., Austral.* 187 FI2
Bedous, *Fr.* 125 S5
Beechey Group *see* Chichi Jima Rettō,
　Japan 163 QII
Beenleigh, *Qnsld., Austral.* 187 HI6
Be'er Menuha, *Israel* 147 L4
Be'er Ora, *Israel* 147 M4
Beersheba *see* Be'ér Sheva', *Israel*
　147 K4
Be'ér Sheva' (Beersheba), *Israel*
　147 K4
Beethoven Peninsula, *Antarctica*
　200 E4

Beeville, *Tex., U.S.* 92 K9
Bega, *N.S.W., Austral.* 187 LI5
Bega, Canalul, *Rom.* 130 D9
Bega, river, *Rom.* 131 DIO
Begejski Kanal, *Serb.* 130 D9
Bègles, *Fr.* 125 Q5
Begusarai, *India* 154 F8
Behagle *see* Laï, *Chad* 175 HII
Behbahān, *Iran* 148 E9
Behchokǫ̀, *N.W.T., Can.* 88 F6
Behring Point, *Bahamas* 96 C7
Behshahr, *Iran* 149 BIO
Bei, river, *Guangdong, China* 159 Q3
Bei'an, *China* 157 BI6
Beida *see* Al Bayḑā', *Lib.* 175 BI2
Beihai, *China* 157 LI3
Beijing (Peking), *Beijing Shi, China*
　158 C6
Beijin Gang, *Guangdong, China*
　159 R2
Beijing Shi, *China* 158 B6
Beilen, *Neth.* 124 EIO
Beiliu, *Guangxi Zhuangzu, China*
　159 QI
Beilun, *Zhejiang, China* 159 K9
Beining, *Liaoning, China* 158 A9
Beinn na Faoghla (Benbecula), island,
　Scot., U.K. 120 F4
Beipan, river, *China* 157 KI2
Beipiao, *Liaoning, China* 158 A8
Beira, *Mozambique* 181 FIO
Beirut *see* Beyrouth, *Leb.* 146 F5
Bei Shan, *China* 156 E9
Beitbridge, *Zimb.* 180 F9
Beït ed Dîne, *Leb.* 146 G5
Beiuş, *Rom.* 131 CIO
Beja, *Port.* 122 H5
Beja, *Tunisia* 174 A9
Bejaïa, *Alg.* 174 A8
Béjar, *Sp.* 122 E7
Bejestān, *Iran* 149 CI2
Bekaa Valley, *Leb.* 146 G5
Bekdash *see* Karabogaz, *Turkm.*
　150 G4
Békés, *Hung.* 127 KI4
Békéscsaba, *Hung.* 127 KI4
Bekily, *Madag.* 181 GI3
Bekkai, *Japan* 162 CI2
Bekobod, *Taj.* 152 E6
Bekobod, *Uzb.* 151 JII
Bekoropoka-Antongo, *Madag.*
　181 FI3
Bekwai, *Ghana* 178 E8
Bela, *Pak.* 153 Q4
Belaga, *Malaysia* 166 G8
Bel Air, *Mauritius* 181 HI6
Belalcázar, *Sp.* 122 H7
Belarus, *Europe* 117 FII
Bela Vista, *Para.* 109 JIO
Belaya, Gora, *Russ.* 137 BI6
Belaya Glina, *Russ.* 135 N9
Belaya Gora, *Russ.* 137 DI4
Belaya Kalitva, *Russ.* 135 M9
Belaya Zemlya, Ostrova, *Russ.* 136 B9
Bełchatów, *Pol.* 127 EI2
Belcheragh, *Afghan.* 152 H4
Belcher Channel, *Can.* 198 K9
Belcher Islands, *Nunavut, Can.* 89 HII
Belcik, *Turk.* 144 D8
Belcoo, *N. Ire., U.K.* 121 L3
Belderg *see* Béal Deirg, *Ire.* 121 L2
Beledweyne, *Somalia* 177 GI4
Belele, *W. Austral., Austral.* 186 G4
Belém, *Braz.* 109 CI2
Belén, *Arg.* 110 E4
Belen, *N. Mex., U.S.* 92 G6
Bélep, Îles, *New Caledonia, Fr.* 190 G7
Belev, *Russ.* 134 H7
Belfast, *N. Ire., U.K.* 121 L5
Belfast Lough, *N. Ire., U.K.* 121 K5

Belfort, *Fr.* 125 LII
Belgaum, *India* 155 K3
Belgica Mountains, *Antarctica*
　201 BI2
Belgium, *Europe* 116 G6
Belgodère, *Fr.* 128 G3
Belgorod, *Russ.* 135 K7
Belgrade *see* Beograd, *Serb.* 130 E9
Belgrano II, station, *Antarctica*
　200 D7
Belinyu, *Indonesia* 166 H5
Belisario Domínguez, Presa, *Mex.*
　95 JIO
Belitung (Billiton), island, *Indonesia*
　166 H6
Belize, *N. Amer.* 87 P7
Belize City, *Belize* 95 HI2
Bel'kachi, *Russ.* 137 GI4
Bel'kovskiy, Ostrov, *Russ.* 137 DI2
Bella Bella, *B.C., Can.* 88 H4
Bellac, *Fr.* 125 N6
Bella Coola, *B.C., Can.* 88 H4
Bellary, *India* 155 K4
Bella Unión, *Uru.* 110 F8
Bella Vista, *Arg.* 110 E5
Bella Vista, *Arg.* 110 F8
Bellavista, *Peru* 108 D4
Belle-Anse, *Haiti* 97 JI2
Belledonne, Chaîne de, mountains, *Fr.*
　125 QIO
Belle Fourche, *S. Dak., U.S.* 92 C8
Belle Fourche, river, *U.S.* 90 C7
Bellegarde, *Fr.* 125 L7
Bellegarde, *Fr.* 125 NIO
Belle-Île, *Fr.* 125 M2
Belle Isle, *Nfld. & Lab., Can.* 89 HI5
Belle Isle, Strait of, *Nfld. & Lab., Can.*
　89 JI5
Bellême, *Fr.* 125 L6
Belleville, *Fr.* 125 N9
Belleville, *Ill., U.S.* 93 FII
Bellew, Mount (An Creagán), *Ire.*
　121 M3
Bellingham, *Wash., U.S.* 92 A3
Bellingshausen, station, *Antarctica*
　200 B3
Bellingshausen Sea, *Antarctica*
　200 F3
Bellinzona, *Switz.* 128 C3
Bello, *Col.* 106 E6
Bellpat, *Pak.* 153 N5
Bell Peninsula, *Nunavut, Can.* 89 FII
Bell Rock (Inchcape), island, *Scot., U.K.*
　120 H8
Bell Sound Isfjorden, *Nor.* 199 FI3
Belluno, *It.* 128 C6
Bell Ville, *Arg.* 110 H6
Belmonte, *Braz.* 109 GI5
Belmonte, *Port.* 122 E5
Belmonte, *Sp.* 123 FIO
Belmopan, *Belize* 95 HI2
Belmullet *see* Béal an Mhuirthead, *Ire.*
　121 L2
Belogorsk, *Russ.* 137 JI5
Belo Horizonte, *Braz.* 109 HI3
Belomorsk, *Russ.* 136 D5
Belorado, *Sp.* 122 C9
Belorechensk, *Russ.* 135 P9
Belo-Tsiribihina, *Madag.* 181 FI3
Beloūsovka, *Kaz.* 151 CI5
Beloye More, *Russ.* 136 D6
Beloye Ozero, *Russ.* 134 D8
Belozersk, *Russ.* 134 D8
Belterra, *Braz.* 109 CIO
Belukha, Gora, *Kaz.* 151 CI6
Belukha, Gora, *Russ.* 136 K8
Belush'ya Guba, *Russ.* 136 D7
Belvedere Marittimo, *It.* 129 LIO
Belvès, *Fr.* 125 Q6
Belvís de la Jara, *Sp.* 122 F8

Belyando, river, *Austral.* 185 FI4
Belyy, *Russ.* 134 G6
Belyy, Ostrov, *Russ.* 136 D8
Bemaraha, plateau, *Madag.* 181 EI3
Bembe, *Angola* 180 B4
Bembibre, *Sp.* 122 B6
Bemidji, *Minn., U.S.* 93 BIO
Benāb, *Iran* 148 B8
Benabarre, *Sp.* 123 CI3
Benalla, *Vic., Austral.* 187 LI3
Benasque, *Sp.* 123 CI3
Benavente, *Sp.* 122 C7
Benbecula *see* Beinn na Faoghla, island,
　Scot., U.K. 120 F4
Bender, *Moldova* 135 M4
Bender Cassim *see* Boosaaso, *Somalia*
　177 EI5
Bendigo, *Vic., Austral.* 187 LI3
Bene Beraq, *Israel* 146 J4
Benetutti, *It.* 129 K3
Benevento, *It.* 128 J9
Bengal, Bay of, *Asia* 140 K9
Bengalūru *see* Bangalore, *India*
　155 L4
Bengara, *Indonesia* 166 F9
Bengbu, *Anhui, China* 158 H6
Benghazi *see* Banghāzī, *Lib.*
　175 BI2
Bengkalis, *Indonesia* 166 G4
Bengkalis, island, *Indonesia*
　166 G4
Bengkayang, *Indonesia* 166 G7
Bengkulu, *Indonesia* 166 J4
Bengo, Baía do, *Angola* 180 B4
Benguela, *Angola* 180 C4
Benguerir, *Mor.* 174 B5
Beni, river, *Bol.* 108 F7
Beni Abbes, *Alg.* 174 C7
Benicarló, *Sp.* 123 EI3
Benidorm, *Sp.* 123 HI2
Benifaió, *Sp.* 123 GI2
Beni Mazâr, *Egypt* 175 CI4
Benin, *Af.* 172 J4
Benin, Bight of, *Af.* 171 K4
Benin City, *Nig.* 179 EII
Beni Ounif, *Alg.* 174 B7
Beni Suef, *Egypt* 175 CI4
Benitses, *Gr.* 132 D4
Benjamin Constant, *Braz.* 108 D6
Benjamin Hill, *Mex.* 94 B4
Benlidi, *Qnsld., Austral.* 187 FI3
Bennett, Ostrov, *Russ.* 137 CI3
Bennett, Lake, *Austral.* 184 F8
Bennett Island, *Russ.* 198 E6
Ben Nevis, peak, *Scot., U.K.* 120 G6
Benneydale, *N.Z.* 189 EI6
Benoud, *Alg.* 174 B7
Bensbach, *P.N.G.* 188 H7
Bensheim, *Ger.* 126 G5
Benson, *Ariz., U.S.* 92 H5
Bent, *Iran* 149 FI3
Benta, *Malaysia* 166 F4
Bentinck Island, *Austral.* 185 CI2
Bentinck Island, *Myanmar* 165 K5
Bentiu, *S. Sudan* 177 EIO
Bentley Subglacial Trench, *Antarctica*
　200 H7
Bentong, *Indonesia* 167 KIO
Bentong, *Malaysia* 165 P7
Benua, *Indonesia* 167 JII
Benue, river, *Nig.* 179 DI2
Benwee Head, *Ire.* 121 L2
Benxi, *Liaoning, China* 158 BIO
Beobwon, *S. Korea* 161 K6
Beograd (Belgrade), *Serb.* 130 E9
Beohari, *India* 154 F6
Beolgyo, *S. Korea* 161 Q7
Beppu, *Japan* 163 K4
Bequia, island, *St. Vincent & the*
　Grenadines 99 GI3

Bera Ndjoko, *Congo* 179 FI5
Berane, *Maced.* 130 G8
Berat, *Alban.* 130 K8
Berau, Teluk, *Indonesia* 188 L4
Berber, *Sudan* 177 CII
Berbera, *Somalia* 177 EI4
Berbérati, *Cen. Af. Rep.* 176 G6
Berbice, river, *Guyana* 107 EI4
Berceto, *It.* 128 E4
Berchtesgaden, *Ger.* 126 J8
Berck, *Fr.* 124 H7
Berdún, *Sp.* 123 CII
Berdyans'k, *Ukr.* 135 M8
Berdychiv, *Ukr.* 135 K4
Berdzor (Laçın), *Azerb.* 145 DI5
Berehove, *Ukr.* 135 LI
Bereina, *P.N.G.* 188 E7
Berenice, *Egypt* 175 DI5
Berens River, *Man., Can.* 88 J9
Beretău, river, *Rom.* 131 BIO
Berezniki, *Russ.* 136 F6
Berga, *Sp.* 123 CI4
Bergama, *Turk.* 144 D2
Bergamo, *It.* 128 C4
Bergara, *Sp.* 123 BIO
Bergen, *Neth.* 124 E9
Bergen, *Nor.* 118 H9
Bergerac, *Fr.* 125 Q6
Bergues, *Fr.* 124 G7
Berhala, Selat, *Indonesia* 166 H5
Bering, Ostrov, *Russ.* 137 DI8
Bering Island, *Russ.* 198 DI
Beringovskiy, *Russ.* 137 BI6
Bering Sea, *Asia, N. Amer.* 84 BI
Bering Strait, *Asia, N. Amer.* 84 C2
Berja, *Sp.* 123 KIO
Berkeley, Cabo, *Ecua.* 106 DI
Berkner Island, *Antarctica* 200 D7
Berlanga de Duero, *Sp.* 123 DIO
Berlevåg, *Nor.* 119 BI4
Berlin, *Ger.* 126 D9
Berlin, Mount, *Antarctica* 200 K7
Bermejito, river, *Arg.* 110 D6
Bermejo, river, *Arg.* 110 E7
Bermeo, *Sp.* 123 BIO
Bermillo de Sayago, *Sp.* 122 D7
Bermuda Islands, *U.K., Atl. Oc.*
 85 LIO
Bern, *Switz.* 128 B2
Bernalda, *It.* 129 KIO
Bernardo de Irigoyen, *Arg.* 110 E9
Bernardo O'Higgins, station,
 Antarctica 200 B3
Bernasconi, *Arg.* 111 K6
Bernau, *Ger.* 126 D9
Bernay, *Fr.* 125 K6
Bernburg, *Ger.* 126 E7
Berner Alpen, *Switz.* 128 B2
Berneray *see* Bearnaraigh, island, *Scot.,*
 U.K. 120 G4
Berneray *see* Eilean Bhearnaraigh,
 island, *Scot., U.K.* 120 F4
Bernier Bay, *Nunavut, Can.* 89 DIO
Bernier Island, *Austral.* 184 G2
Beroroha, *Madag.* 181 FI3
Berre, Étang de, *Fr.* 125 SIO
Berrechid, *Mor.* 174 B6
Berri, *S. Austral., Austral.* 187 KI2
Berry Islands, *Bahamas* 96 B7
Bertholet, Cape, *Austral.* 184 D5
Bertoua, *Cameroon* 179 EI4
Bertraghboy Bay, *Ire.* 121 MI
Beru, island, *Kiribati* 190 D8
Beruniy, *Uzb.* 150 H8
Beruri, *Braz.* 108 C9
Beruwala, *Sri Lanka* 155 P5
Berwick-upon-Tweed, *Eng., U.K.*
 120 J8
Berwyn, mountains, *Wales, U.K.*
 121 N7

Beryslav, *Ukr.* 135 M6
Besalampy, *Madag.* 181 EI3
Besançon, *Fr.* 125 MIO
Beserah, *Malaysia* 165 P8
Besham Qala, *Pak.* 152 J8
Besikama, *Indonesia* 167 LII
Beşiri, *Turk.* 145 FI2
Besni, *Turk.* 144 F9
Beşparmak Dağı, *Turk.* 144 F2
Bessarabia, region, *Moldova* 135 L3
Bessemer, *Ala., U.S.* 93 GI3
Bessines, *Fr.* 125 N6
Bestobe, *Kaz.* 151 BI2
Bestyakh, *Russ.* 137 GI3
Beswick, *N. Terr., Austral.* 186 B9
Betanzos, *Sp.* 122 B5
Betanzos, Ría de, *Sp.* 122 A5
Bethanie, *Namibia* 180 H5
Bethel, *Alas., U.S.* 92 L2
Bethlehem, *S. Af.* 180 H8
Bethlehem *see* Bayt Laḥm, *West Bank*
 146 J4
Beth Shan *see* Bet She'an, *Israel*
 146 H5
Béthune, *Fr.* 124 H7
Betong, *Malaysia* 166 G7
Betong, *Thai.* 165 N7
Betoota, *Qnsld., Austral.* 187 GI2
Bétou, *Congo* 179 FI5
Betpaqdala (Desert), *Kaz.* 151 FII
Betroka, *Madag.* 181 GI4
Bet She'an (Beth Shan), *Israel*
 146 H5
Betul, *India* 154 G5
Beverley, *Eng., U.K.* 121 MIO
Bewcastle, *Eng., U.K.* 121 K8
Bexhill, *Eng., U.K.* 121 RII
Beycesultan, ruins, *Turk.* 144 E4
Bey Dağı, *Turk.* 144 D9
Bey Dağı, *Turk.* 144 E8
Beykoz, *Turk.* 144 C4
Beyla, *Guinea* 178 D6
Bēylul, *Eritrea* 177 DI3
Beyneu, *Uzb.* 150 F6
Beyonēsu Retsugan (Bayonnaise
 Rock), *Japan* 163 L9
Beypazarı, *Turk.* 144 D5
Beyrouth (Beirut), *Leb.* 146 F5
Beyşehir, *Turk.* 144 F5
Beyşehir Gölü, *Turk.* 144 F5
Beytüşşebap, *Turk.* 145 FI3
Bezhetsk, *Russ.* 134 E7
Béziers, *Fr.* 125 S8
Bhadarwah, *India* 153 KIO
Bhadra, *India* 154 D4
Bhadrakh, *India* 154 H8
Bhag, *Pak.* 153 N5
Bhagalpur, *India* 154 F8
Bhakkar, *Pak.* 153 L7
Bhaktapur, *Nepal* 154 E8
Bhamo, *Myanmar* 164 C5
Bhandara, *India* 154 H5
Bhanpura, *India* 154 F4
Bharatpur, *India* 154 E4
Bharatpur, *India* 154 F6
Bharuch, *India* 154 G3
Bhatapara, *India* 154 G6
Bhatarsaigh (Vatersay), island, *Scot.,*
 U.K. 120 G4
Bhatinda, *India* 154 D4
Bhatkal, *India* 155 L3
Bhatpara, *India* 154 G9
Bhavnagar, *India* 154 G2
Bhawanipatna, *India* 154 H7
Bhera, *Pak.* 153 L8
Bhilai, *India* 154 H6
Bhilwara, *India* 154 F3
Bhima, river, *India* 154 J4
Bhimbar, *Pak.* 153 K9
Bhind, *India* 154 E5

Bhinmal, *India* 154 F2
Bhisho, *S. Af.* 180 J8
Bholari, *Pak.* 153 R5
Bhongir, *India* 154 J5
Bhopal, *India* 154 G4
Bhreandáin, Bá (Brandon Bay), *Ire.*
 121 PI
Bhubaneshwar, *India* 154 H8
Bhuj, *India* 154 FI
Bhusawal, *India* 154 H4
Bhutan, *Asia* 143 HIO
Biak, *Indonesia* 188 K4
Biak, island, *Indonesia* 188 K4
Biała Podlaska, *Pol.* 127 DI5
Białogard, *Pol.* 127 BIO
Biały Bór, *Pol.* 127 BII
Białystok, *Pol.* 127 CI5
Bianco, *It.* 129 NIO
Biando, island, *S. Korea* 161 P6
Biaora, *India* 154 F4
Bīārjomand, *Iran* 149 BII
Biaro, island, *Indonesia* 167 GI2
Biarritz, *Fr.* 125 S4
Bias, *Fr.* 125 R4
Biau, *Indonesia* 167 GII
Bibala, *Angola* 180 D4
Bibbiena, *It.* 128 F6
Biberach, *Ger.* 126 J6
Bibi Nani, *Pak.* 153 N5
Bicaz, *Rom.* 131 BI3
Bichänäk Ashyrymy, range, *Arm.*
 145 DI5
Bichvint'a, *Ga.* 145 AII
Bida, *Nig.* 179 DII
Bideford, *Eng., U.K.* 121 R7
Biei, *Japan* 162 CIO
Biel, *Switz.* 128 A2
Bielawa, *Pol.* 127 FII
Bielefeld, *Ger.* 126 D5
Biele Karpaty, mountains, *Czech Rep.,*
 Slovakia 127 HII
Bieler See, *Switz.* 128 A2
Biella, *It.* 128 C2
Bielsa, *Sp.* 123 BI3
Bielsko-Biała, *Pol.* 127 GI2
Bielsk Podlaski, *Pol.* 127 CI5
Bien Hoa, *Viet.* 165 KIO
Bienville, Lac, *Que., Can.* 89 HI2
Biescas, *Sp.* 123 BI2
Big, river, *N.W.T., Can.* 88 C7
Biga, *Turk.* 144 C2
Bigadiç, *Turk.* 144 D3
Big Delta, *Alas., U.S.* 92 K3
Bigeumdo, island, *S. Korea* 161 Q5
Big Falls, *Minn., U.S.* 93 BIO
Biggar, *Sask., Can.* 88 J7
Biggenden, *Qnsld., Austral.* 187 GI6
Bighorn, river, *U.S.* 90 C6
Bighorn Mountains, *U.S.* 90 C7
Big Island, *Nunavut, Can.* 89 FI2
Big Spring, *Tex., U.S.* 92 H8
Big Trout Lake, *Ont., Can.* 89 JIO
Big Trout Lake, *Ont., Can.* 89 JIO
Big Wood Cay, *Bahamas* 96 C7
Bihać, *Bosn. & Herzg.* 130 E5
Bihar Sharif, *India* 154 F8
Bihoro, *Japan* 162 CII
Biinman, bay, *S. Korea* 161 N6
Bijagós, Arquipélago dos, *Guinea-Bissau*
 178 D3
Bijapur, *India* 154 J4
Bijapur, *India* 154 J6
Bījār, *Iran* 148 B8
Bijeljina, *Bosn. & Herzg.* 130 E8
Bijnor, *India* 154 D5
Bikaner, *India* 154 E3
Bikin, *Russ.* 137 JI6
Bikini Atoll, *Marshall Is.* 190 C7
Bīkkū Bīttī, peak, *Lib.* 175 EI2
Bikoro, *D.R.C.* 176 H7

Bilād Banī Bū 'Alī, *Oman* 149 HI3
Bilaspur, *India* 154 G6
Biläsuvar, *Azerb.* 145 DI7
Bila Tserkva, *Ukr.* 135 K5
Bilauktaung Range, *Thai.* 164 H6
Bilbao, *Sp.* 123 BIO
Bileća, *Bosn. & Herzg.* 130 G7
Bilecik, *Turk.* 144 C4
Biłgoraj, *Pol.* 127 FI5
Bilhorod-Dnistrovs'kyy, *Ukr.*
 135 N4
Bilibino, *Russ.* 137 CI5
Bilican Dağları, *Turk.* 145 EI2
Billilla, *N.S.W., Austral.* 187 JI3
Billiluna, *W. Austral., Austral.* 186 D7
Billings, *Mont., U.S.* 92 C6
Billings, *Russ.* 137 BI5
Billiton *see* Belitung, island, *Indonesia*
 166 H6
Billom, *Fr.* 125 P8
Bilma, *Niger* 175 FIO
Biloela, *Qnsld., Austral.* 187 GI5
Bilo Gora, mountains, *Croatia*
 130 C6
Bilohirs'k, *Ukr.* 135 P7
Bilopillya, *Ukr.* 135 K6
Biloxi, *Miss., U.S.* 93 JI2
Biltine, *Chad* 175 GI2
Bilto, *Nor.* 119 CI3
Bilüü, *Mongolia* 156 B8
Bilzen, *Belg.* 124 GIO
Bimberi Peak, *Austral.* 185 LI4
Bimini Islands, *Bahamas* 96 B6
Binaqadi, *Azerb.* 145 CI7
Bindloe *see* Marchena, Isla, *Ecua.*
 106 D2
Bindura, *Zimb.* 180 E9
Binéfar, *Sp.* 123 CI3
Bingen, *Ger.* 126 F5
Bingham, *Me., U.S.* 93 BI7
Binghamton, *N.Y., U.S.* 93 DI5
Bingöl, *Turk.* 145 EII
Bingöl Dağları, *Turk.* 145 DI2
Binhai (Dongkan), *Jiangsu, China*
 158 G8
Binh Khe, *Viet.* 164 HII
Binh Lieu, *Viet.* 164 DIO
Binjai, *Indonesia* 166 F3
Binjai, *Indonesia* 166 F6
Binongko, island, *Indonesia*
 167 JII
Bintan, island, *Indonesia* 166 G5
Bintuhan, *Indonesia* 166 J5
Bintulu, *Malaysia* 166 F8
Binyang, *China* 157 LI2
Binzhou, *Shandong, China* 158 E6
Biobío, river, *Chile* 111 K2
Bioč, peak, *Maced.* 130 G8
Bioko, island, *Atl. Oc.* 171 K5
Biokovo, peak, *Croatia* 130 G6
Bir, *India* 154 J4
Birāk, *Lib.* 175 DIO
Bi'r 'Alī, *Yemen* 148 M8
Birao, *Cen. Af. Rep.* 176 E8
Biratnagar, *Nepal* 154 E8
Birch Mountains, *Alta., Can.* 88 H6
Bird Island *see* Aves, *Venez.* 99 DII
Bird's Head Peninsula *see* Jazirah
 Doberai, *Indonesia* 167 HI4
Birdsville, *Qnsld., Austral.* 187 GII
Birecik, *Turk.* 144 G9
Bîr el 'Abd, *Egypt* 147 K2
Bireun, *Indonesia* 166 F2
Birganj, *Nepal* 154 E7
Bîr Ḥasana, *Egypt* 147 L2
Bīrjand, *Iran* 149 CI2
Birkenhead, *Eng., U.K.* 121 M8
Bîrlad, river, *Rom.* 131 CI5
Birmingham, *Ala., U.S.* 93 GI3
Birmingham, *Eng., U.K.* 121 P9

Bontang, *Indonesia* **166** G9
Bontoc, *Philippines* **167** B10
Bonvouloir Islands, *P.N.G.* **188** C8
Booligal, *N.S.W., Austral.* **187** K13
Boonderoo, *Qnsld., Austral.* **187** E13
Bööntsagaan Nuur, *Mongolia*
  157 D10
Boorabbin, *W. Austral., Austral.*
  186 J5
Boorama, *Somalia* **177** E13
Booroondara, Mount, *Austral.*
  185 J13
Boosaaso (Bender Cassim), *Somalia*
  177 E15
Boothia, Gulf of, *Nunavut, Can.* **88** E9
Boothia Peninsula, *Nunavut, Can.*
  88 D9
Booué, *Gabon* **179** G13
Bopeechee, *S. Austral., Austral.*
  187 H11
Boppard, *Ger.* **126** F5
Bor, *Russ.* **134** F10
Bor, *Serb.* **131** F10
Bor, *Turk.* **144** F7
Bora-Bora, island, *Fr. Polynesia, Fr.*
  191 F12
Borah Peak, *U.S.* **90** C5
Boran, *Kaz.* **151** D16
Boran, region, *Eth.* **177** G12
Borås, *Sweden* **119** K12
Borāzjān, *Iran* **149** E10
Borba, *Braz.* **108** D9
Borba, *Sp.* **122** G5
Borborema, Planalto da, *Braz.*
  109 E16
Borchgrevink Coast, *Antarctica*
  201 M10
Borçka, *Turk.* **145** C12
Bordeaux, *Fr.* **125** Q5
Borden Island, *N.W.T., Can.* **88** B8
Borden Peninsula, *Nunavut, Can.*
  89 D10
Bordertown, *S. Austral., Austral.*
  187 L12
Bordeyri, *Ice.* **118** D3
Bordj Flye Sainte Marie, *Alg.* **174** C6
Bordj le Prieur, *Alg.* **174** E7
Bordj Messouda, *Alg.* **174** C9
Bordj Omar Driss, *Alg.* **174** C9
Boré, *Mali* **174** G6
Boreray, island, *Scot., U.K.* **120** F3
Boreumdo, island, *S. Korea* **161** K5
Borgarnes, *Ice.* **118** E3
Borger, *Neth.* **124** E11
Borger, *Tex., U.S.* **92** G8
Borgholm, *Sweden* **119** K13
Borg Massif, *Antarctica* **200** B9
Borgo San Dalmazzo, *It.* **128** E2
Borgosesia, *It.* **128** C3
Borgou, range, *Benin, Nig.* **179** C10
Borhoyn Tal, *Mongolia* **157** D13
Borisoglebsk, *Russ.* **134** J10
Borisovo Sudskoye, *Russ.* **134** D7
Borjomi, *Ga.* **145** B13
Borkou, region, *Chad* **175** F11
Borlänge, *Sweden* **119** H12
Bormio, *It.* **128** B4
Borneo, island, *Asia* **141** L12
Bornholm, island, *Den.* **119** L12
Bornova, *Turk.* **144** E2
Boro, river, *S. Sudan* **176** F9
Borohora Shan, *China* **156** D7
Boroko, *Indonesia* **167** G11
Boromo, *Burkina Faso* **178** C8
Boronga Islands, *Myanmar* **164** E3
Borotou, *Côte d'Ivoire* **178** D6
Borovichi, *Russ.* **134** E6
Borovo, *Serb.* **130** D8
Borovsk, *Russ.* **134** G7
Borovskoy, *Kaz.* **150** A9

Borroloola, *N. Terr., Austral.* **187** C10
Borşa, *Rom.* **131** B12
Børselv, *Nor.* **119** B13
Borūjerd, *Iran* **148** C9
Boryeong, *S. Korea* **161** M6
Boryslav, *Ukr.* **135** K2
Boryspil', *Ukr.* **135** K5
Borzya, *Russ.* **137** K13
Bosa, *It.* **129** K2
Bosanska Gradiška, *Bosn. & Herzg.*
  130 D6
Bosanski (Šamac), *Bosn. & Herzg.*
  130 E7
Bosanski Petrovac, *Bosn. & Herzg.*
  130 E6
Boscastle, *Eng., U.K.* **121** R6
Bose, *China* **157** L12
Boseong, *S. Korea* **161** Q7
Boshan, *Shandong, China* **158** E6
Bosilegrad, *Serb.* **131** H10
Bosna, river, *Bosn. & Herzg.* **130** E7
Bosnia & Herzegovina, *Europe* **116** J9
Bosobolo, *D.R.C.* **176** G7
Bōsō Hantō, *Japan* **162** J9
Bosporus *see* İstanbul Boğazi, *Turk.*
  144 B4
Bossangoa, *Cen. Af. Rep.* **176** F6
Bossembélé, *Cen. Af. Rep.* **176** F7
Bossut, Cape, *Austral.* **184** D5
Bostan, *Pak.* **153** M5
Bosten Hu, *China* **156** D7
Boston, *Eng., U.K.* **121** N10
Boston, *Mass., U.S.* **93** C16
Boston Mountains, *U.S.* **91** G10
Botany Bay, *Austral.* **185** K15
Botev, peak, *Bulg.* **131** G13
Botevgrad, *Bulg.* **131** G12
Bothnia, Gulf of, *Europe* **114** D9
Boticas, *Port.* **122** D5
Botoşani, *Rom.* **131** A14
Botswana, *Af.* **173** Q7
Bottle Creek, *Turks & Caicos Is., U.K.*
  97 F12
Botwood, *Nfld. & Lab., Can.* **89** J16
Bouaflé, *Côte d'Ivoire* **178** D7
Bouaké, *Côte d'Ivoire* **178** D7
Bouar, *Cen. Af. Rep.* **176** F6
Bougainville, Cape, *Austral.* **184** B7
Bougainville, island, *P.N.G.* **188** A6
Bougouni, *Mali* **174** H5
Bouillon, *Belg.* **124** J9
Bouilly, *Fr.* **125** L9
Bouira, *Alg.* **174** A8
Boulder, *Colo., U.S.* **92** E7
Boulder City, *Nev., U.S.* **92** F4
Boulia, *Qnsld., Austral.* **187** F12
Boulogne, *Fr.* **125** S6
Boulogne-sur-Mer, *Fr.* **124** H7
Bouna, *Côte d'Ivoire* **178** D8
Boundary Peak, *U.S.* **90** E3
Boundiali, *Côte d'Ivoire* **178** C6
Bounty Islands, *N.Z., Pac. Oc.* **190** L8
Bourbon-Lancy, *Fr.* **125** N8
Bourem, *Mali* **174** F7
Bourganeuf, *Fr.* **125** P7
Bourg-en-Bresse, *Fr.* **125** N10
Bourges, *Fr.* **125** M7
Bourget, Lac du, *Fr.* **125** P10
Bourg-Lastic, *Fr.* **125** P7
Bourg-Madame, *Fr.* **125** T7
Bourgneuf, Baie de, *Fr.* **125** M3
Bourg-Saint-Maurice, *Fr.* **125** P11
Bourke, *N.S.W., Austral.* **187** J14
Bournemouth, *Eng., U.K.* **121** R9
Bousso, *Chad* **175** H11
Boutilimit, *Mauritania* **174** F3
Bovalino Marina, *It.* **129** N10
Bowen, *Qnsld., Austral.* **187** E15
Bowling Green, *Ky., U.S.* **93** F13
Bowling Green Bay, *Austral.* **185** D14

Bowman Bay, *Nunavut, Can.* **89** F11
Bowman Glacier, *Antarctica* **200** H9
Bowman Island, *Antarctica* **201** H16
Boxing, *Shandong, China* **158** E7
Boyabat, *Turk.* **144** C7
Boyang, *Jiangxi, China* **159** L6
Boyarka, *Russ.* **137** E10
Boyle (Mainistir na Búille), *Ire.*
  121 L3
Boyne, river, *Ire.* **121** M4
Boyoma Falls, *D.R.C.* **176** H9
Bozashchy Tübegi, *Kaz.* **150** F4
Bozburun, *Turk.* **144** G2
Boz Burun, *Turk.* **144** C3
Bozburun Dağı, *Turk.* **144** F5
Bozcaada, island, *Turk.* **144** C1
Boz Dağ, *Turk.* **144** F3
Bozdoğan, *Turk.* **144** F3
Bozeman, *Mont., U.S.* **92** C6
Bozhou, *Anhui, China* **158** G5
Bozkır, *Turk.* **144** F5
Bozkurt, *Turk.* **144** B7
Bozouls, *Fr.* **125** Q8
Bozoum, *Cen. Af. Rep.* **176** F6
Bozova, *Turk.* **145** F10
Bozüyük, *Turk.* **144** D4
Bra, *It.* **128** D2
Brabant Island, *Antarctica* **200** C3
Brač, island, *Croatia* **130** G6
Bracadale, Loch, *Scot., U.K.* **120** G5
Bracciano, *It.* **128** H6
Bracciano, Lago di, *It.* **128** H6
Brački Kanal, *Croatia* **130** F6
Bracknell, *Eng., U.K.* **121** Q10
Brad, *Rom.* **131** C11
Bradenton, *Fla., U.S.* **93** K14
Brades, *Montserrat, U.K.* **99** C12
Bradford, *Eng., U.K.* **121** M9
Bradford, *Pa., U.S.* **93** D14
Braga, *Port.* **122** D4
Bragado, *Arg.* **110** J7
Bragança, *Port.* **122** C6
Brahmanbaria, *Bangladesh* **154** F10
Brahmapur, *India* **154** H7
Brahmaputra, river, *Asia* **141** H10
Brahmaur, *India* **153** L10
Brăila, *Rom.* **131** D15
Brainerd, *Minn., U.S.* **93** C10
Braintree, *Eng., U.K.* **121** P11
Bramsche, *Ger.* **126** D5
Bramwell, *Qnsld., Austral.* **187** A13
Brancaleone Marina, *It.* **129** N10
Branco, river, *Braz.* **108** B8
Brandenburg, *Ger.* **126** D8
Brandenburg, region, *Ger.* **126** D8
Brandfort, *S. Af.* **180** H8
Brandon, *Man., Can.* **88** K8
Brandon Bay *see* Bhreandáin, Bá, *Ire.*
  121 P1
Brandvlei, *S. Af.* **180** J6
Bransby, *Qnsld., Austral.* **187** H12
Bransfield Strait, *Antarctica* **200** C3
Brantôme, *Fr.* **125** P6
Bras d'Or Lake, *N.S., Can.* **89** K15
Brasileiro, Planalto, *Braz.* **109** G13
Brasília, *Braz.* **109** G12
Brasília Legal, *Braz.* **109** C10
Braşov, *Rom.* **131** D13
Brasstown Bald, *U.S.* **91** G13
Brateş, Lacul, *Rom.* **131** D15
Bratislava (Pressburg), *Slovakia*
  127 J11
Bratsk, *Russ.* **137** J11
Bratskoye Vodokhranilishche, *Russ.*
  137 J11
Braţul Chilia, river, *Rom.* **131** D16
Braunau, *Aust.* **126** J8
Braunschweig (Brunswick), *Ger.*
  126 D7
Braunton, *Eng., U.K.* **121** R7

Brava, island, *Cape Verde* **174** E1
Brava, Costa, *Sp.* **123** C16
Bray (Bré), *Ire.* **121** N5
Bray Island, *Nunavut, Can.* **89** E11
Brazil, *S. Amer.* **104** G7
Brazilian Highlands, *S. Amer.*
  102 G8
Brazos, river, *U.S.* **90** H9
Brazzaville, *Congo* **179** J14
Brčko, *Serb.* **130** E8
Bré *see* Bray, *Ire.* **121** N5
Breaza, *Rom.* **131** D13
Brechin, *Scot., U.K.* **120** G8
Brecknock, Península, *Chile* **111** T3
Breda, *Neth.* **124** G9
Bredasdorp, *S. Af.* **180** K6
Bregalnica, river, *Maced.* **131** H11
Bregenz, *Ger.* **126** J6
Bréhat, Île de, *Fr.* **125** K3
Breiðafjörður, *Ice.* **118** D3
Breid Bay, *Antarctica* **201** A12
Breil-sur-Roya, *Fr.* **125** R12
Breisach, *Fr.* **125** L12
Brejo, *Braz.* **109** C14
Bremen, *Ger.* **126** C6
Bremerhaven, *Ger.* **126** B6
Bremerton, *Wash., U.S.* **92** A3
Brennero, *It.* **128** B5
Brenner Pass, *Aust., It.* **126** K7
Breno, *It.* **128** C4
Brentwood, *Eng., U.K.* **121** Q11
Brescia, *It.* **128** C4
Bressanone, *It.* **128** B6
Bressay, island, *Scot., U.K.* **120** B9
Bressuire, *Fr.* **125** N5
Brest, *Belarus* **134** J2
Brest, *Fr.* **125** K1
Breteuil, *Fr.* **124** J7
Breton, Pertuis, *Fr.* **125** N4
Bretón, Cayo, *Cuba* **96** G6
Breton Sound, *U.S.* **91** J12
Brett, Cape, *N.Z.* **189** B15
Breu, river, *Peru* **108** E9
Breves, *Braz.* **109** C12
Brevoort Island, *Nunavut, Can.*
  89 F13
Brewarrina, *N.S.W., Austral.*
  187 J14
Brewster, Cape *see* Kangikajiip
  Appalia, *Greenland, Den.* **199** J14
Bria, *Cen. Af. Rep.* **176** F8
Briare, *Fr.* **125** M8
Briatico, *It.* **129** M10
Bridgend (Pen-y-bont ar Ogwr),
  Wales, U.K. **121** Q7
Bridgeport, *Conn., U.S.* **93** D16
Bridgetown, *Barbados* **99** G14
Bridgewater, *N.S., Can.* **89** L14
Bridgewater, *Tas., Austral.* **187** L18
Bridgman, Cape, *Greenland, Den.*
  84 B8
Bridgwater, *Eng., U.K.* **121** R8
Bridlington, *Eng., U.K.* **121** L10
Brielle, *Neth.* **124** F9
Brienne-le-Château, *Fr.* **125** L9
Brienza, *It.* **129** K9
Brienzer See, *Switz.* **128** B2
Brig, *Switz.* **128** B2
Brighton, *Eng., U.K.* **121** R10
Brihuega, *Sp.* **123** E10
Brijuni Otoci, island, *Croatia* **130** E4
Brindisi, *It.* **128** J12
Brisbane, *Qnsld., Austral.* **187** H16
Bristol, *Eng., U.K.* **121** Q8
Bristol, *Va., U.S.* **93** F14
Bristol Bay, *U.S.* **90** M2
Bristol Channel, *Wales, U.K.* **121** Q6
British Columbia, *Can.* **88** H4
British Isles, *Europe* **114** E5
Britstown, *S. Af.* **180** J7

Byahoml', *Belarus* **134** G4
Byala, *Bulg.* **131** G15
Byala Slatina, *Bulg.* **131** F12
Byam Martin, Cape, *Nunavut, Can.*
89 C11
Byam Martin Island, *Nunavut, Can.*
88 C9
Byarezina, river, *Belarus* **134** H4
Byaroza, *Belarus* **134** H3
Byblos *see* Jbail, *Leb.* **146** F5
Bydgoszcz, *Pol.* **127** C11
Bykhaw, *Belarus* **134** H5
Bykovo, *Russ.* **135** K11
Bylot Island, *Nunavut, Can.* **89** D10
Byrdbreen, glacier, *Antarctica*
201 B12
Byrd Glacier, *Antarctica* **201** J10
Byrock, *N.S.W., Austral.* **187** J14
Byron, Cape, *Austral.* **185** H16
Byron, Isla, *Chile* **III** Q2
Bytom, *Pol.* **127** F12
Bytów, *Pol.* **127** B11

C

C, Dome, *Antarctica* **201** J13
Caála, *Angola* **180** C5
Caazapá, *Para.* **109** K10
Cabaiguán, *Cuba* **96** F6
Caballones, Cayo, *Cuba* **96** G6
Caballo Reservoir, *U.S.* **90** H6
Cabanatuan, *Philippines* **167** B10
Cabeza del Buey, *Sp.* **122** G7
Cabezas, *Bol.* **108** H8
Cabimas, *Venez.* **106** B8
Cabinda, *Angola* **180** A4
Cabo, *Braz.* **109** E16
Cabo Blanco, *Arg.* **III** P5
Cabo Frio, *Braz.* **109** J14
Cabonga, Réservoir, *Que., Can.* **89** L12
Caboolture, *Qnsld., Austral.* **187** H16
Caborca, *Mex.* **94** B4
Cabo San Lucas, *Mex.* **94** E4
Cabot Strait, *Can.* **84** H10
Cabral, *Dom. Rep.* **97** J13
Cabrera, *Dom. Rep.* **97** H14
Cabrera, island, *Sp.* **123** G15
Cabrera Baja, Sierra de la, *Sp.* **122** C6
Cabril, Barragem do, *Port.* **122** F5
Cabrobó, *Braz.* **109** E15
Cabrón, Cabo, *Dom. Rep.* **97** H14
Čačak, *Serb.* **130** F9
Caccia, Capo, *It.* **129** K2
Cáceres, *Braz.* **109** G10
Cáceres, *Sp.* **122** F6
Cachimbo, *Braz.* **109** E10
Cachoeira, *Braz.* **109** F15
Cachoeira do Sul, *Braz.* **109** L11
Cachoeiro do Itapemirim, *Braz.*
109 J14
Cacine, *Guinea-Bissau* **178** C3
Cacolo, *Angola* **180** C6
Caçu, *Braz.* **109** H11
Caculé, *Braz.* **109** G14
Cacuri, *Venez.* **107** E11
Čadca, *Slovakia* **127** G12
Cadí, Serra del, *Sp.* **123** C14
Cadillac, *Fr.* **125** Q5
Cadillac, *Mich., U.S.* **93** C13
Çadır Dağı, *Turk.* **145** E13
Cadiz, *Philippines* **167** D11
Cádiz, *Sp.* **122** K6
Cádiz, Golfo de, *Sp.* **122** K6
Cádiz, Bahía de, *Sp.* **122** K6
Caen, *Fr.* **125** K5
Caerdydd *see* Cardiff, *Wales, U.K.*
121 Q8
Caergybi *see* Holyhead, *Wales, U.K.*
121 M6
Caernarfon Bay, *Wales, U.K.* **121** N6
Caerphilly, *Wales, U.K.* **121** Q8

Caesarea, ruins, *Israel* **146** H4
Cafayate, *Arg.* **110** D5
Cagayan de Oro, *Philippines* **167** E11
Cagayan Islands, *Philippines* **167** D10
Cagayan Sulu Island, *Philippines*
166 E9
Cagli, *It.* **128** F6
Cagliari, *It.* **129** L3
Cagliari, Golfo di, *It.* **129** L3
Cagnes, *Fr.* **125** R12
Caguamas, Cayo Las, *Cuba* **96** G6
Caguán, river, *Col.* **106** G6
Caguas, *P.R., U.S.* **97** J17
Caha Mountains, *Ire.* **121** Q1
Cahir, *Ire.* **121** P3
Cahora Bassa, Lago de, *Mozambique*
181 D10
Cahore Point, *Ire.* **121** N5
Cahors, *Fr.* **125** Q6
Cahul, *Moldova* **135** N4
Caia, *Mozambique* **181** E11
Caiapônia, *Braz.* **109** G11
Caibarién, *Cuba* **96** E6
Caicara, *Venez.* **107** D10
Caicó, *Braz.* **109** E16
Caicos Islands, *Turks & Caicos Is., U.K.*
87 N10
Caicos Passage, *Bahamas* **97** F11
Caird Coast, *Antarctica* **200** C8
Cairngorm Mountains, *Scot., U.K.*
120 G7
Cairns, *Qnsld., Austral.* **187** C14
Cairo *see* El Qâhira, *Egypt* **175** C14
Cairo, *Ill., U.S.* **93** F12
Caiseal *see* Cashel, *Ire.* **121** N3
Caisleán an Bharraigh *see* Castlebar,
Ire. **121** L2
Caisleán Ghriaire *see* Castlegregory,
Ire. **121** P1
Cajamarca, *Peru* **108** E4
Cajàzeiras, *Braz.* **109** E15
Çakırgöl Dağı, *Turk.* **145** C11
Cakit, river, *Turk.* **144** F7
Çakmak, *Turk.* **144** D5
Çakmak Dağı, *Turk.* **145** D12
Čakovec, *Croatia* **130** C6
Çal, *Turk.* **144** E3
Calabar, *Nig.* **179** E12
Calabozo, *Venez.* **107** C10
Calaburras, Punta de, *Sp.* **122** K8
Calacuccia, *Fr.* **128** H3
Calafat, *Rom.* **131** F11
Calafort Ros Láir *see* Rosslare
Harbour, *Ire.* **121** P5
Calahorra, *Sp.* **123** C11
Calais, *Fr.* **124** G7
Calais, *Me., U.S.* **93** B17
Calalaste, Sierra de, *Arg.* **110** D4
Calalzo, *It.* **128** B6
Calama, *Braz.* **108** E8
Calama, *Chile* **110** C3
Calamar, *Col.* **106** C6
Calamar, *Col.* **106** G7
Calamian Group, *Philippines* **167** D10
Calamocha, *Sp.* **123** E11
Călan, *Rom.* **131** D11
Calanda, *Sp.* **123** E12
Calapan, *Philippines* **167** C10
Călăraşi, *Rom.* **131** E14
Calatayud, *Sp.* **123** D11
Calayan, island, *Philippines* **167** A10
Calbayog, *Philippines* **167** D11
Calcanhar, Ponta do, *Braz.* **109** D16
Calçoene, *Braz.* **109** A12
Calcutta *see* Kolkata, *India* **154** G9
Caldas da Rainha, *Port.* **122** F4
Caldera, *Chile* **110** E3
Çaldıran, *Turk.* **145** E14
Caldwell, *Idaho, U.S.* **92** C4
Caldy Iskand, *Wales, U.K.* **121** Q6

Caledon Bay, *Austral.* **185** B11
Caledonian Canal, *Scot., U.K.* **120** G6
Calf of Man (Yn Cholloo), cape, *Isle of
Man, U.K.* **121** L6
Calgary, *Alta., Can.* **88** J6
Calheta, *Azores, Port.* **122** L3
Cali, *Col.* **106** F5
Calicut *see* Kozhikode, *India* **155** M4
Caliente, *Nev., U.S.* **92** E4
California, *U.S.* **92** D2
California, Golfo de (Cortés, Mar de),
Mex. **94** D4
Calilegua, *Arg.* **110** C5
Cālilibad, *Azerb.* **145** D17
Callabonna, Lake, *Austral.* **185** H12
Callainn *see* Callan, *Ire.* **121** N4
Callan (Callainn), *Ire.* **121** N4
Callao, *Peru* **108** F4
Calliope Range, *Austral.* **185** G16
Calp *see* Calpe, *Sp.* **123** H12
Calpe (Calp), *Sp.* **123** H12
Caltagirone, *It.* **129** P8
Caltanissetta, *It.* **129** P8
ÇaltıBurnu, *Turk.* **144** C9
Calulo, *Angola* **180** C5
Caluso, *It.* **128** D2
Caluula, *Somalia* **177** E15
Calvert Hills, *N. Terr., Austral.* **187** C11
Calvi, *Fr.* **128** G3
Calvinia, *S. Af.* **180** J6
Camabatela, *Angola* **180** B5
Camacupa, *Angola* **180** C5
Camagüey, *Cuba* **96** F7
Camagüey, Archipiélago de, *Cuba*
96 E7
Camajuaní, *Cuba* **96** E5
Camaná, *Peru* **108** G5
Camapuã, *Braz.* **109** H11
Camarat, Cap, *Fr.* **125** S11
Çamardı, *Turk.* **144** F7
Camargo, *Bol.* **108** H8
Camargue, Île de la, *Fr.* **125** S9
Camarón, Cape, *N. Amer.* **85** Q8
Camarones, *Arg.* **III** N5
Camarones, Bahía, *Arg.* **III** N5
Ca Mau, *Viet.* **165** L9
Camballin, *W. Austral., Austral.* **186** D6
Cambodia, *Asia* **143** K11
Camborne, *Eng., U.K.* **121** S6
Cambrai, *Fr.* **124** H8
Cambre, *Sp.* **122** B5
Cambrian Mountains, *Wales, U.K.*
121 P7
Cambridge, *Eng., U.K.* **121** P11
Cambridge, *Jamaica* **96** J7
Cambridge Bay, *Nunavut, Can.* **88** E8
Cambridge Gulf, *Austral.* **184** B7
Cambundi-Catembo, *Angola* **180** C5
Çam Burnu, *Turk.* **144** C9
Camden, *Ark., U.S.* **93** H11
Camden Bay, *U.S.* **90** H3
Camden Sound, *Austral.* **184** C6
Çameli, *Turk.* **144** F3
Camerino, *It.* **128** G7
Cameroon, *Af.* **173** K5
Cameroon Mount, *Cameroon* **179** E12
Cametá, *Braz.* **109** C12
Camiguin, island, *Philippines* **167** A10
Camiguin, island, *Philippines* **167** D11
Caminha, *Port.* **122** C4
Camiri, *Bol.* **108** H8
Camirus, ruins, *Gr.* **133** K15
Camissombo, *Angola* **180** B6
Çamlibel *see* Myrtou, *Cyprus* **133** E15
Camocim, *Braz.* **109** C15
Camooweal, *Qnsld., Austral.* **187** D11
Camopi, river, *Fr. Guiana, Fr.* **107** F17
Camorta Island, *India* **155** N11
Campagnano di Roma, *It.* **128** H6
Campana, *Arg.* **110** H8

Campana, *It.* **129** L11
Campana, Isla, *Chile* **III** Q2
Campanario, Cerro, *Arg., Chile* **110** J3
Campbell, Cape, *N.Z.* **189** G15
Campbell Hill, *U.S.* **91** E13
Campbell Island (Motu Ihupuku), *N.Z.,
Pac. Oc.* **190** M7
Campbell River, *B.C., Can.* **88** J4
Campbell Town, *Tas., Austral.* **187** L18
Campeche, *Mex.* **95** G11
Campechuela, *Cuba* **96** G7
Cam Pha, *Viet.* **164** E10
Campidano, mountains, *It.* **129** L3
Campina Grande, *Braz.* **109** E16
Campinas, *Braz.* **109** J13
Campli, *It.* **128** G7
Campo, *Cameroon* **179** F12
Campoalegre, *Col.* **106** F6
Campobasso, *It.* **128** H8
Campofelice, *It.* **129** N8
Campo Gallo, *Arg.* **110** E6
Campo Grande, *Braz.* **109** H10
Campo Mourão, *Braz.* **109** K11
Campos, *Braz.* **109** J14
Cam Ranh, *Viet.* **164** J11
Cam Ranh, Vung, *Viet.* **165** K11
Camrose, *Alta., Can.* **88** J6
Camsell Portage, *Sask., Can.* **88** G7
Çan, *Turk.* **144** C2
Ca Na, *Viet.* **165** K11
Ca Na, Mui, *Viet.* **165** K11
Canaan, *Trinidad & Tobago* **99** H14
Canacona, *India* **155** K3
Canada, *N. Amer.* **86** G5
Cañada de Gómez, *Arg.* **110** H7
Cañada Honda, *Arg.* **110** G4
Canadian, river, *U.S.* **90** G8
Canadian Shield, *Can.* **84** F5
Çanakkale, *Turk.* **144** C2
Çanakkale Boğazi (Dardanelles), *Turk.*
144 C1
Cananea, *Mex.* **94** B4
Canarias, Islas *see* Canary Islands,
Spain **174** C3
Canarreos, Archipiélago de los, *Cuba*
96 F3
Canary Islands, *Atl. Oc.* **170** F1
Cañas, *C.R.* **95** L14
Canatlán, *Mex.* **94** E6
Canaveral, Cape, *U.S.* **91** J15
Canavieiras, *Braz.* **109** G15
Canberra, *Austral. Capital Terr., Austral.*
187 L14
Cancún, *Mex.* **95** F12
Çandarlı, *Turk.* **144** D2
Çandarli Körfezi, *Turk.* **144** D2
Candás, *Sp.* **122** A7
Candé, *Fr.* **125** M4
Candia *see* Iráklio, *Gr.* **133** M11
Candon, *Philippines* **167** B10
Canea *see* Haniá, *Gr.* **133** L10
Cañete, *Sp.* **123** F11
Canfranc, *Sp.* **123** B12
Cangamba, *Angola* **180** D6
Cangas, *Sp.* **122** C4
Cangas del Narcea, *Sp.* **122** B6
Canguaretama, *Braz.* **109** E16
Cangwu, *Guangxi Zhuangzu, China*
159 Q2
Cangzhou, *Hebei, China* **158** D6
Caniapiscau, Réservoir, *Que., Can.*
89 J13
Caniapiscau, river, *Que., Can.* **89** H13
Canicattì, *It.* **129** P8
Caniles, *Sp.* **123** J10
Canindé, *Braz.* **109** D15
Canipaan, *Philippines* **166** E9
Canjáyar, *Sp.* **123** K10
Çankırı, *Turk.* **144** C7
Canna, island, *Scot., U.K.* **120** G5

Cannae, site, *It.* **128** J10
Cannanore *see* Kannur, *India* **155** M3
Cannes, *Fr.* **125** R12
Canning Hill, *Austral.* **184** H4
Canoas, *Braz.* **109** L11
Canon City, *Colo., U.S.* **92** F7
Canosa di Puglia, *It.* **128** J10
Canouan, island, *St. Vincent & the Grenadines* **99** G13
Canso, Strait of, *N.S., Can.* **89** K15
Cantabria, Sierra de, *Sp.* **123** C10
Cantábrica, Cordillera, *Sp.* **122** B6
Cantalejo, *Sp.* **122** D9
Cantavieja, *Sp.* **123** E12
Canterbury, *Eng., U.K.* **121** Q12
Canterbury Bight, *N.Z.* **189** K13
Can Tho, *Viet.* **165** K9
Cantiles, Cayo, *Cuba* **96** F3
Canto do Buriti, *Braz.* **109** E14
Canton *see* Guangzhou, *Guangdong, China* **159** Q3
Canton, *Ohio, U.S.* **93** D14
Cantù, *It.* **128** C3
Cantwell, *Alas., U.S.* **92** K3
Canumã, *Braz.* **108** C9
Canutama, *Braz.* **108** D8
Cany-Barville, *Fr.* **124** J6
Cao Bang, *Viet.* **164** D9
Caoxian, *Shandong, China* **158** F5
Capayán, *Arg.* **110** F5
Cap Barbas, *W. Sahara, Mor.* **174** D3
Cap-Chat, *Que., Can.* **89** K14
Cape Barren Island, *Austral.* **185** K18
Cape Breton Island, *N.S., Can.* **89** K15
Cape Coast, *Ghana* **178** E8
Cape Dorset, *Nunavut, Can.* **89** F11
Cape Fear, river, *U.S.* **91** F15
Cape Girardeau, *Mo., U.S.* **93** F11
Capenda-Camulembu, *Angola* **180** B6
Cape Palmas, *Liberia* **178** E6
Cape Rodney, *P.N.G.* **188** D8
Capestrano, *It.* **128** H8
Cape Town, *S. Af.* **180** K6
Cape Verde, *Af.* **174** D1
Cape Yakataga, *Alas., U.S.* **92** L4
Cape York Peninsula, *Austral.* **185** A13
Cap-Haïtien, *Haiti* **97** H12
Capistrello, *It.* **128** H7
Capital Hill, *N. Mariana Is., U.S.* **190** B5
Capitán Pablo Lagerenza, *Para.* **108** H9
Capodistria *see* Koper, *Slov.* **130** D4
Capoeira, Corredeira, *Braz.* **109** D10
Capo Rizzuto, Isola di, *It.* **129** M11
Cappadocia, region, *Turk.* **144** E7
Cappamore (An Cheapach Mhór), *Ire.* **121** N3
Cappoquin (Ceapach Choinn), *Ire.* **121** P3
Capraia, Isola di, *It.* **128** G4
Capreol, *Ont., Can.* **89** L11
Caprera, Isola, *It.* **128** J3
Capri, Isola di, *It.* **129** K8
Capricorn Channel, *Austral.* **185** F16
Capricorn Group, *Austral.* **185** F16
Caprivi Strip, region, *Namibia* **180** E7
Cap Rock Escarpment, *U.S.* **90** H8
Captieux, *Fr.* **125** R5
Capua, *It.* **128** J8
Caquetá, river, *Col.* **106** H8
Caracal, *Rom.* **131** F12
Caracaraí, *Braz.* **108** B9
Caracas, *Venez.* **107** B10
Caracol, *Braz.* **109** E14
Carahue, *Chile* **111** K2
Carajás, Serra dos, *Braz.* **109** D11
Caramulo, Serra do, *Port.* **122** E5
Carandotta, *Qnsld., Austral.* **187** E11
Caransebeș, *Rom.* **131** D10

Caratasca, Laguna de, *Hond.* **95** J14
Carauari, *Braz.* **108** D7
Caraúbas, *Braz.* **109** D16
Caravaca de la Cruz, *Sp.* **123** H11
Caravelas, *Braz.* **109** H15
Carballiño, *Sp.* **122** C5
Carballo, *Sp.* **122** B4
Carbón, Laguna del, *Arg.* **111** Q4
Carbonara, Capo, *It.* **129** L3
Carbondale, *Ill., U.S.* **93** F12
Carboneras, *Sp.* **123** K11
Carbonia, *It.* **129** L2
Carbonne, *Fr.* **125** S6
Carcajou, *Alta., Can.* **88** G6
Carcans, Lac de, *Fr.* **125** Q4
Carcasse, Cap, *Haiti* **97** J10
Carcassonne, *Fr.* **125** S7
Carche, peak, *Sp.* **123** H11
Carcross, *Yukon, Can.* **88** E4
Cardamom Mountains, *Cambodia* **164** J8
Cardamum Island *see* Kadmat Island, *India* **155** M2
Cardeña, *Sp.* **122** H8
Cárdenas, *Cuba* **96** E4
Cárdenas, *Mex.* **94** F7
Cardiff (Caerdydd), *Wales, U.K.* **121** Q8
Cardigan (Aberteifi), *Wales, U.K.* **121** P6
Cardigan Bay, *Wales, U.K.* **121** P6
Cardona, *Sp.* **123** C14
Cardwell, *Qnsld., Austral.* **187** D14
Carei, *Rom.* **131** B11
Careiro da Várzea, *Braz.* **108** C9
Carey, Lake, *Austral.* **184** H6
Cargèse, *Fr.* **128** H3
Carhué, *Arg.* **110** J6
Cariati, *It.* **129** L11
Caribbean Sea, *Atl. Oc.* **96** H5
Caribou Mountains, *Can.* **84** F4
Cariñena, *Sp.* **123** D11
Carinhanha, *Braz.* **109** G14
Cariparé, *Braz.* **109** F13
Caripito, *Venez.* **107** B12
Carlin, *Nev., U.S.* **92** D4
Carlingford Lough, *Ire.* **121** L5
Carlisle, *Eng., U.K.* **121** K8
Carlos, Isla, *Chile* **111** S3
Carlos Manuel de Céspedes, *Cuba* **96** F7
Carlow (Ceatharlach), *Ire.* **121** N4
Carlsbad, *N. Mex., U.S.* **92** H7
Carmacks, *Yukon, Can.* **88** E4
Carmagnola, *It.* **128** D2
Carmarthen (Sir Gaerfyrddin), *Wales, U.K.* **121** Q7
Carmarthen Bay, *Wales, U.K.* **121** Q6
Carmaux, *Fr.* **125** R7
Carmen, Isla, *Mex.* **94** D4
Carmen de Bolívar, *Col.* **106** C6
Carmen de Patagones, *Arg.* **111** L6
Carmona, *Sp.* **122** J7
Carnarvon, *Qnsld., Austral.* **187** G14
Carnarvon, *S. Af.* **180** J7
Carnarvon, *W. Austral., Austral.* **186** G2
Carn Domhnach *see* Carndonagh, *Ire.* **121** K4
Carndonagh (Carn Domhnach), *Ire.* **121** K4
Carnegie, *W. Austral., Austral.* **186** G6
Carnegie, Lake, *Austral.* **184** G5
Carney Island, *Antarctica* **200** J6
Carnic Alps, *Aust., It.* **128** B7
Car Nicobar, island, *India* **155** N11
Carnot, *Cen. Af. Rep.* **176** F6
Carnot, Cape, *Austral.* **185** K10
Carnsore Point, *Ire.* **121** P5

Carolina, *Braz.* **109** E13
Caroline Island (Millennium Island), *Kiribati* **191** E12
Caroline Islands, *F.S.M.* **190** D4
Caroní, river, *Venez.* **107** D12
Carora, *Venez.* **106** C8
Carpathian Mountains, *Europe* **114** H9
Carpathos *see* Kárpathos, island, *Gr.* **133** L14
Carpatho-Ukraine, region, *Ukr.* **135** L1
Carpentaria, Gulf of, *Austral.* **185** B11
Carpentras, *Fr.* **125** R10
Carpi, *It.* **128** D5
Carpina, *Braz.* **109** E16
Carpolac, *Vic., Austral.* **187** L12
Carquefou, *Fr.* **125** M4
Carrara, *It.* **128** E4
Carrarang, *W. Austral., Austral.* **186** H2
Carrauntoohil, peak, *Ire.* **121** P1
Carriacou, island, *Grenada* **99** G13
Carrickfergus, *Scot., U.K.* **121** K5
Carrick-on-Shannon (Cora Droma Rúisc), *Ire.* **121** L3
Carrión de los Condes, *Sp.* **122** C8
Carrizal Bajo, *Chile* **110** E3
Carrowmore Lough, *Ire.* **121** L2
Çarşamba, *Turk.* **144** C9
Çarşamba, river, *Turk.* **144** F5
Carson City, *Nev., U.S.* **92** E3
Carson Sink, *U.S.* **90** D3
Cartagena, *Col.* **106** C6
Cartagena, *Sp.* **123** J11
Cartago, *C.R.* **95** L14
Cartago, *Col.* **106** E5
Carter, Mount, *Austral.* **185** B13
Cartier Island, *Austral.* **184** B6
Cartwright, *Nfld. & Lab., Can.* **89** H15
Caruaru, *Braz.* **109** E16
Carúpano, *Venez.* **107** B12
Carutapera, *Braz.* **109** C13
Carvoeiro, *Braz.* **108** C8
Carvoeiro, Cabo, *Port.* **122** F3
Caryapundy Swamp, *Austral.* **185** H13
Casablanca, *Mor.* **174** B6
Casa Grande, *Ariz., U.S.* **92** G5
Casale Monferrato, *It.* **128** D3
Casamance, region, *Senegal* **174** G3
Casanare, river, *Col.* **106** D8
Casarano, *It.* **129** K12
Cascade Range, *U.S.* **90** C2
Cascavel, *Braz.* **109** K11
Cascina, *It.* **128** F5
Cascorro, *Cuba* **96** F7
Casere, *It.* **128** B6
Caserta, *It.* **128** J8
Casey, station, *Antarctica* **201** J16
Casey Bay, *Antarctica* **201** B14
Cashel (Caiseal), *Ire.* **121** N3
Casiguran, *Philippines* **167** B11
Casilda, *Arg.* **110** H7
Casino, *N.S.W., Austral.* **187** H16
Casiquiare, river, *Venez.* **107** F10
Casma, *Peru* **108** E4
Casnewydd *see* Newport, *Wales, U.K.* **121** Q8
Caspe, *Sp.* **123** D12
Casper, *Wyo., U.S.* **92** D7
Caspian Depression, *Asia, Europe* **115** H15
Caspian Sea, *Asia, Europe* **115** H16
Casquets, island, *Channel Is., U.K.* **121** T8
Cassel, *Fr.* **124** H7
Cassiar Mountains, *B.C., Can.* **88** F4

Cassino, *It.* **128** J8
Cassis, *Fr.* **125** S10
Castagneto Carducci, *It.* **128** F5
Castanhal, *Braz.* **109** C13
Castaño Nuevo, *Arg.* **110** G3
Casteggio, *It.* **128** D3
Castelbuono, *It.* **129** N8
Castel di Sangro, *It.* **128** H8
Castelfranco Veneto, *It.* **128** C6
Casteljaloux, *Fr.* **125** R5
Castellabate, *It.* **129** K9
Castellammare, Golfo di, *It.* **129** N7
Castellammare del Golfo, *It.* **129** N7
Castellaneta, *It.* **129** K11
Castelló de la Plana *see* Castellón de la Plana, *Sp.* **123** F12
Castellón de la Plana (Castelló de la Plana), *Sp.* **123** F12
Castelnaudary, *Fr.* **125** S7
Castelnovo ne' Monti, *It.* **128** E4
Castelo Branco, *Port.* **122** F5
Castelo de Bode, Barragem de, *Port.* **122** F5
Castelo de Vide, *Port.* **122** F5
Castelsardo, *It.* **128** J3
Castiglione Messer Marino, *It.* **128** H8
Castille, region, *Sp.* **122** C7
Castillon, *Fr.* **125** S6
Castillos, *Uru.* **110** H10
Castlebar (Caisleán an Bharraigh), *Ire.* **121** L2
Castlebay *see* Bagh a' Chaisteil, *Scot., U.K.* **120** G4
Castlebridge, *Ire.* **121** P5
Castle Douglas, *Scot., U.K.* **121** K7
Castlegregory (Caisleán Ghriaire), *Ire.* **121** P1
Castle Island, *Bahamas* **97** F10
Castlepollard (Baile na gCros), *Ire.* **121** M4
Castlerea (An Caisleán Riabhach), *Ire.* **121** M3
Castlereagh, river, *Austral.* **185** J14
Castletownshend (Baile an Chaisleáin), *Ire.* **121** Q2
Castres, *Fr.* **125** S7
Castries, *Fr.* **125** R9
Castries, *St. Lucia* **99** F13
Castro, *Chile* **111** M2
Castro Daire, *Port.* **122** E5
Castro-Urdiales, *Sp.* **122** B9
Castro Verde, *Port.* **122** J4
Castrovillari, *It.* **129** L10
Castuera, *Sp.* **122** G7
Çat, *Turk.* **145** D12
Çatak, *Turk.* **145** F13
Catalão, *Braz.* **109** H12
Çatalca, *Turk.* **144** B3
Catalina, *Chile* **110** D3
Catalonia, region, *Sp.* **123** C13
Catamarca, *Arg.* **110** F5
Catanduanes, island, *Philippines* **167** C11
Catania, *It.* **129** N9
Catania, Golfo di, *It.* **129** P9
Catania, Piana di, *It.* **129** P9
Catanzaro, *It.* **129** M10
Catarman, *Philippines* **167** C11
Catawba, river, *U.S.* **91** F14
Cat Cays, *Bahamas* **96** B6
Cateel, *Philippines* **167** E12
Catete, *Angola* **180** B4
Cathair na Mart *see* Westport, *Ire.* **121** M2
Cat Island, *Bahamas* **96** C9
Cat Lake, *Ont., Can.* **88** K9
Catoche, Cape, *Mex.* **85** P7
Cato Island, *Austral.* **185** F17
Catria, Monte, *It.* **128** F7

Catriló, *Arg.* **110** J6
Catrimani, *Braz.* **108** B8
Catrimani, river, *Braz.* **108** B8
Catskill Mountains, *U.S.* **91** C16
Cattolica Eraclea, *It.* **129** P7
Cauca, river, *Col.* **106** D6
Caucasus Mountains, *Asia, Europe*
115 J14
Caucete, *Arg.* **110** G4
Caudry, *Fr.* **124** H8
Caulnes, *Fr.* **125** L3
Caungula, *Angola* **180** B6
Cauquenes, *Chile* **110** J2
Caura, river, *Venez.* **107** E11
Caussade, *Fr.* **125** R7
Cauto, river, *Cuba* **96** G8
Cavaillon, *Fr.* **125** R10
Cavalaire, *Fr.* **125** S11
Cavalcante, *Braz.* **109** F13
Cavalese, *It.* **128** C5
Cavalla, river, *Liberia* **178** E6
Cavallo, Île, *Fr.* **128** J3
Cavally, river, *Côte d'Ivoire* **178** E6
Cavan (An Cabhán), *Ire.* **121** L4
Caviana, Ilha, *Braz.* **109** B12
Cavignac, *Fr.* **125** Q5
Cavo, Monte, *It.* **128** H7
Cavour, *It.* **128** D2
Çavuş Burnu, *Turk.* **144** G4
Çavuşçu Gölü, *Turk.* **144** E5
Caxias, *Braz.* **108** D6
Caxias, *Braz.* **109** D14
Caxias do Sul, *Braz.* **109** L11
Caxito, *Angola* **180** B4
Çay, *Turk.* **144** E5
Cayambe, *Ecua.* **106** H4
Cayambe, peak, *Ecua.* **106** H5
Çaycuma, *Turk.* **144** B6
Çayeli, *Turk.* **145** C11
Cayenne, *Fr. Guiana, Fr.* **107** E17
Cayeux-sur-Mer, *Fr.* **124** H7
Cayey, *P.R., U.S.* **97** J17
Çayıralan, *Turk.* **144** D8
Çayirova see Agios Theodoros, *Cyprus*
133 E17
Cayman Brac, island, *Cayman Is., U.K.*
96 H5
Cayman Islands, *U.K.* **96** H5
Caynabo, *Somalia* **177** E14
Cazalla de la Sierra, *Sp.* **122** H7
Cazaux et de Sanguinet, Lac de, *Fr.*
125 Q4
Cazères, *Fr.* **125** S6
Cazombo, *Angola* **180** C7
Cazorla, *Sp.* **122** J9
Ceanannas see Kells, *Ire.* **121** M4
Ceann Trá (Ventry), *Ire.* **121** P1
Ceapach Choinn see Cappoquin, *Ire.*
121 P3
Ceatharlach see Carlow, *Ire.* **121** N4
Cebollar, *Arg.* **110** F4
Cebu, island, *Philippines* **167** D11
Cebu City, *Philippines* **167** D11
Cecil Plains, *Qnsld., Austral.* **187** H15
Cecina, *It.* **128** F5
Cedar, river, *U.S.* **91** D11
Cedar City, *Utah, U.S.* **92** F5
Cedar Rapids, *Iowa, U.S.* **93** D11
Cedeira, *Sp.* **122** A5
Cedillo, Embalse de, *Sp., Port.* **122** F5
Cedros, Isla, *Mex.* **94** C2
Cedros Island, *Mex.* **85** M2
Ceduna, *S. Austral., Austral.* **186** J9
Ceelbuur, *Somalia* **177** G14
Ceerigaabo (Erigavo), *Somalia*
177 E14
Cefalù, *It.* **129** N8
Cegléd, *Hung.* **127** K13
Cehotina, river, *Bosn. & Herzg., Maced.*
130 G8

Cejal, *Col.* **106** F9
Çekerek, *Turk.* **144** D8
Çekerek, river, *Turk.* **144** D8
Celano, *It.* **128** H7
Celanova, *Sp.* **122** C5
Celaya, *Mex.* **94** G7
Celebes see Sulawesi, island, *Indonesia*
167 H10
Celebes Sea, *Asia* **141** L14
Çeleken, *Turkm.* **150** H5
Celje, *Slov.* **130** C5
Cella, *Sp.* **123** E11
Celle, *Ger.* **126** D6
Celtic Sea, *Atl. Oc.* **121** Q4
Çemişgezek, *Turk.* **145** E10
Cenderawasih, Teluk, *Indonesia*
188 K5
Cento, *It.* **128** D5
Central, Cordillera, *Col.* **106** F6
Central, Cordillera, *Dom. Rep.* **97** H13
Central African Republic, *Af.* **173** K7
Central America, *N. Amer.* **85** Q7
Central Brahui Range, *Pak.* **153** N5
Central Greece, region, *Gr.* **132** F7
Central Highlands, *Viet.* **164** J11
Centralia, *Wash., U.S.* **92** B3
Central Lowland, *U.S.* **91** E11
Central Lowlands, *Austral.* **185** E11
Central Makran Range, *Pak.* **153** Q2
Central Range, *P.N.G.* **188** G5
Central Range, *Russ.* **198** C1
Central Siberian Plateau, *Asia*
141 C10
Centre de Flacq, *Mauritius* **181** H16
Cenxi, *Guangxi Zhuangzu, China*
159 Q1
Cephalonia see Kefaloniá, island, *Gr.*
132 F5
Ceprano, *It.* **128** H7
Ceram, island, *Indonesia* **167** J13
Ceram Sea, *Indonesia* **188** M4
Cerbère, *Fr.* **125** T8
Ceredigion see Aberaeron, *Wales, U.K.*
121 P7
Ceres, *Arg.* **110** F6
Ceres, *Braz.* **109** G12
Cerigo see Kíthira, island, *Gr.* **132** K8
Cérilly, *Fr.* **125** N8
Çerkeş, *Turk.* **144** C6
Çermik, *Turk.* **145** F10
Cernavodă, *Rom.* **131** E15
Cerralvo, Isla, *Mex.* **94** E4
Cerrillos, *Arg.* **110** D5
Cerro de Pasco, *Peru* **108** F4
Cerro Sombrero, *Chile* **111** S4
Certaldo, *It.* **128** F5
Cervales, peak, *Sp.* **122** F7
Cervera, *Sp.* **123** D13
Cervera de Pisuerga, *Sp.* **122** B8
Cerveteri, *It.* **128** H6
Cervia, *It.* **128** E6
Cesana Torinese, *It.* **128** D1
Cesar, river, *Col.* **106** C7
Cesarò, *It.* **129** N9
Cesena, *It.* **128** E6
Cesenatico, *It.* **128** E6
Cēsis, *Latv.* **119** J15
České Budějovice, *Czech Rep.*
126 H9
Českomoravská Vrchovina, mountains,
Czech Rep. **127** G10
Český Krumlov, *Czech Rep.* **126** H9
Çeşme, *Turk.* **144** E1
Cetinje, *Maced.* **130** H8
Ceuta, *Sp.* **122** L7
Cévennes, mountains, *Fr.* **125** R9
Cevio, *Switz.* **128** B3
Ceyhan, *Turk.* **144** G8
Ceyhan, river, *Turk.* **144** F8
Ceylanpınar, *Turk.* **145** G11

Chabana, *Japan* **163** Q2
Chablis, *Fr.* **125** L8
Chacao, Canal de, *Chile* **111** M2
Chachapoyas, *Peru* **108** D4
Chacharan, *Pak.* **153** N7
Chachora, *India* **154** F4
Chachro, *Pak.* **153** R7
Chad, *Af.* **172** H6
Chad, Lake (Tchad, Lac), *Chad*
175 G10
Chadan, *Russ.* **136** K9
Chadron, *Nebr., U.S.* **92** D8
Chaeryŏng, *N. Korea* **160** J5
Chaeryŏng, river, *N. Korea* **160** J5
Chafarinas, Islas, *Sp.* **123** M10
Chagai, *Pak.* **153** N3
Chagai Hills, *Pak.* **153** N3
Chagda, *Russ.* **137** G14
Chagoda, *Russ.* **134** D7
Chagyl, *Turkm.* **150** H5
Chahar Bagh, *Afghan.* **152** G4
Chahar Borj, *Afghan.* **152** J2
Chāh Bāhar, *Iran* **149** G13
Chah-e Ab, *Afghan.* **152** G6
Chah-e Kerteh, *Afghan.* **153** L1
Ch'aho, *N. Korea* **160** F9
Ch'ahŭng, *N. Korea* **160** F4
Chaibasa, *India* **154** G8
Ch'ail-bong, peak, *N. Korea* **160** E7
Chai-Nat, *Thai.* **164** H6
Chajarí, *Arg.* **110** G8
Chakar, river, *Pak.* **153** N5
Chakaria, *Bangladesh* **154** G10
Chake Chake, *Tanzania* **177** J12
Chakhansur, *Afghan.* **153** L2
Chakwal, *Pak.* **153** K8
Chalais, *Fr.* **125** P5
Chalap Dalan Range, *Afghan.* **153** K3
Chalhuanca, *Peru* **108** G5
Chaling, *Hunan, China* **159** N3
Chalisgaon, *India* **154** H3
Chalkhi, *Afghan.* **152** J1
Chalkis see Halkída, *Gr.* **132** F9
Challans, *Fr.* **125** M4
Chalon, *Fr.* **125** N9
Châlons-en-Champagne, *Fr.* **125** K9
Châlus, *Fr.* **125** P6
Cham, *Ger.* **126** G8
Chamah, peak, *Malaysia* **165** N7
Chaman, *Pak.* **153** M4
Chaman Bid, *Iran* **149** B11
Chamatang, *India* **153** K12
Chamba, *India* **153** K10
Chambal, river, *India* **154** F4
Chambéry, *Fr.* **125** P10
Chambois, *Fr.* **125** K5
Chamburi Kalat, *Pak.* **153** Q3
Chamical, *Arg.* **110** F5
Chamkani, *Afghan.* **153** K6
Ch'amo Hāyk', *Eth.* **177** F12
Chamoli, *India* **154** D5
Chamonix, *Fr.* **125** P11
Champagne, region, *Fr.* **125** L9
Champagnole, *Fr.* **125** N10
Champasak, *Laos* **164** H9
Champéry, *Switz.* **128** C1
Champlain, Lake, *Can., U.S.* **91** B16
Champotón, *Mex.* **95** G11
Chamrajnagar, *India* **155** M4
Chamzinka, *Russ.* **134** G11
Chañaral, *Chile* **110** E3
Chança, river, *Port., Sp.* **122** J5
Chandigarh, *India* **154** C4
Chandless, river, *Braz.* **108** E6
Chandpur, *Bangladesh* **154** G10
Chandrapur, *India* **154** H5
Chang, Ko, *Thai.* **164** J8
Ch'angam, *N. Korea* **160** J3
Changan, *N. Korea* **160** D8

Changanacheri, *India* **155** N4
Changane, river, *Mozambique*
181 G10
Changbai Shan, *China, N. Korea*
157 D16
Chang Chenmo Range, *China*
152 J12
Changchon, *S. Korea* **161** K8
Changchun, *China* **157** D16
Changde, *Hunan, China* **159** L2
Ch'angdo, *N. Korea* **160** J7
Ch'angdo, *N. Korea* **160** J8
Changdong, *N. Korea* **160** G7
Changdong, *S. Korea* **161** K8
Changfeng, *Anhui, China* **158** H6
Changgang, *N. Korea* **160** D6
Changhua, *Taiwan, China* **159** Q8
Changhŭng, *N. Korea* **160** F8
Changhyŏn, *N. Korea* **160** E9
Changji, *China* **156** D8
Chang Jiang (Yangtze), river, *China*
157 J12
Changjin, *N. Korea* **160** F7
Changjin, river, *N. Korea* **160** D7
Changjin-ho (Chosin Reservoir), *N.
Korea* **160** E7
Changle, *Fujian, China* **159** N8
Changli, *Hebei, China* **158** C7
Changmar, *China* **156** F5
Changnyeong, *S. Korea* **161** P9
Changnyŏn, *N. Korea* **160** J4
Changping, *Beijing Shi, China*
158 B5
Changp'ung, *N. Korea* **160** J6
Ch'angp'yŏng, *N. Korea* **160** E9
Changsha, *Hunan, China* **159** L3
Changshan, *Zhejiang, China* **159** L7
Changshan Qundao, *Liaoning, China*
158 C9
Changshu, *Jiangsu, China* **158** J8
Ch'angsŏng, *N. Korea* **160** E4
Changsu-ho, reservoir, *N. Korea*
160 J5
Changting, *Fujian, China* **159** N5
Changwon, *S. Korea* **161** P9
Changxing, *Zhejiang, China* **158** J8
Changxing Dao, *Liaoning, China*
158 C8
Changyŏn, *N. Korea* **160** J4
Changyuan, *Henan, China* **158** F4
Changzhi, *Shanxi, China* **158** E4
Changzhi, *Shanxi, China* **158** F3
Changzhou, *Jiangsu, China* **158** J8
Chaníon, Kólpos, *Gr.* **133** L10
Channapatna, *India* **155** L4
Channel Country, region, *Austral.*
185 G11
Channel Islands, *U.K.* **121** T8
Channel Islands, *U.S.* **90** G2
Channel-Port aux Basques, *Nfld. &
Lab., Can.* **89** K15
Channel Rock, *Bahamas* **96** E8
Chantada, *Sp.* **122** B5
Chanthaburi, *Thai.* **164** J7
Chantilly, *Fr.* **125** K7
Chantrey Inlet, *Nunavut, Can.* **88** E9
Chaochou, *Taiwan, China* **159** R8
Chaohu, *Anhui, China* **158** J6
Chao Hu, *Anhui, China* **158** J6
Chao Phraya, river, *Thai.* **164** H6
Chaoyang, *Guangdong, China*
159 Q5
Chaoyang, *Liaoning, China* **158** A8
Chaozhou, *Guangdong, China* **159** Q5
Chapadinha, *Braz.* **109** D14
Chapaev, *Kaz.* **150** C5
Chapak Gozar, *Afghan.* **152** H3
Chapala, Lake, *Mex.* **85** P4
Chapala, Lago de, *Mex.* **94** G6
Chapcha, *Bhutan* **154** E9

Cha-Chi

Chapeco, *Braz.* **109** K11
Chapleau, *Ont., Can.* **89** L11
Char, *India* **154** B4
Chara, *Russ.* **137** H13
Chara, river, *Russ.* **137** H13
Charadai, *Arg.* **110** E7
Charagua, *Bol.* **108** H8
Charambirá, Punta, *Col.* **106** F4
Charcot Island, *Antarctica* **200** E4
Chard, *Eng., U.K.* **121** R8
Chardonnières, *Haiti* **97** J10
Charduar, *India* **154** E11
Chari, river, *Af.* **170** J7
Charikar, *Afghan.* **152** J6
Charity, *Guyana* **107** D14
Chärjew *see* Türkmenabat, *Turkm.* **150** J8
Charleroi, *Belg.* **124** H9
Charles, Cape, *U.S.* **91** E16
Charles *see* Santa María, Isla, *Ecua.* **106** F2
Charles Darwin Research Station, *Ecua.* **106** E3
Charles Island, *Nunavut, Can.* **89** F12
Charles Mound, *U.S.* **91** D11
Charles Point, *Austral.* **184** A8
Charleston, *N.Z.* **189** H13
Charleston, *S.C., U.S.* **93** G15
Charleston, *W. Va., U.S.* **93** E14
Charlestown, *St. Kitts & Nevis* **99** C12
Charleville (An Ráth), *Ire.* **121** P3
Charleville, *Qnsld., Austral.* **187** G14
Charleville-Mézières, *Fr.* **124** J9
Charlieu, *Fr.* **125** N9
Charlotte, *N.C., U.S.* **93** G14
Charlotte Amalie, *V.I., U.S.* **99** B10
Charlotte Harbor, *U.S.* **91** K14
Charlottenberg, *Sweden* **119** J11
Charlottesville, *Va., U.S.* **93** E15
Charlottetown, *P.E.I., Can.* **89** K15
Charlotteville, *Trinidad & Tobago* **99** H14
Charlton Island, *Nunavut, Can.* **89** J11
Charolles, *Fr.* **125** N9
Charsadda, *Pak.* **152** J8
Charters Towers, *Qnsld., Austral.* **187** E14
Chartres, *Fr.* **125** L6
Charyeongsanmaek, range, *S. Korea* **161** L7
Chasan, *N. Korea* **160** G5
Chascomús, *Arg.* **110** J8
Chasŏng, *N. Korea* **160** D6
Châteaubriant, *Fr.* **125** L4
Châteaudun, *Fr.* **125** L6
Château-Gontier, *Fr.* **125** L5
Château-la-Vallière, *Fr.* **125** M6
Châteaulin, *Fr.* **125** L2
Châteauneuf-de-Randon, *Fr.* **125** Q8
Châteauneuf-en-Thymerais, *Fr.* **125** K6
Châteauneuf-sur-Loire, *Fr.* **125** L7
Château-Renault, *Fr.* **125** M6
Châteauroux, *Fr.* **125** N7
Château-Thierry, *Fr.* **125** K8
Châteauvillain, *Fr.* **125** L9
Châtel, *Fr.* **125** N11
Châtelet, *Belg.* **124** H9
Châtellerault, *Fr.* **125** N6
Chatham, *Eng., U.K.* **121** Q11
Chatham, *N.B., Can.* **89** K14
Chatham *see* San Cristóbal, Isla, *Ecua.* **106** E3
Chatham Island, *N.Z., Pac. Oc.* **190** K9
Chatham Islands, *N.Z., Pac. Oc.* **190** K9
Châtillon, *Fr.* **125** L9
Châtillon-sur-Indre, *Fr.* **125** M6
Chatra, *India* **154** F7

Chattahoochee, river, *U.S.* **91** H13
Chattanooga, *Tenn., U.S.* **93** G13
Chatyr-Tash, *Kyrg.* **152** E10
Chau Doc, *Viet.* **165** K9
Chauk, *Myanmar* **164** E4
Chaukan Pass, *India, Myanmar* **154** E12
Chaumont, *Fr.* **125** L10
Chaun Bay, *Russ.* **198** E4
Chaunskaya Guba, *Russ.* **137** C15
Chauny, *Fr.* **124** J8
Chaves, *Braz.* **109** B12
Chaves, *Port.* **122** C5
Chaves *see* Santa Cruz, Isla, *Ecua.* **106** E3
Chayek, *Kyrg.* **152** D9
Ch'ayu, *N. Korea* **160** C10
Cheaha Mountain, *U.S.* **91** G13
Cheb, *Czech Rep.* **126** F8
Cheboksarskoye Vodokhranilishche, *Russ.* **134** F11
Cheboksary, *Russ.* **134** F11
Chebsara, *Russ.* **134** D8
Chech, Erg, *Alg., Mali* **174** D7
Chechaktu, *Afghan.* **152** H3
Chechnya, region, *Russ.* **135** P12
Cheduba Island, *Myanmar* **164** F3
Cheektowaga, *N.Y., U.S.* **93** D14
Cheepie, *Qnsld., Austral.* **187** G13
Chehar Borjak, *Afghan.* **153** M2
Cheju *see* Jeju, *S. Korea* **161** S6
Chekichler, *Turkm.* **150** J5
Chelforó, *Arg.* **111** K5
Chełm, *Pol.* **127** E15
Chełmno, *Pol.* **127** C12
Chelmsford, *Eng., U.K.* **121** Q11
Cheltenham, *Eng., U.K.* **121** P9
Chelyabinsk, *Russ.* **136** H6
Chelyuskin, *Russ.* **137** D10
Chelyuskin, Cape, *Russ.* **198** C9
Chemillé, *Fr.* **125** M5
Chemin Grenier, *Mauritius* **181** H15
Chemnitz, *Ger.* **126** F8
Chen, Gora, *Russ.* **198** B4
Chenab, river, *India, Pak.* **153** M7
Chenārān, *Iran* **149** B12
Chengalpattu, *India* **155** L5
Chengbu, *Hunan, China* **159** N1
Chengchow *see* Zhengzhou, *China* **157** G14
Chengde, *Hebei, China* **158** B6
Chengdu, *China* **157** H11
Chengele, *India* **154** D12
Chenghai, *Guangdong, China* **159** Q6
Chengkou, *China* **157** H12
Chengkung, *Taiwan, China* **159** Q9
Chengmai, *China* **157** M13
Chengshan Jiao, *Shandong, China* **158** E9
Chengwu, *Shandong, China* **158** F5
Chengyang *see* Juxian, *Shandong, China* **158** F7
Chennai (Madras), *India* **155** L6
Chenxi, *Hunan, China* **159** M1
Chenzhou, *Hunan, China* **159** N3
Cheom Ksan, *Cambodia* **164** H9
Cheonan, *S. Korea* **161** M7
Cheongdo, *S. Korea* **161** P9
Cheongju, *S. Korea* **161** M7
Cheongsando, island, *S. Korea* **161** R6
Cheongsong, *S. Korea* **161** M9
Cheongyang, *S. Korea* **161** M6
Cheonsuman, bay, *S. Korea* **161** M6
Cheorwon, *S. Korea* **160** J7
Chepén, *Peru* **108** E3
Chepes, *Arg.* **110** G4
Cherbourg-Octeville, *Fr.* **124** J4
Cherepovets, *Russ.* **134** D8
Chergui, Chott ech, *Alg.* **174** B8
Cherkasy, *Ukr.* **135** L5

Cherkessk, *Russ.* **135** P10
Cherlak, *Russ.* **136** J7
Chermenino, *Russ.* **134** D10
Chernaya, *Russ.* **136** E7
Chernihiv, *Ukr.* **134** J5
Cherni Vrŭkh, peak, *Bulg.* **131** H11
Chernivtsi, *Ukr.* **135** L3
Chernobyl' *see* Chornobyl', *Ukr.* **134** J5
Chernogorsk, *Russ.* **136** J9
Chernyakhovsk, *Russ.* **134** G2
Chernyayevo, *Russ.* **137** J14
Chernyshevskiy, *Russ.* **137** G12
Cherokees, Lake of the, *U.S.* **91** F10
Cherokee Sound, *Bahamas* **96** B8
Cherry Island *see* Anuta, *Solomon Is.* **190** F7
Cherskiy, *Russ.* **137** C15
Cherskiy Range, *Russ.* **198** B4
Cherskogo, Khrebet, *Russ.* **137** E14
Cherven Bryag, *Bulg.* **131** G12
Chervonohrad, *Ukr.* **135** K2
Cherykaw, *Belarus* **134** H5
Chesapeake Bay, *U.S.* **91** E15
Chesha Bay, *Russ.* **199** B14
Cheshskaya Guba, *Russ.* **136** D6
Chesht-e Sharif, *Afghan.* **152** J3
Cheshunt, *Eng., U.K.* **121** Q11
Chester, *Eng., U.K.* **121** N8
Chesterfield, *Eng., U.K.* **121** M9
Chesterfield, Îles, *New Caledonia, Fr.* **190** G6
Chesterfield Inlet, *Nunavut, Can.* **89** F10
Chesterton Range, *Austral.* **185** G14
Chetamale, *India* **155** M11
Chetlat Islands, *India* **155** M2
Chetumal, *Mex.* **95** H12
Chetumal Bay, *Mex.* **85** P7
Chetvertyy Kuril'skiy Proliv, *Russ.* **137** F18
Chevanceaux, *Fr.* **125** P5
Cheviot, The, peak, *Eng., U.K.* **120** J8
Cheviot Hills, *Scot., U.K.* **121** K8
Ch'ew Bahir, lake, *Eth.* **177** G12
Cheyenne, *Wyo., U.S.* **92** E7
Cheyenne, river, *U.S.* **90** C8
Cheyne Bay, *Austral.* **184** L5
Chhapra, *India* **154** F7
Chhatarpur, *India* **154** F5
Chhep, *Cambodia* **164** J9
Chhîm, *Leb.* **146** G5
Chhindwara, *India* **154** G5
Chhukha, *Bhutan* **154** E9
Chhung Kompong Saom, bay, *Cambodia* **165** K8
Chi, river, *Thai.* **164** H9
Chiang Mai, *Thai.* **164** F6
Chiang Rai, *Thai.* **164** E6
Chiaromonte, *It.* **129** K10
Chiasso, *Switz.* **128** C3
Chiat'ura, *Ga.* **145** B13
Chiavari, *It.* **128** E3
Chiavenna, *It.* **128** B4
Chiayi, *Taiwan, China* **159** Q8
Chiba, *Japan* **162** J9
Chibemba, *Angola* **180** D4
Chibia, *Angola* **180** D4
Chibougamau, *Que., Can.* **89** K12
Chiburi Shima, *Japan* **162** H5
Chicago, *Ill., U.S.* **93** D12
Chicapa, river, *Angola* **180** B6
Chichagof Island, *U.S.* **90** M5
Chichawatni, *Pak.* **153** M8
Chicheng, *Hebei, China* **158** B5
Chichén Itzá, ruins, *Mex.* **95** G12
Chichester, *Eng., U.K.* **121** R10
Chichester Range, *Austral.* **184** F4

Chichi Jima Rettō (Beechey Group), *Japan* **163** Q11
Chickasha, *Okla., U.S.* **92** G9
Chiclayo, *Peru* **108** E3
Chico, river, *Arg.* **111** N5
Chico, river, *Arg., Chile* **111** R4
Chicomo, *Mozambique* **181** G10
Chicoutimi, *Que., Can.* **89** K13
Chieri, *It.* **128** D2
Chieti, *It.* **128** G8
Chifeng, *Nei Mongol, China* **158** A7
Chignik, *Alas., U.S.* **92** M2
Chihsing Yen, island, *Taiwan, China* **159** R9
Chihuahua, *Mex.* **94** C6
Chihuahuan Desert, *Mex.* **94** C6
Chikan, *Russ.* **137** J11
Chikhachevo, *Russ.* **134** F5
Chikhli, *India* **154** H4
Chilas, *Pak.* **152** J9
Chilaw, *Sri Lanka* **155** N5
Chilca, *Peru* **108** F4
Childress, *Tex., U.S.* **92** G8
Chile, *S. Amer.* **105** N4
Chilecito, *Arg.* **110** F4
Chililabombwe, *Zambia* **180** C8
Chilka Lake, *India* **154** H8
Chillán, *Chile* **110** J2
Chiloé, Isla Grande de, *Chile* **111** M2
Chilpancingo, *Mex.* **94** H8
Chiltern Hills, *Eng., U.K.* **121** Q10
Chilumba, *Malawi* **181** C10
Chilung (Keelung), *Taiwan, China* **159** P9
Chimborazo, peak, *Ecua.* **106** J4
Chimbote, *Peru* **108** E4
Chimboy, *Uzb.* **150** G7
Chimoio, *Mozambique* **181** E10
China, *Asia* **142** G9
Chinandega, *Nicar.* **95** K13
Chincha Alta, *Peru* **108** G4
Chinchilla de Monte Aragón, *Sp.* **123** G11
Chinde, *Mozambique* **181** E11
Chindwin, river, *Myanmar* **164** C4
Chingola, *Zambia* **180** C8
Chinguetti, *Mauritania* **174** E4
Chin Hills, *Myanmar* **164** D3
Chinhoyi, *Zimb.* **180** E9
Chiniot, *Pak.* **153** L8
Chino, *Japan* **162** H8
Chinon, *Fr.* **125** M5
Chinsali, *Zambia* **181** C10
Chinsong, *N. Korea* **160** D6
Chioggia, *It.* **128** D6
Chios *see* Híos, *Gr.* **133** F12
Chios *see* Híos, island, *Gr.* **133** F12
Chipata, *Zambia* **181** D10
Chiping, *Shandong, China* **158** E5
Chiplun, *India* **154** J3
Chippenham, *Eng., U.K.* **121** Q9
Chiquián, *Peru* **108** F4
Chiquimula, *Guatemala* **95** J12
Chiquinquirá, *Col.* **106** E6
Chirchiq, *Uzb.* **151** H11
Chiredzi, *Zimb.* **180** F9
Chirikof Island, *U.S.* **85** S5
Chirinda, *Russ.* **137** F10
Chiriquí, Golfo de, *Pan.* **95** L15
Chiromo, *Malawi* **181** E11
Chirpan, *Bulg.* **131** H13
Chirripo, Cerro, *C.R.* **95** L14
Chisasibi, *Que., Can.* **89** J11
Chishan, *Taiwan, China* **159** R8
Chishtian Mandi, *Pak.* **153** M8
Chisimayu *see* Kismaayo, *Somalia* **177** H13
Chişinău, *Moldova* **135** M4
Chişineu Criş, *Rom.* **131** C10

248

Chita, *Russ.* 137 JI2
Chitado, *Angola* 180 E4
Chitato, *Angola* 180 B6
Chitembo, *Angola* 180 D5
Chitipa, *Malawi* 181 BIO
Chitose, *Japan* 162 DIO
Chitradurga, *India* 155 L4
Chitral, *Pak.* 152 H7
Chitré, *Pan.* 95 LI5
Chittagong, *Bangladesh* 154 GIO
Chittaurgarh, *India* 154 F3
Chittoor, *India* 155 L5
Chitungwiza, *Zimb.* 180 E9
Chiumbe, river, *Angola* 180 B6
Chivasso, *It.* 128 D2
Chivilcoy, *Arg.* 110 H7
Chlef, *Alg.* 174 A8
Ch'o-do, island, *N. Korea* 160 J3
Chodo, island, *S. Korea* 161 R7
Chodzież, *Pol.* 127 CII
Choele Choel, *Arg.* III K5
Ch'ogu, *N. Korea* 160 J8
Chŏgyuryŏng-sanmaek, range, *N. Korea* 160 E5
Choirokoitia, *Cyprus* 133 FI6
Choiseul, island, *Solomon Is.* 190 E6
Choiseul Sound, *Falk. Is., U.K.* III R7
Chŏjak, *N. Korea* 161 K4
Chojna, *Pol.* 126 C9
Chojnice, *Pol.* 127 BII
Chokurdakh, *Russ.* 137 DI4
Cholet, *Fr.* 125 M4
Cholpon-Ata, *Kyrg.* 152 CIO
Ch'ŏlsan, *N. Korea* 160 G3
Choluteca, *Hond.* 95 KI3
Choma, *Zambia* 180 E8
Chomutov, *Czech Rep.* 126 F8
Ch'ŏnam, *N. Korea* 160 H6
Ch'ŏnam, *N. Korea* 160 J7
Chon Buri, *Thai.* 164 J7
Chonchi, *Chile* III M2
Chŏnch'ŏn, *N. Korea* 160 E6
Chone, *Ecua.* 106 H4
Ch'ŏngdan, *N. Korea* 161 K5
Ch'ŏngjin, *N. Korea* 160 CIO
Chŏngju, *N. Korea* 160 G4
Chong Kal, *Cambodia* 164 H8
Chongli, *Hebei, China* 158 B5
Chongming, *Shanghai Shi, China* 158 J9
Chongming Dao, *Shanghai Shi, China* 158 J9
Chŏngp'yŏng, *N. Korea* 160 G7
Chongqing, *China* 157 JI2
Chongqing Shi, *China* 158 JI
Ch'ŏngsŏng, *N. Korea* 160 E4
Chongsŏng, *N. Korea* 160 AIO
Chongyang, *Hubei, China* 159 L4
Chongyi, *Jiangxi, China* 159 N4
Ch'ŏnma, *N. Korea* 160 F4
Ch'ŏnma-san, peak, *N. Korea* 160 F4
Ch'ŏnnae, *N. Korea* 160 G7
Chonogol, *Mongolia* 157 CI4
Chonos, Archipiélago de los, *Chile* III N2
Chonos Archipelago, *S. Amer.* 103 Q4
Ch'ŏnsu, *N. Korea* 160 C9
Chornobyl' (Chernobyl'), *Ukr.* 134 J5
Chornomors'ke, *Ukr.* 135 N6
Chorregon, *Qnsld., Austral.* 187 FI3
Chorrillos, *Peru* 108 F4
Chortkiv, *Ukr.* 135 L3
Ch'ŏrwŏn, *N. Korea* 160 J6
Ch'osan, *N. Korea* 160 E5
Chosin Reservoir see Changjin-ho, *N. Korea* 160 E7
Chos Malal, *Arg.* III K3
Choyang, *N. Korea* 160 F5

Choybalsan, *Mongolia* 157 CI3
Choyr, *Mongolia* 157 CI2
Christchurch, *Eng., U.K.* 121 R9
Christchurch, *N.Z.* 189 JI4
Chri stiansted, *V.I., U.S.* 99 BIO
Christmas Creek, *W. Austral., Austral.* 186 D7
Christmas Island, *Austral.* 166 L5
Christmas Island see Kiritimati, *Kiribati* 191 DII
Chub Cay, *Bahamas* 96 B7
Chubut, river, *Arg.* III M4
Chudleigh Park, *Qnsld., Austral.* 187 DI3
Chudovo, *Russ.* 134 D6
Chudskoye Ozero (Peipus, Lake), *Est., Russ.* 134 D4
Chugach Mountains, *U.S.* 84 E2
Chuginadak, island, *U.S.* 85 T4
Chuhuyiv, *Ukr.* 135 K8
Chuí, *Braz.* 109 MII
Chukai, *Malaysia* 165 P8
Chukchi Peninsula, *Russ.* 198 G3
Chukchi Range, *Russ.* 198 F4
Chukchi Sea, *Asia, N. Amer.* 141 AI2
Chukhloma, *Russ.* 134 EIO
Chukotskiy Poluostrov, *Russ.* 137 AI6
Chukotskoye Nagor'ye, *Russ.* 137 BI5
Chumar, *India* 154 C5
Chumbicha, *Arg.* 110 F5
Chumikan, *Russ.* 137 HI5
Chumphon, *Thai.* 165 K6
Chun'an, *Zhejiang, China* 159 L7
Chuncheon, *S. Korea* 161 K8
Chunggang, *N. Korea* 160 C6
Chunghwa, *N. Korea* 160 H5
Chungju, *S. Korea* 161 L8
Chungjuho, reservoir, *S. Korea* 161 L8
Chungli, *Taiwan, China* 159 P9
Chungp'yŏngjang, *N. Korea* 160 D8
Chŭngsan, *N. Korea* 160 F9
Chŭngsan, *N. Korea* 160 H4
Chungyang Shanmo, *Taiwan, China* 159 Q9
Chunnel, tunnel, *Fr., U.K.* 121 RI2
Chunya, *Tanzania* 177 KII
Chuquibamba, *Peru* 108 G5
Chuquicamata, *Chile* 110 C3
Chur, *Switz.* 128 B4
Churachandpur, *India* 154 FII
Churchill, *Man., Can.* 88 H9
Churchill, Cape, *Man., Can.* 88 H9
Churchill, river, *Man., Can.* 88 H9
Churchill, river, *Nfld. & Lab., Can.* 89 HI4
Churchill Falls, *Nfld. & Lab., Can.* 89 HI4
Churchill Lake, *Sask., Can.* 88 H7
Churchill Mountains, *Antarctica* 201 JIO
Churuguara, *Venez.* 106 B8
Chushul, *India* 154 B5
Chuska Mountains, *U.S.* 90 F6
Chusovoy, *Russ.* 136 G6
Chuuk (Truk Islands), *F.S.M.* 190 C5
Chuzhou, *Anhui, China* 158 H7
Cianjur, *Indonesia* 166 K6
Çiçekdağı, *Turk.* 144 D7
Cide, *Turk.* 144 B6
Ciechanów, *Pol.* 127 CI3
Ciego de Ávila, *Cuba* 96 F6
Ciempozuelos, *Sp.* 122 F9
Ciénaga, *Col.* 106 B6
Cienfuegos, *Cuba* 96 E5
Cieszyn, *Pol.* 127 GI2
Cieza, *Sp.* 123 HII
Çiftlik, *Turk.* 144 F7
Cihanbeyli, *Turk.* 144 E6
Ci jara, Embalse de, *Sp.* 122 G8
Çikës, Maja e, *Alban.* 130 K8

Cilacap, *Indonesia* 166 K6
Çıldır, *Turk.* 145 CI3
Çıldır Gölü, *Turk.* 145 CI3
Cili, *Hunan, China* 159 K2
Cilician Gates, *Turk.* 144 F7
Cill an Dísirt see Killadysert, *Ire.* 121 N2
Cill Chainnigh see Kilkenny, *Ire.* 121 N4
Cill Chaoi see Kilkee, *Ire.* 121 N2
Cill Charthaigh (Kilcar), *Ire.* 121 K3
Cill Choca see Kilcock, *Ire.* 121 M4
Cille Bhrighde, *Scot., U.K.* 120 G4
Cill Mhantáin see Wicklow, *Ire.* 121 N5
Cill Orglan see Killorglin, *Ire.* 121 PI
Cimarron, river, *U.S.* 90 F9
Cimolais, *It.* 128 C6
Cimone, Monte, *It.* 128 E5
Cîmpina, *Rom.* 131 DI3
Cîmpulung, *Rom.* 131 DI3
Çınar, *Turk.* 145 FII
Cinaruco, river, *Venez.* 106 D9
Cincinnati, *Ohio, U.S.* 93 EI3
Cinco Balas, Cayos, *Cuba* 96 G6
Cîndrelu, peak, *Rom.* 131 DI2
Çine, *Turk.* 144 F2
Cinn Mhara see Kinvara, *Ire.* 121 N2
Cintegabelle, *Fr.* 125 S7
Cinto, Monte, *Fr.* 128 G3
Cioara Doiceşti, *Rom.* 131 EI5
Čiovo, island, *Croatia* 130 F5
Çırçır, *Turk.* 144 D9
Circle, *Alas., U.S.* 92 K4
Cirebon, *Indonesia* 166 K6
Cirencester, *Eng., U.K.* 121 Q9
Cisnădie, *Rom.* 131 DI2
Cisneros, *Col.* 106 D6
Cistern Point, *Bahamas* 96 D7
Cittadella, *It.* 128 C6
Città di Castello, *It.* 128 F6
Cittanova, *It.* 129 MIO
Ciucea, *Rom.* 131 BII
Ciudad Acuña, *Mex.* 94 C7
Ciudad Altamirano, *Mex.* 94 H7
Ciudad Bolívar, *Venez.* 107 CII
Ciudad Camargo, *Mex.* 94 D6
Ciudad Cortés, *C.R.* 95 LI4
Ciudad del Carmen, *Mex.* 95 HII
Ciudad del Este, *Para.* 109 KIO
Ciudad Guayana, *Venez.* 107 CI2
Ciudad Guerrero, *Mex.* 94 C5
Ciudad Guzmán, *Mex.* 94 G6
Ciudad Hidalgo, *Mex.* 95 JII
Ciudad Juárez, *Mex.* 94 B6
Ciudad Madero, *Mex.* 94 F8
Ciudad Mante, *Mex.* 94 F8
Ciudad Obregón, *Mex.* 94 D4
Ciudad Piar, *Venez.* 107 DI2
Ciudad Real, *Sp.* 122 G9
Ciudad-Rodrigo, *Sp.* 122 E6
Ciudad Valles, *Mex.* 94 F8
Ciudad Victoria, *Mex.* 94 F8
Ciutadella de Menorca, *Sp.* 123 FI6
Civa Burnu, *Turk.* 144 C9
Civita Castellana, *It.* 128 H6
Civitanova Marche, *It.* 128 F8
Civitavecchia, *It.* 128 H6
Civray, *Fr.* 125 N5
Çivril, *Turk.* 144 E4
Cixian, *Hebei, China* 158 E4
Cizre, *Turk.* 145 FI2
Clacton-on-Sea, *Eng., U.K.* 121 PI2
Clairview, *Qnsld., Austral.* 187 FI5
Clare Island, *Ire.* 121 MI
Clarence, river, *N.Z.* 189 HI4
Clarence Island, *Antarctica* 200 B3
Clarence Town, *Bahamas* 96 E9
Clarie Coast, *Antarctica* 201 MI4
Clarión, Isla, *Mex.* 94 G2

Clarke Island, *Austral.* 185 LI8
Clarke Range, *Austral.* 185 EI5
Clarksburg, *W. Va., U.S.* 93 EI4
Clarksdale, *Miss., U.S.* 93 GII
Clarksville, *Tenn., U.S.* 93 FI2
Clauzetto, *It.* 128 C7
Clayton, *N. Mex., U.S.* 92 F8
Clear Island see Cléire, *Ire.* 121 Q2
Clearwater, *Fla., U.S.* 93 JI4
Clearwater, river, *Sask., Can.* 88 H7
Clearwater Mountains, *U.S.* 90 B5
Cleburne, *Tex., U.S.* 92 H9
Cléire (Clear Island), *Ire.* 121 Q2
Clelles, *Fr.* 125 QIO
Cleopatra Needle, peak, *Philippines* 167 DIO
Clerke Reef, *Austral.* 184 D4
Clermont, *Fr.* 124 J7
Clermont, *Qnsld., Austral.* 187 FI4
Clermont-Ferrand, *Fr.* 125 P8
Cles, *It.* 128 B5
Cleveland, *Ohio, U.S.* 93 DI4
Cleveland Hills, *Eng., U.K.* 121 L9
Clew Bay, *Ire.* 121 L2
Clifden (An Clochán), *Ire.* 121 MI
Clifton Hills, *S. Austral., Austral.* 187 GII
Clingmans Dome, *U.S.* 91 FI4
Clipperton, island, *Fr., Pac. Oc.* 191 CI7
Cliza, *Bol.* 108 H7
Cloates, Point, *Austral.* 184 F2
Cloch na Rón see Roundstone, *Ire.* 121 MI
Clonagh, *Qnsld., Austral.* 187 EI2
Clonakilty Bay, *Ire.* 121 Q2
Cloncurry, *Qnsld., Austral.* 187 EI2
Cloncurry, river, *Austral.* 185 DI2
Cloncurry Plateau, *Austral.* 185 EII
Clonmany (Cluain Maine), *Ire.* 121 K4
Clonmel (Cluain Meala), *Ire.* 121 P3
Cloppenburg, *Ger.* 126 C5
Cloud Peak, *U.S.* 90 C7
Clovis, *N. Mex., U.S.* 92 G8
Cluain Cearbán see Louisburgh, *Ire.* 121 M2
Cluain Maine see Clonmany, *Ire.* 121 K4
Cluain Meala see Clonmel, *Ire.* 121 P3
Cluj-Napoca, *Rom.* 131 CII
Clun, *Eng., U.K.* 121 P8
Cluses, *Fr.* 125 NII
Clusone, *It.* 128 C4
Clutha, river, *N.Z.* 189 LI2
Clyde, Firth of, *Scot., U.K.* 120 J6
Clyde Inlet, *Nunavut, Can.* 89 DI2
Clyde River, *Nunavut, Can.* 89 DI2
Cnossus (Knossos), ruins, *Gr.* 133 MII
Coalcomán, *Mex.* 94 G6
Coal Creek, *N.Z.* 189 LI2
Coalinga, *Calif., U.S.* 92 F2
Coalville, *Eng., U.K.* 121 N9
Coamo, *P.R., U.S.* 97 JI7
Coari, *Braz.* 108 C8
Coari, river, *Braz.* 108 D8
Coastal Plain, *U.S.* 91 JIO
Coast Mountains, *Can., U.S.* 90 L5
Coast Ranges, *U.S.* 90 B2
Coats Island, *Nunavut, Can.* 89 GII
Coats Land, *Antarctica* 200 D8
Coatzacoalcos, *Mex.* 95 HIO
Cobalt, *Ont., Can.* 89 LI2
Cobán, *Guatemala* 95 JII
Cobar, *N.S.W., Austral.* 187 JI4
Cobija, *Bol.* 108 F6
Cobourg Peninsula, *Austral.* 184 A9
Cóbuè, *Mozambique* 181 CIO
Coburg, *Ger.* 126 F7
Coburg Island, *Nunavut, Can.* 89 CIO

Douarnenez, *Fr.* **125** L2
Douarnenez, Baie de, *Fr.* **125** L1
Double Island Point, *Austral.* **185** G16
Double Point, *Austral.* **185** D14
Doubtful Bay, *Austral.* **184** C6
Doubtless Bay, *N.Z.* **189** B14
Doué, *Fr.* **125** M5
Douentza, *Mali* **174** G6
Douglas, *Ariz., U.S.* **92** H5
Douglas, *Ga., U.S.* **93** H14
Douglas (Doolish), *Isle of Man, U.K.* **121** L6
Douglas, *Wyo., U.S.* **92** D7
Douglas, Cabo, *Ecua.* **106** E1
Doullens, *Fr.* **124** H7
Doura, *Mali* **174** G5
Dourados, *Para.* **109** J10
Douro, river, *Port.* **122** D5
Dove Bay, *Greenland, Den.* **84** B9
Dover, *Del., U.S.* **93** E16
Dover, *Eng., U.K.* **121** Q12
Dover, Strait of, *Europe* **114** G6
Dowlatabad, *Afghan.* **152** H3
Dowlatābād, *Iran* **149** F12
Dowlat Yar, *Afghan.* **152** J4
Downpatrick, *N. Ire., U.K.* **121** L5
Downpatrick Head, *Ire.* **121** L2
Dowshi, *Afghan.* **152** H6
Doxáto, *Gr.* **133** B10
Doyang, *S. Korea* **161** R7
Dōzen, island, *Japan* **162** H5
Drâa, Hamada du, *Alg., Mor.* **174** C5
Drâa, Oued, *Alg., Mor.* **174** C5
Drac, Coves del, site, *Sp.* **123** F16
Drăgăneşti-olt, *Rom.* **131** F12
Drăgăşani, *Rom.* **131** E12
Dragon's Mouths, strait, *Trinidad & Tobago, Venez.* **99** J13
Draguignan, *Fr.* **125** R11
Drakensberg, range, *Af.* **171** R8
Dráma, *Gr.* **133** B10
Drammen, *Sweden* **119** J11
Dranov, Ostrov, *Rom.* **131** E16
Dras, *India* **152** J10
Drasan, *Pak.* **152** H8
Drau, river, *Aust.* **126** K8
Drava, river, *Europe* **115** J9
Dravograd, *Slov.* **130** C5
Drépano, Akrotírio, *Gr.* **133** D10
Dresden, *Ger.* **126** E9
Dreux, *Fr.* **125** K6
Drevsjø, *Nor.* **119** G11
Drin, river, *Alban.* **130** H8
Drina, river, *Bosn. & Herzg., Serb.* **130** E8
Drinit, Gjiri I, *Alban.* **130** J8
Driskill Mountain, *U.S.* **91** H11
Drøbak, *Nor.* **119** J11
Drobeta-Turnu Severin, *Rom.* **131** E11
Drogheda (Droichead Átha), *Ire.* **121** M5
Drohobych, *Ukr.* **135** K2
Droichead Átha see Drogheda, *Ire.* **121** M5
Droitwich, *Eng., U.K.* **121** P8
Dronning Louise Land, *Greenland, Den.* **199** H13
Drosh, *Pak.* **152** H7
Drouseia, *Cyprus* **133** F14
Drovyanoy, *Russ.* **136** E8
Drumheller, *Alta., Can.* **88** J6
Drummond Island, *Mich., U.S.* **93** B13
Drummond Range, *Austral.* **185** F14
Druza, Gora, *Russ.* **137** F15
Druzhina, *Russ.* **198** C5
Dryanovo, *Bulg.* **131** G13
Dryden, *Ont., Can.* **88** K9
Drygalski Ice Tongue, *Antarctica* **201** L11

Drygalski Island, *Antarctica* **201** G16
Drygalski Mountains, *Antarctica* **201** A10
Drysdale, river, *Austral.* **184** C7
Dry Tortugas, island, *U.S.* **91** L14
Dschang, *Cameroon* **179** E12
Dörtyol, *Turk.* **144** G8
Döşemealtı, *Turk.* **144** F4
Du, river, *Hubei, China* **158** H2
Duaringa, *Qnsld., Austral.* **187** F15
Duarte, Pico, *Dom. Rep.* **97** J13
Ḍubā, *Saudi Arabia* **148** F4
Dubai, *U.A.E.* **149** G11
Dubăsari, *Moldova* **135** M4
Dubawnt, river, *N.W.T., Can.* **88** G8
Dubawnt Lake, *Nunavut, Can.* **88** F8
Dubbo, *N.S.W., Austral.* **187** K14
Dubh Artach, island, *Scot., U.K.* **120** H5
Dublin, *Ga., U.S.* **93** H14
Dublin (Baile Átha Cliath), *Ire.* **121** M5
Dubna, *Russ.* **134** F8
Dubno, *Ukr.* **135** K3
Dubovka, *Russ.* **135** L11
Dubrovnik (Ragusa), *Croatia* **130** G7
Dubrovytsya, *Ukr.* **134** J3
Dubuque, *Iowa, U.S.* **93** D11
Duc de Gloucester, Îles, *Fr. Polynesia, Fr.* **191** G13
Duchess, *Qnsld., Austral.* **187** E12
Ducie Island, *U.K., Pac. Oc.* **191** G15
Duck Creek, *W. Austral., Austral.* **186** F3
Duc Tho, *Laos* **164** F9
Dudinka, *Russ.* **136** F9
Dudley, *Eng., U.K.* **121** P9
Duero, river, *Sp.* **122** D7
Dufek Coast, *Antarctica* **200** H9
Duff Islands, *Solomon Is.* **190** E7
Dufftown, *Scot., U.K.* **120** F7
Dugi Otok, island, *Croatia* **130** F5
Duifken Point, *Austral.* **185** B12
Duisburg, *Ger.* **126** E4
Duitama, *Col.* **106** E7
Dukla, *Pol.* **127** G14
Dulan, *China* **157** G10
Dulce, Golfo, *C.R.* **95** L14
Dulce, river, *Arg.* **110** F6
Dulce Gulf, *N. Amer.* **85** R8
Dulovo, *Bulg.* **131** F14
Duluth, *Minn., U.S.* **93** B11
Dūmā, *Syr.* **146** G6
Dumai, *Indonesia* **166** G4
Dumaran, island, *Philippines* **167** D10
Dumas, *Tex., U.S.* **92** G8
Dumbarton, *Scot., U.K.* **120** H6
Dumfries, *Scot., U.K.* **121** K7
Dumido, island, *S. Korea* **161** Q8
Dumka, *India* **154** F8
Dumoga Kecil, *Indonesia* **167** G11
Dumont d'Urville, station, *Antarctica* **201** M14
Dumra, *India* **154** E8
Dumyât (Damietta), *Egypt* **175** B14
Dun, *Fr.* **124** J10
Duna, river, *Hung.* **127** J12
Dunaj, river, *Slovakia* **127** J12
Dún an Uchta see Eyrecourt, *Ire.* **121** N3
Dunaújváros, *Hung.* **127** K12
Dunav, river, *Bulg., Rom.* **131** F14
Dunbar, *Qnsld., Austral.* **187** C13
Duncan see Pinzón, Isla, *Ecua.* **106** E2
Duncan Passage, *India* **155** M11
Duncansby Head, *Scot., U.K.* **120** E7
Duncan Town, *Bahamas* **96** F9
Dundalk (Dún Dealgan), *Ire.* **121** L5
Dundalk Bay, *Ire.* **121** L5
Dundas, Lake, *Austral.* **184** K6

Dundas Peninsula, *N.W.T., Can.* **88** C8
Dundas Strait, *Austral.* **184** A9
Dún Dealgan see Dundalk, *Ire.* **121** L5
Dundee, *Scot., U.K.* **120** H8
Dundee Island, *Antarctica* **200** B3
Dundonnell, *Scot., U.K.* **120** F6
Dundrennan, *Scot., U.K.* **121** K7
Dundrum Bay, *N. Ire., U.K.* **121** L5
Dund-Urt, *Mongolia* **157** C12
Dund-Us see Hovd, *Mongolia* **156** C9
Dunedin, *N.Z.* **189** L13
Dunfermline, *Scot., U.K.* **120** H7
Dungarpur, *India* **154** F3
Dungarvan Harbour, *Ire.* **121** P4
Dungeness, *Eng., U.K.* **121** R12
Dungeness, Punta, *Arg.* **111** R4
Dungiven, *N. Ire., U.K.* **121** K4
Dunham River, *W. Austral., Austral.* **186** C7
Dünheger, peak, *China* **156** C8
Dunhua, *China* **157** D16
Dunhuang, *China* **156** E9
Dunkerque (Dunkirk), *Fr.* **124** G7
Dunkineely, *Ire.* **121** K3
Dunkwa, *Ghana* **178** E8
Dunkirk see Dunkerque , *Fr.* **124** G7
Dún Laoghaire, *Ire.* **121** M5
Dún Mánmhaí see Dunmanway, *Ire.* **121** Q2
Dunmanus Bay, *Ire.* **121** Q1
Dunmanway (Dún Mánmhaí), *Ire.* **121** Q2
Dunmore Town, *Bahamas* **96** B8
Dunolly, *Vic., Austral.* **187** L13
Duntroon, *N.Z.* **189** K13
Dunvegan, *Scot., U.K.* **120** F5
Duolun (Dolonnur), *Nei Mongol, China* **158** A6
Duqm, *Oman* **149** J12
Duque de Caxias, *Braz.* **109** J14
Duque de York, Isla, *Chile* **111** R2
Durack, river, *Austral.* **184** C7
Dura Europus, ruins, *Syr.* **146** E11
Durance, river, *Fr.* **125** R11
Durango, *Colo., U.S.* **92** F6
Durango, *Mex.* **94** E6
Durango, *Sp.* **123** B10
Durankulak, *Bulg.* **131** F15
Durant, *Okla., U.S.* **93** G10
Duras, *Fr.* **125** Q5
Durazno, *Uru.* **110** H9
Durban, *S. Af.* **180** J9
Durbuy, *Belg.* **124** H10
Đurđevac, *Croatia* **130** C6
Dureji, *Pak.* **153** Q5
Düren, *Ger.* **126** E4
Durg, *India* **154** H6
Durham, *Eng., U.K.* **121** K9
Durham, *N.C., U.S.* **93** F15
Durlas see Thurles, *Ire.* **121** N3
Durlston Head, *Eng., U.K.* **121** R9
Durness, Kyle of, *Scot., U.K.* **120** E6
Duroy, *Russ.* **137** K13
Durrës, *Alban.* **130** J8
Durrësit, Gjiri I, *Alban.* **130** J8
Dursey Island, *Ire.* **121** Q1
Dursunbey, *Turk.* **144** D3
Durtal, *Fr.* **125** L5
Ḍurumā, *Saudi Arabia* **148** G8
Durusu Gölü, *Turk.* **144** B3
Durūz, Jabal ad, *Syr.* **146** H6
D'Urville, Tanjung, *Indonesia* **188** J4
D'Urville Island, *N.Z.* **189** G15
Duşak, *Turkm.* **150** K7
Dûsh, *Egypt* **175** D14
Dushan, *China* **157** K12
Dushanbe, *Taj.* **152** F6
Dushanzi, *China* **156** D7
Düsseldorf, *Ger.* **126** E4
Duvergé, *Dom. Rep.* **97** J12

Duwayhin, Dawḩat, *Saudi Arabia* **149** G10
Düzce see Achna, *Cyprus* **133** F17
Düzce, *Turk.* **144** C5
Dvina, Severnaya, river, *Russ.* **136** E5
Dwarka, *India* **154** G1
Dyat'kovo, *Russ.* **134** H7
Dyer, Cape, *Nunavut, Can.* **89** E13
Dyer Bay, *N.W.T., Can.* **88** B7
Dyersburg, *Tenn., U.S.* **93** F12
Dynevor Downs, *Qnsld., Austral.* **187** H13
Dzaanhushuu, *Mongolia* **157** C11
Dzag, *Mongolia* **157** C10
Dzangali, *Afghan.* **153** K5
Dzavhan, river, *Mongolia* **156** C9
Dzerzhinsk, *Russ.* **134** F10
Dzhagdy, Khrebet, *Russ.* **137** H15
Dzhankoy, *Ukr.* **135** N6
Dzhardzhan, *Russ.* **137** E12
Dzharty-Rabat, *Taj.* **152** G8
Dzharylhach, Ostriv, *Ukr.* **135** N5
Dzhilandy, *Taj.* **152** G8
Dzhugdzhur, Khrebet, *Russ.* **137** G15
Dzhunkun, *Russ.* **137** G12
Działdowo, *Pol.* **127** C13
Dzibilchaltún, ruins, *Mex.* **95** F11
Dzierżoniów, *Pol.* **127** F11
Dzöölön, *Mongolia* **157** B10
Dzungarian Basin see Junggar Pendi, *China* **156** C8
Dzungarian Gate, *China, Kaz.* **151** E15
Dzuunmod, *Mongolia* **157** C12
Dzvina, river, *Belarus* **134** G5
Dzyarzhynsk, *Belarus* **134** H4

E

Eagle, *Alas., U.S.* **92** K4
Eagle Mountain, *U.S.* **91** B11
Eagle Pass, *Tex., U.S.* **92** J8
Eagle Peak, *U.S.* **90** D3
Easky (Iascaigh), *Ire.* **121** L2
East Anglia, region, *Eng., U.K.* **121** P11
East Anglian Heights, mountains, *Eng., U.K.* **121** P11
East Antarctica, region, *Antarctica* **201** D10
Eastbourne, *Eng., U.K.* **121** R11
East Caicos, island, *Turks & Caicos Is., U.K.* **97** F12
East Cape, *N.Z.* **189** D18
East China Sea, *Asia* **141** G13
East Coast Bays, *N.Z.* **189** C15
Easter Island see Pascua, Isla de, *Chile, Pac. Oc.* **191** H17
Eastern Desert, *Egypt* **175** C15
Eastern Ghats, range, *India* **155** L5
East Falkland, island, *Falk. Is., U.K.* **111** R8
East Frisian Islands, *Ger.* **126** B5
East Isaac, island, *Bahamas* **96** B6
Eastleigh, *Eng., U.K.* **121** R9
East London, *S. Af.* **180** K8
Eastmain, *Que., Can.* **89** J12
Eastmain, river, *Que., Can.* **89** J12
East Pen Island, *Ont., Can.* **89** H10
East Prussia, region, *Pol., Russ.* **127** B13
East Saint Louis, *Ill., U.S.* **93** F11
East Sea see Japan, Sea of, *Asia* **141** F14
East Siberian Sea, *Arctic Ocean* **137** C13
East Timor see Timor-Leste, *Asia* **143** M15
Eau Claire, *Wis., U.S.* **93** C11
Eau Claire, Lac à l', *Que., Can.* **89** H12

Emerald Island, *N.W.T., Can.* **88** B8
Emet, *Turk.* **144** D3
Emilius, Monte, *It.* **128** C2
Emin, *China* **156** C7
Emirau, island, *P.N.G.* **188** C4
Emirdağ, *Turk.* **144** E5
Emir Dağları, *Turk.* **144** E5
Emmen, *Neth.* **124** E11
Empedrado, *Arg.* **110** E8
Empoli, *It.* **128** F5
Emporia, *Kans., U.S.* **93** F10
Empress Augusta Bay, *P.N.G.* **188** A6
Empty Quarter *see* Ar Rub' Al Khālī, *Saudi Arabia* **148** J8
Ems, river, *Ger.* **126** C5
Enard Bay, *Scot., U.K.* **120** E6
'En Boqeq, *Israel* **147** K4
Encarnación, *Para.* **109** K10
Encontrados, *Venez.* **106** C7
Encounter Bay, *Austral.* **185** L11
Ende, *Indonesia* **167** K10
Endeavour Hill, *Austral.* **184** C8
Endeavour Strait, *Austral.* **185** A13
Enderbury Island, *Kiribati* **191** E10
Enderby Land, *Antarctica* **201** C14
Endicott Mountains, *U.S.* **198** J4
Eneabba, *W. Austral., Austral.* **186** J3
Enewetak Atoll, *Marshall Is.* **190** C6
Enez, *Turk.* **144** C1
Enfer, Pointe d', *Martinique, Fr.* **99** E14
Engaño, Cabo, *Dom. Rep.* **97** J15
Engels, *Russ.* **134** J11
Enggano, island, *Indonesia* **166** J4
England, *U.K.* **121** N8
English Channel (La Manche), *Fr., U.K.* **121** S8
English Coast, *Antarctica* **200** F5
'En Hazeva, *Israel* **147** L4
Enid, *Okla., U.S.* **92** F9
Enipéas, river, *Gr.* **132** E7
Eniwa, *Japan* **162** D10
Enkhuizen, *Neth.* **124** E9
Ennadai, *Nunavut, Can.* **88** G8
En Nahud, *Sudan* **176** D9
Ennedi, range, *Chad* **175** F12
Ennell, Lough, *Ire.* **121** M4
Enngonia, *N.S.W., Austral.* **187** H14
Ennis (Inis), *Ire.* **121** N2
Enniscorthy (Inis Córthaidh), *Ire.* **121** P4
Enniskillen (Inis Ceithlann), *N. Ire., U.K.* **121** L4
Ennistimon (Inis Díomáin), *Ire.* **121** N2
Enontekiö, *Fin.* **119** C13
Énos, Óros, *Gr.* **132** G5
Enriquillo, *Dom. Rep.* **97** K13
Enriquillo, Lago, *Dom. Rep.* **97** J12
Enschede, *Neth.* **124** F11
Ensenada, *Mex.* **94** A2
Enshi, *Hubei, China* **159** K1
Ensisheim, *Fr.* **125** L12
Entebbe, *Uganda* **177** H10
Enterprise, *Ala., U.S.* **93** H13
Entinas, Punta, *Sp.* **123** K10
Entrada, Punta, *Arg.* **111** R4
Entrepeñas, Embalse de, *Sp.* **123** E10
Entrèves, *It.* **128** C1
Entroncamento, *Port.* **122** F4
Enugu, *Nig.* **179** E11
Enurmino, *Russ.* **137** A16
Envira, *Braz.* **108** E6
'En Yahav, *Israel* **147** L4
Eochaill *see* Youghal, *Ire.* **121** P3
Eocheongdo, island, *S. Korea* **161** N5
Eolie *see* Lipari, Isole, *It.* **129** M9
Eonyang, *S. Korea* **161** P9
Epanomí, *Gr.* **132** C8
Epéna, *Congo* **179** F15
Epenarra, *N. Terr., Austral.* **187** E10
Épernay, *Fr.* **125** K9

Épernon, *Fr.* **125** K7
Ephesus, ruins, *Turk.* **144** E2
Epidavros, ruins, *Gr.* **132** H8
Épinal, *Fr.* **125** L11
Epirus, region, *Alban., Gr.* **132** E5
Episkopi, *Cyprus* **133** G15
Episkopi Bay, *Cyprus* **133** G15
Epsilon, *Qnsld., Austral.* **187** H12
Epsom, *Eng., U.K.* **121** Q10
Eptachórion, *Gr.* **132** C6
Épuisay, *Fr.* **125** L6
Epukiro, *Namibia* **180** F6
Epu Pel, *Arg.* **111** K5
Equatorial Channel, *Maldives* **155** S2
Equatorial Guinea, *Af.* **173** L5
Erbaa, *Turk.* **144** C9
Erçek, *Turk.* **145** E13
Erçek Gölü, *Turk.* **145** E13
Erciş, *Turk.* **145** E13
Erciyeş Dağı, *Turk.* **144** E8
Érd, *Hung.* **127** J12
Erdaojiang, *Jilin, China* **158** A11
Erdek, *Turk.* **144** C3
Erdemli, *Turk.* **144** G7
Erding, *Ger.* **126** H7
Erebus, Mount, *Antarctica* **201** K10
Erechim, *Braz.* **109** L11
Ereentsav, *Mongolia* **157** B14
Ereğli, *Turk.* **144** C5
Ereğli, *Turk.* **144** F7
Erei, Monti, *It.* **129** P8
Erenhot, *China* **157** D13
Erenköy *see* Kokkina, *Cyprus* **133** E15
Eressós, *Gr.* **133** E12
Erétria, *Gr.* **132** F9
Ereymentaū, *Kaz.* **151** C12
Erfoud, *Mor.* **174** B6
Erfurt, *Ger.* **126** E7
Ergani, *Turk.* **145** E11
Ergedzhey, *Russ.* **137** G12
Ergene, river, *Turk.* **144** B3
Ergun, river, *China* **157** B14
Ergun Youqi, *China* **157** B14
Erhulai, *Liaoning, China* **158** A11
Eriboll, *Scot., U.K.* **120** E6
Eriboll, Loch, *Scot., U.K.* **120** E6
Ericht, Loch, *Scot., U.K.* **120** G6
Erie, *Pa., U.S.* **93** D14
Erie, Lake, *Can., U.S.* **91** D14
Erigavo *see* Ceerigaabo, *Somalia* **177** E14
Erikoússa, island, *Gr.* **132** D4
Erímanthos, Óros, *Gr.* **132** G7
Erimo, *Japan* **162** D11
Erimo Misaki, *Japan* **162** D11
Eriskay *see* Eiriosgaigh, island, *Scot., U.K.* **120** G4
Erisort, Loch, *Scot., U.K.* **120** E5
Erithrés, *Gr.* **132** G9
Eritrea, *Af.* **172** H10
Erkilet, *Turk.* **144** E8
Erlangen, *Ger.* **126** G7
Erldunda, *N. Terr., Austral.* **186** G9
Ermenek, *Turk.* **144** G6
Ermióni, *Gr.* **132** H9
Ermoúpoli, *Gr.* **133** H11
Ernabella, *S. Austral., Austral.* **186** G9
Ernakulam, *India* **155** M4
Ernée, *Fr.* **125** L4
Erode, *India* **155** M4
Eromanga, *Qnsld., Austral.* **187** G13
Er Rachidia, *Mor.* **174** B6
Er Rahad, *Sudan* **177** D10
Erris Head, *Ire.* **121** L2
Erromango, island, *Vanuatu* **190** G7
Ershijiazi, *Liaoning, China* **158** B8
Ertai, *China* **156** C8
Ertis (Irtysh), river, *Kaz.* **151** C13

Ertix, river, *China* **156** C8
Erudina, *S. Austral., Austral.* **187** J11
Eruh, *Turk.* **145** F12
Erzin, *Russ.* **137** K10
Erzincan, *Turk.* **145** D10
Erzurum, *Turk.* **145** D12
Esan Misaki, *Japan* **162** D10
Esashi, *Japan* **162** B10
Esashi, *Japan* **162** D9
Esbjerg, *Den.* **119** L10
Esbo *see* Espoo, *Fin.* **119** H14
Escanaba, *Mich., U.S.* **93** C12
Escárcego, *Mex.* **95** H11
Eschwege, *Ger.* **126** E6
Escocesa, Bahia, *Dom. Rep.* **97** H14
Escuinapa, *Mex.* **94** F5
Escuintla, *Guatemala* **95** J11
Escuintla, *Mex.* **95** J10
Eséka, *Cameroon* **179** F13
Esenguly, *Turkm.* **150** K5
Eşfahān (Isfahan), *Iran* **149** D10
Esfandak, *Iran* **149** F14
Eshkamesh, *Afghan.* **152** H6
Eshkashem, *Afghan.* **152** H7
Esil, *Kaz.* **151** B10
Esil, river, *Kaz.* **151** B10
Esimi, *Gr.* **133** B12
Esker, *Nfld. & Lab., Can.* **89** H13
Eskifjördur, *Ice.* **118** E5
Eskilstuna, *Sweden* **119** J12
Eskimo Lakes, *N.W.T., Can.* **88** D6
Eskipazar, *Turk.* **144** C6
Eskişehir, *Turk.* **144** D4
Esla, river, *Sp.* **122** C7
Eslāmābād, *Iran* **148** C8
Eslam Qal'eh, *Afghan.* **152** J1
Eşler Dağı, *Turk.* **144** F3
Eşme, *Turk.* **144** E3
Esmeralda, *Cuba* **96** F7
Esmeralda, Isla, *Chile* **111** Q2
Esmeraldas, *Ecua.* **106** G4
Esmeraldas, Río, *Ecua.* **106** G4
Esmoriz, *Port.* **122** D4
Espakeh, *Iran* **149** F13
Espalion, *Fr.* **125** Q8
Española, Isla (Hood), *Ecua.* **106** F3
Esperance, *W. Austral., Austral.* **186** K6
Esperance Bay, *Austral.* **184** K6
Esperanza, *Arg.* **110** G7
Esperanza, *Peru* **108** E6
Esperanza, station, *Antarctica* **200** B3
Espichel, Cabo, *Port.* **122** H3
Espiel, *Sp.* **122** H8
Espinhaço, Serra do, *Braz.* **109** H14
Espírito Santo *see* Vila Velha, *Braz.* **109** J14
Espíritu Santo, Isla, *Mex.* **94** E4
Espiritu Santo, island, *Vanuatu* **190** F7
Espoo (Esbo), *Fin.* **119** H14
Esposende, *Port.* **122** D4
Espuña, peak, *Sp.* **123** J11
Espungabera, *Mozambique* **181** F10
Esquel, *Arg.* **111** M3
Esquina, *Arg.* **110** F7
Essaouira, *Mor.* **174** B5
Essen, *Belg.* **124** G9
Essen, *Ger.* **126** E4
Essendon, Mount, *Austral.* **184** G5
Essequibo, river, *Guyana* **107** D14
Essex, Punta, *Ecua.* **106** E1
Essington, Port, *Austral.* **184** A9
Esslingen, *Ger.* **126** H6
Esso, *Russ.* **137** E17
Es Suki, *Sudan* **177** D11
Estonia, *Europe* **117** E10
Estaca de Bares, Punta da, *Sp.* **122** A5
Estacado, Llano, *U.S.* **90** G8

Estación Maritima Antártica, station, *Antarctica* **200** B3
Estados, Isla de los (Staten Island), *Chile* **111** T6
Estahbān, *Iran* **149** E11
Estância, *Braz.* **109** F15
Estats, Pic d', *Sp.* **123** B14
Este, *It.* **128** D6
Estelí, *Nicar.* **95** K13
Estella (Lizarra), *Sp.* **123** B10
Estepona, *Sp.* **122** K7
Estevan, *Sask., Can.* **88** K7
Estrela, Serra da, *Port.* **122** E5
Estrella, peak, *Sp.* **122** H9
Estremoz, *Port.* **122** G5
Esztergom, *Hung.* **127** J12
Etadunna, *S. Austral., Austral.* **187** H11
Étampes, *Fr.* **125** L7
Étaples, *Fr.* **124** H7
Etawah, *India* **154** E5
Ethel Creek, *W. Austral., Austral.* **186** F5
Ethiopia, *Af.* **173** K10
Ethiopian Highlands, *Af.* **170** J10
Etive, Loch, *Scot., U.K.* **120** H6
Etna, peak, *It.* **129** N9
Etolikó, *Gr.* **132** F6
Etorofu *see* Iturup, island, *Russ.* **137** H18
Etosha Pan, *Namibia* **180** E5
Etoumbi, *Congo* **179** G14
Ettlingen, *Ger.* **126** H5
Ettrick, *N.Z.* **189** L12
Eu, *Fr.* **124** J6
Euboea *see* Évia, island, *Gr.* **133** F10
Eucla, *W. Austral., Austral.* **186** J8
Eucla Basin, *Austral.* **184** K6
Eucumbene, Lake, *Austral.* **185** L14
Eudunda, *S. Austral., Austral.* **187** K11
Eufaula Lake, *U.S.* **91** G10
Eugene, *Oreg., U.S.* **92** C2
Eugenia, Punta, *Mex.* **94** C2
Eugenia Point, *Mex.* **85** M2
Eugenio Bustos, *Arg.* **110** H4
Eulo, *Qnsld., Austral.* **187** H13
Eumseong, *S. Korea* **161** M7
Eupen, *Belg.* **124** H10
Euphrates *see* Al Furāt, Firat, river, *Iraq, Syr., Turk.* **148** D7
Eurardy, *W. Austral., Austral.* **186** H3
Eureka, *Calif., U.S.* **92** D2
Eureka, *Nunavut, Can.* **89** B10
Europa, Picos de, *Sp.* **122** B8
Eutin, *Ger.* **126** B7
Eva Downs, *N. Terr., Austral.* **187** D10
Evanston, *Ill., U.S.* **93** D12
Evanston, *Wyo., U.S.* **92** D6
Evansville, *Ind., U.S.* **93** F12
Évdilos, *Gr.* **133** H12
Evensk, *Russ.* **137** D16
Everard, Lake, *Austral.* **185** J10
Everard Park, *S. Austral., Austral.* **186** G9
Everest, Mount (Qomolangma, Sagarmāthā), *China, Nepal* **156** J7
Everett, *Wash., U.S.* **92** A3
Everglades, The, swamp, *U.S.* **91** K15
Evesham, *Eng., U.K.* **121** P9
Évia (Euboea), island, *Gr.* **133** F10
Évian, *Fr.* **125** N11
Évora, *Port.* **122** H5
Évreux, *Fr.* **125** K6
Évros, river, *Gr., Turk.* **133** B12
Evrótas, river, *Gr.* **132** J8
Évry, *Fr.* **125** K7
Evrychou, *Cyprus* **133** F15

French Polynesia, *Fr., Pac. Oc.*
191 G13
Fresnay, *Fr.* 125 L5
Fresnillo, *Mex.* 94 F7
Fresno, *Calif., U.S.* 92 E3
Frévent, *Fr.* 124 H7
Frewena, *N. Terr., Austral.* 187 D10
Freyung, *Ger.* 126 H9
Fri, *Gr.* 133 L14
Fria, *Guinea* 178 C4
Frías, *Arg.* 110 F5
Fridtjof Nansen, Mount, *Antarctica*
200 H9
Friedrichshafen, *Ger.* 126 J6
Friesland, region, *Ger., Neth.*
124 E10
Frissell, Mount, *U.S.* 91 D16
Friza, Proliv, *Russ.* 137 H18
Frobisher Bay, *Nunavut, Can.* 89 F12
Frolovo, *Russ.* 135 K11
Frome, *Eng., U.K.* 121 Q8
Frome, Lake, *Austral.* 185 J12
Frómista, *Sp.* 122 C8
Frontera, *Mex.* 94 D7
Frontera, *Mex.* 95 H10
Frontignan, *Fr.* 125 S9
Front Range, *U.S.* 90 D7
Frosinone, *It.* 128 H7
Frøya, island, *Nor.* 119 F10
Fu, river, *Jiangxi, China* 159 M5
Fua Mulaku, island, *Maldives*
155 S3
Fu'an, *Fujian, China* 159 M8
Fuchuan, *Guangxi Zhuangzu, China*
159 P2
Fucino, Piana del, *It.* 128 H7
Fuding, *Fujian, China* 159 M8
Fuengirola, *Sp.* 122 K8
Fuente de Cantos, *Sp.* 122 H6
Fuentesaúco, *Sp.* 122 D7
Fuerte Olimpo, *Para.* 109 J10
Fuerteventura, island, *Atl. Oc.*
170 F2
Fuga, island, *Philippines* 167 A10
Fugu, *Shaanxi, China* 158 C2
Fuguo *see* Zhanhua, *Shandong, China*
158 D7
Fuhai, *China* 156 C8
Fuidhaigh (Wiay), island, *Scot., U.K.*
120 F4
Fujairah, *U.A.E.* 149 G11
Fuji, *Japan* 162 J8
Fujian, *China* 159 N6
Fujin, *China* 157 B17
Fujisawa, *Japan* 162 J9
Fukagawa, *Japan* 162 C10
Fukuchiyama, *Japan* 162 J6
Fukue, *Japan* 163 L2
Fukue Jima, *Japan* 163 L2
Fukui, *Japan* 162 H7
Fukuoka, *Japan* 163 K3
Fukushima, *Japan* 162 E9
Fukushima, *Japan* 162 G9
Fukushima, Mount, *Antarctica*
201 B12
Fukuyama, *Japan* 162 J5
Fulda, *Ger.* 126 F6
Fuliang, *Jiangxi, China* 159 L6
Fuling, *China* 157 J12
Fumay, *Fr.* 124 J9
Fumel, *Fr.* 125 Q6
Funabashi, *Japan* 162 J9
Funafuti, *Tuvalu* 190 E9
Funan, *Anhui, China* 158 H5
Fundy, Bay of, *Can.* 84 J10
Funhalouro, *Mozambique* 181 G10
Funing, *Jiangsu, China* 158 G8
Funing Wan, *Fujian, China* 159 N8
Funiu Shan, *Henan, China* 158 G2
Funtua, *Nig.* 179 C11

Fuping, *Hebei, China* 158 C4
Fuqing, *Fujian, China* 159 N7
Furano, *Japan* 162 C10
Furmanov, *Russ.* 134 F9
Furneaux Group, *Austral.* 185 K18
Furqlus, *Syr.* 146 F6
Fürstenfeldbruck, *Ger.* 126 H7
Fürstenwalde, *Ger.* 126 D9
Fürth, *Ger.* 126 G7
Furth im Wald, *Ger.* 126 G8
Furukawa, *Japan* 162 G10
Fuscaldo, *It.* 129 L10
Fuse, *Japan* 162 H5
Fushan, *Shandong, China* 158 D8
Fushan, *Shanxi, China* 158 F3
Fushun, *Liaoning, China* 158 A10
Fusio, *Switz.* 128 B3
Fusong, *Jilin, China* 158 A12
Füssen, *Ger.* 126 J6
Futou Hu, *Hubei, China* 159 K4
Futun, river, *Fujian, China* 159 M6
Futuna, island, *Vanuatu* 190 G7
Fuwwah, *Yemen* 148 L9
Fuxin, *Liaoning, China* 158 A9
Fuxingdi, *Liaoning, China* 158 A8
Fuya, *Japan* 162 G9
Fuyang, *Anhui, China* 158 H5
Fuyu, *China* 157 C16
Fuyuan, *China* 157 B17
Fuyun, *China* 156 C8
Fuzhou, *Fujian, China* 159 N7
Fuzhoucheng, *Liaoning, China*
158 C9
Füzuli *see* Karaghbyur, *Azerb.*
145 D16
Fyn, island, *Den.* 119 L11
Fyne, Loch, *Scot., U.K.* 120 H6

G

Gaalkacyo (Galcaio), *Somalia*
177 F14
Gabela, *Angola* 180 C4
Gabes, *Tunisia* 175 B10
Gabes, Gulf of, *Tunisia* 175 B10
Gabon, *Af.* 173 L5
Gaborone, *Botswana* 180 G8
Gabras, *Sudan* 176 E9
Gabriel Vera, *Bol.* 108 H7
Gabrovo, *Bulg.* 131 G13
Gädäbäy, *Azerb.* 145 C15
Gadag, *India* 155 K4
Gadarwara, *India* 154 G5
Gäddede, *Sweden* 119 F11
Gadeokdo, island, *S. Korea* 161 Q9
Gadifuri, island, *Maldives* 155 R2
Gadrut *see* Hadrut, *Azerb.* 145 D16
Gadsden, *Ala., U.S.* 93 G13
Gadwal, *India* 155 K5
Gael Hamke Bay, *Greenland, Den.*
199 H13
Găeşti, *Rom.* 131 E13
Gaeta, *It.* 128 J7
Gaeta, Golfo di, *It.* 128 J7
Gaferut, island, *F.S.M.* 190 C4
Gafsa, *Tunisia* 174 B9
Gagarin, *Russ.* 134 G7
Gagnoa, *Côte d'Ivoire* 178 E7
Gagra, *Ga.* 145 A11
Gaillac, *Fr.* 125 R7
Gaillimh *see* Galway, *Ire.* 121 M2
Gaimán, *Arg.* 111 M5
Gainesville, *Fla., U.S.* 93 J14
Gairdner, Lake, *Austral.* 185 J10
Gaizhou, *Liaoning, China* 158 B9
Gaja Shima, *Japan* 163 N3
Gakuch, *Pak.* 152 H9
Galápagos Islands (Colón, Archipiélago
de), *Ecua.* 106 C2
Galashiels, *Scot., U.K.* 120 J8
Galatás, *Gr.* 132 H9

Galateia (Mehmetçik), *Cyprus*
133 E17
Galaţi, *Rom.* 131 D15
Galatina, *It.* 129 K12
Galatxo, Punta del, *Sp.* 123 E13
Galaxidi, *Gr.* 132 F8
Galcaio *see* Gaalkacyo, *Somalia*
177 F14
Galegu, *Sudan* 177 D11
Galela, *Indonesia* 167 G12
Galena, *Alas., U.S.* 92 K2
Galera, Punta, *Ecua.* 106 G3
Galera, Punta, *Chile* 111 L2
Galera Point, *Trinidad & Tobago*
99 J14
Gali, *Ga.* 145 A12
Galich, *Russ.* 134 E10
Galicia, region, *Pol., Ukr.* 127 F14
Galicia, region, *Sp.* 122 B5
Galilee, Lake, *Austral.* 185 F14
Galilee, Sea of, *Israel* 146 H5
Galina Mine, *W. Austral., Austral.*
186 H3
Galinoporni (Kaleburnu), *Cyprus*
133 E16
Galiwinku, *N. Terr., Austral.* 187 A10
Gallarate, *It.* 128 C3
Galle, *Sri Lanka* 155 P5
Gállego, river, *Sp.* 123 C12
Gallinas, Punta, *Col.* 106 A8
Gallipoli, *It.* 129 K12
Gallipoli, *N. Terr., Austral.* 187 D11
Gallipoli *see* Gelibolu, *Turk.* 144 C2
Gällivare, *Sweden* 119 D13
Galloway, Mull of, cape, *Scot., U.K.*
121 K6
Gallup, *N. Mex., U.S.* 92 G6
Galty Mountains (An Chathair), *Ire.*
121 P3
Galveston, *Tex., U.S.* 93 J10
Galveston Bay, *U.S.* 91 J10
Gálvez, *Arg.* 110 G7
Galwa, *Nepal* 154 D6
Galway (Gaillimh), *Ire.* 121 M2
Galway Bay, *Ire.* 121 M2
Gambaga, *Ghana* 178 C9
Gambell, *Alas., U.S.* 92 K1
Gambia, *Af.* 172 H1
Gambier, Îles, *Fr. Polynesia, Fr.* 191 G14
Gamboma, *Congo* 179 H15
Gamboula, *Cen. Af. Rep.* 176 G9
Gamila *see* Tímfi, Óros, *Gr.* 132 D6
Gamkonora, peak, *Indonesia* 167 G12
Gamlaha, *Indonesia* 167 G13
Gamleby, *Sweden* 119 K13
Gan, island, *Maldives* 155 S2
Gan, river, *Jiangxi, China* 159 N4
Gäncä, *Azerb.* 145 C15
Gandajika, *D.R.C.* 176 K8
Gandava, *Pak.* 153 N5
Gander, *Nfld. & Lab., Can.* 89 J16
Gandhinagar, *India* 154 G2
Gandía, *Sp.* 123 G12
Gang, island, *Maldives* 155 R3
Gan Gan, *Arg.* 111 M4
Ganganagar, *India* 154 D3
Gangapur, *India* 154 E4
Gangawati, *India* 155 K4
Gangdisê Shan, *China* 156 H6
Ganges, *Fr.* 125 R9
Ganges, river, *Asia* 140 H9
Ganges, Mouths of the, *Bangladesh,
India* 154 G9
Ganggu, *S. Korea* 161 M10
Ganggyeong, *S. Korea* 161 N6
Ganghwa, *S. Korea* 161 K6
Gangi, *It.* 129 N8
Gangjin, *S. Korea* 161 Q6
Gangneung, *S. Korea* 161 K9

Gangtok, *India* 154 E9
Ganhyeon, *S. Korea* 161 L8
Gannat, *Fr.* 125 N8
Gannett Peak, *U.S.* 90 D6
Ganquan, *Shaanxi, China* 158 E1
Ganseong, *S. Korea* 160 J9
Gansu, *China* 158 E1
Ganta, *Liberia* 178 D6
Gantgaw, *Myanmar* 164 D3
Gantheaume Bay, *Austral.* 184 H3
Ganyu (Qingkou), *Jiangsu, China*
158 G7
Ganyuskīno, *Kaz.* 150 E4
Ganzhou, *Jiangxi, China* 159 N4
Gao, *Mali* 174 G7
Gao'an, *Jiangxi, China* 159 L5
Gaolan Dao, *Guangdong, China* 159 R3
Gaoligong Shan, *Myanmar* 164 B6
Gaomi, *Shandong, China* 158 E8
Gaoping, *Shanxi, China* 158 F3
Gaoqing, *Shandong, China* 158 E6
Gaotang, *Shandong, China* 158 E5
Gaoua, *Burkina Faso* 178 C8
Gaoual, *Guinea* 178 B4
Gaoyang, *Hebei, China* 158 D5
Gaoyi, *Hebei, China* 158 D4
Gaoyou, *Jiangsu, China* 158 H7
Gaoyou Hu, *Jiangsu, China* 158 H7
Gaozhou, *Guangdong, China* 159 R1
Gap, *Fr.* 125 Q11
Gapado, island, *S. Korea* 161 T5
Gapyeong, *S. Korea* 161 K7
Garabil Belentligi, range, *Turkm.*
150 K8
Garabogaz Aylagy, *Turkm.* 150 H5
Garabogazköl, *Turkm.* 150 H5
Garacad, *Somalia* 177 F15
Garagum, desert, *Turkm.* 150 H6
Garagum Canal, *Turkm.* 150 K8
Garaina, *P.N.G.* 188 E7
Garaliáni, *Gr.* 132 J7
Garanhuns, *Braz.* 109 E16
Garavuti, *Taj.* 152 G5
Garbyang, *India* 154 D6
García de Sola, Embalse de, *Sp.*
122 G7
Garda, Lago di, *It.* 128 C5
Garden City, *Kans., U.S.* 92 F8
Garden Hill, *Man., Can.* 88 J9
Gardiz, *Afghan.* 153 K6
Gardner Pinnacles, island, *Hawaii, U.S.*
191 A10
Gareloi, island, *U.S.* 85 T3
Garessio, *It.* 128 E2
Gargano, Testa del, *It.* 128 H10
Gargano, Promontorio del, *It.* 128 H9
Garhakota, *India* 154 F5
Garies, *S. Af.* 180 J6
Garissa, *Kenya* 177 H12
Garm Ab, *Afghan.* 153 K3
Garmeh Jäjarm, *Iran* 149 B11
Garmisch-Partenkirchen, *Ger.* 126 J7
Garmna (Gorumna Island), *Ire.*
121 M2
Garonne, river, *Fr.* 125 Q5
Garoowe, *Somalia* 177 F15
Garoua, *Cameroon* 179 C14
Garoua Boulaï, *Cameroon* 179 E14
Garron Point, *N. Ire., U.K.* 121 K5
Garrucha, *Sp.* 123 J11
Garrygala, *Turkm.* 150 J6
Garry Lake, *Nunavut, Can.* 88 F8
Garsen, *Kenya* 177 J12
Gartog *see* Markam, *China* 157 J10
Garu, *India* 154 G7
Garub, *Namibia* 180 H5
Garut, *Indonesia* 166 K6
Garve, *Scot., U.K.* 120 F6
Garwa, *India* 154 F7
Gary, *Ind., U.S.* 93 D12

Garzón, *Col.* **106** G6
Gasa, *Bhutan* **154** E9
Gasado, island, *S. Korea* **161** R5
Gascony, region, *Fr.* **125** R5
Gascoyne, river, *Austral.* **184** G4
Gascoyne Junction, *W. Austral.,*
    Austral. **186** G3
Gashagar, *Nig.* **179** B13
Gashua, *Nig.* **179** B13
Gas Hure Hu, *China* **156** F8
Gaspé, *Que., Can.* **89** K14
Gaspé Peninsula, *Que., Can.* **89** K14
Gastonia, *N.C., U.S.* **93** G14
Gastoúni, *Gr.* **132** G6
Gastre, *Arg.* **111** M4
Gata, Cabo de, *Sp.* **123** K10
Gata, Cape, *Cyprus* **133** G15
Gata, Sierra de, *Sp.* **122** E6
Gatchina, *Russ.* **134** D5
Gatehouse of Fleet, *Scot., U.K.*
    121 K7
Gateshead, *Eng., U.K.* **121** K9
Gâtine, Hauteurs de, *Fr.* **125** M4
Gauido, island, *S. Korea* **161** M5
Gausta, peak, *Nor.* **119** J10
Gautheaume Point, *Austral.* **184** D5
Gavarnie, *Fr.* **125** T5
Gaväter, *Iran* **149** G13
Gävbandī, *Iran* **149** F10
Gavdopoúla, island, *Gr.* **133** M10
Gávdos, island, *Gr.* **133** M10
Gävle, *Sweden* **119** H12
Gavrilov Yam, *Russ.* **134** F9
Gávrio, *Gr.* **133** G11
Gawachab, *Namibia* **180** H6
Gawai, *Myanmar* **164** A5
Gawler, *S. Austral., Austral.* **187** K11
Gawler Ranges, *Austral.* **185** J10
Gaya, *India* **154** F8
Gaya, *Nig.* **179** C12
Gaya, *Niger* **174** H8
Gaza City *see* Ghazzah, *Gaza Strip*
    147 K3
Gazak, *Afghan.* **152** J4
Gazak, *Iran* **149** F13
Gazanjyk, *Turkm.* **150** J5
Gaza Strip, *Asia* **147** K3
Gaziantep, *Turk.* **144** G9
Gazimağusa *see* Famagusta, *Cyprus*
    133 E17
Gazipaşa, *Turk.* **144** G5
Gazojak, *Turkm.* **150** H8
Gbadolite, *D.R.C.* **176** G7
Gcuwa, *S. Af.* **180** J8
Gdańsk, *Pol.* **127** B12
Gdańsk, Gulf of, *Europe* **114** F9
Gdov, *Russ.* **134** D4
Gdynia, *Pol.* **127** A12
Gebe, island, *Indonesia* **167** H13
Gebiz, *Turk.* **144** F4
Gebze, *Turk.* **144** C4
Geçitkale *see* Lefkonoiko, *Cyprus*
    133 E17
Gedaref, *Sudan* **177** D11
Gediz, *Turk.* **144** D4
Gediz, river, *Turk.* **144** E2
Gedser, *Den.* **119** M11
Geel, *Belg.* **124** G9
Geelong, *Vic., Austral.* **187** M13
Geelvink Channel, *Austral.* **184** H3
Geesthacht, *Ger.* **126** C7
Geeveston, *Tas., Austral.* **187** M17
Géfira, *Gr.* **132** B8
Gê'gyai (Napug), *China* **156** G5
Geidam, *Nig.* **179** B13
Geilo, *Nor.* **119** H10
Geita, *Tanzania* **177** J10
Gejiu, *China* **157** L11
Gela, *It.* **129** P8
Gela, Golfo di, *It.* **129** P8

Gelam, island, *Indonesia* **166** H7
Gelasa, Selat, *Indonesia* **166** H6
Gelendzhik, *Russ.* **135** P8
Gelibolu (Gallipoli), *Turk.* **144** C2
Gelsenkirchen, *Ger.* **126** E4
Gembloux, *Belg.* **124** H9
Gemena, *D.R.C.* **176** G7
Gemerek, *Turk.* **144** E8
Gemlik, *Turk.* **144** C3
Gemlik Körfezi, *Turk.* **144** C3
Gemona del Friuli, *It.* **128** C7
Gemsa, *Egypt* **175** C15
Genádio, *Gr.* **133** K15
Genalē, river, *Eth.* **177** F12
Genç, *Turk.* **145** E11
Geneina (Al Junaynah), *Sudan*
    176 D8
General Acha, *Arg.* **111** K5
General Alvear, *Arg.* **110** J4
General Carrera, Lago, *Chile* **111** P3
General Conesa, *Arg.* **111** L5
General Eugenio A. Garay, *Para.*
    108 H8
General Güemes, *Arg.* **110** D5
General Guido, *Arg.* **110** J8
General Juan Madariage, *Arg.*
    110 J8
General La Madrid, *Arg.* **111** K7
General Levalle, *Arg.* **110** H6
General Lorenzo Vintter, *Arg.*
    111 L5
General Paz, *Arg.* **110** E8
General Pico, *Arg.* **110** J6
General Pinedo, *Arg.* **110** E7
General Roca, *Arg.* **111** K4
General San Martín, *Arg.* **110** H8
General San Martín, *Arg.* **111** K6
General San Martín, *Arg.* **111** N3
General Santos, *Philippines*
    167 E12
Geneva *see* Genève, *Switz.* **128** B1
Geneva, Lake *see* Léman, Lac,
    Fr., Switz. **125** N11
Genève (Geneva), *Switz.* **128** B1
Genhe, *China* **157** B15
Genil, river, *Sp.* **122** J7
Genisséa, *Gr.* **133** B11
Genk, *Belg.* **124** G10
Genlis, *Fr.* **125** M10
Gennargentu, Monti del, *It.* **129** K3
Genoa *see* Genova, *It.* **128** E3
Génolhac, *Fr.* **125** R9
Genova (Genoa), *It.* **128** E3
Genova, Golfo di, *It.* **128** E3
Genovesa, Isla (Tower), *Ecua.* **106** D3
Gent, *Belg.* **124** G8
Geoado, island, *S. Korea* **161** M5
Geochang, *S. Korea* **161** P8
Geogeumdo, island, *S. Korea* **161** R7
Geographe Bay, *Austral.* **184** K3
Geographe Channel, *Austral.* **184** G2
Geographical Society Ø, island,
    Greenland, Den. **199** H14
Geoje, *S. Korea* **161** Q9
Geojedo, island, *S. Korea* **161** Q9
Geojin, *S. Korea* **160** J9
Geomundo, island, *S. Korea* **161** R7
George, *S. Af.* **180** K7
George, Zemlya, *Russ.* **136** B9
George, Lake, *Austral.* **184** F6
George, Lake, *Austral.* **185** L15
George, river, *Que., Can.* **89** G13
George Land, *Russ.* **199** E11
Georgetown, *Bahamas* **96** D9
George Town, *Cayman Is., U.K.* **96** H4
Georgetown, *Gambia* **174** G3
Georgetown, *Guyana* **107** D14
George Town, *Malaysia* **165** N6
Georgetown, *Qnsld., Austral.*
    187 D13

Georgetown, *S.C., U.S.* **93** G15
Georgetown, *St. Vincent & the
    Grenadines* **99** F13
George Town, *Tas., Austral.* **187** L17
George V Coast, *Antarctica* **201** M12
George VI Sound, *Antarctica* **200** E4
Georgia, *Asia* **142** E5
Georgia, *U.S.* **93** H13
Georgia, Strait of, *B.C., Can.* **88** J4
Georgian Bay, *Can.* **84** J8
Georgīevka, *Kaz.* **151** C15
Georgina, river, *Austral.* **185** E11
Geórgios, Ágios *see* Ro, island, *Gr.*
    133 K17
Geórgios, Ágios, island, *Gr.* **133** H10
Georgiyevsk, *Russ.* **135** P11
Georgiyevskoye, *Russ.* **134** E10
Gera, *Ger.* **126** F8
Gerákion, *Gr.* **132** J8
Geral de Goiás, Serra, *Braz.* **109** G13
Geraldine, *N.Z.* **189** J13
Geraldton, *Ont., Can.* **89** K10
Geraldton, *W. Austral., Austral.* **186** H3
Gérardmer, *Fr.* **125** L11
Gerasa *see* Jarash, *Jordan* **146** J5
Gercüş, *Turk.* **145** F12
Gerdine, Mount, *U.S.* **90** L3
Gerede, *Turk.* **144** C6
Gereshk, *Afghan.* **153** L3
Geretsried, *Ger.* **126** J7
Gerlachovsky Štit, peak, *Slovakia*
    127 G13
Germania Land, *Greenland, Den.* **84** B9
Germany, *Europe* **116** G7
Germering, *Ger.* **126** J7
Germī, *Iran* **148** A8
Gerolakkos, *Cyprus* **133** E16
Geroliménas, *Gr.* **132** K8
Gersthofen, *Ger.* **126** H7
Gêrzê, *China* **156** G6
Gerze, *Turk.* **144** B8
Gesoa, *P.N.G.* **188** F7
Getafe, *Sp.* **122** E9
Getz Ice Shelf, *Antarctica* **200** J6
Geum, river, *S. Korea* **161** N6
Geumdangdo, island, *S. Korea* **161** R7
Geumil, *S. Korea* **161** R7
Geumodo, island, *S. Korea* **161** R8
Geumpang, *Indonesia* **166** F2
Geumsan, *S. Korea* **161** N7
Geumwang, *S. Korea* **161** L7
Geunto, Gora, *Russ.* **137** C16
Gevaş, *Turk.* **145** E13
Gex, *Fr.* **125** N11
Geylegphug, *Bhutan* **154** E10
Geyve, *Turk.* **144** C4
Gezhouba Dam, *Hubei, China* **158** J2
Ghadāmis, *Lib.* **174** C9
Ghaddūwah, *Lib.* **175** D10
Ghana, *Af.* **173** K3
Ghanzi, *Botswana* **180** F7
Gharandal, *Jordan* **147** M4
Ghardaïa, *Alg.* **174** B8
Gharm, *Taj.* **152** F7
Gharo, *Pak.* **153** R5
Gharyān, *Lib.* **175** B10
Ghawdex *see* Gozo, island, *Malta*
    129 Q8
Ghaziabad, *India* **154** D5
Ghazipur, *India* **154** F7
Ghazni, *Afghan.* **153** K5
Ghazzah (Gaza City), *Gaza Strip*
    147 K3
Gheorghieni, *Rom.* **131** C13
Gherla, *Rom.* **131** B12
Ghilarza, *It.* **129** K3
Ghisonaccia, *Fr.* **128** H3
Ghormach, *Afghan.* **152** H3
Ghotki, *Pak.* **153** P6
Ghow Gardan Pass, *Afghan.* **152** J5

Ghurian, *Afghan.* **152** J1
Gia Nghia, *Viet.* **164** J10
Gianitsá, *Gr.* **132** B8
Giannutri, Isola di, *It.* **128** H5
Gia Rai, *Viet.* **165** L9
Giáros, island, *Gr.* **133** H11
Giarre, *It.* **129** N9
Giba, *It.* **129** L3
Gibara, *Cuba* **96** G8
Gibb River, *W. Austral., Austral.*
    186 C7
Gibeon, *Namibia* **180** G5
Gibraleón, *Sp.* **122** J6
Gibraltar, *U.K.* **122** L7
Gibraltar, Strait of, *Af., Europe*
    114 L3
Gibson Desert, *Austral.* **184** F7
Gidar, *Pak.* **153** P4
Giddalur, *India* **155** K5
Gīdolē, *Eth.* **177** F12
Gien, *Fr.* **125** L7
Giesecke Bræer, glacier, *Greenland,
    Den.* **199** K12
Giessen, *Ger.* **126** F5
Gifford, river, *Nunavut, Can.* **89** D10
Gifhorn, *Ger.* **126** D7
Gifu, *Japan* **162** J7
Gigant, *Russ.* **135** N10
Gigha Island, *Scot., U.K.* **120** J5
Giglio, Isola del, *It.* **128** G5
Gijang, *S. Korea* **161** P10
Gijón, *Sp.* **122** A7
Gila, river, *U.S.* **90** G4
Gila Bend, *Ariz., U.S.* **92** G5
Gilbert, river, *Austral.* **185** D13
Gilbert Islands, *Kiribati* **190** D8
Gilberton, *Qnsld., Austral.* **187** D13
Gilbués, *Braz.* **109** E13
Gilf Kebir Plateau, *Egypt* **175** E13
Gilgandra, *N.S.W., Austral.* **187** J14
Gilgit, *Pak.* **152** H9
Gilgit, region, *Pak.* **152** H9
Gilgit, river, *Pak.* **152** H9
Gill, Lough, *Ire.* **121** L3
Gillam, *Man., Can.* **88** H9
Gillen, Lake, *Austral.* **184** G6
Gilles, Lake, *Austral.* **185** K10
Gillette, *Wyo., U.S.* **92** C7
Gilmore Hut, *Qnsld., Austral.*
    187 G13
Gilpeppee, *Qnsld., Austral.* **187** G12
Gima, *Japan* **163** Q1
Gimcheon, *S. Korea* **161** N8
Gimhae, *S. Korea* **161** P9
Gimhwa (Kŭmhwa), *S. Korea* **160** J7
Gimje, *S. Korea* **161** N6
Gimli, *Man., Can.* **88** K8
Gimnyeong, *S. Korea* **161** S6
Gimpo, *S. Korea* **161** K6
Gingin, *W. Austral., Austral.* **186** J4
Gingoog, *Philippines* **167** E12
Gīnīr, *Eth.* **177** F13
Ginowan, *Japan* **163** Q1
Giohar *see* Jawhar, *Somalia* **177** G14
Gioia, Golfo di, *It.* **129** M10
Gioia del Colle, *It.* **128** J11
Gioia Tauro, *It.* **129** M10
Gióna, Óros, *Gr.* **132** F7
Gioúra, island, *Gr.* **133** E10
Giovinazzo, *It.* **128** J10
Gippsland, region, *Austral.* **185** M13
Girab, *India* **154** E2
Girardot, *Col.* **106** F6
Giresun, *Turk.* **145** C10
Girga, *Egypt* **175** D15
Gir Hills, peak, *India* **154** G2
Giridih, *India* **154** F8
Girne *see* Kyrenia, *Cyprus* **133** E16
Girolata, *Fr.* **128** G3
Girona, *Sp.* **123** C15**

Gironde, bay, *Fr.* **125** P4
Gironne, river, *Fr.* **125** P4
Gisborne, *N.Z.* **189** E17
Gissi, *It.* **128** H8
Gitega, *Burundi* **177** J10
Gíthio, *Gr.* **132** J8
Giulianova, *It.* **128** G8
Giurgiu, *Rom.* **131** F13
Givet, *Fr.* **124** H9
Givors, *Fr.* **125** P9
Gizab, *Afghan.* **153** K4
Gizhiga Bay, *Russ.* **198** D3
Gizhuduvan, *Uzb.* **150** J9
Giżycko, *Pol.* **127** B14
Gjakovë (Đakovica), *Kos.* **130** H9
Gjeravica, peak, *Kos.* **130** H9
Gjilan (Gnjilane), *Kos.* **131** H10
Gjirokastër (Argyrus), *Alban.* **130** K9
Gjoa Haven, *Nunavut, Can.* **88** E9
Gjøvik, *Nor.* **119** H11
Gkreko, Cape, *Cyprus* **133** F17
Glace Bay, *N.S., Can.* **89** K15
Glachau, *Ger.* **126** F8
Gladstone, *Qnsld., Austral.* **187** F16
Glåma, river, *Nor.* **119** G11
Glasgow, *Mont., U.S.* **92** B7
Glasgow, *Scot., U.K.* **120** J7
Glazov, *Russ.* **136** F5
Glénan, Îles de, *Fr.* **125** L2
Glenariffe, *N. Ire., U.K.* **121** K5
Glenarm, *N. Ire., U.K.* **121** K5
Glenavy, *N.Z.* **189** K13
Glenayle, *W. Austral., Austral.* **186** G5
Glenbarr, *Scot., U.K.* **120** J5
Glendale, *Calif., U.S.* **92** G3
Glendive, *Mont., U.S.* **92** B7
Glenelg, river, *Austral.* **185** M12
Glengarriff (An Gleann Garbh), *Ire.*
   121 Q2
Glengyle, *Qnsld., Austral.* **187** F12
Glen Innes, *N.S.W., Austral.* **187** J16
Glenmorgan, *Qnsld., Austral.* **187** H15
Glenrothes, *Scot., U.K.* **120** H7
Glenties (Na Gleannta), *Ire.* **121** K3
Glenwood Springs, *Colo., U.S.* **92** E6
Glina, *Croatia* **130** D5
Gliwice, *Pol.* **127** F12
Globe, *Ariz., U.S.* **92** G5
Głogów, *Pol.* **127** E10
Glorenza, *It.* **128** B5
Glossglockner, peak, *Aust.* **126** K8
Gloucester, *Eng., U.K.* **121** P8
Gloucester, *N.S.W., Austral.* **187** K16
Gloucester, *P.N.G.* **188** D6
Glubokiy, *Russ.* **135** M10
Glubokiy, *Russ.* **135** L9
Glūbokoe, *Kaz.* **151** C15
Glynebwy see Ebbw Vale, *Wales, U.K.*
   121 P8
Gmunden, *Aust.* **126** J9
Gniezno, *Pol.* **127** D11
Gnjilane see Gjilan, *Kos.* **131** H10
Goa, *India* **155** K3
Goa, *S. Korea* **161** N8
Goalpara, *India* **154** E10
Goba, *Eth.* **177** F12
Gobabis, *Namibia* **180** F6
Gobernador Duval, *Arg.* **111** K5
Gobernador Gregores, *Arg.* **111** Q3
Gobi, desert, *Asia* **141** F11
Gobō, *Japan* **163** K6
Gobu, *S. Korea* **161** P6
Gochang, *S. Korea* **161** P6
Go Cong, *Viet.* **165** K10
Godalming, *Eng., U.K.* **121** Q10
Godavari, river, *India* **154** J6
Godavari, Mouths of the, *India* **155** K6
Goderville, *Fr.* **124** J6
Godhavn see Qeqertarsuaq, *Greenland,*
   Den. **199** L13

Godhra, *India* **154** G3
Gödöllő, *Hung.* **127** J13
Godoy Cruz, *Arg.* **110** H4
Gods, river, *Man., Can.* **88** J9
Gods Lake, *Man., Can.* **88** J9
Godthåb see Nuuk, *Greenland, Den.*
   199 M14
Godwin Austen see K2, peak, *China,*
   Pak. **152** H10
Goélands, Lac aux, *Que., Can.* **89** H14
Goes, *Neth.* **124** G8
Gogebic Range, *U.S.* **91** B11
Gogeumdo, island, *S. Korea* **161** R6
Gogland, island, *Russ.* **134** D4
Gogrial, *S. Sudan* **176** F9
Gohan, *S. Korea* **161** L9
Goheung, *S. Korea* **161** Q7
Goianésia, *Braz.* **109** G12
Goiânia, *Braz.* **109** G12
Góis, *Port.* **122** E5
Gojōme, *Japan* **162** F9
Gojra, *Pak.* **153** M8
Gokak, *India* **155** K3
Gökdepe, *Turkm.* **150** J6
Gokseong, *S. Korea* **161** P7
Golaghat, *India* **154** E11
Golan Heights, region, *Israel*
   146 H5
Golbahar, *Afghan.* **152** J6
Gold Coast, *Qnsld., Austral.*
   187 H16
Gold Coast, *Ghana* **178** F8
Golden Bay, *N.Z.* **189** G14
Goldfield, *Nev., U.S.* **92** E4
Goldsboro, *N.C., U.S.* **93** F15
Goldsworthy, *W. Austral., Austral.*
   186 E4
Goleniów, *Pol.* **126** C9
Golfito, *C.R.* **95** L14
Golfo Aranci, *It.* **128** J4
Golmud, *China* **156** F9
Golo, river, *Fr.* **128** G3
Golovin, *Alas., U.S.* **92** K2
Golūbovka, *Kaz.* **151** B12
Golyama Kamchiya, river, *Bulg.*
   131 G14
Golyam Perelik, peak, *Bulg.* **131** J12
Goma, *D.R.C.* **177** H10
Gombe, *Nig.* **179** C13
Gomera, island, *Atl. Oc.* **170** F1
Gómez Palacio, *Mex.* **94** E6
Gonābād, *Iran* **149** C12
Gonaïves, *Haiti* **97** H11
Gonam, *Russ.* **137** G14
Gonam, river, *Russ.* **137** H14
Gonâve, Golfe de la, *Haiti* **97** H11
Gonâve, Île de la, *Haiti* **97** J11
Gonbad-e Kāvūs, *Iran* **149** B11
Gonda, *India* **154** E6
Gonder, *Eth.* **177** D12
Gondia, *India* **154** G6
Gondomar, *Port.* **122** D4
Gong'an, *Hubei, China* **159** K3
Gongcheng, *Guangxi Zhuangzu, China*
   159 P1
Gonggar, *China* **156** J8
Gonghe, *China* **157** G10
Gonghui, *Hebei, China* **158** B5
Gongjtang, *Nei Mongol, China* **158** A3
Gongju, *S. Korea* **161** M7
Gonglee, *Liberia* **178** E5
Gongliu, *China* **156** D6
Gongola, river, *Nig.* **179** C13
Gongtang see Damxung, *China*
   156 H8
Gongyi, *Henan, China* **158** G3
Gongzhuling, *China* **157** D16
Góni, *Gr.* **132** D8

González Chaves, *Arg.* **111** K7
Goodenough Island, *P.N.G.* **188** C7
Good Hope, Cape of, *S. Af.* **180** K6
Goodhouse, *S. Af.* **180** H6
Goodland, *Kans., U.S.* **92** E8
Goodlands, *Mauritius* **181** G15
Goodnews Bay, *Alas., U.S.* **92** L1
Goodparla, *N. Terr., Austral.* **186** B9
Goomalling, *W. Austral., Austral.*
   186 J4
Goondiwindi, *Qnsld., Austral.* **187** H15
Goongarrie, Lake, *Austral.* **184** J5
Goose Lake, *U.S.* **90** C3
Gorakhpur, *India* **154** E7
Gordion, ruins, *Turk.* **144** D5
Gordon, Lake, *Austral.* **185** L17
Gordon Downs, *W. Austral., Austral.*
   186 D8
Gordon's, *Bahamas* **97** E10
Gordonvale, *Qnsld., Austral.* **187** C14
Goré, *Chad* **175** J11
Gorē, *Eth.* **177** F11
Gore, *N.Z.* **189** L12
Goreda, *Indonesia* **188** K5
Gorey (Guaire), *Ire.* **121** N5
Gorgān, *Iran* **149** B11
Gorgona, Isla, *Col.* **106** F4
Gorgona, Isola di, *It.* **128** F4
Gori, *Ga.* **145** B14
Goris, *Arm.* **145** D15
Gorizia, *It.* **128** C7
Gor'kovskoye Vodokhranilishche, *Russ.*
   134 F10
Gorlice, *Pol.* **127** G14
Görlitz, *Ger.* **126** E9
Gorna Oryakhovitsa, *Bulg.* **131** G13
Gornja Radgona, *Slov.* **130** C6
Gornji Milanovac, *Serb.* **130** F9
Gorno Altaysk, *Russ.* **136** K8
Gornozavodsk, *Russ.* **137** H17
Gornyak, *Russ.* **136** K8
Gorodets, *Russ.* **134** F10
Gorodishche, *Russ.* **134** H11
Goroka, *P.N.G.* **188** F6
Gorong, Kepulauan, *Indonesia*
   167 J14
Gorontalo, *Indonesia* **167** G11
Gortyn, ruins, *Gr.* **133** M11
Gorumna Island see Garmna, *Ire.*
   121 M2
Goryeong, *S. Korea* **161** P8
Góry Swietokrzyskie, mountains, *Pol.*
   127 E13
Gorzów Wielkopolski, *Pol.* **127** C10
Gosan, *S. Korea* **161** T5
Goschen Strait, *P.N.G.* **188** C8
Gosen, *Japan* **162** G9
Goseong, *S. Korea* **161** K8
Goseong, *S. Korea* **161** Q8
Gosford, *N.S.W., Austral.* **187** K15
Goshogawara, *Japan* **162** E9
Goslar, *Ger.* **126** D7
Gospić, *Croatia* **130** E5
Gosselies, *Belg.* **124** H9
Gostivar, *Maced.* **130** H9
Göteborg, *Sweden* **119** K11
Gotha, *Ger.* **126** E7
Gothèye, *Niger* **174** G7
Gotland, island, *Sweden* **119** K13
Gotō Rettō, *Japan* **163** K2
Gotse Delchev, *Bulg.* **131** J12
Gotska Sandön, island, *Sweden*
   119 J13
Gōtsu, *Japan* **162** J4
Göttingen, *Ger.* **126** E6
Gouin, Réservoir, *Que., Can.* **89** K12
Goulburn, *N.S.W., Austral.* **187** L15
Gould Bay, *Antarctica* **200** D7
Gould Coast, *Antarctica* **200** H9
Goumbou, *Mali* **174** G5

Goundam, *Mali* **174** F6
Gouré, *Niger* **174** G9
Gournay, *Fr.* **124** J7
Gournia, ruins, *Gr.* **133** M12
Gouro, *Chad* **175** F12
Gouzon, *Fr.* **125** N7
Govena, Mys, *Russ.* **137** D17
Govindgarh, *India* **154** F6
Govorovo, *Russ.* **137** E12
Gowd-e Zereh, Dasht-e, *Afghan.*
   153 M1
Gower Peninsula, *Wales, U.K.* **121** Q7
Gowmal Kalay, *Afghan.* **153** L6
Gowon, *S. Korea* **161** P7
Gowrzanak, *Afghan.* **153** K3
Goya, *Arg.* **110** F7
Goyang, *S. Korea* **161** K6
Gozo (Għawdex), island, *Malta*
   129 Q8
Graaff-Reinet, *S. Af.* **180** J7
Gračac, *Croatia* **130** E5
Gračanica, *Bosn. & Herzg.* **130** E7
Gracias a Dios, Cabo, *Nicar.* **95** J14
Graciosa, island, *Azores, Port.* **122** L3
Gradaús, *Braz.* **109** E12
Grafton, *N. Dak., U.S.* **92** B9
Grafton, *N.S.W., Austral.* **187** J16
Graham, *Ont., Can.* **89** K10
Graham Bell, Ostrov, *Russ.* **136** C9
Graham Island, *B.C., Can.* **88** G3
Graham Island, *Can.* **84** D7
Graham Island, *Nunavut, Can.* **89** B10
Graham Island, *U.S.* **84** F2
Graham Land, *Antarctica* **200** C3
Grahamstown, *S. Af.* **180** K8
Graian Alps, *Fr., It.* **128** C1
Grain Coast, *Liberia* **178** E5
Grajaú, *Braz.* **109** D13
Grajewo, *Pol.* **127** B14
Gramat, *Fr.* **125** Q7
Grámos, Óros, *Gr.* **132** C6
Grampian Mountains, *Scot., U.K.*
   120 H6
Granada, *Nicar.* **95** K13
Granada, *Sp.* **122** J9
Gran Altiplanicie Central, plateau, *Arg.*
   111 Q4
Granby, *Que., Can.* **89** L13
Gran Canaria, island, *Spain* **174** C4
Gran Chaco, region, *S. Amer.* **102** K6
Grand, river, *Mich., U.S.* **91** D13
Grand, river, *S. Dak., U.S.* **90** C8
Grand Bahama Island, *Bahamas*
   96 A6
Grand Baie, *Mauritius* **181** G15
Grand Baie, *Mauritius* **181** J15
Grand-Bassam, *Côte d'Ivoire* **178** E7
Grand-Bourg, *Guadeloupe, Fr.* **99** D13
Grand Caicos, island, *Turks & Caicos Is.,*
   U.K. **97** F12
Grandcamp-Maisy, *Fr.* **124** J4
Grand Canal see Da Yunhe, *China*
   159 K8
Grand Canal, *Ire.* **121** M4
Grand Canaria, island, *Atl. Oc.* **170** F1
Grand Canyon, *Ariz., U.S.* **92** F5
Grand Canyon, *U.S.* **90** F5
Grand Cayman, island, *Cayman Is., U.K.*
   96 H4
Grand Cess, *Liberia* **178** E6
Grande, Bahía, *Arg.* **111** R4
Grande, Boca, *Venez.* **107** C13
Grande, Cayo, *Cuba* **96** G6
Grande, Cuchilla, *Uru.* **110** H9
Grande, Cayo, *Venez.* **98** H9

Grande, Salina, *Arg.* III K4
Grande, Corno, *It.* 128 G7
Grande, river, *Arg.* 110 J3
Grande, river, *Arg., Chile* III S4
Grande, river, *Bol.* 108 G8
Grande, river, *Braz.* 109 F13
Grande, river, *Braz.* 109 H12
Grande Cayemite, island, *Haiti* 97 J10
Grande Comore see Njazidja, island,
  Ind. Oc. 171 N11
Grande Prairie, *Alta., Can.* 88 H5
Grand Erg de Blima, *Niger* 175 F10
Grand Erg Occidental, *Alg.* 174 C7
Grand Erg Oriental, *Alg.* 174 C9
Grande Rivière du Nord, *Haiti* 97 H12
Grande Rivière Sud Est, *Mauritius*
  181 H16
Grandes, Salinas, *Arg.* 110 F5
Grande-Terre, island, *Guadeloupe, Fr.*
  99 D13
Grand Falls-Windsor, *Nfld. & Lab., Can.*
  89 J16
Grand Forks, *N. Dak., U.S.* 92 B9
Grand-Gosier, *Haiti* 97 J12
Grand Island, *Nebr., U.S.* 92 E9
Grand Isle, *La., U.S.* 93 J12
Grand Junction, *Colo., U.S.* 92 E6
Grand Lieu, Lac de, *Fr.* 125 M4
Grand Marais, *Minn., U.S.* 93 B11
Grândola, *Port.* 122 H4
Grand Rapids, *Man., Can.* 88 J8
Grand Rapids, *Mich., U.S.* 93 D13
Grand Teton, *U.S.* 90 C5
Grand Turk, island, *Turks & Caicos Is.,*
  U.K. 97 F13
Grandvilliers, *Fr.* 124 J7
Grange (An Ghráinseach), *Ire.* 121 L3
Granite Peak, *Mont., U.S.* 90 C6
Granite Peak, *Nev., U.S.* 90 D4
Granja, *Braz.* 109 C15
Granollers, *Sp.* 123 D14
Grant Island, *Antarctica* 200 K6
Grants, *N. Mex., U.S.* 92 G6
Grants Pass, *Oreg., U.S.* 92 C2
Granville, *Fr.* 125 K4
Granville Lake, *Man., Can.* 88 H8
Grão Mogol, *Braz.* 109 G14
Grasse, *Fr.* 125 R11
Grassholm Island, *Wales, U.K.* 121 Q5
Grass Patch, *W. Austral., Austral.*
  186 K6
Graus, *Sp.* 123 C13
Grave, Pointe de, *Fr.* 125 P4
Gravelbourg, *Sask., Can.* 88 K7
Gravina in Puglia, *It.* 128 J10
Gravois, Pointe-à-, *Haiti* 97 J10
Gray, *Fr.* 125 M10
Grays, *Eng., U.K.* 121 Q11
Graz, *Aust.* 127 K10
Great Abaco Island, *Bahamas* 85 N9
Great Artesian Basin, *Austral.*
  185 F12
Great Australian Bight, *Austral.*
  184 K8
Great Bahama Bank, *Bahamas* 96 C6
Great Barrier Island, *N.Z.* 189 C16
Great Barrier Reef, *Austral.* 185 E16
Great Basin, *U.S.* 90 E4
Great Bear Lake, *N.W.T., Can.* 88 E6
Great Bend, *Kans., U.S.* 92 F9
Great Bernera, island, *Scot., U.K.*
  120 E4
Great Bitter Lake see Murrat el Kubra,
  Buheirat, *Egypt* 147 L1
Great Britain, island, *Scot., U.K.*
  120 H7
Great Channel, *India, Indonesia*
  166 E2
Great Coco Island, *Myanmar* 164 H3
Great Crater, *Israel* 147 K4

Great Dismal Swamp, *U.S.* 91 F16
Great Divide Basin, *U.S.* 90 D6
Great Dividing Range, *Austral.*
  185 L14
Great Driffield, *Eng., U.K.* 121 L10
Greater Antilles, islands, *Caribbean Sea*
  85 P8
Greater Sudbury, *Ont., Can.* 89 L11
Greater Sunda Islands, *Asia* 141 M12
Great Exuma, island, *Bahamas* 96 D9
Great Fall, *Guyana* 107 E13
Great Falls, *Mont., U.S.* 92 B6
Great Guana Cay, *Bahamas* 96 A8
Great Harbour Cay, *Bahamas* 96 B7
Great Inagua Island, *Bahamas* 97 G11
Great Indian Desert (Thar Desert),
  India, Pak. 153 P7
Great Isaac, island, *Bahamas* 96 B6
Great Lake, *Austral.* 185 L17
Great Miami, river, *U.S.* 91 E13
Great Namaland, region, *Namibia*
  180 H5
Great Nicobar, island, *India* 155 P11
Great Orme's Head, *Wales, U.K.*
  121 M7
Great Oyster Bay, *Austral.* 185 L18
Great Pedro Bluff, *Jamaica* 96 K7
Great Pee Dee, river, *U.S.* 91 G15
Great Plains, *U.S.* 90 B7
Great Rift Valley, *Af.* 171 M9
Great Ruaha, river, *Tanzania* 177 K11
Great Sale Cay, *Bahamas* 96 A7
Great Salt Lake, *U.S.* 90 D5
Great Salt Lake Desert, *U.S.* 90 D5
Great Sandy Desert, *Austral.* 184 D6
Great Sandy Desert, *U.S.* 90 C3
Great Sandy Island see Fraser Island,
  Austral. 185 G16
Great Slave Lake, *N.W.T., Can.* 88 F7
Great Smoky Mountains, *U.S.* 91 G14
Great Sound, *Bermuda, U.K.* 97 D12
Great Stirrup Cay, *Bahamas* 96 B7
Great Tenasserim, river, *Myanmar*
  164 J6
Great Victoria Desert, *Austral.*
  184 H7
Great Wall, station, *Antarctica*
  200 B3
Great Wall, *China* 158 B7
Great Western Tiers, mountains,
  Austral. 185 L17
Great Yarmouth, *Eng., U.K.* 121 N12
Great Zab, river, *Turk.* 145 F14
Great Zimbabwe, ruins, *Zimb.* 180 F9
Greci, *It.* 128 J9
Gredos, Sierra de, *Sp.* 122 E7
Greece, *Europe* 117 L10
Greeley, *Colo., U.S.* 92 E7
Greely Fiord, *Nunavut, Can.* 89 B10
Green, Cape, *Austral.* 185 M15
Green, river, *Ky., U.S.* 91 F13
Green, river, *Utah, U.S.* 90 E6
Green Bay, *Wis., U.S.* 93 C12
Green Bay, *U.S.* 91 C12
Green Cay, *Bahamas* 96 D8
Green Head, *Austral.* 184 J3
Green Island, *Jamaica* 96 J7
Green Islands, *P.N.G.* 188 A5
Greenland (Kalaallit Nunaat), *Den.,*
  N. Amer. 86 C9
Greenland, island, *Den.* 84 C8
Greenland Environmental Observatory
  (Summit Camp), station, *Greenland,*
  Den. 199 K13
Green Mountains, *U.S.* 91 C16
Greenock, *Scot., U.K.* 120 J6
Green River, *Wyo., U.S.* 92 D6
Greensboro, *N.C., U.S.* 93 F15
Greenville, *Liberia* 178 E5
Greenville, *Miss., U.S.* 93 H11

Greenville, *S.C., U.S.* 93 G14
Gregory, Lake, *Austral.* 184 G5
Gregory, Lake, *Austral.* 185 H11
Gregory, river, *Austral.* 185 D11
Gregory Lake, *Austral.* 184 E7
Gregory Range, *Austral.* 185 D13
Greifswald, *Ger.* 126 B9
Greiz, *Ger.* 126 F8
Grenada, *N. Amer.* 87 Q12
Grenade, *Fr.* 125 R5
Grenoble, *Fr.* 125 P10
Grenville, *Grenada* 99 G13
Grenville, Cape, *Austral.* 185 A13
Grevená, *Gr.* 132 C6
Grey, Cape, *Austral.* 185 B11
Grey, Mount, *Austral.* 184 J4
Grey Islands, *Nfld. & Lab., Can.* 89 H15
Greylock, Mount, *U.S.* 91 C16
Grey Range, *Austral.* 185 H13
Grezzana, *It.* 128 C5
Gribanovskiy, *Russ.* 134 J10
Griffith, *N.S.W., Austral.* 187 K13
Grim, Cape, *Austral.* 185 L17
Grimsby, *Eng., U.K.* 121 M10
Grímsey, island, *Ice.* 118 D4
Grimshaw, *Alta., Can.* 88 H6
Grimstad, *Nor.* 119 J10
Grindelwald, *Switz.* 128 B2
Grinnell Peninsula, *Nunavut, Can.*
  88 C9
Grintavec, peak, *Slov.* 130 C4
Griquatown, *S. Af.* 180 H7
Grise Fiord, *Nunavut, Can.* 89 C10
Grishkino, *Russ.* 136 H8
Gris-Nez, Cap, *Fr.* 124 H7
Grisslehamn, *Sweden* 119 H13
Gródek, *Pol.* 127 C15
Groenlo, *Neth.* 124 F11
Groix, Île de, *Fr.* 125 L2
Grójec, *Pol.* 127 D13
Gronau, *Ger.* 126 D4
Groningen, *Neth.* 124 E10
Groote Eylandt, island, *Austral.*
  185 B11
Grootfontein, *Namibia* 180 E6
Grosio, *It.* 128 C4
Gros-Morne, *Haiti* 97 H11
Grosseto, *It.* 128 G5
Grossvenediger, peak, *Aust.* 126 K8
Grosvenor Mountains, *Antarctica*
  200 H9
Grotli, *Nor.* 119 G10
Grottaminarda, *It.* 128 J9
Grove Mountains, *Antarctica* 201 E14
Groznyy, *Russ.* 135 P12
Grudovo, *Bulg.* 131 H14
Grudziądz, *Pol.* 127 C12
Gruinard Bay, *Scot., U.K.* 120 F6
Gryazi, *Russ.* 134 J9
Gryazovets, *Russ.* 134 E9
Gryfino, *Pol.* 126 C9
Gök, river, *Turk.* 144 B7
Gökçeada (İmroz), island, *Turk.* 144 C1
Gökova Körfezi, *Turk.* 144 F2
Göksu, river, *Turk.* 144 G6
Göksun, *Turk.* 144 F8
Gölbaşı, *Turk.* 144 D6
Gölbaşı, *Turk.* 144 F9
Gölcük, *Turk.* 144 C4
Göle, *Turk.* 145 C13
Gölköy, *Turk.* 144 C9
Gölpazarı, *Turk.* 144 C4
Gölören, *Turk.* 144 F7
Gönen, *Turk.* 144 C2
Gördes, *Turk.* 144 D3
Görele, *Turk.* 145 C10
Göyçay, *Azerb.* 145 C16
Göynük, *Turk.* 144 C5
Guacanayabo, Golfo de, *Cuba* 96 G7
Guadalajara, *Mex.* 94 G6

Guadalajara, *Sp.* 122 E9
Guadalcanal, *Sp.* 122 H7
Guadalcanal, island, *Solomon Is.*
  190 E6
Guadalquivir, river, *Sp.* 122 J7
Guadalupe, *Mex.* 94 C4
Guadalupe, *Mex.* 94 F7
Guadalupe, Isla de, *Mex.* 94 B1
Guadalupe, Sierra de, *Sp.* 122 G7
Guadalupe, river, *U.S.* 90 J9
Guadalupe Mountains, *U.S.* 90 H7
Guadalupe Peak, *U.S.* 90 H7
Guadarrama, Sierra de, *Sp.* 122 E9
Guadeloupe, islands, *Fr., Lesser*
  Antilles 99 D13
Guadeloupe Passage, *Lesser*
  Antilles 99 C13
Guadiana, Bahía, *Cuba* 96 E1
Guadiana, river, *Port.* 122 J5
Guadix, *Sp.* 122 J9
Guafo, Boca del, *Chile* III N2
Guafo, Isla, *Chile* III N2
Guai, *Indonesia* 167 J16
Guáimaro, *Cuba* 96 G7
Guainía, river, *Col.* 106 F9
Guaíra, *Braz.* 109 K11
Guaire see Gorey, *Ire.* 121 N5
Guajaba, Cayo, *Cuba* 96 F7
Guajará-Mirim, *Braz.* 108 E7
Guajira, Península de la, *Col.* 106 B7
Gualeguay, *Arg.* 110 H4
Gualeguaychú, *Arg.* 110 H8
Gualicho, Salina, *Arg.* III L4
Guallatiri, Volcán, *Chile* 110 A3
Guam, island, *U.S., Pac. Oc.* 190 C4
Guamúchil, *Mex.* 94 E5
Gua Musang, *Malaysia* 165 N7
Gu'an, *Hebei, China* 158 C6
Guanajay, *Cuba* 96 E3
Guanajuato, *Mex.* 94 G7
Guanambi, *Braz.* 109 G14
Guanare, *Venez.* 106 C8
Guanare, river, *Venez.* 106 C9
Guandacol, *Arg.* 110 F4
Guandu, *Guangdong, China* 159 P4
Guane, *Cuba* 96 E2
Guangchang, *Jiangxi, China* 159 N5
Guangdong, *China* 159 Q3
Guangfeng, *Jiangxi, China* 159 L7
Guanghai, *Guangdong, China* 159 R3
Guanghai Wan, *Guangdong, China*
  159 R3
Guangling, *Shanxi, China* 158 C4
Guangning, *Guangdong, China* 159 Q3
Guangrao, *Shandong, China* 158 E7
Guangshan, *Henan, China* 158 J4
Guangshui, *Hubei, China* 158 J4
Guangxi Zhuangzu, *China* 159 Q1
Guangyuan, *China* 157 H12
Guangze, *Fujian, China* 159 M6
Guangzhou (Canton), *Guangdong,*
  China 159 Q3
Guanipa, river, *Venez.* 107 C12
Guanmian Shan, *Chongqing Shi, China*
  158 J1
Guannan (Xin'an), *Jiangsu, China*
  158 G7
Guano, Cayo, *Cuba* 96 F4
Guantánamo, *Cuba* 96 G9
Guantánamo, Bahía de, *Cuba, U.S.*
  96 H9
Guanyang, *Guangxi Zhuangzu, China*
  159 N2
Guanyun (Yinshan), *Jiangsu, China*
  158 G7
Guapí, *Col.* 106 G5
Guaporé, river, *Bol.* 108 F8
Guara, Sierra de, *Sp.* 123 C12
Guaranda, *Ecua.* 106 J4
Guarapuava, *Braz.* 109 K11

Haimen see Taizhou, Zhejiang, China **159** L9
Haimen Wan, Guangdong, China **159** Q6
Hainan, China **157** F12
Hainan, island, China **157** M13
Hainan, China **159** T1
Haines, Alas., U.S. **92** L5
Haines Junction, Yukon, Can. **88** E4
Haiphong, Viet. **164** E10
Haitan Dao, Fujian, China **159** P8
Haiti, N. Amer. **87** P10
Haixing, Hebei, China **158** D6
Haiya, Sudan **177** C11
Haiyan, Zhejiang, China **159** K8
Haiyang (Dongcun), Shandong, China **158** E8
Haizhou, Jiangsu, China **158** G7
Haizhou Wan, Jiangsu, China **158** F7
Hajdúböszörmény, Hung. **127** J14
Hajdúszoboszló, Hung. **127** J14
Hajiki Saki, Japan **162** G8
Haji Pir Pass, India, Pak. **153** K9
Ḩajjah, Yemen **148** L7
Ḩājjīābād, Iran **149** F11
Hajnáčka, Slovakia **127** H13
Hajnówka, Pol. **127** C15
Hajodo, island, S. Korea **161** R5
Hakataramea, N.Z. **189** K13
Hakdam, S. Korea **161** K8
Hakgok, S. Korea **161** K8
Hakha, Myanmar **164** D3
Hakkari, Turk. **145** F13
Hakodate, Japan **162** D9
Haksong, N. Korea **160** F5
Hakui, Japan **162** H7
Hala, Pak. **153** Q5
Ḩalab (Aleppo), Syr. **146** C7
Ḩalabān, Saudi Arabia **148** H7
Halachó, Mex. **95** G11
Halayeb, Egypt **175** E16
Halba, Leb. **146** F5
Halban, Mongolia **157** B10
Halberstadt, Ger. **126** D7
Halcon, Mount, Philippines **167** C10
Haldwani, India **154** D5
Haleʻiwa, Hawaii, U.S. **93** L11
Halfeti, Turk. **144** F9
Halifax, N.S., Can. **89** L15
Halifax, Qnsld., Austral. **187** D14
Halifax Bay, Austral. **185** D14
Halik Shan, China **156** D6
Hálki, Gr. **132** D8
Hálki, island, Gr. **133** K14
Hálki, strait, Gr. **133** K14
Halkída (Chalkis), Gr. **132** F9
Halkidikí, peninsula, Gr. **132** C9
Hall, Aust. **126** K7
Hallasan, peak, S. Korea **161** T6
Hall Basin, Nunavut, Can. **89** A11
Hall Beach, Nunavut, Can. **89** E10
Halle, Belg. **124** H9
Halle, Ger. **126** E8
Hallein, Aust. **126** J8
Halley, station, Antarctica **200** C8
Hallim, S. Korea **161** T5
Hall Islands, F.S.M. **190** C5
Hällnäs, Sweden **119** F13
Hall Peninsula, Nunavut, Can. **89** F13
Halls Creek, W. Austral., Austral. **186** D7
Hallstatt, Aust. **126** J9
Halmahera, island, Indonesia **167** G13
Halmahera Sea, Indonesia **167** H13
Halmeu, Rom. **131** A11
Halmstad, Sweden **119** K12
Halstead, Eng., U.K. **121** P11

Haltdalen, Sweden **119** G11
Haltiatunturi, peak, Nor. **199** D15
Halys see Kızılırmak, river, Turk. **144** C7
Ham, Fr. **124** J8
Hamada, Japan **162** J4
Hamadān, Iran **148** C9
Hamaguir, Alg. **174** B7
Ḩamāh (Hamath), Syr. **146** E6
Hamamatsu, Japan **162** J8
Hamar, Nor. **119** H11
Hamasaka, Japan **162** J6
Ḩamâta, Gebel, Egypt **175** D15
Hamath see Ḩamāh, Syr. **146** E6
Hamatombetsu, Japan **162** B10
Hamburg, Ger. **126** B6
Hamchang, S. Korea **161** M8
Ḩamḍah, Saudi Arabia **148** J7
Ḩamdānah, Saudi Arabia **148** J5
Hämeenlinna, Fin. **119** G14
Hamelin, W. Austral., Austral. **186** H3
Hamelin Pool, Austral. **184** H3
Hameln, Ger. **126** D6
Hamersley Range, Austral. **184** F4
Hamgyŏng-sanmaek, range, N. Korea **160** E9
Hamhŭng, N. Korea **160** F7
Hamhŭng-man, bay, N. Korea **160** G7
Hami (Kumul), China **156** D9
Hamilton, Bermuda, U.K. **97** D12
Hamilton, N.Z. **189** D13
Hamilton, Ont., Can. **89** M12
Hamilton, Scot., U.K. **120** J7
Hamilton, Vic., Austral. **187** M12
Hamilton Inlet, Nfld. & Lab., Can. **89** H15
Hamina, Fin. **119** G15
Hami Pendi, China **156** D9
Hamirpur, India **154** F6
Hamju, N. Korea **160** F7
Hamlí, island, Gr. **133** L13
Hamm, Ger. **126** D5
Hammerfest, Nor. **119** B13
Hampden, N.Z. **189** K13
Hampton Tableland, Austral. **184** J7
Hampyeong, S. Korea **161** Q6
Ḩamrīn, Jabal, Iraq **148** C7
Hāmūn-e Şāberī, lake, Iran **149** D13
Hamyang, S. Korea **161** P8
Ham Yen, Viet. **164** D9
Han, river, China **157** H13
Han, river, S. Korea **161** K6
Hāna, Hawaii, U.S. **93** L12
Hanam, S. Korea **161** K7
Hanam, S. Korea **161** P9
Hanamaki, Japan **162** F10
Hanau, Ger. **126** F5
Hanawa, Japan **162** E9
Hancheng, Shaanxi, China **158** F2
Hanchuan, Hubei, China **159** K4
Hancock, Mich., U.S. **93** B12
Handa Island, Scot., U.K. **120** E6
Handan, Hebei, China **158** E4
Hangayn Nuruu, Mongolia **157** C10
Hanggin Qi, Nei Mongol, China **158** B1
Hangö (Hanko), Fin. **119** H14
Hangu, Pak. **153** K7
Hangu, Tianjin Shi, China **158** C6
Hangzhou, Zhejiang, China **159** K8
Hangzhou Wan, Zhejiang, China **159** K9
Hanhöhiy Uul, Mongolia **156** B9
Hani, Turk. **145** E11
Haniá (Canea, Cydonia), Gr. **133** L10
Hanimadu, island, Maldives **155** P2
Ḩanish al Kabīr, Jazīrat al, Yemen **148** M6
Hanko see Hangö, Fin. **119** H14
Hanle, India **153** K12
Hann, Mount, Austral. **184** C6

Hanna, Alta., Can. **88** J6
Hannover (Hanover), Ger. **126** D6
Hanöbukten, bay, Sweden **119** L12
Hanoi, Viet. **164** E9
Hanover see Hannover, Ger. **126** D6
Hanover, Isla, Chile **111** R2
Hansen Mountains, Antarctica **201** C15
Hantsavichy, Belarus **134** H3
Hanumangarh, India **154** D3
Hanuy, river, Mongolia **157** C11
Hanyang, Hubei, China **159** K4
Hanyuan, China **157** J11
Hanzhong, China **157** H12
Hao, island, Fr. Polynesia, Fr. **191** G13
Haora, India **154** G9
Haparanda, Sweden **119** E14
Hapcheon, S. Korea **161** P8
Hapdeok, S. Korea **161** M6
Hapo, Indonesia **167** G13
Happy Valley-Goose Bay, Nfld. & Lab., Can. **89** H14
Ḩaql, Saudi Arabia **148** E4
Har, Indonesia **167** J14
Ḩaraḍ, Saudi Arabia **148** G9
Harad, Jabal al, Jordan **147** M5
Haradok, Belarus **134** G5
Haradzishcha, Belarus **134** H3
Haranomachi, Japan **162** G10
Harappa, ruins, Pak. **153** M8
Harar, Eth. **177** F16
Harare, Zimb. **180** E9
Har Ayrag, Mongolia **157** C12
Harbin, China **157** C16
Harbours, Bay of, Falk. Is., U.K. **111** R7
Harda, India **154** G4
Hardangerfjorden, Nor. **118** J9
Hardenberg, Neth. **124** E11
Harderwijk, Neth. **124** F10
Hardin, Mont., U.S. **92** C7
Harding, S. Af. **180** J9
Hardy, Península, Chile **111** T4
Hargeysa, Somalia **177** E13
Har Hu, China **157** F10
Haridwar, India **154** D5
Harihari, N.Z. **189** J13
Harij, India **154** F2
Ḩārim, Syr. **146** C6
Haripur, Pak. **153** K8
Harirud, river, Asia **152** J1
Harīrūd, river, Turkm. **150** L7
Harkány, Hung. **127** L12
Harlingen, Neth. **124** E10
Harlingen, Tex., U.S. **92** K9
Harmancık, Turk. **144** D3
Harnai, Pak. **153** M5
Harney Basin, U.S. **90** C4
Harney Peak, U.S. **90** C8
Härnösand, Sweden **119** G12
Har Nuur, Mongolia **156** C9
Haro, Sp. **123** C10
Haroldswick, Scot., U.K. **120** B9
Harpanahalli, India **155** K4
Harper, Liberia **178** E6
Harput, Turk. **145** E10
Harqin, Liaoning, China **158** B7
Harqin Qi, Nei Mongol, China **158** A7
Ḩarrah, Yemen **148** L9
Harrai, India **154** G5
Harran, Turk. **145** G10
Harray, Loch of, Scot., U.K. **120** D7
Harricana, river, Que., Can. **89** K12
Harrington Harbour, Que., Can. **89** J15
Harrington Sound, Bermuda, U.K. **97** D13
Harris, Lake, Austral. **185** J10
Harris, Sound of, Scot., U.K. **120** F4
Harrisburg, Pa., U.S. **93** D15
Harrison, Cape, Can. **84** G10

Harrison Bay, U.S. **90** H3
Harrogate, Eng., U.K. **121** L9
Harry S Truman Reservoir, U.S. **91** F10
Harşit, river, Turk. **145** C10
Harstad, Nor. **119** C12
Hartao, Liaoning, China **158** A9
Hartford, Conn., U.S. **93** D16
Hartland Point, Eng., U.K. **121** R6
Har Us Nuur, Mongolia **156** C9
Harut, river, Afghan. **153** L1
Harūz-e Bālā, Iran **149** D12
Harvey, N. Dak., U.S. **92** B9
Harz, mountains, Ger. **126** E7
Hasanabad, Azerb. **145** D17
Ḩaşānah, Yemen **148** L9
Hasan Dağı, Turk. **144** F7
Ḩasan Langī, Iran **149** F12
Haseo, S. Korea **161** P10
Hashaat, Mongolia **157** D11
Ḩāsik, Oman **149** K11
Hasil, island, Indonesia **167** H13
Hasilpur, Pak. **153** N8
Haskeir see Eilean Hasgeir, island, Scot., U.K. **120** F4
Hassel Sound, Nunavut, Can. **88** B9
Hassi Messaoud, Alg. **174** B9
Hassi R'mel, Alg. **174** B8
Hässleholm, Sweden **119** L12
Hastings, Eng., U.K. **121** R11
Hastings, N.Z. **189** F16
Hastings, Nebr., U.S. **92** E9
Hastings, battlefield, Eng., U.K. **121** R11
Hasvik, Nor. **119** B13
Hataedo, island, S. Korea **161** R4
Hataedo, island, S. Korea **161** R5
Hatay (Antioch), Turk. **144** G8
Haţeg, Rom. **131** D11
Hateruma Jima, Japan **159** Q11
Hatgal, Mongolia **157** B10
Hatherleigh, Eng., U.K. **121** R7
Ḩāṭibah, Ra's, Saudi Arabia **148** H5
Ha Tien, Viet. **165** K9
Ha Tinh, Viet. **164** F9
Hato Mayor, Dom. Rep. **97** J14
Ha Trung, Viet. **164** E9
Hatteras, Cape, U.S. **91** F16
Hattiesburg, Miss., U.S. **93** H11
Hatunuru, Indonesia **167** H13
Hatutu, island, Marquesas Is., Fr. **191** E13
Hatvan, Hung. **127** J13
Hat Yai, Thai. **165** M7
Haud, plateau, Eth. **177** F14
Haugesund, Nor. **118** J9
Haugsdorf, Aust. **127** H12
Hauido, island, S. Korea **161** Q5
Haukeligrend, Nor. **119** J10
Haukipudas, Fin. **119** E14
Haukivesi, lake, Fin. **119** G15
Haulover, Nicar. **95** K14
Hauraki Gulf, N.Z. **189** C15
Hautere see Solander Island, N.Z. **189** M11
Havana see La Habana, Cuba **96** E3
Havant, Eng., U.K. **121** R10
Havel, river, Ger. **126** C8
Havelberg, Ger. **126** C8
Haveli, Pak. **153** M9
Haverfordwest (Hwlffordd), Wales, U.K. **121** Q6
Haverhill, Eng., U.K. **121** P11
Haveri, India **155** K3
Havířov, Czech Rep. **127** G12
Havlíčkův Brod, Czech Rep. **127** G10
Havre, Mont., U.S. **92** B6
Havre-St.-Pierre, Que., Can. **89** J14
Havza, Turk. **144** C8

Hawai'i, *U.S.* **93** K12
Hawai'i, island, *U.S.* **91** M13
Hawaiian Islands, *U.S., Pac. Oc.*
190 A9
Hawangdeungdo, island, *S. Korea*
161 P5
Hawarden, *Wales, U.K.* **121** N8
Hawea, Lake, *N.Z.* **189** K12
Ḥawf, *Yemen* **149** K10
Hāwī, *Hawaii, U.S.* **93** L13
Hawick, *Scot., U.K.* **120** J8
Hawke Bay, *N.Z.* **189** F17
Hawker, *S. Austral., Austral.* **187** J11
Hawkeye Point, *U.S.* **91** D10
Hawr as Suwayqīyah, lake, *Iraq*
148 D8
Hawthorne, *Nev., U.S.* **92** E3
Hay, river, *Alta., Can.* **88** G6
Hay, river, *Austral.* **185** F11
Hayange, *Fr.* **124** J10
Hayes, river, *Man., Can.* **88** H9
Hayes Peninsula, *Greenland, Den.*
84 C7
Hayling Island, *Eng., U.K.* **121** R10
Haymā', *Oman* **149** J12
Haymana, *Turk.* **144** D6
Haynin, *Yemen* **148** L8
Hayrabolu, *Turk.* **144** B2
Hay River, *N.W.T., Can.* **88** G6
Hays, *Kans., U.S.* **92** F9
Haysyn, *Ukr.* **135** L4
Hayvoron, *Ukr.* **135** L4
Hazarajat, region, *Afghan.* **153** K4
Hazard, *Ky., U.S.* **93** F14
Hazar Gölü, *Turk.* **145** E11
Hazar Qadam, *Afghan.* **153** K4
Ḥaẓawẓā' Sabkhat, *Saudi Arabia*
148 D5
Hazebrouck, *Fr.* **124** H7
Hazen Strait, *Can.* **84** C6
Hazro, *Turk.* **145** E11
Head of Bight, *Austral.* **184** J9
Hearst, *Ont., Can.* **89** K11
Hearst Island, *Antarctica* **200** D4
Herat (Hirat), *Afghan.* **152** J2
Heart, river, *U.S.* **90** B8
Heath, Pointe, *Que., Can.* **89** J15
Hebei, *China* **158** D5
Hebel, *Qnsld., Austral.* **187** H14
Hebi, *Henan, China* **158** F4
Hebrides, Sea of the, *Scot., U.K.*
120 G4
Hebron *see* Al Khalīl, *West Bank*
147 K4
Hecate Strait, *B.C., Can.* **88** G3
Hechi, *China* **157** K12
Hecho, *Sp.* **123** B12
Hecla, Cape, *Nunavut, Can.* **89** A10
Heddal, *Nor.* **119** J10
Hédé, *Fr.* **125** L4
Hede *see* Sheyang, *Jiangsu, China*
158 G8
Hede, *Sweden* **119** G11
Hedo Misaki, *Japan* **163** Q2
Heerenveen, *Neth.* **124** E10
Ḥefa (Haifa), *Israel* **146** H4
Hefei, *Anhui, China* **158** J6
Hefeng, *Hubei, China* **159** K1
Hegura Jima, *Japan* **162** G7
Heichengzi, *Liaoning, China* **158** A8
Heide, *Ger.* **126** B6
Heidelberg, *Ger.* **126** G5
Heidenheim, *Ger.* **126** H6
Heihe, *China* **157** B16
Heilbronn, *Ger.* **126** G6
Heilong Jiang, river, *China* **157** B17
Heilprin Glacier, *Greenland, Den.*
199 K11
Heimaey, island, *Ice.* **118** E3
Heinola, *Fin.* **119** G15

Heishan, *Liaoning, China* **158** A9
Heishui, *Liaoning, China* **158** A7
Heisker Islands *see* Na h-Eileanan
Theisgeir, *Scot., U.K.* **120** F4
Hejaz *see* Al Ḥijāz, region, *Saudi Arabia*
148 F4
Hejian, *Hebei, China* **158** D5
Hejing, *China* **156** D7
Hekimhan, *Turk.* **144** E9
Hekla, peak, *Ice.* **118** E3
Hekou, *China* **157** L11
Hekou, *Shandong, China* **158** D7
Helagsfjället, peak, *Sweden* **119** G11
Helena, *Mont., U.S.* **92** B6
Helena *see* Makroníssi, island, *Gr.*
133 G10
Helengili, island, *Maldives* **155** Q3
Helen Island, *Palau* **190** D3
Helgoländer Bucht, *Ger.* **126** B5
Helicon *see* Elikónas, peak, *Gr.* **132** G8
Hell, *Nor.* **119** G11
Hellevoetsluis, *Neth.* **124** F9
Hellín, *Sp.* **123** H11
Hellissandur, *Ice.* **118** D2
Hell-Ville *see* Andoany, *Madag.*
181 D14
Helmand, river, *Afghan.* **153** M2
Helmsdale, *Scot., U.K.* **120** E7
Helsingborg, *Sweden* **119** L12
Helsingfors *see* Helsinki, *Fin.* **119** H15
Helsinki (Helsingfors), *Fin.* **119** H15
Henan, *China* **158** G3
Henashi Zaki, *Japan* **162** E9
Hendaye, *Fr.* **125** S3
Hendek, *Turk.* **144** C5
Henderson Island, *U.K., Pac. Oc.*
191 G15
Hengchun, *Taiwan, China* **159** R8
Hengduan Shan, *China* **156** J9
Hengelo, *Neth.* **124** F11
Hengshan, *Hunan, China* **159** M3
Hengshan, *Shaanxi, China* **158** D1
Heng Shan, *Shanxi, China* **158** C4
Hengshui, *Hebei, China* **158** D5
Hengyang, *Hunan, China* **159** M3
Heniches'k, *Ukr.* **135** N7
Hennebont, *Fr.* **125** L2
Hennigsdorf, *Ger.* **126** D8
Henrietta, Ostrov, *Russ.* **137** B13
Henrietta Island, *Russ.* **198** E6
Henrietta Maria, Cape, *Nunavut, Can.*
89 H11
Henry Kater Peninsula, *Nunavut, Can.*
89 D12
Heping, *Guangdong, China* **159** P4
Hequ, *Shanxi, China* **158** C3
Heráklion *see* Iráklio, *Gr.* **133** M11
Herald, Ostrov, *Russ.* **137** A14
Herald Cays, *Austral.* **185** C15
Herbault, *Fr.* **125** M6
Herbert, *Sask., Can.* **88** K7
Herbert Downs, *Qnsld., Austral.*
187 F11
Hercules Dome, *Antarctica* **200** G9
Hereford, *Eng., U.K.* **121** P8
Hereford, *Tex., U.S.* **92** G8
Hereheretue, island, *Fr. Polynesia, Fr.*
191 G13
Herford, *Ger.* **126** D5
Herisau, *Switz.* **128** A4
Hérisson, *Fr.* **125** N8
Heritage Range, *Antarctica* **200** F7
Herlacher, Cape, *Antarctica* **200** J5
Herlen, river, *Mongolia* **157** C13
Herm, island, *Channel Is., U.K.*
121 T8
Hermannsburg, *N. Terr., Austral.*
186 F9
Hermanus, *S. Af.* **180** K6
Hermit Islands, *P.N.G.* **188** F4

Hermon, Mount, *Leb., Syr.* **146** G5
Hermosillo, *Mex.* **94** C4
Hernando, *Arg.* **110** G5
Hernani, *Sp.* **123** B10
Herne, *Ger.* **126** E5
Herrera, *Arg.* **110** F6
Herrera del Duque, *Sp.* **122** G8
Herrera de Pisuerga, *Sp.* **122** C8
Herschel Island, *Yukon, Can.* **88** C5
Hersónissos Akrotírio, *Gr.* **133** L10
Hertford, *Eng., U.K.* **121** P10
Hervás, *Sp.* **122** E7
Hervey Bay, *Qnsld., Austral.* **187** G16
Hervey Bay, *Austral.* **185** G16
Hervey Islands, *Cook Is., N.Z.* **191** G11
Herzberg, *Ger.* **126** E8
Hesar Range, *Afghan.* **152** J4
Heshun, *Shanxi, China* **158** E4
Heungdeok, *S. Korea* **161** P6
Heunghae, *S. Korea* **161** N10
Heyang, *Shaanxi, China* **158** F2
Heyuan, *Guangdong, China* **159** Q4
Hezār, Kūh-e, *Iran* **149** E12
Heze, *Shandong, China* **158** F5
Hezhou (Babu), *Guangxi Zhuangzu,*
China **159** P2
Hezuo, *China* **157** G11
Hibbing, *Minn., U.S.* **93** B10
Hicacos, Península de, *Cuba* **96** E4
Hickmann, *Arg.* **110** C6
Hicks Bay, *N.Z.* **189** D17
Hidaka Sammyaku, *Japan* **162** D10
Hidalgo del Parral, *Mex.* **94** D6
Hierro, island, *Spain* **174** C3
Higginsville, *W. Austral., Austral.*
186 J5
Highlands, region, *Scot., U.K.* **120** G6
High Level, *Alta., Can.* **88** G6
High Plains, *U.S.* **90** F8
High Point, *U.S.* **91** D16
High Rock, *Bahamas* **96** A7
High Willhays, peak, *Eng., U.K.*
121 R6
Higüero, Punta, *P.R., U.S.* **97** J16
Higüey, *Dom. Rep.* **97** J15
Hiiumaa (Dagö), island, *Est.* **119** J14
Híjar, *Sp.* **123** D12
Ḥijāz, Jabal al, *Saudi Arabia* **148** J6
Hikueru, island, *Fr. Polynesia, Fr.*
191 F13
Hikurangi, peak, *N.Z.* **189** D17
Hildesheim, *Ger.* **126** D6
Hillary Coast, *Antarctica* **201** K10
Hillsborough, *Grenada* **99** G13
Hillsborough, *N. Ire., U.K.* **121** L5
Hillside, *W. Austral., Austral.* **186** E4
Hillston, *N.S.W., Austral.* **187** K13
Hillswick, *Scot., U.K.* **120** B9
Hilo, *Hawaii, U.S.* **93** M13
Hilo Bay, *U.S.* **91** M13
Hilvan, *Turk.* **145** F10
Himadítida, Límni, *Gr.* **132** C7
Himalaya, range, *Asia* **140** G8
Ḥimar, Wādī al, *Syr.* **146** C9
Himatnagar, *India* **154** F3
Himeji, *Japan* **162** J6
Ḥimş (Homs), *Syr.* **146** E6
Hınako, Kepulauan, *Indonesia*
166 G3
Hinche, *Haiti* **97** H12
Hinchinbrook Island, *Austral.*
185 D14
Hindaun, *India* **154** E4
Hindmarsh, Lake, *Austral.* **185** L12
Hindu Kush, range, *Asia* **140** G7
Hines Creek, *Alta., Can.* **88** H5
Hinganghat, *India* **154** H5
Hingol, river, *Pak.* **153** Q3
Hingorja, *Pak.* **153** P5
Hinidan, *Pak.* **153** Q5

Hınıs, *Turk.* **145** D12
Hinlopen Strait, *Nor.* **199** F12
Hinnøya, island, *Nor.* **119** C12
Hinthada, *Myanmar* **164** G4
Híos (Chios), *Gr.* **133** F12
Híos (Chios), island, *Gr.* **133** F12
Hippolytushoef, *Neth.* **124** E9
Hirado Shima, *Japan* **163** K3
Hiranai, *Japan* **162** E10
Hira Se, island, *Japan* **163** M3
Hirat *see* Herat, *Afghan.* **152** J2
Hirata, *Japan* **162** J5
Hirfanlı Barajı, *Turk.* **144** E6
Hiroo, *Japan* **162** D11
Hirosaki, *Japan* **162** E9
Hiroshima, *Japan* **163** K5
Hirson, *Fr.* **124** J9
Hîrşova, *Rom.* **131** E15
Hisarönü, *Turk.* **144** B6
Ḥismá, desert, *Jordan, Saudi Arabia*
148 E4
Hispaniola, island, *N. Amer.* **85** P10
Ḥisyah, *Syr.* **146** E6
Hita, *Japan* **163** K4
Hitachi, *Japan* **162** H9
Hitadu, island, *Maldives* **155** R2
Hitadu, island, *Maldives* **155** S2
Hitoyoshi, *Japan* **163** L3
Hitra, island, *Nor.* **119** F10
Hiva Oa, island, *Marquesas Is., Fr.*
191 E13
Hizan, *Turk.* **145** F13
Hjälmaren, lake, *Sweden* **119** J13
Hjørring, *Den.* **119** K11
Hkakabo Razi, peak, *Myanmar*
164 A5
Hlohovec, *Slovakia* **127** H12
Hlukhiv, *Ukr.* **134** J6
Hlybokaye, *Belarus* **134** G4
Hněvkovice, *Czech Rep.* **127** G10
Hnúšt'a, *Slovakia* **127** H13
Ho, *Ghana* **178** E9
Hoa Binh, *Viet.* **164** E9
Hoai An, *Viet.* **164** H11
Hoanib, river, *Namibia* **180** E4
Hoare Bay, *Nunavut, Can.* **89** E13
Hoban, *N. Korea* **160** E7
Hobart, *Tas., Austral.* **187** L18
Hobbs, *N. Mex., U.S.* **92** H7
Hobbs Coast, *Antarctica* **200** K6
Hoboksar, *China* **156** C7
Hobq Shamo, *Nei Mongol, China*
158 B1
Hobro, *Den.* **119** K11
Hobyo, *Somalia* **177** F15
Ho Chi Minh City (Saigon), *Viet.*
165 K10
Hŏch'ŏn, river, *N. Korea* **160** D8
Hochstetterbugt, fjord, *Greenland, Den.*
84 C7
Hochstetter Forland, region,
Greenland, Den. **199** H13
Hodgson Downs, *N. Terr., Austral.*
187 C10
Hódmezővásárhely, *Hung.* **127** K13
Hodo, *N. Korea* **160** G7
Hodonín, *Czech Rep.* **127** H11
Hodrogö, *Mongolia* **157** B10
Hoech'ang, *N. Korea* **160** H6
Hoedic, Île, *Fr.* **125** M3
Hoedspruit, *S. Af.* **180** G9
Hoenggando, island, *S. Korea*
161 S5
Hoengseong, *S. Korea* **161** L8
Hoeryŏng, *N. Korea* **160** B10
Hoeyang, *N. Korea* **160** H7
Hof, *Ger.* **126** F7
Höfdakaupstaður, *Ice.* **118** D4
Höfn, *Ice.* **118** E4
Hofsjökull, glacier, *Ice.* **118** E4

Hog Cay, *Bahamas* **96** D9
Hoggar *see* Ahaggar, range, *Alg.*
  174 E8
Hohenems, *Ger.* **126** J6
Hohe Tauern, mountains, *Aust.*
  126 K8
Hohhot, *Nei Mongol, China* **158** B3
Hoh Xil Shan, *China* **156** F7
Hoi An, *Viet.* **164** G11
Hokitika, *N.Z.* **189** H13
Hokkaidō, island, *Japan* **162** D11
Hola Prystan', *Ukr.* **135** N6
Holbrook, *Ariz., U.S.* **92** G5
Hold with Hope, cape, *Greenland, Den.*
  199 H14
Holguín, *Cuba* **96** G8
Hollick-Kenyon Plateau, *Antarctica*
  200 G6
Hollum, *Neth.* **124** D10
Hollywood, *Fla., U.S.* **93** K15
Holman, *N.W.T., Can.* **88** D7
Hólmavík, *Ice.* **118** D3
Holme Bay, *Antarctica* **201** D15
Holm Land, *Greenland, Den.* **199** G12
Holot Ḥaluẓa, desert, *Israel* **147** K3
Holroyd, river, *Austral.* **185** B13
Holstebro, *Den.* **119** L10
Holsteinborg *see* Sisimiut, *Greenland,*
  Den. **199** M13
Holsworthy, *Eng., U.K.* **121** R6
Holy Cross, *Alas., U.S.* **92** L2
Holyhead (Caergybi), *Wales, U.K.*
  121 M6
Holy Island (Lindisfarne), *Eng., U.K.*
  120 J9
Holy Island, *Wales, U.K.* **121** N6
Hombori, *Mali* **174** G6
Homburg, *Ger.* **126** G4
Home Bay, *Nunavut, Can.* **89** D12
Homer, *Alas., U.S.* **92** L3
Homestead, *Fla., U.S.* **93** K15
Hommalinn, *Myanmar* **164** C4
Homnabad, *India* **154** J4
Homs *see* Ḥimṣ, *Syr.* **146** E6
Homyel', *Belarus* **134** J5
Honam, *N. Korea* **160** D10
Honavar, *India* **155** K3
Honaz, *Turk.* **144** F3
Honda, *Col.* **106** E6
Hondo, *Japan* **163** L3
Honduras, *N. Amer.* **87** Q7
Honduras, Gulf of, *Belize, Guatemala,*
  Hond. **95** J12
Hønefoss, *Nor.* **119** H11
Hong (Red), river, *Viet.* **164** D8
Hong'an, *Hubei, China* **158** J4
Hongcheon, *S. Korea* **161** K8
Hongdo, island, *S. Korea* **161** Q4
Hong Gai, *Viet.* **164** E10
Honggong, *Guangdong, China* **159** P3
Honggun, *N. Korea* **160** E8
Honghai Wan, *Guangdong, China*
  159 R4
Honghu, *Hunan, China* **159** K4
Hong Hu, *Hubei, China* **159** K3
Hongjiang, *Hunan, China* **159** M1
Hong Kong, *Hong Kong S.A.R., China*
  159 R4
Hong Kong (Xianggang), S.A.R., *China*
  159 R4
Hongliu, river, *Nei Mongol, China*
  158 D1
Hongliuyuan, *China* **156** E9
Hongning *see* Wulian, *Shandong, China*
  158 F7
Hongnong, *S. Korea* **161** P6
Hongor, *Mongolia* **157** C13
Hongseong, *S. Korea* **161** M6
Hongshan, *Nei Mongol, China* **158** A7
Hongshui, river, *China* **157** L12

Hongwŏn, *N. Korea* **160** F8
Hongwŏn-man, bay, *N. Korea* **160** F8
Hongyang, *Guangdong, China* **159** Q5
Hongze, *Jiangsu, China* **158** H7
Hongze Hu, *Jiangsu, China* **158** H7
Honiara, *Solomon Is.* **190** E6
Honiton, *Eng., U.K.* **121** R8
Honjō, *Japan* **162** F9
Honoka'a, *Hawaii, U.S.* **93** M13
Honolulu, *Hawaii, U.S.* **93** L12
Hon Quan, *Viet.* **165** K10
Honshū, island, *Japan* **162** H5
Hood *see* Española, Isla, *Ecua.*
  106 F3
Hood, Mount, *U.S.* **90** B3
Hood Point, *Austral.* **184** L5
Hoogeveen, *Neth.* **124** E10
Hook Head, *Ire.* **121** P4
Hoonah, *Alas., U.S.* **92** L5
Hooper, Cape, *Nunavut, Can.* **89** E12
Hooper Bay, *Alas., U.S.* **92** L1
Hoorn, *Neth.* **124** E9
Hoosier Hill, *U.S.* **91** E13
Hopa, *Turk.* **145** C12
Hope, *Ark., U.S.* **93** H10
Hope, Cape, *Nunavut, Can.* **88** D7
Hope, Lake, *Austral.* **184** K5
Hope, Point, *U.S.* **198** H4
Hopedale, *Nfld. & Lab., Can.* **89** H14
Hope Island, *Nor.* **199** E13
Hopelchén, *Mex.* **95** G11
Hope Point, *Myanmar* **164** H5
Hopetoun, *W. Austral., Austral.* **186** K5
Hope Town, *Bahamas* **96** A8
Hopetown, *S. Af.* **180** J7
Hopewell Islands, *Nunavut, Can.*
  89 H11
Hopkins, Lake, *Austral.* **184** F8
Horasan, *Turk.* **145** D12
Hordil Sarïdag, *Mongolia* **157** B10
Horgos, *Serb.* **130** C9
Hörh Uul, *Mongolia* **157** E11
Horinger, *Nei Mongol, China* **158** B3
Horki, *Belarus* **134** H5
Horlick Mountains, *Antarctica*
  200 G8
Horlivka, *Ukr.* **135** L8
Ḥormak, *Iran* **149** E13
Hormuz, Strait of, *Iran, Oman* **149** F11
Horn, Cape *see* Hornos, Cabo de, *Chile*
  111 T5
Hornavan, lake, *Sweden* **119** E12
Hornby Hill, *Nunavut, Can.* **88** E7
Horne, Îles de, *Fr., Pac. Oc.* **190** F9
Hornos, Cabo de (Horn, Cape), *Chile*
  111 T5
Horodnya, *Ukr.* **134** J5
Horodyshche, *Ukr.* **135** L5
Horo Shan, *China* **156** D7
Horqueta, *Para.* **109** J10
Horsham, *Eng., U.K.* **121** R6
Horsham, *Vic., Austral.* **187** L12
Horta, *Azores, Port.* **122** L2
Horten, *Nor.* **119** J11
Horton, river, *N.W.T., Can.* **88** D6
Horvat 'Avedat (Eboda), ruins, *Israel*
  147 L4
Hosdrug, *India* **155** L3
Hoshab, *Pak.* **153** Q3
Hoshangabad, *India* **154** G5
Hoste, Isla, *Chile* **111** T4
Hosur, *India* **155** L4
Hot, *Thai.* **164** F6
Hotan, *China* **156** F5
Hotan, river, *China* **156** E6
Hot Springs, *Ark., U.S.* **93** G11
Hot Springs, *S. Dak., U.S.* **92** D8
Hottah Lake, *N.W.T., Can.* **88** E6
Hotte, Massif de la, *Haiti* **97** J10
Hottentot Bay, *Namibia* **180** H5

Houat, Île, *Fr.* **125** M3
Houayxay, *Laos* **164** E7
Houffalize, *Belg.* **124** H10
Houlton, *Me., U.S.* **93** B17
Houlung, *Taiwan, China* **159** P8
Houma, *La., U.S.* **93** J11
Houma, *Shanxi, China* **158** F2
Hourtin, *Fr.* **125** Q4
Houston, *Tex., U.S.* **93** J10
Houtman Abrolhos, *Austral.* **184** J3
Hovd (Dund-Us), *Mongolia* **156** C9
Hovd, *Mongolia* **157** D11
Hovd, river, *Mongolia* **156** B9
Hovgaard Ø, islands, *Greenland, Den.*
  199 I12
Hövsgöl, *Mongolia* **157** D12
Hövsgöl Nuur, *Mongolia* **157** B11
Howar, Wadi, *Sudan* **176** C9
Howard Lake, *N.W.T., Can.* **88** G8
Howe, Cape, *Austral.* **185** M15
Howland Island, *U.S., Pac. Oc.* **190** D9
Ho Xa, *Viet.* **164** G10
Hoxud, *China* **156** D7
Hoy, island, *Scot., U.K.* **120** D7
Høyanger, *Nor.* **118** H9
Hoyerswerda, *Ger.* **126** E9
Hozat, *Turk.* **145** E10
Hpa-an, *Myanmar* **164** G5
Hradec Králové, *Czech Rep.* **127** F10
Hrazdan, river, *Arm.* **145** D14
Hrebenne, *Pol.* **127** F15
Hrissí, island, *Gr.* **133** M12
Hrissoúpoli, *Gr.* **133** B11
Hristianí, island, *Gr.* **133** K11
Hrodna, *Belarus* **134** H2
Hron, river, *Slovakia* **127** H13
Hrubieszów, *Pol.* **127** E15
Hsiaohungtou Yü, *Taiwan, China*
  159 R9
Hsi-hseng, *Myanmar* **164** E5
Hsinchu, *Taiwan, China* **159** P9
Hsinhua, *Taiwan, China* **159** Q8
Hsinying, *Taiwan, China* **159** Q8
Hsipaw, *Myanmar* **164** D5
Huachi, *China* **157** G12
Huacho, *Peru* **108** F4
Huade, *Nei Mongol, China* **158** A4
Huadian, *China* **157** D16
Hua Hin, *Thai.* **164** J6
Huahine, island, *Fr. Polynesia, Fr.*
  191 F12
Huai, river, *Anhui, China* **158** H6
Huai'an, *Hebei, China* **158** B4
Huai'an, *Jiangsu, China* **158** H7
Huai'ancheng, *Hebei, China* **158** B4
Huaibei, *Anhui, China* **158** G6
Huaibin, *Henan, China* **158** H5
Huaihua, *Hunan, China* **159** M1
Huaiji, *Guangdong, China* **159** Q2
Huailai, *Hebei, China* **158** B5
Huainan, *Anhui, China* **158** H6
Huaining, *Anhui, China* **159** K6
Huairen, *Shanxi, China* **158** C4
Huai Yang, *Thai.* **165** K6
Huaiyin, *Jiangsu, China* **158** H7
Huaiyuan, *Anhui, China* **158** H6
Huajuapan de León, *Mex.* **94** H8
Hualfín, *Arg.* **110** E4
Hualian *see* Hualien, *Taiwan, China*
  159 Q9
Hualien (Hualian), *Taiwan, China*
  159 Q9
Huallaga, river, *Peru* **108** E4
Huambo, *Angola* **180** C5
Huancané, *Peru* **108** G6
Huancavelica, *Peru* **108** F5
Huancayo, *Peru* **108** F5
Huang (Yellow), river, *China* **157** F13
Huangchuan, *Henan, China* **158** J5
Huanggang, *Hubei, China* **159** K4

Huanggang Shan, *Fujian, China*
  159 M6
Huanghua, *Hebei, China* **158** D6
Huanglong (Shipu), *Shaanxi, China*
  158 F1
Huangmao Jian, peak, *Zhejiang, China*
  159 M7
Huangpu, *Guangdong, China* **159** Q3
Huangqi Hai, *Nei Mongol, China*
  158 B4
Huangshan, *Anhui, China* **159** K7
Huang Shan, *Anhui, China* **159** K7
Huangshi, *Hubei, China* **159** K5
Huangtang Hu, *Hubei, China* **159** K4
Huangxian, *Shandong, China* **158** D8
Huangyan, *Zhejiang, China* **159** L9
Huang (Yellow), Mouth of the,
  Shandong, China **158** D7
Huangzhu, *Hainan, China* **159** T1
Huanren, *Liaoning, China* **158** B11
Huanta, *Peru* **108** F5
Huantai (Suozhen), *Shandong, China*
  158 E7
Huánuco, *Peru* **108** E4
Huanxian, *China* **157** F12
Huara, *Chile* **110** B3
Huaral, *Peru* **108** F4
Huaraz, *Peru* **108** E4
Huarmey, *Peru* **108** F4
Huarong, *Hunan, China* **159** L3
Huasco, *Chile* **110** F2
Hua Shan, *Shaanxi, China* **158** G2
Huashaoying, *Hebei, China* **158** B5
Huashi Shan, *Guangdong, China*
  159 P4
Huatabampo, *Mex.* **94** D4
Huaura, *Peru* **108** F4
Huaxian, *Henan, China* **158** F4
Hubei, *China* **158** J3
Hubei Kou, pass, *Shaanxi, China*
  158 H1
Hubli, *India* **155** K3
Hudiksvall, *Sweden* **119** G12
Hudson, river, *U.S.* **91** D16
Hudson Bay, *Sask., Can.* **88** J8
Hudson Bay, *Nunavut, Can.* **89** G10
Hudson Strait, *Nunavut, Can.* **89** F12
Hue, *Viet.* **164** G10
Huehuetenango, *Guatemala* **95** J11
Huelma, *Sp.* **122** J9
Huelva, *Sp.* **122** J6
Huesca, *Sp.* **123** C12
Huéscar, *Sp.* **123** J10
Hughenden, *Qnsld., Austral.* **187** E13
Hughes, *Alas., U.S.* **92** K3
Hughes Bay, *Antarctica* **200** C3
Hugh Town, *Eng., U.K.* **121** S5
Hugli, river, *India* **154** G9
Hui'an, *Fujian, China* **159** P7
Huichang, *Jiangxi, China* **159** P5
Hŭich'ŏn, *N. Korea* **160** F5
Huidong, *Guangdong, China* **159** Q4
Huilai, *Guangdong, China* **159** Q5
Huimin, *Shandong, China* **158** E6
Huinca Renancó, *Arg.* **110** H5
Hŭisaek-pong, peak, *N. Korea*
  160 D7
Huitong, *Hunan, China* **159** M1
Huixian, *Henan, China* **158** F4
Huiyang, *Guangdong, China* **159** R4
Huizhou, *Guangdong, China* **159** Q4
Hukawng Valley, *Myanmar* **164** B5
Hulan, *China* **157** C16
Ḥulayfā', *Saudi Arabia* **148** F6
Hulin, *China* **157** C17
Hulingol, *China* **157** C14
Hulst, *Neth.* **124** G9
Huludao (Jinxi), *Liaoning, China*
  158 B8
Hulun Nur, *China* **157** B14

Hulyaypole, *Ukr.* **135** M7
Huma, *China* **157** A16
Humacao, *P.R., U.S.* **97** J17
Humahuaca, *Arg.* **110** C5
Humaitá, *Braz.* **108** D8
Humansdorp, *S. Af.* **180** K7
Ḥumar, *U.A.E.* **149** H10
Humbe, *Angola* **180** E5
Humber, river, *Eng., U.K.* **121** M10
Humboldt, *Sask., Can.* **88** J7
Humboldt, river, *U.S.* **90** D4
Humboldt Glacier see Sermersuaq,
   Greenland, Den. **199** J11
Hūmedān, *Iran* **149** G13
Humen, *Guangdong, China* **159** R3
Humenné, *Slovakia* **127** H14
Humphreys Peak, *U.S.* **90** G5
Hūn, *Lib.* **175** C11
Hun, river, *Liaoning, China* **158** B9
Húnaflói, bay, *Ice.* **118** D3
Hunan, *China* **159** M2
Hunedoara, *Rom.* **131** D11
Hungary, *Europe* **116** J9
Hŭngbong, *N. Korea* **160** F7
Hungerford, *Qnsld., Austral.* **187** H13
Hŭngnam, *N. Korea* **160** G7
Hungund, *India* **155** K4
Hunjiang, *China* **157** D16
Hunstanton, *Eng., U.K.* **121** N11
Hunsur, *India* **155** L4
Hunt, *Mongolia* **157** C10
Hunter, island, *Vanuatu* **190** G8
Hunter Islands, *Austral.* **185** K17
Huntington, *W. Va., U.S.* **93** E14
Huntly, *N.Z.* **189** D15
Huntly, *Scot., U.K.* **120** F8
Huntsville, *Ala., U.S.* **93** G13
Huntsville, *Tex., U.S.* **93** J10
Hunucmá, *Mex.* **95** G11
Hunyuan, *Shanxi, China* **158** C4
Hunza, region, *Pak.* **152** H9
Huocheng, *China* **156** C6
Huojia, *Henan, China* **158** F4
Huon, Île, *New Caledonia, Fr.* **190** F7
Huong Hoa, *Viet.* **164** G10
Huon Gulf, *P.N.G.* **188** E6
Huon Peninsula, *P.N.G.* **188** E6
Huoqiu, *Anhui, China* **158** H5
Huoshan, *Anhui, China* **158** J5
Hupo, *S. Korea* **161** M10
Hurdiyo, *Somalia* **177** E15
Hurghada, *Egypt* **175** D15
Hurmagai, *Pak.* **153** P3
Huron, *S. Dak., U.S.* **92** C9
Huron, Lake, *Can., U.S.* **91** C13
Húsavík, *Ice.* **118** D4
Huşi, *Rom.* **131** C15
Huslia, *U.S.* **198** J4
Husum, *Ger.* **126** A6
Hutag, *Mongolia* **157** B11
Hutchinson, *Kans., U.S.* **92** F9
Huthi, *Thai.* **164** G6
Hutuo, river, *Shanxi, China* **158** D4
Huvadu see Suvadiva Atoll, island,
   Maldives **155** R2
Huy, *Belg.* **124** H10
Hüyük, *Turk.* **144** F5
Huzhou, *Zhejiang, China* **159** K8
Hvammstangi, *Ice.* **118** D3
Hvannadalshnúkur, peak, *Ice.*
   199 H16
Hvar (Pharus), island, *Croatia*
   130 G6
Hvarski Kanal, *Croatia* **130** G6
Hveragerdi, *Ice.* **118** E3
Hvítá, river, *Ice.* **118** E3
Hwaaksan, peak, *S. Korea* **161** K7
Hwacheon, *S. Korea* **160** J7
Hwadae, *N. Korea* **160** E10
Hwajeon, *S. Korea* **161** N9

Hwajin, *N. Korea* **160** H4
Hwange, *Zimb.* **180** E8
Hwangjin, *N. Korea* **160** D10
Hwangju, *N. Korea* **160** H5
Hwangsuwŏn, *N. Korea* **160** E8
Hwap'yŏng, *N. Korea* **160** D6
Hwaseong, *S. Korea* **161** L6
Hwasŏng, *N. Korea* **160** D10
Hwasun, *S. Korea* **161** Q6
Hwayang, *S. Korea* **161** P9
Hwlffordd see Haverfordwest, *Wales,
   U.K.* **121** Q6
Hyangsan, *N. Korea* **160** F5
Hyargas Nuur, *Mongolia* **156** B9
Hydaburg, *Alas., U.S.* **92** M6
Hyden, *W. Austral., Austral.* **186** K5
Hyderabad, *India* **154** J5
Hyderabad, *Pak.* **153** R5
Hydra see Ídra, island, *Gr.* **132** H9
Hyeolli, *S. Korea* **161** K8
Hyères, *Fr.* **125** S11
Hyères, Îles d' (Or, Les Îles d'), *Fr.*
   125 S11
Hyesan, *N. Korea* **160** D8
Hyŏlli, *N. Korea* **160** J7
Hyrra Banda, *Cen. Af. Rep.* **176** F8
Hyrynsalmi, *Fin.* **119** E15

Í

Ía, *Gr.* **133** K11
Iaco, river, *Braz.* **108** E6
Ialomiţa, river, *Rom.* **131** E14
Iamara, *P.N.G.* **188** G7
Iar Connaught, region, *Ire.* **121** M2
Iascaigh see Easky, *Ire.* **121** L2
Iaşi, *Rom.* **131** B14
Íasmos, *Gr.* **133** B11
Iauaretê, *Braz.* **108** B6
Ibadan, *Nig.* **179** D10
Ibagué, *Col.* **106** F6
Ibarra, *Ecua.* **106** H4
Ibb, *Yemen* **148** M7
Iberá, Laguna, *Arg.* **110** F8
Iberia, *Peru* **108** F6
Iberian Peninsula, *Europe* **114** K4
Ibipetuba, *Braz.* **109** F13
Ibiza see Eivissa, *Sp.* **123** G14
Ibiza (Ivisa), island, *Sp.* **123** G14
Iblei, Monti, *It.* **129** P9
Ibn Hani', Ra's, *Syr.* **146** D5
Ibo, *Mozambique* **181** C12
Iboperenda, *Bol.* **108** H8
Ibotirama, *Braz.* **109** F14
Ibrā', *Oman* **149** H12
Ibra, Wadi, *Sudan* **176** E8
'Ibrī, *Oman* **149** H12
Ibusuki, *Japan* **163** M3
Ica, *Peru* **108** G5
Içá, river, *Braz.* **108** C6
Ica, river, *Peru* **108** G5
Içana, *Braz.* **108** B7
Içana, river, *Braz.* **108** B7
İçel (Mersin), *Turk.* **144** G7
Iceland, *Europe* **116** A5
Ichchapuram, *India* **154** H7
Icheon, *S. Korea* **161** L7
Ichikawa, *Japan* **162** J9
Ichinohe, *Japan* **162** E10
Ichinomiya, *Japan* **162** J7
Ichinoseki, *Japan* **162** F10
Ichinskaya Sopka, *Russ.* **137** E17
Ichinskiy, *Russ.* **137** E17
Ichnya, *Ukr.* **135** K6
Ich'ŏn, *N. Korea* **160** F5
Ich'ŏn, *N. Korea* **160** J6
Icó, *Braz.* **109** D15
Iconium see Konya, *Turk.* **144** F6
Icoraci, *Braz.* **109** C12
Idah, *Nig.* **179** D11

Idaho, *U.S.* **92** B4
Idaho Falls, *Idaho, U.S.* **92** C5
Idanha-a-Nova, *Port.* **122** F5
'Idd el Ghanam, *Sudan* **176** E8
Ideriyn, river, *Mongolia* **157** C10
Idfu, *Egypt* **175** D15
Idi, *Indonesia* **166** F3
Ídi, Óros (Psiloreítis), *Gr.* **133** M11
İdil, *Turk.* **145** F12
Idiofa, *D.R.C.* **176** J7
Idlib, *Syr.* **146** D6
Ídra, *Gr.* **132** H9
Ídra (Hydra), island, *Gr.* **132** H9
Idracowra, *N. Terr., Austral.* **186** F9
Ieper (Ypres), *Belg.* **124** H8
Ierápetra, *Gr.* **133** M12
Ierissós, *Gr.* **132** C9
Ifalik Atoll, *F.S.M.* **190** C4
Ife, *Nig.* **179** D10
Iferouâne, *Niger* **174** F9
Ifjord, *Nor.* **119** B13
Iforas, Adrar des, *Mali* **174** F7
Igara Paraná, river, *Col.* **106** H7
Igarka, *Russ.* **136** F9
Igatpuri, *India* **154** H3
Iğdır, *Turk.* **145** D14
Iglesias, *It.* **129** L2
Igli, *Alg.* **174** C7
Igloolik, *Nunavut, Can.* **89** E10
'Igma, Gebel el, *Egypt* **147** N2
Ignalina, *Lith.* **119** K16
İğneada, *Turk.* **144** B3
İğneada Burnu, *Turk.* **144** B3
Igoumenítsa, *Gr.* **132** D5
Igrim, *Russ.* **136** F7
Iguaçu, Cataratas do, *Arg., Braz.*
   110 D10
Iguala, *Mex.* **94** H8
Igualada, *Sp.* **123** D14
Iguatu, *Braz.* **109** D15
Iguéla, *Gabon* **179** H12
Iguidi, Erg, *Alg., Mauritania* **174** D5
Iharaña (Vohemar), *Madag.*
   181 D15
Ihavandiffulu Atoll, *Maldives*
   155 P2
Ihavandu, island, *Maldives* **155** P2
Ihbulag, *Mongolia* **157** D13
Iheya Rettō, *Japan* **163** Q1
Iheya Shima, *Japan* **163** Q1
Ihosy, *Madag.* **181** F14
Ihu, *P.N.G.* **188** F7
Ihwa, *S. Korea* **161** L6
Ii, *Fin.* **119** E14
Iida, *Japan* **162** J8
Iisalmi, *Fin.* **119** F15
Ijevan, *Arm.* **145** C14
Ijill, Sebkhet, *Mauritania* **174** D4
Ijin-man, bay, *N. Korea* **160** C11
IJmuiden, *Neth.* **124** F9
IJsselmeer, bay, *Neth.* **124** E9
Ijuí, *Braz.* **109** L11
Ikanbujmal, *China* **156** E8
Ikare, *Nig.* **179** D11
Ikaría, island, *Gr.* **133** H12
Ikela, *D.R.C.* **176** H8
Ikerasassuaq (Prins Christian Sound),
   Greenland, Den. **199** M15
Ikertivaq, bay, *Greenland, Den.*
   199 L15
Ikhtiman, *Bulg.* **131** H12
Iki, island, *Japan* **163** K3
İkizdere, *Turk.* **145** C11
Ikopa, river, *Madag.* **181** E14
Ikorodu, *Nig.* **179** E10
Iksan, *S. Korea* **161** N6
Ilagan, *Philippines* **167** B10
Ilave, *Peru* **108** G6
Iława, *Pol.* **127** B12
Ilbilbie, *Qnsld., Austral.* **187** E15

Ile, river, *Kaz.* **151** F13
Île-à-la-Crosse, *Sask., Can.* **88** H7
Ilebo, *D.R.C.* **176** J7
Ilemi Triangle, region, *Kenya*
   177 G11
Ilfracombe, *Wales, U.K.* **121** Q7
Ilgaz, *Turk.* **144** C7
Ilgaz Dağları, *Turk.* **144** C7
Ilgın, *Turk.* **144** E5
Ílhavo, *Port.* **122** E4
Ilhéus, *Braz.* **109** G15
Ilhéus Formigas, island, *Azores, Port.*
   122 M4
Ili, river, *China* **156** D6
Iliamna Lake, *U.S.* **90** L2
İliç, *Turk.* **145** D10
Ilica, *Turk.* **145** D12
Iligan, *Philippines* **167** E11
Ilinden, *Bulg.* **131** J12
Illapel, *Chile* **110** G3
Illéla, *Niger* **174** G8
Illichivs'k, *Ukr.* **135** N5
Illinois, *U.S.* **93** E11
Illinois, river, *U.S.* **91** E11
Illinois Peak, *U.S.* **90** B5
Illizi, *Alg.* **174** D9
Illo, *S. Korea* **161** Q6
Il'men', Ozero, *Russ.* **134** E6
Ilmenau, *Ger.* **126** F7
Ilo, *Peru* **108** H6
Iloilo, *Philippines* **167** D11
Ilorin, *Nig.* **179** D10
Ilovik, island, *Croatia* **130** E4
Ilpyeong, *S. Korea* **161** R6
Il'pyrskiy, *Russ.* **137** D16
Ilulissat (Jakobshavn), *Greenland, Den.*
   199 L13
Imabari, *Japan* **163** K5
Imabetsu, *Japan* **162** E9
Imatra, *Fin.* **119** G16
Imbert, *Dom. Rep.* **97** H13
Imese, *D.R.C.* **176** G7
Īmī, *Eth.* **177** F13
Imías, *Cuba* **97** H10
İmişli, *Azerb.* **145** D16
Imjado, island, *S. Korea* **161** Q5
Immarna, *S. Austral., Austral.* **186** J9
Imola, *It.* **128** E6
Imotski, *Croatia* **130** F6
Imperatriz, *Braz.* **109** D13
Imperia, *It.* **128** E2
Imperial Valley, *U.S.* **90** G4
Imperieuse Reef, *Austral.* **184** D4
Impfondo, *Congo* **179** F15
Imphal, *India* **154** F11
İmralı, island, *Turk.* **144** C3
İmranlı, *Turk.* **145** D10
İmroz see Gökçeada, island, *Turk.*
   144 C1
Imsan, *N. Korea* **160** E7
Imsil, *S. Korea* **161** P7
Imtān, *Syr.* **146** J6
Ina, *Japan* **162** J8
Inaccessible Island, *Atl. Oc.* **171** S2
Inamba Jima, *Japan* **163** K9
In Amenas see I-n-Amenas, *Alg.*
   174 C9
I-n-Amenas (In Amenas), *Alg.*
   174 C9
I-n-Amguel, *Alg.* **174** E8
Inanwatan, *Indonesia* **167** H14
Inari, *Fin.* **119** C14
Inari, lake, *Fin.* **119** C14
Inca, *Sp.* **123** F15
Inca de Oro, *Chile* **110** E3
İncekum Burnu, *Turk.* **144** G7
İncesu, *Turk.* **144** E8
Inchcape see Bell Rock, island, *Scot.,
   U.K.* **120** H8
Incheon (Inch'ŏn), *S. Korea* **161** L6

Inch Island, *Ire.* **121** K4

Inchnadamph, *Scot., U.K.* **120** E6

Inch'ŏn *see* Incheon, *S. Korea* **161** L6

Indawgyi Lake, *Myanmar* **164** C5

Indefatigable *see* Santa Cruz, Isla, *Ecua.* **106** E3

Independence Fjord, *Greenland, Den.* **199** G11

Ĭnderbor, *Kaz.* **150** D5

India, *Asia* **142** J8

Indiana, *U.S.* **93** E12

Indianapolis, *Ind., U.S.* **93** E13

Indigirka, river, *Russ.* **137** D14

Indija, *Serb.* **130** E9

Indira Point, *India* **155** P12

Indochina Peninsula, *Asia* **141** J11

Indonesia, *Asia* **143** L12

Indore, *India* **154** G4

Indravati, river, *India* **154** H6

Indus, river, *India, Pak.* **153** H7

Indus, Mouths of the, *Pak.* **153** R5

Ĭnebolu, *Turk.* **144** B7

Ĭnegöl, *Turk.* **144** D4

I-n-Eker, *Alg.* **174** D8

Ineu, *Rom.* **131** C10

Ingal, *Niger* **174** F9

Ingende, *D.R.C.* **176** H7

Ingeniero Guillermo N. Juárez, *Arg.* **110** C6

Ingeniero Jacobacci, *Arg.* **111** L4

Ingeniero Luiggi, *Arg.* **110** J5

Ingham, *Qnsld., Austral.* **187** D14

Inglefield Land, *Greenland, Den.* **199** J11

Ingolstadt, *Ger.* **126** H7

Ingomar, *S. Austral., Austral.* **187** H10

Ingraj Bazar, *India* **154** F9

Ingrid Christensen Coast, *Antarctica* **201** E15

Ingwiller, *Fr.* **125** K12

Inhambane, *Mozambique* **181** G11

Inharrime, *Mozambique* **181** G10

Inírida, *Col.* **106** F9

Inírida, river, *Col.* **106** F9

Inis *see* Ennis, *Ire.* **121** N2

Inis Ceithlann *see* Enniskillen, *N. Ire., U.K.* **121** L4

Inis Córthaidh *see* Enniscorthy, *Ire.* **121** P4

Inis Díomáin *see* Ennistimon, *Ire.* **121** N2

Inis Eoáin *see* Inishannon, *Ire.* **121** Q2

Inis Gé Theas (Inishkea South), island, *Ire.* **121** L1

Inis Gé Thuaidh (Inishkea North), island, *Ire.* **121** L1

Inishannon (Inis Eoáin), *Ire.* **121** Q2

Inishbofin, island, *Ire.* **121** M1

Inisheer *see* Inis Oírr, island, *Ire.* **121** N2

Inishkea North *see* Inis Gé Thuaidh, island, *Ire.* **121** L1

Inishkea South *see* Inis Gé Theas, island, *Ire.* **121** L1

Inishmaan *see* Inis Meáin, island, *Ire.* **121** N2

Inishmore *see* Árainn, island, *Ire.* **121** N2

Inishmurray, island, *Ire.* **121** L3

Inishowen, Head, *Ire.* **121** K4

Inishshark, island, *Ire.* **121** M1

Inishtrahull (Inis Trá Tholl), island, *Ire.* **120** J4

Inis Meáin (Inishmaan), island, *Ire.* **121** N2

Inis Oírr (Inisheer), island, *Ire.* **121** N2

Inis Trá Tholl *see* Malin Head, cape, *Ire.* **120** J4

Inis Trá Tholl *see* Inishtrahull, island, *Ire.* **120** J4

Inje, *S. Korea* **161** K8

Injune, *Qnsld., Austral.* **187** G15

Inkerman, *Qnsld., Austral.* **187** C12

Inland Niger Delta, *Mali* **174** G6

Inland Sea, *Japan* **163** K5

Inlet, *Nfld. & Lab., Can.* **89** H14

Inn, river, *Ger.* **126** H8

Innamincka, *S. Austral., Austral.* **187** H12

Inner Hebrides, islands, *Scot., U.K.* **120** H5

Inner Mongolia, region, *China* **157** D13

Inner Sound, *Scot., U.K.* **120** F5

Innisfail, *Qnsld., Austral.* **187** D14

Innsbruck, *Aust.* **126** K7

Inongo, *D.R.C.* **176** H7

Inowrocław, *Pol.* **127** C12

I-n-Salah, *Alg.* **174** D8

Insan, *N. Korea* **160** J5

Insar, *Russ.* **134** H11

Inscription, Cape, *Austral.* **184** G2

Insein, *Myanmar* **164** G4

Ĭnönü, *Turk.* **144** D4

Instow, *Eng., U.K.* **121** R7

Inta, *Russ.* **199** A13

Intendente Alvear, *Arg.* **110** J6

International Falls, *Minn., U.S.* **93** B10

Interview Island, *India* **155** L11

Inthanon, Doi, *Thai.* **164** F5

Intiyaco, *Arg.* **110** F7

Inubō Zaki, *Japan* **162** J10

Inukjuak, *Que., Can.* **89** H11

Inuvik, *N.W.T., Can.* **88** D5

Inuya, river, *Peru* **108** F5

Inverbervie, *Scot., U.K.* **120** G8

Invercargill, *N.Z.* **189** L11

Inverell, *N.S.W., Austral.* **187** J15

Invermoriston, *Scot., U.K.* **120** G6

Invershin, *Scot., U.K.* **120** F6

Investigator Strait, *Austral.* **185** L10

Inza, *Russ.* **134** H11

Inzhavino, *Russ.* **134** J10

Inzia, river, *D.R.C.* **176** J6

Ioánina, *Gr.* **132** D6

Iō Jima, *Japan* **163** M3

Ioma, *P.N.G.* **188** D7

Iona, island, *Scot., U.K.* **120** H5

Ionian Sea, *Europe* **114** L9

Iony, Ostrov (Saint Jona Island), *Russ.* **137** G16

Iori, river, *Azerb.* **145** C15

Íos, *Gr.* **133** J11

Íos, island, *Gr.* **133** J11

Iōtori Shima, *Japan* **163** P2

Iowa, *U.S.* **93** D10

Iowa, river, *U.S.* **91** D11

Ipáti, *Gr.* **132** F7

Ipatovo, *Russ.* **135** N10

Ipiales, *Col.* **106** G5

Ipixuna, *Braz.* **108** D6

Ipixuna, river, *Braz.* **108** E5

Ipoh, *Malaysia* **165** N7

Iporá, *Braz.* **109** G12

İpsala, *Turk.* **144** C2

Ipswich, *Eng., U.K.* **121** P12

Iput', river, *Russ.* **134** H6

Iqaluit, *Nunavut, Can.* **89** F12

Iqe, *China* **156** F9

Iquique, *Chile* **110** B3

Iquitos, *Peru* **108** D5

Iracoubo, *Fr. Guiana, Fr.* **107** E16

Ĭrafshān, *Iran* **149** F13

Iraio, ruins, *Gr.* **133** G13

Iráklia, island, *Gr.* **133** J12

Iráklio (Heráklion, Candia), *Gr.* **133** M11

Iran, *Asia* **142** G6

Ĭrānshahr, *Iran* **149** F13

Irapuata, *Mex.* **94** G7

Iraq, *Asia* **142** F5

Irayel', *Russ.* **136** E6

Irazú, Volcán, *C.R.* **95** L14

Irbe Strait, *Est., Latv.* **119** J14

Irbid (Arbela), *Jordan* **146** H5

Ireland (Éire), *Europe* **116** F4

Ireland, island, *Europe* **121** P2

Iret', *Russ.* **137** E16

Irian Jaya, region, *Indonesia* **188** J5

Irimi, *Indonesia* **188** L4

Iringa, *Tanzania* **177** K11

Iriomote Jima, *Japan* **159** P11

Iriri, river, *Braz.* **109** D11

Irīsal, Rhiy di-, *Yemen* **149** M11

Irish Sea, *Ire., U.K.* **121** N5

Irkeshtam, *Kyrg.* **152** F9

Irkutsk, *Russ.* **137** K11

Irmauw, *Indonesia* **167** K14

Iroise, bay, *Fr.* **125** L1

Iron Gate Dam, *Rom., Serb.* **131** E11

Iron Mountain, *Mich., U.S.* **93** C12

Ironwood, *Mich., U.S.* **93** B11

Irpin', *Ukr.* **135** K5

Irrawaddy *see* Ayeyarwady, river, *Myanmar* **164** D4

Irsina, *It.* **128** J10

Irtysh *see* Ertis, river, *Kaz.* **151** C13

Irtysh, river, *Russ.* **136** G7

Iruña *see* Pamplona, *Sp.* **123** B11

Irvine, *Scot., U.K.* **120** J6

Isabela, *P.R., U.S.* **97** J16

Isabela, *Philippines* **167** E11

Isabela, Cabo, *Dom. Rep.* **97** H13

Isabela, Isla (Albemarle), *Ecua.* **106** E2

Isabela, Canal, *Ecua.* **106** E2

Isabela de Sagua, *Cuba* **96** E5

Isachsen Mount, *Antarctica* **201** B12

Ísafjörđur, *Ice.* **118** D3

Isahaya, *Japan* **163** L3

Isa Khel, *Pak.* **153** K7

Isar, river, *Ger.* **126** H7

Íscar, *Sp.* **122** D8

Ischia, Isola d', *It.* **129** K8

Isdu, island, *Maldives* **155** R3

Ise, *Japan* **163** K7

Isen Saki, *Japan* **163** P2

Iseo, Lago d', *It.* **128** C4

Isère, Pointe, *Fr. Guiana, Fr.* **107** E16

Isernia, *It.* **128** H8

Ise Wan, *Japan* **162** J7

Isfahan *see* Eşfahān, *Iran* **149** D10

Isfara, *Taj.* **152** E7

Ishigaki Jima, *Japan* **159** P11

Ishikari Wan, *Japan* **162** C9

Ishim, *Russ.* **136** H7

Ishim, river, *Russ.* **136** H7

Ishim Steppe, *Kaz.* **151** A10

Ishinomaki, *Japan* **162** G10

Ishinomaki Wan, *Japan* **162** G10

Ishkuman, *Pak.* **152** H9

Ishpeming, *Mich., U.S.* **93** B12

Işık Dağı, *Turk.* **144** C6

Işıkveren, *Turk.* **145** F13

Isili, *It.* **129** L3

Isimu, *Indonesia* **167** G11

Isiro, *D.R.C.* **176** G9

Isisford, *Qnsld., Austral.* **187** F13

Iskandar, *Uzb.* **151** H11

Iskele *see* Trikomo, *Cyprus* **133** E17

İskenderun, *Turk.* **144** G8

İskenderun Körfezi, *Turk.* **144** G8

İskilip, *Turk.* **144** C7

Iskŭr, river, *Bulg.* **131** F12

Iskushuban, *Somalia* **177** E15

İslâhiye, *Turk.* **144** G8

Islamabad, *Pak.* **153** K8

Islamkot, *Pak.* **153** R7

Island Lagoon, *Austral.* **185** J11

Islands, Bay of, *N.Z.* **189** B15

Islay, island, *Scot., U.K.* **120** J5

Ismâ'ilîya, *Egypt* **147** L1

Isna, *Egypt* **175** D15

Isoka, *Zambia* **181** C10

Isonzo, river, *It.* **128** C7

Isparta, *Turk.* **144** F4

Ispas, *Turkm.* **150** J8

Ispikan, *Pak.* **153** Q2

İspir, *Turk.* **145** C12

Israel, *Asia* **142** F4

Isrīyah, ruins, *Syr.* **146** E7

Issano, *Guyana* **107** E13

Issime, *It.* **128** C2

Issoudun, *Fr.* **125** M7

Ist, island, *Croatia* **130** E4

İstanbul (Constantinople), *Turk.* **144** C3

İstanbul Boğazi (Bosporus), *Turk.* **144** B4

Istaravshan (Ŭroteppa), *Taj.* **152** E6

Istiéa, *Gr.* **132** E9

Isto, Mount, *U.S.* **90** J4

Istres, *Fr.* **125** S10

Istria, peninsula, *Croatia* **130** D4

Itabaianinha, *Braz.* **109** F15

Itabuna, *Braz.* **109** G15

Itacoatiara, *Braz.* **108** C9

Itaetê, *Braz.* **109** F14

Itaipú Dam, *Braz., Para.* **109** K10

Itaituba, *Braz.* **109** C10

Itajaí, *Braz.* **109** K12

Italia, Gran Sasso d', *It.* **128** G7

Italia, Monte, *Chile* **111** T4

Italy, *Europe* **116** K8

Itamarati, *Braz.* **108** D7

Itambé, Pico de, *Braz.* **109** H14

Itanagar, *India* **154** E11

Itapetinga, *Braz.* **109** G14

Itapipoca, *Braz.* **109** D15

Itapiranga, *Braz.* **109** C10

Itasca, Lake *see* Mississippi, Source of the, *U.S.* **91** B10

Itatupã, *Braz.* **109** B12

Itéa, *Gr.* **132** F8

Iténez, river, *Bol.* **108** F8

Itezhi-Tezhi, Lake, *Zambia* **180** D8

Ithaca, *N.Y., U.S.* **93** C15

Ithaca *see* Itháki, island, *Gr.* **132** F5

Itháki (Vathý), *Gr.* **132** F5

Itháki (Ithaca), island, *Gr.* **132** F5

Ítilo, *Gr.* **132** J8

Itiquira, river, *Braz.* **109** G10

Itō, *Japan* **162** J9

Itoman, *Japan* **163** Q1

Ittiri, *It.* **129** K3

Ittoqqortoormiit (Scoresbysund), *Greenland, Den.* **199** H14

Itu Aba Island, *Spratly Is.* **166** D8

Ituí, river, *Braz.* **108** D6

Ituiutaba, *Braz.* **109** H12

Ituni, *Guyana* **107** E14

Iturama, *Braz.* **109** H12

Iturup (Etorofu), island, *Russ.* **137** H18

Ituxi, river, *Braz.* **108** E7

Ituzaingó, *Arg.* **110** E9

Itzehoe, *Ger.* **126** B6

Iul'tin, *Russ.* **137** B15

Ivaí, river, *Braz.* **109** J11

Ivalo, *Fin.* **119** C14

Ivanhoe, *N.S.W., Austral.* **187** K13

Ivanić Grad, *Croatia* **130** D6

Ivanjica, *Serb.* **130** F9

Ivano-Frankivs'k, *Ukr.* **135** L2

Ivanovo, *Russ.* **134** F9

Ivatsevichy, *Belarus* **134** H3

Ivaylovgrad, *Bulg.* **131** J14

Ivdel', *Russ.* **136** F6
Ivisa *see* Ibiza, island, *Sp.* **123** G14
Ivittuut, *Greenland, Den.* **199** M14
Ivory Coast *see* Côte d'Ivoire, *Af.*
　172 J2
Ivory Coast, *Côte d'Ivoire* **178** E7
Ivrea, *It.* **128** C2
Ivujivik, *Que., Can.* **89** G11
Iwaki, *Japan* **162** H10
Iwakuni, *Japan* **163** K4
Iwamizawa, *Japan* **162** C10
Iwanuma, *Japan* **162** G10
Iwate, *Japan* **162** F10
Iwo, *Nig.* **179** D10
Iwo Jima *see* Iwo To, island, *Japan*
　163 R10
Iwŏn, *N. Korea* **160** F9
Iwon-man, bay, *N. Korea* **160** F9
Iwo To (Iwo Jima), island, *Japan*
　163 R10
Ixtapa, *Mex.* **94** H7
Iyo, *Japan* **163** K5
Iž, island, *Croatia* **130** F5
Īzadkhvāst, *Iran* **149** D10
Izamal, *Mex.* **95** G12
Izbica, *Pol.* **127** D12
Izena Shima, *Japan* **163** Q1
Izhevsk, *Russ.* **136** G5
Izmayil, *Ukr.* **135** N4
İzmir (Smyrna), *Turk.* **144** E2
İzmit *see* Kocaeli, *Turk.* **144** C4
İznik (Nicaea), *Turk.* **144** C4
İznik Gölü, *Turk.* **144** C4
Izra', *Syr.* **146** H5
Izu Hantō, *Japan* **162** J8
Izuhara, *Japan* **163** K3
Izumo, *Japan* **162** J5
Izu Shotō, *Japan* **163** K9
Izvestiya Tsik Islands, *Russ.* **199** C10
Izyaslav, *Ukr.* **135** K3
Izyum, *Ukr.* **135** L8

Jabalpur, *India* **154** G5
Jabal Shammar, region, *Saudi Arabia*
　148 F6
Jabal Zuqar, Jazīrat, *Yemen* **148** M6
Jabbūl, *Syr.* **146** D7
Jabbūl, Sabkhat al, *Syr.* **146** D7
Jabiru, *N. Terr., Austral.* **186** B9
Jablah, *Syr.* **146** E5
Jablaničko Jezero, *Bosn. & Herzg.*
　130 F7
Jablonec, *Czech Rep.* **127** F10
Jaboatão, *Braz.* **109** E16
Jäbrayyl *see* Kurakhtin, *Azerb.*
　145 D16
Jabuka, island, *Croatia* **130** G5
Jaca, *Sp.* **123** C12
Jacareacanga, *Braz.* **109** D10
Jaciparaná, *Braz.* **108** E8
Jackson, *Miss., U.S.* **93** H12
Jackson, *Tenn., U.S.* **93** G12
Jackson, Ostrov, *Russ.* **136** B9
Jackson Bay, *N.Z.* **189** J11
Jackson Lake, *U.S.* **90** C6
Jacksonville, *Fla., U.S.* **93** H14
Jacmel, *Haiti* **97** J12
Jacobabad, *Pak.* **153** P6
Jacquinot Bay, *P.N.G.* **188** C6
Jadraque, *Sp.* **123** E10
Jaén, *Peru* **108** D3
Jaén, *Sp.* **122** J9
Jaeundo, island, *S. Korea* **161** Q5
Jaewondo, island, *S. Korea* **161** Q5
Ja'farābād, *Iran* **148** A8
Jaffa, Cape, *Austral.* **185** L11
Jaffna, *Sri Lanka* **155** M5
Jafr, Qā' al, *Jordan* **147** L6
Jagaedo, island, *S. Korea* **161** R6

Jagdalpur, *India* **154** J6
Jagdaqi, *China* **157** B15
Jāghir Bāzār, *Syr.* **146** C11
Jaghjagh, river, *Syr.* **146** C11
Jagodina, *Serb.* **131** F10
Jagraon, *India* **154** C4
Jagtial, *India* **154** J5
Jaguarão, *Braz.* **109** M11
Jahanabad, *India* **154** F7
Jahorina, peak, *Bosn. & Herzg.* **130** F7
Jahrom, *Iran* **149** E10
Jaicós, *Braz.* **109** E14
Jaigarh, *India* **154** J3
Jaintiapur, *Bangladesh* **154** F10
Jaipur, *India* **154** E4
Jaisalmer, *India* **154** E2
Jajpur, *India* **154** H8
Jakar, *Bhutan* **154** E10
Jakarta, *Indonesia* **166** K6
Jakhau, *India* **154** F1
Jakobshavn *see* Ilulissat, *Greenland,*
　Den. **199** L13
Jakobshavn Isbræ, glacier, *Greenland,*
　Den. **199** L13
Jakobstad (Pietarsaari), *Fin.*
　119 F14
Jalaid Qi, *China* **157** C15
Jalalabad, *Afghan.* **152** J7
Jalal-Abad, *Kyrg.* **152** E8
Jalandhar, *India* **154** C4
Jala Nur, *China* **157** B14
Jalasjärvi, *Fin.* **119** G14
Jalaun, *India* **154** E5
Jaldak, *Afghan.* **153** L4
Jaleswar, *India* **154** G8
Jalgaon, *India* **154** H4
Jalingo, *Nig.* **179** D13
Jalkot, *Pak.* **152** J8
Jalón, river, *Sp.* **123** D11
Jalor, *India* **154** F3
Jalpaiguri, *India* **154** E9
Jālq, *Iran* **149** F14
Jáltipan, *Mex.* **95** H10
Jaluit Atoll, *Marshall Is.* **190** D7
Jamaame, *Somalia* **177** H13
Jamaica, *N. Amer.* **87** P9
Jamaica Cay, *Bahamas* **96** E9
Jamalpur, *Bangladesh* **154** F10
Jaman Pass, *Taj.* **152** G9
Jambi, *Indonesia* **166** H5
Jambusar, *India* **154** G2
James *see* San Salvador, Isla, *Ecua.*
　106 D2
James, river, *S. Dak., U.S.* **90** C9
James, river, *Va., U.S.* **91** E15
James Bay, *Nunavut, Can.* **89** J11
James Range, *Austral.* **184** F9
James Ross Island, *Antarctica* **200** C3
Jamestown, *N. Dak., U.S.* **92** B9
Jamestown, *N.Y., U.S.* **93** D14
Jamestown, *S. Austral., Austral.*
　187 K11
Jammu, *India* **154** C4
Jamnagar, *India* **154** G1
Jampur, *Pak.* **153** N7
Jämsä, *Fin.* **119** G14
Jamshedpur, *India* **154** G8
Jamuna, river, *Bangladesh* **154** F9
Janaúba, *Braz.* **109** G14
Jan Bulaq, *Afghan.* **152** H5
Jand, *Pak.* **153** K8
Jandaq, *Iran* **149** C11
Jandiatuba, river, *Braz.* **108** D6
Jandola, *Pak.* **153** L7
Jangaon, *India* **154** J5
Jangdo, island, *S. Korea* **161** R7
Jangdong, *S. Korea* **161** Q7
Jangeru, *Indonesia* **166** H9
Janggye, *S. Korea* **161** P7
Janghang, *S. Korea* **161** N6

Jangheung, *S. Korea* **161** Q6
Janghowon, *S. Korea* **161** L7
Jangipur, *India* **154** F9
Jangpyeong, *S. Korea* **161** K9
Jangsando, island, *S. Korea* **161** Q5
Jangseong, *S. Korea* **161** P6
Jangsu, *S. Korea* **161** P7
Jani Kheyl, *Afghan.* **153** K5
Janīn, *West Bank* **146** H4
Jan Mayen, island, *Greenland, Den.*
　84 B10
Janów Lubelski, *Pol.* **127** F14
Jansenville, *S. Af.* **180** J7
Januária, *Braz.* **109** G13
Jaora, *India* **154** F3
Japan, *Asia* **143** F14
Japan, islands, *Asia* **141** F14
Japan, Sea of (East Sea), *Asia*
　141 F14
Japurá, *Braz.* **108** C7
Japurá, river, *Braz.* **108** C7
Jarābulus, *Syr.* **146** C7
Jaramillo, *Arg.* **111** P5
Jaranwala, *Pak.* **153** L9
Jarash (Gerasa), *Jordan* **146** J5
Jardim, *Braz.* **109** J10
Jardines de la Reina, islands, *Cuba*
　96 G6
Jargalant, *Mongolia* **157** C10
Jargalant, *Mongolia* **157** C14
Jargalant Hayrahan, peak, *Mongolia*
　156 C9
Jarghan, *Afghan.* **152** H4
Jari, river, *Braz.* **109** B11
Jarocin, *Pol.* **127** D11
Jarosław, *Pol.* **127** F15
Järvenpää, *Fin.* **119** G15
Jarvis Island, *U.S., Pac. Oc.* **191** D11
Järvsö, *Sweden* **119** G12
Jashpurnagar, *India* **154** G7
Jāsk, *Iran* **149** G12
Jasło, *Pol.* **127** G14
Jason Islands, *Falk. Is., U.K.* **111** R7
Jason Peninsula, *Antarctica* **200** C3
Jasper, *Alta., Can.* **88** H5
Jastrowie, *Pol.* **127** C11
Jastrzębie-Zdrój, *Pol.* **127** G12
Jászberény, *Hung.* **127** J13
Jataí, *Braz.* **109** H11
Jati, *Pak.* **153** R5
Jatibonico, *Cuba* **96** F6
Jatobal, *Braz.* **109** D12
Jaú, river, *Braz.* **108** C8
Jauaperi, river, *Braz.* **108** B9
Jaunpur, *India* **154** F7
Java (Jawa), island, *Asia* **166** K6
Javari, river, *Braz.* **108** D5
Java Sea, *Asia* **141** M12
Jávea (Xàbia), *Sp.* **123** G13
Javhlant *see* Uliastay, *Mongolia*
　157 C10
Jawa *see* Java, island, *Indonesia* **166** K6
Jawhar (Giohar), *Somalia* **177** G14
Jawi, *Indonesia* **166** H6
Jawoldo, island, *S. Korea* **161** L5
Jaworzno, *Pol.* **127** F12
Jaya, Puncak, *Indonesia* **188** J5
Jayapura, *Indonesia* **188** H4
Jayawijaya, Pegunungan, *Indonesia*
　188 J5
Jazirah Doberai (Bird's Head
　Peninsula), *Indonesia* **167** H14
Jaz Mūrīān, Hāmūn-e, *Iran* **149** F12
Jbail (Byblos), *Leb.* **146** F5
Jdaïdet Ghazīr, *Leb.* **146** F5
Jeanette, Ostrov, *Russ.* **137** B13
Jean Marie River, *N.W.T., Can.* **88** F6
Jeannette Island, *Russ.* **198** E6
Jean-Rabel, *Haiti* **97** H11
Jebba, *Nig.* **179** D10

Jebel Alí, *U.A.E.* **149** G11
Jebri, *Pak.* **153** P4
Jebus, *Indonesia* **166** H5
Jecheon, *S. Korea* **161** L8
Jeddah, *Saudi Arabia* **148** H5
Jędrzejów, *Pol.* **127** F13
Jefferson, Mount, *Nev., U.S.* **92** E4
Jefferson City, *Mo., U.S.* **93** F11
Jef Jef el Kebir, desert, *Chad*
　175 E12
Jega, *Nig.* **179** B10
Jégun, *Fr.* **125** R6
Jeju (Cheju), *S. Korea* **161** S6
Jeju-Do, island, *S. Korea* **161** S5
Jeju Strait, *S. Korea* **161** S6
Jelbart Ice Shelf, *Antarctica* **200** A9
Jelenia Góra, *Pol.* **127** F10
Jelgava (Mitau), *Latv.* **119** K15
Jemaja, island, *Indonesia* **166** G5
Jember, *Indonesia* **166** K8
Jembongan, island, *Malaysia* **166** E9
Jeminay, *China* **156** C7
Jena, *Ger.* **126** E7
Jengish Chokusu (Pobedy, Pik, Victory
　Peak), *Kyrg.* **152** D12
Jens Munk Island, *Nunavut, Can.*
　89 E11
Jenu, *Indonesia* **166** H7
Jeogu, *S. Korea* **161** Q9
Jeongeup, *S. Korea* **161** P6
Jeongnim, *S. Korea* **161** N9
Jeongok, *S. Korea* **161** K7
Jeongseon, *S. Korea* **161** L9
Jeonju, *S. Korea* **161** N7
Jequié, *Braz.* **109** G15
Jequitinhonha, river, *Braz.* **109** G14
Jerantut, *Malaysia* **165** P8
Jerba Island, island, *Tunisia* **175** B10
Jérémie, *Haiti* **97** J10
Jeremoabo, *Braz.* **109** F15
Jerez de la Frontera, *Sp.* **122** K6
Jerez de los Caballeros, *Sp.* **122** H6
Jericho *see* Arīḥā, *West Bank* **146** J4
Jerid, Shott el, *Tunisia* **174** B9
Jerimoth Hill, *U.S.* **91** C16
Jerome, *Idaho, U.S.* **92** D5
Jerramungup, *W. Austral., Austral.*
　186 K5
Jersey, island, *Channel Is., U.K.* **121** T9
Jersey City, *N.J., U.S.* **93** D16
Jerusalem, *Israel* **146** J4
Jervis *see* Rábida, Isla, *Ecua.* **106** E2
Jervis Bay, *Austral.* **185** L15
Jervis Bay Territory, *Austral.* **187** L15
Jerzu, *It.* **129** L3
Jesenice, *Slov.* **130** C4
Jeseník, *Czech Rep.* **127** F11
Jesi, *It.* **128** F7
Jessore, *Bangladesh* **154** G9
Jesús María, *Arg.* **110** G5
Jetpur, *India* **154** G2
Jeungdo, island, *S. Korea* **161** Q5
Jeungpyeong, *S. Korea* **161** M7
Jeypore, *India* **154** J7
Jezercë, Maja, *Alban.* **130** H8
Jezioro Shiardwy, *Pol.* **127** B14
Jezzîne, *Leb.* **146** G5
Jhalawar, *India* **154** F4
Jhal Jhao, *Pak.* **153** Q4
Jhang, *Pak.* **153** L8
Jhansi, *India* **154** F5
Jharsuguda, *India* **154** G7
Jhatpat, *Pak.* **153** P5
Jhelum, *Pak.* **153** K9
Jhelum, river, *Pak.* **153** L8
Jhimpir, *Pak.* **153** R5
Jhudo, *Pak.* **153** R6
Jhunjhunun, *India* **154** E4
Jiahe, *Hunan, China* **159** N3
Jialing, river, *China* **157** H12

Kawthoung, *Myanmar* 165 K5
Kaya, *Burkina Faso* 178 B8
Kaya, *Indonesia* 166 G9
Kayan, river, *Indonesia* 166 G9
Kayapınar, *Turk.* 145 F12
Kayes, *Congo* 179 J14
Kayes, *Mali* 174 G4
Kaymaz, *Turk.* 144 D5
Kaynar, *Turk.* 144 E8
Kaysatskoye, *Russ.* 135 K12
Kayser Gebergte, *Suriname*
    107 F15
Kayseri, *Turk.* 144 E8
Kazach'ye, *Russ.* 137 D13
Kazakhstan, *Asia* 142 E7
Kazakh Uplands, *Kaz.* 151 C11
Kazan', *Russ.* 134 F12
Kazan, river, *Nunavut, Can.* 88 F9
Kazan Rettō *see* Volcano Islands, *Japan*
    163 R10
Kazanskaya, *Russ.* 135 K9
Kazarman, *Kyrg.* 152 D9
Kazbek, peak, *Ga.* 145 A14
Kaz Dağı, *Turk.* 144 D2
Kāzerūn, *Iran* 149 E10
Kazi Ahmad, *Pak.* 153 Q5
Kazimierz Dolny, *Pol.* 127 E14
Kazincbarcika, *Hung.* 127 H13
Kaztalovka, *Kaz.* 150 C4
Kazym Mys, *Russ.* 136 F7
Kéa (Tziá), island, *Gr.* 133 H10
Kea, Mauna, *U.S.* 91 M13
Kea'au, *Hawaii, U.S.* 93 M13
Keadu, island, *Maldives* 155 Q3
Kealaikahiki Channel, *U.S.* 91 L12
Kearney, *Nebr., U.S.* 92 E9
Keban, *Turk.* 145 E10
Kebnekaise, peak, *Sweden* 119 D12
Kech, river, *Pak.* 153 Q2
Keçiborlu, *Turk.* 144 F4
Kecskemét, *Hung.* 127 K13
Kediri, *Indonesia* 166 K7
Kédougou, *Senegal* 174 G4
Kędzierzyn-Koźle, *Pol.* 127 F12
Keele, river, *N.W.T., Can.* 88 E5
Keele Peak, *Yukon, Can.* 88 E5
Keelung *see* Chilung, *Taiwan, China*
    159 P9
Keer-weer, Cape, *Austral.* 185 B12
Keetmanshoop, *Namibia* 180 H6
Kefaloniá (Cephalonia), island, *Gr.*
    132 F5
Kéfalos, *Gr.* 133 J14
Kefaluka, *Turk.* 144 F2
Keflavík, *Ice.* 118 E3
Kegen, *Kaz.* 151 G14
Keg River, *Alta., Can.* 88 G6
Keheili, *Sudan* 177 C10
Kehl, *Ger.* 126 H5
Keila, *Est.* 119 H15
Keitele, lake, *Fin.* 119 F14
Keith, *Scot., U.K.* 120 F8
Keith Arm, *N.W.T., Can.* 88 E6
Kékes, peak, *Hung.* 127 J13
Kekirawa, *Sri Lanka* 155 N6
Kekra, *Russ.* 137 G15
Kekri, *India* 154 E4
Kel, *Pak.* 152 J9
K'elafo, *Eth.* 177 F13
Kelai, island, *Maldives* 155 P2
Kelan, *Shanxi, China* 158 C3
Kelang, *Malaysia* 165 P7
Kelang, island, *Indonesia* 167 J12
Këlcyrë, *Alban.* 130 K9
Keleft, *Afghan.* 152 G4
Kelheim, *Ger.* 126 H7
Kelkit, *Turk.* 145 D10
Kelkit, river, *Turk.* 144 C9
Keller Lake, *N.W.T., Can.* 88 E6
Kellet, Cape, *N.W.T., Can.* 88 C7

Kells (Ceanannas), *Ire.* 121 M4
Kells, Rhinns of, *Scot., U.K.* 121 K7
Kélo, *Chad* 175 H11
Kelowna, *B.C., Can.* 88 J5
Kelso, *Wash., U.S.* 92 B3
Keluang, *Malaysia* 165 Q8
Kem', *Russ.* 136 D5
Kema, *Indonesia* 167 G12
Kemah, *Turk.* 145 D10
Kemaliye, *Turk.* 145 E10
Kemasik, *Malaysia* 165 N8
Kemer, *Turk.* 144 C2
Kemer, *Turk.* 144 F3
Kemer, *Turk.* 144 G3
Kemer, *Turk.* 144 G4
Kemerovo, *Russ.* 136 J9
Kemi, *Fin.* 119 E14
Kemijärvi, *Fin.* 119 D14
Kemijärvi, lake, *Fin.* 119 D14
Kemijoki, river, *Fin.* 119 C14
Kemlya, *Russ.* 134 G11
Kemmerer, *Wyo., U.S.* 92 D6
Kemp Coast, *Antarctica* 201 C15
Kempendyay, *Russ.* 137 G12
Kemp Peninsula, *Antarctica* 200 D5
Kemps Bay, *Bahamas* 96 D7
Kempsey, *N.S.W., Austral.* 187 J16
Kempten, *Ger.* 126 J6
Kenai, *Alas., U.S.* 92 L3
Kenai Peninsula, *U.S.* 84 E2
Kendal, *Eng., U.K.* 121 L8
Kendall, Cape, *Nunavut, Can.* 89 F10
Kendari, *Indonesia* 167 J11
Kendawangan, *Indonesia* 166 H7
Kendikolu, island, *Maldives* 155 P2
Kendrapara, *India* 154 H8
Këndrevicës, Maja e, *Alban.* 130 K8
Kenema, *Sierra Leone* 178 D5
Kéngkok, *Laos* 164 G9
Kengtung, *Myanmar* 164 E6
Kenhardt, *S. Af.* 180 H6
Kenitra, *Mor.* 174 A6
Kenli, *Shandong, China* 158 D7
Kenmare (Neidín), *Ire.* 121 P2
Kenmore, *Scot., U.K.* 120 H7
Kennebec, river, *U.S.* 91 B16
Kennedy Channel, *Nunavut, Can.*
    89 A11
Kennedy Entrance, *U.S.* 90 L3
Keno Hill, *Yukon, Can.* 88 E5
Kenora, *Ont., Can.* 88 K9
Kenosha, *Wis., U.S.* 93 D12
Kent Peninsula, *Nunavut, Can.* 88 E8
Kentucky, *U.S.* 93 F12
Kentucky, river, *U.S.* 91 E13
Kentucky Lake, *U.S.* 91 F12
Kenya, *Af.* 173 L10
Kenya, Mount, *Kenya* 177 H12
Keonjhargarh, *India* 154 G8
Kep, *Cambodia* 165 K9
Kepi, *Indonesia* 188 H6
Kępno, *Pol.* 127 E11
Keppel Bay, *Austral.* 185 F16
Kepsut, *Turk.* 144 D3
Keramotí, *Gr.* 133 B11
Keran, *Pak.* 152 J9
Kerang, *Vic., Austral.* 187 L13
Kerch, *Ukr.* 135 N7
Kerchenskiy Proliv, *Ukr.* 135 P7
Kerempe Burnu, *Turk.* 144 B6
Keren, *Eritrea* 177 D12
Keri, *Gr.* 132 H5
Kerikeri, *N.Z.* 189 B15
Kerinci, peak, *Indonesia* 166 H4
Kerki *see* Atamyrat, *Turkm.* 150 K9
Kerkíni, *Gr.* 132 B8
Kerkínis, Límni, *Gr.* 132 B9
Kérkira, *Gr.* 132 D4
Kérkira (Corfu, Corcyra), island, *Gr.*
    132 D4

Kermadec Islands, *N.Z., Pac. Oc.*
    190 H9
Kermān, *Iran* 149 E12
Kermānshāh, *Iran* 148 C8
Kermānshāhān, *Iran* 149 D11
Kéros, island, *Gr.* 133 J12
Kerrobert, *Sask., Can.* 88 J7
Kerry Head, *Ire.* 121 N1
Kertamulia, *Indonesia* 166 H6
Keryneia Range, *Cyprus* 133 E16
Keşan, *Turk.* 144 C2
Keşap, *Turk.* 145 C10
Kesennuma, *Japan* 162 F10
Keshem, *Afghan.* 152 H6
Keshīt, *Iran* 149 E12
Keshod, *India* 154 G1
Keşiş Dağı, *Turk.* 145 D11
Keskal, *India* 154 H6
Keskin, *Turk.* 144 D6
Kes'ma, *Russ.* 134 E8
Keszthely, *Hung.* 127 K11
Ketanda, *Russ.* 137 F15
Ketaun, *Indonesia* 166 J4
Ketchikan, *Alas., U.S.* 92 M6
Kete Krachi, *Ghana* 178 D9
Keti Bandar, *Pak.* 153 R5
Kettering, *Eng., U.K.* 121 P10
Keul', *Russ.* 137 H11
Keweenaw Peninsula, *U.S.* 91 B12
Key, Lough, *Ire.* 121 L3
Keyano, *Que., Can.* 89 J12
Keystone Lake, *U.S.* 91 G10
Key West, *Fla., U.S.* 93 L15
Kežmarok, *Slovakia* 127 G13
Khabarovsk, *Russ.* 137 J16
Khābūr, river, *Syr.* 146 C11
Khada Hills, *Afghan.* 153 L4
Khadyzhensk, *Russ.* 135 P9
Khailino, *Russ.* 137 D16
Khairpur, *Pak.* 153 N8
Khairpur, *Pak.* 153 P6
Khakhar', *Russ.* 137 G15
Khalatse, *India* 154 B4
Khalūf, *Oman* 149 J12
Khambhaliya, *India* 154 G1
Khambhat, Gulf of, *India* 154 G2
Khamgaon, *India* 154 H4
Khamīs Mushayṭ, *Saudi Arabia*
    148 K6
Kham Khowrki, *Afghan.* 153 K2
Khammouan, *Laos* 164 G9
Khamr, *Yemen* 148 L7
Khanabad, *Afghan.* 152 H6
Khān Abū Shāmāt, *Syr.* 146 G6
Khanai, *Pak.* 153 M5
Khanaqa, *Afghan.* 152 H4
Khānaqīn, *Iraq* 148 C7
Khān az Zābīb, *Jordan* 147 K5
Khanderi Island, *India* 154 J2
Khandwa, *India* 154 G4
Khandyga, *Russ.* 137 F14
Khanewal, *Pak.* 153 M8
Khangarh, *Pak.* 153 P8
Khaniadhana, *India* 154 F5
Khanka, Ozero, *Russ.* 137 K16
Khanozai, *Pak.* 153 M5
Khanpur, *Pak.* 153 N7
Khān Shaykhūn, *Syr.* 146 D6
Khan Tängiri (Lord of the Sky), *Kyrg.*
    152 C12
Khantayskoye, Ozero, *Russ.*
    137 F10
Khanty-Mansiysk, *Russ.* 136 G7
Khān Yūnis, *Gaza Strip* 147 K3
Khapalu, *Pak.* 152 J10
Kharabali, *Russ.* 135 M12
Kharagpur, *India* 154 G8
Kharan, *Pak.* 153 N4
Kharānaq, *Iran* 149 D11
Kharasavey, Mys, *Russ.* 136 E8

Khârga Oasis, *Egypt* 175 D14
Khargon, *India* 154 G4
Khargŭsh, *Taj.* 152 G8
Kharian, *Pak.* 153 K9
Khariar, *India* 154 H7
Kharimkotan, island, *Russ.* 137 G18
Khärk, island, *Iran* 148 E9
Kharkiv, *Ukr.* 135 K7
Kharlovka, *Russ.* 136 C6
Kharmanli, *Bulg.* 131 H13
Kharovsk, *Russ.* 134 D9
Khartoum, *Sudan* 177 D10
Khartoum North, *Sudan* 177 D10
Kharyyalakh, *Russ.* 137 F11
Khasavyurt, *Russ.* 135 P12
Khash, *Afghan.* 153 L2
Khāsh, *Iran* 149 E13
Khash, river, *Afghan.* 153 K3
Khash Desert, *Afghan.* 153 L2
Khashuri, *Ga.* 145 B13
Khasi Hills, *India* 154 F10
Khaskovo, *Bulg.* 131 H13
Khatanga, *Russ.* 137 E10
Khatanga Gulf, *Russ.* 198 B8
Khatangskiy Zaliv, *Russ.* 137 E11
Khātūnīyah, *Syr.* 146 C11
Khatyrka, *Russ.* 137 C16
Khaval, *Afghan.* 152 H4
Khavda, *India* 154 F1
Khaybar, Ḥarrat, *Saudi Arabia*
    148 G5
Khaydarkan, *Kyrg.* 152 E7
Khemmarat, *Thai.* 164 G9
Khenjan, *Afghan.* 152 H6
Kherson, *Ukr.* 135 N6
Kherwara, *India* 154 F3
Kheta, *Russ.* 137 E10
Khewari, *Pak.* 153 Q5
Kheyrabad, *Afghan.* 152 H5
Khimki, *Russ.* 134 G8
Khipro, *Pak.* 153 Q6
Khiri Ratthanikhom, *Thai.* 165 L6
Khiwa, *Uzb.* 150 H7
Khlevnoye, *Russ.* 134 J8
Khmel'nyts'kyy, *Ukr.* 135 L3
Khoai, Hon, *Viet.* 165 L9
Khocho, *Russ.* 137 F14
Khodzhakala, *Turkm.* 150 J6
Khojak Pass, *Pak.* 153 M4
Khokhol'skiy, *Russ.* 134 J8
Khokhropar, *Pak.* 153 Q7
Khok Kloi, *Thai.* 165 L5
Kholm, *Afghan.* 152 H5
Kholm, *Russ.* 134 F5
Kholmsk, *Russ.* 137 H17
Không, *Laos* 164 H9
Khôngxédôn, *Laos* 164 H9
Khonuu, *Russ.* 198 C5
Khoper, river, *Russ.* 134 J10
Khorāsān, region, *Iran* 149 C11
Khormaleq, *Afghan.* 153 L2
Khorol, *Ukr.* 135 K6
Khorramābād, *Iran* 148 C9
Khorugh, *Taj.* 152 G7
Khost (Khowst), *Afghan.* 153 K6
Khost, *Pak.* 153 M5
Khowst *see* Khost, *Afghan.* 153 K6
Khoy, *Iran* 148 A7
Khoyniki, *Belarus* 134 J5
Khrenovoye, *Russ.* 135 K9
Khromtaū, *Kaz.* 150 C7
Khudabad, *Pak.* 153 M9
Khuiala, *India* 154 E2
Khujand, *Taj.* 152 E6
Khŭjayli, *Uzb.* 150 G7
Khulkhuta, *Russ.* 135 N12
Khulna, *Bangladesh* 154 G9
Khunjerab Pass, *China, Pak.*
    152 G10

Kouango, *Cen. Af. Rep.* **176** F7
Koudougou, *Burkina Faso* **178** B8
Koufália, *Gr.* **132** B8
Koufoníssi, island, *Gr.* **133** JI2
Koufoníssi, island, *Gr.* **133** MI3
Koufós, *Gr.* **133** DIO
Kouilou, river, *Congo* **179** HI3
Koukdjuak, Great Plain of the, *Nunavut, Can.* **89** EI2
Kouklia, *Cyprus* **133** FI5
Koúla, peak, *Gr.* **133** AII
Koulamoutou, *Gabon* **179** GI3
Koulen, *Cambodia* **164** J9
Koulikoro, *Mali* **174** G5
Koumra, *Chad* **175** JII
Kourou, *Fr. Guiana, Fr.* **107** EI7
Kouroussa, *Guinea* **178** C5
Koussi, Emi, *Chad* **175** FII
Koutiala, *Mali* **174** H5
Kouvola, *Fin.* **119** GI5
Kovel', *Ukr.* **134** J2
Kovic, Baie, *Que., Can.* **89** GII
Kovin, *Serb.* **130** E9
Kovrov, *Russ.* **134** F9
Kovur, *India* **155** K5
Kowanyama, *Qnsld., Austral.* **187** CI3
Kowloon see Jiulong, *Hong Kong S.A.R., China* **159** R4
Kowŏn, *N. Korea* **160** G7
Koyda, *Russ.* **136** D6
Koytendag, *Turkm.* **150** K9
Koyuk, *Alas., U.S.* **92** K2
Koyukuk, river, *U.S.* **90** J3
Koyulhisar, *Turk.* **144** D9
Kozan, *Turk.* **144** F8
Kozáni, *Gr.* **132** C7
Kozel'sk, *Russ.* **134** H7
Kozhasay, *Kaz.* **150** D6
Kozhikode (Calicut), *India* **155** M4
Kozjak, peak, *Maced.* **131** JIO
Kozlovka, *Russ.* **135** K9
Kozlu, *Turk.* **144** B5
Kozluk, *Turk.* **145** EI2
Koz'modem'yansk, *Russ.* **134** FII
Kōzu Shima, *Japan* **163** K9
Kozyatyn, *Ukr.* **135** K4
Kpalimé, *Togo* **178** D9
Krabi, *Thai.* **165** M6
Kra Buri, *Thai.* **165** K6
Kragerø, *Nor.* **119** JIO
Kragujevac, *Serb.* **130** F9
Kra, Isthmus of, *Myanmar, Thai.* **165** K6
Kraków, *Pol.* **127** FI3
Kralendijk, *Bonaire, Neth.* **98** G7
Kraljevo, *Serb.* **130** F9
Král'ovský Chlmec, *Slovakia* **127** HI4
Kramators'k, *Ukr.* **135** L8
Kramfors, *Sweden* **119** GI2
Kranídi, *Gr.* **132** H9
Kranj, *Slov.* **130** C4
Krasavino, *Russ.* **136** E5
Krasino, *Russ.* **199** BI2
Kraśnik, *Pol.* **127** EI4
Krasnoarmeysk see Tayynsha, *Kaz.* **151** AII
Krasnoarmeysk, *Russ.* **136** G3
Krasnoarmeyskaya, *Russ.* **135** N8
Krasnodar, *Russ.* **135** P9
Krasnogorsk, *Russ.* **137** HI7
Krasnogvardeyskoye, *Russ.* **135** NIO
Krasnohrad, *Ukr.* **135** L7
Krasnokamensk, *Russ.* **137** KI3
Krasnoslobodsk, *Russ.* **135** LII
Krasnovishersk, *Russ.* **136** F6
Krasnoyarsk, *Russ.* **137** JIO
Krasnyy Dolginets, *Kaz.* **150** F4
Krasnyye Baki, *Russ.* **134** FII
Krasnyy Kholm, *Russ.* **134** E8

Krasnyy Luch, *Ukr.* **135** M9
Krasnyy Yar, *Russ.* **135** KII
Kratie, *Cambodia* **164** J9
Kraul Mountains, *Antarctica* **200** B8
Kraulshavn see Nuussuaq, *Greenland, Den.* **199** KI2
Kray Lesa, *Russ.* **137** CI4
Krefeld, *Ger.* **126** E4
Kremastí, *Gr.* **133** KI5
Kremastón, Technití Límni, *Gr.* **132** E6
Kremen, peak, *Croatia* **130** E5
Kremenchuk, *Ukr.* **135** L6
Kremenchuts'ke Vodokhranilishche, *Ukr.* **135** L6
Kremenets', *Ukr.* **135** K3
Krems, *Aust.* **127** HIO
Krest Bay, *Russ.* **198** G3
Kréstena, *Gr.* **132** H7
Kresty, *Russ.* **137** EIO
Kretinga, *Latv.* **119** KI4
Kreuzlingen, *Switz.* **128** A3
Kribi, *Cameroon* **179** FI2
Krim, peak, *Slov.* **130** C4
Krims'ke Hory, mountains, *Ukr.* **135** P6
Krishna, river, *India* **155** K4
Krishnagiri, *India* **155** L5
Krishnanagar, *India* **154** G9
Kristiansand, *Nor.* **119** KIO
Kristianstad, *Sweden* **119** LI2
Kristiansund, *Nor.* **119** GIO
Kristinestad, *Fin.* **119** GI3
Kríti (Crete), island, *Gr.* **133** MIO
Krk, *Croatia* **130** D4
Krnov, *Pol.* **127** FII
Kroken, *Nor.* **119** EII
Krolevets', *Ukr.* **134** J6
Kromy, *Russ.* **134** J7
Krong Koh Kong, *Cambodia* **165** K8
Kronotskaya Sopka, *Russ.* **137** EI7
Kronshtadt, *Russ.* **134** D5
Kroonstad, *S. Af.* **180** H8
Kropotkin, *Russ.* **135** N9
Krosno, *Pol.* **127** GI4
Krosno Odrzańskie, *Pol.* **127** DIO
Krotoszyn, *Pol.* **127** EII
Krstača, peak, *Maced., Serb.* **130** G9
Krui, *Indonesia* **166** J5
Krumovgrad, *Bulg.* **131** JI3
Krung Thep (Bangkok), *Thai.* **164** J7
Krupá, *Czech Rep.* **126** F9
Krupište, *Maced.* **131** HIO
Krupki, *Belarus* **134** G5
Kruševac, *Serb.* **131** FIO
Krutets, *Russ.* **134** D8
Kruzof Island, *U.S.* **90** M5
Krychaw, *Belarus* **134** H5
Krylovskaya, *Russ.* **135** N9
Krymsk, *Russ.* **135** P8
Kryvichy, *Belarus* **134** G4
Kryvyy Rih, *Ukr.* **135** M6
Ksar el Kebir, *Mor.* **174** A6
Köpekkayası Burnu, *Turk.* **144** B6
Köprü, river, *Turk.* **144** F5
Köyceğiz, *Turk.* **144** F3
Kuala Abang, *Brunei* **166** F8
Kuala Belait, *Brunei* **166** F8
Kuala Berang, *Malaysia* **165** N8
Kuala Dungun, *Malaysia* **165** N8
Kualakapuas, *Indonesia* **166** H8
Kuala Kerai, *Malaysia* **165** N7
Kualakurun, *Indonesia* **166** H8
Kuala Lumpur, *Malaysia* **165** P7
Kualamanjual, *Indonesia* **166** H7
Kuala Nerang, *Malaysia* **166** E4
Kuala Rompin, *Malaysia* **165** P8
Kuala Terengganu, *Malaysia* **165** N8
Kualatungkal, *Indonesia* **166** H5
Kuam-ho, reservoir, *N. Korea* **161** K5

Kuancheng, *Hebei, China* **158** B7
Kuandian, *Liaoning, China* **158** BIO
Kuanshan, *Taiwan, China* **159** Q9
Kuantan, *Malaysia* **165** P8
Kubbum, *Sudan* **176** E8
Kubenskoye, Ozero, *Russ.* **134** D8
Kuchaman, *India* **154** E3
Kuching, *Malaysia* **166** G7
Kuchinoerabu Jima, *Japan* **163** M3
Kuchino Shima, *Japan* **163** N3
Kuchnay Darvishan, *Afghan.* **153** M3
Kuçovë, *Alban.* **130** K8
Küçüksu, *Turk.* **145** EI2
Kud, river, *Pak.* **153** Q4
Kudara, *Taj.* **152** F8
Kudat, *Malaysia* **166** E9
Kudremukh, peak, *India* **155** L3
Kudu, *N. Korea* **160** F5
Kudu Kyuyel', *Russ.* **137** GI3
Kufra Oasis see Al Jawf, *Lib.* **175** DI3
Kufstein, *Aust.* **126** J8
Kuglugtuk, *Nunavut, Can.* **88** E7
Kugul'ta, *Russ.* **135** NIO
Kūhak, *Iran* **149** FI4
Kuh-e Sangan, peak, *Afghan.* **153** K4
Kuh-e Sayyad, *Afghan.* **152** H3
Kuhmo, *Fin.* **119** EI5
Kui Buri, *Thai.* **164** J6
Kuikuina, *Nicar.* **95** JI4
Kuiseb, river, *Namibia* **180** G5
Kuitan, *Guangdong, China* **159** Q5
Kuito, *Angola* **180** C5
Kuiu Island, *U.S.* **90** M5
Kuivaniemi, *Fin.* **119** EI4
Kujang, *N. Korea* **160** F5
Kuji, *Japan* **162** EIO
Kuju, *Japan* **163** K4
Kukës, *Alban.* **130** H9
Kŭktong, *N. Korea* **160** DIO
Kula, *Serb.* **130** D8
Kula, *Turk.* **144** E3
Kula Gangri, peak, *Bhutan* **154** DIO
Kūlagīno, *Kaz.* **150** D5
Kulaura, *Bangladesh* **154** FIO
Kul'chi, *Russ.* **137** GI6
Kuldīga, *Latv.* **119** KI4
Kule, *Botswana* **180** G6
Kulebaki, *Russ.* **134** GIO
Kulin, *W. Austral., Austral.* **186** K4
Kulkuduk, *Uzb.* **150** G8
Kulmbach, *Ger.* **126** F7
Kŭlob, *Taj.* **152** G6
Kulp, *Turk.* **145** EI2
Kulu, *Turk.* **144** E6
Kulumadau, *P.N.G.* **188** B7
Kulunda, *Russ.* **136** J8
Kuma, river, *Russ.* **135** NI2
Kumagaya, *Japan* **162** H9
Kumai, *Indonesia* **166** H7
Kumai, Teluk, *Indonesia* **166** J7
Kumamoto, *Japan* **163** L3
Kumano, *Japan* **163** K7
Kumano Nada, *Japan* **163** K7
Kumanovo, *Maced.* **131** HIO
Kuman Range, *Myanmar* **164** B5
Kumara Junction, *N.Z.* **189** HI3
Kumarina Mine, *W. Austral., Austral.* **186** G4
Kumarl, *W. Austral., Austral.* **186** K5
Kumasi, *Ghana* **178** D8
Kumawa, Pegunungan, *Indonesia* **188** L5
Kumba, *Cameroon* **179** EI2
Kumbakonam, *India* **155** M5
Kumbe, *Indonesia* **167** LI7
Kŭmch'ŏn, *N. Korea* **160** H7
Kŭmch'ŏn, *N. Korea* **160** J6
Kume Jima, *Japan* **163** QI
Kŭmgang, *N. Korea* **160** J8

Kŭmgang-san, peak, *N. Korea* **160** J8
Kŭmhwa see Gimhwa, *S. Korea* **160** J7
Kumo, *Nig.* **179** CI3
Kumphawapi, *Thai.* **164** G8
Kŭmsŏng see Kimhwa, *N. Korea* **160** J7
Kumta, *India* **155** K3
Kumtag Shamo, *China* **156** E8
Kumul see Hami, *China* **156** D9
Kŭmya, *N. Korea* **160** G7
Kŭmya-man see Yŏnghŭng-man, bay, *N. Korea* **160** H7
Kumylzhenskaya, *Russ.* **135** KIO
Kumzār, *Oman* **149** FII
Kunahandu, island, *Maldives* **155** R2
Kunashir (Kunashiri), island, *Russ.* **137** HI8
Kunashiri see Kunashir, island, *Russ.* **137** HI8
Kundapura (Coondapoor), *India* **155** L3
Kundar, river, *Afghan.* **153** L6
Kundian, *Pak.* **153** L7
Kunduz see Kondoz, *Afghan.* **152** H6
Kunene, river, *Namibia* **180** E4
Kungsbacka, *Sweden* **119** KII
Kungurtug, *Russ.* **137** KIO
Kunié see Pins, Île des, *New Caledonia, Fr.* **190** G7
Kunlon, *Myanmar* **164** D6
Kunlun Shan, *China* **156** F5
Kunlun Shankou, *China* **156** G9
Kunming, *China* **157** KII
Kunnamkulam, *India* **155** M4
Kunshan, *Jiangsu, China* **158** J8
Kununurra, *W. Austral., Austral.* **186** C8
Kunyu Shan, *Shandong, China* **158** E9
Kuopio, *Fin.* **119** FI5
Kupa, river, *Croatia, Slov.* **130** D5
Kupang, *Indonesia* **167** LII
Kupino, *Russ.* **136** J7
Kupreanof Island, *U.S.* **90** M5
Kup''yans'k, *Ukr.* **135** L8
Kuqa, *China* **156** D6
Kür (Kura), river, *Azerb.* **145** DI7
Kura, river, *Azerb., Ga.* **145** DI7
Kurakhtin (Jäbrayyl), *Azerb.* **145** DI6
Kura Lowland, *Azerb.* **145** CI6
Kūrān Dap, *Iran* **149** FI3
Kurashassayskiy, *Kaz.* **150** C6
Kurashiki, *Japan* **162** J5
Kurayoshi, *Japan* **162** J5
Kurbağa Gölü, *Turk.* **144** E7
Kürchatov, *Kaz.* **151** CI3
Kürdämir, *Azerb.* **145** CI6
Kur Dili, cape, *Azerb.* **145** DI7
Kurdistan, region, *Iran, Iraq, Turk.* **145** FII
Kurduna, *Pak.* **153** M5
Kurduvadi, *India* **154** J3
Kürdzhali, *Bulg.* **131** JI3
Kure, *Japan* **163** K5
Küre, *Turk.* **144** B7
Kure Atoll, *Hawaii, U.S.* **190** A9
Kuressaare, *Est.* **119** JI4
Kureyka, *Russ.* **136** F9
Kurgan, *Russ.* **136** H6
Kurganinsk, *Russ.* **135** P9
Kuria Muria Islands see Khurīyā Murīyā, Jazā'ir, *Oman* **149** KI2
Kuri Bay, *W. Austral., Austral.* **186** C6
Kuridala, *Qnsld., Austral.* **187** EI2
Kurikka, *Fin.* **119** FI4
Kuril Islands see Kuril'skiye Ostrova, *Russ.* **137** GI8
Kuril'sk, *Russ.* **137** HI8
Kuril'skiye Ostrova (Kuril Islands), *Russ.* **137** GI8

Liepāja, *Latv.* 119 K14
Lier, *Belg.* 124 G9
Lieshan, *Anhui, China* 158 G6
Liestal, *Switz.* 128 A2
Liffey, river, *Ire.* 121 M4
Lifford (Leifear), *Ire.* 121 K4
Lifou (Leifear), island, *New Caledonia, Fr.* 190 G7
Lightning Ridge, *N.S.W., Austral.* 187 H14
Ligneuville, *Belg.* 124 H10
Ligny-en-Barrois, *Fr.* 125 K10
Ligurian Sea, *It.* 128 F3
Lihir, island, *P.N.G.* 188 B5
Lihir Group, *P.N.G.* 188 B5
Līhue, *Hawaii, U.S.* 93 L11
Lijiang, *China* 157 K10
Lijin, *Shandong, China* 158 D7
Likasi, *D.R.C.* 176 L9
Likupang, *Indonesia* 167 G12
L'Île-Bouchard, *Fr.* 125 M6
L'Île-Rousse, *Fr.* 128 G3
Liling, *Hunan, China* 159 M3
Lille, *Fr.* 124 H8
Lillehammer, *Nor.* 119 H11
Lillesand, *Nor.* 119 K10
Lillie Glacier, *Antarctica* 201 M11
Lillooet, *B.C., Can.* 88 J4
Lilongwe, *Malawi* 181 D10
Lilo Viejo, *Arg.* 110 E6
Lim, river, *Serb.* 130 F8
Lima, *Ohio, U.S.* 93 E13
Lima, *Peru* 108 F4
Lima, river, *Port.* 122 C4
Liman, *Russ.* 135 N12
Liman Beren, lake, *Russ.* 135 M11
Limarí, Río, *Chile* 110 G2
Limavady, *N. Ire., U.K.* 121 K4
Limbara, Monte, *It.* 128 J3
Limbdi, *India* 154 G2
Limbe, *Cameroon* 179 F12
Limbé, *Haiti* 97 H12
Limburg, *Ger.* 126 F5
Limeira, *Braz.* 109 J12
Limenária, *Gr.* 133 C10
Limerick (Luimneach), *Ire.* 121 N3
Limfjorden, lake, *Den.* 119 K10
Limia, river, *Sp.* 122 C5
Limín see Thássos, *Gr.* 133 B11
Liminka, *Fin.* 119 E14
Limmen Bight, *Austral.* 185 B10
Límni, *Gr.* 132 F9
Límni Kastorías, *Gr.* 132 C6
Límnos (Lemnos), island, *Gr.* 133 D11
Limoges, *Fr.* 125 P6
Limón, *C.R.* 95 L14
Limon, Mount, *Mauritius* 181 J15
Limone Piemonte, *It.* 128 E2
Limoux, *Fr.* 125 S7
Limpopo, river, *Botswana, Mozambique, S. Af.* 181 G10
Līnah, *Saudi Arabia* 148 E7
Lin'an, *Zhejiang, China* 159 K8
Linapacan, island, *Philippines* 167 D10
Linares, *Chile* 110 J3
Linares, *Mex.* 94 E8
Linares, *Sp.* 122 H9
Linariá, *Gr.* 133 F10
Lincang, *China* 157 L10
Linchuan, *Jiangxi, China* 159 M5
Lincoln, *Arg.* 110 H6
Lincoln, *Eng., U.K.* 121 M10
Lincoln, *Nebr., U.S.* 93 E10
Lincoln Heights, region, *Eng., U.K.* 121 M10
Lincoln Island, *China* 166 B8
Lincoln Sea, *Greenland, Den.* 84 B7
Linda Downs, *Qnsld., Austral.* 187 E11
Lindau, *Ger.* 126 J6
Linden, *Guyana* 107 D14

Lindenow Fjord see Kangerlussuatsiaq, *Greenland, Den.* 199 M15
Lindesnes, point, *Nor.* 119 K10
Lindi, *Tanzania* 177 L12
Lindisfarne see Holy Island, *Eng., U.K.* 120 J9
Lindo Monte, river, *Para.* 108 J9
Líndos, *Gr.* 133 K15
Line Islands, *Kiribati* 191 D12
Linfen, *Shanxi, China* 158 E3
Lingao, *China* 157 M13
Lingbao, *Henan, China* 158 G2
Lingbi, *Anhui, China* 158 H6
Lingchuan, *Guangxi Zhuangzu, China* 159 N1
Lingen, *Ger.* 126 C5
Lingga, island, *Indonesia* 166 H5
Lingga, Kepulauan, *Indonesia* 166 G5
Lingou, *Shanxi, China* 158 C4
Ling Qu, *Guangxi Zhuangzu, China* 159 N1
Lingshan Dao, *Shandong, China* 158 F8
Lingshan Wan, *Shandong, China* 158 F8
Linguère, *Senegal* 174 F3
Lingui, *Guangxi Zhuangzu, China* 159 P1
Lingxian, *Shandong, China* 158 E6
Lingyuan, *Liaoning, China* 158 B7
Linhai, *Zhejiang, China* 159 L9
Linhares, *Braz.* 109 H14
Linhe, *China* 157 E12
Linjiang, *Jilin, China* 158 A12
Linköping, *Sweden* 119 J12
Linli, *Hunan, China* 159 L2
Linnhe, Loch, *Scot., U.K.* 120 H6
Linqing, *Shandong, China* 158 E5
Linquan, *Anhui, China* 158 H5
Linshu, *Shandong, China* 158 G7
Lintao, *China* 157 G11
Linxi, *Hebei, China* 158 C7
Linxi, *Hebei, China* 158 E5
Linxia, *China* 157 G11
Linxian, *Shanxi, China* 158 D2
Linxiang, *Hunan, China* 159 L4
Linyi, *Shaanxi, China* 158 F2
Linyi, *Shandong, China* 158 F7
Linying, *Henan, China* 158 G4
Linz, *Aust.* 126 H9
Linzhou, *Henan, China* 158 F4
Linzi, *Shandong, China* 158 E7
Lio Matoh, *Malaysia* 166 F8
Lions, Gulf of, *Europe* 114 J6
Lions Den, *Zimb.* 180 E9
Lios nag Cearrbhach see Lisburn, *N. Ire., U.K.* 121 L5
Lios Tuathail see Listowel, *Ire.* 121 P2
Liot Point, *N.W.T., Can.* 88 C7
Liouesso, *Congo* 179 G14
Lipa, *Philippines* 167 C10
Lipari, Isola, *It.* 129 M9
Lipari, Isole (Eolie), *It.* 129 M9
Lipetsk, *Russ.* 134 J9
Lipno, *Pol.* 127 C12
Lipova, *Rom.* 131 C10
Lipsí, *Gr.* 133 H13
Lipsí, island, *Gr.* 133 H13
Liptovský Mikuláš, *Slovakia* 127 G13
Lipu, *Guangxi Zhuangzu, China* 159 P1
Lipu Lekh Pass, *China, India* 154 D6
Liri, river, *It.* 128 J7
Līsakovsk, *Kaz.* 150 B8
Lisala, *D.R.C.* 176 G7
Lisboa (Lisbon), *Port.* 122 G4
Lisbon see Lisboa, *Port.* 122 G4
Lisburn (Lios nag Cearrbhach), *N. Ire., U.K.* 121 L5
Lisburne, Cape, *U.S.* 198 H4
Liscannor Bay, *Ire.* 121 N2

Li Shan, *Shanxi, China* 158 F3
Lishi, *Shanxi, China* 158 D2
Lishui, *Zhejiang, China* 159 L8
Lisianski Island, *Hawaii, U.S.* 190 A9
Lisieux, *Fr.* 125 K5
Liski, *Russ.* 135 K9
L'Isle-sur-la-Sorgue, *Fr.* 125 R10
Lismore, *N.S.W., Austral.* 187 H16
Lismore, *Vic., Austral.* 187 M12
Lismore, island, *Scot., U.K.* 120 H6
Lissa see Vis, island, *Croatia* 130 G5
Lister, Mount, *Antarctica* 201 K10
Litang, *China* 157 J10
Litani, river, *Fr. Guiana, Fr., Suriname* 107 F16
Lîtâni, river, *Leb.* 146 G4
Lit-et-Mixe, *Fr.* 125 R4
Lithuania, *Europe* 117 F10
Líthino, Akrotírio, *Gr.* 133 M11
Litóhoro, *Gr.* 132 C8
Little Abaco Island, *Bahamas* 96 A7
Little Andaman, island, *India* 155 M11
Little Barrier Island, *N.Z.* 189 C15
Little Bitter Lake see Murrat el Sughra, Buheirat, *Egypt* 147 L1
Little Cayman, island, *Cayman Is., U.K.* 96 H5
Little Coco Island, *Myanmar* 164 H3
Little Exuma, island, *Bahamas* 96 D9
Littlehampton, *Eng., U.K.* 121 R10
Little Inagua Island, *Bahamas* 97 F11
Little Minch, The, strait, *Scot., U.K.* 120 F4
Little Missouri, river, *U.S.* 90 B8
Little Nicobar, island, *India* 155 N11
Little Rock, *Ark., U.S.* 93 G11
Little San Salvador, island, *Bahamas* 96 C9
Little Sitkin, island, *U.S.* 85 S2
Liuchiu Yü, *Taiwan, China* 159 R8
Liuhe, *Jilin, China* 158 A11
Liulin, *Shanxi, China* 158 D2
Liuwa Plain, *Zambia* 180 D7
Liuzhou, *China* 157 K13
Livadi, *Gr.* 133 H10
Livadiá, *Gr.* 132 F8
Livádia, *Gr.* 133 K14
Līvāni, *Latv.* 119 K16
Liverpool, *Eng., U.K.* 121 M8
Liverpool, *N.S., Can.* 89 L14
Liverpool Bay, *N.W.T., Can.* 88 D6
Liverpool Range, *Austral.* 185 K15
Lívingston, *Guatemala* 95 J12
Livingston, *Mont., U.S.* 92 C6
Livingstone, *Zambia* 180 E8
Livingston Island, *Antarctica* 200 C3
Livny, *Russ.* 134 J8
Livorno (Leghorn), *It.* 128 F4
Livron, *Fr.* 125 Q10
Līwā, region, *U.A.E.* 149 H11
Liwale, *Tanzania* 177 L12
Liwonde, *Malawi* 181 D11
Lixian, *Hunan, China* 159 K2
Lixin, *Anhui, China* 158 H5
Liyang, *Jiangsu, China* 158 J7
Li Yubu, *S. Sudan* 176 F9
Lizard Point, *Eng., U.K.* 121 S6
Lizarra see Estella, *Sp.* 123 B10
Ljubljana, *Slov.* 130 C4
Ljusdal, *Sweden* 119 G12
Llamara, Salar de, *Chile* 110 B3
Llandrindod see Llandrindod Wells, *Wales, U.K.* 121 P7
Llandrindod Wells (Llandrindod), *Wales, U.K.* 121 P7
Llanes, *Sp.* 122 A8
Llano de la Magdalena, region, *Mex.* 94 E3

Llano Estacado (Staked Plain), *U.S.* 85 L4
Llanos, plain, *S. Amer.* 102 D3
Llanquihue, Lago, *Chile* 111 L2
Llavorsí, *Sp.* 123 C13
Lleida, *Sp.* 123 D13
Llerena, *Sp.* 122 H7
Lleyn Peninsula, *Wales, U.K.* 121 N6
Llica, *Bol.* 108 H7
Llívia, *Sp.* 123 C14
Llodio, *Sp.* 123 B10
Lloydminster, *Alta., Sask., Can.* 88 J6
Llucmajor, *Sp.* 123 F15
Llyswen, *Wales, U.K.* 121 P7
Lo, river, *Viet.* 164 D9
Loa, Mauna, *U.S.* 91 M13
Loa, river, *Chile* 110 B3
Loaita Island, *Spratly Is.* 166 D8
Lobamba, *Swaziland* 180 H9
Lobatse, *Botswana* 180 G8
Lobería, *Arg.* 111 K8
Lobería, *Arg.* 111 M6
Lobito, *Angola* 180 C4
Lobitos, *Peru* 108 D3
Lobo, *Indonesia* 167 J15
Lobos, *Arg.* 110 J7
Lobos Bahamas, Cay, *Bahamas* 96 E7
Lobuya, *Russ.* 137 D14
Locana, *It.* 128 C2
Locarno, *Switz.* 128 C3
Lochcarron, *Scot., U.K.* 120 F6
Lochearnhead, *Scot., U.K.* 120 H7
Loch Garman see Wexford, *Ire.* 121 P5
Lochgilphead, *Scot., U.K.* 120 H6
Lochmaddy see Loch na Madadh, *Scot., U.K.* 120 F4
Loch na Madadh (Lochmaddy), *Scot., U.K.* 120 F4
Lochy, Loch, *Scot., U.K.* 120 G6
Lockhart River, *Qnsld., Austral.* 187 B13
Locminé, *Fr.* 125 L3
Locri, *It.* 129 N10
Lod (Lydda), *Israel* 146 J4
Lodeynoye Pole, *Russ.* 134 C6
Lodhran, *Pak.* 153 N8
Lodi, *It.* 128 D4
Lodja, *D.R.C.* 176 J8
Lodwar, *Kenya* 177 G11
Łódź, *Pol.* 127 D12
Loei, *Thai.* 164 G7
Lofoten, islands, *Nor.* 119 D11
Lofty Range, *Austral.* 184 F4
Logan, *Utah, U.S.* 92 D5
Logan, Mount, *Yukon, Can.* 88 E3
Logashkino, *Russ.* 137 C14
Logoniégué, *Burkina Faso* 178 C7
Logroño, *Sp.* 123 C10
Lohardaga, *India* 154 G7
Loharghat, *India* 154 E10
Lohne, *Ger.* 126 C5
Loi Mwe, *Myanmar* 164 E6
Loire, river, *Fr.* 125 M4
Loja, *Ecua.* 106 K4
Loja, *Sp.* 122 J8
Loji, *Indonesia* 167 H12
Lokhwabe, *Botswana* 180 G7
Lokitaung, *Kenya* 177 G11
Loknya, *Russ.* 134 F5
Lokoja, *Nig.* 179 D11
Lokolama, *D.R.C.* 176 J7
Lokomo, *Cameroon* 179 F14
Lokoro, river, *D.R.C.* 176 J7
Loks Land, island, *Nunavut, Can.* 89 F13
Lol, river, *S. Sudan* 176 E9
Lolland, island, *Den.* 119 L11
Lom, *Bulg.* 131 F11
Lom, *Nor.* 119 G10
Lomami, river, *D.R.C.* 176 H8

Loma Mountains, *Guinea, Sierra Leone* **178** C5
Lombadina, *W. Austral., Austral.* **186** C5
Lombez, *Fr.* **125** S6
Lomblen, island, *Indonesia* **167** KII
Lombok, island, *Indonesia* **166** K9
Lombok, Selat, *Indonesia* **166** K9
Lomé, *Togo* **178** E9
Lomela, *D.R.C.* **176** H8
Lomela, river, *D.R.C.* **176** H8
Lomié, *Cameroon* **179** FI4
Lomond, Loch, *Scot., U.K.* **120** H6
Lomonosov, *Russ.* **134** D5
Lomphat, *Cambodia* **164** JIO
Lompoc, *Calif., U.S.* **92** F2
Łomża, *Pol.* **127** CI4
Lon, Hon, *Viet.* **164** JII
Lonauli, *India* **154** J3
Loncoche, *Chile* **III** L2
Loncopué, *Arg.* **III** K3
London, *Eng., U.K.* **121** QII
London, *Ont., Can.* **89** MII
Londonderry (Derry), *N. Ire., U.K.* **121** K4
Londonderry, Cape, *Austral.* **184** B7
Londonderry, Isla, *Chile* **III** T3
Londrina, *Braz.* **109** JII
Longa, river, *Angola* **180** C4
Long Beach, *Calif., U.S.* **92** G3
Long Cay (Fortune Island), *Bahamas* **97** EIO
Longchuan, *Guangdong, China* **159** Q5
Long Eaton, *Eng., U.K.* **121** N9
Longeau, *Fr.* **125** LIO
Longford (An Longfort), *Ire.* **121** M3
Longglat, *Indonesia* **166** G9
Longhai, *Fujian, China* **159** P6
Longhua, *Hebei, China* **158** B6
Longhui, *Hunan, China* **159** M2
Longido, *Tanzania* **177** JII
Longiram, *Indonesia* **166** H9
Long Island, *Bahamas* **97** EIO
Long Island, *N.Y., U.S.* **93** DI6
Long Island, *Nunavut, Can.* **89** JII
Long Island, *P.N.G.* **188** E6
Long Island Sound, *U.S.* **91** DI6
Longjiang, *China* **157** CI5
Longjing, *China* **157** DI7
Longju, *India* **154** DII
Longjuzhai *see* Danfeng, *Shaanxi, China* **158** G2
Longkou, *Shandong, China* **158** D8
Longlac, *Ont., Can.* **89** KIO
Longmen, *Guangdong, China* **159** Q4
Longmont, *Colo., U.S.* **92** E7
Longnan, *Jiangxi, China* **159** P4
Longnawan, *Indonesia* **166** G8
Longquan, *Zhejiang, China* **159** M7
Long Range Mountains, *Can.* **84** HIO
Longreach, *Qnsld., Austral.* **187** FI3
Longshan, *Hunan, China* **159** KI
Longsheng, *Guangxi Zhuangzu, China* **159** NI
Longs Peak, *U.S.* **90** E7
Long Strait, *Russ.* **198** G4
Longview, *Tex., U.S.* **93** HIO
Longview, *Wash., U.S.* **92** B3
Longwy, *Fr.* **124** JIO
Longxi, *China* **157** GII
Longxian, *China* **157** GI2
Long Xuyen, *Viet.* **165** K9
Longyan, *Fujian, China* **159** P6
Longyearbyen, *Nor.* **199** FI2
Long'yugan, *Russ.* **136** F8
Lonquimay, *Chile* **III** K3
Lons-le-Saunier, *Fr.* **125** NIO
Lookout, Cape, *U.S.* **91** FI6
Lookout, Point, *Austral.* **185** HI6

Loongana, *W. Austral., Austral.* **186** J7
Loop Head, *Ire.* **121** NI
Lop, *China* **156** F5
Lopatino, *Russ.* **134** H7
Lopatka, Mys, *Russ.* **137** FI8
Lop Buri, *Thai.* **164** H7
Lopez, Cap, *Gabon* **179** GI2
Lop Nur, *China* **156** E8
Lopphavet, bay, *Nor.* **119** BI2
Lora, Hamun-i-, *Pak.* **153** N3
Loralai, *Pak.* **153** M6
Lorca, *Sp.* **123** JII
Lord Howe Island, *Austral., Pac. Oc.* **190** H6
Lord of the Sky *see* Khan Tängiri, *Kyrg.* **152** CI2
Lordsburg, *N. Mex., U.S.* **92** H6
Loreto, *Bol.* **108** G8
Loreto, *Braz.* **109** DI3
Loreto, *Mex.* **94** D4
Lorica, *Col.* **106** C5
Lorient, *Fr.* **125** L2
Lorimers, *Turks & Caicos Is., U.K.* **97** FI2
Lormes, *Fr.* **125** M8
Lormi, *India* **154** G6
Lorn, Firth of, *Scot., U.K.* **120** H5
Lornel, Pointe de, *Fr.* **124** H7
Lörrach, *Ger.* **126** J4
Lorraine, *Qnsld., Austral.* **187** DI2
Lorraine, region, *Fr.* **125** KIO
Los Alamos, *N. Mex., U.S.* **92** G7
Los Andes, *Chile* **IIO** H3
Los Angeles, *Calif., U.S.* **92** G3
Los Ángeles, *Chile* **III** K2
Los Blancos, *Arg.* **IIO** C6
Los Cerrillos, *Arg.* **IIO** G5
Los Corrales, *Sp.* **122** B9
Los Frailes, islands, *Venez.* **99** HII
Los Hermanos, islands, *Venez.* **99** HII
Lošinj, island, *Croatia* **130** E4
Los Lagos, *Chile* **III** L2
Los Loros, *Chile* **IIO** E3
Los Mochis, *Mex.* **94** D4
Los Palacios, *Cuba* **96** E2
Lospalos, *Timor-Leste* **167** KI2
Los Roques, Islas, *Venez.* **107** BIO
Lossiemouth, *Scot., U.K.* **120** F7
Los Teques, *Venez.* **107** BIO
Los Testigos, islands, *Venez.* **99** HI2
Losuia, *P.N.G.* **188** D7
Los Vilos, *Chile* **IIO** G3
Los Yébenes, *Sp.* **122** F9
Lot, river, *Fr.* **125** R6
Lota, *Chile* **III** K2
Lotagipi Swamp, *Kenya* **177** GII
Lot's Wife *see* Sōfu Gan, island, *Japan* **163** N9
Lou, island, *P.N.G.* **188** E4
Louang-Namtha, *Laos* **164** E7
Louangphrabang, *Laos* **164** E7
Loubomo *see* Dolisie, *Congo* **179** JI3
Loudéac, *Fr.* **125** L3
Loudi, *Hunan, China* **159** M2
Loudun, *Fr.* **125** M5
Loué, *Fr.* **125** L5
Louga, *Senegal* **174** F3
Lougheed Island, *Nunavut, Can.* **88** B9
Louhans, *Fr.* **125** NIO
Louisa Downs, *W. Austral., Austral.* **186** D7
Louisburgh (Cluain Cearbán), *Ire.* **121** M2
Louisiade Archipelago, *P.N.G.* **188** B8
Louisiana, *U.S.* **93** HII
Louisville, *Ky., U.S.* **93** FI3
Louis-XIV, Pointe, *Que., Can.* **89** JII
Loukouo, *Congo* **179** HI4
Loulay, *Fr.* **125** P5
Loulé, *Port.* **122** J4

Loup, river, *U.S.* **90** E9
Lourdes, *Fr.* **125** S5
Lourdes-de-Blanc-Sablon, *Que., Can.* **89** HI5
Lousã, *Port.* **122** F5
Louth, *Eng., U.K.* **121** MIO
Loutrá Eleftherón, *Gr.* **133** BIO
Loutrá Epidsoú, *Gr.* **132** F8
Loutráki, *Gr.* **132** E9
Loutráki, *Gr.* **132** G8
Loutrá Smokóvou, *Gr.* **132** E7
Louviers, *Fr.* **125** K6
Lovea, *Cambodia* **164** J8
Lovech, *Bulg.* **131** GI2
Lovelock, *Nev., U.S.* **92** D3
Lovere, *It.* **128** C4
Low, Cape, *Nunavut, Can.* **89** FIO
Lowell, *Mass., U.S.* **93** CI6
Lower Guinea, *Af.* **171** L5
Lower Hutt, *N.Z.* **189** GI5
Lower Lough Erne, *Ire.* **121** L3
Lower Peninsula, *U.S.* **91** CI3
Lower Post, *B.C., Can.* **88** F5
Lower Red Lake, *U.S.* **91** BIO
Lowestoft, *Eng., U.K.* **121** NI2
Łowicz, *Pol.* **127** DI3
Lowkhi, *Afghan.* **153** L2
Loyal, Loch, *Scot., U.K.* **120** E6
Loyalty Islands, *New Caledonia, Fr.* **190** G7
Loyew, *Belarus* **134** J5
Loyola, Punta, *Arg.* **III** R4
Loznica, *Serb.* **130** E8
Lozova, *Ukr.* **135** L7
Lu, river, *Shaanxi, China* **158** DI
Luama, river, *D.R.C.* **176** J9
Lu'an, *Anhui, China* **158** J6
Luan, river, *Hebei, China* **158** B7
Luancheng, *Hebei, China* **158** D4
Luanchuan, *Henan, China* **158** G2
Luanco, *Sp.* **122** A7
Luanda, *Angola* **180** B4
Luang Prabang Range, *Laos* **164** F7
Luangwa, *Zambia* **180** D9
Luangwa, river, *Zambia* **180** D9
Luanping, *Hebei, China* **158** B6
Luanshya, *Zambia* **180** C9
Luanxian, *Hebei, China* **158** C7
Luapula, river, *Af.* **171** N8
Luarca, *Sp.* **122** A6
Luau, *Angola* **180** C7
Luba, *Eq. Guinea* **179** FI2
Lubāns Ezers, lake, *Latv.* **119** JI6
Lubang Island, *Philippines* **167** CIO
Lubango, *Angola* **180** D4
Lubao, *D.R.C.* **176** J9
Lubartów, *Pol.* **127** EI4
Lübbenau, *Ger.* **126** D9
Lubbock, *Tex., U.S.* **92** H8
Lübeck, *Ger.* **126** B7
Lubero, *D.R.C.* **177** HIO
Lubéron, Montagne Du, *Fr.* **125** RIO
Lubin, *Pol.* **127** EIO
Lublin, *Pol.* **127** EI4
Lubliniec, *Pol.* **127** FI2
Lubny, *Ukr.* **135** K6
Lubok Antu, *Malaysia* **166** G7
Luboten, peak, *Kos.* **130** H9
Lubu, *Guangdong, China* **159** Q2
Lubuagan, *Philippines* **167** BIO
Lubudi, *D.R.C.* **176** L9
Lubuklinggau, *Indonesia* **166** J4
Lubumbashi (Elisabethville), *D.R.C.* **176** L9
Lucaya, *Bahamas* **96** A6
Lucca, *It.* **128** F5
Lucea, *Jamaica* **96** J7
Luce Bay, *Scot., U.K.* **121** K6
Lucena, *Philippines* **167** CIO
Lucena, *Sp.* **122** J8

Lučenec, *Slovakia* **127** HI3
Lucera, *It.* **128** H9
Lucerne, Lake of *see* Vierwaldstätter See, *Switz.* **128** B3
Luchegorsk, *Russ.* **137** JI6
Lucheng, *Shanxi, China* **158** E4
Lucie, river, *Suriname* **107** FI4
Lucipara, Kepulauan, *Indonesia* **167** JI2
Lucira, *Angola* **180** D4
Lucknow, *India* **154** E6
Lucknow, *Qnsld., Austral.* **187** FI2
Lücongpo, *Hubei, China* **158** JI
Lucy Creek, *N. Terr., Austral.* **187** EIO
Luda Kamchiya, river, *Bulg.* **131** GI4
Ludborough, *Eng., U.K.* **121** MIO
Lüdenscheid, *Ger.* **126** E5
Lüderitz, *Namibia* **180** H5
Ludhiana, *India* **154** C4
Ludogorsko Plato, mountains, *Bulg.* **131** FI4
Ludus, *Rom.* **131** CI2
Ludwigsburg, *Ger.* **126** H6
Ludwigshafen, *Ger.* **126** G5
Luebo, *D.R.C.* **176** J7
Luena, *Angola* **180** C6
Lüeyang, *China* **157** HI2
Lufeng, *Guangdong, China* **159** Q5
Lufkin, *Tex., U.S.* **93** HIO
Luga, *Russ.* **134** E5
Lugano, *Switz.* **128** C3
Lugenda, river, *Mozambique* **181** CII
Lugo, *It.* **128** E6
Lugo, *Sp.* **122** B5
Lugoj, *Rom.* **131** DIO
Lugovoy, *Russ.* **136** G7
Luhans'k, *Ukr.* **135** L9
Luhuo, *China* **157** HIO
Luiana, river, *Angola* **180** E7
Luichow Peninsula *see* Leizhou Bandao, *Guangdong, China* **159** SI
Luimneach *see* Limerick, *Ire.* **121** N3
Luing, island, *Scot., U.K.* **120** H5
Luino, *It.* **128** C3
Luitpold Coast, *Antarctica* **200** D8
Luján, *Arg.* **IIO** H7
Lujiang, *Anhui, China* **158** J6
Luke, Mount, *Austral.* **184** H4
Lukenie, river, *D.R.C.* **176** J7
Lukolela, *D.R.C.* **176** H6
Lukovit, *Bulg.* **131** GI2
Łuków, *Pol.* **127** DI4
Lukulu, *Zambia* **180** D7
Luleå, *Sweden* **119** EI3
Lüleburgaz, *Turk.* **144** B2
Lules, *Arg.* **IIO** E5
Lüliang Shan, *Shanxi, China* **158** E2
Lulong, *Hebei, China* **158** C7
Lulonga, river, *D.R.C.* **176** H7
Lulua, river, *D.R.C.* **176** K8
Lumajangdong Co, *China* **156** G6
Luman, *Afghan.* **153** K5
Lumbala N'guimbo, *Angola* **180** D6
Lumberton, *N.C., U.S.* **93** GI5
Lumbo, *Mozambique* **181** DI2
Lumbrales, *Sp.* **122** E6
Lumbres, *Fr.* **124** H7
Lumding, *India* **154** EII
Lumi, *P.N.G.* **188** G5
Lumu, *Indonesia* **167** HIO
Lumut, *Malaysia* **165** P7
Lunavada, *India* **154** G3
Lundazi, *Zambia* **181** CIO
Lundu, *Malaysia* **166** G7
Lundy Island, *Eng., U.K.* **121** R6
Lüneburg, *Ger.* **126** C7
Lüneburger Heide, region, *Ger.* **126** C7
Lunéville, *Fr.* **125** KII
Lunggar, *China* **156** H6

Mahuva, *India* 154 H2
Maibong, *India* 154 F11
Maicao, *Col.* 106 B7
Maîche, *Fr.* 125 M11
Maicuru, river, *Braz.* 109 B11
Maida, *It.* 129 M10
Maidenhead, *Eng., U.K.* 121 Q10
Maiduguri, *Nig.* 179 C13
Maigh Chromtha see Macroom, *Ire.*
121 P2
Maigualida, Serra, *Venez.* 107 E11
Maihar, *India* 154 F6
Maikoor, island, *Indonesia* 188 L6
Mailly-le-Camp, *Fr.* 125 K9
Mailsi, *Pak.* 153 M8
Main, river, *Ger.* 126 G7
Mai-Ndombe, Lac, *D.R.C.* 176 H7
Maine, Gulf of, *Atl. Oc.* 91 C17
Maine, *U.S.* 93 B16
Maingkwan, *Myanmar* 164 B5
Main Island (Bermuda Island),
Bermuda, U.K. 97 D13
Mainistir Fhear Maí see Fermoy, *Ire.*
121 P3
Mainistir Laoise see Abbeyleix, *Ire.*
121 N4
Mainistir na Búille see Boyle, *Ire.*
121 L3
Mainistir na Féile see Abbeyfeale, *Ire.*
121 P2
Mainland, island, *Scot., U.K.* 120 B9
Mainland, island, *Scot., U.K.* 120 D7
Mainoru, *N. Terr., Austral.* 187 B10
Maintirano, *Madag.* 181 E13
Mainz, *Ger.* 126 F5
Maio, island, *Cape Verde* 174 E2
Maiquetía, *Venez.* 107 B10
Maire, Estrecho de Le, *Chile* 111 T5
Maisí, *Cuba* 97 G10
Maisí, Punta de, *Cuba* 97 G10
Maiskhal, island, *Bangladesh* 154 G10
Maitland, *N.S.W., Austral.* 187 K15
Maitri, station, *Antarctica* 201 A11
Maíz, Islas del, *Nicar.* 95 K14
Maizhokunggar, *China* 156 H8
Maizuru, *Japan* 162 J6
Majene, *Indonesia* 167 J10
Majī, *Eth.* 177 F11
Majorca see Mallorca, island, *Sp.*
123 F16
Majuro, *Marshall Is.* 190 C8
Makale, *Indonesia* 167 J10
Makalu, peak, *Nepal* 154 E8
Makarov, *Russ.* 137 H17
Makarovo, *Russ.* 137 H11
Makar'yev, *Russ.* 134 E10
Makassar (Ujungpandang), *Indonesia*
167 J10
Makassar Strait, *Indonesia* 166 H9
Makatea, island, *Fr. Polynesia, Fr.*
191 F12
Make Jima, *Japan* 163 M3
Makemo, island, *Fr. Polynesia, Fr.*
191 F13
Makeni, *Sierra Leone* 178 D4
Makgadikgadi Pans, *Botswana* 180 F8
Makhachkala, *Russ.* 136 H2
Makhad, *Pak.* 153 K8
Makhado, *S. Af.* 180 G9
Makhambet, *Kaz.* 150 D5
Makhfar al Buşayyah, *Iraq* 148 E8
Maki, *Indonesia* 167 J15
Makīnsk, *Kaz.* 151 B11
Makiyivka, *Ukr.* 135 M8
Makkah (Mecca), *Saudi Arabia*
148 H5
Makkovik, *Nfld. & Lab., Can.* 89 H14
Makó, *Hung.* 127 L14
Makokou, *Gabon* 179 G13
Makoua, *Congo* 179 G14

Makrá, island, *Gr.* 133 K12
Makrakómi, *Gr.* 132 E7
Makrana, *India* 154 E3
Makran Coast Range, *Pak.* 153 Q2
Makrínitsa, *Gr.* 132 E8
Makroníssi (Helena, Eléni), island, *Gr.*
133 G10
Mākū, *Iran* 148 A7
Makung, *Taiwan, China* 159 Q8
Makunudu Atoll (Malcolm), *Maldives*
155 P2
Makurazaki, *Japan* 163 M3
Makurdi, *Nig.* 179 D12
Mâl, *Mauritania* 174 F4
Mala see Mallow, *Ire.* 121 P3
Malabar Coast, *India* 155 M3
Malabo, *Eq. Guinea* 179 F12
Malabuñgan, *Philippines* 166 E9
Malacca, *Malaysia* 165 Q7
Malacca, Strait of, *Indonesia, Malaysia*
165 N5
Malacky, *Slovakia* 127 H11
Maladzyechna, *Belarus* 134 G4
Málaga, *Col.* 106 D7
Málaga, *Sp.* 122 K8
Malagón, *Sp.* 122 G9
Málainn Mhóir (Malin More), *Ire.*
121 K3
Malaita, island, *Solomon Is.* 190 E6
Malakal, *S. Sudan* 177 E10
Malakanagiri, *India* 154 J6
Malakand, *Pak.* 152 J8
Malakula, island, *Vanuatu* 190 F7
Malang, *Indonesia* 166 K8
Malanje, *Angola* 180 B5
Malanville, *Benin* 179 C10
Malar, *Pak.* 153 Q3
Mälaren, lake, *Sweden* 119 J13
Malargüe, *Arg.* 110 J3
Malaspina Glacier, *U.S.* 198 L3
Malatya, *Turk.* 145 E10
Mala Vyska, *Ukr.* 135 L5
Malawi, *Af.* 173 N9
Malawi, Lake (Nyasa, Lake), *Af.*
181 C11
Malayagiri, peak, *India* 154 G8
Malaya Vishera, *Russ.* 134 E6
Malaybalay, *Philippines* 167 E12
Malāyer, *Iran* 148 C9
Malay Peninsula, *Asia* 141 K11
Malaysia, *Asia* 143 L11
Malazgirt, *Turk.* 145 E13
Malbork, *Pol.* 127 B12
Malcolm, *W. Austral., Austral.* 186 H5
Malcolm see Makunudu Atoll, *Maldives*
155 P2
Malcolm, Point, *Austral.* 184 K6
Maldegem, *Belg.* 124 G8
Malden Island, *Kiribati* 191 E12
Maldive Islands, *Maldives* 155 Q2
Maldives, *Asia* 142 L7
Maldonado, *Uru.* 110 J9
Maldonado, Punta, *Mex.* 94 J8
Malè, *It.* 128 B5
Male see Maale, *Maldives* 155 Q3
Maléas, Akrotírio, *Gr.* 132 K9
Male Atoll, *Maldives* 155 Q3
Malebo, Pool, *D.R.C.* 176 J6
Malegaon, *India* 154 H3
Malemba-Nkulu, *D.R.C.* 176 K8
Malessína, *Gr.* 132 F8
Malgobek, *Russ.* 135 P11
Malhão, Serra do, *Port.* 122 J4
Malhargarh, *India* 154 F3
Mali, *Af.* 172 J2
Mali, river, *Myanmar* 164 B5
Mália, *Gr.* 133 M12
Mali Drvenik, island, *Croatia* 130 F5
Mali Kyun, *Myanmar* 164 J5
Malili, *Indonesia* 167 H10

Malindi, *Kenya* 177 J12
Malin Head (Inis Trá Tholl), cape, *Ire.*
120 J4
Malin More see Málainn Mhóir, *Ire.*
121 K3
Malkapur, *India* 154 H4
Malkara, *Turk.* 144 C2
Malki, *Russ.* 137 F17
Korab, Mal, *Alban.* 130 H9
Malko Tŭrnovo, *Bulg.* 131 H15
Mallacoota, *Vic., Austral.* 187 M14
Mallacoota Inlet, *Austral.* 185 M14
Mallawi, *Egypt* 175 C14
Mallorca (Majorca), island, *Sp.*
123 F16
Mallow (Mala), *Ire.* 121 P3
Malmand Range, *Afghan.* 153 K3
Malmberget, *Sweden* 119 D13
Malmesbury, *S. Af.* 180 K6
Malmö, *Sweden* 119 L12
Maloelap Atoll, *Marshall Is.* 190 C8
Maloja, *Switz.* 128 B4
Maloshuyka, *Russ.* 136 D5
Måløy, *Nor.* 118 G9
Malpelo, Isla de, *Col, Pac. Oc.* 193 D16
Malpelo Island, *S. Amer.* 102 D1
Malta, *Europe* 116 M8
Malta, *Mont., U.S.* 92 B7
Malta, island, *Malta* 129 Q8
Maltahöhe, *Namibia* 180 G5
Malton, *Eng., U.K.* 121 L10
Maluku see Moluccas, islands,
Indonesia 167 H12
Malung, *Sweden* 119 H12
Malvan, *India* 155 K3
Malvinas, Islas see Falkland Islands,
Falk. Is., U.K. 111 S7
Malyn, *Ukr.* 135 K4
Malyye Karmakuly, *Russ.* 136 D7
Malyy Lyakhovskiy, Ostrov, *Russ.*
137 D13
Mamberamo, *Indonesia* 188 J4
Mamfé, *Cameroon* 179 E12
Mamiña, *Chile* 110 B3
Mamoiada, *It.* 129 K3
Mamoré, river, *Bol.* 108 F7
Mamoriá, *Braz.* 108 E7
Mamou, *Guinea* 178 C4
Mamoudzou, *Fr.* 181 C14
Mampong, *Ghana* 178 D8
Mamuju, *Indonesia* 167 H10
Man, *Côte d'Ivoire* 178 D6
Man, Isle of (Ellan Vannin), *U.K.*
121 L6
Mana, *Fr. Guiana, Fr.* 107 E16
Mana, river, *Fr. Guiana, Fr.* 107 E16
Manacapuru, *Braz.* 108 C9
Manacor, *Sp.* 123 F15
Manado, *Indonesia* 167 G11
Managua, *Nicar.* 95 K13
Managua, Lago de, *Nicar.* 95 K13
Manaia, *N.Z.* 189 F15
Manakara, *Madag.* 181 F14
Manakau, peak, *N.Z.* 189 H14
Manākhah, *Yemen* 148 L7
Mana La, *India* 154 C5
Manam, island, *P.N.G.* 188 F5
Manama see Al Manāmah, *Bahrain*
148 F9
Manamadurai, *India* 155 N5
Mananjary, *Madag.* 181 F14
Manapouri, Lake, *N.Z.* 189 L11
Manas, *China* 156 D7
Manatí, *Cuba* 96 F8
Manatí, *P.R., U.S.* 97 J17
Manaus, *Braz.* 108 C9
Manavgat, *Turk.* 144 G5
Manbij, *Syr.* 146 C7

Manchester, *Eng., U.K.* 121 M8
Manchester, *N.H., U.S.* 93 C16
Manchhar Lake, *Pak.* 153 Q5
Manchuria see Dongbei, region, *China*
157 C16
Manciano, *It.* 128 G5
Mand, *Pak.* 153 Q1
Mand, river, *Iran* 149 F10
Manda, *Tanzania* 177 L11
Mandai, *Pak.* 153 N5
Mandal, *Mongolia* 157 C12
Mandal, *Nei Mongol, China* 158 A2
Mandal, *Nor.* 119 K10
Mandala, Puncak, *Indonesia* 188 H5
Mandalay, *Myanmar* 164 D4
Mandalgovĭ, *Mongolia* 157 D12
Mandalī, *Iraq* 148 C8
Mandan, *N. Dak., U.S.* 92 B8
Mandapeta, *India* 154 J6
Mandara Mountains, *Cameroon, Nig.*
179 C14
Mandeb, Bab el, *Yemen, Djibouti*
148 M6
Mandel, *Afghan.* 153 K1
Mandera, *Kenya* 177 G13
Mandeville, *Jamaica* 96 J7
Mandi, *India* 154 C4
Mandi Burewala, *Pak.* 153 M8
Mandimba, *Mozambique* 181 D11
Mandioli, island, *Indonesia* 167 H12
Mandla, *India* 154 G6
Mandora, *W. Austral., Austral.* 186 E5
Mándra, *Gr.* 132 G9
Mandráki, *Gr.* 133 J14
Mandritsa, *Bulg.* 131 J14
Mandritsara, *Madag.* 181 D15
Mandsaur, *India* 154 F3
Mandu, island, *Maldives* 155 Q2
Mandurah, *W. Austral., Austral.*
186 K4
Manduria, *It.* 129 K11
Mandvi, *India* 154 G1
Manfredonia, *It.* 128 H10
Manfredonia, Golfo di, *It.* 128 H10
Manga, *Braz.* 109 G14
Manga, region, *Niger* 175 G10
Mangabeiras, Chapada das, *Braz.*
109 E13
Mangaia, island, *Cook Is., N.Z.*
191 G11
Mangalia, *Rom.* 131 F15
Mangalore, *India* 155 L3
Mangareva, island, *Fr. Polynesia, Fr.*
191 G14
Mangeigne, *Chad* 175 H12
Mangghystaū, *Kaz.* 150 F4
Manghit, *Uzb.* 150 G7
Mangnai, *China* 156 F8
Mangoche, *Malawi* 181 D11
Mangoky, river, *Madag.* 181 F13
Mangole, island, *Indonesia* 167 H12
Mangqystaū Shyghanaghy, *Kaz.*
150 F4
Mangrol, *India* 154 G1
Manguchar, *Pak.* 153 N4
Mangueira, Lagoa, *Braz.* 109 M11
Manguinho, Ponta do, *Braz.* 109 F16
Mangut, *Russ.* 137 K12
Mangyeong, *S. Korea* 161 N6
Manhattan, *Kans., U.S.* 92 E9
Manhŭng, *N. Korea* 160 C6
Mani, peninsula, *Gr.* 132 J8
Mania, river, *Madag.* 181 F14
Maniamba, *Mozambique* 181 C10
Manica, *Mozambique* 181 E10
Manicoré, *Braz.* 108 D9
Manicouagan, Réservoir, *Que., Can.*
89 J13
Maniḟah, *Saudi Arabia* 148 F9
Manifold, Cape, *Austral.* 185 F16

Manihi, island, *Fr. Polynesia, Fr.*
 191 FI3
Manihiki Atoll, *Cook Is., N.Z.* **191** FII
Manila, *Philippines* **167** CIO
Manila Bay, *Philippines* **167** CIO
Manily, *Russ.* **137** DI6
Maningrida, *N. Terr., Austral.* **187** AIO
Manipa, island, *Indonesia* **167** JI2
Manisa, *Turk.* **144** E2
Manitoba, *Can.* **88** J9
Manitoba, Lake, *Man., Can.* **88** K8
Manizales, *Col.* **106** E6
Manja, *Madag.* **181** FI3
Manjaedo, island, *S. Korea* **161** R4
Manjimup, *W. Austral., Austral.* **186** L4
Manjra, river, *India* **154** J4
Mankato, *Minn., U.S.* **93** CIO
Manlleu, *Sp.* **123** CI4
Manmad, *India* **154** H3
Manna, *Indonesia* **166** J4
Mannar, Gulf of, *India, Sri Lanka*
 155 N5
Mannheim, *Ger.* **126** G5
Mannu, Capo, *It.* **129** K2
Manoa, *Bol.* **108** E7
Man-of-War Cay, *Bahamas* **96** E9
Manokwari, *Indonesia* **188** L4
Manono, *D.R.C.* **176** K9
Manoron, *Myanmar* **165** K6
Mano Wan, *Japan* **162** G8
Man O'War Cay, *Bahamas* **96** A8
Manp'o, *N. Korea* **160** D6
Manra, island, *Kiribati* **191** EIO
Manresa, *Sp.* **123** DI4
Mansa, *Zambia* **180** C9
Mansehra, *Pak.* **152** J8
Mansel Island, *Nunavut, Can.* **89** GII
Mansfield, *Eng., U.K.* **121** N9
Mansfield, *Vic., Austral.* **187** LI3
Mansfield, Mount, *U.S.* **91** BI6
Mansle, *Fr.* **125** P5
Manta, *Ecua.* **106** H3
Mant'ap-san, peak, *N. Korea* **160** E9
Mantes-la-Jolie, *Fr.* **125** K7
Manti, *Utah, U.S.* **92** E5
Mantova, *It.* **128** D5
Mantua, *Cuba* **96** EI
Mantuan Downs, *Qnsld., Austral.*
 187 FI4
Manturovo, *Russ.* **134** EIO
Mäntyluoto, *Fin.* **119** GI4
Manú, *Peru* **108** F6
Manuae, island, *Fr. Polynesia, Fr.*
 191 FI2
Manu'a Islands, *Amer. Samoa, U.S.*
 191 FIO
Manui, island, *Indonesia* **167** JIII
Manukau, *N.Z.* **189** DI5
Manus, island, *P.N.G.* **188** E4
Manvers, Port, *Nfld. & Lab., Can.*
 89 GI4
Manych Gudilo, Ozero, *Russ.*
 135 NIO
Manzai, *Pak.* **153** L7
Manzanares, *Sp.* **122** G9
Manzanillo, *Cuba* **96** G8
Manzanillo, *Mex.* **94** G6
Manzanillo Bay, *Haiti* **97** HI2
Manzanillo Bay, *Mex.* **85** P4
Manzhouli, *China* **157** BI4
Manzil, *Pak.* **153** N2
Mao, *Chad* **175** GII
Mao, *Dom. Rep.* **97** HI3
Maodianzi, *Liaoning, China* **158** BIO
Maoke, Pegunungan, *Indonesia*
 188 J5
Maoming, *Guangdong, China* **159** RI
Maothail *see* Mohill, *Ire.* **121** L3
Mapai, *Mozambique* **181** FIO
Mapi, *Indonesia* **188** H6

Mapia, Kepulauan (Saint David
 Islands), *Indonesia* **188** L3
Mapimí, Bolsón de, *Mex.* **85** N4
Maprik, *P.N.G.* **188** G5
Mapuera, river, *Braz.* **108** B9
Maputo, *Mozambique* **181** GIO
Maputo, Baía de, *Mozambique*
 181 GIO
Maqat, *Kaz.* **150** D5
Maqellarë, *Alban.* **130** J9
Maqên, *China* **157** GIO
Maqnā, *Saudi Arabia* **148** E4
Maqshūsh, *Saudi Arabia* **148** G5
Maquan, river, *China* **156** H7
Maquela do Zombo, *Angola* **180** A5
Maquinchao, *Arg.* **III** L4
Mar, *Russ.* **137** GI2
Mara, *Guyana* **107** DI4
Mara, *India* **154** DII
Maraã, *Braz.* **108** C7
Marabá, *Braz.* **109** DI2
Maracá, Ilha de, *Braz.* **109** BI2
Maracaibo, *Venez.* **106** B7
Maracaibo, Lago de, *Venez.* **106** C7
Maracaju, *Braz.* **109** JIO
Maracanã, *Braz.* **109** CI3
Maracay, *Venez.* **106** B9
Marādah, *Lib.* **175** CI2
Maradi, *Niger* **174** G9
Marado, island, *S. Korea* **161** T5
Marāghah, Sabkhat, *Syr.* **146** D7
Marāgheh, *Iran* **148** B8
Maragogipe, *Braz.* **109** FI5
Marahuaca, Cerro, *Venez.* **107** FIO
Marajó, Baía de, *Braz.* **109** BI2
Marajó, Ilha de, *Braz.* **109** BI2
Marakei, island, *Kiribati* **190** D8
Maralal, *Kenya* **177** HI2
Maralinga, *S. Austral., Austral.* **186** J9
Marambio, station, *Antarctica* **200** B3
Maran, *Malaysia* **165** P8
Maranboy, *N. Terr., Austral.* **186** B9
Maranchón, *Sp.* **123** EIO
Marand, *Iran* **148** A8
Marang, *Malaysia* **165** N8
Maranhão, Barragem do, *Port.* **122** G5
Marañón, river, *Peru* **108** D4
Marans, *Fr.* **125** N4
Marargiu, Capo, *It.* **129** K2
Mara Rosa, *Braz.* **109** FI2
Maraş *see* Varosha, *Cyprus* **133** FI7
Mărăşeşti, *Rom.* **131** DI4
Maratea, *It.* **129** KIO
Marathon, battlefield, *Gr.* **133** GIO
Marathónas, *Gr.* **133** GIO
Marathus *see* 'Amrīt, ruins, *Syr.*
 146 E5
Maraú, *Braz.* **109** GI5
Marāveh Tappeh, *Iran* **149** AII
Maraza, *Azerb.* **145** CI7
Marbella, *Sp.* **122** K8
Marble Bar, *W. Austral., Austral.*
 186 E4
Marburg, *Ger.* **126** E5
Marchena, Isla (Bindloe), *Ecua.*
 106 D2
Marchena, Canal de, *Ecua.* **106** D2
Mar Chiquita, Laguna, *Arg.* **110** F6
Marciana, *It.* **128** G4
Marckolsheim, *Fr.* **125** LI2
Marcos Juárez, *Arg.* **110** G6
Marcus Island *see* Minami Tori Shima,
 Jap., Pac. Oc. **190** A6
Marcy, Mount, *U.S.* **91** CI6
Mardan, *Pak.* **152** J8
Mar del Plata, *Arg.* **III** K8
Mardie, *W. Austral., Austral.* **186** E3
Mardin, *Turk.* **145** FII
Maré, island, *New Caledonia, Fr.*
 190 G7

Marea de Portillo, *Cuba* **96** H8
Marechal Taumaturgo, *Braz.* **108** E5
Maree, Loch, *Scot., U.K.* **120** F5
Mareeba, *Qnsld., Austral.* **187** CI4
Marennes, *Fr.* **125** P4
Marettimo, Isola, *It.* **129** N6
Mareuil, *Fr.* **125** P6
Marfa, *Tex., U.S.* **92** J7
Marfa, Massif de, *Chad* **175** GI2
Margaret River, *W. Austral., Austral.*
 186 L3
Margarita, Isla de, *Venez.* **99** HII
Margat Castle *see* Qal'at al Marqab,
 ruins, *Syr.* **146** E5
Margeride, Monts de la, *Fr.* **125** Q8
Margherita di Savoia, *It.* **128** JIO
Marghita, *Rom.* **131** BIO
Margow Desert, *Afghan.* **153** M2
Marguerite Bay, *Antarctica* **200** D4
Marhanets', *Ukr.* **135** M7
Mari, ruins, *Syr.* **146** FII
Maria, Îles, *Fr. Polynesia, Fr.* **191** GI2
María Elena, *Chile* **110** C3
Mariánské Lázně, *Czech Rep.*
 126 G8
Marías, Islas, *Mex.* **94** F5
Maria van Diemen, Cape, *N.Z.*
 189 BI4
Ma'rib, *Yemen* **148** L7
Maribor, *Slov.* **130** C5
Maridi, *S. Sudan* **177** GIO
Marié, river, *Braz.* **108** C7
Marie Byrd Land, *Antarctica*
 200 H6
Marie-Galante, island, *Guadeloupe, Fr.*
 99 DI3
Mariehamn (Maarianhamina), *Fin.*
 119 HI3
Mariel, *Cuba* **96** E3
Mariental, *Namibia* **180** G6
Marietta, *Ga., U.S.* **93** GI3
Marigot, *Haiti* **97** JI2
Marigot, St.-Martin, *Fr.* **99** BI2
Marijampolė, *Lith.* **119** LI5
Marília, *Braz.* **109** JI2
Marillana, *W. Austral., Austral.*
 186 F4
Marinduque, island, *Philippines*
 167 CII
Maringá, *Braz.* **109** JII
Maringa, river, *D.R.C.* **176** H7
Marinha Grande, *Port.* **122** F4
Marino, *It.* **128** H7
Marion, *Ohio, U.S.* **93** DI3
Maripa, *Venez.* **107** DII
Marisa, *Indonesia* **167** GII
Mariscal Estigarribia, *Para.* **108** J9
Maritime Alps, *Fr., It.* **128** EI
Maritsa, river, *Bulg.* **131** HI3
Mariupol', *Ukr.* **135** M8
Marivan, *Iran* **148** C8
Mariyets, *Russ.* **134** FI2
Marjayoûn, *Leb.* **146** G5
Marka (Merca), *Somalia* **177** GI4
Markam (Gartog), *China* **157** JIO
Markandeh, ruins, *Afghan.* **152** J5
Markermeer, bay, *Neth.* **124** E9
Markham, Mount, *Antarctica*
 201 JIO
Markham Bay, *Nunavut, Can.* **89** FI2
Markit, *China* **156** E5
Markópoulo, *Gr.* **132** G5
Markovo, *Russ.* **137** CI6
Marks, *Russ.* **134** JI2
Marle, *Fr.* **124** J8
Marmande, *Fr.* **125** Q5
Marmara, island, *Turk.* **144** C3
Marmara Denizi, sea, *Turk.* **144** C3
Marmaraereğlisi, *Turk.* **144** C3
Marmara Gölü, *Turk.* **144** E3

Marmári, *Gr.* **133** GIO
Marmaris, *Turk.* **144** F3
Marmelos, river, *Braz.* **108** D8
Marmolada, peak, *It.* **128** B6
Marmolejo, *Sp.* **122** H8
Marmora, Punta La, *It.* **129** K3
Marne, river, *Fr.* **125** K9
Marne au Rhin, Canal de la, *Fr.*
 125 KII
Maroa, *Venez.* **107** FIO
Maroantsetra, *Madag.* **181** DI5
Marobee Range, *Austral.* **185** KI3
Marol, *Pak.* **152** JIO
Maromokotro, peak, *Madag.*
 181 DI5
Maroni, river, *Fr. Guiana, Fr., Suriname*
 107 EI6
Marónia, *Gr.* **133** BII
Maroochydore, *Qnsld., Austral.*
 187 HI6
Marotiri (Bass, Îlots de), *Fr. Polynesia,
 Fr.* **191** HI3
Maroua, *Cameroon* **179** CI4
Marovoay, *Madag.* **181** DI4
Márpissa, *Gr.* **133** JII
Marqaköl, *Kaz.* **151** CI6
Marquesas Islands, *Fr., Pac. Oc.*
 191 EI3
Marquesas Keys, *U.S.* **91** LI5
Marquette, *Mich., U.S.* **93** BI2
Marra, Jebel, *Sudan* **176** D8
Marrakech, *Mor.* **174** B5
Marrawah, *Tas., Austral.* **187** LI7
Marree, *S. Austral., Austral.* **187** HII
Marromeu, *Mozambique* **181** EII
Marrupa, *Mozambique* **181** DII
Marsá al Burayqah, *Lib.* **175** CI2
Marsabit, *Kenya* **177** GI2
Marsala, *It.* **129** N6
Marsciano, *It.* **128** G6
Marseille, *Fr.* **125** SIO
Marsfjället, peak, *Sweden* **119** EI2
Marshall, river, *Austral.* **185** FIO
Marshall Islands, *Pac. Oc.* **190** C8
Marsh Harbour, *Bahamas* **96** A8
Marsh Island, *U.S.* **91** JII
Mars-la-Tour, *Fr.* **125** KIO
Martaban, Gulf of, *Myanmar*
 164 G5
Martapura, *Indonesia* **166** J8
Martha's Vineyard, island, *U.S.*
 91 CI7
Martí, *Cuba* **96** G7
Martigny, *Switz.* **128** C2
Martigues, *Fr.* **125** SIO
Martin, *S. Dak., U.S.* **92** D8
Martin, *Slovakia* **127** HI2
Martinique, island, *Fr., Lesser Antilles*
 99 EI3
Martinique Passage, *Lesser Antilles*
 99 EI3
Martinsville, *Va., U.S.* **93** FI5
Martos, *Sp.* **122** J9
Martuni, *Arm.* **145** DI4
Martuni (Xocavand), *Azerb.*
 145 DI6
Maru, island, *Indonesia* **188** M6
Ma'ruf, *Afghan.* **153** L5
Marutea, island, *Fr. Polynesia, Fr.*
 191 GI4
Marvão, *Port.* **122** F5
Marv Dasht, *Iran* **149** EIO
Marwah, *Afghan.* **152** J2
Mary, *Turkm.* **150** K8
Maryborough, *Qnsld., Austral.*
 187 GI6
Maryland, *U.S.* **93** EI5
Maryport, *Eng., U.K.* **121** K7
Marzo, Cabo, *Col.* **106** D5
Marzūq, *Lib.* **175** DIO

Marzūq, Şaḥrā', *Lib.* **175** D10
Masada, ruins, *Israel* **147** K4
Masai Steppe, *Tanzania* **177** J11
Masallı, *Azerb.* **145** D17
Masamba, *Indonesia* **167** H10
Masan, *N. Korea* **160** J6
Masan, *S. Korea* **161** P9
Masasi, *Tanzania* **177** L12
Masaya, *Nicar.* **95** K13
Masbate, *Philippines* **167** C11
Masbate, island, *Philippines* **167** D11
Mascara, *Alg.* **174** A7
Masein, *Myanmar* **164** C4
Masela, island, *Indonesia* **167** K13
Maseru, *Lesotho* **180** H8
Mash'abbe Sade, *Israel* **147** K4
Mashhad, *Iran* **149** B12
Mashkai, river, *Pak.* **153** P4
Mashkel, river, *Pak.* **153** P2
Mashkel, Hamun-i-, *Pak.* **153** P2
Mashki Chah, *Pak.* **153** N2
Masi-Manimba, *D.R.C.* **176** J7
Masin, *Indonesia* **167** K16
Masira *see* Maşīrah, Jazīrat, *Oman* **149** J13
Maşīrah, Khalīj, *Oman* **149** J12
Maşīrah, Jazīrat (Masira), *Oman* **149** J13
Masisea, *Peru* **108** E5
Masjed Soleymān, *Iran* **148** D9
Mask, Lough, *Ire.* **121** M2
Maskanah (Meskéné), *Syr.* **146** D8
Maslenica, *Croatia* **130** E5
Maslen Nos, *Bulg.* **131** H15
Masoala, Presqu'île de, *Madag.* **181** D15
Mason Bay, *N.Z.* **189** M11
Mason City, *Iowa, U.S.* **93** D10
Masqaţ (Muscat), *Oman* **149** G12
Massa, *Congo* **179** H14
Massachusetts, *U.S.* **93** C16
Massafra, *It.* **129** K11
Massakory, *Chad* **175** G11
Massa Marittima, *It.* **128** G5
Massangena, *Mozambique* **181** F10
Massawa *see* Mits'iwa, *Eritrea* **177** D12
Massay, *Fr.* **125** M7
Massenya, *Chad* **175** H11
Masset, *B.C., Can.* **88** G3
Massiac, *Fr.* **125** Q8
Massif Central, mountains, *Fr.* **125** P7
Massinga, *Mozambique* **181** G10
Masson Island, *Antarctica* **201** G16
Mastābah, *Saudi Arabia* **148** J5
Maşṭağa, *Azerb.* **145** C18
Masterton, *N.Z.* **189** G16
Mástiho, Akrotírio, island, *Gr.* **133** G12
Mastuj, *Pak.* **152** H8
Mastung, *Pak.* **153** N4
Mastūrah, *Saudi Arabia* **148** H5
Masty, *Belarus* **134** H3
Masuda, *Japan* **162** J4
Masvingo, *Zimb.* **180** F9
Maşyāf, *Syr.* **146** E6
Mat, river, *Alban.* **130** J8
Matadi, *D.R.C.* **176** J5
Matagalpa, *Nicar.* **95** K13
Matagami, *Que., Can.* **89** K12
Matagorda Bay, *U.S.* **91** K10
Mataiva, island, *Fr. Polynesia, Fr.* **191** F12
Matak, island, *Indonesia* **166** F6
Matala, *Gr.* **133** M11
Matale, *Sri Lanka* **155** N6
Matam, *Senegal* **174** F3
Matamoros, *Mex.* **94** E9
Matane, *Que., Can.* **89** K14
Matanzas, *Cuba* **96** E4

Matapás *see* Ténaro, Akrotírio, cape, *Gr.* **132** K8
Matara, *Sri Lanka* **155** P6
Mataram, *Indonesia* **166** K9
Mataranka, *N. Terr., Austral.* **186** B9
Mataró, *Sp.* **123** D15
Matasiri, island, *Indonesia* **166** J9
Matatiele, *S. Af.* **180** J9
Matcha, *Taj.* **152** F6
Mateguá, *Bol.* **108** F8
Matehuala, *Mex.* **94** F7
Matera, *It.* **129** K10
Matese, mountains, *It.* **128** J8
Mátészalka, *Hung.* **127** J15
Matfors, *Sweden* **119** G12
Mathráki, island, *Gr.* **132** D4
Mathura, *India* **154** E5
Mati, *Philippines* **167** E12
Matianxu, *Hunan, China* **159** N3
Matiere, *N.Z.* **189** E15
Matli, *Pak.* **153** R6
Matlock, *Eng., U.K.* **121** N9
Matochkin Shar, *Russ.* **136** D8
Matochkin Shar Strait, *Russ.* **199** C12
Matosinhos, *Port.* **122** D4
Matou, *Taiwan, China* **159** Q8
Maţraḥ, *Oman* **149** G12
Maţrûḥ, *Egypt* **175** C13
Matsu, island, *Taiwan, China* **159** N8
Matsubara, *Japan* **163** P2
Matsue, *Japan* **162** J5
Matsumoto, *Japan* **162** H8
Matsuyama, *Japan* **163** K5
Matterhorn, peak, *It., Switz.* **128** C2
Matthew, island, *Vanuatu* **190** G8
Matthews Peak, *U.S.* **90** F6
Matthew's Ridge, *Guyana* **107** D13
Matthew Town, *Bahamas* **97** G11
Maţţī, Sabkhat, *Saudi Arabia, U.A.E.* **149** H10
Mattili, *India* **154** J6
Mattinata, *It.* **128** H10
Matua, *Indonesia* **166** H7
Matua, island, *Russ.* **137** G18
Maturín, *Venez.* **107** C12
Maúa, *Mozambique* **181** D11
Maubara, *Timor-Leste* **167** K12
Maubeuge, *Fr.* **124** H9
Maude, *N.S.W., Austral.* **187** K13
Maués, *Braz.* **109** C10
Maughold Head (Kione Maghal), cape, *Isle of Man, U.K.* **121** L7
Maui, island, *U.S.* **91** L12
Mauke, island, *Cook Is., N.Z.* **191** G11
Maukme, *Myanmar* **164** E5
Maule, Río, *Chile* **110** J2
Mauléon, *Fr.* **125** M5
Maullín, *Chile* **111** M2
Maumee, river, *U.S.* **91** D13
Maumusson, Pertuis de, *Fr.* **125** P4
Maun, *Botswana* **180** F7
Maunaloa, *Hawaii, U.S.* **91** L12
Maungdaw, *Myanmar* **164** E2
Maunoir, Lac, *N.W.T., Can.* **88** D6
Maupihaa, island, *Fr. Polynesia, Fr.* **191** F12
Mau Ranipur, *India* **154** F5
Maures, Monts des, *Fr.* **125** S11
Mauriac, *Fr.* **125** Q7
Maurice, Lake, *Austral.* **184** H9
Mauritania, *Af.* **172** H4
Mauritania, region, *Af.* **170** H2
Mauritius, *Af.* **181** G15
Mauron, *Fr.* **125** L3
Maury Bay, *Antarctica* **201** L15
Mauvezin, *Fr.* **125** R6
Mavinga, *Angola* **180** D6
Mavroli, *Cyprus* **133** F14
Mawarīd, 'Urūq al, *Yemen* **148** K9
Mawlamyine, *Myanmar* **164** G5

Mawlite, *Myanmar* **164** C3
Mawlu, *Myanmar* **164** C4
Mawqaq, *Saudi Arabia* **148** F6
Mawshij, *Yemen* **148** M6
Mawson, station, *Antarctica* **201** D15
Mawson Coast, *Antarctica* **201** D15
Mawson Escarpment, *Antarctica* **201** E14
Mawson Peninsula, *Antarctica* **201** M12
Maxixe, *Mozambique* **181** G10
May, Isle of, *Scot., U.K.* **120** H8
Mayabandar, *India* **155** L11
Mayaguana Island, *Bahamas* **97** E11
Mayaguana Passage, *Bahamas* **97** E11
Mayagüez, *P.R., U.S.* **97** J16
Mayāmey, *Iran* **149** B11
Mayang-do, island, *N. Korea* **160** F8
Maydān Ikbiz, *Syr.* **146** C6
Maydh, *Somalia* **177** E14
Maydī, *Yemen* **148** L6
Mayenne, *Fr.* **125** L5
Mayfa'ah, *Yemen* **148** M8
Maykop, *Russ.* **135** P9
Mayluu-Suu, *Kyrg.* **152** D8
Mayneside, *Qnsld., Austral.* **187** F13
Mayno Gytkino, *Russ.* **137** B16
Mayo, *Yukon, Can.* **88** E4
Mayo, Cerro, *Chile* **111** R3
Mayo Faran, *Nig.* **179** D13
Mayo Ndaga, *Nig.* **179** D13
Mayorga, *Sp.* **122** C7
Mayotte, island, *Ind. Oc.* **171** N11
May Pen, *Jamaica* **96** K7
Mayreau, island, *St. Vincent & the Grenadines* **99** G13
Mayumba, *Gabon* **179** H13
Mazabuka, *Zambia* **180** D8
Mazagan *see* El Jadida, *Mor.* **174** B5
Mazagão, *Braz.* **109** B12
Mazamet, *Fr.* **125** S7
Mazara del Vallo, *It.* **129** N6
Mazar-e Sharif, *Afghan.* **152** H5
Mazari Pass, *Pak.* **153** N3
Mazarrón, Golfo de, *Sp.* **123** J11
Mazaruni, river, *Guyana* **107** D13
Mazatán, *Mex.* **94** C4
Mazatenango, *Guatemala* **95** J11
Mazatlán, *Mex.* **94** E5
Mazgirt, *Turk.* **145** E11
Mazıdağı, *Turk.* **145** F11
Mazirbe, *Latv.* **119** J14
Mazotos, *Cyprus* **133** F16
Mazrub, *Sudan* **177** D10
Mazyr, *Belarus* **134** J4
Mazzarino, *It.* **129** P8
Mbabane, *Swaziland* **180** H9
Mbaïki, *Cen. Af. Rep.* **176** G7
Mbakaou Reservoir, *Cameroon* **179** E13
Mbala, *Zambia* **180** B9
Mbale, *Uganda* **177** H11
Mbalmayo, *Cameroon* **179** F13
Mbamba Bay, *Tanzania* **177** L11
Mbandaka, *D.R.C.* **176** H7
Mbang, Mountains, *Cameroon* **179** D14
M'banza Congo, *Angola* **180** A4
Mbanza-Ngungu, *D.R.C.* **176** J6
Mbarara, *Uganda* **177** H10
Mbari, river, *Cen. Af. Rep.* **176** F8
Mbé, *Cameroon* **179** D14
Mbeya, *Tanzania* **177** K11
Mbini, *Eq. Guinea* **179** F12
Mbout, *Mauritania* **174** F4
Mbuji-Mayi, *D.R.C.* **176** K8
Mburucuyá, *Arg.* **110** E8
Mbuyuni, *Tanzania* **177** K11
McAlester, *Okla., U.S.* **93** G10
McAllen, *Tex., U.S.* **92** K9

McArthur, river, *Austral.* **185** C10
McArthur River, *N. Terr., Austral.* **187** C10
McCook, *Nebr., U.S.* **92** E8
McDermitt, *Nev., U.S.* **92** D4
McGill, *Nev., U.S.* **92** E4
McGrath, *Alas., U.S.* **92** K2
Mchinji, *Malawi* **181** D10
Mckean Island, *Kiribati* **190** E9
McKinley, Mount (Denali), *U.S.* **90** K3
McLeod Bay, *N.W.T., Can.* **88** F7
M'Clintock Channel, *Nunavut, Can.* **88** D9
M'Clintock Inlet, *Nunavut, Can.* **89** A10
M'Clure Strait, *N.W.T., Can.* **88** C7
McMurdo, station, *Antarctica* **201** K10
McMurdo Sound, *Antarctica* **201** K10
Mdennah, region, *Alg., Mali, Mauritania* **174** D6
Mead, Lake, *U.S.* **90** F4
Meadow, *W. Austral., Austral.* **186** H3
Meadow Lake, *Sask., Can.* **88** J7
Meander River, *Alta., Can.* **88** G6
Meaux, *Fr.* **125** K8
Mecatina Little, river, *Que., Can.* **89** J14
Mecca *see* Makkah, *Saudi Arabia* **148** H5
Mechelen, *Belg.* **124** G9
Mecitözü, *Turk.* **144** C8
Mecklenburger Bucht, *Ger.* **126** B7
Mecúfi, *Mozambique* **181** D12
Mecula, *Mozambique* **181** C11
Medan, *Indonesia* **166** F3
Médea, *Alg.* **174** A8
Medellín, *Col.* **106** E6
Medford, *Oreg., U.S.* **92** C2
Medgidia, *Rom.* **131** E15
Media Luna, Cayo, *Cuba* **96** G7
Medicine Bow Mountains, *U.S.* **90** D7
Medicine Hat, *Alta., Can.* **88** K6
Medina *see* Al Madīnah, *Saudi Arabia* **148** G5
Medinaceli, *Sp.* **123** D10
Medina del Campo, *Sp.* **122** D8
Medina de Pomar, *Sp.* **122** B9
Medina de Rioseco, *Sp.* **122** C8
Medina Sidonia, *Sp.* **122** K7
Medinipur, *India* **154** G8
Mediterranean Sea, *Af., Asia, Europe* **114** L6
Mednogorsk, *Russ.* **136** H5
Mednyy, Ostrov, *Russ.* **137** D18
Médoc, mountains, *Fr.* **125** P4
Mêdog, *China* **156** J9
Medvezh'i Ostrova (Bear Islands), *Russ.* **137** C14
Medvezh'yegorsk, *Russ.* **136** D5
Meekatharra, *W. Austral., Austral.* **186** G4
Meerut, *India* **154** D5
Mēga, *Eth.* **177** G12
Mega, *Indonesia* **167** H14
Megálo Horió, *Gr.* **133** K14
Megalópoli, *Gr.* **132** H7
Mégara, *Gr.* **132** G9
Meghri, *Arm.* **145** E15
Megiddo, *Israel* **146** H4
Megion, *Russ.* **136** G8
Megísti (Kastellórizon), island, *Gr.* **133** K17
Mehadia, *Rom.* **131** E10
Mehamn, *Nor.* **119** A13
Mehar, *Pak.* **153** P5
Meharry, Mount, *Austral.* **184** F4
Mehmetçik *see* Galateia, *Cyprus* **133** E17

Mehola, *West Bank* 146 J5
Mehrīz, *Iran* 149 D11
Mehtar Lam, *Afghan.* 152 J7
Mei, river, *China* 159 P5
Meiganga, *Cameroon* 179 D14
Meighan Island, *Nunavut, Can.* 88 B9
Meihekou, *Jilin, China* 158 A11
Meiktila, *Myanmar* 164 E4
Meiningen, *Ger.* 126 F7
Meissen, *Ger.* 126 E9
Meitan, *China* 157 J12
Meizhou, *Guangdong, China* 159 P5
Meizhou Wan, *Fujian, China* 159 P7
Mejillones, *Chile* 110 C3
Mejillones del Sur, Bahía de, *Chile* 110 C3
Mékambo, *Gabon* 179 G14
Mek'elē, *Eth.* 177 D12
Mekerrhane, Sebkha, *Alg.* 174 D7
Mekhtar, *Pak.* 153 M6
Meknès, *Mor.* 174 B6
Mekong, river, *Asia* 141 K11
Mekong River Delta, *Viet.* 165 L10
Mekoryuk, *Alas., U.S.* 92 L1
Melanesia, islands, *Pac. Oc.* 190 D4
Melbourne, *Fla., U.S.* 93 J15
Melbourne, *Vic., Austral.* 187 M13
Melbourne, Mount, *Antarctica* 201 L11
Mele, Capo, *It.* 128 E2
Melegnano, *It.* 128 D3
Melekeok, *Palau* 190 C3
Melenki, *Russ.* 134 G9
Melfi, *Chad* 175 H11
Melfi, *It.* 128 J9
Melfort, *Sask., Can.* 88 J7
Melgar de Fernamental, *Sp.* 122 C8
Melide, *Sp.* 122 B5
Meligalás, *Gr.* 132 H7
Melilla, *Sp.* 123 M10
Melinka, *Chile* 111 N2
Melipilla, *Chile* 110 H3
Melita *see* Mljet, island, *Croatia* 130 G6
Melitopol', *Ukr.* 135 M7
Mellansel, *Sweden* 119 F13
Melle, *Fr.* 125 N5
Melle, *Ger.* 126 D5
Mělník, *Czech Rep.* 126 F9
Melo, *Uru.* 110 G9
Melolo, *Indonesia* 167 L10
Melos *see* Mílos, island, *Gr.* 133 J10
Melrose, *S. Austral., Austral.* 187 K11
Mels, *Switz.* 128 B4
Meltaus, *Fin.* 119 D14
Meluan, *Malaysia* 166 G7
Melun, *Fr.* 125 K7
Melvich, *Scot., U.K.* 120 E7
Melville, *Sask., Can.* 88 K7
Melville, Cape, *Austral.* 185 B14
Melville, Lake, *Nfld. & Lab., Can.* 89 H14
Melville Bay, *Austral.* 185 A11
Melville Bugt *see* Qimusseriarsuaq, bay, *Greenland, Den.* 84 D8
Melville Hills, *N.W.T., Nunavut, Can.* 88 D7
Melville Island, *Austral.* 184 A8
Melville Island, *Nunavut, Can.* 88 C8
Melville Peninsula, *Nunavut, Can.* 89 E10
Melvin, Lough, *Ire.* 121 L3
Memba, *Mozambique* 181 D12
Memboro, *Indonesia* 167 L10
Memmingen, *Ger.* 126 J6
Memphis, *Tenn., U.S.* 93 G12
Mena, *Ukr.* 134 J6
Menai Strait, *Wales, U.K.* 121 N6
Ménaka, *Mali* 174 G7

Mende, *Fr.* 125 Q8
Mendī, *Eth.* 177 E11
Mendi, *P.N.G.* 188 F6
Mendip Hills, *Eng., U.K.* 121 Q8
Mendocino, Cape, *U.S.* 90 D2
Mendoza, *Arg.* 110 H4
Menetés, *Gr.* 133 L14
Mengcheng, *Anhui, China* 158 H6
Mengen, *Turk.* 144 C6
Mengene Dağı, *Turk.* 145 E14
Mengshan, *Guangxi Zhuangzu, China* 159 P1
Mengyin, *Shandong, China* 158 F6
Menindee, *N.S.W., Austral.* 187 J12
Menkere, *Russ.* 137 F12
Menominee, river, *U.S.* 91 C12
Menongue, *Angola* 180 D5
Menor, Mar, *Sp.* 123 J12
Menorca (Minorca), island, *Sp.* 123 F16
Men'shikova, Mys, *Russ.* 136 D7
Mentawai, Kepulauan, *Indonesia* 166 H3
Menton, *Fr.* 125 R12
Menyamya, *P.N.G.* 188 E7
Menzies, *W. Austral., Austral.* 186 J5
Menzies, Mount, *Antarctica* 201 D14
Me'ona, *Israel* 146 H4
Meppel, *Neth.* 124 E10
Meppen, *Ger.* 126 C5
Mequinenza, Embalse de, *Sp.* 123 D12
Meramangye, Lake, *Austral.* 184 H9
Merampit, island, *Indonesia* 167 F12
Merano, *It.* 128 B5
Meratus, Pegunungan, *Indonesia* 166 J8
Merauke, *Indonesia* 188 H7
Merca *see* Marka, *Somalia* 177 G14
Mercan Dağları, *Turk.* 145 D11
Mercara, *India* 155 L4
Merced, *U.S.* 90 F3
Mercedes, *Arg.* 110 F8
Mercedes, *Arg.* 110 H5
Mercedes, *Arg.* 110 H7
Mercedes, *Uru.* 110 H8
Merceditas, *Chile* 110 F3
Mercy, Cape, *Nunavut, Can.* 89 E13
Mercy Bay, *N.W.T., Can.* 88 C7
Meredith, Lake, *U.S.* 90 G8
Mereeg, *Somalia* 177 G14
Merefa, *Ukr.* 135 L7
Mergenevo, *Kaz.* 150 C5
Mergui Archipelago, *Myanmar* 164 J5
Meriç, *Turk.* 144 B2
Meriç, river, *Turk.* 144 C2
Mérida, *Mex.* 95 G11
Mérida, *Sp.* 122 G6
Mérida, *Venez.* 106 C8
Mérida, Cordillera de, *Venez.* 106 C8
Meridian, *Miss., U.S.* 93 H12
Meringur, *Vic., Austral.* 187 K12
Merir, island, *Palau* 188 M1
Merkine, *Lith.* 119 L15
Mermaid Reef, *Austral.* 184 D4
Meroe, ruins, *Sudan* 177 C11
Merolia, *W. Austral., Austral.* 186 H6
Merowe, *Sudan* 177 C10
Merredin, *W. Austral., Austral.* 186 J4
Merrick Mountains, *Antarctica* 200 E5
Merrimack, river, *U.S.* 91 C16
Merritt Island, *Fla., U.S.* 93 J15
Mersa Fat'ma, *Eritrea* 177 D12
Merseburg, *Ger.* 126 E8
Mersey, river, *Eng., U.K.* 121 M8
Mersin *see* İçel, *Turk.* 144 G7
Mersing, *Malaysia* 165 P8
Merta Road, *India* 154 E3
Merthyr Tudful *see* Merthyr Tydfil, *Wales, U.K.* 121 Q7

Merthyr Tydfil (Merthyr Tudful), *Wales, U.K.* 121 Q7
Mértola, *Port.* 122 J5
Mertz Glacier, *Antarctica* 201 M13
Mertz Glacier Tongue, *Antarctica* 201 M13
Méru, *Fr.* 125 K7
Meru, *Kenya* 177 H12
Merzifon, *Turk.* 144 C8
Merzig, *Ger.* 126 G4
Mesa, *Ariz., U.S.* 92 G5
Mesabi Range, *U.S.* 91 B11
Mesach Mellet, region, *Lib.* 175 D10
Mescit Tepe, peak, *Turk.* 145 D12
Me Shima, *Japan* 163 L2
Meskéné *see* Maskanah, *Syr.* 146 D8
Mesocco, *Switz.* 128 B3
Mesopotamia, region, *Iraq* 148 B6
Messarás, Kó, *Gr.* 133 M11
Messene, ruins, *Gr.* 132 H7
Messina, *It.* 129 N9
Messina, *S. Af.* 180 F9
Messina, Stretto di, *It.* 129 N9
Messíni, *Gr.* 132 J7
Messiniakóos Kólpos, *Gr.* 132 J7
Messolóngi, *Gr.* 132 F6
Mestá, *Gr.* 133 G12
Mestia, *Ga.* 145 A13
Mestre, *It.* 128 D6
Mesudiye, *Turk.* 144 C9
Meta, river, *Col., Venez.* 106 D9
Meta Incognita Peninsula, *Nunavut, Can.* 89 F12
Metán, *Arg.* 110 D5
Metaponto, *It.* 129 K11
Metaxádes, *Gr.* 133 A12
Meteora, ruins, *Gr.* 132 D7
Méthana, *Gr.* 132 H9
Methánon, island, *Gr.* 132 H9
Methóni, *Gr.* 132 J7
Metković, *Croatia* 130 G7
Metlili Chaamba, *Alg.* 174 B8
Mets Beverratap (Dalidag), peak, *Azerb.* 145 D15
Métsovo, *Gr.* 132 D6
Mettur Dam, *India* 155 M4
Metz, *Fr.* 125 K10
Meulan, *Fr.* 125 K7
Meuse, river, *Belg., Fr.* 124 H9
Mexiana, Ilha, *Braz.* 109 B12
Mexicali, *Mex.* 94 A3
Mexico, *N. Amer.* 87 N4
Mexico, Gulf of, *N. Amer.* 91 K11
Mexico City, *Mex.* 94 G8
Meyanodas, *Indonesia* 188 M7
Meydan Shahr, *Afghan.* 152 J6
Meymaneh, *Afghan.* 152 H3
Meyrargues, *Fr.* 125 R10
Mezdra, *Bulg.* 131 G12
Mezen', *Russ.* 136 D6
Mezen', river, *Russ.* 136 E6
Mezhdusharskiy, Ostrov, *Russ.* 136 D7
Mézidon-Canon, *Fr.* 125 K5
Mézin, *Fr.* 125 R5
Mezőtúr, *Hung.* 127 K14
Mezzolombardo, *It.* 128 C5
Mi, river, *Hunan, China* 159 N4
Miahuatlán, *Mex.* 94 J9
Miajadas, *Sp.* 122 G7
Miami, *Fla., U.S.* 93 K15
Miami Beach, *Fla., U.S.* 93 K15
Mianchi, *Henan, China* 158 F3
Mīāndoāh, *Iran* 148 B8
Miandrivazo, *Madag.* 181 E13
Mīāneh, *Iran* 148 B8
Miani Hor, bay, *Pak.* 153 Q4
Mianrud, *Pak.* 153 P3
Mianwali, *Pak.* 153 L7
Mianyang, *China* 157 H11

Miaodao Liedao, islands, *Shandong, China* 158 D8
Miao'er Shan, *Guangxi Zhuangzu, China* 159 N1
Miaoli, *Taiwan, China* 159 P9
Miarinarivo, *Madag.* 181 E14
Miass, *Russ.* 136 G5
Michalovce, *Slovakia* 127 H14
Miches, *Dom. Rep.* 97 J15
Michigan, *U.S.* 93 C12
Michigan, Lake, *U.S.* 91 C12
Michurinsk, *Russ.* 134 H9
Micronesia, islands, *Pac. Oc.* 190 C4
Midai, island, *Indonesia* 166 G6
Midang, *N. Korea* 160 J6
Middelburg, *Neth.* 124 G8
Middelburg, *S. Af.* 180 J7
Middle Andaman, island, *India* 155 L11
Middle Bight, *Bahamas* 96 D7
Middlemarch, *N.Z.* 189 L12
Middlesbrough, *Eng., U.K.* 121 L9
Middleton, *Qnsld., Austral.* 187 E12
Middleton Ponds, *N. Terr., Austral.* 186 F9
Midelt, *Mor.* 174 B6
Midi, Canal du, *Fr.* 125 S6
Midland, *Tex., U.S.* 92 H8
Midu, island, *Maldives* 155 S2
Midway Islands, *U.S., Pac. Oc.* 190 A9
Midyat, *Turk.* 145 F12
Midžor, peak, *Bulg., Serb.* 131 G11
Międzyrzecz, *Pol.* 127 D10
Miélan, *Fr.* 125 S5
Mielec, *Pol.* 127 F14
Miercurea-Ciuc, *Rom.* 131 C13
Mieres, *Sp.* 122 B7
Miguel Calmon, *Braz.* 109 F15
Migyaunglaung, *Myanmar* 164 H5
Mihalıççık, *Turk.* 144 D5
Mijas, *Sp.* 122 K8
Mijek, *W. Sahara, Mor.* 174 D4
Mikhaylovka, *Russ.* 135 K10
Mikkeli, *Fin.* 119 G15
Míkonos, *Gr.* 133 H11
Míkonos, island, *Gr.* 133 H12
Mikrí Préspa, Límni, *Gr.* 132 B6
Mikun', *Russ.* 136 E6
Mikura Jima, *Japan* 163 K9
Miladummadulu Atoll, *Maldives* 155 P2
Milagro, *Ecua.* 106 J4
Milan *see* Milano, *It.* 128 D3
Milano (Milan), *It.* 128 D3
Milas, *Turk.* 144 F2
Milazzo, Capo di, *It.* 129 N9
Milbank, *S. Dak., U.S.* 93 C10
Mildenhall, *Eng., U.K.* 121 P11
Mildura, *Vic., Austral.* 187 K12
Miles, *Qnsld., Austral.* 187 G15
Miles City, *Mont., U.S.* 92 B7
Mileto, *It.* 129 M10
Miletto, Monte, *It.* 128 J8
Miletus, ruins, *Turk.* 144 F2
Milford Haven (Aberdaugleddau), *Wales, U.K.* 121 Q6
Milford Sound, *N.Z.* 189 K11
Milgun, *W. Austral., Austral.* 186 G4
Mili Atoll, *Marshall Is.* 190 D8
Miliés, *Gr.* 132 E9
Milikapiti, *N. Terr., Austral.* 186 A8
Milingimbi, *N. Terr., Austral.* 187 A10
Milk, Wadi el, *Sudan* 177 C10
Milk, river, *U.S.* 90 B6
Mil'kovo, *Russ.* 137 E17
Millau, *Fr.* 125 R8
Mille Lacs Lake, *U.S.* 91 C10
Millennium Island *see* Caroline Island, *Kiribati* 191 E12
Millerovo, *Russ.* 135 L9

Moncton, *N.B., Can.* **89** KI4
Mondego, Cabo, *Port.* **122** E4
Mondego, river, *Port.* **122** E4
Mondeodo, *Indonesia* **167** JII
Mondolfo, *It.* **128** F7
Mondoñedo, *Sp.* **122** A6
Mondovì, *It.* **128** E2
Mondragone, *It.* **128** J8
Mondy, *Russ.* **137** KII
Monemvassía, *Gr.* **132** J8
Monestier-de-Clermont, *Fr.* **125** QIO
Monfalcone, *It.* **128** C7
Monforte, *Port.* **122** G5
Monforte de Lemos, *Sp.* **122** C5
Mongalla, *S. Sudan* **177** FIO
Mongbwalu, *D.R.C.* **177** GIO
Mong Cai, *Viet.* **164** DIO
Mongers Lake, *Austral.* **184** J4
Monggŭmp'o, *N. Korea* **160** J3
Mongo, *Chad* **175** HII
Mongolia, *Asia* **143** FIO
Mongororo, *Chad* **175** HI2
Mongoy, *Russ.* **137** JI2
Mongton, *Myanmar* **164** E6
Mongu, *Zambia* **180** D7
Monistrol-sur-Loire, *Fr.* **125** P9
Monito, island, *P.R., U.S.* **97** JI6
Monitor Range, *U.S.* **90** E4
Monkey Point *see* Mono Point, *N. Amer.* **85** Q8
Monkira, *Qnsld., Austral.* **187** FI2
Mono, Punta, *Nicar.* **95** KI4
Mono Lake, *U.S.* **90** E3
Monóolithos, *Gr.* **133** KI5
Mono Point (Monkey Point), *N. Amer.* **85** Q8
Monopoli, *It.* **128** JII
Monreal del Campo, *Sp.* **123** EII
Monroe, *La., U.S.* **93** HII
Monrovia, *Liberia* **178** E5
Monschau, *Ger.* **126** F4
Mönsterås, *Sweden* **119** KI3
Montagnes Noires, *Fr.* **125** L2
Montalbán, *Sp.* **123** EI2
Montalegre, *Port.* **122** C5
Montalto di Castro, *It.* **128** G6
Montana, *Bulg.* **131** GII
Montana, *U.S.* **92** B6
Montargil, Barragem de, *Port.* **122** G4
Montargis, *Fr.* **125** L8
Montastruc-la-Conseillère, *Fr.* **125** R7
Montauban, *Fr.* **125** R6
Montbard, *Fr.* **125** M9
Montbéliard, *Fr.* **125** MII
Montblanc, *Sp.* **123** DI3
Montbrison, *Fr.* **125** P9
Montceau-les-Mines, *Fr.* **125** N9
Montchanin, *Fr.* **125** N9
Mont-de-Marsan, *Fr.* **125** R5
Montdidier, *Fr.* **124** J7
Monteagle, Mount, *Antarctica* **201** LII
Monte Bello Islands, *Austral.* **184** E3
Montebelluna, *It.* **128** C6
Monte Carlo, *Monaco* **125** RI2
Monte Caseros, *Arg.* **110** F8
Montech, *Fr.* **125** R6
Monte Comán, *Arg.* **110** H4
Monte Cristi, *Dom. Rep.* **97** HI2
Montecristo, Isola di, *It.* **128** G4
Monte Dinero, *Arg.* **111** R4
Montefiascone, *It.* **128** G6
Montego Bay, *Jamaica* **96** J7
Montego Bay, bay, *Jamaica* **96** J7
Montehermoso, *Sp.* **122** F6
Montejinni, *N. Terr., Austral.* **186** C9
Montejunto, Serra de, *Port.* **122** G3
Montélimar, *Fr.* **125** Q9
Montemarciano, *It.* **128** F7

Montemayor, Meseta de, *Arg.* **111** N5
Montemorelos, *Mex.* **94** E8
Montemor-o-Novo, *Port.* **122** G4
Montemuro, peak, *Port.* **122** D5
Montendre, *Fr.* **125** P5
Montenegro, *Europe* **116** K9
Monte Plata, *Dom. Rep.* **97** JI4
Montepuez, *Mozambique* **181** CI2
Monte Quemado, *Arg.* **110** D6
Montereau, *Fr.* **125** L8
Monterey, *Calif., U.S.* **92** E2
Monterey Bay, *U.S.* **90** E2
Montería, *Col.* **106** C5
Monterotondo, *It.* **128** H6
Monterrey, *Mex.* **94** E8
Monte San Savino, *It.* **128** F6
Monte Santu, Capo di, *It.* **129** K4
Montes Claros, *Braz.* **109** GI4
Montese, *It.* **128** E5
Montevarchi, *It.* **128** F6
Montevideo, *Uru.* **110** J9
Montfaucon, *Fr.* **125** Q9
Montgenèvre, *Fr.* **125** QII
Montgomery, *Ala., U.S.* **93** HI3
Monthey, *Switz.* **128** BI
Monti, *It.* **128** J3
Monticello, *Utah, U.S.* **92** F6
Montichiari, *It.* **128** D4
Montijo, *Port.* **122** G4
Montijo, *Sp.* **122** G6
Montilla, *Sp.* **122** J8
Montivilliers, *Fr.* **124** J5
Mont-Joli, *Que., Can.* **89** KI4
Mont-Louis, *Fr.* **125** T7
Montluçon, *Fr.* **125** N7
Montmarault, *Fr.* **125** N8
Montmirail, *Fr.* **125** K8
Monto, *Qnsld., Austral.* **187** GI6
Montoro, *Sp.* **122** H8
Montpelier, *Idaho, U.S.* **92** D6
Montpelier, *Vt., U.S.* **93** CI6
Montpellier, *Fr.* **125** R9
Montpon-Ménestérol, *Fr.* **125** Q5
Montréal, *Fr.* **125** S7
Montréal, *Que., Can.* **89** LI3
Montreuil-Bellay, *Fr.* **125** M5
Montreux, *Switz.* **128** BI
Montrevault, *Fr.* **125** M4
Montrichard, *Fr.* **125** M6
Montrose, *Colo., U.S.* **92** E6
Montrose, *Scot., U.K.* **120** G8
Montsalvy, *Fr.* **125** Q7
Montsec, Serra del, *Sp.* **123** CI3
Montserrat, island, *U.K.* **99** CI2
Montserrat, Monestir de, site, *Sp.* **123** DI4
Monts Otish, *Que., Can.* **89** JI3
Monveda, *D.R.C.* **176** G8
Monywa, *Myanmar* **164** D4
Monza, *It.* **128** C3
Monze, *Zambia* **180** D8
Monzón, *Sp.* **123** CI3
Mooloogool, *W. Austral., Austral.* **186** G4
Mööng Hsu, *Myanmar* **164** D5
Mööng Köung, *Myanmar* **164** D5
Mööng Nawng, *Myanmar* **164** D5
Mööng Pan, *Myanmar* **164** E5
Moora, *W. Austral., Austral.* **186** J4
Moore, Lake, *Austral.* **184** J4
Moorea, island, *Fr. Polynesia, Fr.* **191** FI2
Moore's Island, *Bahamas* **96** B7
Moorhead, *Minn., U.S.* **93** BIO
Moors, The, region, *Scot., U.K.* **121** K6
Moosehead Lake, *U.S.* **91** BI7
Moose Jaw, *Sask., Can.* **88** K7
Moose Lake, *Minn., U.S.* **93** CII

Moosonee, *Ont., Can.* **89** KII
Mootwingee, *N.S.W., Austral.* **187** JI2
Mopti, *Mali* **174** G6
Moqor, *Afghan.* **153** K5
Moquegua, *Peru* **108** H6
Mor, Glen, *Scot., U.K.* **120** G6
Mora, *Sweden* **119** HI2
Morača, river, *Maced.* **130** G8
Moradabad, *India* **154** D5
Móra d'Ebre, *Sp.* **123** DI3
Mora de Rubielos, *Sp.* **123** FI2
Moraleja, *Sp.* **122** F6
Moraleja del Vino, *Sp.* **122** D7
Morane, island, *Fr. Polynesia, Fr.* **191** GI4
Morant Cays, *Jamaica* **96** K9
Morant Point, *Jamaica* **96** K8
Morar, Loch, *Scot., U.K.* **120** G5
Morava, river, *Czech Rep.* **127** GII
Moravia, region, *Czech Rep.* **127** GII
Morawhanna, *Guyana* **107** CI3
Moray Firth, *Scot., U.K.* **120** F7
Morbi, *India* **154** G2
Morbihan, Golfe du, *Fr.* **125** L3
Mörbylånga, *Sweden* **119** KI3
Morcenx, *Fr.* **125** R4
Mor Dağı, *Turk.* **145** FI4
Mordovo, *Russ.* **134** J9
Mordyyakha, *Russ.* **136** E8
Moreau, river, *U.S.* **90** C8
Morebeng, *S. Af.* **180** G9
Morecambe, *Eng., U.K.* **121** L8
Morecambe Bay, *Eng., U.K.* **121** L8
Moree, *N.S.W., Austral.* **187** JI5
Morelia, *Mex.* **94** G7
Morella, *Qnsld., Austral.* **187** FI3
Morella, *Sp.* **123** EI2
Morena, *India* **154** E5
Morena, Sierra, *Sp.* **122** H7
Morenci, *Ariz., U.S.* **92** G6
Moreni, *Rom.* **131** EI3
Morere, *N.Z.* **189** EI7
Moresby Island, *B.C., Can.* **88** G3
Moreton, *Qnsld., Austral.* **187** BI3
Moreton Bay, *Austral.* **185** HI6
Moreton Island, *Austral.* **185** HI6
Moreuil, *Fr.* **124** J7
Morez, *Fr.* **125** NIO
Morfou Bay, *Cyprus* **133** EI5
Morgan, *S. Austral., Austral.* **187** KII
Morganito, *Venez.* **106** E9
Morgat, *Fr.* **125** LI
Morges, *Switz.* **128** BI
Morgex, *It.* **128** CI
Mori, *China* **156** D8
Mori, *Japan* **162** D9
Moriah, Mount, *U.S.* **90** E5
Morihong Shan, *Liaoning, China* **158** AIO
Morin Dawa, *China* **157** BI5
Morioka, *Japan* **162** FIO
Morjärv, *Sweden* **119** EI3
Mor Khun, *Pak.* **152** H9
Morkoka, river, *Russ.* **137** FI2
Morlaas, *Fr.* **125** S5
Morlaix, *Fr.* **125** K2
Mormanno, *It.* **129** KIO
Mornington, *Qnsld., Austral.* **187** GI6
Mornington, Isla, *Chile* **111** R2
Mornington Island, *Austral.* **185** CI2
Moro, *Pak.* **153** Q5
Morocco, *Af.* **172** F3
Morogoro, *Tanzania* **177** KI2
Moro Gulf, *Philippines* **167** EII
Morombe, *Madag.* **181** FI3
Morón, *Arg.* **110** H8
Morón, *Cuba* **96** F6
Mörön, *Mongolia* **157** BIO

Morona, river, *Peru* **108** D4
Morondava, *Madag.* **181** FI3
Morón de la Frontera, *Sp.* **122** J7
Moroni, *Comoros* **181** CI3
Morotai, island, *Indonesia* **167** GI3
Moroto, *Uganda* **177** GII
Morozovsk, *Russ.* **135** LIO
Morpará, *Braz.* **109** FI4
Morpeth, *Eng., U.K.* **120** J9
Morphou (Güzelyurt), *Cyprus* **133** EI5
Morrinhos, *Braz.* **109** HI2
Morris Jesup, Cape, *Greenland, Den.* **84** B8
Morrosquillo, Golfo de, *Col.* **106** C5
Morrumbene, *Mozambique* **181** GIO
Morshansk, *Russ.* **134** H9
Morsi, *India* **154** H5
Mortagne, *Fr.* **125** K6
Mortara, *It.* **128** D3
Morteau, *Fr.* **125** MII
Morteros, *Arg.* **110** G6
Mortlock Islands, *F.S.M.* **188** BI
Mortyq, *Kaz.* **150** C6
Moruga, *Trinidad & Tobago* **99** JI3
Mururoa, island, *Fr. Polynesia, Fr.* **191** GI4
Morvan, Monts du, *Fr.* **125** M9
Morven, *Qnsld., Austral.* **187** GI4
Morven, peak, *Scot., U.K.* **120** G8
Morvern, peninsula, *Scot., U.K.* **120** H5
Mosal'sk, *Russ.* **134** G7
Moscos Islands, *Myanmar* **164** H5
Moscow *see* Moskva, *Russ.* **134** G8
Moscow Canal, *Russ.* **134** F8
Moscow University Ice Shelf, *Antarctica* **201** KI5
Mose, Cape, *Antarctica* **201** LI5
Mosel, river, *Ger.* **126** F4
Moshi, *Tanzania* **177** JI2
Mosjøen, *Nor.* **119** EII
Moskva (Moscow), *Russ.* **134** G8
Moskva, *Taj.* **152** G6
Moskva, river, *Russ.* **134** G7
Mosonmagyaróvár, *Hung.* **127** JII
Mosquitia, region, *Hond.* **95** JI4
Mosquito Cays, *Hond.* **85** Q8
Mosquitos, Golfo de los, *Pan.* **95** LI5
Moss, *Nor.* **119** JII
Mossaka, *Congo* **179** GI5
Mossburn, *N.Z.* **189** LII
Mossel Bay, *S. Af.* **180** K7
Mossendjo, *Congo* **179** HI3
Mossman, *Qnsld., Austral.* **187** CI4
Mossoró, *Braz.* **109** DI6
Most, *Czech Rep.* **126** F9
Mostaganem, *Alg.* **174** A7
Mostar, *Bosn. & Herzg.* **130** G7
Mostardas, *Braz.* **109** MII
Mosteiros, *Azores, Port.* **122** L4
Møsting, Cape, *Greenland, Den.* **199** LI5
Móstoles, *Sp.* **122** E9
Mosul *see* Al Mawşil, *Iraq* **148** B7
Motaba, river, *Congo* **179** FI5
Mota del Cuervo, *Sp.* **123** GIO
Mota Khan, *Afghan.* **153** K6
Motala, *Sweden* **119** JI2
Motane *see* Mohotani, island, *Marquesas Is., Fr.* **191** FI4
Motherwell, *Scot., U.K.* **120** J7
Motril, *Sp.* **122** K9
Motru, *Rom.* **131** EII
Motru, river, *Rom.* **131** EII
Mott, *N. Dak., U.S.* **92** C8
Motta Misaki, *Japan* **162** D9
Motu, river, *N.Z.* **189** EI7
Motueka, *N.Z.* **189** GI4

Musa Khel Bazar, *Pak.* **153** M6
Musala, peak, *Bulg.* **131** H11
Musan, *N. Korea* **160** B9
Musandam, Ra's, *Oman* **149** F12
Musa Qal'eh, *Afghan.* **153** L3
Musaymīr, *Yemen* **148** M7
Muscat *see* Masqaṭ, *Oman* **149** G12
Musgrave, Port, *Austral.* **185** A13
Musgrave Ranges, *Austral.* **184** G9
Mushie, *D.R.C.* **176** J6
Mushuray *see* Wazah Khwah, *Afghan.*
  153 L5
Muskegon, *Mich., U.S.* **93** D12
Muskegon, river, *U.S.* **91** D12
Muskingum, river, *U.S.* **91** E14
Muskogee, *Okla., U.S.* **93** G10
Muslimbagh, *Pak.* **153** M5
Muslimīyah, *Syr.* **146** C7
Musmar, *Sudan* **177** C11
Musoma, *Tanzania* **177** H11
Mussau, island, *P.N.G.* **188** D4
Mussau Islands, *P.N.G.* **188** D4
Musselburgh, *Scot., U.K.* **120** J8
Musselshell, river, *U.S.* **90** B6
Mussuma, *Angola* **180** D7
Mustafakemalpaşa, *Turk.* **144** C3
Mustahīl, *Eth.* **177** F14
Mustang, *Nepal* **154** D7
Musters, Lago, *Arg.* **111** N3
Mustique, island, *St. Vincent & the*
  Grenadines **99** G13
Musu, *N. Korea* **160** B10
Musudan, *N. Korea* **160** E10
Mûṭ, *Egypt* **175** D14
Mut, *Turk.* **144** G6
Mutá, Ponta do, *Braz.* **109** G15
Mutarara, *Mozambique* **181** E10
Mutare, *Zimb.* **181** E10
Muting, *Indonesia* **188** H7
Mutki, *Turk.* **145** E12
Mutnovskaya Sopka, *Russ.* **137** F17
Mutoray, *Russ.* **137** G10
Mutsu, *Japan* **162** E10
Mutsu Wan, *Japan* **162** E10
Muttaburra, *Qnsld., Austral.* **187** F13
Muturi, *Indonesia* **188** L4
Mu Us Shamo (Ordos), *Nei Mongol,*
  China **158** C1
Muxía, *Sp.* **122** B4
Mŭynoq, *Uzb.* **150** G7
Muzaffarabad, *Pak.* **152** J9
Muzaffargarh, *Pak.* **153** M7
Muzaffarnagar, *India* **154** D5
Muzaffarpur, *India* **154** E8
Muztag, peak, *China* **156** F5
Muztag Feng, *China* **156** F7
Mwali (Mohéli), island, *Ind. Oc.*
  171 N11
Mwanza, *Tanzania* **177** J11
Mweka, *D.R.C.* **176** J8
Mwene-Ditu, *D.R.C.* **176** K8
Mwenezi, *Zimb.* **180** F9
Mweru, Lake, *D.R.C., Zambia* **180** B9
Mwinilunga, *Zambia* **180** C7
Myaksa, *Russ.* **134** E8
Myanaung, *Myanmar* **164** F4
Myanmar (Burma), *Asia* **143** J10
Mycenae, ruins, *Gr.* **132** G8
Myebon, *Myanmar* **164** E3
Myeik, *Myanmar* **164** J6
Myingyan, *Myanmar* **164** D4
Myitkyinā, *Myanmar* **164** B5
Myitta, *Myanmar* **164** H5
Mykolayiv, *Ukr.* **135** M5
Mymensingh, *Bangladesh* **154** F10
Mynbulaq, *Uzb.* **150** G8
Mynydd Preseli, peak, *Wales, U.K.*
  121 P6
Myohaung, *Myanmar* **164** E3
Myohyang-san, peak, *N. Korea* **160** F6

Myohyang-sanmaek, range, *N. Korea*
  160 F6
Myŏngch'ŏn, *N. Korea* **160** D10
Myoungmya, *Myanmar* **164** G4
Myrdal, *Nor.* **119** H10
Mýrdalsjökull, glacier, *Ice.* **118** E3
Myrhorod, *Ukr.* **135** K6
Myrtle Beach, *S.C., U.S.* **93** G15
Myrtou (Çamlibel), *Cyprus* **133** E15
Mysore, *India* **155** L4
Mysovaya, *Russ.* **137** D14
Mys Shmidta, *Russ.* **137** B15
Mys Zhelaniya, *Russ.* **136** D9
Myszyniec, *Pol.* **127** C13
My Tho, *Viet.* **165** K10
Mytilene *see* Mitilíni, *Gr.* **133** E13
Mytishchi, *Russ.* **134** G8
Mzuzu, *Malawi* **181** C10

N

Nā'ālehu, *Hawaii, U.S.* **93** M13
Nabatîyé et Tahta, *Leb.* **146** G5
Nabeul, *Tunisia* **175** A10
Nabire, *Indonesia* **188** K5
Na Blascaodaí (Blasket Island), *Ire.*
  121 P1
Nablus *see* Nāblus, *West Bank* **146** J4
Nāblus (Nablus), *West Bank* **146** J4
Nabq Bay, site, *Egypt* **147** P3
Nacala, *Mozambique* **181** D12
Nacaome, *Hond.* **95** J12
Nachingwea, *Tanzania* **177** L12
Náchod, *Czech Rep.* **127** F10
Nachvak Fiord, *Nfld. & Lab., Can.*
  89 G13
Nacogdoches, *Tex., U.S.* **93** H10
Nacozari de García, *Mex.* **94** C4
Nadale, island, *Maldives* **155** S2
Nadiad, *India* **154** G3
Nădlac, *Rom.* **130** C9
Nadvoitsy, *Russ.* **136** D5
Nadym, *Russ.* **136** F8
Naenarodo, island, *S. Korea* **161** R7
Naesu, *S. Korea* **161** M7
Náfpaktos, *Gr.* **132** F7
Náfplio, *Gr.* **132** H8
Nafūsah, Jabal, *Lib.* **175** B10
Nag, *Pak.* **153** P3
Naga, *Indonesia* **167** K10
Naga City, *Philippines* **167** C11
Naga Hills, *India* **154** E12
Nagano, *Japan* **162** H8
Nagaoka, *Japan* **162** G8
Nagaon, *India* **154** E11
Nagar Parkar, *Pak.* **153** R7
Nagasaki, *Japan* **163** L3
Nagaur, *India* **154** E3
Nagēlē, *Eth.* **177** F12
Nagercoil, *India* **155** N4
Nagir, *Pak.* **152** H9
Na Gleannta *see* Glenties, *Ire.* **121** K3
Nago, *Japan* **163** Q1
Nagorno-Karabakh, region, *Azerb.*
  145 C16
Nagoya, *Japan* **162** J7
Nagpur, *India* **154** H5
Nagqu, *China* **156** H8
Nagwŏn, *N. Korea* **160** F8
Nagykanizsa, *Hung.* **127** L11
Nagyŏn, *N. Korea* **160** J4
Naha, *Japan* **163** Q1
Nahanni Butte, *N.W.T., Can.* **88** F5
Na h-Eileanan Flannach (Flannan
  Isles), *Scot., U.K.* **120** E4
Na h-Eileanan Mora (Shiant Islands),
  Scot., U.K. **120** F5
Na h-Eileanan Theisgeir (Heisker or
  Monach Islands), *Scot., U.K.* **120** F4
Nahuei Huapí, Lago, *Arg.* **111** L3
Nā'īn, *Iran* **149** D10

Nain, *Nfld. & Lab., Can.* **89** G14
Nainpur, *India* **154** G6
Nairn, *Scot., U.K.* **120** F7
Nairobi, *Kenya* **177** H12
Najafābād, *Iran* **149** D10
Najd, region, *Saudi Arabia* **148** F6
Nájera, *Sp.* **123** C10
Najin *see* Rajin, *N. Korea* **160** B11
Najin-man, bay, *N. Korea* **160** B11
Najrān, *Saudi Arabia* **148** K7
Najrān, oasis, *Saudi Arabia* **148** K7
Naju, *S. Korea* **161** Q6
Nakadōri Jima, *Japan* **163** K2
Nakagusuku Wan (Buckner Bay),
  Japan **163** Q1
Naka Kharai, *Pak.* **153** R4
Nakamura, *Japan* **163** L5
Nakano, *Japan* **162** H8
Nakano Shima, *Japan* **162** H5
Nakano Shima, *Japan* **163** N3
Naka Shibetsu, *Japan* **162** C12
Nakatane, *Japan* **163** M4
Nakatombetsu, *Japan* **162** B10
Nakatsu, *Japan* **163** K4
Nakdong, river, *S. Korea* **161** P9
Nakfa, *Eritrea* **177** C12
Nakhl, *Egypt* **147** M2
Nakhodka, *Russ.* **137** K16
Nakhon Phanom, *Thai.* **164** G9
Nakhon Ratchasima, *Thai.* **164** H7
Nakhon Sawan, *Thai.* **164** H6
Nakhon Si Thammarat, *Thai.* **165** L6
Nakina, *Ont., Can.* **89** K10
Nakło nad Notecią, *Pol.* **127** C11
Naknek, *Alas., U.S.* **92** L2
Nakodar, *India* **154** C4
Nakuru, *Kenya* **177** H11
Nal, *Pak.* **153** P4
Nalayh, *Mongolia* **157** C12
Nal'chik, *Russ.* **135** P11
Nalgonda, *India* **154** J5
Nallıhan, *Turk.* **144** D5
Nālūt, *Lib.* **175** B10
Nam, river, *S. Korea* **161** P8
Namak, Kavīr-e, *Iran* **149** C12
Namak, Daryācheh-ye, *Iran* **149** C10
Namakzar, Lake, *Afghan., Iran* **153** K1
Namanga, *Kenya* **177** J11
Namangan, *Uzb.* **151** H12
Namapa, *Mozambique* **181** D12
Namatanai, *P.N.G.* **188** B5
Nambour, *Qnsld., Austral.* **187** H16
Nam Can, *Viet.* **165** L9
Nam Co, *China* **156** H8
Namdae, river, *N. Korea* **160** D9
Nam Dinh, *Viet.* **164** E9
Namgia, *India* **154** C5
Namhae, *S. Korea* **161** Q8
Namhaedo, island, *S. Korea* **161** Q8
Namhŭng, *N. Korea* **160** E6
Namib Desert, *Af.* **171** P6
Namibe, *Angola* **180** D4
Namibia, *Af.* **173** P6
Namiquipa, *Mex.* **94** C5
Namji, *S. Korea* **161** P9
Namlea, *Indonesia* **167** J12
Nam Ngum Dam, *Laos* **164** F8
Namoi, river, *Austral.* **185** J15
Namonuito Atoll, *F.S.M.* **190** C5
Namorik Atoll, *Marshall Is.* **190** D7
Nampa, *Idaho, U.S.* **92** C4
Nampala, *Mali* **174** G5
Namp'o, *N. Korea* **160** H4
Nampō Shotō, *Japan* **163** L10
Nampula, *Mozambique* **181** D12
Namsen, river, *Nor.* **119** F11
Namsê Pass, *China, Nepal* **154** D7
Namsos, *Nor.* **119** F11
Nam Tok, *Thai.* **164** H6
Namtsy, *Russ.* **137** F13

Namtu, *Myanmar* **164** D5
Namur, *Belg.* **124** H9
Namutoni, *Namibia* **180** E5
Namwon, *S. Korea* **161** P7
Namwon, *S. Korea* **161** T6
Namyang, *N. Korea* **160** E10
Namyang, *S. Korea* **161** Q7
Nan, *Thai.* **164** F7
Nan, river, *Hubei, China* **158** H2
Nan, river, *Thai.* **164** F7
Nanaimo, *B.C., Can.* **88** J4
Nanam, *N. Korea* **160** C10
Nan'an, *Fujian, China* **159** P7
Nanao, *Japan* **162** H7
Nanatsu Shima, *Japan* **162** G7
Nanchang, *Jiangxi, China* **159** L5
Nanchangshan Dao, *Shandong, China*
  158 D8
Nancheng, *Jiangxi, China* **159** M6
Nanchong, *China* **157** H12
Nancowry Island, *India* **155** N11
Nancy, *Fr.* **125** K10
Nanda Devi, peak, *India* **154** D6
Nanded, *India* **154** H4
Nandgaon, *India* **154** H3
Nandurbar, *India* **154** G3
Nandyal, *India* **155** K5
Nanfeng, *Jiangxi, China* **159** M5
Nanfengmian, peak, *Hunan, China*
  159 N4
Nanga Parbat, peak, *Pak.* **152** J9
Nangapinoh, *Indonesia* **166** H7
Nangaraun, *Indonesia* **166** G8
Nangatayap, *Indonesia* **166** H7
Nangin, *Myanmar* **165** K5
Nangis, *Fr.* **125** K8
Nangnim, *N. Korea* **160** E7
Nangnim-ho, reservoir, *N. Korea*
  160 E7
Nangnim-san, peak, *N. Korea* **160** F6
Nangnim-sanmaek, range, *N. Korea*
  160 E6
Nangong, *Hebei, China* **158** E5
Nangqên (Xangda), *China* **156** H9
Nangtud, Mount, *Philippines* **167** D11
Nanguan, *Shanxi, China* **158** E3
Nanjing, *Fujian, China* **159** P6
Nanjing, *Jiangsu, China* **158** J7
Nankang, *Jiangxi, China* **159** N4
Nankoku, *Japan* **163** K5
Nan Ling, *Hunan, Guangdong, China*
  159 P3
Nanma *see* Yiyuan, *Shandong, China*
  158 F7
Nannine, *W. Austral., Austral.* **186** H4
Nanning, *China* **157** L12
Nanpan, river, *China* **157** K12
Nanpiao, *Liaoning, China* **158** B8
Nanping, *Fujian, China* **159** N7
Nanri Dao, *Fujian, China* **159** P8
Nansan Dao, *Guangdong, China* **159** S1
Nansei Shotō (Ryukyu Islands), *Japan*
  163 Q2
Nansen Sound, *Nunavut, Can.* **88** A9
Nanshan Island, *Spratly Is.* **166** D9
Nansi Hu, *Shandong, China* **158** F6
Nant, *Fr.* **125** R8
Nantes, *Fr.* **125** M4
Nantong, *Jiangsu, China* **158** J8
Nantou, *Taiwan, China* **159** Q8
Nantucket Island, *U.S.* **91** C17
Nantulo, *Mozambique* **181** C12
Nantwich, *Eng., U.K.* **121** N8
Nānu'alele Point, *U.S.* **91** L12
Nanumanga, island, *Tuvalu* **190** E8
Nanumea, island, *Tuvalu* **190** E8
Nanuque, *Braz.* **109** H14
Nanusa, Kepulauan, *Indonesia*
  167 F12
Nanutarra, *W. Austral., Austral.* **186** F3

Nanwan Shuiku, *Henan, China* **158** J4
Nanxian, *Hunan, China* **159** L3
Nanxiong, *Guangdong, China* **159** P4
Nanyang, *Henan, China* **158** H3
Nanzhang, *Hubei, China* **158** J3
Nanzhao, *Henan, China* **158** H3
Nao, Cabo de la, *Sp.* **123** G13
Naococane, Lac, *Que., Can.* **89** J13
Naomid Plain, *Afghan.* **153** K1
Náousa, *Gr.* **132** B7
Napier, *N.Z.* **189** F16
Napier Downs, *W. Austral., Austral.*
  186 C6
Napier Mountains, *Antarctica*
  200 B15
Naples *see* Napoli, *It.* **128** J8
Napo, river, *S. Amer.* **102** E2
Napoli (Naples), *It.* **128** J8
Napoli, Golfo di, *It.* **128** J8
Napug *see* Gê'gyai, *China* **156** G5
Napuka, island, *Fr. Polynesia, Fr.*
  191 F13
Nâqoûra, *Leb.* **146** H4
Nara, *Japan* **162** J7
Nara, *Mali* **174** G5
Nara, river, *Pak.* **153** R6
Naracoorte, *S. Austral., Austral.*
  187 L12
Narang, *Afghan.* **152** J7
Narasannapeta, *India* **154** J7
Narathiwat, *Thai.* **165** M7
Narayanganj, *Bangladesh* **154** F10
Narbonne, *Fr.* **125** S8
Narborough *see* Fernandina, Isla, *Ecua.*
  106 E1
Narcondam Island, *India* **155** L12
Nardò, *It.* **129** K12
Narew, river, *Pol.* **127** C14
Narib, *Namibia* **180** G5
Narin, *Nei Mongol, China* **158** C2
Narlı, *Turk.* **144** F9
Narmada, river, *India* **154** G3
Narnaul, *India* **154** E4
Narndee, *W. Austral., Austral.* **186** H4
Narni, *It.* **128** G6
Narodnaya, Gora, *Russ.* **136** F7
Narooma, *N.S.W., Austral.* **187** L15
Narowal, *Pak.* **153** L9
Narowlya, *Belarus* **134** J5
Narrabri, *N.S.W., Austral.* **187** J15
Narrandera, *N.S.W., Austral.* **187** L14
Narran Lake, *Austral.* **185** J14
Narrogin, *W. Austral., Austral.* **186** K4
Narsarsuaq, *Greenland, Den.* **199** M15
Narsinghgarh, *India* **154** F4
Narsipatnam, *India* **154** J7
Nartës, Laguna e, *Alban.* **130** K8
Nartháki, Oros, *Gr.* **132** E8
Nartkala, *Russ.* **135** P11
Narva, *Est.* **119** H16
Narvik, *Nor.* **119** C12
Narvskoye Vodokhranilishche, *Russ.*
  134 D4
Narwietooma, *N. Terr., Austral.* **186** F9
Nar'yan Mar, *Russ.* **136** E7
Naryn, *Kyrg.* **152** D10
Naryn, *Russ.* **137** K10
Naryn, river, *Kyrg.* **152** D8
Naryn Khuduk, *Russ.* **135** N12
Narynqol, *Kaz.* **151** G15
Naryn Qum, *Kaz.* **150** D4
Näs, *Sweden* **119** G12
Nasarawa, *Nig.* **179** D12
Nasca, *Peru* **108** G5
Na Sceirí *see* Skerries, *Ire.* **121** M5
Nashua, *N.H., U.S.* **93** C16
Nashville, *Tenn., U.S.* **93** F13
Našice, *Croatia* **130** D7

Näsijärvi, lake, *Fin.* **119** G14
Nasik, *India* **154** H3
Nasir, *S. Sudan* **177** F11
Nasirabad, *India* **154** E3
Naso, *It.* **129** N9
Nassau, *Bahamas* **96** C7
Nassau, island, *Cook Is., N.Z.* **191** F10
Nasser, Lake, *Egypt* **175** E15
Nässjö, *Sweden* **119** K12
Nastapoka Islands, *Nunavut, Can.*
  89 H12
Nata, *Botswana* **180** F8
Natal, *Braz.* **109** D16
Natal, *Indonesia* **166** G3
Natal'inskiy, *Russ.* **137** C17
Naţanz, *Iran* **149** C10
Natara, *Russ.* **137** E12
Natashquan, *Que., Can.* **89** J14
Natashquan, river, *Que., Can.* **89** J14
Natchez, *Miss., U.S.* **93** H11
Natchitoches, *La., U.S.* **93** H11
National City, *Calif., U.S.* **92** G3
Natitingou, *Benin* **178** C9
Natividad, Isla, *Mex.* **94** C2
Natividade, *Braz.* **109** F13
Natkyizin, *Myanmar* **164** H5
Nattavaara, *Sweden* **119** D13
Natuna Besar, island, *Indonesia*
  166 F6
Natuna Besar, Kepulauan (Bunguran
  Utara), *Indonesia* **166** F6
Natuna Selatan, Kepulauan (Bunguran
  Selatan), *Indonesia* **166** G6
Naturaliste, Cape, *Austral.* **184** K3
Naturno, *It.* **128** B5
Naukot, *Pak.* **153** R6
Naungpale, *Myanmar* **164** F5
Nauroz Kalat, *Pak.* **153** N4
Nauru, *Pac. Oc.* **190** D7
Naushahra, *India* **153** K9
Naushahro Firoz, *Pak.* **153** Q5
Nauta, *Peru* **108** D5
Nautla, *Mex.* **94** G9
Navabelitsa, *Belarus* **134** J5
Navadwip, *India* **154** G9
Navahrudak, *Belarus* **134** H3
Navalmoral de la Mata, *Sp.* **122** F7
Navan (An Uaimh), *Ire.* **121** M4
Navapolatsk, *Belarus* **134** G4
Navarin, Mys, *Russ.* **137** B16
Navarino, Isla, *Chile* **III** T5
Navarrenx, *Fr.* **125** S4
Navassa Island, *U.S.* **96** J9
Navia, *Sp.* **122** A6
Năvodari, *Rom.* **131** E15
Navoiy, *Uzb.* **150** J9
Navojoa, *Mex.* **94** D4
Navrongo, *Ghana* **178** C8
Navsari, *India* **154** H3
Nawá, *Syr.* **146** H5
Nawabshah, *Pak.* **153** Q5
Nawada, *India* **154** F8
Nawah, *Afghan.* **153** L5
Nawalgarh, *India* **154** E4
Nawāşīf, Ḥarrat, *Saudi Arabia* **148** H6
Naxçıvan, *Azerb.* **145** D15
Naxçıvan, region, *Azerb.* **145** D15
Náxos, *Gr.* **133** J11
Náxos, island, *Gr.* **133** J12
Naxos, site, *It.* **129** N9
Nayak, *Afghan.* **152** J4
Nāy Band, *Iran* **149** D12
Nayoro, *Japan* **162** B10
Nay Pyi Taw, *Myanmar* **164** E4
Nazaré, *Braz.* **109** F15
Nazaré, *Port.* **122** F4
Nazareth *see* Naẕerat, *Israel* **146** H4
Nazas, *Mex.* **94** E6
Naze, *Japan* **163** P2
Naze, The, cape, *Eng., U.K.* **121** P12

Naẕerat (Nazareth), *Israel* **146** H4
Nāzīk, *Iran* **148** A7
Nazik Gölü, *Turk.* **145** E12
Nazilli, *Turk.* **144** E3
Nazımiye, *Turk.* **145** E11
Naziya, *Russ.* **134** D6
Nazran', *Russ.* **135** Q12
Nazrēt, *Eth.* **177** F12
N'dalatando, *Angola* **180** B5
Ndélé, *Cen. Af. Rep.* **176** F7
Ndendé, *Gabon* **179** H13
Ndeni *see* Nendo, island, *Solomon Is.*
  190 F7
N'Djamena, *Chad* **175** H11
Ndola, *Zambia* **180** C9
Nea Epidavros, *Gr.* **132** H9
Neagh, Lough, *N. Ire., U.K.* **121** K5
Neale, Lake, *Austral.* **184** F8
Néa Mihanióna, *Gr.* **132** C8
Nea Moni, site, *Gr.* **133** F12
Néa Moudaniá, *Gr.* **132** C9
Neápoli, *Gr.* **132** C6
Neápoli, *Gr.* **132** K8
Neapolis *see* Kavála, *Gr.* **133** B10
Near Islands, *U.S.* **85** S2
Néa Zíhni, *Gr.* **132** B9
Nebine Creek, *Austral.* **185** H14
Neblina, Pico da, *Braz., Venez.*
  107 G10
Nebraska, *U.S.* **92** D8
Nebrodi, Monti, *It.* **129** N8
Neches, river, *U.S.* **91** J10
Neckar, river, *Ger.* **126** H5
Neckarboo Range, *Austral.* **185** K13
Necker Island, *Hawaii, U.S.* **191** A10
Necochea, *Arg.* **III** K8
Needles, *Calif., U.S.* **92** G4
NEEM Camp *see* North Greenland
  Eemian Ice, station, *Greenland, Den.*
  199 J12
Neftçala, *Azerb.* **145** D17
Nefteyugansk, *Russ.* **136** G7
Negeribatin, *Indonesia* **166** J5
Negev, region, *Israel* **147** L4
Negoiul, peak, *Rom.* **131** D12
Negomane, *Mozambique* **181** C12
Negombo, *Sri Lanka* **155** P5
Negotin, *Serb.* **131** F11
Negra, Laguna, *Uru.* **110** H10
Negra, Punta, *Peru* **108** D3
Negreira, *Sp.* **122** B4
Negreşti-oaş, *Rom.* **131** A11
Negril, *Jamaica* **96** J6
Negritos, *Peru* **108** D3
Negro, river, *Guatemala* **95** J11
Negro, river, *S. Amer.* **102** E6
Negros, island, *Philippines* **167** D11
Negru Vodă, *Rom.* **131** F15
Nehbandān, *Iran* **149** D13
Nehe, *China* **157** B15
Neiba, *Dom. Rep.* **97** J13
Neiba, Bahía de, *Dom. Rep.* **97** J13
Neiden, *Nor.* **119** B14
Neidín *see* Kenmare, *Ire.* **121** P2
Nei Mongol, *China* **158** B1
Nei Mongol Gaoyuan, *Nei Mongol,
  China* **158** A1
Neiqiu, *Hebei, China* **158** E4
Neiva, *Col.* **106** F6
Neixiang, *Henan, China* **158** H3
Neksø, *Den.* **119** L12
Nekurandu, island, *Maldives* **155** P2
Nelemnoye, *Russ.* **137** D15
Nelidovo, *Russ.* **134** F6
Nel'kan, *Russ.* **137** G15
Nellore, *India* **155** K5
Nelson, *B.C., Can.* **88** J5
Nelson, *Eng., U.K.* **121** M8
Nelson, *N.Z.* **189** G14

Nelson, Cape, *Austral.* **185** M12
Nelson, river, *Man., Can.* **88** H9
Nelson, Estrecho, *Chile* **III** R2
Nelson House, *Man., Can.* **88** H8
Néma, *Mauritania* **174** F5
Neman, *Russ.* **134** G2
Nembrala, *Indonesia* **167** L11
Neméa, *Gr.* **132** G8
Nemiscau, *Que., Can.* **89** K12
Nemrut Dagh, ruins, *Turk.* **145** F10
Nemrut Gölü, *Turk.* **145** E12
Nemunas, river, *Lith.* **119** L14
Nemuro, *Japan* **162** C12
Nemuro Strait, *Japan* **162** C12
Nen, river, *China* **157** B15
Nenagh (An tAonach), *Ire.* **121** N3
Nenana, *Alas., U.S.* **92** K3
Nendo (Ndeni), island, *Solomon Is.*
  190 F7
Nenjiang, *China* **157** B15
Neosho, river, *U.S.* **91** F10
Néos Marmarás, *Gr.* **132** C9
Nepa, *Russ.* **137** H11
Nepal, *Asia* **142** H9
Nepalganj, *Nepal* **154** E6
Nephi, *Utah, U.S.* **92** E5
Nephin Beg, peak, *Ire.* **121** L2
Neptune Range, *Antarctica* **200** E8
Nerchinsk, *Russ.* **137** J13
Nerchinskiy Zavod, *Russ.* **137** J13
Nerekhta, *Russ.* **134** E9
Neretva, river, *Bosn. & Herzg.* **130** G7
Neretvanski Kanal, *Croatia* **130** G6
Neriquinha, *Angola* **180** D7
Néris, *Fr.* **125** N8
Nerja, *Sp.* **122** K9
Nerpo, *Russ.* **137** H12
Nerrima, *W. Austral., Austral.* **186** D6
Nerva, *Sp.* **122** J6
Neskaupstadur, *Ice.* **118** E5
Ness, Loch, *Scot., U.K.* **120** F7
Néstos, river, *Gr.* **133** A10
Netanya, *Israel* **146** J4
Netherdale, *Qnsld., Austral.* **187** E15
Netherlands, *Europe* **116** F7
Nettilling Lake, *Nunavut, Can.* **89** E12
Netzahualcóyotl, *Mex.* **94** G8
Neuberg, *Ger.* **126** H7
Neubrandenburg, *Ger.* **126** C8
Neuchâtel, *Switz.* **128** B1
Neuchâtel, Lac de, *Switz.* **128** B1
Neufchâteau, *Belg.* **124** J10
Neufchâteau, *Fr.* **125** L10
Neumagen, *Ger.* **126** F4
Neumayer, station, *Antarctica*
  200 A9
Neumünster, *Ger.* **126** B6
Neun, river, *Laos* **164** E8
Neunkirchen, *Aust.* **127** J10
Neunkirchen, *Ger.* **126** G4
Neuquén, *Arg.* **III** K4
Neuquén, river, *Arg.* **III** K3
Neuruppin, *Ger.* **126** C8
Neuschwanstein, site, *Ger.* **126** J7
Neuse, river, *U.S.* **91** F15
Neusiedler See, *Aust., Hung.* **127** J11
Neuss, *Ger.* **126** E4
Neustadt, *Ger.* **126** G5
Neustrelitz, *Ger.* **126** C8
Neu-Ulm, *Ger.* **126** H6
Neuvic, *Fr.* **125** Q6
Neuwied, *Ger.* **126** F5
Nevada, *U.S.* **92** E3
Nevada, Sierra, *Sp.* **122** K9
Nevada, Sierra, *U.S.* **90** E3
Nevel', *Russ.* **134** F5
Never, *Russ.* **137** H14
Nevers, *Fr.* **125** M8
Nevinnomyssk, *Russ.* **135** P10
Nevis, island, *St. Kitts & Nevis* **99** C12

Olympos (Olympus, Mount), *Cyprus* **133** FI5
Olympus, Mount *see* Olympos, *Cyprus* **133** FI5
Olympus, Mount *see* Ulu Dağ, *Turk.* **144** C3
Olympus *see* Ólimbos, Óros, *Gr.* **132** C8
Olympus, Mount, *U.S.* **90** A3
Olyutorskiy, Mys, *Russ.* **137** CI7
Olyutorskiy Zaliv, *Russ.* **137** DI7
Ōma, *Japan* **162** D9
Ōmagari, *Japan* **162** F9
Omagh (An Ómaigh), *N. Ire., U.K.* **121** L4
Omaha, *Mo., U.S.* **93** EIO
Omaha Beach, *Fr.* **124** J5
Omaja, *Cuba* **96** G8
Oman, *Asia* **142** J5
Oman, Gulf of, *Asia* **140** H6
Ōma Zaki, *Japan* **162** D9
Omboué (Fernan Vaz), *Gabon* **179** HI2
Ombu, *China* **156** H7
Omchak, *Russ.* **137** EI5
Omdurman, *Sudan* **177** DIO
Omegna, *It.* **128** C3
Omeo, *Vic., Austral.* **187** MI4
Ometepec, *Mex.* **94** J8
Omihi, *N.Z.* **189** JI4
Omodeo, Lago, *It.* **129** K3
Omolon, *Russ.* **137** DI5
Omolon, river, *Russ.* **137** DI5
Omsk, *Russ.* **136** H7
Omsukchan, *Russ.* **137** DI5
Ōmu, *Japan* **162** BIO
Omul, peak, *Rom.* **131** DI3
Ōmuta, *Japan* **163** K3
Oña, *Sp.* **122** B9
Oncativo, *Arg.* **110** G6
Ondangwa, *Namibia* **180** E5
Ondjiva, *Angola* **180** E5
Ondo, *Nig.* **179** DII
Ondor Sum, *Nei Mongol, China* **158** A4
One and Half Degree Channel, *Maldives* **155** R2
Onega, *Russ.* **136** D5
Onega, river, *Russ.* **136** D5
Oneida Lake, *U.S.* **91** CI5
Onekotan, island, *Russ.* **137** FI8
Oneşti, *Rom.* **131** CI4
Onezhskoye Ozero, *Russ.* **134** C7
Ongarue, *N.Z.* **189** EI5
Ongcheon, *S. Korea* **161** M9
Ongjin, *N. Korea* **161** K4
Ongjin-man, bay, *N. Korea* **161** K4
Ongniud Qi, *China* **157** DI4
Ongole, *India* **155** K5
Oni, *Ga.* **145** AI3
Onich, *Scot., U.K.* **120** G6
Onilahy, river, *Madag.* **181** GI3
Onishika, *Japan* **162** CIO
Onitsha, *Nig.* **179** EII
Oniwaki, *Japan* **162** B9
Ŏnjin-sanmaek, range, *N. Korea* **160** H6
Onjŏng, *N. Korea* **160** H8
Ōno, *Japan* **162** H7
Ono-i-lau, island, *Fiji* **190** G9
Onomichi, *Japan* **162** J5
Onon, *Mongolia* **157** BI3
Onon, *Mongolia* **157** CI3
Onon, river, *Mongolia* **157** BI3
Onsan, *S. Korea* **161** PIO
Onsen, *Japan* **162** J6
Onslow, *W. Austral., Austral.* **186** F3
Onsŏng, *N. Korea* **160** AIO
Ont'an, *N. Korea* **160** AIO
Ontario, *Can.* **89** KIO
Ontario, *Oreg., U.S.* **92** C4

Ontario, Lake, *Can., U.S.* **91** CI4
Ontinyent, *Sp.* **123** GI2
Ōnuma, *Japan* **162** D9
Oobagooma, *W. Austral., Austral.* **186** C6
Oodaap Qeqertaa (Oodaaq Ø), island, *Greenland, Den.* **199** GII
Oodaaq Ø *see* Oodaap Qeqertaa, island, *Greenland, Den.* **199** GII
Oodnadatta, *S. Austral., Austral.* **187** GIO
Oolloo, *N. Terr., Austral.* **186** B9
Oostende (Ostend), *Belg.* **124** G8
Oosterschelde, bay, *Neth.* **124** G8
Opava, *Czech Rep.* **127** GII
Opelousas, *La., U.S.* **93** JII
Open Bay, *P.N.G.* **188** C5
Ophthalmia Range, *Austral.* **184** F4
Opinaca, river, *Ont., Que., Can.* **89** JI2
Opochka, *Russ.* **134** F5
Opole, *Pol.* **127** FII
Oporto *see* Porto, *Port.* **122** D4
Opotiki, *N.Z.* **189** DI7
Oppdal, *Nor.* **119** GIO
Opunake, *N.Z.* **189** FI5
Opuwo, *Namibia* **180** E4
Or, Côte d', escarpment, *Fr.* **125** M9
Or, Les Îles d' *see* Hyères, Îles d', *Fr.* **125** SII
Or, river, *Kaz.* **150** C7
Oradea, *Rom.* **131** BIO
Orai, *India* **154** F5
Oral, *Kaz.* **150** B5
Oran, *Alg.* **174** A7
Ŏrang, *N. Korea* **160** DIO
Orange, *Fr.* **125** RIO
Orange, *N.S.W., Austral.* **187** KI5
Orange, *Tex., U.S.* **93** JIO
Orange, Cabo, *Braz.* **109** AII
Orange, river, *Namibia, S. Af.* **180** H6
Orangeburg, *S.C., U.S.* **93** GI4
Orange Cay, *Bahamas* **96** C6
Orange Walk, *Belize* **95** HI2
Oranienburg, *Ger.* **126** C8
Oranjemund, *Namibia* **180** H5
Oranjestad, *Aruba, Neth.* **98** G6
Oranjestad, *St. Eustatius, Neth.* **99** CI2
Oraviţa, *Rom.* **131** EIO
Orbe, *Switz.* **128** BI
Orbetello, *It.* **128** G5
Orbost, *Vic., Austral.* **187** MI4
Orcadas Base, station, *Antarctica* **200** A3
Orce, *Sp.* **123** JIO
Ohrid, Lake, *Alban., Maced.* **130** J9
Orchila, Isla, *Venez.* **107** BIO
Ord, Mount, *Austral.* **184** C6
Ord, river, *Austral.* **184** C8
Ordes, *Sp.* **122** B5
Ordos *see* Mu Us Shamo, desert, *Nei Mongol, China* **158** CI
Ord River, *W. Austral., Austral.* **186** C8
Ord River Dam, *Austral.* **184** C8
Ordu, *Turk.* **144** C9
Ordubad, *Azerb.* **145** EI5
Ordzhonikidze, *Ukr.* **135** M6
Örebro, *Sweden* **119** JI2
Oregon, *U.S.* **92** C2
Orekhovo-Zuyevo, *Russ.* **134** G8
Orel, *Russ.* **134** H7
Orellana, *Peru* **108** E5
Orellana, Embalse de, *Sp.* **122** G7
Ore Mountains, *Czech Rep., Ger.* **126** F8
Ören, *Turk.* **144** F2
Orenburg, *Russ.* **136** H4
Orense *see* Ourense, *Sp.* **122** C5
Örenşehir, *Turk.* **144** E9
Orepuki, *N.Z.* **189** LII
Orestiáda, *Gr.* **133** AI3

Oreti, river, *N.Z.* **189** LII
Orfanoú, Kólpos, *Gr.* **133** CIO
Orford Ness, *Eng., U.K.* **121** PI2
Organyà, *Sp.* **123** CI3
Orgaz, *Sp.* **122** F9
Orgun, *Afghan.* **153** K6
Orhangazi, *Turk.* **144** C4
Orhei, *Moldova* **135** M4
Orhon (Orkhon), river, *Mongolia* **157** CII
Oricum *see* Orikon, site, *Alban.* **130** K8
Oriental, Cordillera, *Col.* **106** F6
Oriente, *Arg.* **111** K7
Orihuela, *Sp.* **123** HI2
Orikhiv, *Ukr.* **135** M7
Orikon (Oricum), site, *Alban.* **130** K8
Orinduik, *Guyana* **107** EI3
Orinoco, river, *S. Amer.* **102** C5
Oristano, *It.* **129** K3
Oristano, Golfo di, *It.* **129** L2
Oriximiná, *Braz.* **109** CIO
Orizaba, Pico de, *Mex.* **94** G9
Orjen, peak, *Croatia* **130** G7
Orkanger, *Nor.* **119** GIO
Orkhon *see* Orhon, river, *Mongolia* **157** CII
Orkney Islands, *Scot., U.K.* **120** D8
Orlando, *Fla., U.S.* **93** JI5
Orléans, *Fr.* **125** L7
Ormara, *Pak.* **153** R3
Ormara, Ras, *Pak.* **153** R3
Orménio, *Gr.* **133** AI2
Ormoc, *Philippines* **167** DII
Örnsköldsvik, *Sweden* **119** FI3
Orobie, Alpi, *It.* **128** C4
Orobie, *Col.* **106** E8
Oroluk Atoll, *F.S.M.* **190** C6
Oromia, region, *Eth.* **177** FI2
Orona, island, *Kiribati* **191** EIO
Oronsay, island, *Scot., U.K.* **120** H5
Orontes *see* Al 'Āş, river, *Syr.* **146** D6
Oropesa, *Sp.* **122** F7
Oroqen, *China* **157** BI5
Orós, *Braz.* **109** DI5
Orosei, *It.* **129** K4
Orosei, Golfo di, *It.* **129** K4
Orosháza, *Hung.* **127** KI4
Orsa, *Sweden* **119** HI2
Orsha, *Belarus* **134** G5
Orshanka, *Russ.* **134** FI2
Orsk, *Russ.* **136** H5
Orsogna, *It.* **128** H8
Orşova, *Rom.* **131** EIO
Orta, *Turk.* **144** C6
Ortaca, *Turk.* **144** F3
Orta Nova, *It.* **128** J9
Ortegal, Cabo, *Sp.* **122** A5
Ortepah, *Afghan.* **152** H3
Orthez, *Fr.* **125** S4
Ortigueira, *Sp.* **122** A5
Ortisei, *It.* **128** B6
Ortles, mountains, *It.* **128** B5
Ortón, river, *Bol.* **108** F7
Ortona, *It.* **128** G8
Orto Surt, *Russ.* **137** GI3
Orūmīyeh, *Iran* **148** B7
Orune, *It.* **129** K3
Oruro, *Bol.* **108** H7
Oruzgan, *Afghan.* **153** K4
Orvieto, *It.* **128** G6
Oryakhovo, *Bulg.* **131** FI2
Osa, Península de, *C.R.* **95** LI4
Ōsaka, *Japan* **162** J6
Osakarovka, *Kaz.* **151** CI2
Ōsaka Wan, *Japan* **162** J6
Osan, *S. Korea* **161** L7
Osan, *S. Korea* **161** R5
Oscar II Coast, *Antarctica* **200** C3

Oschiri, *It.* **128** J3
Oscoda, *Mich., U.S.* **93** CI3
Ösel *see* Saaremaa, island, *Est.* **119** JI4
Osen, *Nor.* **119** FIO
Oseo, *S. Korea* **161** Q9
Osh, *Kyrg.* **152** E8
Oshawa, *Ont., Can.* **89** MI2
Ō Shima, *Japan* **162** E9
Ō Shima, *Japan* **162** J9
O Shima, *Japan* **163** L2
Ō Shima, *Japan* **163** K7
Oshkosh, *Wis., U.S.* **93** CI2
Oshogbo, *Nig.* **179** DIO
Oshta, *Russ.* **134** C7
Oshwe, *D.R.C.* **176** J7
Osijek, *Croatia* **130** D8
Osimo, *It.* **128** F7
Osin, *S. Korea* **161** P7
Oskarshamn, *Sweden* **119** KI3
Öskemen (Ust' Kamenogorsk), *Kaz.* **151** CI5
Oskoba, *Russ.* **137** HIO
Oslo, *Nor.* **119** JII
Osmanabad, *India* **154** J4
Osmancık, *Turk.* **144** C7
Osmaniye, *Turk.* **144** G8
Osnabrück, *Ger.* **126** D5
Osorno, *Chile* **111** L2
Osorno, *Sp.* **122** C8
Osorno, Volcán, *Chile* **111** L2
Ossa, Mount, *Austral.* **185** LI7
Óssa, Óros, *Gr.* **132** D8
Ossa de Montiel, *Sp.* **123** GIO
Ostashkov, *Russ.* **134** F6
Ostend *see* Oostende, *Belg.* **124** G8
Østerdalen, region, *Nor.* **119** GII
Osterholz-Scharmbeck, *Ger.* **126** C6
Östersund, *Sweden* **119** GI2
Östhammar, *Sweden* **119** HI3
Ostiglia, *It.* **128** D5
Ostrava, *Pol.* **127** GI2
Ostróda, *Pol.* **127** BI3
Ostrogozhsk, *Russ.* **135** K9
Ostrołęka, *Pol.* **127** CI4
Ostrov, *Russ.* **134** E4
Ostrowiec Świętokrzyski, *Pol.* **127** EI4
Ostrów Mazowiecka, *Pol.* **127** CI4
Ostrów Wielkopolski, *Pol.* **127** EII
Osŭm, river, *Bulg.* **131** GI3
Ōsumi Kaikyō, *Japan* **163** M3
Ōsumi Shotō, *Japan* **163** M3
Osuna, *Sp.* **122** J7
Oswestry, *Eng., U.K.* **121** N8
Oświęcim (Auschwitz), *Pol.* **127** FI2
Ōta, *Japan* **162** H9
Otaki, *N.Z.* **189** GI5
Otar, *Kaz.* **151** GI3
Otare, Cerro, *Col.* **106** G7
Otaru, *Japan* **162** C9
Otavalo, *Ecua.* **106** H4
Otavi, *Namibia* **180** F5
O.T. Downs, *N. Terr., Austral.* **187** CIO
Oţelu Roşu, *Rom.* **131** DIO
Otgon Tenger Uul, *Mongolia* **157** CIO
Othoní, island, *Gr.* **132** D4
Óthris, Óros, *Gr.* **132** E8
Otjiwarongo, *Namibia* **180** F5
Otobe, *Japan* **162** D9
Otog Qi, *Nei Mongol, China* **158** CI
Otoineppu, *Japan* **162** BIO
Otoni Teófilo, *Braz.* **109** HI4
Otradnoye, *Russ.* **137** FI7
Otranto, *It.* **129** KI2
Otranto, Strait of, *Europe* **114** L9
Ōtsu, *Japan* **162** DII
Ōtsu, *Japan* **162** J7
Ottawa, *Ont., Can.* **89** LI2

Preston, *Utah, U.S.* **92** D5
Preto, *Braz.* **109** JI2
Pretoria (Tshwane), *S. Af.* **180** G8
Préveza, *Gr.* **132** E5
Pribilof Islands, *U.S.* **85** S4
Priboj, *Serb.* **130** F8
Priboj, *Serb.* **131** GIO
Příbram, *Czech Rep.* **126** G9
Price, *Utah, U.S.* **92** E6
Price, Cape, *India* **155** LI2
Prichard, *Ala., U.S.* **93** HI2
Priekule, *Latv.* **119** KI4
Prieska, *S. Af.* **180** J7
Priestley Glacier, *Antarctica* **201** LII
Prieta, Peña, *Sp.* **122** B8
Prievidza, *Slovakia* **127** HI2
Prijedor, *Bosn. & Herzg.* **130** E6
Prijepolje, *Serb.* **130** G8
Prilep, *Maced.* **131** JIO
Primorsko Akhtarsk, *Russ.* **135** N8
Prince Albert, *S. Af.* **180** K7
Prince Albert, *Sask., Can.* **88** J7
Prince Albert Mountains, *Antarctica* **201** KII
Prince Albert Peninsula, *N.W.T., Can.* **88** C7
Prince Albert Sound, *N.W.T., Can.* **88** D7
Prince Alfred, Cape, *N.W.T., Can.* **88** C7
Prince Charles Foreland, region, *Nor.* **199** FI2
Prince Charles Island, *Nunavut, Can.* **89** EII
Prince Charles Mountains, *Antarctica* **201** DI4
Prince Edward Island, *Can.* **89** KI5
Prince Frederick Harbour, *Austral.* **184** C6
Prince George, *B.C., Can.* **88** H5
Prince Gustaf Adolf Sea, *Nunavut, Can.* **88** B8
Prince Harald Coast, *Antarctica* **201** BI3
Prince of Wales, Cape, *U.S.* **90** KI
Prince of Wales Island, *Austral.* **185** AI3
Prince of Wales Island, *Nunavut, Can.* **88** D9
Prince of Wales Island, *U.S.* **90** M5
Prince of Wales Strait, *N.W.T., Can.* **88** C7
Prince Olav Coast, *Antarctica* **201** BI3
Prince Patrick Island, *N.W.T., Can.* **88** B8
Prince Regent Inlet, *Nunavut, Can.* **89** DIO
Prince Rupert, *B.C., Can.* **88** G4
Princess Astrid Coast, *Antarctica* **201** AIO
Princess Charlotte Bay, *Austral.* **185** BI3
Princess Elisabeth, station, *Antarctica* **201** AI2
Princess Martha Coast, *Antarctica* **200** B8
Princess Ragnhild Coast, *Antarctica* **201** AI2
Princeton, *B.C., Can.* **88** J4
Prince William Sound, *U.S.* **90** L3
Príncipe, island, *Atl. Oc.* **171** L5
Príncipe da Beira, *Braz.* **108** F8
Prins Christian Sound *see* Ikerasassuaq, *Greenland, Den.* **199** MI5
Prior, Cabo, *Sp.* **122** A5
Pripyat' *see* Pryp'yat', river, *Belarus, Ukr.* **134** J3

Prishtina *see* Prishtinë, *Kos.* **130** G9
Prishtinë (Priština, Prishtina), *Kos.* **130** G9
Prislop, Pasul, *Rom.* **131** BI2
Priština *see* Prishtinë, *Kos.* **130** G9
Pritzwalk, *Ger.* **126** C8
Privas, *Fr.* **125** Q9
Privol'noye, *Russ.* **137** FI7
Privolzhsk, *Russ.* **134** E9
Privolzhskaya Vozvyshennost', mountains, *Russ.* **135** KII
Privolzhskiy, *Russ.* **134** JII
Prizren, *Kos.* **130** H9
Probolinggo, *Indonesia* **166** K8
Prodromi, *Cyprus* **133** FI4
Progress, *Russ.* **137** JI5
Progress 2, station, *Antarctica* **201** EI5
Prokhladnyy, *Russ.* **135** PII
Prokhod Sveti Nikola, pass, *Bulg.* **131** FII
Prokópi, *Gr.* **132** F9
Prokop'yevsk, *Russ.* **136** J9
Prokuplje, *Serb.* **131** GIO
Proletarsk, *Russ.* **135** MIO
Promíri, *Gr.* **132** E9
Propriá, *Braz.* **109** FI6
Propriano, *Fr.* **128** H3
Proserpine, *Qnsld., Austral.* **187** EI5
Prossatsáni, *Gr.* **133** BIO
Prostějov, *Czech Rep.* **127** GII
Próti, island, *Gr.* **132** J6
Provadiya, *Bulg.* **131** GI5
Provence, region, *Fr.* **125** RIO
Providence, *R.I., U.S.* **93** CI6
Providencia, Isla de, *Col.* **95** JI5
Providenciales, island, *Turks & Caicos Is., U.K.* **97** FI2
Providenciya, *Russ.* **137** AI6
Provo, *Utah, U.S.* **92** E5
Prudhoe Bay, *Alas., U.S.* **92** H3
Prudhoe Bay, *U.S.* **90** H3
Prudnik, *Pol.* **127** FII
Prüm, *Ger.* **126** F4
Prune Island *see* Palm Island, *St. Vincent & the Grenadines* **99** GI3
Pruszcz Gdański, *Pol.* **127** BI2
Pruszków, *Pol.* **127** DI3
Prut, river, *Moldova, Rom.* **131** CI5
Pruzhany, *Belarus* **134** H2
Prvić, island, *Croatia* **130** E4
Prydz Bay, *Antarctica* **201** EI5
Pryluky, *Ukr.* **135** K6
Pryp'yat' (Pripyat'), river, *Belarus, Ukr.* **134** J3
Przemyśl, *Pol.* **127** GI5
Przheval'sk *see* Karakol, *Kyrg.* **152** CII
Psahná, *Gr.* **132** F9
Psará, *Gr.* **133** FI2
Psará, island, *Gr.* **133** FI2
Psathoúra, island, *Gr.* **133** DIO
Psérimos, island, *Gr.* **133** JI4
Psiloreítis *see* Ídi, Óros, *Gr.* **133** MII
Pskov, *Russ.* **134** E4
Pskovskoye Ozero, *Est., Russ.* **134** E4
Ptolemaída, *Gr.* **132** C7
Ptuj, *Croatia* **130** C5
Pua, *Thai.* **164** F7
Puán, *Arg.* **111** K6
Pucallpa, *Peru* **108** E5
Puca Urco, *Peru* **108** C5
Pucheng, *Fujian, China* **159** M7
Pucheng, *Shaanxi, China* **158** FI
Pucioasa, *Rom.* **131** EI3
Puck, *Pol.* **127** AI2
Pudasjärvi, *Fin.* **119** EI4
Pudimoe, *S. Af.* **180** H7
Pudu, *Indonesia* **166** H4
Puducherry (Pondicherry), *India* **155** M5

Pudukkottai, *India* **155** M5
Puebla, *Mex.* **94** G8
Puebla de Guzmán, *Sp.* **122** J5
Puebla de Sanabria, *Sp.* **122** C6
Pueblo, *Colo., U.S.* **92** F7
Puente-Genil, *Sp.* **122** J8
Pu'er, *China* **157** LIO
Puerto Acosta, *Bol.* **108** G6
Puerto Aisén, *Chile* **111** N3
Puerto América, *Peru* **108** D4
Puerto Ángel, *Mex.* **94** J9
Puerto Armuelles, *Pan.* **95** LI4
Puerto Ayacucho, *Venez.* **107** EIO
Puerto Ayora, *Ecua.* **106** E2
Puerto Bahía Negra, *Para.* **108** H9
Puerto Baquerizo Moreno, *Ecua.* **106** E3
Puerto Barrios, *Guatemala* **95** JI2
Puerto Belgrano, *Arg.* **111** K6
Puerto Berrío, *Col.* **106** D6
Puerto Cabello, *Venez.* **106** B9
Puerto Cabezas, *Nicar.* **95** JI4
Puerto Carreño, *Col.* **107** DIO
Puerto Chicama, *Peru* **108** E3
Puerto Coig, *Arg.* **111** R4
Puerto Colombia, *Col.* **106** B6
Puerto Cortés, *Hond.* **95** JI2
Puerto Cumarebo, *Venez.* **106** B9
Puerto del Rosario, *Spain* **174** C4
Puerto de Mazarrón, *Sp.* **123** JII
Puerto de Nutrias, *Venez.* **106** D9
Puerto de Pajares, peak, *Sp.* **122** B7
Puerto Deseado, *Arg.* **111** P5
Puerto Etén, *Peru* **108** E3
Puerto Heath, *Bol.* **108** F7
Puerto Jiménez, *C.R.* **95** LI4
Puerto La Concordia, *Col.* **106** F7
Puerto La Cruz, *Venez.* **107** BII
Puerto La Paz, *Arg.* **110** C6
Puerto Lápice, *Sp.* **122** G9
Puerto Leguízamo, *Col.* **106** H6
Puerto Libertad, *Mex.* **94** B3
Puertollano, *Sp.* **122** H8
Puerto Lobos, *Arg.* **111** M5
Puerto López, *Col.* **106** F7
Puerto Madryn, *Arg.* **111** M5
Puerto Maldonado, *Peru* **108** F6
Puerto Manatí, *Cuba* **96** F8
Puerto Montt, *Chile* **111** M2
Puerto Morelos, *Mex.* **95** GI2
Puerto Natales, *Chile* **111** R3
Puerto Obaldía, *Pan.* **95** LI7
Puerto Padre, *Cuba* **96** F8
Puerto Páez, *Venez.* **107** DIO
Puerto Peñasco, *Mex.* **94** B3
Puerto Pinasco, *Para.* **109** JIO
Puerto Pirámides, *Arg.* **111** M5
Puerto Plata, *Dom. Rep.* **97** HI3
Puerto Portillo, *Peru* **108** E5
Puerto Princesa, *Philippines* **167** DIO
Puerto Rico, *U.S.* **97** JI7
Puerto Rico, island, *U.S.* **85** PII
Puerto San Carlos, *Chile* **111** P3
Puerto San Julián, *Arg.* **111** Q5
Puerto Santa Cruz, *Arg.* **111** Q4
Puerto Suárez, *Bol.* **109** HIO
Puerto Tres Palmas, *Para.* **108** J9
Puerto Vallarta, *Mex.* **94** G6
Puerto Velasco Ibarra, *Ecua.* **106** F2
Puerto Villamil, *Ecua.* **106** E2
Puerto Wilches, *Col.* **106** D6
Puerto Williams, *Chile* **111** T5
Pueyrredón, Lago, *Arg.* **111** P3
Puget Sound, *U.S.* **90** A3
Pugŏ, *N. Korea* **160** CIO
Puigcerdà, *Sp.* **123** CI4
Puig Major, peak, *Sp.* **123** FI5
Puigmal d'Err, peak, *Sp.* **123** CI4
Pujehun, *Sierra Leone* **178** D5
Pujiang, *Zhejiang, China* **159** L8

Pujŏn, *N. Korea* **160** E7
Pujŏn, river, *N. Korea* **160** E7
Pujŏn-ho, reservoir, *N. Korea* **160** E7
Pukaki, Lake, *N.Z.* **189** JI2
Pu'er, *China* **157** LIO
Pukapuka, island, *Fr. Polynesia, Fr.* **191** FI3
Pukapuka Atoll (Danger Islands), *Cook Is., N.Z.* **191** FIO
Pukchin, *N. Korea* **160** F5
Pukch'ŏng, *N. Korea* **160** F8
Pula *see* Nyingchi, *China* **156** J9
Pula (Pola), *Croatia* **130** E4
Pula, *It.* **129** M3
Pula, Capo di, *It.* **129** M3
Pulandian, *Liaoning, China* **158** C9
Pulandian Wan, *Liaoning, China* **158** C9
Pulap Atoll, *F.S.M.* **190** C5
Puławy, *Pol.* **127** EI4
Pulepu, *Liaoning, China* **158** BII
Puli, *Taiwan, China* **159** Q9
Pulicat Lake, *India* **155** L6
Puliyangudi, *India* **155** N4
Puliyankulam, *Sri Lanka* **155** N6
Pullman, *Wash., U.S.* **92** B4
Pulo Anna, island, *Palau* **188** MI
Pulog, Mount, *Philippines* **167** BIO
Pülümür, *Turk.* **145** DII
Pulusuk, island, *F.S.M.* **190** C5
Puluwat Atoll, *F.S.M.* **190** C5
Puná, Isla, *Ecua.* **106** J4
Punakha, *Bhutan* **154** E9
Punan, *Indonesia* **166** G9
Punch, *India* **154** B3
Pune, *India* **154** J3
P'ungch'ŏn *see* Kwail, *N. Korea* **160** J4
P'ungch'ŏn, *N. Korea* **160** G3
Punggi, *S. Korea* **161** M9
P'unggye, *N. Korea* **160** D9
P'ungsan, *N. Korea* **160** BIO
P'ungsŏ, *N. Korea* **160** E8
P'ungsŏ-ho, reservoir, *N. Korea* **160** E8
Punitaqui, *Chile* **110** G3
Puno, *Peru* **108** G6
Punta Alta, *Arg.* **111** K6
Punta Arenas, *Chile* **111** S4
Punta Cana, *Dom. Rep.* **97** JI5
Punta del Este, *Uru.* **110** J9
Punta Delgada, *Arg.* **111** M6
Punta Gorda, *Belize* **95** HI2
Punta Prieta, *Mex.* **94** C3
Puntarenas, *C.R.* **95** LI4
Punta Umbría, *Sp.* **122** J6
Puntland, region, *Somalia* **177** FI5
Punto Fijo, *Venez.* **106** B8
Puntudo, Cerro, *Arg.* **111** Q4
Pup'yŏng, *N. Korea* **160** G7
Puqi, *Hubei, China* **159** K4
Puquio, *Peru* **108** G5
Puranpur, *India* **154** D6
Purari, river, *P.N.G.* **188** F6
Purdy Islands, *P.N.G.* **188** E5
Puri, *India* **154** H8
Purmerend, *Neth.* **124** E9
Purna, river, *India* **154** H4
Purnia, *India* **154** F8
Pursat, *Cambodia* **164** J8
Purt ny h-Inshey *see* Peel, *Isle of Man, U.K.* **121** L6
Purus, river, *Braz.* **108** D8
Puryŏng, *N. Korea* **160** CIO
Pusad, *India* **154** H4
Pusan *see* Busan, *S. Korea* **161** Q9
Pushkin, *Russ.* **134** D5
Pushkino, *Russ.* **134** JI2
Pusht-I-Rud, region, *Afghan.* **153** L2
Puta, *Azerb.* **145** CI7
Putao, *Myanmar* **164** A5

Red Rocks Point, *Austral.* 184 J7
Redruth, *Eng., U.K.* 121 S6
Red Sea, *Af., Asia* 140 G4
Ree, Lough, *Ire.* 121 M3
Reeds, Plain of, *Viet.* 165 K9
Reedy Glacier, *Antarctica* 200 H8
Reefton, *N.Z.* 189 H13
Refahiye, *Turk.* 145 D10
Regensburg (Ratisbon), *Ger.* 126 H8
Reggane, *Alg.* 174 D7
Reggio di Calabria, *It.* 129 N10
Reggio nell'Emilia, *It.* 128 E5
Reghin, *Rom.* 131 C12
Régina, *Fr. Guiana, Fr.* 107 E17
Regina, *Sask., Can.* 88 K7
Rehoboth, *Namibia* 180 G5
Reid River, *Qnsld., Austral.* 187 E14
Reigate, *Eng., U.K.* 121 Q10
Reims, *Fr.* 124 J9
Reina Adelaida, Archipiélago, *Chile*
   III S2
Reindeer Lake, *Man., Sask., Can.*
   88 H8
Reinga, Cape, *N.Z.* 189 A14
Reinosa, *Sp.* 122 B8
Reliance, *N.W.T., Can.* 88 F7
Remada, *Tunisia* 175 B10
Remanso, *Braz.* 109 E14
Remarkables, The, peak, *N.Z.*
   189 K12
Remedios, *Cuba* 96 E6
Remeshk, *Iran* 149 F12
Rémire, *Fr. Guiana, Fr.* 107 E17
Remiremont, *Fr.* 125 L12
Remontnoye, *Russ.* 135 N11
Rendsburg, *Ger.* 126 B6
Rengat, *Indonesia* 166 H4
Reni, *Ukr.* 135 N4
Renmark, *S. Austral., Austral.*
   187 K12
Rennell, island, *Solomon Is.* 190 F6
Rennes, *Fr.* 125 L4
Rennick Glacier, *Antarctica* 201 M11
Reno, *Nev., U.S.* 92 D3
Renqiu, *Hebei, China* 158 D5
Repetek, *Turkm.* 150 J8
Republican, river, *U.S.* 90 E9
Repulse Bay, *Nunavut, Can.* 89 E10
Repulse Bay, *Austral.* 185 E15
Requena, *Peru* 108 D5
Requena, *Sp.* 123 G11
Reşadiye, *Turk.* 144 D9
Reshteh-ye Alborz (Elburz Mountains),
   Iran 148 B9
Resia, *It.* 128 B5
Resistencia, *Arg.* 110 E8
Reşiţa, *Rom.* 131 D10
Resolute, *Nunavut, Can.* 88 C9
Resolution Island, *Can.* 84 F9
Resolution Island, *N.Z.* 189 L10
Réthimno, *Gr.* 133 L10
Reti, *Pak.* 153 P6
Reus, *Sp.* 123 D13
Reutlingen, *Ger.* 126 H6
Reval *see* Tallinn, *Est.* 119 H15
Revelstoke, *B.C., Can.* 88 J5
Revigny, *Fr.* 125 K9
Revillagigedo, Islas, *Mex.* 94 G3
Revillagigedo Island, *U.S.* 90 M6
Revsbotn, *Nor.* 119 B13
Rewa, *India* 154 F6
Rey, *Iran* 149 C10
Rey, Isla del, *Pan.* 95 L16
Rey Bouba, *Cameroon* 179 D14
Reyes, *Bol.* 108 G7
Reyes, Point, *U.S.* 90 E2
Reyhanlı, *Turk.* 144 G8
Reykjavík, *Ice.* 118 E3
Reynosa, *Mex.* 94 E8
Rēzekne, *Latv.* 119 J16

Rgotina, *Serb.* 131 F10
Rhaetian Alps, *Aust., Switz.* 128 B4
Rheine, *Ger.* 126 D5
Rhiconich, *Scot., U.K.* 120 E6
Rhine, river, *Europe* 114 G7
Rhinelander, *Wis., U.S.* 93 C11
Rhino Camp, *Uganda* 177 G10
Rhinocolura *see* El 'Arîsh, *Egypt*
   147 K2
Rho, *It.* 128 C3
Rhode Island, *U.S.* 93 C16
Rhodes *see* Ródos, *Gr.* 133 K15
Rhodes *see* Ródos, island, *Gr.* 133 K15
Rhodope Mountains, *Bulg., Gr.*
   133 A10
Rhône, river, *Fr.* 125 Q9
Rhône au Rhin, Canal du, *Fr.* 125 L11
Rhum, Sound of, *Scot., U.K.* 120 G5
Rhumsaa *see* Ramsey, Isle of Man, *U.K.*
   121 L6
Rhydargaeau, *Wales, U.K.* 121 P7
Rhyl, *Wales, U.K.* 121 M7
Rhynie, *Scot., U.K.* 120 G8
Riachão, *Braz.* 109 E13
Ría de Pontevedra, *Sp.* 122 C4
Riang, *India* 154 E11
Riaño, *Sp.* 122 B8
Riasi, *India* 153 K9
Riau, Kepulauan, *Indonesia* 166 G5
Riaza, *Sp.* 122 D9
Ribadeo, *Sp.* 122 A6
Riba-roga, Pantà de, *Sp.* 123 D13
Ribáuè, *Mozambique* 181 D11
Ribeira Grande, *Azores, Port.* 122 L4
Ribeirão, *Braz.* 109 J12
Ribera, *It.* 129 N7
Riberalta, *Bol.* 108 F7
Ribes de Freser, *Sp.* 123 C14
Riblah, *Syr.* 146 F6
Ribniţa, *Moldova* 135 M4
Ribnitz-Damgarten, *Ger.* 126 B8
Riccione, *It.* 128 E7
Richards Bay, *S. Af.* 180 H9
Richardson Mountains, *N.W.T., Yukon,*
   Can. 88 D5
Richfield, *Utah, U.S.* 92 E5
Richland, *Wash., U.S.* 92 B4
Richmond, *N.S.W., Austral.* 187 K15
Richmond, *Qnsld., Austral.* 187 E13
Richmond, *S. Af.* 180 J7
Richmond, *Va., U.S.* 93 E15
Ricobayo, Embalse de, *Sp.* 122 D7
Ridà', *Yemen* 148 L7
Ridanna, *It.* 128 B5
Ridder (Leninogorsk), *Kaz.* 151 C15
Ridgecrest, *Calif., U.S.* 92 F3
Riding Rocks, *Bahamas* 96 C6
Riesa, *Ger.* 126 E8
Rieti, *It.* 128 G7
Rieumes, *Fr.* 125 S6
Rieupeyroux, *Fr.* 125 R7
Riez, *Fr.* 125 R11
Rīga, *Latv.* 119 J15
Riga, Gulf of, *Europe* 115 E10
Rīgān, *Iran* 149 E12
Rigestan, desert, *Afghan.* 153 M3
Riglos, *Sp.* 123 C12
Rigo, *P.N.G.* 188 E8
Rigolet, *Nfld. & Lab., Can.* 89 H14
Rig Rig, *Chad* 175 G10
Riiser-Larsen Ice Shelf, *Antarctica*
   200 B8
Riiser-Larsen Peninsula, *Antarctica*
   201 A13
Rijeka (Fiume), *Croatia* 130 D4
Rijeka Crnojevića, *Maced.* 130 H8
Rikubetsu, *Japan* 162 C11
Rikuzentakata, *Japan* 162 F10
Rila, mountains, *Bulg.* 131 H11
Rilly, *Fr.* 125 K9

Rimā', Jabal ar, *Jordan* 146 J6
Rimah, Wādī ar, river, *Saudi Arabia*
   148 F6
Rimatara, island, *Fr. Polynesia, Fr.*
   191 G12
Rimavská Sobota, *Slovakia* 127 H13
Rimini, *It.* 128 E6
Rîmnicu Sărat, *Rom.* 131 D14
Rimouski, *Que., Can.* 89 K13
Rinconada, *Arg.* 110 C5
Rincón de la Victoria, *Sp.* 122 K8
Rincón del Bonete, Lago, *Uru.* 110 G9
Rincón del Guanal, Punta, *Cuba* 96 F3
Ringbu, *Nor.* 119 H11
Ringdom Gompa, *India* 152 J10
Ringkøbing, *Den.* 119 L10
Ringvassøy, island, *Nor.* 119 C12
Rinía, island, *Gr.* 133 H11
Rio, *Gr.* 132 F7
Riobamba, *Ecua.* 106 J4
Rio Branco, *Braz.* 108 E7
Río Bravo del Norte *see* Rio Grande,
   Mex., U.S. 94 B6
Río Bueno, *Chile* III L2
Río Cauto, *Cuba* 96 G8
Río Cuarto, *Arg.* 110 H5
Rio de Janeiro, *Braz.* 109 J14
Río Gallegos, *Arg.* III R4
Rio Grande, *Braz.* 109 M11
Río Grande, *Chile* III S5
Rio Grande (Río Bravo del Norte),
   Mex., U.S. 94 B6
Ríohacha, *Col.* 106 B7
Riom, *Fr.* 125 P8
Río Mulatos, *Bol.* 108 H7
Río Muni, region, *Eq. Guinea*
   179 G12
Rioni, river, *Ga.* 145 B13
Rio Tejo, Foz do, *Port.* 122 G3
Rio Verde, *Braz.* 109 H12
Río Verde, *Chile* III S4
Río Verde, *Mex.* 94 F7
Rio Verde de Mato Grosso, *Braz.*
   109 H10
Rio Vouga, Foz do, *Port.* 122 E4
Rioz, *Fr.* 125 M10
Ripoll, *Sp.* 123 C14
Ripon, *Eng., U.K.* 121 L9
Risâfe *see* Ar Ruşâfah, ruins, *Syr.*
   146 E7
Riscle, *Fr.* 125 R5
Rishikesh, *India* 154 D5
Rishiri Tō, *Japan* 162 B9
Rishon LeẔiyyon, *Israel* 146 J4
Rîşnov, *Rom.* 131 D13
Risør, *Nor.* 119 J10
Ritchie's Archipelago, *India* 155 L11
Ritscher Upland, *Antarctica* 200 B9
Rivadavia, *Chile* 110 F3
Riva del Garda, *It.* 128 C5
Riva di Tures, *It.* 128 B6
Rivas, *Nicar.* 95 K13
Rive-de-Gier, *Fr.* 125 P9
Rivera, *Uru.* 110 G9
River Cess, *Liberia* 178 E5
Riverina, *W. Austral., Austral.* 186 J5
Riverina, region, *Austral.* 185 L13
Riverside, *Calif., U.S.* 92 G3
Riversleigh, *Qnsld., Austral.* 187 D11
Riverton, *Man., Can.* 88 K9
Riverton, *Wyo., U.S.* 92 D6
Rivesaltes, *Fr.* 125 T8
Riviera, region, *Fr., It.* 128 F1
Rivière des Anguilles, *Mauritius*
   181 H15
Rivière-du-Loup, *Que., Can.* 89 K13
Rivière du Rempart, *Mauritius*
   181 H15
Rivière Noire, Piton de la, *Mauritius*
   181 H15

Rivne, *Ukr.* 135 K3
Rivoli, *It.* 128 D2
Riwoqê, *China* 156 H9
Riyadh *see* Ar Riyāḍ, *Saudi Arabia*
   148 G8
Rize, *Turk.* 145 C11
Rizhao, *Shandong, China* 158 F7
Rizokarpaso (Dipkarpaz), *Cyprus*
   133 D18
Rizzuto, Capo, *It.* 129 M11
Ro (Ágios Geórgios), island, *Gr.*
   133 K17
Roa, *Sp.* 122 D9
Road Town, *V.I., U.K.* 99 B10
Roan Cliffs, *U.S.* 90 E6
Roanne, *Fr.* 125 P9
Roanoke, *Va., U.S.* 93 F14
Roanoke, river, *U.S.* 91 F15
Roaringwater Bay, *Ire.* 121 Q2
Robāţ-e Khān, *Iran* 149 C11
Robat-e Khoshk Aveh, *Afghan.* 153 K2
Robāţ-e Posht-e Bādām, *Iran* 149 D11
Robe, *S. Austral., Austral.* 187 L12
Robert-Bourassa, Réservoir, *Que.,*
   Can. 89 J12
Robert Glacier, *Antarctica* 201 C15
Roberts Butte, *Antarctica* 201 L12
Roberts Mountain, *U.S.* 90 L1
Robertsport, *Liberia* 178 D5
Robeson Channel, *Nunavut, Can.*
   89 A11
Róbinson Crusoe, Isla, *Chile, Pac. Oc.*
   193 J16
Robinson Range, *Austral.* 184 G4
Robinson River, *N. Terr., Austral.*
   187 C11
Robinvale, *Vic., Austral.* 187 K12
Roboré, *Bol.* 108 H9
Robson, Mount, *B.C., Can.* 88 H5
Roca Partida, Isla, *Mex.* 94 G3
Rocas, Atol das, *Braz.* 109 D16
Roccadaspide, *It.* 129 K9
Rocca San Casciano, *It.* 128 E6
Roccastrada, *It.* 128 G5
Rocha, *Uru.* 110 H9
Rochdale, *Eng., U.K.* 121 M8
Rochedo, *Braz.* 109 H10
Rochefort, *Belg.* 124 H10
Rochefort, *Fr.* 125 P4
Rocheservière, *Fr.* 125 M4
Rochester, *Eng., U.K.* 121 K8
Rochester, *Eng., U.K.* 121 Q11
Rochester, *Minn., U.S.* 93 C11
Rochester, *N.Y., U.S.* 93 C15
Rock, river, *U.S.* 91 D12
Rockall, island, *U.K.* 199 J18
Rockefeller Plateau, *Antarctica*
   200 J7
Rockford, *Ill., U.S.* 93 D12
Rockhampton, *Qnsld., Austral.*
   187 F15
Rockingham, *W. Austral., Austral.*
   186 K4
Rockingham Bay, *Austral.* 185 D14
Rock Island, *Ill., U.S.* 93 D11
Rock Springs, *Wyo., U.S.* 92 D6
Rocky Mountains, *Can., U.S.* 90 A5
Roddickton, *Nfld. & Lab., Can.* 89 H15
Rodeo, *Arg.* 110 F3
Rodez, *Fr.* 125 R7
Rodonit, Kepi I, *Alban.* 130 J8
Ródos (Rhodes), *Gr.* 133 K15
Ródos (Rhodes), island, *Gr.* 133 K15
Roebourne, *W. Austral., Austral.* 186 E3
Roebuck Bay, *Austral.* 184 D5
Roermond, *Neth.* 124 G10
Roeselare, *Belg.* 124 G7
Roes Welcome Sound, *Nunavut, Can.*
   89 F10
Rogagua, Lago, *Bol.* 108 F7

Sabaneta, *Dom. Rep.* **97** HI3
Sabang, *Indonesia* **167** GIO
Şabanözü, *Turk.* **144** C6
Sabaya, *Bol.* **108** H7
Şāberī, Hāmūn-e, *Afghan.* **153** LI
Şabḩā, *Jordan* **146** J6
Sabhā, *Lib.* **175** DIO
Sabinal, Cayo, *Cuba* **96** F7
Sabiñánigo, *Sp.* **123** CI2
Sabinas Hidalgo, *Mex.* **94** D8
Sabine, river, *U.S.* **91** JII
Sable, Cape, *N.S., Can.* **89** LI4
Sable, Cape, *U.S.* **91** KI5
Sable Island, *N.S., Can.* **89** LI5
Sabres, *Fr.* **125** R4
Sabrina Coast, *Antarctica* **201** KI5
Sabtang, island, *Philippines* **167** AIO
Sabugal, *Port.* **122** E6
Sabuk, *S. Korea* **161** L9
Sabunçu, *Azerb.* **145** CI8
Sabura, *Pak.* **153** M5
Şabyā, *Saudi Arabia* **148** K6
Sabzak Pass, *Afghan.* **152** J2
Sabzevār, *Iran* **149** BI2
Sacaca, *Bol.* **108** H7
Sacedón, *Sp.* **123** EIO
Săcel, *Rom.* **131** BI2
Săcele, *Rom.* **131** DI3
Sacheon, *S. Korea* **161** Q8
Sachigo, river, *Ont., Can.* **89** JIO
Sachs Harbour, *N.W.T., Can.* **88** C7
Sacile, *It.* **128** C6
Sacramento, *Calif., U.S.* **92** E2
Sacramento, river, *U.S.* **90** D2
Sacramento Mountains, *U.S.* **90** H7
Sacramento Valley, *U.S.* **90** D2
Sacré-Coeur, *Que., Can.* **89** KI3
Şa'dah, *Yemen* **148** K7
Saddle Peak, *India* **155** LII
Şadḩ, *Oman* **149** KII
Sadiqabad, *Pak.* **153** P7
Sadiya, *India* **154** DI2
Sado, island, *Japan* **162** G8
Sado, river, *Port.* **122** H4
Sadon, *Myanmar* **164** C5
Sadovoye, *Russ.* **135** MII
Saebyŏl, *N. Korea* **160** AII
Sae Islands, *P.N.G.* **188** F4
Saelices, *Sp.* **123** FIO
Saengildo, island, *S. Korea* **161** R6
Şafājah, region, *Saudi Arabia* **148** F5
Saffar Kalay, *Afghan.* **153** M3
Säffle, *Sweden* **119** JII
Safford, *Ariz., U.S.* **92** H5
Safi, *Mor.* **174** B5
Şāfītā, *Syr.* **146** E5
Safonovo, *Russ.* **134** G6
Safranbolu, *Turk.* **144** C6
Saga (Gya'gya), *China* **156** H6
Saga, *Japan* **163** K3
Sagae, *Japan* **162** G9
Sagaing, *Myanmar* **164** D4
Sagami Nada, *Japan* **162** J9
Sagar, *India* **154** F5
Sagar, *India* **155** L3
Sagarejo, *Ga.* **145** BI4
Sagarmāthā *see* Everest, Mount, *China, Nepal* **156** J7
Saghyz, *Kaz.* **150** D6
Saghyz, river, *Kaz.* **150** D5
Saginaw, *Mich., U.S.* **93** CI3
Saginaw Bay, *U.S.* **91** CI3
Saglek Bay, *Nfld. & Lab., Can.* **89** GI3
Sagone, *Fr.* **128** H3
Sagone, Golfe de, *Fr.* **128** H3
Sagra, peak, *Sp.* **123** HIO
Sagres, Ponta de, *Port.* **122** J4
Sagu, *Myanmar* **164** E4
Sagua de Tánamo, *Cuba* **96** G9
Sagua la Grande, *Cuba* **96** E5

Sagunt *see* Sagunto, *Sp.* **123** FI2
Sagunto (Sagunt), *Sp.* **123** FI2
Saḩāb, *Jordan* **146** J5
Sahagún, *Sp.* **122** C8
Şaḩam, *Oman* **149** GI2
Sahamalaza, Baie de, *Madag.* **181** DI4
Sahara, *Japan* **162** D9
Sahara, desert, *Af.* **170** G2
Saharanpur, *India* **154** D5
Saharsa, *India* **154** F8
Şahbuz, *Azerb.* **145** DI5
Sahel, region, *Af.* **170** J3
Sahiwal, *Pak.* **153** L8
Sahiwal, *Pak.* **153** M8
Şaḩrā al Ḩijārah, region, *Iraq* **148** E7
Şahtaxtı, *Azerb.* **145** DI4
Sahuaripa, *Mex.* **94** C5
Sahyŏn, *N. Korea* **160** J6
Sai, *Japan* **162** E9
Sai Buri, *Thai.* **165** M7
Saïda, *Alg.* **174** A7
Saïda (Sidon), *Leb.* **146** G4
Sa'īdābād *see* Sīrjān, *Iran* **149** EII
Saidapet, *India* **155** L6
Saidor, *P.N.G.* **188** E6
Saidu, *Pak.* **152** J8
Saignes, *Fr.* **125** P7
Saigon *see* Ho Chi Minh City, *Viet.* **165** KIO
Saiki, *Japan* **163** L4
Sailolof, *Indonesia* **167** HI3
Saimaa, lake, *Fin.* **119** GI5
Saimbeyli, *Turk.* **144** F8
Saindak, *Pak.* **153** NI
Saint Abb's Head, *Scot., U.K.* **120** J8
Saint-Agrève, *Fr.* **125** Q9
Saint-Aignan, *Fr.* **125** M6
Saint Albans, *Eng., U.K.* **121** QIO
Saint-Amand, *Fr.* **124** H8
Saint-Amand-Montrond, *Fr.* **125** N7
Saint-Amans-Soult, *Fr.* **125** S7
Saint-Ambroix, *Fr.* **125** R9
Saint Andrews, *N.Z.* **189** KI3
Saint Andrews, *Scot., U.K.* **120** H8
Saint Ann's Bay, *Jamaica* **96** J7
Saint Anthony, *Nfld. & Lab., Can.* **89** HI5
Saint-Aubin-d'Aubigné, *Fr.* **125** L4
Saint-Aubin-du-Cormier, *Fr.* **125** L4
Saint-Augustin, *Que., Can.* **89** JI5
Saint Augustine, *Fla., U.S.* **93** JI5
Saint Austell, *Eng., U.K.* **121** S6
Saint Austell Bay, *Eng., U.K.* **121** S6
Saint-Avold, *Fr.* **125** KIO
Saint-Barthélemy (St. Barts), island, *Fr., Lesser Antilles* **99** BI2
Saint Barts *see* Saint-Barthélemy, island, *Fr., Lesser Antilles* **99** BI2
Saint Bees Head, *Eng., U.K.* **121** L7
Saint-Brieuc, *Fr.* **125** K3
Saint-Cannat, *Fr.* **125** RIO
Saint-Cernin, *Fr.* **125** Q7
Saint-Chély-d'Apcher, *Fr.* **125** Q8
Saint Clair, Lake, *Can., U.S.* **91** DI3
Saint-Claude, *Fr.* **125** NIO
Saint Clears, *Wales, U.K.* **121** Q6
Saint Cloud, *Minn., U.S.* **93** CIO
Saint Combs, *Scot., U.K.* **120** F8
Saint Croix, island, *V.I., U.S.* **97** KI8
Saint Croix, river, *U.S.* **91** CII
Saint David Islands *see* Mapia, Kepulauan, *Indonesia* **188** L3
Saint David's Head, *Wales, U.K.* **121** P6
Saint David's Island, *Bermuda, U.K.* **97** DI3
Saint-Denis, *Fr.* **125** N4
Saint-Denis, *Fr.* **125** K7
Saint-Dié, *Fr.* **125** LII
Saint-Dizier, *Fr.* **125** K9

Saint Elias, Mount, *Can., U.S.* **90** L4
Saint Elias Mountains, *Can., U.S.* **90** L4
Saint-Éloy-les-Mines, *Fr.* **125** N8
Sainte-Marie, *Martinique, Fr.* **99** EI3
Sainte Marie, Cap, *Madag.* **181** GI3
Sainte-Maxime, *Fr.* **125** SII
Saintes, *Fr.* **125** P5
Sainte-Suzanne, *Fr.* **125** L5
Saint-Étienne, *Fr.* **125** P9
Saint-Étienne-du-Rouvray, *Fr.* **124** J6
Saint Eustatius (Statia), island, *Neth., Lesser Antilles* **99** CI2
Saint-Fargeau, *Fr.* **125** M8
Saint Finan's Bay, *Ire.* **121** PI
Saint-Firmin, *Fr.* **125** QII
Saint-Florent, Golfe de, *Fr.* **128** G3
Saint-Florentin, *Fr.* **125** L8
Saint-Flour, *Fr.* **125** Q8
Saint Francis, river, *U.S.* **91** GII
Saint George, *Bermuda, U.K.* **97** DI3
Saint George, *Qnsld., Austral.* **187** HI5
Saint George, *Utah, U.S.* **92** F5
Saint George, Cape, *P.N.G.* **188** B5
Saint George Basin, *Austral.* **184** C6
Saint George Island, *U.S.* **85** S4
Saint George's, *Grenada* **99** GI3
Saint George's Channel, *India* **155** NII
Saint George's Channel, *Ire.* **121** P5
Saint George's Channel, *P.N.G.* **188** B5
Saint George's Island, *Bermuda, U.K.* **97** DI3
Saint-Germain, *Fr.* **125** K7
Saint-Germain-des-Vaux, *Fr.* **124** J4
Saint-Gildas, Pointe de, *Fr.* **125** M3
Saint-Girons, *Fr.* **125** S6
Saint-Guénolé, *Fr.* **125** LI
Saint Helena, island, *Atl. Oc.* **171** P3
Saint Helena Bay, *S. Af.* **180** J6
Saint Helens, *Eng., U.K.* **121** M8
Saint Helens, Mount, *U.S.* **90** B3
Saint Helier, *Channel Is., U.K.* **121** T9
Saint-Hilaire-du-Harcouët, *Fr.* **125** K4
Saint-Hippolyte, *Fr.* **125** MII
Saint-Hyacinthe, *Que., Can.* **89** LI3
Saint Ives Bay, *Eng., U.K.* **121** S5
Saint-Jean, Lac, *Que., Can.* **89** KI3
Saint-Jean-d'Angély, *Fr.* **125** P5
Saint-Jean-de-Losne, *Fr.* **125** MIO
Saint-Jean-de-Luz, *Fr.* **125** S4
Saint-Jean-de-Maurienne, *Fr.* **125** PII
Saint-Jean-de-Monts, *Fr.* **125** N3
Saint-Jean-Pied-de-Port, *Fr.* **125** S4
Saint John, *N. Dak., U.S.* **92** B9
Saint John, *N.B., Can.* **89** LI4
Saint John, island, *V.I., U.S.* **99** BIO
Saint John, river, *U.S.* **91** AI6
Saint John's, *Antigua and Barbuda* **99** CI3
Saint John's, *Nfld. & Lab., Can.* **89** JI6
Saint Jona Island *see* Iony, Ostrov, *Russ.* **137** GI6
Saint Joseph, *Mo., U.S.* **93** EIO
Saint Joseph, *Trinidad & Tobago* **99** JI3
Saint Joseph, Lake, *Can.* **84** H6
Saint-Junien, *Fr.* **125** P6
Saint Kilda, island, *Scot., U.K.* **120** F3
Saint Kitts, island, *St. Kitts & Nevis* **99** CI2
Saint Kitts and Nevis, *N. Amer.* **87** PII
Saint Kliment Ohridski, station, *Antarctica* **200** C2

Saint-Laurent du Maroni, *Fr. Guiana, Fr.* **107** EI6
Saint Lawrence, Gulf of, *Que., Can.* **89** KI5
Saint Lawrence, river, *Can., U.S.* **91** CI5
Saint Lawrence Island, *U.S.* **90** KI
Saint-Lô, *Fr.* **125** K4
Saint-Louis, *Fr.* **125** LI2
Saint Louis, *Mo., U.S.* **93** FII
Saint-Louis, *Senegal* **174** F3
Saint-Louis du Nord, *Haiti* **97** HII
Saint-Loup, *Fr.* **125** LII
Saint Lucia, *N. Amer.* **87** PI2
Saint Lucia, Lake, *S. Af.* **181** HIO
Saint Lucia Channel, *Lesser Antilles* **99** FI3
Saint-Lys, *Fr.* **125** S6
Saint Magnus Bay, *Scot., U.K.* **120** B9
Saint-Maixent, *Fr.* **125** N5
Saint-Malo, *Fr.* **125** K4
Saint-Malo, Golfe de, *Fr.* **125** K3
Saint-Marc, *Haiti* **97** HII
Saint-Marc, Canal de, *Haiti* **97** JII
Saint-Marcel, Mont, *Fr. Guiana, Fr.* **107** FI7
Saint-Martin, *Fr.* **125** R9
Saint-Martin, island, *Fr., Lesser Antilles* **99** BI2
Saint Martin's, island, *Eng., U.K.* **121** S5
Saint Marys, *Tas., Austral.* **187** LI8
Saint Mary's, island, *Eng., U.K.* **121** S5
Saint Mary's Bay, *Nfld. & Lab., Can.* **89** JI6
Saint Mary's Loch, *Scot., U.K.* **120** J7
Saint-Mathieu, *Fr.* **125** P6
Saint-Mathieu, Pointe de, *Fr.* **125** KI
Saint Matthew Island, *U.S.* **84** CI
Saint-Maurice, river, *Que., Can.* **89** KI3
Saint-Méen-le-Grand, *Fr.* **125** L3
Saint Michael, *Alas., U.S.* **92** K2
Saint-Nazaire, *Fr.* **125** M3
Saint-Omer, *Fr.* **124** H7
Saint-Palais, *Fr.* **125** S4
Saint Paul, *Minn., U.S.* **93** CIO
Saint-Paulien, *Fr.* **125** Q9
Saint Paul Island, *U.S.* **85** S4
Saint-Péray, *Fr.* **125** Q9
Saint Peter Port, *Channel Is., U.K.* **121** T8
Saint Petersburg, *Fla., U.S.* **93** JI4
Saint Petersburg *see* Sankt-Peterburg, *Russ.* **134** D5
Saint-Pierre-de-Chignac, *Fr.* **125** Q6
Saint-Pierre-le-Moûtier, *Fr.* **125** N8
Saint-Pierre & Miquelon, islands, *Fr., N. Amer.* **89** KI6
Saint-Pons, *Fr.* **125** S8
Saint-Quay-Portrieux, *Fr.* **125** K3
Saint-Quentin, *Fr.* **124** J8
Saint-Quentin, Pointe de, *Fr.* **124** H7
Saint-Raphaël, *Fr.* **125** SII
Saint-Savin, *Fr.* **125** N6
Saint-Sernin, *Fr.* **125** R8
Saint-Servan, *Fr.* **125** K4
Saint-Sever, *Fr.* **125** R5
Saint Thomas, island, *V.I., U.S.* **99** BIO
Saint Truiden, *Belg.* **124** H9
Saint Tudwal's Islands, *Wales, U.K.* **121** N6
Saint Vincent and the Grenadines, *N. Amer.* **87** PI2
Saint Vincent Gulf, *Austral.* **185** KII
Saint Vincent Passage, *Lesser Antilles* **99** FI4
Saint Vith, *Belg.* **124** HIO
Saint-Vivien, *Fr.* **125** P4

Saipan, island, *N. Mariana Is., U.S.* **190** B5
Sairang, *India* **154** F11
Saito, *Japan* **163** L4
Saivomuotka, *Sweden* **119** C13
Sajama, Nevado, *Bol.* **108** H7
Sajyang Pass, *China, Myanmar* **157** K10
Sakaiminato, *Japan* **162** J5
Sakākah, *Saudi Arabia* **148** E6
Saka Kalat, *Pak.* **153** P3
Sakakawea, Lake, *U.S.* **90** B8
Sakami, *Que., Can.* **89** J12
Sakami, Lac, *Que., Can.* **89** J12
Sakami, river, *Que., Can.* **89** J12
Sakania, *D.R.C.* **176** L9
Sakarya, *Turk.* **144** C4
Sakarya, river, *Turk.* **144** C4
Sakata, *Japan* **162** F9
Sakçagöze, *Turk.* **144** F9
Sakchu, *N. Korea* **160** F4
Sakhalin, Ostrov, *Russ.* **137** G16
Sakhar, *Afghan.* **153** K3
Şäki, *Azerb.* **145** C16
Sakon Nakhon, *Thai.* **164** G8
Sakrand, *Pak.* **153** Q5
Saky, *Ukr.* **135** P6
Sal, Cay, *Bahamas* **96** D5
Sal, island, *Cape Verde* **174** D2
Sal, Cayo de, *Venez.* **98** H9
Sala, *Sweden* **119** H12
Sala Consilina, *It.* **129** K9
Salada, Laguna, *Mex.* **94** A3
Salada, Gran Laguna, *Arg.* **III** N4
Saladas, *Arg.* **110** E7
Saladillo, *Arg.* **110** J7
Salado, river, *Arg.* **110** F6
Salado, river, *Arg.* **110** J5
Salado, river, *Arg.* **110** J8
Salaga, *Ghana* **178** D9
Salal, *Chad* **175** G11
Salala, *Sudan* **177** B11
Salālah, *Oman* **149** K11
Salamanca, *Chile* **110** G3
Salamanca, *Mex.* **94** G7
Salamanca, *Sp.* **122** E7
Salamína, *Gr.* **132** G9
Salamis, *Gr.* **132** G9
Salamis, ruins, *Cyprus* **133** E17
Salamīyah, *Syr.* **146** E6
Salang Tunnel, *Afghan.* **152** J6
Salas, *Sp.* **122** A7
Salas de los Infantes, *Sp.* **122** C9
Salatiga, *Indonesia* **166** K7
Salavan, *Laos* **164** H10
Salavat, *Russ.* **136** G5
Salaverry, *Peru* **108** E3
Salawati, island, *Indonesia* **167** H13
Sala y Gómez, island, *Chile, Pac. Oc.* **191** H17
Sal, Cay, *Bahamas* **96** D5
Salbris, *Fr.* **125** M7
Salda Gölü, *Turk.* **144** F4
Saldaña, *Sp.* **122** C8
Saldanha, *S. Af.* **180** K6
Sale, *Vic., Austral.* **187** M14
Salebabu, island, *Indonesia* **167** F12
Salekhard, *Russ.* **136** F7
Salem, *India* **155** M5
Salem, *Oreg., U.S.* **92** B3
Salemi, *It.* **129** N7
Salerno, *It.* **129** K9
Salerno, Golfo di, *It.* **129** K8
Salford, *Eng., U.K.* **121** M8
Salgótarján, *Hung.* **127** J13
Salgueiro, *Braz.* **109** E15
Salida, *Colo., U.S.* **92** F7
Salies-du-Salat, *Fr.* **125** S6
Şalīf, *Yemen* **148** L6
Salihli, *Turk.* **144** E3

Salihorsk, *Belarus* **134** H4
Salima, *Malawi* **181** D10
Salina, *Kans., U.S.* **92** F9
Salina, Isola, *It.* **129** M9
Salinas, *Calif., U.S.* **92** E2
Salinas, *Ecua.* **106** J3
Saline, river, *U.S.* **91** G11
Saline di Volterra, *It.* **128** F5
Salines, Cap de ses, *Sp.* **123** G15
Salines, Point, *Grenada* **99** H13
Salinópolis, *Braz.* **109** B13
Salisbury, *Eng., U.K.* **121** R9
Salisbury, Ostrov, *Russ.* **136** B9
Salisbury Downs, *N.S.W., Austral.* **187** J13
Salisbury Island, *Nunavut, Can.* **89** F11
Salisbury Plain, *Eng., U.K.* **121** Q9
Şalkhad, *Syr.* **146** H6
Sallent, *Sp.* **123** C14
Sallfelden, *Aust.* **126** J8
Salluit, *Que., Can.* **89** G11
Salmās, *Iran* **148** A7
Salmon, *Idaho, U.S.* **92** C5
Salmon, river, *U.S.* **90** B4
Salmon River Mountains, *U.S.* **90** C5
Salo, *Fin.* **119** H14
Salò, *It.* **128** C5
Salobelyak, *Russ.* **134** E12
Salon, *Fr.* **125** R10
Salonga, river, *D.R.C.* **176** H7
Salonica *see* Thessaloníki, *Gr.* **132** C8
Salonta, *Rom.* **131** C10
Salou, Cap de, *Sp.* **123** E14
Salpausselkä, region, *Fin.* **119** G15
Salqīn, *Syr.* **146** D6
Sal'sk, *Russ.* **135** N10
Salsomaggiore Terme, *It.* **128** D4
Salt, *Sp.* **123** C15
Salt, river, *U.S.* **90** G5
Salta, *Arg.* **110** D5
Saltash, *Eng., U.K.* **121** R7
Saltburn by the Sea, *Eng., U.K.* **121** L9
Salt Cay, *Turks & Caicos Is., U.K.* **97** F13
Salt Desert *see* Kavīr, Dasht-e, *Iran* **149** C10
Saltee Islands, *Ire.* **121** P4
Saltfjorden, *Nor.* **119** D11
Saltillo, *Mex.* **94** E7
Salt Lake City, *Utah, U.S.* **92** D5
Salto, *Uru.* **110** G8
Salton Sea, *U.S.* **90** G3
Salt Range, *Pak.* **153** K8
Saluda, river, *U.S.* **91** G14
Salūm, *Egypt* **175** C13
Saluzzo, *It.* **128** D2
Salvación, Bahía, *Chile* **III** R2
Salvador (Bahia), *Braz.* **109** F15
Salvador, Port, *Falk. Is., U.K.* **III** R7
Salwá, *Saudi Arabia* **148** G9
Salween *see* Nu, river, *Asia* **141** J10
Salyan, *Azerb.* **145** D17
Salzbrunn, *Namibia* **180** G6
Salzburg, *Aust.* **126** J8
Salzgitter, *Ger.* **126** D7
Salzwedel, *Ger.* **126** C7
Šamac *see* Bosanski, *Bosn. & Herzg.* **130** E7
Samā'il, *Oman* **149** H12
Samaipata, *Bol.* **108** H8
Samâlût, *Egypt* **175** C14
Samaná, *Dom. Rep.* **97** H14
Samaná, Bahia de, *Dom. Rep.* **97** H14
Samaná, Cabo, *Dom. Rep.* **97** H14
Samana Cay (Atwood), *Bahamas* **97** E10
Samandağı (Seleucia), *Turk.* **144** G8
Samangan (Aybak), *Afghan.* **152** H5
Samani, *Japan* **162** D11

Samar, island, *Philippines* **167** D12
Samara, *Russ.* **136** G4
Samarai, *P.N.G.* **188** C8
Samaria Gorge, site, *Gr.* **133** M10
Samarinda, *Indonesia* **166** H9
Samarqand, *Uzb.* **151** J10
Sāmarrā', *Iraq* **148** C7
Samar Sea, *Philippines* **167** C11
Samarskoe, *Kaz.* **151** C15
Şamaxı, *Azerb.* **145** C17
Samba, *India* **154** C4
Sambalpur, *India* **154** G7
Sambava, *Madag.* **181** D15
Sambir, *Ukr.* **135** K2
Samboja, *Indonesia* **166** H9
Sambong, *N. Korea* **160** B10
Samborombón, Bahía, *Arg.* **110** J8
Samburg, *Russ.* **136** F8
Samch'a-do, island, *N. Korea* **160** G3
Samcheok, *S. Korea* **161** L10
Samdari, *India* **154** E3
Same, *Tanzania* **177** J12
Samer, *Fr.* **124** H7
Samgi, *N. Korea* **160** E8
Samhae, *N. Korea* **160** C11
Samho, *N. Korea* **160** F8
Sámi, *Gr.* **132** G5
Sami, *Pak.* **153** Q2
Samīm, Umm as, *Oman, Saudi Arabia* **149** H11
Samjiyŏn, *N. Korea* **160** C8
Şamkir, *Azerb.* **145** C15
Samnak, *N. Korea* **160** E5
Samnangjin, *S. Korea* **161** P9
Samnye, *S. Korea* **161** N7
Samo, *P.N.G.* **188** B5
Samoa, *Pac. Oc.* **190** F9
Samoa Islands, *Pac. Oc.* **191** F10
Samokov, *Bulg.* **131** H11
Sámos, *Gr.* **133** G14
Sámos, island, *Gr.* **133** G13
Samothrace *see* Samothráki, island, *Gr.* **133** C11
Samothráki, *Gr.* **133** C12
Samothráki (Samothrace), island, *Gr.* **133** C11
Sampacho, *Arg.* **110** H5
Sampit, *Indonesia* **166** H8
Sam'po, *N. Korea* **160** D10
Samp'o, *N. Korea* **160** D7
Sampwe, *D.R.C.* **176** K9
Sam Rayburn Reservoir, *U.S.* **91** H10
Samrong, *Cambodia* **164** H8
Samsan, *N. Korea* **161** K4
Samsŏ, *N. Korea* **160** D7
Samsŏk, *N. Korea* **160** H5
Sam Son, *Viet.* **164** E9
Samsu, *N. Korea* **160** D8
Samsun, *Turk.* **144** C8
Samu, *Indonesia* **166** H9
Samui, Ko, *Thai.* **165** L6
Samundri, *Pak.* **153** M8
Samur, *Afghan.* **153** L1
Samut Prakhan, *Thai.* **164** J7
Samut Songkhram, *Thai.* **164** J6
Samyang, *N. Korea* **160** H6
San, *Japan* **163** P2
San, *Mali* **174** G6
San, river, *Cambodia* **164** H10
San, river, *Pol.* **127** F15
Şan'ā' (Sanaa), *Yemen* **148** L7
Sana, river, *Bosn. & Herzg.* **130** E6
Sanaa *see* Şan'ā', *Yemen* **148** L7
San Adrián, Cabo, *Sp.* **122** A4
SANAE IV, station, *Antarctica* **200** A9
Şanafīr, island, *Egypt* **147** Q3
San Agustín, *Col.* **106** G5
San Agustin, Cape, *Philippines* **167** E12

Sanak Islands, *U.S.* **85** S4
Sanām, *Saudi Arabia* **148** H7
San Ambrosio, Isla, *Chile, Pac. Oc.* **193** H16
San Ambrosio Island, *Pac. Oc.* **103** L2
Sanana, island, *Indonesia* **167** H12
Sanandaj, *Iran* **148** C8
San Andés Tuxtla, *Mex.* **94** H9
San Andres, Isla de, *Col.* **95** K15
San Andrés del Rabanedo, *Sp.* **122** B7
San Andrés Island, *Col., N. Amer.* **85** Q8
San Andres Mountains, *U.S.* **90** H6
San Andros, *Bahamas* **96** C7
San Angelo, *Tex., U.S.* **92** H8
San Antonio, *Chile* **110** H3
San Antonio, *Tex., U.S.* **92** J9
San Antonio, Cabo, *Arg.* **110** J8
San Antonio, Cabo de, *Cuba* **96** F1
San Antonio, Mount, *U.S.* **90** G3
San Antonio, Punta, *Mex.* **94** B2
San Antonio, river, *U.S.* **90** J9
San Antonio de los Cobres, *Arg.* **110** D4
San Antonio Oeste, *Arg.* **III** L5
Sanāw, *Yemen* **149** K10
Sanawad, *India* **154** G4
San Benedetto del Tronto, *It.* **128** G8
San Benedicto, Isla, *Mex.* **94** G3
San Bernardino, *Calif., U.S.* **92** G3
San Bernardino Strait, *Philippines* **167** C11
San Bernardo, *Chile* **110** H3
San Blas, *Mex.* **94** D5
San Blas, Cape, *U.S.* **91** J13
San Blas, Archipiélago de, *Pan.* **95** L16
San Blas, Punta, *Pan.* **95** L16
San Borja, *Bol.* **108** G7
San Candido, *It.* **128** B6
San Carlos, *Arg.* **110** D5
San Carlos, *Philippines* **167** D11
San Carlos, *Venez.* **106** C7
San Carlos, *Venez.* **106** C9
San Carlos de Bariloche, *Arg.* **III** L3
San Carlos de Bolívar, *Arg.* **110** J7
San Carlos de Río Negro, *Venez.* **107** G10
Sancheong, *S. Korea* **161** P8
Sánchez, *Dom. Rep.* **97** H14
Sanchor, *India* **154** F2
Sanchung, *Taiwan, China* **159** P9
Sanchursk, *Russ.* **134** F11
San Clemente, *Sp.* **123** G10
San Clemente, island, *U.S.* **90** G3
San Cristóbal, *Arg.* **110** F7
San Cristóbal, *Cuba* **96** E3
San Cristóbal, *Dom. Rep.* **97** J14
San Cristóbal, *Venez.* **106** D7
San Cristóbal, Isla (Chatham), *Ecua.* **106** E3
San Cristobal, island, *Solomon Is.* **190** F6
San Cristóbal de Las Casas, *Mex.* **95** H10
Sancti Spíritus, *Cuba* **96** F6
Sancy, Puy de, *Fr.* **125** P8
Sand, *Nor.* **119** J10
Sanda Island, *Scot., U.K.* **121** K5
Sandakan, *Malaysia* **166** F9
San Daniele del Friuli, *It.* **128** C7
Sanday, island, *Scot., U.K.* **120** D8
Sand Cay, *India* **155** M2
Sanderson, *Tex., U.S.* **92** J8
Sandes, *Nor.* **118** J9
Sand Hills, *U.S.* **90** D8
San Diego, *Calif., U.S.* **92** G3
San Diego, Cabo, *Chile* **III** T5
San Diego de los Baños, *Cuba* **96** E2

Tas Tumus, *Russ.* **137** FI3
Tatabánya, *Hung.* **127** JI2
Tatakoto, island, *Fr. Polynesia, Fr.* **191** FI4
Tatarbunary, *Ukr.* **135** N4
Tatarsk, *Russ.* **136** H7
Tatarskiy Proliv, *Russ.* **137** HI6
Tateyama, *Japan* **162** J9
Tathlina Lake, *N.W.T., Can.* **88** F6
Tathlīth, *Saudi Arabia* **148** J7
Tatkon, *Myanmar* **164** E4
Tatnam, Cape, *Man., Can.* **89** HIO
Tatry, mountains, *Slovakia* **127** GI3
Tattershall, *Eng., U.K.* **121** NIO
Tatuí, *Braz.* **109** JI2
Tatvan, *Turk.* **145** EI2
Tauá, *Braz.* **109** DI5
Taubaté, *Braz.* **109** JI3
Taumarunui, *N.Z.* **189** EI5
Taumatawhakatangihangakoauauota-
    mateapokaiwhenuakitanatahu, peak,
    N.Z. **189** GI6
Taum Sauk Mountain, *U.S.* **91** FII
Taunggok, *Myanmar* **164** F3
Taunggyi, *Myanmar* **164** E5
Taungoo, *Myanmar* **164** F4
Taungup Pass, *Myanmar* **164** F4
Taunsa, *Pak.* **153** M7
Taunton, *Eng., U.K.* **121** R8
Taupo, *N.Z.* **189** EI6
Taupo, Lake, *N.Z.* **189** EI6
Tauragè, *Lith.* **119** LI5
Tauranga, *N.Z.* **189** DI6
Taurus *see* Toros Dağlari, *Turk.* **144** F5
Taūshyq, *Kaz.* **150** F4
Tauste, *Sp.* **123** CII
Tauy Bay, *Russ.* **198** C2
Tavan Bogd Uul *see* Youyi Feng, *Mongolia* **156** B8
Tavannes, *Switz.* **128** A2
Tavas, *Turk.* **144** F3
Tavda, *Russ.* **136** G6
Taverna, *It.* **129** MIO
Taverner Bay, *Nunavut, Can.* **89** EII
Tavernes, *Fr.* **125** RII
Tavernes de la Valldigna, *Sp.* **123** GI2
Taveuni, island, *Fiji* **190** F9
Tavropoú, Límni, *Gr.* **132** E6
Tavşanlı, *Turk.* **144** D4
Tawai, *India* **154** DI2
Tawang, *India* **154** EIO
Tawau, *Malaysia* **166** F9
Tawi Tawi, island, *Philippines* **167** FIO
Tawu, *Taiwan, China* **159** R9
Taxco, *Mex.* **94** H8
Taxkorgan, *China* **156** E4
Tay, Firth of, *Scot., U.K.* **120** H8
Tay, Loch, *Scot., U.K.* **120** H7
Tayan, *Indonesia* **166** H7
Tayandu, Kepulauan, *Indonesia* **167** JI4
Tāybād, *Iran* **149** CI3
Taygonos, Poluostrov, *Russ.* **137** DI6
Taylakova, *Russ.* **136** G7
Taylor Glacier, *Antarctica* **201** KII
Taymā', *Saudi Arabia* **148** F5
Taymyr, Poluostrov, *Russ.* **137** EIO
Taymyr, Ozero, *Russ.* **137** EIO
Tay Ninh, *Viet.* **165** KIO
Taypaq, *Kaz.* **150** D5
Tayshet, *Russ.* **137** JIO
Taytay, *Philippines* **167** DIO
Tayynsha (Krasnoarmeysk), *Kaz.* **151** AII
Taz, river, *Russ.* **136** F9
Taza, *Mor.* **174** B6
Tazawako, *Japan* **162** F9
Tazovskiy, *Russ.* **136** F8

Tazovskiy Poluostrov, *Russ.* **136** F8
Taz Peninsula, *Russ.* **199** AII
Tba P'arvani, *Ga.* **145** BI3
Tbilisi *see* T'bilisi, *Ga.* **145** BI4
T'bilisi (Tbilisi), *Ga.* **145** BI4
Tchabal Gangdaba, range, *Cameroon* **179** DI3
Tchad, Lac *see* Chad, Lake, *Chad* **175** GIO
Tchibanga, *Gabon* **179** HI3
Tchin-Tabaradène, *Niger* **174** G8
Tczew, *Pol.* **127** BI2
Te Anau, *N.Z.* **189** LII
Te Anau, Lake, *N.Z.* **189** KII
Teberda, *Russ.* **135** QIO
Tébessa, *Alg.* **174** A9
Tebingtinggi, *Indonesia* **166** F3
Techirghiol, *Rom.* **131** FI5
Techla, *W. Sahara, Mor.* **174** E3
Tecka, *Arg.* **111** N3
Tecomán, *Mex.* **94** G6
Tecpan, *Mex.* **94** H7
Tecuala, *Mex.* **94** F6
Tecuci, *Rom.* **131** DI4
Teel, *Mongolia* **157** CIO
Tefé, *Braz.* **108** C8
Tefé, river, *Braz.* **108** D7
Tefenni, *Turk.* **144** F4
Tegal, *Indonesia* **166** K6
Tegucigalpa, *Hond.* **95** JI3
Te Hapua, *N.Z.* **189** AI4
Tehek Lake, *Nunavut, Can.* **88** F9
Tehrān, *Iran* **149** BIO
Tehuacán, *Mex.* **94** H9
Tehuantepec, *Mex.* **94** J9
Tehuantepec, Golfo de, *Mex.* **95** JIO
Tehuantepec, Istmo de, *Mex.* **95** HIO
Teignmouth, *Eng., U.K.* **121** R7
Tejen, *Turkm.* **150** K7
Tejenstroy, *Turkm.* **150** K7
Te Karaka, *N.Z.* **189** EI7
Tekax, *Mex.* **95** GI2
Tekeli, *Kaz.* **151** FI4
Tekes, *China* **156** D6
Tekirdağ, *Turk.* **144** C2
Tekirova, *Turk.* **144** G4
Tekkali, *India* **154** J7
Tekman, *Turk.* **145** DI2
Teknaf, *Bangladesh* **154** HII
T'elavi, *Ga.* **145** BI4
Tel Aviv-Yafo, *Israel* **146** J4
Telefomin, *P.N.G.* **188** G6
Telegraph Creek, *B.C., Can.* **88** F4
Telén, *Arg.* **110** J5
Teles Pires (São Manuel), river, *Braz.* **109** EIO
Tel Lakhish, ruins, *Israel* **147** K4
Teller, *Alas., U.S.* **92** KI
Tellicherry *see* Thalassery, *India* **155** M3
Telloh *see* Lakash, ruins, *Iraq* **148** D8
Tell Tayinat, ruins, *Turk.* **144** G8
Telsen, *Arg.* **111** M4
Telšiai, *Lith.* **119** KI4
Telukbutun, *Indonesia* **166** F6
Telukdalem, *Indonesia* **166** G3
Teluk Intan, *Malaysia* **165** P7
Tema, *Ghana* **178** E9
Tematagi, island, *Fr. Polynesia, Fr.* **191** GI3
Tembagapura, *Indonesia* **167** JI5
Tembenchi, *Russ.* **137** GIO
Témbi, valley, *Gr.* **132** D8
Temerin, *Serb.* **130** D8
Temerloh, *Malaysia* **165** P8
Teminabuan, *Indonesia* **188** M4
Teminikov, *Russ.* **134** GIO
Temirtaū, *Kaz.* **151** CI2
Temoe, island, *Fr. Polynesia, Fr.* **191** GI4

Temple, *Tex., U.S.* **92** J9
Temple Bay, *Austral.* **185** AI3
Temryuk, *Russ.* **135** N8
Temryukskiy Zaliv, *Russ.* **135** N8
Temse, *Belg.* **124** G9
Temuco, *Chile* **111** L2
Temuka, *N.Z.* **189** KI3
Tena, *Ecua.* **106** H5
Tenali, *India* **155** K6
Ténaro, Akrotírio (Taenarum, Matapás), *Gr.* **132** K8
Tenasserim, *Myanmar* **164** J6
Tenasserim, region, *Myanmar* **164** H5
Tenby, *Wales, U.K.* **121** Q6
Tende, *Fr.* **125** RI2
Ten Degree Channel, *India* **155** MII
Tendō, *Japan* **162** G9
Tendürek Dağı, *Turk.* **145** DI4
Ténéré, desert, *Niger* **174** E9
Tenerife, island, *Atl. Oc.* **170** FI
Tengchong, *China* **157** KIO
Tengiz, oilfield, *Kaz.* **150** E5
Tengiz Köli, *Kaz.* **151** CII
Tengxian, *Guangxi Zhuangzu, China* **159** QI
Tengzhou, *Shandong, China* **158** F6
Tenkasi, *India* **155** N4
Tenke, *D.R.C.* **176** L9
Tenkodogo, *Burkina Faso* **178** C9
Tennant Creek, *N. Terr., Austral.* **187** DIO
Tennessee, *U.S.* **93** GI2
Tennessee, river, *U.S.* **91** GI2
Tenos *see* Tínos, island, *Gr.* **133** HII
Tenosique, *Mex.* **95** HII
Tenterfield, *N.S.W., Austral.* **187** JI6
Teora, *It.* **128** J9
Tepe, peak, *Kos., Serb.* **131** GIO
Tepe Musyan, ruins, *Iran* **148** D8
Tepic, *Mex.* **94** F6
Téra, *Niger* **174** G7
Teraina (Washington Island), *Kiribati* **191** DII
Teramo, *It.* **128** G8
Teratak, *Indonesia* **166** H7
Tercan, *Turk.* **145** DII
Terceira, island, *Azores, Port.* **122** L3
Terekhovka, *Belarus* **134** J5
Terekli Mekteb, *Russ.* **135** PI2
Terekty, *Kaz.* **151** DI6
Terenos, *Braz.* **109** HIO
Teresina, *Braz.* **109** DI4
Terhazza, ruins, *Mali* **174** D6
Termas de Río Hondo, *Arg.* **110** E5
Terme, *Turk.* **144** C9
Termini Imerese, *It.* **129** N8
Termini Imerese, Golfo di, *It.* **129** N8
Términos, Laguna de, *Mex.* **95** HII
Termita, *Russ.* **135** NI2
Termiz, *Uzb.* **151** KIO
Termoli, *It.* **128** H9
Ternate, *Indonesia* **167** GI2
Terneuzen, *Neth.* **124** G8
Terni, *It.* **128** G7
Ternitz, *Aust.* **127** JIO
Ternopil', *Ukr.* **135** K3
Terrace, *B.C., Can.* **88** G4
Terracina, *It.* **128** J7
Terralba, *It.* **129** L3
Terrassa, *Sp.* **123** DI4
Terrebonne Bay, *U.S.* **91** JI2
Terre Haute, *Ind., U.S.* **93** EI2
Tersakan Gölü, *Turk.* **144** E6
Terschelling, island, *Neth.* **124** D9
Tertenia, *It.* **129** L3
Teru, *Pak.* **152** H8
Teruel, *Sp.* **123** EII
Teseney, *Eritrea* **177** DII
Teshekpuk Lake, *U.S.* **90** H3
Teshikaga, *Japan* **162** CII

Teshio, *Japan* **162** BIO
Teshio, river, *Japan* **162** BIO
Teshio Sanchi, range, *Japan* **162** CIO
Tesiyn, river, *Mongolia* **157** BIO
Teslić, *Bosn. & Herzg.* **130** E7
Teslin, *Yukon, Can.* **88** F4
Tesovo Netyl'skiy, *Russ.* **134** D6
Tessalit, *Mali* **174** E7
Tessaoua, *Niger* **174** G9
Tetas, Punta, *Chile* **110** C3
Tete, *Mozambique* **181** DIO
Te Teko, *N.Z.* **189** DI6
Tetere, *Russ.* **137** HII
Teteven, *Bulg.* **131** GI2
Tetford, *Eng., U.K.* **121** MIO
Tétouan, *Mor.* **174** A6
Tetovo-Skopje, *Maced.* **130** H9
Tetyushi, *Russ.* **134** GI2
Teuco, river, *Arg.* **110** D7
Teulada, *It.* **129** M3
Teulada, Capo, *It.* **129** M3
Teuri Tō, *Japan* **162** B9
Tevere (Tiber), river, *It.* **128** G6
Teverya (Tiberias), *Israel* **146** H5
Tewantin, *Qnsld., Austral.* **187** HI6
Texarkana, *Ark., Tex., U.S.* **93** HIO
Texas, *U.S.* **92** H8
Texas City, *Tex., U.S.* **93** JIO
Texel, island, *Neth.* **124** E9
Texoma, Lake, *U.S.* **90** G9
Teykovo, *Russ.* **134** F9
Teylan, *Afghan.* **152** H3
Teywarah, *Afghan.* **153** K3
Tezpur, *India* **154** EII
Tfaritiy, *W. Sahara, Mor.* **174** D5
Thabana Ntlenyana, peak, *Lesotho* **180** J9
Thabaung, *Myanmar* **164** G4
Thaga Pass, *India* **154** C5
Thagyettaw, *Myanmar* **164** J5
Thai Binh, *Viet.* **164** EIO
Thai Hoa, *Viet.* **164** F9
Thailand, *Asia* **143** KII
Thailand, Gulf of, *Asia* **165** K7
Thai Nguyen, *Viet.* **164** D9
Thal, *Pak.* **153** K7
Thalabarivat, *Cambodia* **164** J9
Thalassery (Tellicherry), *India* **155** M3
Thal Desert, *Pak.* **153** L7
Thale Luang, lake, *Thai.* **165** M6
Thamarīt, *Oman* **149** KII
Thames, river, *Eng., U.K.* **121** QII
Thamūd, *Yemen* **148** K9
Thana, *Pak.* **153** N3
Thandaung, *Myanmar* **164** F5
Thane, *India* **154** H2
Thanet, island, *Eng., U.K.* **121** QI2
Thanh Hoa, *Viet.* **164** E9
Thanh Tri, *Viet.* **165** L9
Thanjavur (Tanjore), *India* **155** M5
Thanlwin (Salween), river, *Myanmar* **164** D6
Tharabwin, *Myanmar* **164** J6
Thar Desert *see* Great Indian Desert, *India, Pak.* **153** P7
Thargomindah, *Qnsld., Austral.* **187** HI3
Tharros, site, *It.* **129** K2
Tharthār, Lake, *Iraq* **148** C7
Tha Sala, *Thai.* **165** L6
Thássos (Limín), *Gr.* **133** BII
Thaton, *Myanmar* **164** G5
Thatta, *Pak.* **153** R5
Thau, Bassin de, *Fr.* **125** S9
Thaungdut, *Myanmar* **164** C4
Thayawthadanngyi Kyun, *Myanmar* **164** J5
Thayet, *Myanmar* **164** F4
The Alley, *Jamaica* **96** K7

Velikiye Luki, *Russ.* **134** F5
Velikiy Novgorod, *Russ.* **134** E6
Velikonda Range, *India* **155** K5
Veliko Tŭrnovo, *Bulg.* **131** GI3
Vélingara, *Senegal* **174** G3
Velingrad, *Bulg.* **131** HI2
Velizh, *Russ.* **134** G5
Velletri, *It.* **128** H7
Vellore, *India* **155** L5
Velopoúla, island, *Gr.* **132** J9
Vel'sk, *Russ.* **136** E5
Véna, *Gr.* **133** BII
Venable Ice Shelf, *Antarctica* **200** F5
Venado Tuerto, *Arg.* **110** H6
Vena Park, *Qnsld., Austral.* **187** DI2
Vendàome, *Fr.* **125** L6
Vendas Novas, *Port.* **122** G4
Veneta, Laguna, bay, *It.* **128** D6
Venétiko, island, *Gr.* **132** J7
Venezia (Venice), *It.* **128** D6
Venezuela, *S. Amer.* **104** C4
Venezuela, Golfo de, *Venez.* **106** B8
Vengurla, *India* **155** K3
Veniaminof, Mount, *U.S.* **90** M2
Venice *see* Venezia, *It.* **128** D6
Venice, Gulf of, *Europe* **114** J8
Venkatapuram, *India* **154** J6
Venlo, *Neth.* **124** GIO
Vennesund, *Nor.* **119** EII
Venosa, *It.* **128** JIO
Venray, *Neth.* **124** GIO
Ventimiglia, *It.* **128** F2
Ventotene, Isola, *It.* **128** J7
Ventoux, Mont, *Fr.* **125** RIO
Ventry *see* Ceann Trá, *Ire.* **121** PI
Ventspils, *Latv.* **119** JI4
Ventuari, river, *Venez.* **107** EIO
Vera, *Arg.* **110** F7
Vera, *Sp.* **123** JII
Vera, Bahía, *Arg.* **III** N5
Veracruz, *Mex.* **94** G9
Veraval, *India* **154** GI
Verbania, *It.* **128** C3
Vercelli, *It.* **128** D3
Verçinin Tepesi, peak, *Turk.* **145** CII
Verdalsøra, *Nor.* **119** FII
Verde, Cay, *Bahamas* **96** F9
Verde, Península, *Arg.* **III** L6
Verde, Arroyo, *Arg.* **III** M5
Verdigris, river, *U.S.* **91** FIO
Verdun, *Fr.* **125** KIO
Vereeniging, *S. Af.* **180** H8
Verga, Cap, *Guinea* **178** C4
Vergara, *Uru.* **110** HIO
Vergato, *It.* **128** E5
Vergina, ruins, *Gr.* **132** C8
Vergt, *Fr.* **125** Q6
Véria, *Gr.* **132** C7
Verín, *Sp.* **122** C5
Verkhneimbatsk, *Russ.* **136** G9
Verkhneye Penzhino, *Russ.* **137** CI6
Verkhnyaya Amga, *Russ.* **137** GI3
Verkhovansk, *Russ.* **198** B5
Verkhovazh'ye, *Russ.* **134** C9
Verkhov'ye, *Russ.* **134** J8
Verkhoyanskiy Khrebet, *Russ.* **137** EI3
Vermelho, river, *Braz.* **109** GII
Vermenton, *Fr.* **125** M8
Vérmio, Óros, *Gr.* **132** B7
Vermont, *U.S.* **93** CI6
Vernadsky, station, *Antarctica* **200** C3
Vernal, *Utah, U.S.* **92** E6
Verneuil, *Fr.* **125** K6
Vernon, *Fr.* **125** K6
Vernon, *Tex., U.S.* **92** G9
Vero Beach, *Fla., U.S.* **93** JI5
Verona, *It.* **128** D5

Versailles, *Fr.* **125** K7
Vertientes, *Cuba* **96** F7
Verzy, *Fr.* **125** K9
Vescovato, *Fr.* **128** G3
Veselyy, *Russ.* **137** HI2
Vesoul, *Fr.* **125** LIO
Vesterålen, islands, *Nor.* **119** CII
Vestfjorden, *Nor.* **119** DII
Vestfold Hills, *Antarctica* **201** EI5
Vestmanna, *Faroe Is., Den.* **118** G6
Vestmannaeyjar (Westman Islands), *Ice.* **118** E3
Veststraumen Glacier, *Antarctica* **200** B8
Vestvågøy, island, *Nor.* **119** DII
Vesuvio, Monte, *It.* **128** J8
Ves'yegonsk, *Russ.* **134** E8
Vetapalem, *India* **155** K6
Vetralla, *It.* **128** G6
Veules-les-Roses, *Fr.* **124** J6
Vevaru, island, *Maldives* **155** Q3
Vezhen, peak, *Bulg.* **131** GI2
Vezirköprü, *Turk.* **144** C8
Viacha, *Bol.* **108** G7
Viana do Bolo, *Sp.* **122** C6
Viana do Castelo, *Port.* **122** C4
Viangchan (Vientiane), *Laos* **164** F8
Viareggio, *It.* **128** F4
Viborg, *Den.* **119** LIO
Vibo Valentia, *It.* **129** MIO
Vibraye, *Fr.* **125** L6
Vic, *Sp.* **123** CI4
Vic, Étang de, *Fr.* **125** S9
Vic-en-Bigorre, *Fr.* **125** S5
Vicente Guerrero, *Mex.* **94** B2
Vicenza, *It.* **128** C6
Vic-Fézensac, *Fr.* **125** R5
Vichada, river, *Col.* **106** E9
Vichuga, *Russ.* **134** F9
Vichy, *Fr.* **125** N8
Vicksburg, *Miss., U.S.* **93** HII
Vicovu De Sus, *Rom.* **131** AI3
Victor, Mount, *Antarctica* **201** BI2
Victor Harbor, *S. Austral., Austral.* **187** LII
Victoria, *B.C., Can.* **88** J4
Victoria, *Chile* **110** B3
Victoria, *Chile* **III** K2
Victoria, *Seychelles* **181** AI7
Victoria, *Tex., U.S.* **92** J9
Victoria, Lake, *Kenya, Tanzania, Uganda* **177** HII
Victoria, Mount, *Myanmar* **164** E3
Victoria, Mount, *P.N.G.* **188** E7
Victoria, river, *Austral.* **184** C8
Victoria, river, *Austral.* **187** MI3
Victoria Falls, *Zimb.* **180** E8
Victoria Falls, *Zambia, Zimb.* **180** E8
Victoria Island, *Nunavut, Can.* **88** D8
Victoria Land, *Antarctica* **201** LII
Victoria River Downs, *N. Terr., Austral.* **186** C8
Victoria Strait, *Nunavut, Can.* **88** E9
Victorica, *Arg.* **110** G7
Victorica, *Arg.* **110** J5
Victory Downs, *N. Terr., Austral.* **186** G4
Victory Peak *see* Jengish Chokusu, *Kyrg.* **152** DI2
Vicuña, *Chile* **110** F3
Videle, *Rom.* **131** EI3
Vidigueira, *Port.* **122** H5
Vidin, *Bulg.* **131** FII
Vidisha, *India* **154** G5
Vidzy, *Belarus* **134** G4
Viedma, *Arg.* **III** L6
Viedma, Lago, *Arg.* **III** Q3
Vielha, *Sp.* **123** BI3
Vienna *see* Wien, *Aust.* **127** JIO

Vienne, *Fr.* **125** PIO
Vientiane *see* Viangchan, *Laos* **164** F8
Vieques, island, *P.R., U.S.* **97** JI8
Vierwaldstätter See (Lucerne, Lake of), *Switz.* **128** B3
Vierzon, *Fr.* **125** M7
Vieste, *It.* **128** HIO
Vietnam, *Asia* **143** KI2
Viet Tri, *Viet.* **164** E9
Vieux-Boucau, *Fr.* **125** R4
Vieux Fort, *St. Lucia* **99** FI3
Vigan, *Philippines* **167** BIO
Vigía Chico, *Mex.* **95** GI2
Vignemale, Pic de, *Fr.* **125** T5
Vigo, *Sp.* **122** C4
Vigo, Ría de, *Sp.* **122** C4
Vihari, *Pak.* **153** M8
Viipuri *see* Vyborg, *Russ.* **134** C5
Vijayawada, *India* **155** K6
Vík, *Ice.* **118** E3
Vikhorevka, *Russ.* **137** JII
Vikhren, peak, *Bulg.* **131** HII
Vikna, *Nor.* **119** FII
Vila Bela da Santíssima Trindade, *Braz.* **108** G9
Vila Bittencourt, *Braz.* **108** C6
Vila de Moura, *Port.* **122** H5
Vila de Sagres, *Port.* **122** J4
Vila do Bispo, *Port.* **122** J4
Vila do Conde, *Port.* **122** D4
Vilafranca del Penedès, *Sp.* **123** DI4
Vila Franca do Campo, *Azores, Port.* **122** M4
Vilagarcía de Arousa, *Sp.* **122** B4
Vila Murtinho, *Braz.* **108** E7
Vilanculos, *Mozambique* **181** FII
Vila Nova de Gaia, *Port.* **122** D4
Vila Nova de Milfontes, *Port.* **122** J4
Vilanova i la Geltrú, *Sp.* **123** DI4
Vila Real, *Port.* **122** D5
Vila-real de los Infantes, *Sp.* **123** FI2
Vilar Formoso, *Port.* **122** E6
Vila Velha, *Braz.* **109** AI2
Vila Velha (Espírito Santo), *Braz.* **109** JI4
Vila Velha de Rodão, *Sp.* **122** F5
Vilhelmina, *Sweden* **119** FI2
Vilhena, *Braz.* **108** F9
Viljandi, *Est.* **119** JI5
Vil'kitskogo, Proliv, *Russ.* **137** DIO
Villa Ahumada, *Mex.* **94** C6
Villa Alberdi, *Arg.* **110** E5
Villa Ángela, *Arg.* **110** E7
Villa Atuel, *Arg.* **110** H4
Villablino, *Sp.* **122** B7
Villa Cañás, *Arg.* **110** H6
Villacarrillo, *Sp.* **122** H9
Villacastĺn, *Sp.* **122** E8
Villach, *Aust.* **126** K9
Villacidro, *It.* **129** L3
Villa Dolores, *Arg.* **110** G5
Villafranca de los Barros, *Sp.* **122** H6
Villafranca di Verona, *It.* **128** D4
Villaguay, *Arg.* **110** G8
Villa Guillermina, *Arg.* **110** E7
Villahermosa, *Mex.* **95** HIO
Villa Krause, *Arg.* **110** G4
Villalba, *Sp.* **122** B5
Villalonga, *Arg.* **III** L6
Villamar, *It.* **129** L3
Villa María, *Arg.* **110** G6
Villa Martín, *Bol.* **108** J7
Villamartín, *Sp.* **122** K7
Villamontes, *Bol.* **108** J8
Villa Nueva, *Arg.* **110** H4
Villanueva, *Mex.* **94** F6
Villanueva de Córdoba, *Sp.* **122** H8
Villanueva del Fresno, *Sp.* **122** H5
Villanueva de los Infantes, *Sp.* **122** G9
Villa Ocampo, *Arg.* **110** F7

Villa Regina, *Arg.* **III** K4
Villarosa, *It.* **129** N8
Villarrica, *Chile* **III** L3
Villarrica, Lago, *Chile* **III** L3
Villarrobledo, *Sp.* **123** GIO
Villatobas, *Sp.* **122** F9
Villa Unión, *Arg.* **110** F3
Villa Unión, *Mex.* **94** F5
Villavicencio, *Col.* **106** F7
Villaviciosa, *Sp.* **122** A7
Villazón, *Bol.* **108** J7
Villedieu-les-Poêles, *Fr.* **125** K4
Villefranche, *Fr.* **125** P9
Villefranche-de-Lauragais, *Fr.* **125** S7
Villefranche-de-Rouergue, *Fr.* **125** R7
Villemaur, *Fr.* **125** L8
Villena, *Sp.* **123** HI2
Villeneuve-Saint-Georges, *Fr.* **125** K7
Villeneuve-sur-Lot, *Fr.* **125** R6
Villerupt, *Fr.* **124** JIO
Villeurbanne, *Fr.* **125** PIO
Villingen-Schwenningen, *Ger.* **126** J5
Villupuram, *India* **155** M5
Vilnius, *Lith.* **119** LI6
Vilyuy, river, *Russ.* **137** FI3
Vilyuysk, *Russ.* **137** FI2
Vilyuyskoye Vodokhranilishche, *Russ.* **137** FI2
Vimoutiers, *Fr.* **125** K5
Viña del Mar, *Chile* **110** H3
Vinaròs, *Sp.* **123** EI3
Vincennes Bay, *Antarctica* **201** JI6
Vindelälven, river, *Sweden* **119** EI2
Vindeln, *Sweden* **119** FI3
Vindhya Range, *India* **154** G4
Vindrey, *Russ.* **134** HIO
Vinh, *Viet.* **164** F9
Vinhais, *Port.* **122** C6
Vinh Chau, *Viet.* **165** L9
Vinh Long, *Viet.* **165** K9
Vinkovci, *Croatia* **130** D8
Vinnytsya, *Ukr.* **135** L4
Vinson Massif, *Antarctica* **200** F6
Vinukonda, *India* **155** K5
Vipiteno, *It.* **128** B5
Viqueque, *Timor-Leste* **167** KI2
Vir, *Taj.* **152** G8
Vir, island, *Croatia* **130** E5
Virac, *Philippines* **167** CII
Virachei, *Cambodia* **164** HIO
Viranşehir, *Turk.* **145** FII
Virawah, *Pak.* **153** R7
Virden, *Man., Can.* **88** K8
Vire, *Fr.* **125** K4
Vîrfurile, *Rom.* **131** CII
Virgin Gorda, island, *V.I., U.K.* **99** BII
Virginia, *U.S.* **93** FI5
Virginia Beach, *Va., U.S.* **93** FI6
Virginia Falls, *N.W.T., Can.* **88** F5
Virgin Islands, *Caribbean Sea* **99** BIO
Virovitica, *Croatia* **130** D7
Virrat, *Fin.* **119** GI4
Virtsu, *Est.* **119** JI5
Virú, *Peru* **108** E4
Virudunagar, *India* **155** N4
Vis (Lissa), island, *Croatia* **130** G5
Visalia, *Calif., U.S.* **92** F3
Visayan Sea, *Philippines* **167** DII
Visby, *Sweden* **119** KI3
Viscount Melville Sound, *Nunavut, Can.* **88** C8
Višegrad, *Bosn. & Herzg.* **130** F8
Viseu, *Port.* **122** E5
Vişeu De Sus, *Rom.* **131** BI2
Vishakhapatnam, *India* **154** J7
Viški Kanal, *Croatia* **130** G5
Viso, Monte, *It.* **128** DI
Viso del Marqués, *Sp.* **122** H9

Washington, *U.S.* **92** A3
Washington, D.C., *U.S.* **93** E15
Washington, Cape, *Antarctica* **201** L11
Washington, Mount, *U.S.* **91** B16
Washington Island *see* Teraina, *Kiribati* **191** D11
Washita, river, *U.S.* **90** G9
Washuk, *Pak.* **153** P3
Wasior, *Indonesia* **167** H15
Waskaganish, *Que., Can.* **89** K12
Waswanipi, Lac, *Que., Can.* **89** K12
Watampone, *Indonesia* **167** J10
Water Cay, *Bahamas* **96** E9
Water Cays, *Bahamas* **96** D7
Waterford (Port Láirge), *Ire.* **121** P4
Waterford Harbour, *Ire.* **121** P4
Waterloo, *Iowa, U.S.* **93** D11
Waterloo, *N. Terr., Austral.* **186** C8
Waterman, Isla, *Chile* **III** T4
Watertown, *N.Y., U.S.* **93** C15
Watertown, *S. Dak., U.S.* **93** C9
Watford, *Eng., U.K.* **121** Q10
Watling *see* San Salvador, island, *Bahamas* **97** D10
Watsa, *D.R.C.* **177** G10
Watson, *S. Austral., Austral.* **186** J9
Watson Lake, *Yukon, Can.* **88** F5
Wattwil, *Switz.* **128** A3
Watubela, Kepulauan, *Indonesia* **188** M5
Wau, *P.N.G.* **188** E7
Wau, *S. Sudan* **176** F9
Wauchope, *N. Terr., Austral.* **187** E10
Waukarlycarly, Lake, *Austral.* **184** E5
Waukegan, *Ill., U.S.* **93** D12
Wausau, *Wis., U.S.* **93** C11
Wave Hill, *N. Terr., Austral.* **186** C8
Wawa, *Ont., Can.* **89** L11
Wāw al Kabīr, *Lib.* **175** D11
Way, Lake, *Austral.* **184** G5
Wayamli, *Indonesia* **167** G13
Wayaobu *see* Zichang, *Shaanxi, China* **158** E1
Waycross, *Ga., U.S.* **93** H14
Wazah, *Afghan.* **153** K6
Wazah Khwah (Mushuray), *Afghan.* **153** L5
Wazirabad, *Pak.* **153** L9
We, island, *Indonesia* **166** E2
Weald, The, region, *Eng., U.K.* **121** R11
Weary Bay, *Austral.* **185** C14
Webi Jubba, river, *Somalia* **177** G13
Weda, *Indonesia* **167** G12
Weda, Teluk, *Indonesia* **167** G13
Weddell Island, *Falk. Is., U.K.* **III** R7
Weddell Sea, *Antarctica* **200** C6
Wedemark, *Ger.* **126** D6
Weert, *Neth.* **124** G10
Wee Waa, *N.S.W., Austral.* **187** J15
Węgorzewo, *Pol.* **127** B14
Wei, river, *China* **157** G12
Wei, river, *Shaanxi, China* **158** G1
Wei, river, *Shandong, China* **158** E5
Weichang, *Hebei, China* **158** A6
Weiden, *Ger.* **126** G8
Weifang, *Shandong, China* **158** E7
Weihai, *Shandong, China* **158** D9
Weihui, *Henan, China* **158** F4
Weilheim, *Ger.* **126** J7
Weilmoringle, *N.S.W., Austral.* **187** H14
Weimar, *Ger.* **126** E7
Weinan, *Shaanxi, China* **158** G1
Weining, *China* **157** K11
Weinsberger Wald, *Aust.* **127** H10
Weipa, *Qnsld., Austral.* **187** B13
Weishan, *Shandong, China* **158** G6
Weishi, *Henan, China* **158** G4
Weissenburg, *Ger.* **126** H7
Weissenfels, *Ger.* **126** E8

Weixi, *China* **157** J10
Wejherowo, *Pol.* **127** A11
Weldiya, *Eth.* **177** E12
Weligama, *Sri Lanka* **155** P6
Welkom, *S. Af.* **180** H8
Wellesley Islands, *Austral.* **185** C12
Wellin, *Belg.* **124** H9
Wellington, *N.S.W., Austral.* **187** K14
Wellington, *N.Z.* **189** G15
Wellington, Isla, *Chile* **III** Q2
Wellington, Lake, *Austral.* **185** M14
Wellington Bay, *Nunavut, Can.* **88** E8
Wells, *Nev., U.S.* **92** D4
Wells, Lake, *Austral.* **184** G6
Wels, *Aust.* **126** J9
Welshpool, *Wales, U.K.* **121** N8
Wenatchee, *Wash., U.S.* **92** A4
Wenchang, *Hainan, China* **159** T1
Wencheng, *Zhejiang, China* **159** M8
Wenchi, *Ghana* **178** D8
Wendeng, *Shandong, China* **158** E9
Wendesi, *Indonesia* **167** H15
Wenjiao, *Hainan, China* **159** T1
Wenling, *Zhejiang, China* **159** L9
Wenman *see* Wolf, Isla, *Ecua.* **106** C1
Wenshan, *China* **157** L11
Wenshang, *Shandong, China* **158** F6
Wentworth, *N.S.W., Austral.* **187** K12
Wenxi, *Shanxi, China* **158** F2
Wenxian, *China* **157** H11
Wenzhou, *Zhejiang, China* **159** M8
Werdau, *Ger.* **126** F8
Werdēr, *Eth.* **177** F14
Werder, *Ger.* **126** D8
Weri, *Indonesia* **188** L5
Weser, river, *Ger.* **126** C5
Wessel Islands, *Austral.* **185** A10
Wessex, region, *Eng., U.K.* **121** R8
West Antarctica, region, *Antarctica* **200** G6
West Bank, *Asia* **146** J4
West Burra, island, *Scot., U.K.* **120** C9
West Caicos, island, *Turks & Caicos Is., U.K.* **97** F12
West Cape Howe, *Austral.* **184** L4
West End, *Bahamas* **96** A6
West End Point, *Cayman Is., U.K.* **96** H5
Westerland, *Ger.* **126** A6
Western, river, *Nunavut, Can.* **88** E8
Western Australia, *Austral.* **186** F4
Western Desert, *Egypt* **175** C13
Western Ghats, range, *India* **154** J3
Western Plateau, *Austral.* **184** F5
Western Sahara, *Af.* **172** F2
Westerschelde, bay, *Neth.* **124** G8
West Falkland, island, *Falk. Is., U.K.* **III** R7
West Frisian Islands, *Neth.* **124** D9
West Ice Shelf, *Antarctica* **201** F16
West Indies, islands, *N. Amer.* **85** N9
West Lafayette, *Ind., U.S.* **93** E12
Westman Islands *see* Vestmannaeyjar, *Ice.* **118** E3
West Memphis, *Ark., U.S.* **93** G11
West Nicholson, *Zimb.* **180** F9
Weston Super Mare, *Eng., U.K.* **121** Q8
West Palm Beach, *Fla., U.S.* **93** K15
West Point, *Austral.* **185** K10
Westport (Cathair na Mart), *Ire.* **121** M2
Westport, *N.Z.* **189** H13
Westray, island, *Scot., U.K.* **120** D7
Westray Firth, *Scot., U.K.* **120** D8
West Siberian Plain, *Asia* **140** D9
West Virginia, *U.S.* **93** E14
Westwood Downs, *N.S.W., Austral.* **187** J12

West Wyalong, *N.S.W., Austral.* **187** K14
West York Island, *Spratly Is.* **166** D8
Wetar, island, *Indonesia* **167** K12
Wetaskiwin, *Alta., Can.* **88** J6
Wetzlar, *Ger.* **126** F5
Wewak, *P.N.G.* **188** F5
Wexford (Loch Garman), *Ire.* **121** P5
Wexford Harbour, *Ire.* **121** P5
Weyburn, *Sask., Can.* **88** K7
Weyer, *Aust.* **126** J9
Weymouth, *Eng., U.K.* **121** R8
Weymouth, Cape, *Austral.* **185** B13
Whakapunake, peak, *N.Z.* **189** E17
Whakatane, *N.Z.* **189** D17
Whale Cay, *Bahamas* **96** B7
Whale Cove, *Nunavut, Can.* **88** G9
Whalsay, island, *Scot., U.K.* **120** B9
Whangamata, *N.Z.* **189** D16
Whangarei, *N.Z.* **189** C15
Wheeler Peak, *N. Mex., U.S.* **90** F7
Wheeler Peak, *Nev., U.S.* **90** E4
Wheeling, *W. Va., U.S.* **93** E14
Whidbey, Point, *Austral.* **185** K10
Whiddy Island, *Ire.* **121** Q2
Whinham, Mount, *Austral.* **184** G8
Whiporie, *N.S.W., Austral.* **187** J16
Whitby, *Eng., U.K.* **121** L10
White, Lake, *Austral.* **184** E8
White, river, *Ark., U.S.* **91** G11
White, river, *Ind., U.S.* **91** E12
White, East Fork, river, *Ind., U.S.* **91** E13
White, river, *S. Dak., U.S.* **90** D8
White Butte, *U.S.* **90** C8
White Cliffs, *N.S.W., Austral.* **187** J13
Whitehaven, *Eng., U.K.* **121** L7
Whitehorse, *Yukon, Can.* **88** E4
White Island, *Antarctica* **201** B14
White Island, *Nunavut, Can.* **89** F10
Whitemark, *Tas., Austral.* **187** K18
White Mountains, *U.S.* **91** C16
White Nile *see* El Bahr el Abyad, river, *S. Sudan, Sudan* **177** E10
White Sea, *Europe* **115** B12
Whithorn, *Scot., U.K.* **121** K6
Whitmore Mountains, *Antarctica* **200** G7
Whitney, Mount, *U.S.* **90** F3
Whittier, *Alas., U.S.* **92** L3
Wholdaia Lake, *N.W.T., Can.* **88** G8
Whyalla, *S. Austral., Austral.* **187** K11
Wiay *see* Fuidhaigh, island, *Scot., U.K.* **120** F4
Wichita, *Kans., U.S.* **92** F9
Wichita Falls, *Tex., U.S.* **92** G9
Wichita Mountains, *U.S.* **90** G9
Wick, *Scot., U.K.* **120** E7
Wickenburg, *Ariz., U.S.* **92** G5
Wicklow (Cill Mhantáin), *Ire.* **121** N5
Wicklow Head, *Ire.* **121** N5
Wicklow Mountains, *Ire.* **121** N5
Wide Bay, *P.N.G.* **188** B6
Widnes, *Eng., U.K.* **121** M8
Wido, island, *S. Korea* **161** P5
Wieleń, *Pol.* **127** C10
Wieluń, *Pol.* **127** E12
Wien (Vienna), *Aust.* **127** J10
Wiener Neustadt, *Aust.* **127** J10
Wieprz, river, *Pol.* **127** E14
Wiesbaden, *Ger.* **126** F5
Wigan, *Eng., U.K.* **121** M8
Wight, Isle of, *Eng., U.K.* **121** R9
Wigtown Bay, *Scot., U.K.* **121** K7
Wil, *Switz.* **128** A3
Wilberforce, Cape, *Austral.* **185** A11
Wilcannia, *N.S.W., Austral.* **187** J13
Wilczek, Zemlya, *Russ.* **136** C9
Wilde Bay, *Austral.* **185** G16
Wildespitze, peak, *Aust.* **126** K7

Wilhelm, Mount, *P.N.G.* **188** F6
Wilhelm II Coast, *Antarctica* **201** G16
Wilhelmina Gebergte, *Suriname* **107** F15
Wilhelmshaven, *Ger.* **126** B5
Wilkes-Barre, *Pa., U.S.* **93** D15
Wilkes Land, *Antarctica* **201** L13
Wilkins Coast, *Antarctica* **200** D4
Willamette, river, *U.S.* **90** B3
Willcox, *Ariz., U.S.* **92** H5
Willemstad, *Curaçao, Neth.* **98** G7
Willeroo, *N. Terr., Austral.* **186** C9
William, Mount, *Austral.* **185** L12
William Creek, *S. Austral., Austral.* **187** H10
Williams, *Ariz., U.S.* **92** G5
Williams Island, *Bahamas* **96** C6
Williams Lake, *B.C., Can.* **88** H4
Williamson Glacier, *Antarctica* **201** J15
Williamsport, *Pa., U.S.* **93** D15
Willis Islets, *Coral Sea Is. Terr., Austral.* **190** F5
Williston, *N. Dak., U.S.* **92** B8
Williston Lake, *B.C., Can.* **88** G4
Willmar, *Minn., U.S.* **93** C10
Willowlake, river, *N.W.T., Can.* **88** F6
Willowra, *N. Terr., Austral.* **186** E9
Wilmington, *Del., U.S.* **93** D15
Wilmington, *N.C., U.S.* **93** G15
Wilson Hills, *Antarctica* **201** M12
Wilsons Promontory, peninsula, *Austral.* **185** M13
Wiluna, *W. Austral., Austral.* **186** G5
Winchester, *Eng., U.K.* **121** R9
Wind, river, *Yukon, Can.* **88** D5
Windhoek, *Namibia* **180** F5
Windorah, *Qnsld., Austral.* **187** G13
Wind River Range, *U.S.* **90** C6
Windsor, *Eng., U.K.* **121** Q10
Windsor, *Ont., Can.* **89** M11
Windward Islands, *Caribbean Sea* **85** P12
Windward Passage, *Cuba, Haiti* **97** H10
Wini, *Indonesia* **167** L11
Winisk, river, *Ont., Can.* **89** J10
Winneba, *Ghana* **178** E9
Winnebago, Lake, *U.S.* **91** C12
Winnemucca, *Nev., U.S.* **92** D4
Winnipeg, *Man., Can.* **88** K8
Winnipeg, Lake, *Man., Can.* **88** J8
Winnipegosis, *Man., Can.* **88** K8
Winnipesaukee, Lake, *U.S.* **91** C16
Winona, *Minn., U.S.* **93** C11
Winsen, *Ger.* **126** C7
Winslow, *Ariz., U.S.* **92** G5
Winston-Salem, *N.C., U.S.* **93** F14
Winterswijk, *Neth.* **124** F11
Winterthur, *Switz.* **128** A3
Winton, *Qnsld., Austral.* **187** F13
Wippra, *Ger.* **126** E7
Wiralong, *N.S.W., Austral.* **187** K13
Wirrulla, *S. Austral., Austral.* **187** J10
Wisbech, *Eng., U.K.* **121** N11
Wisconsin, *U.S.* **93** C11
Wisconsin, river, *U.S.* **91** D11
Wiseman, *Alas., U.S.* **92** J3
Wisła, river, *Pol.* **127** B12
Wismar, *Ger.* **126** B7
Wissembourg, *Fr.* **125** K12
Witham, *Eng., U.K.* **121** P11
Wittenberg, *Ger.* **126** D8
Wittenberge, *Ger.* **126** C7
Wittenoom, *W. Austral., Austral.* **186** F4
Wittlich, *Ger.* **126** F4
Wittstock, *Ger.* **126** C8
Witu Islands, *P.N.G.* **188** D5

Xiuwu, *Henan, China* **158** F4
Xiuyan, *Liaoning, China* **158** B10
Xixia, *Henan, China* **158** H2
Xixian, *Henan, China* **158** H4
Xizhong Dao, *Liaoning, China* **158** C8
Xizhou Shan, *Shanxi, China* **158** D4
Xızı, *Azerb.* **145** C17
Xocavand *see* Martuni, *Azerb.*
  145 D16
Xorkol, *China* **156** F8
Xuan'en, *Hubei, China* **159** K1
Xuanhua, *Hebei, China* **158** B5
Xuan Loc, *Viet.* **165** K10
Xuanwei, *China* **157** K11
Xuanzhou, *Anhui, China* **159** K7
Xuchang, *Henan, China* **158** G4
Xudat, *Azerb.* **145** B17
Xuddur, *Somalia* **177** G13
Xudun, *Somalia* **177** E14
Xun, river, *Guangxi Zhuangzu, China*
  159 Q1
Xun, river, *Shaanxi, China* **158** H1
Xunke, *China* **157** B16
Xunwu, *Jiangxi, China* **159** P5
Xunyang, *Shaanxi, China* **158** H1
Xupu, *Hunan, China* **159** M1
Xuwen, *China* **157** M13
Xuyi, *Jiangsu, China* **158** H7
Xuzhou, *Jiangsu, China* **158** G6
Xylofagou, *Cyprus* **133** F17

Y
Ya'an, *China* **157** J11
Yablonovyy Khrebet, *Russ.* **137** J12
Yabrūd, *Syr.* **146** F6
Yacimiento Río Turbio, *Arg.* **111** R3
Yacuiba, *Bol.* **108** J8
Yacyretá Dam, *Para.* **109** K10
Yadgir, *India* **154** J4
Yadong, *China* **156** J7
Yaeyama Rettō, *Japan* **159** P11
Yafi, *Indonesia* **188** H5
Yağca, *Turk.* **144** F4
Yaguajay, *Cuba* **96** E6
Yahyalı, *Turk.* **144** F8
Yaita, *Japan* **162** H9
Yakacık, *Turk.* **144** G8
Yakapınar, *Turk.* **144** G8
Yakeshi, *China* **157** B15
Yakima, *Wash., U.S.* **92** B3
Yakishiri Jima, *Japan* **162** B10
Yakmach, *Pak.* **153** N3
Yakoma, *D.R.C.* **176** G8
Yakossi, *Cen. Af. Rep.* **176** F8
Yaksha, *Russ.* **136** F6
Yaku Shima, *Japan* **163** M3
Yakutat, *Alas., U.S.* **92** L4
Yakutat Bay, *U.S.* **90** L4
Yakutsk, *Russ.* **137** F13
Yala, *Sri Lanka* **155** P6
Yala, *Thai.* **165** M7
Yalata, *S. Austral., Austral.* **186** J9
Yalgoo, *W. Austral., Austral.* **186** H4
Yallock, *N.S.W., Austral.* **187** K13
Yalong, river, *China* **157** J10
Yalova, *Turk.* **144** C4
Yalta, *Ukr.* **135** P6
Yalu, river, *China* **158** B11
Yalvaç, *Turk.* **144** E5
Yamagata, *Japan* **162** G9
Yamaguchi, *Japan* **163** K4
Yamal, Poluostrov, *Russ.* **136** E8
Yamas, *Indonesia* **167** J17
Yamato Glacier, *Antarctica* **201** B12
Yamato Mountains *see* Queen Fabiola
  Mountains, *Antarctica* **201** B13
Yambio, *S. Sudan* **176** G9
Yambol, *Bulg.* **131** G14
Yamdena, island, *Indonesia* **188** M7
Yamethinn, *Myanmar* **164** E4

Yamm, *Russ.* **134** E4
Yammaw, *Myanmar* **164** B5
Yamma Yamma, Lake, *Austral.*
  185 G12
Yamoussoukro, *Côte d'Ivoire* **178** D7
Yan, river, *Shaanxi, China* **158** E2
Yana, Gulf of, *Russ.* **198** C6
Yana, river, *Russ.* **137** E13
Yanagawa, *Japan* **163** K3
Yan'an, *Shaanxi, China* **158** E1
Yanbu' al Baḥr, *Saudi Arabia* **148** G5
Yancheng, *Jiangsu, China* **158** H8
Yanchuan, *Shaanxi, China* **158** E2
Yandal, *W. Austral., Austral.* **186** H5
Yandeearra, *W. Austral., Austral.*
  186 E4
Yandoon, *Myanmar* **164** G4
Yandu, *Jiangsu, China* **158** H8
Yangcheng, *Shanxi, China* **158** F3
Yangchun, *Guangdong, China* **159** R2
Yangdŏk, *N. Korea* **160** H6
Yanggang, *N. Korea* **160** E5
Yanggao, *Shanxi, China* **158** B4
Yanggu, *S. Korea* **160** J8
Yanggu, *Shandong, China* **158** F5
Yanghŭng, *N. Korea* **160** D9
Yanghwa-man, bay, *N. Korea* **160** F8
Yangi Qal'eh, *Afghan.* **152** H3
Yangi Qal'eh, *Afghan.* **152** G6
Yangjiang, *Guangdong, China* **159** R2
Yangju, *S. Korea* **161** K7
Yangmei, *Taiwan, China* **159** P9
Yangmingshan, *Taiwan, China* **159** P9
Yangming Shan, *Hunan, China* **159** N2
Yangon (Rangoon), *Myanmar* **164** G4
Yangpo, *S. Korea* **161** N10
Yangqu, *Shanxi, China* **158** D3
Yangquan, *Shanxi, China* **158** D4
Yangsan, *S. Korea* **161** P9
Yangshan, *Guangdong, China* **159** P3
Yangshuo, *Guangxi Zhuangzu, China*
  159 P1
Yangtze, river, *Asia* **141** G12
Yangtze, Mouth of the, *Shanghai Shi,*
  China **158** J9
Yangtze Gorges, *Chongqing Shi, China*
  158 J1
Yangxin, *Hubei, China* **159** K5
Yangxin, *Shandong, China* **158** D6
Yangyang, *S. Korea* **161** K9
Yangyuan, *Hebei, China* **158** B4
Yangzhou, *Jiangsu, China* **158** H7
Yanji, *China* **157** D17
Yankton, *S. Dak., U.S.* **92** D9
Yanliang, *Shaanxi, China* **158** F1
Yanling, *Hunan, China* **159** N4
Yano-Indigirskaya Nizmennost', *Russ.*
  137 D13
Yano-Oymyakonskoye Nagor'ye, *Russ.*
  137 E13
Yanqi, *China* **156** D7
Yanrey, *W. Austral., Austral.* **186** F3
Yanshan, *Jiangxi, China* **159** M6
Yan Shan, *Hebei, China* **158** B7
Yanskiy, *Russ.* **137** E13
Yanskiy Zaliv, *Russ.* **137** D13
Yantabulla, *N.S.W., Austral.* **187** H13
Yantai, *Shandong, China* **158** D9
Yantra, river, *Bulg.* **131** F13
Yanzhou, *Shandong, China* **158** F6
Yao, *Japan* **162** J6
Yaoundé, *Cameroon* **179** F13
Yapen, island, *Indonesia* **188** K4
Yapen, Selat, *Indonesia* **188** K4
Yapero, *Indonesia* **188** J5
Yap Islands, *F.S.M.* **190** C4
Yaqui, river, *Mex.* **94** C4
Yara, *Cuba* **96** G8
Yaraka, *Qnsld., Austral.* **187** G13
Yaralıgöz, peak, *Turk.* **144** B7

Yaransk, *Russ.* **134** E12
Yardımcı Burnu, *Turk.* **144** G4
Yardymly, *Azerb.* **145** E17
Yarí, river, *Col.* **106** G7
Yarīm, *Yemen* **148** M7
Yarkant, river, *China* **156** E5
Yarle Lakes, *Austral.* **184** J9
Yarlung Zangbo (Brahmaputra), river,
  China **156** J8
Yarma, *Turk.* **144** F6
Yarmouth, *N.S., Can.* **89** L14
Yaroslavl', *Russ.* **134** E9
Yarozero, *Russ.* **134** D8
Yarraden, *Qnsld., Austral.* **187** B13
Yarraloola, *W. Austral., Austral.* **186** E3
Yarrowmere, *Qnsld., Austral.* **187** E14
Yartsevo, *Russ.* **134** G6
Yarumal, *Col.* **106** D6
Yashkul', *Russ.* **135** N12
Yasin, *Pak.* **152** H8
Yasinza'i Kalay, *Afghan.* **153** M3
Yasothon, *Thai.* **164** G8
Yass, *N.S.W., Austral.* **187** L14
Yasun Burnu, *Turk.* **144** C9
Yata, river, *Bol.* **108** F7
Yatağan, *Turk.* **144** F3
Yatakala, *Niger* **174** G7
Yathkyed Lake, *Nunavut, Can.* **88** G8
Yatsushiro, *Japan* **163** L3
Yauca, *Peru* **108** G5
Yauco, *P.R., U.S.* **97** J17
Yaupi, *Ecua.* **106** J5
Yavarí, river, *Peru* **108** D5
Yavatmal, *India* **154** H5
Yaviza, *Pan.* **95** L17
Yawatahama, *Japan* **163** K5
Yawri Bay, *Sierra Leone* **178** D4
Yaylâdağı, *Turk.* **144** H8
Yaynangyoung, *Myanmar* **164** E4
Yazd, *Iran* **149** D11
Yazdān, *Iran* **149** C13
Yazılıkaya, *Turk.* **144** D4
Yazlıca Dağı, *Turk.* **145** F13
Yazman, *Pak.* **153** N8
Yazoo, river, *U.S.* **91** H11
Ye, *Myanmar* **164** H5
Yebyu, *Myanmar* **164** H5
Yecheng, *China* **156** E5
Yecheon, *S. Korea* **161** M9
Yecla, *Sp.* **123** H11
Yeeda, *W. Austral., Austral.* **186** D6
Yefremov, *Russ.* **134** H8
Yei, *D.R.C.* **177** G10
Yekaterinburg, *Russ.* **136** G6
Yekateriny, Proliv, *Russ.* **137** H18
Yelan', *Russ.* **135** K11
Yelan Kolenovskiy, *Russ.* **135** K9
Yelets, *Russ.* **134** J8
Yélimané, *Mali* **174** G4
Yelizavety, Mys, *Russ.* **137** G16
Yell, island, *Scot., U.K.* **120** B9
Yellandu, *India* **154** J6
Yellow *see* Huang, river, *China*
  157 F13
Yellowknife, *N.W.T., Can.* **88** F7
Yellow, Mouth of the *see* Huang,
  Mouth of the, *Shandong, China*
  158 D7
Yellow Sea, *Asia* **141** G13
Yellowstone, river, *U.S.* **90** B7
Yellowstone Lake, *U.S.* **90** C6
Yell Sound, *Scot., U.K.* **120** B9
Yel'sk, *Belarus* **134** J4
Yelwa, *Nig.* **179** C10
Yemanzhelinsk, *Russ.* **136** H6
Yemen, *Asia* **142** J4
Yenakiyeve, *Ukr.* **135** M8
Yen Bai, *Viet.* **164** D9
Yendi, *Ghana* **178** C9
Yengisar, *China* **156** E5

Yeniçağa, *Turk.* **144** C5
Yenice, *Turk.* **144** D6
Yenice, river, *Turk.* **144** E8
Yeniceoba, *Turk.* **144** E6
Yeni Erenköy *see* Yialousa, *Cyprus*
  133 E17
Yenişehir, *Turk.* **144** C4
Yenisey, river, *Russ.* **136** G9
Yenisey Gulf, *Russ.* **199** B10
Yeniseysk, *Russ.* **136** H9
Yeniseyskiy Zaliv, *Russ.* **136** E9
Yen Minh, *Viet.* **164** D9
Yenyuka, *Russ.* **137** H13
Yeola, *India* **154** H3
Yeo Lake, *Austral.* **184** H6
Yeoncheon, *S. Korea* **160** J7
Yeondo, island, *S. Korea* **161** R8
Yeongam, *S. Korea* **161** Q6
Yeongcheon, *S. Korea* **161** N9
Yeongchun, *S. Korea* **161** R6
Yeongdeok, *S. Korea* **161** M10
Yeongdong, *S. Korea* **161** N8
Yeonggwang, *S. Korea* **161** P6
Yeongheungdo, island, *S. Korea* **161** L6
Yeongjongdo, island, *S. Korea* **161** L6
Yeongju, *S. Korea* **161** M9
Yeongwol, *S. Korea* **161** L9
Yeongyang, *S. Korea* **161** M9
Yeonil, *S. Korea* **161** N10
Yeoryang, *S. Korea* **161** L9
Yeosan, *S. Korea* **161** N7
Yeoseodo, island, *S. Korea* **161** S6
Yeosu, *S. Korea* **161** Q7
Yeovil, *Eng., U.K.* **121** R8
Yeppoon, *Qnsld., Austral.* **187** F16
Yerbogachen, *Russ.* **137** G11
Yerema, *Russ.* **137** H11
Yerevan, *Turk.* **145** D14
Yerköy, *Turk.* **144** D7
Yeroham, *Israel* **147** K4
Yershov, *Russ.* **134** J12
Yesan, *S. Korea* **161** M6
Yeşilhisar, *Turk.* **144** E7
Yeşilırmak, river, *Turk.* **144** C8
Yeşilkent, *Turk.* **144** G8
Yeşilova, *Turk.* **144** F4
Yesŏng, river, *N. Korea* **160** J6
Yessentuki, *Russ.* **135** P11
Yessey, *Russ.* **137** F11
Ye-u, *Myanmar* **164** D4
Yeu, Île d', *Fr.* **125** N3
Yevlax, *Azerb.* **145** C16
Yevpatoriya, *Ukr.* **135** P6
Yexian, *Henan, China* **158** G4
Yeysk, *Russ.* **135** N8
Ygatimí, *Para.* **109** J10
Yí, river, *Uru.* **110** H9
Yialias, river, *Cyprus* **133** F16
Yialousa (Yeni Erenköy), *Cyprus*
  133 E17
Yibin, *China* **157** J11
Yichang, *Hubei, China* **159** K2
Yicheng, *Hubei, China* **158** J3
Yichuan, *Henan, China* **158** G3
Yichun, *Jiangxi, China* **159** M4
Yifeng, *Jiangxi, China* **159** L4
Yilan, *China* **157** C17
Yıldız Dağları, *Turk.* **144** B3
Yıldızeli, *Turk.* **144** D9
Yinan, *Shandong, China* **158** F7
Yinchuan, *China* **157** F12
Yindarlgooda, Lake, *Austral.* **184** J6
Yindi, *W. Austral., Austral.* **186** J6
Yingcheng, *Hubei, China* **158** J4
Yingde, *Guangdong, China* **159** Q3
Yingkou, *Liaoning, China* **158** B9
Yingshan, *Hubei, China* **159** K5
Yingshang, *Anhui, China* **158** H5
Yingtan, *Jiangxi, China* **159** M6
Yingxian, *Shanxi, China* **158** C4

Zarautz, *Sp.* **123** B10
Zaraysk, *Russ.* **134** G8
Zaraza, *Venez.* **107** C11
Zard, Kūh-e, *Iran* **148** D9
Zaria, *Nig.* **179** C12
Zárkos, *Gr.* **132** D7
Zărneşti, *Rom.* **131** D13
Zaruma, *Ecua.* **106** K4
Żary, *Pol.* **127** E10
Zaskar Mountains, *Asia* **153** K11
Zatish'ye, *Russ.* **137** D15
Zatobyl, *Kaz.* **150** B9
Zatoka, *Ukr.* **135** N5
Zavolzhsk, *Russ.* **134** E9
Zawiercie, *Pol.* **127** F12
Zāwiyat Masūs, *Lib.* **175** C12
Zawr, Ra's az, *Saudi Arabia* **148** F9
Zayaki Jangal, *Pak.* **153** P4
Zaysan, *Kaz.* **151** D16
Zaysan Köli, *Kaz.* **151** D15
Zayü, *China* **156** J9
Zdolbuniv, *Ukr.* **135** K3
Zeča, island, *Croatia* **130** E4
Zednes, peak, *Mauritania* **174** D4
Zefat, *Israel* **146** H5
Zeil, Mount, *Austral.* **184** F9
Zeist, *Neth.* **124** F9
Zelenchukskaya, *Russ.* **135** P10
Zelenodol'sk, *Russ.* **134** F12
Zelenoe, *Kaz.* **150** D5
Zelenogorsk, *Russ.* **134** D5
Zelenogradsk, *Russ.* **134** F1
Zelenokumsk, *Russ.* **135** P11
Železná Ruda, *Czech Rep.* **126** H8
Železnik, *Serb.* **130** E9
Zelzate, *Belg.* **124** G8
Zemetchino, *Russ.* **134** H10
Zemio, *Cen. Af. Rep.* **176** G8
Zemongo, *Cen. Af. Rep.* **176** F8
Zencirli, site, *Turk.* **144** G9
Zengcheng, *Guangdong, China* **159** Q4
Zenica, *Bosn. & Herzg.* **130** F7
Zeni Su, island, *Japan* **163** K8
Zenobia, ruins, *Syr.* **146** D9
Žepče, *Bosn. & Herzg.* **130** E7
Zereh Depression, *Afghan.* **153** M1
Zermatt, *Switz.* **128** C2
Zernez, *Switz.* **128** B4
Zernograd, *Russ.* **135** M9
Zestap'oni, *Ga.* **145** B13
Zetland see Shetland Islands, *Scot., U.K.*
   120 B9
Zeya, *Russ.* **137** H14
Zgharta, *Leb.* **146** F5
Zgierz, *Pol.* **127** D12
Zgorzelec, *Pol.* **127** E10
Zhabdün, *China* **156** H6
Zhalpaqtal, *Kaz.* **150** C4
Zhaltyr, *Kaz.* **151** C11
Zhamo see Bomi, *China* **156** J9
Zhanatal, *Kaz.* **150** F8
Zhang, river, *Henan, China* **158** E4
Zhangaly, *Kaz.* **150** E4
Zhangaözen, *Kaz.* **150** G5
Zhanga Qazan, *Kaz.* **150** C4
Zhangaqorghan, *Kaz.* **151** G10
Zhangatas, *Kaz.* **151** G11
Zhangbei, *Hebei, China* **158** B5
Zhangjiajie, *Hunan, China* **159** L1
Zhangjiakou, *Hebei, China* **158** B5
Zhangjiapan see Jingbian, *Shaanxi,*
   China **158** D1
Zhangping, *Fujian, China* **159** P6
Zhangpu, *Fujian, China* **159** Q6
Zhangqiu, *Shandong, China* **158** E6
Zhangshu (Qingjiang), *Jiangxi, China*
   159 M5
Zhangwu, *Liaoning, China* **158** A9
Zhangye, *China* **157** F10
Zhangzhou, *Fujian, China* **159** P6

Zhangzi, *Shanxi, China* **158** F3
Zhanhua (Fuguo), *Shandong, China*
   158 D7
Zhanjiang, *Guangdong, China* **159** S1
Zhanyi, *China* **157** K11
Zhao'an, *Fujian, China* **159** Q6
Zhaodong, *China* **157** C16
Zhaojue, *China* **157** J11
Zhaoping, *Guangxi Zhuangzu, China*
   159 P1
Zhaoqing, *Guangdong, China* **159** Q3
Zhaosu, *China* **156** D6
Zhaotong, *China* **157** J11
Zhaoxian, *Hebei, China* **158** D5
Zhaoyuan, *Shandong, China* **158** E8
Zhapo, *Guangdong, China* **159** R2
Zhaqsy, *Kaz.* **151** B10
Zhari Mamco, lake, *China* **156** H6
Zharkamys, *Kaz.* **150** D6
Zharkent, *Kaz.* **151** F14
Zharma, *Kaz.* **151** D14
Zharmysh, *Kaz.* **150** F5
Zhashui (Qianyou), *Shaanxi, China*
   158 G1
Zhaslyk, *Uzb.* **150** F6
Zhayrang, *Kaz.* **151** D11
Zhayylma, *Kaz.* **150** C8
Zhayyq (Ural), river, *Kaz.* **150** D5
Zhdanov, *Azerb.* **145** D16
Zhecheng, *Henan, China* **158** G5
Zhejiang, *China* **159** L8
Zhelaniya, Cape, *Russ.* **199** C11
Zhelezīnka, *Kaz.* **151** A12
Zheleznodorozhnyy, *Russ.* **136** E6
Zheleznogorsk, *Russ.* **134** J7
Zheleznovodsk, *Russ.* **135** P11
Zhem, river, *Kaz.* **150** E6
Zhemgang, *Bhutan* **154** E10
Zhen'an (Yongle), *Shaanxi, China*
   158 G1
Zhengding, *Hebei, China* **158** D4
Zhenghe, *Fujian, China* **159** M7
Zhenglan Qi, *Nei Mongol, China*
   158 A5
Zhengning, *Gansu, China* **158** F1
Zhengxiangbai Qi see Qagan Nur,
   Nei Mongol, China **158** A5
Zhengyang, *Henan, China* **158** H4
Zhengzhou, *Henan, China* **158** G4
Zhenjiang, *Jiangsu, China* **158** J7
Zhenping, *Henan, China* **158** H3
Zhenping, *Shaanxi, China* **158** J1
Zhenwudong see Ansai, *Shaanxi, China*
   158 E1
Zhenxiong, *China* **157** J11
Zherdevka, *Russ.* **134** J9
Zherong, *Fujian, China* **159** M8
Zhetiqara, *Kaz.* **150** B8
Zhezqazghan, *Kaz.* **151** E10
Zhicheng, *Hubei, China* **159** K2
Zhidan (Bao'an), *Shaanxi, China*
   158 E1
Zhigansk, *Russ.* **137** F12
Zhilaya Kosa, *Kaz.* **150** E5
Zhil'gur, *Russ.* **137** G13
Zhilinda, *Russ.* **137** E11
Zhlobin, *Belarus* **134** H5
Zhmerynka, *Ukr.* **135** L4
Zhob, *Pak.* **153** L6
Zhob, river, *Pak.* **153** L6
Zhokhova, Ostrov, *Russ.* **137** C13
Zhongfang, *Hunan, China* **159** M1
Zhongshan, *Guangdong, China* **159** R3
Zhongshan, *Guangxi Zhuangzu, China*
   159 P2
Zhongshan, station, *Antarctica*
   201 E15
Zhongtiao Shan, *Shanxi, China* **158** F2
Zhongwei, *China* **157** F11
Zhongxian, *China* **157** H12

Zhongxiang, *Hubei, China* **158** J3
Zhosaly, *Kaz.* **150** F9
Zhoucun, *Shandong, China* **158** E6
Zhoukou, *Henan, China* **158** G4
Zhouning, *Fujian, China* **159** M7
Zhoushan, *Zhejiang, China* **159** K9
Zhoushan Dao, *Zhejiang, China*
   159 K9
Zhoushan Qundao, *Zhejiang, China*
   159 K9
Zhoutuozi, *Liaoning, China* **158** A9
Zhovtneve, *Ukr.* **135** M5
Zhu (Pearl River), *Guangdong, China*
   159 R3
Zhuanghe, *Liaoning, China* **158** C10
Zhucheng, *Shandong, China* **158** F7
Zhuhai, *Guangdong, China* **159** R3
Zhuji, *Zhejiang, China* **159** K8
Zhukovka, *Belarus* **134** H6
Zhumadian, *Henan, China* **158** H4
Zhuolu, *Hebei, China* **158** B5
Zhuozhou, *Hebei, China* **158** C5
Zhupanovo, *Russ.* **137** E17
Zhuryn, *Kaz.* **150** D7
Zhushan, *Hubei, China* **158** H2
Zhuxi, *Hubei, China* **158** H1
Zhuzhou, *Hunan, China* **159** M3
Zhympity, *Kaz.* **150** C5
Zi, river, *Hunan, China* **159** L2
Ziarat, *Pak.* **153** M5
Zibak, *Afghan.* **152** H7
Zibo, *Shandong, China* **158** E7
Zicavo, *Fr.* **128** H3
Zichang (Wayaobu), *Shaanxi, China*
   158 E1
Zielona Góra, *Pol.* **127** D10
Zigana Geçidi, pass, *Turk.* **145** C10
Zigar, *Taj.* **152** G7
Zigey, *Chad* **175** G11
Zigong, *China* **157** J11
Ziguinchor, *Senegal* **174** G3
Zile, *Turk.* **144** D8
Žilina, *Slovakia* **127** G12
Zillah, *Lib.* **175** C11
Zima, *Russ.* **137** J11
Zimbabwe, *Af.* **173** P8
Zimnicea, *Rom.* **131** F13
Zimovniki, *Russ.* **135** M10
Zinder, *Niger* **174** G9
Zinjibār, *Yemen* **148** M7
Žirje, island, *Croatia* **130** F5
Zirndorf, *Ger.* **126** G7
Zittau, *Ger.* **126** F9
Živinice, *Bosn. & Herzg.* **130** E7
Ziway Hāyk', *Eth.* **177** F12
Zixi, *Jiangxi, China* **159** M6
Zixing, *Hunan, China* **159** N3
Ziyamet see Leonarisso, *Cyprus*
   133 E17
Ziyuan, *Guangxi Zhuangzu, China*
   159 N1
Zizhou, *Shaanxi, China* **158** D2
Zlarin, island, *Croatia* **130** F5
Zlatoust, *Russ.* **136** G5
Zlatoustovsk, *Russ.* **137** H15
Zlín, *Czech Rep.* **127** G11
Złotów, *Pol.* **127** C11
Zmari Sar, peak, *Afghan.* **153** M4
Zmeica, Lacul, *Rom.* **131** E16
Zmeinogorsk, *Russ.* **136** K8
Zmiyev, *Ukr.* **135** L7
Zmiyinyy, Ostriv, *Ukr.* **135** N5
Znamenka, *Kaz.* **151** C14
Znamensk, *Russ.* **134** G1
Znam'yanka, *Ukr.* **135** L6
Znojmo, *Czech Rep.* **127** H10
Zoetermeer, *Neth.* **124** F9
Zofar, *Israel* **147** L4
Zofingen, *Switz.* **128** A2

Zoigê, *China* **157** G11
Zolochiv, *Ukr.* **135** K2
Zolochiv, *Ukr.* **135** K7
Zolotaya Gora, *Russ.* **137** H14
Zolotonosha, *Ukr.* **135** L5
Zomba, *Malawi* **181** D11
Zongga see Gyirong, *China* **156** H6
Zongo, *D.R.C.* **176** G7
Zonguldak, *Turk.* **144** B5
Zonza, *Fr.* **128** H3
Zor Dağ, *Turk.* **145** D14
Zorkol Lake, *Taj.* **152** G9
Zorritos, *Peru* **108** D3
Zouar, *Chad* **175** E11
Zoucheng, *Shandong, China* **158** F6
Zouping, *Shandong, China* **158** E6
Zoushi, *Hunan, China* **159** L2
Zrenjanin (Petrovgrad), *Serb.* **130** D9
Zubayr, Jazā'ir az, *Yemen* **148** L5
Zubovo, *Russ.* **134** D8
Zubtsov, *Russ.* **134** F7
Zuera, *Sp.* **123** C12
Zufār, region, *Oman* **149** K11
Zug, *Switz.* **128** A3
Zugdidi, *Ga.* **145** B12
Zugspitze, peak, *Aust.* **126** J7
Zululand, region, *S. Af.* **180** H9
Žumberačka Gora, peak, *Slov.* **130** D5
Zumberge Coast, *Antarctica* **200** F6
Zumbo, *Mozambique* **180** D9
Zunhua, *Hebei, China* **158** B6
Zunyi, *China* **157** J12
Zuoquan, *Shanxi, China* **158** E4
Zuoyun, *Shanxi, China* **158** C3
Zuoz, *Switz.* **128** B4
Zürich, *Switz.* **128** A3
Zur Kowt, *Afghan.* **153** K6
Zuru, *Nig.* **179** C11
Žut, island, *Croatia* **130** F5
Zutphen, *Neth.* **124** F10
Zuwārah, *Lib.* **175** B10
Zvenyhorodka, *Ukr.* **135** L5
Zvishavane, *Zimb.* **180** F9
Zvolen, *Slovakia* **127** H12
Zvornik, *Bosn. & Herzg.* **130** E8
Zwettl, *Aust.* **127** H10
Zwickau, *Ger.* **126** F8
Zwolle, *Neth.* **124** E10
Zygi, *Cyprus* **133** F16
Zyrya, *Azerb.* **145** C18
Zyryanka, *Russ.* **137** D15
Zyryanovo, *Russ.* **136** G9
Zyryanovsk, *Kaz.* **151** C15

Acknowledgments

World Thematic Section

World Thematics Intro (opener)
pp. 20–21

GRAPHICS
ANTHROPOSPHERE: Félix Pharand-Deschênes, Globaïa.
http://globaia.org

Paleogeography
pp. 22–23

CONSULTANTS
Robert Tilling
Volcano Hazards Team, U.S. Geological Survey (USGS)

Ron Blakey
Colorado Plateau Geosystems

GRAPHICS
PALEOGEOGRAPHIC MAPS: Ron Blakey, Colorado Plateau Geosystems, Inc.

GEOLOGIC TIME GRAPH:
International Commission on Stratigraphy. *International Chronostratigraphic Chart,* August 2012. http://www.stratigraphy.org

Tectonics
pp. 24–25

CONSULTANT
Robert Tilling
Volcano Hazards Team,
U.S. Geological Survey (USGS)

GRAPHICS
MAP: Smithsonian Institution, Global Volcanism Program. http://www.volcano.si.edu/world

Muller, R. D., M. Sdrolias, C. Gaina, and W. R. Roest. 2008. "Age, spreading rates, and spreading asymmetry of the world's ocean crust." *Geochem. Geophys. Geosyst.,* 9, Q04006, doi:10.1029/2007GC001743.

USGS National Earthquake Information Center (NEIC): http://earthquake.usgs.gov/regional/neic

EARTH'S INTERIOR: Tibor G. Tóth

GEOLOGIC PROCESSES: Susan Sanford

Earth's Surface
pp. 26–27

CONSULTANT
Mike Slattery
Texas Christian University

MAP DATA: Natural Earth CleanTOPO2: http://www.naturalearthdata.com

Land Cover
pp. 28–29

CONSULTANTS
**Mark Friedl and
Damien Sulla-Menashe**
Global Land Cover Project,
Boston University

SATELLITE IMAGES
GLOBAL LAND COVER: Boston University Department of Geography and Environment Global Land Cover Project. Source data provided by NASA's Moderate Resolution Imaging Spectroradiometer.

Oceans
pp. 30–31

CONSULTANTS
Benjamin S. Halpern
Nat. Ctr. for Ecological Analysis and Synthesis

S. Bradley Moran and Lewis Rothstein
University of Rhode Island

GRAPHICS
HUMAN IMPACT: Halpern, B.S., S. Walbridge, K.A. Selkoe, C.V. Kappel, F. Micheli, C. D'Agrosa, J. Bruno, K.S. Casey, C. Ebert, H.E. Fox, R. Fujita, D. Heinemann, H.S. Lenihan, E.M.P. Madin, M. Perry, E. Selig, M. Spalding, R. Steneck, and R. Watson. "A global map of human impact on marine ecosystems." *Science* 319: 948–952, 2008.

SEA SURFACE TEMPERATURES: Gene Carl Feldman, NASA/Goddard Space Flight Center Aqua-MODIS

Fresh Water
pp. 32–33

GRAPHICS
MAP: National Geographic Magazine. 2010. *Water: A Special Issue.* Sources: World Wildlife Fund; Igor A. Shiklomanov, State Hydrological Institute, Russia; USGS; University of Kassel Center for Environmental Systems Research, Germany; National Snow and Ice Data Center, University of Colorado.

WATER WITHDRAWALS, BY SECTOR: UNESCO. "Managing Water under Uncertainty and Risk, The United Nations World Water Development Report 4," 2012, p. 443.

MAPPING IRRIGATION: Food and Agricultural Organization of the United Nations (FAO)2008.

WATER AVAILABILITY: Gleick, Peter. 2006. *The World's Water: The Biennial Report on Freshwater Resources.* Island Press, 2006.

SAFE DRINKING WATER: World Health Organization. 2012. "Proportion of population using improved drinking water sources (%), 2010."

Climate
pp. 34–35

GRAPHICS
CLIMATE ZONES: © National Geographic Society

CHANGING OF THE SEASONS: © National Geographic Society

SATELLITE IMAGES
Images originally created for the GLOBE program by NOAA's National Geophysical Data Center, Boulder, Colorado, U.S.A.
AVERAGE TEMPERATURE: National Center for Environmental Prediction (NCEP); National Center for Atmospheric Research (NCAR); National Weather Service (NWS)

AVERAGE PRECIPITATION: Global Precipitation Climatology Project (GPCP); International Satellite Land Surface Climatology Project (ISLSCP)

Climate Change
pp. 36–37

GRAPHICS
HUMAN VULNERABILITY TO CLIMATE CHANGE (MAP): Maplecroft. 2013. Climate Change Vulnerability Index. http://www.maplecroft.com

RISING TEMPERATURES AND CO_2: NOAA/NCDC: Global Climate Change Indicators. http://www.ncdc.noaa.gov/indicators

DIMINISHING ICE AND SEA LEVEL RISE (IMAGE): NASA. 2012. "Arctic Sea Ice Hits Smallest Extent in Satellite Era." http://www.nasa.gov/topics/earth/features/2012-seaicemin.html

ICE SHEET CONTRIBUTIONS TO GLOBAL SEA LEVEL: NASA/ESA/Planetary visions.

ETHICAL CONSIDERATIONS: Patz JA, Campbell-Lendrum D, Holloway T, Foley, JA. Impact of regional climate change on human health. *Nature* (cover) (2005); 438: 310–317.

COUNTRIES WITH THE HIGHEST LEVELS OF GREENHOUSE GAS EMISSIONS: UNdata. 2013. Millennium Development Goals Database, United Nations Statistics Division. data.un.org

COUNTRIES THAT WILL SUFFER THE MOST DUE TO CLIMATE CHANGE: DARA. 2012. Climate Vunerability Monitor, 2nd ed. http://daraint.org/climate-vulnerability-monitor/climate-vulnerability-monitor-2012

Natural Hazards
pp. 38–39

GENERAL REFERENCES
The United Nations Office for Disaster Risk Reduction (UNISDR). "Impacts of Disasters since the 1992 Rio de Janeiro Earth Summit." 2012. http://www.unisdr.org

The OFDA/CRED International Disaster Database, EM-DAT. http://www.emdat.be

United Nations Department of Economic and Social Affairs/Population Division. 2012. *UN World Urbanization Prospects, the 2011 Revision.* http://esa.un.org/unup

The Center for Research on Epidemiology of Disasters. http://www.cred.be

GRAPHICS
MAP/HIGHEST MORTALITY RISK DISASTER HOT SPOTS: Dilley, Maxx, et al. 2005. "Natural disaster hotspots: A global risk analysis." The World Bank and Columbia University.

MAP/TROPICAL CYCLONE PATHS, VULNERABLE COASTS: UNEP/GRID-Europe/UNISDR. PREVIEW Global Risk Data Platform, 2012. http://preview.grid.unep.ch

MAP/CITIES: United Nations Department of Economic and Social Affairs/Population Division. 2012. *UN World Urbanization Prospects, the 2011 Revision.* http://esa.un.org/unup

Human Impact
pp. 40–41

CONSULTANT
Erle C. Ellis
University of Maryland,
Baltimore County

GENERAL REFERENCE
Ellis, E. C. 2011. "Anthropogenic transformation of the terrestrial biosphere." *Proceedings of the Royal Society A: Mathematical, Physical and Engineering Science* 369:1010–1035.

GRAPHICS
MAP AND GRAPH: Ellis, E. C., K. Klein Goldewijk, S. Siebert, D. Lightman, and N. Ramankutty. 2010. "Anthropogenic transformation of the biomes, 1700 to 2000." *Global Ecology and Biogeography* 19:589–606. DOI: 10.1111/j.1466-8238.2010.00540.x

Population: Density and Growth
pp. 42–43

GRAPHICS
POPULATION DENSITY: Oak Ridge National Laboratory (ORNL); Edward A. Bright, Phillip R. Coleman, Amy N. Rose. June 2012. LandScan 2011™.

United Nations Department of Economic and Social Affairs/Population Division. 2012. *UN World Urbanization Prospects, the 2011 Revision.* http://esa.un.org/unup

Population: Demographics
pp. 44–45

GENERAL REFERENCES
FERTILITY, LIFE EXPECTANCY, AND PROJECTED POPULATION: Population Reference Bureau. DataFinder: PRB's Hub for U.S. and International Data. http://www.prb.org/DataFinder.aspx

MIGRATION: *The World Factbook.* Washington, DC:

Central Intelligence Agency. https://www.cia.gov/library/publications/the-world-factbook/index.html

POPULATION PYRAMIDS: International Data Base (IDB), U.S. Census Bureau.

Urbanization: Megacities
pp. 46–47

GENERAL REFERENCE
United Nations Department of Economic and Social Affairs/Population Division. 2012. *UN World Urbanization Prospects, the 2011 Revision.* http://esa.un.org/unup

GRAPHICS
MAP: *World Urbanization Prospects, the 2011 Revision.* File 6: "Average Annual Rate of Change of the Urban Population by Major Area, Region and Country, 1950–2050 (percent)."

GRAPHS: *World Urbanization Prospects, the 2011 Revision.* Figure 1 and Table 4.

Urbanization: Other Cities
pp. 48–49

GENERAL REFERENCE
United Nations Department of Economic and Social Affairs/Population Division. 2012. *UN World Urbanization Prospects, the 2011 Revision.* http://esa.un.org/unup

GRAPHICS
MAP: *World Urbanization Prospects, the 2011 Revision.* File 12: "Population of Urban Agglomerations with 750,000 Inhabitants or More in 2011, by Country, 1950–2025 (thousands)."

GRAPHS: *World Urbanization Prospects, the 2011 Revision.* Table 5 and Figure 5.

Health and Education
pp. 50–51

CONSULTANT
Ruth Levine
Center for Global Development

GENERAL REFERENCES
United Nations. 2012. *The Millennium Development Goals Report, 2012.* http://ww.un.org/millenniumgoals

Education Policy and Data Center: www.epdc.org

GRAPHICS
INCOME LEVELS: 2013. The World Bank. Country and Lending Groups. http://data.worldbank.org

ACCESS TO IMPROVED SANITATION: Adapted from *WHO Water Supply and Sanitation Monitoring Mid-Term Report, 2004.*

NUTRITION: FAO, WFP and IFAD. *The State of Food Insecurity in the World 2012: Economic growth is necessary but not sufficient to accelerate reduction of hunger and malnutrition.* 2012. Rome, FAO.

HIV/AIDS: UN AIDS data. http://www.unaids.org/en/dataanalysis/datatools/aidsinfo

GLOBAL DISEASE BURDEN AND CAUSES OF DEATH: World Health Organization. WHO Mortality Database; Mortality and Global Burden of Disease (GBD), 2012. http://www.who.int

MORTALITY RATES, UNDER AGE FIVE: United Nations Statistics Division/UNdata. 2012. Children under five mortality rate per 1,000 live births. http://data.un.org

MATERNAL MORTALITY RATIOS: Trends in Maternal Mortality: 1990–2010. Estimates Developed by WHO, UNICEF, UNFPA and the World Bank. http://data.worldbank.org

ADULT LITERACY: UNESCO Institute for Statistics. Literacy and Educational Attainment. http://stats.uis.unesco.org/unesco

SCHOOL ENROLLMENT FOR GIRLS: UNICEF. *The State of the World's Children 2012.* Table 5: Education. http://www.unicef.org/sowc2012/statistics.php

DEVELOPING HUMAN CAPITAL: Adapted from Human Capital Projections developed by Education Policy and Data Center.

Human Development
pp. 52–53

GENERAL REFERENCES
United Nations Development Programme (UNDP). *Human Development Report 2011.*

United Nations Development Programme (UNDP). *Human Development Report 2013.*

Human Development Reports website. http://hdr.undp.org/en

GRAPHICS
HUMAN DEVELOPMENT INDEX (MAP) AND HDI RANKINGS OVER TIME (GRAPH): UNDP Human Development Reports website. http://hdr.undp.org/en/statistics

Human Migration
pp. 54–55

GENERAL REFERENCES
The UN Refugee Agency (UNHCR). UNHCR Global Trends 2011 web presentation. http://www.unhcr.org/pages/4fd9a0676.html

UNHCR Statistics & Operational Data. http://www.unhcr.org/pages/49c3646c4d6.html

Refworld. UNHCR. http://www.unhcr.org/cgi-bin/texis/vtx/refworld/rwmain

U.S. Census Bureau, 2009–2011. American Community Survey.

Additional population information from UNdata and various government census departments.

FORCED MIGRATION: UNHCR/Governments. 2012. Table 2. Refugees, asylum-seekers, internally displaced persons (IDPs), returnees (refugees and IDPs), stateless persons, and others of concern to UNHCR by origin, end-2011.

Languages
pp. 56–57

CONSULTANTS
Bill Dickson
Global Mapping International (GMI)

Stephen Huffman

GRAPHICS
LANGUAGE FAMILIES: Global Mapping International (GMI) and SIL International. World Language Mapping System, version 3.2.1.

SMALL LANGUAGES GET SMALLER: Anderson, Gregory and K. David Harrison. 2007. Language Hotspots - Global Trends. http://www.swarthmore.edu/SocSci/langhotspots/globaltrends.html

WORLD POPULATION AND LANGUAGES BY REGION: Loh, Jonathan and Dave Harmon. 2013. Data from Gordon, R.G. (ed.), 2005. *Ethnologue: Languages of the World,* Fifteenth edition. Dallas, Tex.: SIL International.

VANISHING LANGUAGES: Living Tongues Institute for Endangered Languages/National Geographic. Language Hotspots map. http://travel.nationalgeographic.com/travel/enduring-voices

Religion
pp. 58–59

CONSULTANT
Todd Johnson
Gordon-Conwell Theological Seminary

GENERAL REFERENCES
Johnson, Todd M. and Brian J. Grim, eds. *World Religion Database.* Leiden/Boston: Brill. http://www.worldreligiondatabase.org/wrd_default.asp

CIA World Factbook: https://www.cia.gov/library/publications/the-world-factbook

Economy
pp. 60–61

GENERAL REFERENCES
CIA World Factbook. https://www.cia.gov/library/publications/the-world-factbook

OECD Factbook 2013: *Economic, Environmental and Social Statistics.* Table 8: Value added by activity. http://www.oecd-ilibrary.org/economics/oecd-factbook-2013_factbook-2013-en

World Bank data. http://data.worldbank.org

GRAPHICS
VALUE ADDED BY SECTOR AND REGION: United Nations Industrial Development Organization (UNIDO). 2010. *Structural Change in the World Economy: Main Features and Trends.* Figures 1b and 2b.

Trade
pp. 62–63

GENERAL REFERENCES
World Trade Organization. 2012. *International Trade Statistics 2012.* http://www.wto.org/english/res_e/statis_e/its2012_e/its12_toc_e.htm

United Nations Conference on Trade and Development: www.unctad.org

World Bank data. http://data.worldbank.org

GRAPHICS
GROWTH OF WORLD TRADE: World Trade Organization. *International Trade Statistics 2012.* Table A1, World merchandise exports, production and gross domestic product, 1950–2011.

TRADE BLOCS: World Trade Organization. *International Trade Statistics 2012.* Regional integration agreements, pp. 188–189.

Food
pp. 64–65

CONSULTANTS
Food and Agriculture Organization of the United Nations (FAO)

GENERAL REFERENCE
Food and Agriculture Organization of the United Nations (FAO) Statistics Division: http://faostat.fao.org

GRAPHICS
MAIN MAP: Monfreda, C., N. Ramankutty, and J.A. Foley. 2008. Farming the planet. Part 2: Geographic distribution of crop areas, yields, physiological types, and net primary production in the year 2000. *Global Biogeochemical Cycles* 22, GB1022, doi:10.1029/2007GB002947. http://www.earthstat.org

CALORIC SUPPLY: FAOSTAT Food Balance Sheets. http://faostat.fao.org.

WORLD AGRICULTURAL PRODUCTION: FAOSTAT. http://faostat.fao.org

FISHING AND AQUACULTURE: FAO. *The State of World Fisheries and Aquaculture 2012.* Figure 1.

Energy
pp. 66–67

GENERAL REFERENCES
International Energy Agency (IEA). World Energy Outlook. http://www.iea.org

Energy Information Administration, U.S. Department of Energy. http://www.eia.gov

Acknowledgments

GRAPHICS

ENERGY CONSUMPTION, BY LEADING SOURCE: Energy Information Administration, U.S. Department of Energy: http://www.eia.gov/cfapps/ipdbproject/IEDIndex3.cfm

GLOBAL PRODUCTION, BY FUEL TYPE AND REGION: International Energy Agency (IEA). 2012. *Key World Energy Statistics,* pages 6 and 8.

RENEWABLE LEADERS: Energy Information Administration, U.S. (EIA). Table: Renewable Electric Generation by Type (billion kilowatt hours), Year 2011.

Mineral Resources

pp. 68–69

CONSULTANT

Philip Brown
University of Wisconsin–Madison

GENERAL REFERENCES

World Trade Organization (WTO)

World Mineral Production, British Geological Survey

MAIN MAP: Statistics Database, World Trade Organization (WTO). http://www.wto.org

WORLD MINERAL PRODUCTION: USGS Mineral Commodity Summaries, 2012: http://minerals.usgs.gov/minerals/pubs/mcs/; Mineral Fund Advisory, www.mineralprices.com

WORLD SHARE OF PRODUCTION: USGS Mineral Commodity Summaries, 2012.

Protected Areas

pp. 70–71

GENERAL REFERENCE

UNEP-WCMC, World Database on Protected Areas: http://www.unep-wcmc.org/wdpa

GRAPHICS

MAIN MAP: IUCN and UNEP-WCMC (2013) The World Database on Protected Areas (WDPA) Cambridge, UK: UNEP- WCMC. Available at: http://www.protectedplanet.net. March 2013 Monthly Release.

Biodiversity Hotspots, Conservation International. http://www.conservation.org

BIOME PROTECTION: *Confronting a Biome Crisis: Global Disparities of Habitat Loss and Protection,* Hoekstra et al, 2005.

TRACKING CONSERVATION: IUCN and UNEP-WCMC. 2012. The World Database on Protected Areas (WDPA). Cambridge, UK: UNEP-WCMC.

CHARTING THREATENED SPECIES: IUCN. 2012. *The IUCN Red List of Threatened Species. Version 2012.2.* http://www.iucnredlist.org

Environmental Stress

pp. 72–73

GENERAL REFERENCES

Ozone Processing Team at NASA/Goddard Space Flight Center: http://ozoneaq.gsfc.nasa.gov

Energy Information Administration. U.S. Department of Energy: www.eia.doe.gov

Natural Resources Conservation Service: www.nrcs.usda.gov

United Nations Environment Programme-World Conservation and Monitoring Program (UNEP-WCMC): http://www.unep-wcmc.org

GRAPHICS

DESERTIFICATION: World Resources Institute. Millennium Ecosystem Assessment, 2005. *Ecosystems and Human Well-Being, Desertification Synthesis.* Fig. 7.1.

DEFORESTATION: World Resources Institute. Millennium Ecosystem Assessment, 2005. *Ecosystems and Human Well-Being, General Synthesis.* Fig. 1.4.

AIR POLLUTION: Aaron van Donkelaar, Dalhousie University. MODIS and MISR data, NASA.

WATER SCARCITY: International Water Management Institute (IWMI), Colombo, Sri Lanka. 2006. *Insights from the Comprehensive Assessment of Water Management in Agriculture.*

ENVIRONMENTAL PERFORMANCE RANKINGS: Environmental Performance Index, Yale Center for Environmental Law & Policy, Yale University: http://epi.yale.edu

CARBON EMISSIONS: International Energy Agency (IEA). *CO$_2$ Emissions from Fuel Combustion (2012 Edition).* Paris: http://www.iea.org

Transportation

pp. 74–75

GENERAL REFERENCES

Globaïa: http://globaia.org

International Organization of Motor Vehicle Manufacturers: http://oica.net

Maersk Line: http://www.maerskline.com

GRAPHICS

MAIN MAP: Image by Félix Pharand-Deschênes, Globaïa, 2013. www.globaia.org. Data sources: Paved and Unpaved Roads, Pipelines, Railways & VMap0, National Geospatial-Intelligence Agency, September 2000. Shipping Lanes: NOAA's SEAS BBXX database, from 14.10.2004 to 15.10.2005. Air Networks: International Civil Aviation Organization statistics. Urban Areas: naturalearthdata.com. Submarine Cables: Greg Mahlknecht's Cable Map. Earth texture maps: Tom Patterson. Anthropocene Indicators: Global Change and the Earth System: A Planet Under Pressure, Steffen, W., Sanderson, A., Jäger, J., Tyson, P.D., Moore III, B., Matson, P.A., Richardson, K., Oldfield, F., Schellnhuber, H.-J., Turner II, B.L., Wasson, R.J. Springer Verlag, Heidelberg, Germany, 1st ed. 2004, 2nd printing, 2005, pp. 132–133.

WORLD'S BUSIEST AIRPORTS: Airports Council International: http://www.aci.aero

SHIPPING THE WORLD'S GOODS: *World's Top Container Ports,* The Journal of Commerce: http://www.joc.com

CHARTING INTERNATIONAL TOURISM: United Nations World Tourism Organization (UNWTO): http://www2.unwto.org

Globalization

pp. 76–77

GENERAL REFERENCE

KOF Index of Globalization: http://globalization.kof.ethz.ch

GRAPHICS

MAIN MAP: KOF Index of Globalization 2013; Dreher, Axel (2006): "Does Globalization Affect Growth? Evidence from a new Index of Globalization." *Applied Economics 38,* 10: 1091-1110. Updated in: Dreher, Axel, Noel Gaston and Pim Martens (2008), *Measuring Globalisation—Gauging its Consequences* (New York: Springer). http://globalization.kof.ethz.ch

TRANSNATIONAL CORPORATIONS: United Nations Conference on Trade and Development (UNCTAD). http://unctad.org

OFFSHORE SERVICES: *The Offshore Services Global Value Chain,* Center on Globalization, Governance & Competitiveness (CGGC), Duke University, 2010.

Digital Connectivity

pp. 78–79

GENERAL REFERENCES

TeleGeography: http://www.telegeography.com

International Telecommunication Union: http://www.itu.int

GRAPHICS

MAPS: Used by permission from TeleGeography; http://www.telegeography.com

MOBILE SUBSCRIPTIONS ON THE RISE: International Telecommunication Union, ITU World Telecommunication/ICT Indicators database

Time Zones

pp. 80–81

GENERAL REFERENCES

CIA World Factbook. https://www.cia.gov/library/publications/the-world-factbook

http://tycho.usno.navy.mil/tzones.html

http://www.timeanddate.com

Continental Section

Continent openers

GLOBES: GTOPO30, USGS EROS Data Center, 2000; ETOPO1/Amante and Eakins, 2009; Natural Earth: http://www.naturalearthdata.com

Antarctica

pp. 200–201

CONSULTANT

Jill E. Caldwell
National Geomagnetism Program,
U.S. Geological Survey

GENERAL REFERENCE

Antarctic Digital Database, British Antarctic Survey http://www.add.scar.org

Sea Ice Extent

pp. 202–203

National Snow and Ice Data Center: http://nsidc.org

Flags and Facts; Pie Charts

CONSULTANT

Whitney Smith
Flag Research Center

GENERAL REFERENCES

CIA World Factbook. https://www.cia.gov/library/publications/the-world-factbook

International Monetary Fund (IMF). 2012. World Economic Outlook Databases. http://www.imf.org

United Nations Department of Economic and Social Affairs/Population Division. 2012. *UN World Urbanization Prospects, the 2011 Revision.* http://esa.un.org/unup

Physical and Political Maps

Bureau of the Census, U.S. Department of Commerce
Bureau of Land Management, U.S. Department of the Interior
Central Intelligence Agency (CIA)
National Geographic Maps
National Geospatial-Intelligence Agency (NGA)
National Park Service, U.S. Department of the Interior
Office of the Geographer, U.S. Department of State
U.S. Board on Geographic Names (BGN)
U.S. Geological Survey, U.S. Department of the Interior

Land Cover and Population Maps

LAND COVER: Natural Earth. http://www.naturalearthdata.com

POPULATION DENSITY: LandScan™ Global Population Database. Oak Ridge National Laboratory. Under license from UT-Battelle, under U.S. Department of Energy (DOE) Contract No. DE-AC05-00OR22725.

Appendix Section

Major Cities of the World
pp. 210–211

United Nations Department of Economic and Social Affairs/ Population Division. 2012. *UN World Urbanization Prospects, the 2011 Revision.* http://esa.un.org/unup

World Temperature and Rainfall
pp. 218–227

NOAA/National Climatic Data Center; Climate Normals 1961-1990. http://www.ncdc.noaa.gov/

Principal References

CIA (Central Intelligence Agency)
https://www.cia.gov

CIESIN
http://www.ciesin.org

Conservation International
http://www.conservation.org

Energy Information Agency
http://www.eia.doe.gov

Food and Agriculture Organization of the UN
http://www.fao.org

International Monetary Fund
http://www.imf.org

NASA (National Aeronautics and Space Administration)
http://www.nasa.gov

NOAA (National Atmospheric and Oceanic Administration)
http://www.noaa.gov

NCDC (National Climatic Data Center)
http://www.ncdc.noaa.gov

NGDC (National Geophysical Data Center)
http://www.ngdc.noaa.gov

PRB (Population Reference Bureau)
http://www.prb.org

United Nations
http://www.un.org

UN Conference on Trade and Development
http://www.unctad.org

UN Development Programme
http://www.undp.org

UN Educational, Cultural, and Scientific Organization
http://www.unesco.org

UNEP-WCMC
http://www.unep-wcmc.org

UN Millennium Development Goals
http://www.un.org/millenniumgoals

UN Population Division
http://www.unpopulation.org

UN Refugee Agency
http://www.unhcr.org

UN Statistics Division
http://unstats.un.org

U.S. Board on Geographic Names
http://geonames.usgs.gov

U.S. Census Bureau
http://www.census.gov

USGS (U.S. Geological Survey)
http://www.usgs.gov

World Bank
http://www.worldbank.org

World Health Organization
http://www.who.int

World Trade Organization
http://www.wto.org

WWF (World Wildlife Fund)
http://www.worldwildlife.org

Photo Credits

24 (UP), Frans Lanting/Corbis; 24 (CTR), James P. Blair/National Geographic Stock; 24 (LO), Frans Lanting/National Geographic Stock; 26, Diehm/Getty Images; 27 (UP), Frank Krahmer/Getty Images; 27 (UP CTR), John W. Banagan/Getty Images; 27 (LO CTR), Momatiuk - Eastcott/Corbis; 27 (LO), Jeremy Woodhouse/Corbis; 28 (UP LE), Tom and Pat Leeson/Science Source; 28 (UP RT), Michael Nichols/National Geographic Stock; 28 (LO-a), Stephen J. Krasemann/Science Source; 28 (LO-b), Rod Planck/Science Source; 28 (LO-c), James Steinberg/Science Source; 28 (LO-d), Matthew C. Hansen; 28 (LO-e), Gregory G. Dimijian/Science Source; 28 (LO-f), Sharon G. Johnson Edell; 28 (LO-g), Adam Burton/Robert Harding World Imagery/Corbis; 29 (a), Rod Planck/Science Source; 29 (b), James Randklev/Getty Images; 29 (c), George Steinmetz/Corbis; 29 (d), Jim Richardson/National Geographic Stock; 29 (e), Steve McCurry/National Geographic Image Collection; 29 (f), George Steinmetz/National Geographic Image Collection; 29 (g), B. & C. Alexander/Science Source; 31 (UP), Brandon Cole; 31 (UP CTR), Chris Newbert/Minden Pictures/National Geographic Stock; 31 (LO CTR), Kaz Mori/Getty Images; 31 (LO), Jean Guichard/Corbis; 32 (UP), Konstantin Mikhailov/Foto Natura/Minden Pictures/Getty Images; 32 (CTR), Jenny E. Ross/Corbis; 32 (LO), Kevin Fleming/Corbis; 34 (UP), Winfried Wisniewski/Foto Natura/Minden Pictures/Getty Images; 34 (CTR), Yevgen Timashov/beyond/Corbis; 34 (LO), Michael Melford/National Geographic Stock; 37 (UP), Charlie Mahoney/Corbis; 37 (CTR), Rinie Van Meurs/Foto Natural Minden Pictures/National Geographic Stock; 37 (LO), Annie Griffiths/National Geographic Stock; 38 (UP), Yang Hoe-Seong/AFP/Getty Images; 38 (CTR), Anthony Asael/Art in All of Us/Corbis; 38 (LO), Rick D'Elia/Corbis; 40 (LE), Qilai Shen/epa/Corbis; 40 (CTR), Frank Chen/Getty Images; 40 (RT), Sara Winter/Getty Images; 42, Martin Puddy/Corbis; 47 (UP), Jane Sweeney/JAI/Corbis; 47 (UP CTR), Navid Baraty; 47 (LO CTR), Julian Love/JAI/Corbis; 47 (LO), SeanPavonePhoto/Shutterstock.com; 49 (UP), David Laronde/Corbis; 49 (UP CTR), John W. Banagan/Getty Images; 49 (LO CTR), Robert Mandel/Shutterstock; 49 (LO), Ian Trower/Robert Harding World Imagery/Corbis; 52 (LE), Barbara Walton/epa/Corbis; 52 (CTR), Jochen Schlenker/Robert Harding World Imagery/Corbis; 52 (RT), Francis Dean/Corbis; 54 (LE), Qilai Shen/In Pictures/Corbis; 54 (CTR), Stan Honda/Pool/Reuters/Corbis; 54 (RT), Ton Koene/Visuals Unlimited/Corbis; 56 (UP), Paul Souders/Corbis; 56 (CTR), Catherine Karnow/Corbis; 56 (LO), Lynn Johnson/National Geographic Stock; 58 (UP), Piti Anchaleesahakorn/Demotix/Corbis; 58 (UP CTR), Sylvain Sonnet/Corbis; 58 (CTR), Amit Dave/Reuters/Corbis; 58 (LO CTR), Moemen Faiz/APA Images/ZUMAPRESS.com/Corbis; 58 (LO), Donald Nausbaum/Robert Harding/Corbis; 60 (UP), Paulo Fridman/Bloomberg via Getty Images; 60 (CTR), Mauro Ujetto/Demotix/Corbis; 60 (LO), Hendrik Schmidt/epa/Corbis; 62 (UP), AP Photo/Andy Wong; 62 (CTR), Kenichiro Seki/Xinhua Press/Corbis; 62 (LO), AP Photo/Yves Logghe; 64 (UP), AP Photo/Charlie Riedel; 64 (CTR), Reuters/Romeo Ranoco; 64 (LO), Bertrand Rieger/Hemis/Corbis; 67 (UP), Herbert Kehrer/imagebroker/Corbis; 67 (UP CTR), Xiao Yijiu/Xinhua Press/Corbis; 67 (LO CTR), Sergio Pitamitz/Corbis; 67 (LO), Kevin Steele/Aurora Photos/Corbis; 68 (UP), Bloomberg via Getty Images; 68 (CTR), William Hong/Reuters/Corbis; 68 (LO), Ilya Naymushin/Reuters/Corbis; 70 (UP), Peter Walton Photography/Getty Images; 70 (CTR), Marc Muench/Getty Images; 70 (LO), Peter Barritt/SuperStock/Corbis; 72 (LE), Dave Reede/First Light/Getty Images; 72 (LE CTR), Paulo Fridman/Corbis; 72 (RT CTR), Adrian Bradshaw/epa/Corbis; 72 (RT), Lin Yiguang/Xinhua Press/Corbis; 73, Andre Kudyusov/Getty Images; 74 (UP), Jay Dickman/Corbis; 74 (CTR), Teun van den Dries/Getty Images; 74 (LO), David Nunuk/All Canada Photos/Getty Images; 76 (UP), Eightfish/Getty Images; 76 (CTR), AP Photo/Geert Vanden Wijngaert; 76 (LO), Bloomberg via Getty Images; 78 (UP), Jens Buettner/epa/Corbis; 78 (UP CTR), Carl Walsh/Aurora Photos/Corbis; 78 (LO CTR), Justin Guariglia/Corbis; 78 (LO), Saeed Khan/AFP/Getty Images.

Printed and bound by Toppan Printing Co., (H.K.) Ltd.

NATIONAL GEOGRAPHIC

Global Atlas

Published by the National Geographic Society

John M. Fahey, *Chairman of the Board and Chief Executive Officer*

Declan Moore, *Executive Vice President; President, Publishing and Travel*

Melina Gerosa Bellows, *Executive Vice President; Chief Creative Officer, Books, Kids, and Family*

Book Division

Hector Sierra, *Senior Vice President and General Manager*

Janet Goldstein, *Senior Vice President and Editorial Director*

Jonathan Halling, *Design Director, Books and Children's Publishing*

Marianne R. Koszorus, *Design Director, Books*

R. Gary Colbert, *Production Director*

Jennifer A. Thornton, *Director of Managing Editorial*

Susan S. Blair, *Director of Photography*

Meredith C. Wllcox, *Director, Administration and Rights Clearance*

National Geographic Maps

Charles D. Regan, Jr., *Senior Vice President, General Manager*

Daniel J. Ortiz, *Vice President, Publisher*

Kevin P. Allen, *Vice President, Production Services*

Staff for This Atlas

Carl Mehler, *Project Editor and Director of Maps*

Juan José Valdés, *The Geographer and Director of Editorial and Research*

Matthew W. Chwastyk, Mike McNey, Gregory Ugiansky, XNR Productions, *Map Research and Production*

Maureen J. Flynn, Julie A. Ibinson, Regina Peregoy, *Map Editors*

K.M. Kostyal, *Writer*

Victoria Garret Jones, Laura McCormick, Jennifer Conrad Seidel *Text Editors*

Kyle S. Mackie, Alexander Pommer, Gloriana Sojo Lara, *Map Interns*

Manufacturing and Quality Management

Phillip L. Schlosser, *Senior Vice President*

Chris Brown, *Vice President, NG Book Manufacturing*

George Bounelis, *Vice President, Production Services*

Robert L. Barr, Nicole Elliott, and Rachel Faulise *Managers*

CELEBRATING
‹125›
Y E A R S

The National Geographic Society is one of the world's largest nonprofit scientific and educational organizations. Founded in 1888 to "increase and diffuse geographic knowledge," the Society works to inspire people to care about the planet. National Geographic reflects the world through its magazines, television programs, films, music and radio, books, DVDs, maps, exhibitions, live events, school publishing programs, interactive media and merchandise. *National Geographic* magazine, the Society's official journal, published in English and 33 local-language editions, is read by more than 60 million people each month. The National Geographic Channel reaches 435 million households in 37 languages in 173 countries. National Geographic Digital Media receives more than 19 million visitors a month. National Geographic has funded more than 10,000 scientific research, conservation and exploration projects and supports an education program promoting geography literacy.

For more information, visit www.nationalgeographic.com.

For more information, please call 1-800-NGS LINE (647-5463) or write to the following address:

National Geographic Society
1145 17th Street N.W.
Washington, D.C. 20036-4688 U.S.A.

For information about special discounts for bulk purchases, please contact National Geographic Books Special Sales: ngspecsales@ngs.org

For rights or permissions inquiries, please contact National Geographic Books Subsidiary Rights: ngbookrights@ngs.org

ISBN 978-1-4262-1201-7

Printed in Hong Kong
13/THK/1